ELEVEN DAYS
IN AUGUST

Also by Matthew Cobb

THE RESISTANCE: THE FRENCH FIGHT
AGAINST THE NAZIS

ELEVEN DAYS IN AUGUST

The Liberation of Paris in 1944

MATTHEW COBB

**SIMON &
SCHUSTER**

London · New York · Sydney · Toronto · New Delhi

A CBS COMPANY

First published in Great Britain by Simon & Schuster UK Ltd, 2013
This paperback edition published by Simon & Schuster UK Ltd, 2014
A CBS COMPANY

1 3 5 7 9 10 8 6 4 2

Simon & Schuster UK Ltd
1st Floor
222 Gray's Inn Road
London WC1X 8HB.

www.simonandschuster.co.uk

Simon & Schuster Australia, Sydney
Simon & Schuster India, New Delhi

A CIP catalogue record for this book is available
from the British Library

ISBN: 978-0-85720-318-2
ISBN: 978-0-85720-319-9 (ebook)

Typeset by M Rules
Printed and bound by CPI Group (UK) Ltd, Croydon, CR0 4YY

For Lauren and Evie, a tale of your city

Contents

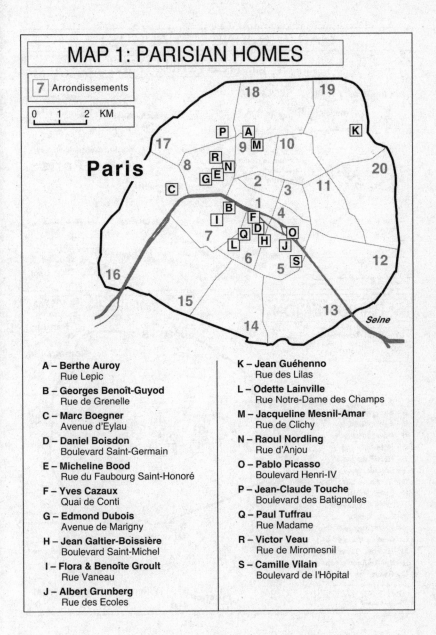

MAP 1: PARISIAN HOMES

7 Arrondissements

0   1   2   KM

Paris

18   19

17   P   A   K

9   M

8   R   10

E   N

C   2   3   11   20

B   1

I   F   4

7   Q   D   O

L   H   J

6   S   12

5

16

15   13   Seine

14

A – **Berthe Auroy**
Rue Lepic

B – **Georges Benoît-Guyod**
Rue de Grenelle

C – **Marc Boegner**
Avenue d'Eylau

D – **Daniel Boisdon**
Boulevard Saint-Germain

E – **Micheline Bood**
Rue du Faubourg Saint-Honoré

F – **Yves Cazaux**
Quai de Conti

G – **Edmond Dubois**
Avenue de Marigny

H – **Jean Galtier-Boissière**
Boulevard Saint-Michel

I – **Flora & Benoîte Groult**
Rue Vaneau

J – **Albert Grunberg**
Rue des Ecoles

K – **Jean Guéhenno**
Rue des Lilas

L – **Odette Lainville**
Rue Notre-Dame des Champs

M – **Jacqueline Mesnil-Amar**
Rue de Clichy

N – **Raoul Nordling**
Rue d'Anjou

O – **Pablo Picasso**
Boulevard Henri-IV

P – **Jean-Claude Touche**
Boulevard des Batignolles

Q – **Paul Tuffrau**
Rue Madame

R – **Victor Veau**
Rue de Miromesnil

S – **Camille Vilain**
Boulevard de l'Hôpital

MAP 2: 6 JUNE – 21 AUGUST

WESTERN FRONT

Allied advances
German defences
🅢 German HQ

6 June

Utah Beach
Bayeux
30 June
La Roche-Guyon 🅢
Mantes
Saint-Germain-en-Laye 🅢
Paris 🅢
21 August
Falaise pocket
1 August
Argentan
Rambouillet
Avranches
16 August
9 August
Chartres
Sens
0   50   100 KM
Le Mans
21 August

PARIS REGION

☐ Arrondissements
🅢 German HQ

La Chapelle
Drancy
Pantin
Paris
Romainville

A
J
D
M
Bois de Boulogne
F
H
Montreuil
B
K
C
E
O
I
G
N
L

A – Batignolles
B – Ecole Militaire
C – Hôtel de Ville
D – Hôtel Majestic 🅢
E – Hôtel Matignon
F – Hôtel Meurice 🅢
G – Jardin du Luxembourg 🅢
H – Palais Royal
I – Place Saint-Michel
J – Porte Maillot
K – Préfecture de Police
L – Quai de la Gare
M – Rue des Saussaies 🅢
N – Sainte-Agonie convent
O – Senate 🅢

Marne
Montrouge
Ivry
Seine
Vitry
0 1 2 KM
Villeneuve-Saint-Georges
Fresnes

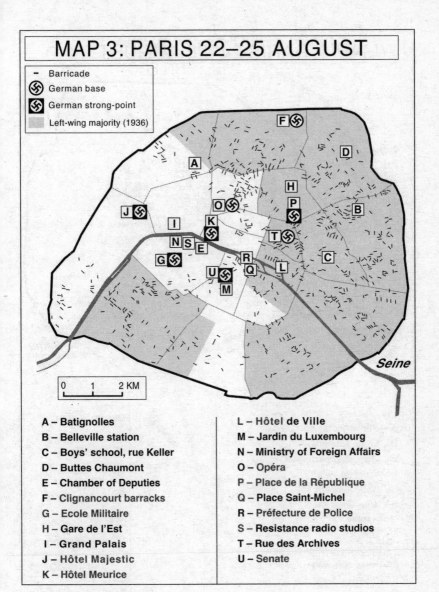

MAP 3: PARIS 22–25 AUGUST

- — Barricade
- ⌖ German base
- ⌖ German strong-point
- ▨ Left-wing majority (1936)

F⌖ German base

D

A

H
P⌖

J⌖

B

O⌖

I
K⌖

T⌖

N S E

C

G⌖

R
Q

L

U⌖

M

Seine

0   1   2 KM

A – Batignolles
B – Belleville station
C – Boys' school, rue Keller
D – Buttes Chaumont
E – Chamber of Deputies
F – Clignancourt barracks
G – Ecole Militaire
H – Gare de l'Est
I – Grand Palais
J – Hôtel Majestic
K – Hôtel Meurice

L – Hôtel de Ville
M – Jardin du Luxembourg
N – Ministry of Foreign Affairs
O – Opéra
P – Place de la République
Q – Place Saint-Michel
R – Préfecture de Police
S – Resistance radio studios
T – Rue des Archives
U – Senate

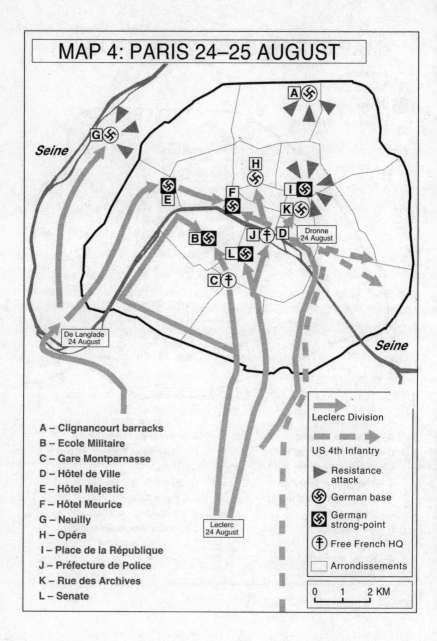

MAP 4: PARIS 24–25 AUGUST

Seine

Seine

De Langlade
24 August

Dronne
24 August

Leclerc
24 August

A – Clignancourt barracks
B – Ecole Militaire
C – Gare Montparnasse
D – Hôtel de Ville
E – Hôtel Majestic
F – Hôtel Meurice
G – Neuilly
H – Opéra
I – Place de la République
J – Préfecture de Police
K – Rue des Archives
L – Senate

Leclerc Division

US 4th Infantry

Resistance attack

German base

German strong-point

Free French HQ

Arrondissements

0   1   2 KM

Dramatis personae

2e—DB Free French 2nd Armoured Division
Colonel Pierre Billotte
Colonel Alain de Boissieu
Colonel Paul de Langlade
Captain Raymond Dronne
General Philippe Leclerc
Lieutenant Suzanne Torrès, Rochambeau Ambulance Brigade

Allies
Colonel Claude Arnould ('Ollivier'), JADE-AMICOL MI6 circuit
General Omar Bradley, US Army
Colonel George Bruce, OSS
Captain Adrien Chaigneau, Jedburgh Team AUBREY
General Leonard Gerow, US Army
Sergeant Ivor Hooker, Jedburgh Team AUBREY
Captain Guy Marchant, Jedburgh Team AUBREY
General George S. Patton, US Army

Collaborators
René Bouffet, Prefect of the Seine
Robert Brasillach, writer
Amédée Bussière, Prefect of Police
Marcel Déat, fascist politician
Pierre Drieu La Rochelle, writer
Philippe Henriot, journalist
Max Knipping, northern leader of the Milice
Pierre Laval, Prime Minister
Lucien Rébatet, journalist
Pierre Taittinger, President of the Paris Council

Free French

Georges Boris, London head of propaganda

General Jacques Delmas ('Chaban'), National Military Delegate

Francis-Louis Closon, BCRA

Marcel Flouret, Prefect of the Seine

General Koenig, Commander of the Free French Army

Charles Luizet, Prefect of Police

Alexandre Parodi, General Delegate

Edgard Pisani, Luizet's aide

Roland Pré ('Oronte'), Regional Military Delegate

Germans

Otto Abetz, German ambassador to France

Lieutenant Dankwart Graf von Arnim, aide to von Choltitz

Emil 'Bobby' Bender, German intelligence, British agent

Lieutenant-General Wilhelm von Boineburg, military commander of Paris

General Dietrich von Choltitz, military commander of Greater Paris

Private Walter Dreizner, military electrician, photographer

Colonel Jay, Ordnance officer to von Choltitz

Field Marshal von Kluge, German commander in the West

Field Marshal Model, German commander in the West

SS General Carl Oberg, SS chief in Paris

Lieutenant Erich 'Riki' Posch-Pastor, German officer, British agent

General Hans Speidel, Chief of Staff of Army Group B

Quartermaster Robert Wallraf

Neutrals

René Naville, Swiss legate

Rolf Nordling, brother of Raoul

Raoul Nordling, Swedish Consul General

Others

Ernest Hemingway, writer

Philippe Herriot, ex-President of the National Assembly

P. G. Wodehouse, writer

Parisians

Berthe Auroy, retired schoolteacher
Georges Benoît-Guyod, retired officer
Andrzej Bobkowski, Polish exile
Marc Boegner, Protestant priest
Daniel Boisdon, lawyer
Micheline Bood, teenage schoolgirl
Yves Cazaux, civil servant
Simone de Beauvoir, writer
Edmond Dubois, Swiss journalist
Jean Galtier-Boissière, journalist
Benoîte Groult, single woman, sister of Flora
Flora Groult, schoolgirl
Albert Grunberg, hairdresser
Jean Guéhenno, schoolteacher
Odette Lainville, housewife
Jacqueline Mesnil-Amar, housewife
Pierre Patin, railway engineer
Pablo Picasso, artist
Claude Roy, journalist
Jean-Paul Sartre, writer
Jean-Claude Touche, student
Paul Tuffrau, university lecturer
Victor Veau, retired surgeon
Camille Vilain, poet

Résistants

André Amar, Organisation Juive de Combat
Major Armand ('Spiritualist'), SOE
Georges Bidault, President of the Conseil National de la Résistance
Claire Chevrillon, Parodi's coder
Captain Roger Cocteau ('Gallois'), FFI
René Courtin, Secretary-General for the Economy
General Dassault, Front National
Georges Dukson, FFI
Marie-Madeleine Fourcade, ALLIANCE

Colonel Pierre Georges ('Fabien'), FTP

Léo Hamon, Ceux de la Résistance representative on CPL

Maurice Kriegel ('Valrimont'), member of COMAC

Marie-Helène Lefaucheux, OCM representative on CPL

Pierre Lefaucheux, OCM head of Paris FFI until July 1944

Colonel Tessier de Marguerittes ('Lizé'), FFI

Commander Raymond Massiet ('Dufresnes'), FFI regional chief of staff

Doctor Monod, FFI

Bernard Pierquin, Resistance medical service

Jean Sainteny ('Dragon'), ALLIANCE

Colonel Henri Tanguy ('Rol'), regional FFI commander

Madeline Riffaud, FFI

Roger Stéphane, FFI

Charles Tillon, FTP

Pierre Villon, communist, member of COMAC

Count Jean de Vogüé ('Vaillant'), member of COMAC

Glossary

AMGOT	Allied Military Government of Occupied Territories
2e DB	Deuxième Division Blindée (Free French 2nd Armoured Division), Free French Army / Third US Army
BCRA	Bureau Central de Renseignements et d'Action – Free French Intelligence Service
Ceux de la Résistance	Resistance group, based mainly in Paris region
CGT	Conféderation Générale du Travail – General Labour Confederation
CNR	Conseil National de la Résistance – the Resistance leadership
COMAC	Comité d'Action Militaire – the Resistance military leadership
CPL	Comité Parisien de la Libération – leadership of the Parisian Resistance
FFI	Forces Françaises de l'Intérieur – armed wing of the Resistance
Free French	Generic term for supporters of de Gaulle and of the Provisional Government
FTP	Franc-Tireurs et Partisans – Communist Party armed group
Libération-Nord	Resistance group based in the north of France
OCM	Organisation Civile et Militaire – right-wing Resistance group
OSS	Office of Strategic Services – US intelligence organisation
mairie	Town hall

Milice	French fascist paramilitary organisation that specialised in fighting the Resistance
PCF	Parti Communiste Français – French Communist Party
SHAEF	Supreme Headquarters of the Allied Expeditionary Force
SOE	Special Operations Executive – secret British military organisation

Introduction

On 14 June 1940, when the German Army marched into Paris without a shot being fired, over a dozen people took their lives in despair.[1] Less than ten days later, the French government surrendered. The battle of France, which had begun in earnest six weeks earlier, had been brief, but bloody: over 300,000 French soldiers had been killed or wounded in the fighting, and nearly 2 million had been taken prisoner.

Under the terms of the armistice, France was divided up, with the industrial north, including Paris, placed under direct German administration and occupation. For the next four years the Germans stamped the city with their Nazi presence. Official buildings were draped with massive swastika flags; French road signs were replaced with instructions in German gothic script; café terraces and public transport were packed with the grey-green uniforms of German troops. While some urbane Nazis hobnobbed with unprincipled French artists and intellectuals, swilling champagne in the nightclubs and discussing philosophy over cups of tea, tens of thousands of German administrators and soldiers based in the capital oversaw the systematic pillaging of France's wealth, and the oppression and exploitation of the entire population. Rationing and shortages affected every aspect of life in the city, as the massive German military machine sucked resources like some vast parasite slowly destroying its host. The Germans spun a web of spies across the face of the capital; its centre was the Paris Gestapo headquarters on the rue des Saussaies, where French men and women were beaten, tortured and killed. The Gestapo were aided by the French police, who rounded up thousands of Parisian Jews and then deported them to Germany. After 1942, those Jews that remained in the city were forced to wear the yellow Star of David.

In the south of France, which was not initially occupied by the Germans, the octogenarian Marshal Pétain led a nominally sovereign

government, based in the spa town of Vichy. Pétain, who was in his
dotage, coined the infamous term that marked this period in history:
collaboration. As well as Pétain and the other collaborators, there were
also committed fascists and anti-Semites who revelled in the triumph of
the Nazis and wanted to see collaboration taken to an even higher level.
These people, who included journalists, writers and politicians, tended
to be based in Paris rather than Vichy. During the occupation the capital became a hothouse world in which the fascists plotted to take power
from Pétain and his prime minister, Laval, and where their vile views
were reinforced by the proximity of their jackbooted idols. From
November 1942 the Germans occupied the southern zone of France,
too, and all semblance of independence for Vichy disappeared.
Although Pétain and his collaborationist government remained as an
increasingly futile façade, real power in France always lay in the hands
of the Germans, who were based in Paris.[2]

Paris is not only the capital and the traditional seat of the French
government, it has its own local administration and municipal police
forces. In 1944, Paris was also the seat of the regional administration –
the Seine département, which covered both the city and its suburbs. At
the time there were ninety French départements, each of roughly
equivalent size. In each département there was a representative of central government, called the Prefect; he had authority over all the civil
servants in the region, and also acted as an interface between the government and the local councils. Paris was divided into twenty local
areas or arrondissements, each with their own town hall or *mairie* and,
before the war, an elected local council. The capital also contained two
police forces: the municipal police, under the control of the Paris
council, and the national police operating in the city, who were controlled by the Prefect of Police (not to be confused with the Prefect).
Policing in the rural areas surrounding the city was the responsibility of
French gendarmes, who were part of the Army.

Paris combined a glorious architectural heritage in the centre and the
west of the city with sordid working-class slums in the north and the
east. Densely populated, with a substantial Jewish and immigrant population (many of whom had fled Russian pogroms, the Nazi invasion of
Poland or the rise of fascism in Italy and Spain), Paris was still an indus-

trial centre, with factories and workshops all over the north, east and parts of the south of the city. It was surrounded by a sea of industrial suburbs, full of engineering factories, many linked with the railways, and the vast Renault and Citroën car plants that sprawled across the south-western edge of the city. As well as the workers in the Paris factories and small workshops, there were tens of thousands of clerks working in the capital, employed by private companies or the government, earning just enough to buy what food they could find in the markets that existed in every neighbourhood. The markets got food from the immense abbatoirs at La Villette on the north-eastern edge of the city, or from the bustling wholesale market at Les Halles, right in the very centre of the capital. As the war continued, food supplies became increasingly restricted, and the black market flourished.

*

Even before France fell, General Charles de Gaulle was in London, broadcasting on the BBC and calling for French resistance to the occupation. De Gaulle had in mind continued military struggle by sections of the French Army, but this proved a vain hope, and only a few thousand troops joined de Gaulle's 'Free French' in London.[3] However, another form of 'resistance' soon appeared – underground Resistance groups were created, with Paris as one of the first and most important centres of their activity. These groups had a wide variety of political views and also differed over the kind of action they felt ought to be taken against the Germans; despite being lumped under the title 'the Resistance', in reality they never formed a cohesive whole. Nevertheless, in Paris, as elsewhere in France, for many people the Resistance shaped the course of the occupation, providing a voice of opposition by publishing underground newspapers, working with Allied secret agents, and even for a period shooting soldiers and throwing bombs in a vain attempt to terrorise the immense German military machine.[4]

After the tragic destruction in summer 1943 of a Paris-based group of Allied agents belonging to the Special Operations Executive (SOE), the Allies focused their attention outside of the capital, and by 1944 underground work against the Germans in Paris was very much left to the Free French and to the Resistance.[5] Throughout the occupation, Paris was the scene of a series of disputes within the Resistance over what should be done to fight the Germans, with what means and under whose command. These arguments were amplified by the very real danger involved in carrying out underground activity, which created awful tensions and magnified minor differences. There was also an important difference between the activists in the Resistance and the Paris representatives of the Free French, who were widely seen as simply wanting to wait for the Allied armies to arrive. This difference not only related to means, it was also about ends. Most of the Paris Resistance organisations were not on the same political wavelength as the Free French. Indeed, many Resistance fighters in the capital and its region were close to the communists. Although all the groups came to accept de Gaulle as the Resistance figurehead, few of them were in favour of him taking power after the liberation of the country. The Resistance felt it should play an important role, but this was not at all how de Gaulle saw matters – by 1943 he was in charge of a provisional government in Algiers, and he intended to take control of France once the country had been liberated.

Ultimately, the fate of France would be decided in Downing Street and the White House: the US and British Allies controlled all the levers of economic and military power. Although de Gaulle had undoubted popular support in France, the whole of the French ruling elite supported Pétain's collaborationist government – not one leading industrialist, banker or military leader came over to the Free French. De Gaulle's movement was entirely financed by handouts or loans from the Allies, while the Free French armed forces were completely integrated with the Allies and depended entirely on Allied tactical and logistical support when they carried out their operations. As a result, the fiercely independent de Gaulle had to count on the goodwill of Roosevelt, Churchill and, to a lesser extent, Stalin, while the three leaders saw France as merely part of the map of Europe, the future of which would be decided by the Allies, not by the French themselves. Throughout the war, de Gaulle's relationship with the Allies remained stormy, and in the run-up to D-Day in June 1944 the Americans and the British prepared to take charge of France themselves, through an Allied Military Government of

Occupied Territories (AMGOT). There were therefore three contending forces struggling for the future of France – the Allies, the Free French and the Resistance – and each had a different vision of what a post-war France should look like. The outcome of this three-way conflict was not determined in advance, and it was not certain that it would be peaceful. Paris came to symbolise that struggle, and the battle for Paris that took place in August 1944 played a decisive part in determining the future of the country.

*

In the spring of 1944, Paris was exhausted by nearly four years of occupation. The winter had been long and hard, and with food scarce people were thin and malnourished. Although bombing raids on railway lines and German military installations in France indicated that the Allies were preparing the ground for an invasion, the end of the occupation still seemed far off. Furthermore, in Vichy there were growing signs that the fascists were gaining the upper hand in their slow and complex power struggle against Prime Minister Laval, as Joseph Darnand, the leader of the fascist Milice (militia), a French paramilitary organisation that specialised in fighting the Resistance, was made Minister of the Interior. Some sections of French society welcomed this. As well as the fringe of murderous fascists, there was also a large group of traditional nationalists, many of them fervent Catholics, who were devoted to Pétain; they feared communists and Jews, and indeed anyone who they felt might threaten their conservative world. Unlike the killers and torturers who fought for the fascist cause, these passive collaborationists were a kind of human dust that could be blown away by events, if the wind of history was strong enough.

Against this backdrop, the liberation of Paris included a series of clashes involving all of the forces at play in the city – the Resistance, the Free French, the Allies, the Germans, the collaborationist politicians and the French fascists. But above all, liberation engaged the ordinary men, women and even children of Paris who had been subjected to four years of occupation. In the heat of August 1944, they would finally be able to settle accounts with the Germans and their French allies. In telling this dramatic story, I have emphasised the personal experiences of people from all these groups, as they all, in their different ways, contributed to how events unfolded. Diaries, eye-witness accounts and contemporary documents, many of them previously unpublished, provide a glimpse of life in Paris in those momentous days by presenting the individual voices of both historic figures and little-known 'ordinary' people, many of whom turn out to be extraordinary.[6] Pictures, film, sound files and information relating to the events and people described here can be found at elevendaysinaugust.com.

Exactly when the fight to liberate Paris began is a matter of debate – a good case could be made for 10 August or for 19 August. I have chosen 15 August and have described in detail the eleven days in August that followed: the ten days of heightened struggle and the first day after the Germans were defeated, which was of major political importance and had a symbolism that is still felt in France today.

I lived in Paris for eighteen years; my daughters were born there. It is a city that shaped much of my outlook on life and is still part of me, ten years after leaving. In the summer it is particularly beautiful, with the golden late-afternoon light and the sound of swifts screeching around the courtyards and along the banks of the Seine.[7] Even the occasionally oppressive heat and its sudden release through dramatic thunderstorms have their beauty. It was like that in August 1944, too, but then German troops were occupying the city, there were barricades in the streets and the Parisians were rising up against a vicious army of occupation. Thousands of people died in the fighting, most of them civilians. This book will take you back to that time, to its moments of glory and horror. I hope it will excite you, move you and above all inspire you.

Manchester, September 2012

Prelude

April 1944: Bombers

Parisian medical student Bernard Pierquin writes in his diary: 'My activity in the Resistance continues, silently and without any fanfares. Two or three times a week I carry medicine and bandages in my bicycle saddle-bag; they are for the underground emergency medical centres we have set up in Paris in case of an insurrection ... We are anxiously awaiting the Allied invasion: as it gets closer, everyone realises the risks of battle. Already there have been so many victims, and in the future there will be even more, and we will not be able to expect any protection from the Allies. They will attack, they will destroy, they will massacre, they will do everything that is necessary to win. That's war, and war is horrible.'[1]

Thursday 20 April

Shortly after midnight, there was a faint rumbling in the Paris sky that grew gradually louder. Then the air-raid sirens wailed and people leapt from their beds and hurried to the nearest shelter – either the cellar of their building or the closest Métro station. All over the city, anti-aircraft guns fired into the black sky, punching lines of light into the darkness. On the northern border of the capital, eerie red flares drifted down above the massive railway yards at La Chapelle, showing the Allied bombers where to strike. Millions of thin strips of aluminium foil floated on the air, confusing German radar and fluttering down onto the roofs and pavements below. The first squadrons flew in from the south, dropping thousands of bombs, some of them weighing half a ton. The planes came in six waves, four minutes apart. As smoke and dust drifted over the target, more flares were dropped, but they were carried by the wind and soon they marked a wide area of the northern and eastern suburbs. And so the bombs rained down there, too, as a second attack came from north to south. Over two hundred aircraft were involved in the operation.[2]

For Jean Guéhenno, a schoolteacher, the bombs seemed to start falling as soon as the sirens sounded: 'There was no time to find shelter. We stayed in our fragile building, with the windows open, and could do nothing but watch the show. Magnificent, but frightening. Man is incredibly powerful and stupid.'[3] Sixty-four-year-old Berthe Auroy could not appreciate the magnificence, as her apartment in the 18th arrondissement was directly under the bombs. Terrified by the scale of the bombardment, she decided to seek shelter with her neighbours in the apartment above:

> I open the door onto the stairway and recoil in horror. The staircase seems to be surrounded by flames. It makes terrible cracking noises, it shakes with each explosion. I don't dare go up the ten steps. I go back to my shaking bed. Normally, a raid doesn't last very long. But the earth has been shaking for half an hour already; surely the nightmare must end soon ... The electricity goes off. I light a candle. The bombing is still very intense. An hour! This torture has been going on for a whole hour! Have they decided to destroy the whole of Paris?[4]

Albert Grunberg, a 46-year-old Jewish hairdresser, did not have the opportunity to find shelter. For the previous eighteen months Grunberg had been hiding with his brother Sami in the attic of his building in the Latin Quarter. He had not gone outside once, and almost none of his neighbours knew he was there. There was no question of joining them in the safety of the cellars.[5] Grunberg was eight kilometres away from the target[6] but was nevertheless horrified by the bombardment:

> It lasted two hours, from midnight to 2 o'clock. For the first time everyone in the building went into the cellar, except Sami and me of course. It was awful! We held onto each other in the corridor. The doors and fanlights were wide open. The whole building shook ...

We saw things we will never forget: flares so bright you could read a newspaper, tracer bullets, salvos of anti-aircraft fire and shrapnel falling in the rue des Ecoles and the rue Monge. Bits of metal rained down into the courtyard, and onto the fanlights of the kitchen and the bedroom.[7]

By 01:30 it was over. The bombers returned back to base, with a minimal loss of only six aircraft.

On the ground, however, the losses were immense. One thousand two hundred and sixty-five tons of high explosive had been dropped. The railway yards were pitted with craters; the rails were 'twisted like skis, locomotives thrown on top of each other in monstrous copulation'.[8] In the surrounding areas the devastation was terrible: 670 people had been killed – 372 of them in smashed buildings in Montmartre. Among the dead were a teacher from the boys' school on the rue Sainte-Isaure and her two children. Two pupils from the school were also killed, and most of the windows and doors in the school building were blown out.[9] Some were lucky: 4530 people in Montmartre were eventually pulled alive out of the debris, having made it safely to the cellars while their buildings collapsed on top of them in a night of noise, destruction and horror.[10]

Wednesday 26 April

Marshal Pétain came to Paris to honour those killed on the night of the 20th. Although Pétain had been the head of the French State since France capitulated to Germany in June 1940, in all that time he had not set foot in the capital. Three days earlier, Pétain had celebrated his eighty-eighth birthday. He was semi-senile and unable to keep much in his mind for very long, so his encounter with the Parisian public was planned down to the last detail. At 11:00, Pétain and his entourage arrived in front of Notre Dame, where a memorial Mass was said for the dead of the La Chapelle raid. Around four thousand people crowded into the Gothic cathedral, including Prime Minister Pierre Laval and SS General Carl Oberg. Then Pétain was driven the short distance to the

Hôtel de Ville; after a meal with various dignitaries and celebrities, he walked out onto a specially built dais in front of the building, where he was acclaimed by about ten thousand invited participants. The children in the front rows were particularly enthusiastic – they had been given the day off school.[11] An impressed adolescent wrote: 'The place de l'Hôtel de Ville and the rue de Rivoli are covered in people. People are grouped together, perched on the lampposts; others have clambered onto cars that are drowning in the crowd.'[12] Pétain made an anodyne speech and then was whisked off to visit injured victims, before leaving the city and returning to Vichy. That evening, Albert Grunberg, seething with rage in his attic refuge, wrote in his diary: 'The Radio Paris announcer, not bothering to disguise his joy and triumph, has just announced that the awful old man who goes by the name of Pétain is in Paris. Every time things are going badly for his Hun friends, he's always ready to help them ... Despite his best efforts since he surrendered, Pétain hadn't completely degraded himself; well, he's just gone the whole hog in coming to sully the soil of revolutionary Paris.'[13]

Two days later, Pétain made a radio broadcast in which he denounced the promised liberation of France by the Allies and praised 'the defence of the continent by Germany'. The old man was not always lucid, but when he was, he knew he was on the side of Germany. The next time Pétain visited Paris would be in July 1945 – to face charges of treason.

1

June–July: Hope

Tuesday 6 June, D-Day. For Benoîte Groult, a young woman whose hus-
band, a Resistance fighter, had recently died of his wounds, there is now a
reason to hope again: 'There are already 180,000 men on the Continent.
What an amazing exploit. It is a technical and human epic that already
resembles a legend. This time, it has happened; hope is no longer in
heaven, it is within our walls.'[1]

On D-Day the Allies assembled the largest invasion force ever, changing
the course of history and sending a wave of hope through the whole of
occupied Europe as Allied soldiers stepped onto French soil. But many
French men and women felt that hope was not enough – they wanted to
transform hope into action, into an uprising. In 1942, General de
Gaulle had proclaimed that 'National liberation cannot be separated
from national insurrection,' but two years later both the Free French
and the Allies were convinced that liberation should be the work of the
Allied troops, not the French population.[2] Although D-Day was accompanied by a coordinated surge of Resistance action aimed at German
supply lines, there was no national insurrection. The scattered spontaneous uprisings that did occur after D-Day were met with savagery by
the Germans, who were at first able to engage the Allies in a bloody
stalemate in northern Normandy and on the Cotentin peninsula. The
population of France soon realised that liberation was not a certainty,
and that Allied progress would be slow and hard.

Nevertheless, the invasion was a cause for rejoicing and optimism,
and it gave Parisian film-makers Albert Mahuzier and Gaston Madru the

confidence to record an amazing stunt. They were both members of a
Resistance 'escape line' that helped downed Allied airmen to escape
occupied Europe, and they decided to film some Allied airmen before
they were exfiltrated. With incredible audacity, Mahuzier and Madru
decided to film them in the streets of occupied Paris, to show the world
how the French were resisting the German occupation.[3] On a beautiful
June day, Madru, who had an official permit to make films, set up his
equipment on top of a car and followed Mahuzier and three airmen –
a Scottish fighter pilot called Stewart, and two Americans – as they
walked around a city crawling with German soldiers on leave. At
Trocadero, there was a large group of German troops relaxing on the
esplanade opposite the Eiffel Tower, so Mahuzier boldly walked his trio
among them; they were also filmed standing next to a smart German
officer who was wearing his ceremonial dagger, in front of a German
road-sign indicating the route to the front, and, most audaciously, by
one of the bookstalls on the banks of the Seine, where Stewart cheekily
took a copy of Hitler's *Mein Kampf* from a German officer. At the end of
an adrenalin-filled afternoon, they all had a well-deserved beer in a bar
on the boulevard Saint-Germain.[4]

*

On Wednesday 14 June 1944, four years to the day since the Germans
entered Paris, Charles de Gaulle visited the small Normandy town of
Bayeux, which had recently been liberated by the Allies. The Americans
and the British had been extremely wary about letting him make the
trip from the Free French headquarters in Algiers, for throughout the
war de Gaulle's relationship with the Allies had been stormy, and the
Free French leader's natural stubbornness had been strengthened by
his complete financial and military dependence on the Americans and
the British.[5] Against all expectations, de Gaulle received an overwhelming welcome. There was genuine joy on the faces of those who
crowded the streets to see the man who, up until then, had been nothing more than a voice on the BBC.[6] The very real support expressed by
the crowds of ordinary French men and women showed that de Gaulle
was seen by the bulk of the French population as their leader – for the

moment, at least. The rapturous welcome dissipated the Allies' dreams of bypassing the Free French, whom they still did not officially recognise as the Provisional Government of France. At the end of an eventful day, de Gaulle returned to Britain, leaving the Allies with much to ponder.

While de Gaulle was lapping up the applause in Bayeux, there was a furious row in Paris between the military leaders of the Resistance and the Parisian representatives of the Free French. Not for the first time, the three members of the Comité d'Action Militaire (Committee of Military Action – COMAC) were arguing with the Free French Délégué Militaire National (National Military Delegate), Jacques Delmas ('Chaban'), over who was in control of Resistance action. Chaban was an athletic, confident and good-looking 29-year-old, who had recently been promoted by de Gaulle to the rank of general despite being a civil servant by profession.[7] Urbane and suave, Chaban did his best to placate or neuter the three COMAC firebrands, but the two sides did not agree on what exactly should be done to fight the Germans, to what end, and under whose command.[8]

This time Chaban's task was extremely hard, as he had to explain that General Koenig, the commander of the Free French Army (under whose command the armed wing of the Resistance nominally came), had ordered the Resistance to avoid large-scale confrontation with the Germans and to limit guerrilla attacks as much as possible, because the Allied advance was progressing slowly.[9] Furthermore, there would be no more supplies parachuted to the Resistance until the August full moon – over six weeks away. The members of COMAC protested that these measures ran counter to their view that it was necessary to attack the Germans wherever possible. Chaban was sympathetic, but could do nothing, as everything was in the hands of London, which was the heart of the Allied war machine.

Tensions were further heightened because two of the three members of COMAC were politically suspect in the eyes of the Gaullists: 30-year-old insurance agent Maurice Kriegel (code name 'Valrimont') was close to the Communist Party, while 43-year-old Pierre Villon was a hardened Communist Party full-time worker (he did not bother with a code name). The third member of COMAC, Count Jean de Vogüé (code name 'Vaillant'), was hardly any better from a Free French point of view. Although he was a right-wing naval officer, aristocrat and businessman, de Vogüé was also in favour of an insurrection, but in the image of the French Revolution of 1789, not the Bolshevik Revolution of 1917.[10] The radical forces of the Resistance wanted a mass, popular insurrection to drive out the Germans and take power; the Gaullists wanted the Resistance and the population to act as passive participants in de Gaulle's triumphant entry into Paris. These two forces were on a collision course. However, even if all the Resistance leaders and rank-and-file had wanted to launch an uprising, the numbers simply did not add up. By the middle of August it was claimed there were around 35,000 Resistance fighters in the Paris region, but their armament was pitiful – 166 machine guns, 825 revolvers, 562 shotguns and rifles and only 192 grenades. There were neither heavy weapons nor explosives.[11] They would not be able to beat the German Army with such a weak arsenal.

Until the beginning of June, Pierre Lefaucheux, a staunch Gaullist, had been the Paris regional leader of the Resistance fighters – now known collectively as the Forces Françaises de l'Intérieur (FFI), or more popularly as 'les Fifis'.[12] Although the FFI were now considered to be part of the Free French Army, under the nominal leadership of General Koenig, their chain of command was entirely entwined with the structures of the Resistance inside France. In many ways, the FFI was the armed wing of the Resistance, or rather of the Resistance groups: each underground organisation retained control over its armed fighters while at the same time accepting the orders of the FFI command.

A shift in the balance of power within the FFI leadership of the Paris region occurred when Lefaucheux was arrested in June and was replaced by 36-year-old Henri Tanguy (code name 'Rol'), a communist who had fought with the International Brigades during the Spanish Civil War.[13] Given that the communists claimed to have about 20,000 fighters in the Paris region, this might have indicated that the Communist Party had a tight grip on all Resistance armed actions in the area.[14] However, none of the four local leaders of the Paris FFI was a communist, nor were any of the key members of Rol's staff.[15] Furthermore, 10,000 fighters in the region were linked to de Vogüé's group, Ceux de la Résistance ('The Men of the Resistance'), and constituted a counterweight to any potential communist coup.[16] In fact, the communists were never going to try to seize power – eight years earlier, in June 1936, the French communists had accepted that the massive strike wave that rocked the country would not lead to revolution, and by meekly following the twists and turns of the USSR as it made an alliance with Hitler in 1939, the party leadership had shown that it had no independence. Whatever rank and file members of the Communist Party might have believed or hoped, the party high-ups would not sanction a revolutionary movement or an attempt to seize power unless they had the approval of Moscow. When Roosevelt, Churchill and Stalin met at the Tehran conference of 1943, the Soviet leader had agreed that France would remain under Western control after the war, and his followers in France were wedded to Moscow's view of the world. Nevertheless, the existence of so many different political and military forces within the Paris Resistance meant that the Free French had a hard time trying to control events on the ground.

*

Shortly before dawn on 28 June, over a dozen armed Resistance fighters crept towards the Ministry of Information on the rue de Solférino at the western end of the boulevard Saint-Germain.[17] They disarmed the two police guards outside the ministry and cut the telephone wires to the building. Their target was the Vichy Minister of Information, Philippe Henriot, and their orders were to kidnap him. If that proved impossible, they were to kill him. Twenty-two-year-old Charles Gonard ('Morlot') and two comrades tricked their way into Henriot's first-floor apartment. But Henriot made a grab for their guns and was immediately shot; severely wounded, he fell to the floor and another burst of machine-gun fire killed him. With that the three men left; downstairs, their comrades asked, 'What happened?' 'He resisted, so I shot him,' said Morlot. The whole operation had taken thirteen minutes.[18]

Henriot's assassination – the first armed action in Paris for months – was a major coup for the Resistance. From the beginning of the year, Henriot had appeared twice a day on Radio Paris, spewing his anti-Semitic bile and attracting large audiences.[19] The Free French were so concerned about Henriot's influence that in their broadcasts on the BBC they had openly called for him to be killed. As the Free French comedian Pierre Dac put it in one programme: 'Monsieur Henriot, when you are dead you will perhaps have an inscription on your gravestone, and it will read: "Philippe Henriot, he died for Germany, killed by French bullets". And now, sleep well Monsieur Henriot . . . if you can.'[20]

The news of Henriot's death shocked the country, unnerving leading collaborators.[21] Fascist journalist Lucien Rebatet, who had been carrying a gun for protection, now supplemented his arsenal with a large Army revolver and a grenade: 'I won't let myself be gunned down empty-handed like poor old Henriot,' he wrote.[22] Although a section of the population was disturbed by the brutality of the assassination, many rejoiced.[23] Hidden in his attic room, Albert Grunberg wrote: 'Nothing but good news today. First of all, that scab Philippe Henriot was executed this morning by patriots . . . We'll never again hear Hitler's lackey spew his venom several times a day on all the Hun radios of Occupied France . . . To pay for his crimes against France, that bastard ought to have been roasted over a slow fire, but he can't complain as he was rubbed out in a second.'[24]

Vichy generated as much propaganda as they could from the assassination, plastering Paris with Henriot's portrait and the slogan: 'He told the truth – they killed him!' Even after his death, Henriot's broadcasts continued, as Radio Paris took to repeating his programmes *ad nauseam* – 'The traitor Henriot might be dead, but that doesn't stop him from continuing to give us earache,' grumbled Grunberg in his diary.[25] The French state paid for Henriot's funeral, which took place at Notre Dame and was celebrated by the Archbishop of Paris, Cardinal Suhard, in the presence of all the leading figures of occupation and collaboration except Pétain.[26]

Following Henriot's assassination, Vichy's fascist paramilitary organisation, the Milice, launched a frenzied wave of reprisals, murdering people associated with the Resistance all over the country.[27] Probably the most notable victim was Georges Mandel, who had been the Minister of the Interior in June 1940, and as a Jewish politician was a

Milice hate figure. At the beginning of July 1944, Mandel was transferred from a German prison to the Santé prison in the south of the
French capital. A mere three hours after he entered the Santé, Mandel
was taken away by Milice leader Max Knipping and a group of henchmen, who killed him in the Fontainebleau forest, south of Paris.[28]
Mandel had no illusions about his fate, as shown by his parting words to
the Santé prison governor: 'Dying is nothing. But it is sad to die before
seeing the country liberated.'[29]

In the past, the Resistance had refused to be intimidated by the
Germans' vicious campaign of reprisals, such as the murder of French
hostages following the assassination of German soldiers, even when
hundreds of Frenchmen were killed.[30] Similarly, the murder of Georges
Mandel did not alter the Resistance campaign against leading collaborators. Three days after the death of Mandel, on a slightly chilly Monday
morning, four young men left Paris in a car, headed for the western
suburb of Puteaux. They were members of a Communist Party hit-
squad, and their target was the collaborationist Mayor of Puteaux,
Georges Barthélemy, although they were not certain what their man
looked like. André Calvès recalled what happened when he went up to
his target:

'Are you Monsieur Barthélemy?' I asked. 'No,' he replied. He was
pale. My thoughts raced. Of course he'd say 'No'. 'Show me your
papers,' I said. At the same time, I thought to myself, 'Idiot – now
you've given him the chance to draw a gun. Watch out!' He put his
hand inside his jacket then looked as though he was about to run off.
His whole body seemed to tremble. It was only now that I could fire.
Without realising it, I emptied the whole magazine into him before he
fell to the ground. Théo got up from the bench nearby and fired, too,
from eight to ten metres. From the car, thirty metres away, our mates,
who were covering us, also opened fire ... Théo and I ran to the car.
I loaded another magazine and gave everyone a cigarette to calm
their nerves. Outside we could see people's noses pressed up against
nearby windows. In the newspaper the next day they said that 'one of
the killers calmly handed out cigarettes after the murder'. I was anything but calm![31]

The assassination of Barthélemy was followed by another attack: on 13 July, in the southern suburb of Thiais, Resistance fighters shot two German soldiers, injuring one and killing the other.[32] This resurgence of Resistance activity in Paris alarmed the Germans – it seemed that the Allied bridgehead in Normandy was giving the Resistance renewed confidence. Walter Dreizner, a rank-and-file German soldier based in the French capital, wrote glumly in his diary: 'Hundreds of fetching Parisian women zip though the city on their smart bicycles. Their flimsy clothes float behind them like flags. The cafés are full, the theatres are full. Paris is alive ... But Paris is increasingly becoming a trap for the Germans. There are more and more assassinations. Soldiers in uniform are in constant danger. The enemy is invisible. He is waiting in ambush.'[33]

*

Before the war, 14 July had been the day of national celebration, marking the anniversary of the storming of the Bastille in 1789 with dancing and fireworks. From 1940 the festival had been banned by the Germans, along with the French flag and the singing of the 'Marseillaise'. Now Bastille Day was to be a public holiday again, although the motivation was to save money on salaries, and all public celebrations remained illegal.[34] Not that there was much to celebrate: the massive commercial dislocation caused by the war in Normandy and the incessant bombing raids on the railways were beginning to affect food supplies. Berthe Auroy wrote in her diary, mixing infuriation and good humour: 'Out of 10 grocery shops, nine are closed, and the tenth is more or less empty. NOTHING TO SELL! Except, here and there, on a small shelf, a bunch of parsley or fresh mint ... We have been officially warned: Parisians will experience days of famine. Without the railways, we can no longer expect to receive the tons of vegetables they need to feed the capital ... And then there's the cruellest of all the hardships that could be inflicted on the French: wine – there's no more wine getting through!'[35]

In response to such complaints, the Comité Parisien de la Libération (Parisian Liberation Committee – CPL), which grouped together all Resistance groups in the region and endeavoured to lead them, decided to organise demonstrations on 14 July to protest against the occupation.

They even called for 'major acts of sabotage and executions of traitors and Huns' in and around Bastille Day.[36] This had the support of the national leadership of the Resistance, the Conseil National de la Résistance (CNR – National Resistance Council), although not all its component parts supported the idea. On 7 July, Daniel Mayer of the Socialist Party made a bold prediction: 'the CNR will come out of this severely weakened: either the call will not be followed and the CNR will look foolish ... or it will be heeded and the tragic and pointless reprisals and massacres that result will hit the best fighters.'[37]

In fact, the 14 July protests were a huge success for the Paris Resistance and a pleasant surprise for those like Mayer who continually warned of the dangers of reprisals whenever action was proposed. Hundreds of people demonstrated in the suburbs of Nanterre, Clichy, Puteaux and Villeneuve-Saint-Georges, while forbidden tricolour flags were hoisted in most towns – in the northern suburb of Aulnay-sous-Bois around forty people marched to the war memorial, carrying flags and singing the 'Marseillaise', before the German police fired shots and arrested two people. All over the capital people wore red, white and blue, showing their opposition to the occupation and their hope for the future. They marched from Belleville up the steep hill to the Pyrénées Métro station, they marched at the Place de l'Etoile, they marched around the Latin Quarter.[38] Tens of thousands of people took part, far surpassing anything seen in the capital since the beginning of the occupation.[39] Something important was happening.

The Latin Quarter demonstration made a strong impression on one man even though he could not participate. Albert Grunberg wrote in his diary:

I was pacing up and down in my kitchen when I heard the sounds of the 'Marseillaise' being sung by hundreds and hundreds of people. Then I head the chant 'Bread! Bread!' It had to be a patriotic demonstration. Around 17:00, M. Chabanaud [a neighbour] came and brought me one of the tens of thousands of leaflets that had been thrown in the air by the demonstrators ... Mme Oudard [the concierge] came to see me, draped with a huge tricolour flag, like most of the passers-by. She told me it had been magnificent and that there had been demonstrations all over Paris. Policemen followed the demonstrators and warned them when the Milice threatened to get too close.[40]

The sympathetic attitude of the Parisian police was also noted by the Resistance.[41] When the police turned up at the Belleville demonstration, protestors started chanting 'Police, join us!' and, at a rally at the picturesque place de la Contrescarpe in the 5th arrondissement, the police sang the 'Marseillaise'.[42] Even though the demonstrations were illegal, very few people were arrested. This was an important develop-ment, showing that the police, who for four years had been loyal servants of the occupation, were starting to waver.[43] However, not all sec-tions of the police were so benign. Shortly before the Belleville demonstration began, members of the Brigades Spéciales, the police anti-Resistance squad, shot dead the trade union leader Yves Toudic and severely wounded one of his comrades.[44]

One the most significant demonstrations took place in Choisy-le-Roi, part of the string of working-class suburbs that stretch south-east of Paris along the Seine and the railway lines. Demonstrators from these towns – Ivry, Vitry, Choisy-le-Roi, Thiais and Villeneuve-Saint-Georges, many of them railway workers – converged on the statue of Rouget de Lisle, the author of the 'Marseillaise', in Choisy. In a daring move, the local Resistance group led the demonstration, driving a car carrying a captured German heavy machine gun. As the march approached the statue, German troops opened fire and arrested a number of demon-strators, including several railway workers.[45] The demonstration dissolved into chaos, as marchers scattered and ran through nearby gardens.[46] Over the next week, as it became clear that many railway workers had been arrested during the demonstration, unrest spread through the railway depots, culminating in strikes at the Ivry and Vitry railway workshops on Wednesday 19 July.[47] Workers at both sites returned to work only when management promised to get the men released. But despite further strikes and meetings addressed by armed speakers from the Resistance, the men remained in prison.

On 23 July there was a seven-hour strike at the Villeneuve-Saint-Georges depot as railway workers demanded the release of the prisoners. When a delegation of seven strikers went to see management to discuss the issue, they were all arrested by the Gestapo, increasing tension throughout the Paris railway network. Four days later, on 27 July, at the Noisy-le-Sec depot in the north-eastern suburbs, the local Resistance took over the canteen and held a 500-strong meeting, protected by thirteen armed men, which led to an afternoon strike in support of the immediate needs of the railway workers (food, clothing and housing). This series of strikes and disputes that rolled around the railways in the Paris region was yet another sign of an imminent shift in power. For the previous four years, the Germans and their French collaborators had been able to dominate every aspect of life. That was beginning to change, but there was a long way to go: the men from Vitry and from Villeneuve, along with thirty-six other railway workers, were still in prison nearly a month later.[48]

Prison could be a very dangerous place. On the evening of 14 July, a riot broke out at the Santé prison. The reasons behind the disturbance are still unclear, but no Resistance prisoners were involved. The men of the paramilitary Milice quelled the rebellion with their usual bloody and vindictive enthusiasm. The next day, after rudimentary and profoundly unjust 'trials', they executed twenty-eight prisoners.[49] The fascist Milice were growing daily more confident, more independent of state control, and more vicious.

*

As the 14 July demonstrations took place in Paris and the suburbs, the century's greatest artist was at work in his attic studio on the rue des Grands Augustins, in the heart of the capital. Pablo Picasso positioned a jug, a glass and a lemon on a table, and examined them in the light that came through the window. Over the next twelve days, the 62-year-old Picasso painted eight versions of exactly the same composition, although mid-way through the series he sliced the lemon in half. The paintings were all in his cubist style, breaking the forms up into their fundamental lines, showing shadows and textures as huge angular blocks of colour. Then, on 27 July, Picasso abruptly turned his attention to a tomato plant that was growing in the studio, and produced two exquisite drawings in blue crayon, the first delicate and naturalistic, the second exploring the shapes of the leaves, revealing abstract forms.

This was the studio in which Picasso had painted his anti-war masterpiece, *Guernica*, in 1937. He lived in the French capital throughout the occupation, untroubled by the Germans despite his left-wing views, quietly producing around two thousand works, none of which was explicitly about the war, suggesting that he was not engaged by events.[50] Although Picasso did not paint the occupation in any literal form, as he said shortly afterwards: 'I have no doubt that the war is in these paintings I have done.'[51] As July wore into August, his work began to change as the situation in Paris crept into his art.

*

On Thursday 20 July, deep in the forest of north-east Poland, Adolf Hitler was discussing the state of the war with some of his closest military advisors, including Colonel Claus von Stauffenberg and General Walter Warlimont. Shortly before 13:00, von Stauffenberg left the room; Warlimont described what happened next: 'In a flash the map room became a scene of stampede and destruction. At one moment was to be seen a set of men and things which together formed a focal point of world events; at the next there was nothing but wounded men groaning, the acrid smell of burning, and charred fragments of maps and papers fluttering in the wind.'[52]

Seeing the pall of smoke rising from the shattered building, the man who had planted the bomb, von Stauffenberg, assumed that Operation Valkyrie had succeeded and that Hitler was dead. He sped to Berlin, where the next phase of the coup was to take place involving important sections of the German army.[53] In fact Hitler had been only slightly wounded and as that news came through, the coup in Berlin collapsed.[54] But although the *putsch* failed – Hitler survived, the war continued and most of the conspirators were executed – in one place, for a few brief hours, the coup succeeded.

Shortly before 16:00, news of the bomb attack reached Paris via a coded telephone call. Walter Bargatzky, a young Army lawyer who was part of the plot, grabbed a bewildered colleague and urged him: 'Always think back on this moment – it is the most important in the whole war.'[55] General Stülpnagel, the military commander of occupied France and one of the plot leaders, told his officers that the SS had carried out a coup in Berlin – this was the cover story that had been agreed in order to dupe Hitler loyalists. Stülpnagel then instructed Lieutenant-General von Boineburg, the military commander of Paris, to arrest all the members of the SS in the city. Anyone who resisted was to be shot.[56] Bargatzky described how the mutiny was set in motion: 'Stülpnagel, three floors below me, is handing out the orders that have been ready for months. The telephone connection with the Reich is to be interrupted, and the functionaries of the security service, down to its lowest officials, are to be arrested.'[57]

Shortly afterwards, teenager Micheline Bood was at home in her mother's apartment overlooking the rue Faubourg Saint-Honoré. Intrigued by the sound of German being spoken in hushed tones on the street below, she and her mother went to their balcony:

> We saw a long convoy of lorries, with no lights, going from the rue du Cirque towards the avenue Matignon; then we saw loads of German soldiers getting out, taking care not to make too much noise ... We thought 'yet another raid', but instead the soldiers formed up in single file while their officers continued to give orders in lowered voices. They skirted round the place Beauvau before heading off towards the rue des Saussaies with fixed bayonets, their bodies hunched as though they were preparing to attack.[58]

Shortly afterwards, a surprised French policeman noted that tanks were surrounding the SS building on avenue Foch: 'a Gestapo officer turned up on a bicycle; straight away a German soldier pointed his machine gun at him, while another removed the officer's pistol. The officer was then taken off to a nearby German lorry, which contained other members of the Gestapo ... Several lorries containing the arrested Germans drove off down the boulevard Lannes, to an unknown destination.'[59] In less than an hour, over 1200 Germans had been arrested, including the head of the SS in France, General Carl Oberg, who was beside himself with rage as troops burst into his office.[60]

The Supreme Field Commander in France, Field Marshal von Kluge, had known of the plot for some time, but had carefully refused to endorse it. Wanting to be certain of success, he would support the coup only if Hitler were dead.[61] At around 18:00 von Kluge swept into his headquarters at La Roche-Guyon, a beautiful castle on a bend in the Seine mid-way between Paris and Rouen. He was told first that Hitler had been killed, then that the assassination attempt had failed and that the Führer was alive. Faced with this confusion, von Kluge immediately summoned von Stülpnagel from Paris. By the time von Stülpnagel arrived at 20:00, von Kluge was certain that Hitler was alive and he began furiously distancing himself from any involvement.[62] Lieutenant-Colonel von Hofacker, von Stauffenberg's cousin and the lynchpin of the Paris conspiracy, made an impassioned plea to von Kluge: 'Field Marshal, your word and honour are under fire. In your hands lies the fate of millions of Germans and the honour of the Army.'[63] But von Kluge would not budge and refused to be involved in any way. When asked one final time if he would support the coup, von Kluge replied – 'Yes, if the pig were dead!'[64]

The conspirators knew that was the end of the matter: without von Kluge's support, the Paris *putsch* would collapse.[65] Even if the circumstances were dire, the niceties still had to be observed, so Kluge ordered dinner to be served. As von Kluge's aide later recalled: 'They ate by candlelight, as if they sat in a house just visited by death.'[66] When a dejected von Stülpnagel left shortly before 23:00, von Kluge relieved him of his duties and gave him a final piece of advice that both men would have done well to follow: 'Swap your uniform for civvies and disappear!'[67]

Once von Stülpnagel was back in Paris, he set about undoing the *putsch*, ordering his officers to release the SS men. At around 02:00 the next morning there was a tense meeting between von Stülpnagel and his erstwhile prisoner Oberg, in the presence of the German ambassador to France, Otto Abetz. A few floors above them, Walter Bargatzky prayed for events to take a different course: 'Even now, everything could have been saved. The general would only have had to rise and shoot Oberg and Abetz beside him. But a fatal quality hampers him: his intelligence. Clearly, too clearly, he sees thousands shrinking back from the risk, as Kluge did ... And the same resignation inhibits us from going down to the general from where we are, on the fourth floor.'[68]

And so the *putsch* came to an end, with a whimper. To reassure the rank-and-file troops and to maintain a veneer of German unity, it was agreed that the attempted coup would be described as 'an exercise'. The erstwhile enemies toasted the agreement in champagne and a jovial Oberg left the Hôtel Raphael in the early hours.[69] Von Stülpnagel was recalled to Berlin the next day, his fate sealed. On the journey back, he attempted suicide but succeeded only in blinding himself. He was hanged in Plötzensee prison on 30 August.

The next day, the Parisian press parroted the Nazi lie that the troops had been on an exercise. The Resistance was not fooled, however, and on 22 July a Socialist Party leaflet described the events in Paris under the headline 'The disintegration of Nazism – Wehrmacht against Gestapo'.[70] Even Albert Grunberg, hiding in his attic on the rue des Ecoles, knew what had really happened – more or less. His concierge had hurried to see him, proud to be the first to tell him of the 'pitched battle' that had taken place between the Gestapo and the Wehrmacht. No matter how exaggerated this gossip might have been, for Grunberg and for many others, this remarkable event was a sign of hope: for a few hours, the Nazi machine had been at war with itself.

*

The chaotic situation in the German ranks that followed the attempt on Hitler's life raised the question of what would happen when German control of the city finally disintegrated. In Algiers, Free French agent Francis-Louis Closon outlined three possible scenarios: fighting between Allied and German troops in the city ('very unlikely'), gradual withdrawal of the Germans from Paris coupled with action by guerrilla groups, or a straightforward German collapse in the face of an insurrection. Above all, Closon was concerned about how the Free French could control the population once an insurrection had begun. He outlined the Gaullists' nightmare scenario in a series of clipped phrases: 'Revolutionary ferment. Highly charged atmosphere. Uprising of the suburbs and possible anti-communist reactions ... Highly probable occupation of all big factories, the workers will refuse to obey collaborationist bosses or management.'[71]

For the moment, however, the Germans remained firmly in control and none of these issues was pressing. On 27 July, the Gestapo arrested two men at La Muette Métro station in the 16th arrondissement. One of them, Alain de Beaufort, tried to flee. Shots rang out; he was wounded in the foot and captured. De Beaufort's arrest was a serious blow to the Resistance – he was in charge of all air drops in the northern zone. His comrade, André Rondenay, was an even bigger catch for the Germans – for three months he had been the Military Delegate for the northern zone, one rank below Chaban in the Free French hierarchy in occupied France. When he was captured, Rondenay was on his way to meet Chaban; if he had been followed, the Germans could have made a clean sweep of the Free French military leadership in Paris.[72] Both de Beaufort and Rondenay were taken off to Fresnes prison, where they were tortured. Two years earlier, Rondenay had been a prisoner in Colditz; after repeatedly attempting to escape, he was transferred to Lübeck, from where he successfully escaped to London, following an amazing journey across Nazi Germany, through occupied France, Spain and Portugal. There would be no escape from Fresnes.[73]

*

For over a year, 32-year-old SS officer Hauptsturmführer Alois Brunner had been commander of the Drancy internment camp for Jews in the north-east suburbs of Paris. Under Brunner's command, the Drancy camp plumbed new depths of depravity. He insisted that all food and medical supplies for the inmates should come from the Jewish community itself, through a stooge organisation set up by Vichy, the Union Générale des Israélites de France (UGIF – General Union of French Jews). The UGIF collaborated with Brunner and his goons in tracking down family members of Drancy internees and bringing them to the camp; if they did not surrender, Brunner tortured their loved ones.[74] As a former UGIF leader put it after the war: 'Brunner ... is the very model of the degenerate Nazi with the bearing of a mad sadist.'[75]

On the evening of 21 July, Brunner found that he was still several hundred people short of his monthly deportation quota to the death camps in Germany. So he sent his men to raid six UGIF orphanages, arresting 215 children; the next night they picked up another 27 infants and also arrested around 30 adults working for the UGIF.[76] All of these people were taken to Drancy to be put on a rail convoy to Germany. When the train left Drancy for Auschwitz on 31 July, it carried 1,300 people, including 327 children. As soon as they arrived 726 people were gassed; only 209 survived the camp and returned to France.[77] The youngest person on the train was a baby called Alain Blumberg. He was two weeks old. He did not survive.

2

Early August: Breakout

Tuesday 1 August. Pierre Bourdan, a journalist embedded with the Free French Army, writes: 'Over the past four years, some of us have had brief contacts with France. These furtive visits were almost painful, mere fleeting landfalls from a boat moored offshore. But tonight we truly return to France. In the cool night, the sea air accompanies us across the fields of Normandy; although we cannot see much in the darkness, the smell of France is reassuring, an unmistakable sign that we are home.'[1]

Early in the morning of 1 August, soldiers of the Free French 2nd Armoured Division or 'Deuxième Division Blindée' (2e DB) stepped onto 'Utah Beach' in Normandy. Although some French troops had been involved in the D-Day landings nearly two months earlier, this was the first time that a unit of the Free French Army landed on home soil. They were accompanied by the Rochambeau medical group, composed primarily of female ambulance drivers, nicknamed 'Les Rochambelles'. Lieutenant Suzanne Torrès spent the voyage across the Channel smoking cigarettes, filing her nails and losing substantial of amounts of money at poker, before passing the night and much of the next day moored off the coast, watching vehicles being unloaded in a swelling sea. Then, after hours of waiting, the moment came. As Torrès recalled: 'Night is falling and, with queasy stomachs, we finally set foot on the sand of "Utah" Beach. Instantly, our feeling of joy overwhelms everything else ... it is the kind of moment that occurs rarely in your life. Before jumping into my vehicle, I scoop up some sand and press it against my cheek ... I could almost eat it!'[2]

The 2e DB was not just another set of soldiers. None of them knew it, but they had been chosen to be the first Free French troops to enter Paris. The 2e DB had been transferred from Morocco to England at the end of April 1944, and assigned to General Patton's Third US Army. In other words, although this was a 15,000-strong Free French unit, commanded by General Leclerc (hence 'the Leclerc Division'), it was part of the US Army. Its orders, weaponry and supplies – even its uniforms – were American.[3] The division commander's real name was not Leclerc but Philippe de Hauteclocque – like many Resistance fighters and Free French soldiers, he had adopted a *nom de guerre* to protect his family in France.[4] Tall and gaunt with a toothbrush moustache, Leclerc was a 41-year-old aristocrat and career officer who walked with a cane – an affectation rather than a medical requirement – and was utterly loyal to de Gaulle, whom he joined in June 1940. The men and women of the 2e DB shared that loyalty. A small number of them had escaped from France to join de Gaulle; others were in Britain when France surrendered. But the vast majority were from France's African colonies – either white settlers or indigenous black or Arab men who had joined up as the group fought its way across North Africa.[5] After their first major success at Kufra, deep in the southern Libyan desert in 1941, Leclerc and his men swore a solemn oath not to lay down their arms until the French tricolour flag flew over Strasbourg cathedral.[6] Most of these men had never set foot in France, let alone Strasbourg, yet the symbolic power of the French Empire, the loyalty it inspired among sections of the indigenous populations, and their certainty that they were French, had led them to join up and risk their lives.

Although the black and Arab men of the French colonies were convinced that they were just as French as de Gaulle or Leclerc, the Allies did not agree. At the beginning of the year, US Major General Walter Bedell Smith, Chief of Staff at the Supreme Headquarters of the Allied Expeditionary Force (SHAEF), had insisted that only 'white personnel' should be involved in the liberation of Paris, even if it meant ethnically cleansing the Leclerc Division.[7] In the end, the thousands of North African soldiers were not actually removed from the 2e DB, nor were 400 Spaniards, many of them exiled republicans, who had joined up to continue the fight against fascism after the end of the Spanish Civil

War.[8] But there were no French West African soldiers among the thousands of 2e DB men who landed on Utah Beach at the beginning of August. Furthermore, all the US soldiers who were eventually involved in the liberation of Paris were from white regiments (the US Army systematically segregated its units at this time).[9] The freedoms the Allies brought to France were not yet for everyone.

In the weeks following D-Day, men and machines poured endlessly onto the Normandy beaches. By the end of July the Allied armies were nearly 1 million strong. New ports and roads were built to maintain the flow to the front, but the fighting was hard and progress was slow. However, at the end of July the Allies launched a massive land and air offensive against the German lines and, on the evening of 31 July, US troops finally succeeded in taking Avranches south of the Cotentin peninsula, opening the way eastwards to Paris. Field Marshal von Kluge confided to his colleagues: 'Gentlemen, this breakthrough means for us and the German people the beginning of a decisive and bitter end. I see no remaining possibility of halting this ongoing attack.'[10] Von Kluge was right. Within a little more than a week, the Allies had progressed 200 km and had liberated Le Mans, approximately halfway to Paris from the Normandy beaches. The speed of the advance kindled new hope in the hearts of the Parisians, who were finding life increasingly harsh. On Sunday 6 August Protestant priest Marc Boegner wrote in his diary: 'New restrictions: we will have gas only from 12:15 to 12:30 at lunchtime and in the evening from 19:20 to 20:30. The Métro will be shut from 11:00 to 15:00. Working hours will have to be adapted to this new situation. The week that is beginning will undoubtedly be one of the most extraordinary in history. The week that has just finished has left us stunned. The Americans have advanced 300 km with their tanks and the Russians have taken the war onto German soil.'[11]

*

In the first week of August the military situation in the west grew increasingly serious for the Germans. The Allies pushed eastwards, then turned north at Alençon, beginning a pincer movement towards the town of Falaise, with the aim of trapping the German armies in

Normandy. Caught in what became known as the 'Falaise pocket', surrounded on all sides by overwhelming forces and with no air support, the Germans soon found their food, ammunition and fuel supplies rapidly dwindling. Unless they could find a way to escape, they were doomed.

A few dozen kilometres to the south, away from the fighting, Colonel David Bruce, London head of the US intelligence agency the Office of Strategic Services (OSS – the forerunner of the CIA), was setting up his headquarters in Le Mans. Bruce had found the town in good shape: the buildings were undamaged, food supplies were plentiful and the population was in good spirits. Because farmers had no way of getting their produce to the Paris region, they were happy to supply the townsfolk of Le Mans and the thousands of Allied soldiers with some excellent food and wine. Two things struck Colonel Bruce that day. Driving into Le Mans he was amazed by the scale of the Allied supply lines – fuel, ammunition and rations were continuously transported along the road, together with engineers to repair infrastructure and communication lines. The logistics of the Allied advance were mind-boggling. For example, every day the 16,000 men of the US 3rd Armoured Division – less than 2 per cent of the total number of Allied soldiers in Normandy – required 60,000 gallons of fuel, 35 tons of food and an even greater tonnage of ammunition.[12] All this had to be brought from the landing beaches up to the front line, creating the elongated supply lines that Bruce noted in his diary. The other event he recorded was more sombre. He learned that six of his French intelligence agents had headed for Paris but had been arrested by the Germans. Five of them were interrogated and executed. The sixth agent, a young man in his mid-twenties, managed to escape back to Le Mans, but was profoundly shocked and disturbed by his experience. Directly or indirectly, Bruce had been responsible for all these people. Three days later, he was shown graphic evidence of the fate of his five agents: 'I saw the photographs and they were horrible. They had all, including the woman, been shot through the groin and the stomach.'[13]

*

On Monday 7 August, General Dietrich von Choltitz was ushered into Hitler's presence. Von Choltitz (pronounced 'Kol-titz') was a short and plump 49-year-old, with thin lips and a small mouth – US military historian Martin Blumenson said that he 'looked like a nightclub comedian'.[14] Just two days earlier von Choltitz had been on the Western Front, trying to get his men to hold the line as the US Army crashed its way out of the Cotentin peninsula. Then, out of the blue, he received orders to cross the continent and meet Hitler in Poland. Von Choltitz was not a member of the Nazi Party and had never seen the Führer in person. The atmosphere at Hitler's headquarters was tense, von Choltitz told a colleague: 'One was looked at very suspiciously ... there was an SS man behind every tree.'[15] The Führer turned out not to be the brilliant leader portrayed by Nazi propaganda, but rather 'a fat, broken-down old man' still suffering from the physical and mental effects of the 20 July assassination attempt.[16] As von Choltitz told some of his German comrades: 'You couldn't shake hands properly. His paws were all swollen and septic. He then started making me a forty-five-minute speech. I had to bite my tongue to keep myself from bursting.'[17]

During the interview – or monologue – Hitler instructed von Choltitz to take command of Paris and to transform the city from a pleasure-dome for troops on leave into a garrison prepared to fight to the end.[18] The Führer's written orders stated: 'All non-essential German administrative services and all individuals who are not required to be in Paris should be evacuated as soon as possible ... The territory of Greater Paris must be protected against any act of rebellion, of subversion or sabotage.'[19] With that, von Choltitz was dismissed and dispatched by train to Paris. He had been given unprecedented command over both Wehrmacht and SS troops, as well as over all parts of the Nazi Party, along with the powers of the commander of a besieged fort. The message could not have been clearer: von Choltitz was to defend the city as a vital military base. He had been chosen for this task because he was prepared to carry out even the most difficult orders. In a secret conversation with a colleague, von Choltitz confessed what he had done during the Crimean campaign of 1941–2: 'The worst job I ever carried out – which however I carried out with great consistency – was the liquidation of the Jews. I carried out this order *down to the very last detail.*'[20]

While admitting his role in the extermination of the Jews in the Crimea, von Choltitz claimed that he also knew all about the 20 July plot in advance – the main participants were 'all friends of mine', he boasted.[21] His fellow officers recognised these contradictions. They said he was 'two-faced; when with Nazis he is "150%" for Hitler and when with anti-Nazis he is all against him'. Worse, they said he was 'a thoroughly uncongenial fellow ... he played the big man ... a cunning fellow ... sly'.[22] Sometimes, their opinions of him verged on the ridiculous, as when one German officer stated: 'I haven't seen him since we were at school together and nobody liked him then ... He used to be the dirtiest little pig in the whole school. He was smelly. I know everyone used to say: "Go away, you stink." He was filthy and lazy to the last degree.'[23] The best that was said about von Choltitz by his comrades was that he was 'a nice fellow; but, as a soldier, a dud'.[24] Perhaps the most perceptive view came from an Allied officer who observed him closely: 'a cinema-type German officer, fat, coarse, bemonocled and inflated with a tremendous sense of his own importance'.[25]

Hitler not only changed the Paris command, he also ordered a new tactic on the battlefield. Early in the morning of 7 August, German forces on the Western Front launched a massive attack to retake the town of Mortain, thirty-five kilometres east of Avranches. Hitler's order deployed his usual crazed rhetoric and showed a typically poor grasp of military reality: 'Continue the attack recklessly to the sea, regardless of the risk ... The greatest daring, determination and imagination must give wings to all echelons of command. Each and every man must believe in victory.'[26]

The offensive failed after only two days, at the cost of thousands of lives and the destruction of nearly a hundred German tanks. Any sensible commander would have drawn the same conclusion as Field Marshal von Kluge had done a week earlier, and would have ordered a rapid retreat to safety. Hitler carried on regardless, wasting men and materiel. Less than three weeks later, Lieutenant-General Elfeldt complained about 'the madness at Mortain of thrusting towards Avranches with six Panzer Divisions which weren't Panzer Divisions any longer. It was just madness. The High Command wouldn't listen to our reports on the strength of our forces.'[27] For Hitler, the cause of the inevitable failure of the Mortain offensive was simple: 'the attack failed because Field Marshal von Kluge wanted it to fail,' he spat.[28] The Führer had given von Choltitz the task of defending Paris against the oncoming Allied armies; that encounter was getting closer.

*

For weeks, the Resistance leaders had been complaining about Chaban, the National Military Delegate – the Resistance had not received enough weapons from the Allies, and they felt Chaban was responsible. On 9 August, an increasingly frustrated Rol wrote a bleak letter to COMAC, (the Resistance military leadership), and to the Free French Military Delegation: 'As far as Paris is concerned, I am unable to ensure the security of the main services – water, gas, electricity, telegraph, telephone, transport, food supplies, etc. Because the FFI has no weapons, the Parisian population is at serious risk from the Huns who will inevitably fall back on Paris. The FFI and all patriots are determined to fight with all their force. They will take weapons from the enemy. The question is, will the Military Delegation give them weapons?'[29] At one level, this was a fair criticism: Chaban had control of all supply drops, and he consistently refused to press London to deliver more arms for the Resistance. In reality, even if Chaban had done everything that Rol wanted, the result would probably have been the same. The Free French and the Allies had long ago agreed to strictly control the supply of light weapons to the Resistance, for fear that those weapons might be used not only against the Germans. They were particularly suspicious of Resistance forces that might be influenced by the Communist Party.[30] When General Koenig had asked the Allies to drop 40,000 Sten guns to the Resistance in the Paris region, the British Foreign Office blocked the request because 'there will always be the temptation to put them to mischievous uses should political passions be inflamed when the war is over.'[31]

Chaban's civilian counterpart was Alexandre Parodi, de Gaulle's 'Délégué Général' (General Delegate) in occupied France who was a minister in the Provisional Government. Unlike the dashing Chaban, Parodi was an austere, balding 43-year-old civil servant who had spent the whole of the occupation in Paris, planning for the moment when the Free French would set up their government in the capital.[32] He had to deal with the operators of the Comité Parisien de la Libération (CPL), the political leadership of the Resistance in the Paris region.[33] Parodi's task was made more difficult because Paris was both the capital, and therefore the focus of all Free French preparations for taking power, and also a city with its own local government and a centuries-old tradition of revolution that was at odds with the Gaullist project. Half the members of the CPL were members of or sympathetic to the Communist Party – the President of the CPL, 31-year-old André Tollet, was a communist trade unionist, and there were also representatives from both the Communist Party and the Front National, the broadly based Resistance organisation the Communist Party had set up in 1941 (there is no connection with the modern French far-right party of the same name).[34] As a supposedly neutral civil servant, Parodi's duty was to carry out the instructions of de Gaulle's Provisional Government in Algiers. Whenever the views of the government clashed with those of the Parisian Resistance (which was often), Parodi had to find a way through the thicket of opposition and ensure that de Gaulle's will prevailed.

At the beginning of August, however, Parodi found himself on the same side as the Resistance and on a collision course with Algiers. In a firm message to his Free French comrades, Parodi criticised their policy of trying to break COMAC's control over the FFI fighters, noting that this would divide those who were loyal to Algiers from those who followed the Resistance. Above all, like so many Free French plans drawn up from afar, it was completely impractical. 'In non-liberated areas,' Parodi told his comrades, 'COMAC is the only body that can really lead the FFI.'[35] Algiers made no reply. The next day, Parodi sent yet another message to Algiers on his debate with the CPL over 'who should lead operations in the liberation of Paris'. Parodi's message closed with a plea to his comrades on the other side of the Mediterranean: 'You must give us your confidence and your support in this affair so that we can come to an agreement and the Government's authority can be maintained. Could you please send us instructions?'[36] Again there was no reply.

Two days later, Parodi met with the CPL and they all finally agreed that the CPL 'alone has the authority to lead the national insurrection

in the region and receive the Allies in Paris'.[37] Parodi sent an enthusiastic account of this decision to Algiers ('we have completely settled the
problem of the seizure of power in Paris') and for once there was an
immediate response from the Minister of the Interior, the veteran
Resistance leader Emmanuel d'Astier.[38] The minister was scathing: 'The
General asked me to communicate his surprise regarding the content of
the telegram concerning the liberation of Paris ... There can be no
question of divesting ourselves of any power.'[39]

Had he received this reply, Parodi would no doubt have gone dutifully back to the CPL for yet another round of arguments, and might
not have later behaved as he did. But he never got the message. At the
beginning of August the complex communications web between Paris,
London and Algiers collapsed, for reasons that are unknown. In truth,
communication was always a source of tension, because of the delays
inherent in the system – coded messages from Paris were broadcast to
Britain; they were then decoded and recoded in London, and finally
sent on to Algiers by telegram, in batches that could represent over a
week's correspondence from France. This produced a frustrating delay:
a message sent from France could take at least a week to reach Algiers.
Messages from Algiers or London, however, were immediately received
in Paris, reinforcing the impression in Paris that those safe in Britain
and North Africa were engaged in a one-way conversation, not listening
to those on the ground.[40]

During the communications problem that occurred in August, trans-
missions from Paris got through as normal – that is, with the habitual
delays – but no messages were received in the capital for at least two
weeks.[41] Even de Gaulle's secret instructions to Parodi, sent on 31 July,
were never received. The Free French leader had said: 'Always speak
loud and clear in the name of the State. The numerous acts of our glorious Resistance are the means by which the nation fights for its
salvation. The State is above all these manifestations and actions.'[42] In
fact, this piece of Gaullist rhetoric would have been useless for dealing
with the razor-sharp factional minds that Parodi encountered in some
Resistance meetings. He was better off on his own.

*

On 7 August, Colonel Rol issued an order to all FFI fighters in the Paris region, beginning with a perceptive description of the military and political situation in the capital:

> The main characteristic of the Allied offensive is that the Wehrmacht is completely unable to resist in the current theatre of operations. In the Paris region, there is nothing to indicate that the enemy has decided to carry out a determined resistance; but this situation could change with the arrival of German troops in the Parisian basin and it could transform the area into a zone of deadly combat. The Allied offensive, the precarious situation of the Wehrmacht and the recent events of 14 July 1944 all indicate that we are on the eve of an insurrection in our region.[43]

That evening, Rol's position appeared to get support from a most unlikely quarter: General de Gaulle himself. Broadcasting from Algiers, de Gaulle said: 'Everyone can fight. Everyone must fight. Those who are able should join the FFI. Everyone else, wherever they may be, can help our fighters. In the countryside, in the factory, in the workshop, in the office, at home, in the street, whether you are imprisoned, deported or a prisoner of war, you can always weaken the enemy or prepare that which will weaken him.'[44]

In Paris, Chaban and Parodi were surprised by de Gaulle's speech, which suggested that the population should immediately go on strike and join the FFI in fighting the Germans. With the Allied armies racing towards Paris, everything that the two Free French delegates were working towards looked as if it would actually happen – so long as their actions were coordinated with those of de Gaulle. But this latest speech could wreck everything, by encouraging the very people that Chaban and Parodi had spent their time trying to restrain. Indeed, even some members of the Delegation were beginning to think that an insurrection would be a good idea, as shown by a letter sent to Emmanuel d'Astier by Parodi's aide, Léon Morandat ('Yvon'): 'The atmosphere in Paris has changed quickly over the last few days. We expect the American tanks to arrive any day now. We are feverishly getting ready to launch the national insurrection soon enough for the *résistants* to be able to welcome them.'[45]

Nearly two weeks earlier, it had been agreed that Chaban would fly to London during the August full moon to finalise preparations for the liberation of the city. His visit had now become vital.[46] As General von Choltitz, the new German commander of Paris, sat in a train rattling its way westwards towards the French capital, Chaban ran across a moonlit field north of Lyons and clambered into a twin-engine RAF Hudson aeroplane bound for London.[47]

Chaban spent the next two days in the Free French intelligence headquarters in Hill Street, trying to convince his comrades that if the Allies did not arrive in Paris soon, there would be an appalling massacre. Two things prompted Chaban's fears. A few days earlier the Paris Delegation had been contacted by a Resistance agent in Metz, who had overhead Gestapo officers being ordered to make their way to Paris to take charge of 1500 political prisoners. These prisoners were to be murdered, either *en route* or when they arrived at Metz.[48] Everyone in Paris accepted that this was a very real threat. Hundreds of Resistance and Free French prisoners were apparently in danger of being massacred. Important as this was, Chaban was preoccupied by what was happening in a similar situation on the other side of the continent, in Warsaw.

On 1 August, the Warsaw Resistance – the Home Army – had risen against the German occupiers, in order to set up a pro-Western government before the arrival of the Soviet armed forces, who were advancing from the East.[49] The Home Army seem to have expected that if the Germans found themselves caught between an insurrection in the city and the rapidly advancing Russians, they would leave. But the Germans did not leave – they stood and fought. On the first day of the insurrection, around 2000 Resistance fighters were killed. An enraged Himmler gave orders to destroy the city and kill every inhabitant, and the SS were sent into the western suburbs of the city, where in a couple of days they killed up to 50,000 people.[50] Thousands died as rebel-held districts in the city were bombarded by aircraft and by artillery fire. After the first week, an awful, bloody war of attrition set in, with the poorly armed rebels facing the destructive might of the German Army. Meanwhile, the Soviet armed forces, instead of arriving at Warsaw as the leaders of the insurrection had expected, lingered in the East, giving the Germans a free hand to kill the USSR's political opponents.

Although the full horror of what was happening in Warsaw was not known at the time – not even by the Allies – ordinary people in both France and London knew that a terrible battle was raging in the centre of Warsaw, and that the Germans were crushing the Polish Resistance.[51] This was what haunted Chaban. For weeks he and Parodi, together with the more cautious elements in the Resistance, had countered suggestions of Resistance action by repeatedly emphasising the danger of German reprisals. It had almost become a reflex. The situation in Warsaw vindicated their fears, but the Free French outpost in London did not have the authority to take any decisions, and lacked the connections and influence required to convince the Allied command to change tactics. All that Chaban and his London comrades could do was urge Algiers one more time to come up with a solution that would resolve the tensions between the Resistance and the Free French in Paris: 'the lack of instructions for Paris is a serious problem, given that this situation is both the most pressing and the only one that presents any real difficulties,' they wrote.[52] Yet again, there was no reply.

In the evening of 10 August, Andrzej Bobkowski, a Polish exile living in Paris, discussed the situation in Warsaw with two fellow countrymen. They were all bitter about what was happening – 'It takes away our pleasure at the fact that the occupation here may soon be over,' Bobkowski wrote in his diary. In the twilight, the three of them went for a walk by the side of the Seine: 'The sun has set; night is falling. The black towers of Notre Dame stand out against a pink sky that shimmers and changes colour. The Eiffel Tower floats in the distance, as if in a fog. A pleasant coolness rises from the water. There is a grinding sound from the street as a steel giant goes by, covered with tree branches. It is a solitary German Tiger tank, and it disappears into the night. Blue flames burst from its massive exhausts, sending sparks into the sky.'[53]

*

After years of deprivation because of rationing and German pillaging, conditions in Paris were becoming precarious. Important areas of the countryside around the capital, which supplied the 4 million inhabitants of the capital with their food, were ravaged by the war, and rail and road transport were disrupted. At the beginning of August, the Red Cross delegate in Paris published a report describing the cumulative effects of malnutrition on the inhabitants of the capital. Bread supplies were at around 60 per cent of their pre-war levels, milk supplies had plunged to a mere 12 per cent, meat consumption was down to 20 per cent and vegetable supplies had plummeted to 10 per cent of their levels in 1939. Around 25,000 babies were undernourished, and mortality due to tuberculosis was soaring, particularly among the young. Compared with the same period in 1943, typhoid cases in the city had nearly tripled, scarlet fever cases had increased by 25 per cent, while the number of measles cases had more than doubled.[54] 'The capital is threatened with famine,' the report declared.[55]

Food may also have been on Picasso's mind when he began a painting of the tomato plant in his attic studio.[56] Over the next ten days he would paint nine identically sized canvases depicting the plant, chronicling the daily changes and experimenting with form, colour and light.[57] One interpretation of this series of pictures would be that the green fruits of the plant promise life, while the red tomatoes show the potential of what is to come, and that the whole series deals with the imminent liberation of Paris. A more prosaic view – which does not contradict the other, and which is supported by the fact that the number of fruit declined as the series progressed – is that Picasso liked eating tomatoes. Most of the tomato plant paintings show strong light and vivid colours, but in the painting of 7 August, the sky just visible through the window is dull and yellow, and the light in the room is flat and without contrast. That afternoon the capital was covered by a thick bank of coppery grey cloud drifting from the north as petrol depots at Saint-Ouen were destroyed in an Allied air-raid.[58] The war was getting into Picasso's pictures.

*

When General von Choltitz arrived in Paris, he spent much of his first day negotiating the handover from his predecessor, von Boineburg.[59] Hitler's primary order for Paris was immediately put into effect, and the Germans began preparing to evacuate the administrative services from the capital. Scouts were sent eastwards towards the frontier to find new offices for the thousands of German administrators. The evacuation plans created a logistical nightmare: there were simply not enough vehicles available. The Army was throwing everything it had westwards towards the front, while the vehicles owned by Parisians had long been pillaged.[60] Many German offices began to destroy their archives, hoping the flames would erase the horrors of four years of occupation. Jacqueline Mesnil-Amar noted in her diary: 'On the place de la Concorde, on rue Boissy-d'Anglas, from the Hôtel Crillon and all the other German offices, flakes of ash rain from the sky, falling on our faces, our hair, our arms.'[61]

One of von Choltitz's first actions was to try to intimidate the population by ordering his men to march through the city in a display of force. Parisian civil servant Yves Cazaux noted various troop movements in his diary, but was not sure what they meant: 'At the moment there is a great deal of agitation in Paris ... A cannon is pointed towards the Lion de Belfort statue in the rue Denfert-Rocherau near the Observatory ... Artillery sections are moving down the avenue d'Orléans, towards Concorde ... Large numbers of troops are marching down the Champs-Elysées, passing by rue Royale, boulevard Malesherbes; there are all sorts of forces – infantry, tanks and anti-aircraft guns.'[62] Cazaux's bemused response was not exactly what von Choltitz had in mind, but few Parisians were struck by the event and even the collaborationist press did not make much of it.[63] The parade got only a brief mention in Marcel Déat's fascist daily, *L'Oeuvre*: 'Saturday 12 August, the General von Choltitz, military governor of Paris, deployed part of the German troops stationed in the capital on an emergency exercise, at the end of which they returned to barracks.'[64]

Von Choltitz also tried to intimidate his subordinates. He removed General Erwin Vierow from command of German troops to the south and west of Paris, despite Vierow's familiarity with the conditions in the area.[65] This was just one of many changes in command that affected the Paris region in July and August, each of which further weakened the German forces. As Colonel Kurt Hesse put it three years later: 'The effected removals of the military commander in France, General of the Inf. von Stülpnagel, the commander of Great-Paris, General von

Boineburg, Major General Bremer and later on the commander in chief for the West, Field Marshal von Kluge, in the course of the events and their substitution by personalities that were not familiar with the difficult situation of Paris, brought about conditions that were considered as extremely disadvantageous for the ensuing mission.'[66]

Von Choltitz soon realised that Paris was ill-prepared for an enemy assault. The defences comprised a series of anti-aircraft ('flak') batteries and a total of 36 heavy and 220 medium or light cannons.[67] Designed for use against an aerial offensive, these weapons could also be employed against tanks and ground forces, but they were not adequately protected and would be vulnerable to any major attack.[68] The flak batteries were backed up by sections of the 325th Security Division – 6000 men, split into four regiments of poorly armed, mainly non-motorised troops. However, one of those four regiments was miles away on the coast and so was useless for all practical purposes, while another protected the Grande Ceinture railway line 15 km around the capital. Alongside the remaining 3000 members of the 325th, there were another 17,000 German soldiers in Paris, most of them having minor security or administrative duties, many of them not young and few of them battle-hardened.[69] The only other force at von Choltitz's command was an armoured group that had been cobbled together by von Boineburg, composed of fourteen old tanks (captured French tanks and pre-war Panzer 1s) and eighteen Panhard scout cars.[70] Von Boineburg himself later admitted these forces were 'weak'.[71]

Inside the capital, the Germans had reinforced concrete defences and thirty-two bunkered *Stützpunkte* ('strong-points') at strategic locations like the Senate building (the upper house of Parliament) or the German administrative centre at the place de l'Opéra, which were well defended and had sufficient supplies to hold out for a month. These defences would deter infantry but would not be able to resist a concerted armoured attack. The explanation for these apparently lightweight defensive preparations was that the Germans had been expecting a civilian insurrection rather than an attack by an Allied armoured column; the 'defence of Paris' was focused purely on internal threats. This was not unreasonable: throughout the occupation, Paris had been the centre of both sporadic large-scale civil disobedience, such as a student demonstration on 11 November 1940, and occasional waves of urban guerrilla action in which individual German soldiers were assassinated.[72] This was expected to increase after D-Day.[73] Kurt Hesse wrote: 'Heavy arms – artillery, tanks – were not to [be] expected on the side of the Resistance, but then it was likely that they had in great numbers submachine guns, small arms, hand grenades and also incendiary material.'[74]

As well as continuing to prepare for an armed confrontation with the Resistance, the Germans now had to deal with the perspective of a pitched battle on the western approaches to the French capital. Hitler might have wanted Paris to be defended at all costs, but he had not provided the means. The commander of the German 1st Army headquarters at Fontainebleau gave this damning description of the Paris garrison: 'No combat troops, units lacking solid structure as well as uniform leadership and training. Insufficient armament. AA [anti-aircraft] detachments not equipped with necessary means of observation and signal equipment for ground-fighting. For the most not mobile. In view of the particular difficulties of fighting in a large city and the material superiority of the enemy, any real resistance on the part of the Paris Mil[itary] District could not be expected.'[75] Daniel Boisdon, a 60-year-old lawyer and member of the Libération-Nord Resistance group, gained a similar impression of the military situation around Paris on 10 August. Boisdon had been in Bourges, 200 km south of Paris, and was trying to return to his home in the capital. He eventually got a lift with a butcher, who invited him for a meal on the way:

I ate a piece of beef the like of which I hadn't tasted for several months and we became the best of friends. In the Paris suburbs we dropped in on the mother of one of the drivers, opened a bottle of Pouilly and drank to the defeat of the Huns. By 20:00 I was at the Pont d'Austerlitz. Throughout our journey we had seen that the Germans were leaving. And what a departure! Their lorries were loaded with all sorts of things, including old furniture and sewing machines. Every now and again, hidden in the woods, we came across a piece of artillery or a few tanks. But very few troops. Certainly nothing that could resist a mass attack.[76]

The fact that the Paris region was not well defended did not mean that there would not be a battle. As the Allied armies advanced, retreating German units would be pushed in front of them. Hitler had insisted that Paris was to be the point at which that retreat would halt. The position of Paris at the heart of all road and rail routes back to Germany meant that the Allies would come to the gates of the capital, and the Germans would have to fight or flee. All indications were that they would fight. As Yves Cazaux walked past place du Châtelet he saw a column of Tiger tanks clanking their way south down the boulevard Sebastopol before turning left with a grinding sound and heading south-eastwards along the Seine: 'The tanks are camouflaged with branches, they move clumsily. The massive machines turn slowly, with a series of slow movements. The Parisian tarmac is being seriously damaged by this long column of more than 25 tanks.'[77] At lunchtime, 57-year-old university lecturer Paul Tuffrau strolled down to the sun-filled Jardin du Luxembourg, now completely closed to civilians. He found French labourers at the north-west corner of the park building a strange platform into the ripped-up paving stones. As they ate their lunch he asked them what the structure was for. 'A cannon' was the simple reply. Similar work was going on outside the Senate building, just up the road. The Germans were digging in. From time to time German fighter planes roared low over the city.[78]

*

Frustrated by the lack of action, the communist leadership of the armed Resistance group, the Franc-Tireurs et Partisans (FTP – Sharpshooters and Partisans), issued a call to arms. Drafted by regional FTP leader Charles Tillon, and then amended by Communist Party youth leaders Albert Ouzoulias and Pierre Georges ('Colonel Fabien'), the document was entitled 'Forward to the Battle of Paris'. FTP units were immediately to cut all German lines of communication, attack the enemy forces, get all workers to cease working for the enemy and join the FTP, culminating in an armed insurrection:

> Together with groups of patriotic militias, smash the repressive apparatus of the traitors and the enemy. Exterminate the agents of the

Gestapo ... Attack and destroy police roadblocks manned by the French and the German police on major roads and in the cities. Lay siege to the arms depots and attack them. Distribute seized arms to the patriots ... Francs-Tireurs et Partisans of the Parisian region, make de Gaulle's slogan EVERYONE TO BATTLE the cry of the Paris uprising. Officers and Parisian soldiers of the Francs-Tireurs et Partisans, forward to the national insurrection. March to the sound of guns![79]

This might appear to confirm the worst fears of those who suspected the communists were planning to seize power, but this was not the case. Over the next few days there were no signs of any increase in FTP armed activity, for the simple reason that they did not have enough weapons. Nor was there any mass influx into the FTP, because they did not have the broad support they imagined they had. In some senses, this revolutionary rhetoric represented the high point of direct communist influence over the Paris insurrection. The FTP forces in the Paris region were now under the orders of the FFI, and had adopted an outlook that was similar to that of the whole Resistance: 'Our slogan must be to respond to General de Gaulle with all our strength by opening the road to Paris for the Allies.'[80] The 10 August call to arms was apparently the last attempt by the FTP leaders to intervene independently in the impending struggle for the capital. In the days that followed, they issued no independent orders, nor did they carry out any independent actions; everything was left in the hands of Colonel Rol, the undisputed leader of the FFI.[81]

3

Mid-August: Build-up

On Thursday 10 August, Protestant priest Marc Boegner writes in his diary: 'A beautiful day, the most beautiful that we have had this summer. Paris is full of lorries, of hastily camouflaged cars of all kinds. They are waiting for nightfall before leaving. People "in the know" claim that Pétain will be here on Saturday. Laval is already here. They say that the newspapers will be moving to Vittel or Nancy. Part of the German embassy has apparently already moved out. It's odd, there are people moving in and moving out!' [1]

As the sun rose on 10 August, around 500 workers went into the Noisy-le-Sec railway depot and stayed there, refusing to work, protesting against their low pay and poor working conditions, and against the continued imprisonment of some of their comrades following the 14 July events. The Germans were occupying the country, now the railway workers were occupying their workplace. A sprawling tangle of lines on the north side of the main Paris–Strasbourg line, Noisy was a central part of the rail network. All trains heading towards Germany passed through Noisy, and many of the locomotives that hauled those trains were housed and maintained there. Two weeks earlier, the depot had seen the last spasm of the strikes that began on 14 July; now it was at the beginning of a new and decisive wave of industrial unrest. [2]

In a carefully planned movement organised by the banned trade union the CGT (Conféderation Générale du Travail – General Labour Confederation), railway workers were going on strike all over the region, and soon twenty-five depots were affected. This was not de

Gaulle's 'national insurrection', but it did show a shift in the balance of power. A railway worker described what happened in his Montrouge workshop: 'Around 09:00, armed men arrived and called us out on strike. We wanted the liberation of the hostages arrested on 14 July, a pay increase and food reserves. Everyone walked out. Some of us were sent to other depots to spread the movement. Pickets were set up at the gates of the workshops.'[3] The strike did not immediately take hold everywhere. At Mantes-la-Jolie, to the north-west of Paris, Louis Racaud recalled how although many drivers followed the call to cease work and disable their locomotives, others refused: 'My mate Léon said, "I don't get involved in politics. I'm going back to the canteen."'[4] At the Villeneuve-Saint-Georges depot, which still had seven of its workers held captive by the Germans, the strike was a flop.[5] A local activist, protected by armed FTP fighters, spoke to three consecutive shifts of workers in the canteen but to no avail – the workers refused to go on strike.[6] That night the regional CGT leader, 'Véry', tried to put a positive spin on the mood in the depot by describing it as 'undecided'.[7]

Even if the massive Villeneuve depot was not taking action, the movement had a major impact. The number of trains on the Grande Ceinture line around the Paris region fell from thirty-two to eighteen, with seventy-four trains stuck on the tracks, waiting to pass.[8] All commuter traffic was halted: the Parisian stations were closed and passengers from Versailles had to walk the thirteen kilometres into the capital. In the late afternoon, Yves Cazaux called the headquarters of the state-owned railway company, the SNCF, to find out what was going on, but there was no reply.[9]

Over the next few days, the Germans responded to the strike, seizing hostages from among strikers across the region. At the La Chapelle depot, where sixteen workers were arrested and threatened with execution, the strikers returned to work. At the nearby Batignolles depot, where hundreds of workers were occupying the workshops, the strikers decided to go home rather than run the risk of being taken hostage by the Germans. At Noisy, where the movement had begun, troops took hostages and threatened to kill them if the strikers did not go back to work. Although the strike was temporarily halted at Noisy, rail traffic did not return to normal: all the Noisy steam locomotives were cold as the drivers had dumped the red-hot contents of the fireboxes onto the tracks.[10]

At the Gare Saint-Lazare, the management decided to run a number of suburban electric trains, arguing that if the service looked vaguely normal, the Germans might free the hostages. Pierre Patin, an engineer in his twenties, gingerly volunteered for the job, despite his fears that breaking the strike might compromise his Resistance work and that the train might be attacked by the Allies or the Resistance. To Patin's amazement, there were actually passengers waiting at the stations he stopped at, and for eight hours he buzzed back and forth along the suburban lines that stretched westwards towards the rumble of distant artillery fire, singing strike songs and feeling 'both very patriotic and very revolutionary'.[11]

A handful of militants at Villeneuve-Saint-Georges met to see how they could revive the flagging momentum of the strike in their workplace. Véry, the regional union organiser, explained the next day: 'I decided to stay at Villeneuve to organise the work of the union militants, because things were pretty anarchic. On Sunday morning, I gathered together the leaders of the railway workers, and we decided to use diplomacy, force and sabotage to keep the strike alive.'[12] By the afternoon of 13 August, around 300 German soldiers had turned up to intimidate the workers. They succeeded, and the strike stalled. The next day, which was a public holiday, Véry reported wearily: 'The "strike" is effective because all the railway workers are on holiday.'[13]

Elsewhere it was the strikers who were doing the threatening: one strike committee leaflet read 'Death to those who drive trains', while at La Villette, on the north-eastern edge of Paris, a driver and fireman were menaced by armed men until they refused to drive their convoy. At Montrouge, shots were exchanged between gendarmes and strikers, and at nearby Bercy a ninety-six-ton steam engine was driven into a turntable pit, putting the equipment – and the locomotive – out of action for the duration.[14]

Responding to pressure from railway managers, the government asked the Germans to free all fifty-two railwaymen hostages, including sixteen who had been arrested on 14 July, to help end the strike.[15] It appears that the Germans accepted this, as the SNCF was told that all the hostages would be released, with the exception of those who were arrested following the demonstrations of 14 July, and that their cases would be re-examined if the strike ended.[16]

In some depots, the strikers began to return to work. At the Jules-Coutant workshop in Ivry the police reported there were few strikers: 'The workforce in this workshop, showing their goodwill, hopes that the eight workers arrested following a strike will soon be freed ... It can be assumed that if they are not freed, there will be more strike action.'[17] Elsewhere, threats from the Resistance against strike-breakers meant that railwaymen were prepared to go back to work only if they were protected by the police.[18]

The significance of the rail strike was not lost on the Parisian population. Bernard Pierquin wrote in his diary: 'We are waiting for the insurrection, but when will it happen? At the moment, the Huns are moving out; the requisitioned hotels are emptying. There are no obvious signs of defence in the streets. But there is a warning sign of the fight to come: all the railways are on strike.'[19] The Germans may have thought that matters were settled, but as Pierquin implied, it was only the beginning.

*

On Sunday 6 August, Raoul Nordling, the Swedish Consul General in Paris, went to see a German military judge. Nordling, a portly 62-year-old with a moustachioed, jowly face and stick-like legs, had lived in France most of his life and was used to dealing with the Germans: he was on the board of the Swedish ball-bearing manufacturer, SKF, which had a major plant in Ivry, south-east of Paris, and which supplied the Germans.[20] The German judge told Nordling of his concern for the hundreds of political prisoners in Fresnes prison, given that ninety French prisoners had been executed in Caen prison as the Germans prepared to evacuate. In particular, the judge warned Nordling of the threat to a member of the Swedish consul's family who was in Fresnes prison, accused of sheltering Allied airmen.[21]

Worried for his relative and for the other political prisoners, Nordling contacted two acquaintances in the German administration who had previously helped him free a friend from prison. One of the men, Erich 'Riki' Posch-Pastor, was a dashing 26-year-old aristocratic Austrian officer, described by an anti-fascist friend as 'a first-rate, extraordinarily helpful companion, cheerful, high-spirited and constantly on the look-out to put down the great German Wehrmacht'.[22] Nordling's other contact, Emil 'Bobby' Bender, was a young-looking man in his forties who was a member of German military intelligence.[23] Nordling's humanitarian concerns were drawing him into a complex web of espionage and influence; although he did not know it, both Posch-Pastor and Bender were in fact working for British intelligence. Over the next three weeks they were always at Nordling's side, playing an essential, hidden role in the dramatic events that unfolded.

On a more official level, Nordling attempted to discuss the situation of the prisoners with Pierre Laval, but was told that the prime minister was unavailable.[24] Nordling then telephoned the German ambassador, Otto Abetz.[25] At first, the ambassador was in a buoyant mood, claiming that there was no threat to the prisoners because the German counter-attack in the west had transformed the military situation. But when Nordling mentioned the case of a professor who had been arrested because he refused to name students involved in the Resistance, the Nazi's urbane mask slipped and he snarled furiously that the university was a nest of assassins that should be burnt down, and that the Gestapo was far too nice to such people. When Nordling asked Abetz whether he condoned the murder of the prisoners in Caen two months earlier, the German was chillingly callous: shooting them was the only solution, he said.[26] This reinforced Nordling's fears – the prisoners were clearly in mortal danger.

Having got nowhere with Abetz, Nordling met with René Naville, a Swiss diplomat, and discussed what could be done to save the prisoners. Naville suggested that all the prisons in Paris and its surrounding region could be put under the protection of the Red Cross, which he also represented. The Germans might accept the idea if there were some guarantee about the treatment of the German garrison in Paris. So Naville went to the German embassy, where he discovered that Ambassador Abetz was busy making preparations to leave the capital, and was too preoccupied to see him. An aide suavely told him that the issue had been drawn to the attention of SS General Oberg, who was dealing with the matter.[27] Meanwhile, Nordling had finally secured a meeting with Laval, but the prime minister was too focused on his politicking to properly take in anything that Nordling said. The prisoners would have to wait until he had been able to see Abetz, Laval explained. Nordling left with nothing more than the promise of yet another meeting.

As Chaban had explained in London, the Free French and the Resistance had also heard that the prisoners were in danger, but they could not agree on the best course of action. Despite the urgency of the situation, Parodi insisted on his habitual justification for doing nothing: 'Everyone agrees,' he said in a message to London, 'that it would be impossible to attack the prisons without provoking a widespread massacre.' Instead, Parodi suggested that Eisenhower should broadcast a threat to the Germans, warning them they would be tried for war crimes if any of the prisoners were harmed.[28] A discussion by COMAC of the prisoners' situation showed that 'everyone' did not agree with Parodi: the three members of COMAC sent a telegram to London requesting that enough automatic weapons and grenades to arm 1000 men be immediately parachuted into the Paris region, 'to enable us to carry out plans to free the prisoners'.[29] There was no reply, and no weapons arrived.

*

The collaborators in local and national government began to worry what would become of them in the event of an Allied victory. Members of the Senate had the idea of setting up a new parliamentary assembly that might be looked on positively by the Allies, and would prevent the Gaullists from taking power. These politicians not only had an acute instinct for self-preservation, they were also profoundly fearful of what might come with liberation, something even worse than the triumph of the Free French: 'We must at all costs avoid Paris falling into the hands of a Communist revolutionary committee,' they wrote.[30] The chairman of the Paris municipal council, Pierre Taittinger, drew similar conclusions and argued that Laval and Pétain should immediately bring the government to Paris, so they could negotiate with the USA when the Allies arrived.[31] When this idea was put to Pétain, the old man prevaricated and then naïvely said he would ask the Germans for permission.

Prime Minister Pierre Laval was more lucid, and more desperate, and leapt at the idea – he would find a way of negotiating with the Allies, thereby saving his skin and stopping de Gaulle from taking power. Laval knew that his time in office might soon be over: the fascist politicians Marcel Déat and Jacques Doriot, and the head of the Milice, Joseph Darnand, were planning to remove him from power.[32] The Germans had not yet given the green light to a coup against Laval, partly because of the fluidity of the military situation, but above all because there was no mass political support for an openly fascist government – a coup would merely create unnecessary instability. The French fascists were too deluded to recognise this reality and continued to live in cloud cuckoo land – Doriot and a henchman sat in a hunting lodge near Metz, imagining which ministerial positions they would give their cronies if they were in government.[33] Although Laval was equally deluded in his own way, he was determined to make his own pipedream come true. On the evening of 8 August he left Vichy for Paris, taking his wife and daughter with him. He would never return.[34]

When Laval arrived in Paris the next morning, he headed straight for the prime minister's official residence in the Hôtel Matignon, in the 7th arrondissement. He explained his plan to the Paris municipal council and the regional government, the Conseil Général of the Seine (the members of both bodies were all Vichy appointees). Laval said he would ensure that the Allies and the Germans declared Paris an 'open city' that would be neither defended nor attacked, just like Rome two months earlier. Edouard Herriot, who had been President of the National Assembly in June 1940, and was now in a prison hospital in Nancy following a nervous breakdown, would be brought back to Paris to preside over a National Assembly meeting. If the timing were right, the assembly would be in session when the Allied armies arrived, thereby short-circuiting de Gaulle's claim to power.

On paper, this plan had a lot going for it. The Americans were deeply suspicious of de Gaulle, whom they considered unreliable, and of the Resistance, which they saw as tainted by the participation of the communists. Moreover, Herriot, an international figure who had been prime minister three times before the war, was a personal friend of both Roosevelt and Stalin. The scheme had been hatched nearly four months earlier by one of Laval's close associates, André Enfière.[35] Enfière had subsequently made several trips to Berne in Switzerland where the US spy chief Allen Dulles assured him that such a transitional government would have the support of President Roosevelt.[36] For Laval, the most important thing about the plan was that he would be at the heart of events: 'The Germans will be evacuating Paris in a matter of weeks, if not days. My place is here. I have come back to Paris. I will stay here whatever happens,' he told the assembled politicians.[37]

And so on 13 August a convoy of six large cars swept out of the Hôtel Matignon and headed eastwards to Nancy. Early the next morning the convoy was back in Paris, carrying Laval's precious cargo: Herriot, the man who could stop de Gaulle. At 05:00, the Prefect of the Seine département, René Bouffet, who had his offices and his official apartment in the Hôtel de Ville, was summoned down to the courtyard, still wearing his dressing gown. There he found Laval, Ambassador Abetz, and Monsieur and Madame Edouard Herriot. Laval's plan was taking shape, and the presence of Abetz indicated it had German backing. Herriot was still the President of the National Assembly, but he could not stay in his official residence as it was occupied by a high-ranking Luftwaffe officer. Laval decided that until the German could be persuaded to vacate the premises, Herriot would have to remain in the Hôtel de Ville and should not receive any guests. Even though Pierre Taittinger had ordered Herriot's room to be decorated with a massive bouquet of red and blue flowers (the colours of the capital), it was still effectively a prison cell.[38]

In Vichy, Laval's project was making Pétain's entourage increasingly uncomfortable, as it threatened to make the marshal and his cronies irrelevant. To regain the initiative, Admiral Gabriel Auphan – the man who ordered the scuttling of the French fleet at Toulon in 1942 – was sent to Paris on Pétain's behalf with instructions to negotiate with the Allies and the Free French and ensure an orderly transfer of power.[39] Although in reality the Resistance and the Free French had lost too many people and made too many sacrifices to accept such a proposal when they were on the verge of seizing power, the Allies might indeed be interested in Pétain's ploy – it would give them yet another opportunity to undermine de Gaulle. Auphan arrived in Paris on the evening of the 11th, and the next day he sent Algiers a message explaining his mission. Auphan was ignored and met with silence.[40]

Parodi was also alarmed by Laval's manoeuvres and sent an urgent message to Algiers asking how soon de Gaulle would arrive in Paris, what would be the General Delegate's powers in the intervening period, and above all what he should do in the meantime. Shortly afterwards, Parodi sent another message explaining that he had heard 'from a highly reliable source' that Pétain was discussing a transfer of power with an American general, and that Vichy was highly confident that the manoeuvre would succeed. Parodi closed with a bitter remark: 'Once again, I ask for instructions and I draw your attention to the fact that you have not sent any weapons to arm the forces that are under the direct control of the Delegation.'[41] It would be a week before Algiers sent Parodi a bland reply about Laval's manoeuvres, simply telling him not to worry. By this time Paris would be on the verge of insurrection, Laval and Pétain long gone. The weapons never arrived.[42]

As the world of collaboration began to disintegrate, fascist writer Pierre Drieu La Rochelle drew some drastic conclusions. On 7 August, he wrote in his diary: 'Hitler pleases me no end, despite his mistakes, his ignorance and his blunders. He presented me with my political ideal: physical pride, style, prestige, warrior heroism – even the romantic desire to give oneself totally, to destroy oneself in a headstrong gesture, uncontrolled, excessive and fatal.'[43] Four days later, Drieu took this model literally: in the afternoon he went for a walk in the Tuileries gardens, drank a half-bottle of champagne then returned home to his tidy apartment, where he tried to commit suicide with poison. He failed.[44]

*

Like many other Parisians, middle-aged housewife Odette Lainville decided to write a diary to record the historic events that she could sense were imminent.[45] In her first entry she described how she went to church early in the morning, then dyed some sheets red and blue to make a massive tricolour flag that she planned to drape over her balcony when liberation came. Her work complete, Odette went out for a walk: 'I went down to be in the cool shadow of the trees in the Jardin du Luxembourg, near the irises, not far from the old statues and the delightful merry-go-round. One of the main alleys is full of German lorries that have escaped from the Front, cluttered with tanks and ammunition; the Huns have set up a kind of park that is shut off by chains and barbed wire.'[46] In the heart of Paris, the Germans were following Hitler's orders and readying themselves for the inevitable Allied onslaught.

As Drieu La Rochelle was trying to kill himself, there was another air-raid alert in the capital. Sheltering under some trees by the side of the Seine, Odette watched a stricken Allied bomber falling to earth, leaving a zigzag of smoke behind it, followed by tiny white dots – parachutes. Closer to the scene, Spanish exile Victoria Kent saw the terrible aftermath: German anti-aircraft guns fired at the airmen, hitting at least one of them.[47] Around 18:00, after sewing her dyed sheets together, Odette rode her bike to the other side of Paris, nipping in between speeding German lorries laden down with the most diverse booty: 'a pile of mattresses as high as the Eiffel Tower', a piano, cases and cases of Moët & Chandon champagne. Despite the real risk of being knocked off her bike by a lorry, Madame Lainville felt only one thing: 'It's marvellous! They really are moving out. They are shoving each other out of the way; it's crazy. I am so happy!'[48] When she got home, Odette took up her pen and celebrated the completion of her flag by writing a poem dedicated 'to my old sewing machine':

Rattle on, my machine, through the blue
Rattle on, my machine, through the red and white, too.
Our hearts are leaping, victorious
    Gently rocked by three colours
    Soon to feel glorious ...
Rattle on, my machine, through the blue
Rattle on, my machine, through the red and white, too...
    Glory to the Allies,
    Glory to our nation!

In my heart you are as one
As I pray for liberation ...[49]

In the midst of the preparations and the politicking, ordinary life continued. Swiss journalist Edmond Dubois went to a small church on the Left Bank to attend a marriage that was marked by the conditions within the capital. Because there was no electricity, the organ did not work and the hymns had to be sung unaccompanied. Because of the food shortages, there was no reception and the newlyweds were fêted in the sacristy. And because of the fuel shortages, the couple went off on their honeymoon by bicycle. They may not have got very far – German soldiers in the place de la République were stopping passing cyclists and simply stealing their bicycles in order to flee.

*

In the early hours of 12 August, three B-24 Liberator bombers took off from Harrington aerodrome in Northamptonshire. Painted matt black, the planes carried containers full of weapons and supplies, and three men in civilian clothes: Jedburgh Team AUBREY. 'Jedburghs' were joint military operations composed of three agents from Free France and Britain or the USA. Their mission was to carry out guerrilla warfare behind German lines, in conjunction with local Resistance movements. Of the ninety-nine Jedburgh missions sent into France in the summer of 1944, only one – AUBREY – had Paris in its sights.[50]

At around 01:55, the three men parachuted into a large field about thirty-five kilometres north-east of Paris. They were Captain Guy Marchant and Sergeant Ivor Hooker of the Special Operations Executive (SOE), and Captain Adrien Chaigneau of the Free French Intelligence Service, the BCRA.[51] They were to aid an underground group or 'circuit' set up by SOE to the north-east of Paris, which was called SPIRITUALIST after the code name of its leader.[52] Marchant reported: 'We all landed well (although the descent seemed faster than usual) and were met on the field (near Le Plessis-Belleville) by Major Armand ('Spiritualist') in person. We walked with him to St Pathus while the remainder of the reception committee dealt with the containers and packages ... We accompanied Major Armand to M. Leridan's house where we ate, conversed and drank champagne until the early hours of the morning.'[53]

Team AUBREY was not the first clandestine Allied mission to Paris – throughout the war there had been a series of operations in the capital to support Resistance activity or collect intelligence. In 1944 there were a number of joint British, French and US operations known as SUSSEX; these were based in two Parisian cafés and worked with some of the armed Resistance groups in the countryside around Paris.[54] The most important Allied operations in Paris at this time were completely secret, their existence unknown to more than a handful of people. These were two British intelligence circuits: JADE-AMICOL and ALLIANCE. JADE-AMICOL was part of MI6 and was based in the dilapidated Sainte-Agonie convent on the rue de la Santé on the southern edge of the 6th arrondissement. In August 1944 its leader was Colonel Claude Arnould ('Ollivier'), a 45-year-old who had been involved in the French intelligence services before the war. Ollivier had set up JADE-AMICOL in the Bordeaux region, together with 30-year-old Philip Keun, and its headquarters had moved to Paris at the end of 1942. Henriette Frédé, Mother Superior of the dozen nuns who lived in the convent, was a willing participant in Ollivier's work, enlisting her nuns to help carry messages, and above all hiding the radio transmitter and the vital coding sheets.[55]

ALLIANCE, the largest single intelligence circuit in occupied France, was another MI6 group and was run by Marie-Madeleine Fourcade. It was called 'Noah's Ark' by the Germans because of the animal codenames used by its agents.[56] Fourcade had spent the first part of 1944 in London, but insisted on returning to France at the beginning of July.[57] After being arrested by the Germans and dramatically escaping from prison in Aix-en-Provence, Fourcade made her way north and arrived in Paris at the beginning of August.[58] She was installed in a smart flat a stone's throw from the Eiffel Tower, and was quickly given a morale-boosting makeover: 'In Paris, I had to look like a Parisian. Raven-black hair, an Hermès twin-set in beige corduroy (bought in a sale), a pair of large shoes and one of those shoulder bags like a bus conductor's satchel that all the women were carrying. I felt so unrecognisable that I was no longer afraid of being discovered. All of a sudden, I felt my strength returning.'[59] And with that, she began a round of meetings with ALLIANCE agents in Paris, beginning with Jean Sainteny ('Dragon'), who had also recently escaped from the hands of the Germans. The ALLIANCE and JADE-AMICOL circuits were both active in Paris, and were both attached to MI6, but it appears they knew nothing of each other's work, even though earlier in the year Sainteny and Colonel Ollivier of JADE-AMICOL had returned from London on the same aeroplane.[60]

*

At 02:00 on 12 August, while Jedburgh Team AUBREY was swilling champagne, buses and lorries stopped at two sites in Paris, on either side of the Seine. German soldiers and French members of the Milice poured into the nearby buildings and began to herd men and women into the lorries, hitting them with rifle butts, kicking and punching them. Then tarpaulins were pulled over the vehicles, and they drove off into the darkness.

Unknown to most Parisians, the Drancy internment camp had three 'annexes' in the centre of Paris. Jews were not only interned in these buildings, they were also put into forced labour there, as components of a macabre scheme called *Möbel Aktion* (Operation Furniture). This involved stealing household effects from French Jews and shipping the loot to Germany where the Nazi hierarchy took the richest pickings and what remained was supposedly distributed to the victims of Allied bombing raids. The role of the hundreds of internees in Paris was to sort the material that had been seized, parcel it up and load it ready for deportation. Sometimes they found themselves handling personal effects that belonged to their own family members. During the occupation 69,619 apartments were pillaged, and 26,984 railway wagons filled with stolen goods trundled down the tracks eastwards.[61] The last train of *Möbel Aktion* material was assembled on 2 August. It was made up of 52 wagons, 5 of them packed full of 148 cases containing works of art by Monet, Dufy, Cézanne and others. However, because of the chaos caused by Allied bombing raids on the railway network and the effects of the rail strike, the train got only as far as the northern suburb of Aubervilliers, where it was put into a siding. It was not until mid-October that the cases were finally moved to safety in Paris.[62]

Around 500 internees who had been dragooned into *Möbel Aktion* lived and worked in the three Paris 'annexes' of Drancy. Two of the annexes were conveniently close to railway stations – the Levitan furniture store on the rue Faubourg Saint-Martin near the Gare de l'Est, and two warehouses on the quai de la Gare, next to the Gare d'Austerlitz. At the third site, on rue de Bassano in the wealthy 16th arrondissement, a few dozen internees worked as tailors and seamstresses, making German uniforms. Concerned by the Allied advance, SS officer Alois Brunner, commander of Drancy, was preparing for evacuation and had ordered the Jews in the Parisian camps to be brought back to Drancy so they could be sent off to Germany – this was the reason for the terrifying night raids.[63] Some of the prisoners from Levitan were transported in a Parisian bus, accompanied by armed members of the Milice; Michèle Bonnet recalled what happened as the loaded bus moved off: 'I pressed the button. In a conditioned response, the driver stopped. Everyone panicked. I helped as many people as possible to get off … Just as I was about to jump, the bus started up again. A member of the Milice grabbed me by the arm. I had with me a nightdress wrapped around a 1 kg tin of food; furious, I swung it round and gave him a good crack on the head. Then I was in the street, running.'[64]

*

For the Jews who remained at liberty in Paris, the situation was becoming alarming. While it seemed probable that liberation was at hand, it was likely that things would get worse before they got better. This was why Odette Lainville received a visit from one of her daughter's friends, who was involved in sheltering Jews. Earlier in the year, Odette and her husband, Robert, had agreed to hide Jewish children if needed. Now was the time. Suzanne (five years old) and Adèle (aged twelve), Turkish Jews who lived in the Marais, were brought to Odette's apartment in the early evening. Their father had fled Paris and was now in a prison camp in the south of France. Their mother, distraught with worry, had allowed them to go to the relative safety of the 6th arrondissement, just the other side of the Seine.

The girls were soon settled in, running up and down the long balcony, getting lost in the corridors, and playing with Odette's daughters' old toys. Then it was time for bed, as Odette recorded in her diary: 'Adèle, the eldest, says a very polite "Goodnight". Little Suzanne, very emotional, throws her arms around my neck. They really need a mum at that age – I am overjoyed that I have been accepted so quickly.'[65] The next morning, the girls woke early, so Odette took them out to do some shopping. But as soon as they left the building they bumped into one of the few neighbours Odette did not trust. 'Are these your little relatives?' the woman asked; Odette mumbled something about helping their mother out. 'Oh, the little one does have frizzy hair,' said the eagle-eyed busybody. 'Yes, Madame, just like me,' retorted Odette. Even though the Germans were leaving, Odette could take no chances; nowhere was safe.[66]

*

In the small hours of the morning of 14 August, Suzanne Torrès of the 'Rochambelle' ambulance group ordered her small convoy to halt. They were on a narrow forest road five kilometres south of Argentan, and a ferocious artillery battle was going on around them. With her group completely unprotected – it was composed only of ambulances and a single half-track vehicle – Torrès felt it would be safer to hide in the woods. Suddenly, out of the darkness loomed the vague shape of an enormous tank, which came clanking to a stop less than thirty metres in front of them. When Torrès heard German being spoken she realised they were trapped. After warning her comrades to stay in their vehicles, she strode towards some shadowy figures and demanded to be taken to their commanding officer. A Frenchman from Alsace, who had been conscripted into the German Army and found himself with the armoured column, was brought in to act as an interpreter, and the commander of the German column boasted to Torrès that the German offensive was going brilliantly and that the Allies were beaten. The interpreter duly translated this, but added: 'That's all lies – we're trying to escape under the cover of darkness.' When the German officer explained that Torrès and her group would be taken prisoner, the young Frenchwoman lost her temper, gesticulating and invoking the Geneva Convention, pointing out that they were merely women and that their vehicles would surely slow down the column's advance. After some discussion, the Germans agreed they would not take the women with them, on condition that Torrès agreed not to move for two hours. When the deal was done, six massive tanks and twelve armoured vehicles rumbled past the Rochambelles' convoy, belching exhaust fumes.

As soon as the German column had disappeared into the darkness, Torrès ordered her drivers to start their vehicles and they quickly headed off towards Mortrée, five kilometres to the east, to find the camp of her commanding officer, Colonel de Langlade. Some of Torrès' colleagues complained that she had broken her word; she was more interested in reporting the position of the German tanks. She burst into the camp and dragged a bleary eyed de Langlade from his bed. The artillery was alerted, maps were brandished and as soon as day broke, a scout plane was sent up. The enemy column was soon localised and destroyed.[67] Torrès and her comrades had a lucky escape, but many of the 2e DB's soldiers were not so fortunate: during the fighting to close the Falaise pocket, 141 men of the 2e DB were killed, 78 were missing and 618 were wounded, while 52 of their tanks had been destroyed.[68]

While the 2e DB was involved in fighting to contain the Germans, General Patton, commander of the Third US Army, of which the Leclerc Division was a tiny part, ordered half of the XV US Army Corps to drive eastwards to the Seine, with Paris on the horizon. Furious, Leclerc wrote to Patton demanding to know when the French troops could join in the advance on the capital. 'It's political' was Patton's laconic reply.[69] In fact, it was simpler than that: Paris was not on Patton's radar. He had no immediate intention of taking the city. It had been decided by Eisenhower that the Allied armies would circle around the French capital and harry the enemy eastwards, leaving the German garrison cooped up with millions of Parisians.

*

In the afternoon of 14 August, General von Choltitz had his first meeting with Field Marshal von Kluge and the two men discussed the plans for the defence of Paris.[70] Once the evacuation of non-essential forces was complete there would be around 20,000 Germans in the capital, together with the anti-aircraft units and about thirty armoured vehicles of one kind or another. These forces would clearly be unable to defend the city against the kind of massive army being assembled in the west, but they would easily be sufficient to restrain an unarmed civilian population. The flak units were disposed in a ring around Paris and preparations were made to face the Allied onslaught. Staff officers were told they could not leave the city without the express approval of von Kluge; in an atmosphere permeated with evacuation and flight, it was essential that the commanders should give an example to their troops.[71] However, von Kluge was a realist: the weakness of the defences, coupled with the critical supply situation, meant that the garrison would be unable to withstand a siege of more than a few days. Von Choltitz, as commander of the city, was ordered 'to resist as long as possible and to remain in Paris until the end'.[72]

Ambassador Abetz was also preoccupied by the growing menace of the Allied advance. In a secret message to Berlin, which was retransmitted to the Allies by the US spy Fritz Kolbe, Abetz recounted the latest twists in Laval's scheme to call a meeting of the National Assembly, focusing on the fate of Pétain, who Abetz felt was the key to continued German control over France. The imminence of an Allied landing in the south of France, and the growing strength of the Resistance in the region around Vichy, raised the possibility that Pétain could be either captured by the Allies, or even assassinated. Abetz cynically explained to his masters:

> The summoning of the National Assembly is to the Reich's advantage in this instance. However, it is of secondary importance whether it is really allowed to meet. Aside from the propaganda value this will afford us against dissidents, Communists and Roosevelt, the summoning of the National Assembly provides us with the only chance to get Pétain out of Vichy of his own volition, and in this way to keep the legality of the French Government on our side, should the Anglo-Americans further occupy France.[73]

At midday on 14 August, Alexandre Parodi went to Professor Victor Veau's apartment for lunch. Veau was a retired surgeon who had pioneered the treatment of cleft palate, and was now intimately connected to the highest circles of the Resistance through his good friend Louis Pasteur Vallery-Radot. 'PVR', as he was known, was the grandson of Louis Pasteur and the founder of the Comité medical de la Résistance, the clandestine system for treating wounded Resistance fighters. For over a year PVR had been hiding from the Germans, living in Veau's first-floor apartment at the junction of the boulevard Haussmann and the rue de Miromesnil, in the 9th arrondissement. PVR held meetings there and regularly entertained Resistance leaders together with Veau, who claimed he did not understand much of what was said because he did not know people's code names, and was not interested in the internal politics of the Resistance. At lunch, Veau, PVR and Parodi ate an expensive joint of beef and discussed the political situation. PVR and Parodi dismissed Laval's manoeuvres as doomed to failure, but they were concerned that the US would look to the Vichy collaborators as their preferred political partners, and that the Resistance and de Gaulle would be sidelined.[74] The Allied armies were advancing rapidly, but even the highest ranks of the Resistance were uncertain about what would happen next.

Over the previous five days Parodi, Valrimont and Chaban's second-in-command, General Ely, had thrashed out a compromise agreement in the long-running dispute between COMAC and the Free French over who had ultimate control over the FFI. COMAC was designated as 'the supreme command of the FFI in France', but at the same time this power was 'delegated from General Koenig'. The Free French military delegates, who were described as mere 'liaison officers', would put all their weapons, materiel and finances at the disposition of the FFI, but the FFI would follow the orders of General Koenig. There was enough there for Valrimont to claim later that 'all the positions defended by the Resistance were contained within it', but in reality nothing fundamental had changed, and the Free French retained the upper hand. There was no sudden surge of arms from the military delegates, and above all there was a get-out clause: if there was a major disagreement between COMAC and Chaban, then COMAC's decision would be suspended for up to five days while the CNR decided the matter.[75] This procedure undoubtedly satisfied COMAC, because it gave the Resistance the final say; but in the heat of battle, five days could be an eternity, and during that time Chaban would be in charge. Rather than unambiguously resolving the issue of who would have the final say, the text merely put off the question. Within a week, that lack of clarity, coupled with fast-moving events, created an atmosphere of uncertainty that had a decisive impact on the course of the Paris insurrection.

*

In London, Free French agent Georges Boris was trying to get Algiers to decide how it would react to an insurrection in Paris. He sent the last of his increasingly desperate messages, using terms that were even more clairvoyant than he realised: 'if the Provisional government does not give any indications or advice to Paris, the movement will begin without the authorisation of the government.'[76] That was exactly what was about to happen.

On the morning of Sunday 13 August, a group of Resistance fighters met in an apartment on rue Vulpian in the southern part of the city. All the men were members of a Resistance group in the Paris police that was linked to the Front National and thereby to the Communist Party. Although the Paris police had faultlessly carried out the anti-Semitic and repressive orders of Vichy, including a notorious round-up of Jews in 1942, there were several Resistance groups within the police force, some engaged in sabotage or in running escape lines for stranded Allied airmen, others working with Allied intelligence circuits.[77] At around 11:00, the meeting was interrupted by the news that the Germans had disarmed and arrested policemen in three northern sub-urbs.[78] Alarmed by the implication that the German Army was now targeting the police force, the meeting immediately decided to call for an all-out police strike from the morning of Tuesday 15 August. However, the Front National had an influence over less than 10 per cent of the 20,000 Paris policemen. For the call to be effective, the other police Resistance organisations would have to be brought on board.[79] Contacts were made with the Socialist Party's group, Police et Patrie, who agreed to print 20,000 leaflets calling for a strike, and a meeting was arranged with representatives of a third, Gaullist, Resistance group called Honneur de la Police, to take place the following day.

The Resistance was not alone in reacting so rapidly to the disarming of the police by the Germans. Fearing that this marked the beginning of a move against the whole police force, the Paris police headquarters, the Préfecture de Police, immediately ordered all policemen off the streets and out of uniform. Some perplexed Parisians noticed the protest – Victor Veau mused in his diary: 'The police guarding the police station are wearing civilian clothes. What does it mean?'[80] By 13:30 the police were back on the beat, after the Director of the Paris Municipal Police, Emile Hennequin, had sent a telegram to all the police stations assuring them that the incident was due to 'a misinterpretation by some local German services' and that the Germans would immediately rectify their mistake.[81]

But the disarming of the police was no mistake. On the same day, Milice leader Max Knipping sent a letter to the head of the gendarmerie, stating that the gendarmes in the Paris region would be disarmed, and that arms would henceforth be distributed to groups of volunteers who would patrol alongside members of the Milice.[82] With the approval of the Germans, the French fascists were preparing for combat in Paris. Suspicious of the police, obsessed with their campaign against Laval, who was notionally in charge of the government that commanded the police and the gendarmerie, the fascists and their German masters were trying to ensure that only the utterly loyal would have access to weapons. If the operation went well, they would short-circuit any opposition and would have a reliable police force at their beck and call. If it went badly, there would be a civil war in the capital.[83]

At 14:00 on Monday 14 August, the three police Resistance groups – Front National de la Police, Police et Patrie and Honneur de la Police – met in an apartment on rue Chapon, a narrow street on the northern edge of the Marais district. The meeting began with a brief discussion of Laval's scheme involving Herriot. Honneur et Police, the group most closely linked to the Gaullists, were particularly excited by this, so it was decided to let them deal with the affair – they immediately began planning to kidnap Herriot. The meeting then moved on to discussing the real issue: the proposed strike. There was bad news as the leaders of Police et Patrie had got cold feet, and had not printed the 20,000 leaflets as promised.[84] In a familiar refrain, their representative explained they were worried about the reprisals that might occur if the movement failed.[85] The Front National representative held two trump cards, however. First, he pointed out that by taking action the police force would be able to cleanse itself of the crimes committed by the Brigades Spéciales – the police squad that had targeted the Resistance during the occupation. Then he handed over to Colonel Rol, who was attending the meeting as regional leader of the FFI. Rol made clear that since he was not a policeman he could not express an opinion about the strike, but he deftly pointed out that the FFI had called for workers to stop working for the enemy, which implicitly included strike action by the police. With that, the argument was won, and the meeting voted unanimously for a strike, to begin the next day. A leaflet was produced carrying an 'order' (not a 'call') from the three Resistance organisations for a strike of all Paris policemen, warning that those who did not obey would 'be considered to be traitors and collaborators'.[86] On the other side of the leaflet was a declaration from Rol, who instructed policemen not to help the enemy in any way and threatened those who did not join the strike: 'You will refuse to participate in the arrests of patriots, raids, roadblocks, identity checks, holding prisoners, etc. You will help the FFI kill all those who, by not following these orders, are continuing to serve the enemy.'[87]

The Comité Parisien de la Libération also changed gear in its preparations for the insurrection. In a new round of instructions to the local liberation committees in the region, the CPL described what should be done with collaborators. Those to be arrested included hardline fascists and members of the Milice, important Vichy collaborators, leaders of the fascist political parties, and, more vaguely, those individuals 'whose attitude and speech have been particularly outrageous over the last few months ... in this task as in all others involved in the insurrection, it is popular rule that must be victorious and assert itself'.[88] In some cases, of course, 'popular rule' could be a recipe for personal score-settling and profound injustice. But the stakes were high – the Milice and their German masters had a terrifying track record of murderous violence and intimidation. They would have to be taken off the streets by any means necessary and dealt with by the legal system once peace was restored.

Posters issued by Rol's subordinate, Raymond Massiet ('Dufresne'), appeared on the walls of the capital calling for a 'general mobilisation' of all FFI members in the Paris region. Dufresne was a member of Ceux de la Résistance and, like his comrade de Vogüé, he was an ardent advocate of insurrection.[89] This was not yet a call for an uprising, but it was the penultimate step towards that goal.

Even those far removed from the military preparations on either side could sense the scale of the imminent conflict. Jewish housewife Jacqueline Mesnil-Amar wrote in her diary:

> The heat is heavy, grey and suffocating. Right now we can often hear the sound of artillery fire from the west . . . A kind of silent oppression weighs on the city, the café terraces are full, but people barely speak. The Parisians are waiting. The women are wearing their light-coloured summer dresses, very full – that's the way they're worn this summer (yes, people are still interested in fashion!), with their hair loose. Many of these women look beautiful, but if you observe them closely, you can see that their faces are drawn, their eyes are feverish and that nervous fatigue has hollowed out their features. The difficult daily struggle to find food, getting about on a bicycle, work, children, fighting for their family, has worn out these women, producing an underlying fever that has left cruel lines underneath the makeup . . . The city is like a pressure cooker, the temperature is slowly rising. Will we be declared an open city? Will they lay siege to Paris? Alone in the great Parisian silence, birds sing in the trees, children play in the squares, while old people, indifferent to the madness of the world, doze on park benches.[90]

4

Tuesday 15 August:
Turning-point

BBC journalist Godfrey Talbot broadcasts from the south of France: 'Our air armada was a tremendous sight. Tow-planes and gliders, four abreast in one great procession a mile or two long, flying at 2000 feet high in the blue sky, with fighter cover glinting and whirling overhead and the placid blue sea below ... I saw fourteen gliders land beautifully, close together, in one not-too-big field, half grass, half ploughed. They raised just a dust cloud, and then they stopped and out came men. And we, we wheeled and back we went, our plane and the tow-planes, and still unopposed, back over the coast, a Riviera coast that was lovely, beautiful there in the hot sun. Still not a shot, still not a soul to be seen, not a vehicle, not a movement. This is a great day, a new assault on the enemy in great strength. Great things are happening in the area between Nice and Marseilles.'[1]

Operation DRAGOON – the Allied invasion of the French Mediterranean coast – was not quite as peaceful as Talbot's bird's-eye view suggested. A fleet of over 600 vessels, including six battleships and four aircraft carriers, lay offshore. For two hours before the first Allied boot touched a Provençal beach, the German defences were subject to a ferocious air and naval bombardment, shaking the earth for miles around. At one point, 400 naval guns fired 16,000 shells in less than twenty minutes. The landings took place on a thirty-five-mile strip of coast to the east of Toulon, and were made by the Seventh US Army, backed up by de Gaulle's 1st French Army. The Allies were relieved to discover that the German defences that had survived the bombardment were relatively light and easily disposed of. German naval forces and the Luftwaffe in Provence had been severely weakened by Allied attacks and by a series of bad choices by the German High Command, who had moved men and machinery away from the region, perhaps trying to second guess Allied intentions or to meet the Allied offensive in Italy. Although the number of soldiers on each side was roughly comparable – 250,000 Allied men and around 210,000 Germans – the situation in the air was completely skewed: there were fewer than 200 German aircraft of all types in the region, compared to over 4000 in the US attack force. That statistic alone shows the inevitability of Allied victory over Germany.[2]

By the end of the day, thousands of men were dead – mainly Germans – and the Allies were in control of the beachhead. The Allies were ready to split into two groups: one to move west along the coast, dealing with German forces in Toulon and Marseille before moving north along the Rhône valley, the other to head through the stunning foothills of the Alps, driving along the winding *Route Napoleon* – the same mountain road that Napoleon's forces had followed in 1815.[3] All along their way the Allies were helped by the Resistance who harried the retreating Germans, provided intelligence to the advancing Allies, and launched insurrections to help ensure liberation. In less than a month, far ahead of schedule, the Allied armies, supported and aided by the Resistance, had liberated the whole of France, except for its north-east corner. The unravelling of the German occupation of France began in earnest with the landings in Provence. It is hardly surprising that on 31 August Hitler confided to two of his closest advisors: '15 August was the worst day of my life.'[4]

In Paris, news of the Allied landings spread quickly. The BBC announced it at lunchtime, and soon the cafés were buzzing. There were already plenty of reasons to be happy about the military situation – the whole of Brittany was liberated, with the exception of a few pockets, such as Brest, which would not fall for another month; American troops were in the suburbs of Blois and Orléans, and above all, the Allies had taken Chartres, a mere ninety kilometres south-west of Paris. With the Allies now fighting on two fronts, liberation seemed certain.

The proximity of the Allied armies to Paris led to a sharp increase in German air activity in the region. At lunchtime there was a massive aerial dogfight over Rambouillet, mid-way between Chartres and Paris, which saw the destruction of eighteen Allied and German aircraft. In the late afternoon, Allied raids on Luftwaffe airfields near Versailles wrecked planes on the ground, leading the Germans to withdraw at least one of their squadrons to the relative safety of the southern suburbs.[5]

Sensing that the situation around Paris was reaching a tipping-point, Leclerc again pestered Patton for orders to move on the capital. Patton became somewhat irritated, as he confided to his diary that night: 'Leclerc came in very much excited. He said, among other things, that if he were not allowed to advance on Paris, he would resign. I told him in my best French that he was a baby and ... that I had left him in the most dangerous place [at the front]. We parted friends.'[6] The 2e DB stayed where it was, around Argentan, moving to close the German exit from the Falaise pocket, which was now like a U on its side with the 2e DB near its open, eastern end. They were doing vital work for the Allied cause, but they were still over 150 km from where they wanted to be: Paris.

*

In Paris, economic life was grinding to a halt. The Métro was closed; households would have electricity for only an hour a day after 22:30.[7] It was impossible for anyone who had to travel more than a few kilometres to carry on working.[8] The most visible sign of the growing crisis was the police strike, which began with the morning shift, as planned. The word had been spread the previous evening and every police service was affected, including the emergency service and the police guarding the prisons.[9] Those who had not got the message learnt what was going on when they turned up for work. Sometimes, striking officers were not clear whose instructions they were following – a couple of policemen told Yves Cazaux that some colleagues had told them either to go home or to change out of uniform, but they were unsure whether these men were from the Resistance or the Prefect of Police.[10]

Posters were put up outside each police station, explaining the reasons for the strike; passers-by gathered to find out what was happening. Paul Tuffrau left his apartment near the Jardin du Luxembourg to see what was going on: the rue Jean-Bart police station was shut, while the commissariat at place Saint-Sulpice was completely empty. A passer-by told him that on the nearby rue d'Assas they had seen fifty policemen marching silently in civilian clothes, but wearing their official white belts and brandishing their truncheons, carrying a placard reading 'Death to the Prefect of Police'.[11] Not far away, in the police station at Saint-Germain, the commanding officer, a notorious collaborator called Turpeau, tried to convince his men to work as normal. Officer Le Rousès cut him short: 'You are the *ex*-Divisional Officer; you are no longer in command here. We obey only the orders of our Resistance leaders and of Algiers, until the Germans have left.' 'They're still here,' snapped Turpeau. 'Not for long,' replied Le Rousès.[12]

As the police strike took hold, supported by 95 per cent of the morning shift, the Prefect of Police, Amédée Bussière, desperately organised a series of meetings with rank-and-file police officers.[13] In the Mairie (town hall) of the 6th arrondissement, Bussière addressed over 300 policemen, all in civilian clothes, many in shirt-sleeves because of the heat. He pointed out the improvements he had made to their conditions – more cigarettes, free meals, a canteen and so on – but then played the moral card, reminding them that they had not deserted their posts in 1940 when the Germans arrived, and exhorting them not to do so when the Germans were on the point of leaving. Above all, he warned them against the 'incalculable consequences' of going on strike. None of this had any effect. In the afternoon, in an attempt to appease the strikers, Bussière sacked Hennequin, the hated Director of the Municipal Police. That made no difference, either.[14] Under the hot August sun, there had been a political earthquake: the police had changed sides.[15]

Paradoxically, this development alarmed Alexandre Parodi and in an urgent message to Algiers, which got badly garbled in transmission, he warned that the city was growing increasingly tense. Once again he underlined the danger of 'bloody reprisals' by the German commanders, urging the Free French to make a new appeal to the population 'in order to prevent a premature uprising'.[16] But by the time the message was received in Algiers, a week had passed and the uprising was in full swing.

The police strike had an immediate effect on Laval's scheme to stop the Gaullists from taking power in Paris. As well as urging Herriot to call a meeting of the National Assembly, Laval had been trying to persuade Pétain to be in Paris when the Allies arrived. However, by late afternoon Laval was forced to accept that the police strike could lead to a decisive shift in the situation by hastening the disintegration of state power in the capital. Laval felt that the moment had passed when Pétain could surf on a wave of popular acclaim and defuse the threat of insurrection. Equally important, Laval learnt from Darnand, the Vichy Minister of the Interior, that the Milice was going to be concentrated in the main cities, principally Paris and Lyons.[17] This was yet another sign that the French fascists were trying to take over law enforcement and were organising for civil war. They wanted to ensure that nothing happened in the major conurbations that might go against their plans, which were aimed against Laval and his scheme for a compromise with the Americans. Events were slipping out of Laval's grasp.

The Resistance plot to kidnap Herriot, hatched the previous day, proved short-lived. André Enfière, who had first come up with the idea of bringing Herriot to Paris, heard of the scheme from a friend in the Resistance and immediately telephoned Laval and told him that there were plans to 'assassinate' Herriot. With Laval's agreement, an elite squad of heavily armed policemen, who had not joined the strike, was sent to the Hôtel de Ville to guard Herriot's apartment. Then Enfière contacted Georges Bidault, the head of the CNR, and warned him that any attempt to kidnap Herriot would be vigorously resisted. In the late afternoon, as Honneur et Police were putting the finishing touches to their plan that allegedly involved 300 men, Bidault and the leader of Honneur et Police discussed the situation with Parodi in a café behind the Ecole Militaire. As always whenever Parodi was involved, prudence prevailed, and the project was abandoned.[18] Rather than support direct action, Parodi merely informed Algiers that he 'hoped it would be possible' to let Herriot know that the Resistance did not want the National Assembly to meet.[19] The upshot was that Laval was free to continue with his scheming and the heavily armed police squad remained in the Hôtel de Ville.

As Parodi prevaricated, the growing tension in the region led the two main military forces of the Resistance – the FFI and the communist-led FTP – to move their headquarters into the capital. The day before, Colonel Rol had decided to split the FFI centre into two and locate them in the inner southern suburbs – one in Malakoff, the other in Montrouge – to respond rapidly to the changing situation. On the morning of 15 August, Rol met with his FTP comrade Pierre Le Queinnec and emphasised that the insurrection was not far off. Surprisingly, Le Queinnec was hostile to the move towards open conflict, and Rol had to forcefully explain that any hesitation in coming into the open could lead to decisive opportunities being missed. This was an accurate diagnosis of the problem that now faced all wings of the Resistance. The reflexes of secrecy had been burnt into Resistance fighters over the previous four years; stepping out of the shadows into the light of day was now proving just as difficult as going underground had been.[20] Meanwhile, Rol's wife Cécile, accompanied by her mother, brought guns and equipment from their house in the southern suburb of Antony. Cécile's mother pushed a pram containing Rol's son Jean, together with a typewriter and a machine gun; the pair walked past the German checkpoints without encountering any difficulty, then Cécile got on a bicycle together with her precious load, leaving her mother to take the baby back home.[21]

The leadership of the FTP was making similar moves. Their military headquarters had been based in Charles Tillon's house in the sleepy village of Chevreuse, twenty-five kilometres to the south-west of the capital; now it was to be moved to the heart of events. But getting to Paris was a problem. Tillon, his wife Colette and a comrade were preparing their bicycles for the long ride to their new urban base, and were loading them up with parcels of documents and weapons when a dozen German troops arrived and began setting up a machine-gun nest at the cross-roads outside the house. The soldiers were distracted by the offer of beer, which they gratefully drank in the shade of a nearby tree. Meanwhile, Tillon and his two comrades clambered onto their bicycles and made their way to Paris, dodging German patrols.[22]

To make it absolutely clear which way the wind was blowing, the leader of the Communist Party, Jacques Duclos, wrote an article in the party's underground newspaper, *L'Humanité*, which was the closest anyone had come to calling for an insurrection: 'Men and women of Paris, young and old, everyone must fight, by any means, and make our great capital city, the heart of France, the site of a popular insurrection and an insurrectional general strike. This will help us win the battle of Paris and will hasten the time when the whole of France will be free.'[23]

This kind of statement was exactly what the more authoritarian wing of the Free French Delegation in Paris feared. In a letter to Emmanuel d'Astier in Algiers, Léon Morandat outlined the differences within the Delegation; Regional Military Delegate Roland Pré ('Oronte') was in favour of 'order at any price' and was preparing for armed confrontation with Resistance insurgents. Morandat himself had a completely different position: he was prepared to take a gamble and to call on the Parisian population to rise up. Morandat recognised that this was 'dangerous', but his reasoning was quite logical: 'an uprising of the Parisian population is inevitable, and if it is not we who lead it, then it will take place against us. We will have to be strong in order to lead it, and not to be led by it. That is why the General must be here as soon as Paris is liberated.' Predictably, Parodi had not decided which approach he agreed with – 'temperamentally he is with Oronte, but he has a good political sense, and despite everything he understands the advantages of our position and feels it is inevitable,' wrote Morandat.[24]

Morandat did not know it, but he was on a similar wavelength to Chaban, who had arrived in Le Mans after a three-day journey from London. In Le Mans, Chaban had seen the local FFI fighters being rapidly replaced by army officers who for years had done nothing to help the Resistance but had recently taken their uniforms out of mothballs and were now trying to take command. Chaban sensed that this would cause problems, and in a letter to General Koenig – the nominal head of the FFI – Chaban insisted that as long as the FFI were helping the Allied offensive, 'they should keep their organisation and their leaders ... If we do not act in this way, we will have internal difficulties that can only lead the Allies to change their attitude.'[25] In other words, if a strictly military conception of liberation were applied, with the Free French Army rapidly sidelining the FFI, there could be armed confrontations with parts of the Resistance which would undermine the Free French's claim to enjoy the full support of the French population, and might lead the Allies to think again about whether the Free French should form the government of liberated France.

*

Conscious of the power of propaganda in cowing the public, von Choltitz made his first declaration to the Parisian population. He recognised that food, electricity and gas supplies were problematic – how could he deny it? – but he claimed this was due to 'sabotage'. In a statement that was widely reproduced in the collaborationist press, Choltitz told the population, and the Resistance, what he would do: 'Order will be imposed with the greatest possible determination. The food supplies of the Parisian population depend on order.'[26] The article spelt it out: 'In case of sabotage, attacks or riots, the Military Governor von Choltitz is determined to immediately apply the most severe, indeed the most brutal, means of repression. The proximity of the front line places particular responsibilities on the German Military Authorities, and justifies this intransigent attitude. All means that repress disorder, including the harshest, will be employed ... Everything necessary will be done to maintain order and to pitilessly repress disorder.'[27]

Von Choltitz prepared to put his threat into action; Berlin had ordered him to destroy the dozens of bridges in Paris and the suburbs to block the Allied advance – a week earlier, the Germans in Florence had destroyed every bridge over the Arno, with the exception of the historic ponte Vecchio. Because most of the bridges across the Seine and the Loire to the west and south of the French capital had already been destroyed, the only direct route eastwards would soon pass through the centre of Paris. To ensure that von Choltitz had the means to carry out this order, Hitler had dispatched an ordnance battalion, which was billeted in the Senate building under the watchful eye of German quartermaster Robert Wallraf. As Wallraf settled the men in, he talked to their commanding officer, a squat and surly man, sunburnt from months of campaigning. When Wallraf asked whether the task of destroying so many bridges was daunting, the officer boasted that his unit had already carried out similar missions on the Eastern Front, in Stalingrad, Kiev and Kharkov, without any problem. The order would certainly require a huge amount of explosive, but that was already at hand in the form of several hundred torpedoes that the German Navy had stored in a disused road tunnel at Saint-Cloud. To expedite matters, von Choltitz ordered lorries to be put at the disposal of the ordnance battalion to transport the torpedoes from the western suburbs into the city centre.[28]

For the second day running, von Choltitz met von Kluge and the other commanders in the massive German command bunker at Saint-Germain-en-Laye, to discuss the preparations for the defence and eventual destruction of the city.[29] After the war, Lieutenant-General Bodo Zimmermann, who was not present at the meeting, claimed that von Kluge and von Choltitz agreed not to defend the city by house-to-house fighting in order 'to avoid destruction and loss of life'.[30] If this decision was taken, it seems unlikely to have been based on a humanitarian desire to protect Paris or its population. A more probable justification would have been a sober estimate of the morale and battle-readiness of the German garrison, coupled with secret doubts at the highest level – two weeks later, von Choltitz admitted in a private conversation: 'I have been a defeatist for the last two years, and I no longer feel optimistic about the outcome of the war.'[31]

After the meeting, von Kluge left Army Group B headquarters to meet with General Eberbach at Nécy, eight kilometres south-east of Falaise, and discuss the increasingly serious situation on the Western Front. But von Kluge never arrived, and the alarm bells began to ring in Hitler's headquarters in Poland. Hitler's paranoid suspicions about von Kluge's loyalty flared once again, and rumours spread that Kluge had gone over to the Allies.[32] Eberbach received an urgent message: 'Establish whereabouts of Field Marshal Kluge. Report back every hour.'[33] For the next twelve hours the Wehrmacht vainly scoured the Normandy front for signs of their leader. Eventually, around midnight, von Kluge turned up at Eberbach's command post. An Allied fighter plane had attacked his car and he had lost all radio contact; he had spent much of the day hiding in a ditch while Allied aircraft buzzed overhead, and then found himself on roads jammed with the chaos of retreating German vehicles. Back in Poland the damage was done. Hitler was convinced that von Kluge was untrustworthy and made preparations to replace him with a commander who looked and behaved like a cartoon Nazi, bullet head, monocle and all: the utterly loyal Field Marshal Walter Model.

In Paris, wild rumours began to circulate. The newspapers claimed that there was an American general at the Hôtel de Ville, negotiating with the Laval government.[34] According to Léon Morandat, it was not a 'general' but a US 'diplomat' who was discussing with Laval.[35] Hidden in his attic, Albert Grunberg not only heard this rumour, he was even told that Paris would be declared an open city, policed by three different forces (French, German and American).[36] For Marc Boegner, who was generally well informed, the only thing preventing an agreement between the Americans and the Germans was the extent of the planned German retreat: the Germans wanted to retreat five kilometres from Paris, whereas the Americans apparently wanted them back sixty kilometres.[37] There is no evidence that any such discussions were taking place or that a US general or diplomat was in Paris at this time.[38]

More truthful than any of these fantasies was the gossip that writer Jean Galtier-Boissière recorded in his diary: the 'collabos' were getting frightened, while the bankers and bosses were trembling with fear, convinced that each night would bring a communist coup.[39] The accuracy of some of these rumours is shown by the behaviour of the fascist Marcel Déat. The man who had been a hero during World War I lost his nerve as the Paris sky was filled with the continuous rumble of distant artillery fire.[40] Keeping one eye on the moment when he would have to flee the capital, Déat incessantly demanded to be updated on the number of vehicles and the amount of fuel at his disposition. Appropriately, he noted with satisfaction in his diary that a stylish hearse had been requisitioned for his escape.[41]

*

As the collaborators prepared to leave Paris, the Allies sent their men into the city. With London's agreement, Guy Marchant and Adrien Chaigneau of the Jedburgh Team AUBREY, accompanied by the French SOE agent 'Spiritualist' (Major Armand), made their way to the capital from their base to the north-east of Paris.[42] The journey, by bicycle, was uneventful. Marchant was given Spanish papers, as his French was too poor to enable him to pass for a native; Chaigneau was provided with French papers and a precious motorcycle, and he began organising the scattered FFI forces that were part of the SPIRITUALIST circuit. The third member of the team, radio operator Ivor Hooker, had contracted mumps, so he stayed back at base, relaying messages to London every day or so. SPIRITUALIST's previous SOE radio operator, Eileen Nearne, had been arrested by the Gestapo in July; although she had been able to convince the Germans that she was simply a French girl mixed up in something that was way over her head, she was still locked up in Fresnes prison.

AUBREY's instructions stated that if they were arrested, Marchant, Chaigneau and Hooker would be considered as 'soldiers in uniform performing ordinary military duties'. That was all very reassuring, but they were not wearing uniforms and there was little doubt that if they were arrested they would be shot as spies.[43] Despite this very real danger, Marchant moved around Paris, sometimes sleeping at Major Armand's apartment, sometimes returning to their base in the countryside. Marchant's report on food supplies in the capital revealed the classic situation of a city in wartime: although there was rationing, virtually anything could be obtained on the black market: 'In the restaurants there was no shortage of food or wine. Better meals could be obtained than anywhere in London – at a price. A lunch of hors-d'oeuvres, Camembert cheese and peaches for three people cost around 4000 francs. Nevertheless all restaurants were crowded.'[44] For ordinary people such luxuries were mere dreams. In many neighbourhoods it was impossible to cook at home as the gas supply was cut completely, so the city council planned to set up communal kitchens.[45] Because of the lack of fuel and flour, the bakers announced they would not be able to bake bread.[46] Even water was becoming scarce. The water pressure was reduced, and all over the city Parisians began collecting water in bottles and baths, adding drops of potassium permanganate to sterilise it, turning it purple in the process.[47]

The tenth birthday of Jacqueline Mesnil-Amar's daughter Sylvie was on 15 August, so she had to have some kind of party. Her only friend still in Paris was duly invited round and the two girls played in a desultory fashion. In a lowered voice, the friend's mother started asking Jacqueline whether there was any news of André, Jacqueline's husband, who had been arrested on 18 July for his involvement in a Jewish Resistance organisation and was being held in Fresnes prison. Little Sylvie stiffened slightly and paid attention to what the two grown-ups were saying as she carried on playing; Jacqueline had not told her daughter that André was in prison, preferring to tell her stories about his bravery in the Resistance. In her diary that night, Jacqueline worried about the effect the situation was having on Sylvie and all the other children: 'They listen, then they play, then they look at us without saying anything, then they play again ... Does she really believe the stories we tell her? Above all, does she want to believe them?'

One evening in autumn 1943, Sylvie had been present when the Gestapo raided her grandmother's apartment; she had hidden under the covers, pretending to be asleep. 'She never spoke about it,' wrote Jacqueline in her diary. 'What do our children know of our terror? They are so close, but also so distant; so often, they leave us, abandoning the world of adults for their life in an eternal present.' Inevitably, the adult world impinged on Sylvie, who displaced her fears into dreams that disconcerted and upset her mother, such as the one about her 2-year-old cousin, Zabeth: 'You know, Mummy, I dreamt that they put Zabeth in a big box at the station, and they wrote "Deportation" on it in big letters. What does it mean?'[48]

All across the Paris region, thousands of prisoners were about to discover the answer to Sylvie's question. At Fresnes prison, shortly after a breakfast of soup, the prisoners were ordered out of their cells and into a massive hall where there was a roll call. Around 1500 men and women were then led out and loaded into dozens of buses and lorries, guarded by SS soldiers who continually threatened them with guns. The prisoners were ordered to sit down with their heads bowed and not to look up as the convoy crossed Paris. Resistance fighter André Rougeyron recalled: 'What a contrast: as we were going towards our deaths, thousands of people were enjoying the August sunshine and sitting idly at sidewalk cafés. A few noticed us, and I remember seeing, through the slats in the side of the truck, some horror-stricken Parisians watching our convoy pass by. A few women were weeping.'[49]

The same scene was repeated in prisons across the Paris region – la Santé, Cherche-Midi, Romainville, Compiègne; Resistance prisoners were loaded up and taken to Pantin railway station on the north-east edge of the capital. As the vehicles went through Paris, prisoners threw notes for loved ones onto the street, desperately hoping that a passer-by would deliver the message to its destination. One note that did get to its addressee, thanks to the help of the prison bus driver, was written by Virginia d'Albert-Lake, an American living in France who had been arrested for helping Allied airmen. As she was taken from Romainville Virgina wrote hopefully to a friend: 'The entire prison is being evacuated this morning to an unknown destination. Thank you for the parcel which arrived yesterday. It was a lovely one and brought me much pleasure. My fifteen days have passed very agreeably. It's very sad to be obliged to leave when the others are so near. But what can we do? Morale is high and I'm in good health. I am one of three hundred women leaving the prison. My love to all, especially to my darling. See you soon! Virginia.'[50] Along with Virginia and André, over 2200 men and women were literally treated like animals by the Germans: they were herded onto the broad bricked surface of the *quai aux bestiaux* – the cattle platform – at Pantin goods station and then corralled in groups of up to 120 into cattle wagons, where they were so tightly packed no one could sit down. There was a meagre supply of water that was soon exhausted, and a single central pan acted as a stinking toilet. The heavy wooden doors were slid shut and then padlocked, leaving the prisoners in semi-darkness and fetid, stifling heat. They waited there all day under the baking August sun. Convoy I-264 was being assembled; its twin destinations were the concentration camps at Buchenwald (for the men) and Ravensbrück (for the women).

One of the prisoners taken onto the train was SOE agent Georges Clément, who had been caught by the Gestapo in Le Mans two days before the Allies liberated the city. At Pantin, he dropped a scrap of paper marked with the name and address of Andrée Goubillon, whose café sheltered SUSSEX agents passing through Paris. The note, which was duly transmitted to Madame Goubillon, read: 'Have been arrested. Leaving for Germany. I can forget about resting. In friendship.' Clément was executed at Mauthausen a month later.[51]

All over Paris, families were alerted to the imminent deportation of their loved ones, and scores of mothers, daughters and sisters flocked to Pantin, carrying food or simply good wishes. Over half a century later, Geneviève Savreux, who was a child at the time, recalled rushing with her mother to the station to catch a glimpse of her father, Resistance fighter Robert Savreux. She was able to wait on the platform near her father's wagon: 'All afternoon I stayed near Daddy, despite the German guards. I was wearing a beige pleated skirt with a red blouse and a belt with laces that Daddy had bought me. In the end, the SS made us leave. I can still hear the whistle of the train when it left.'[52] Geneviève never saw her father again.

Madame Guilhamon heard her son, Paul, was being deported on a train from the Gare de l'Est, so she went there, only to discover that the convoy would in fact be leaving from Pantin. She managed to borrow a bicycle from a railway worker and pedalled her way to the eastern suburb. There she was eventually able to say goodbye to Paul. Madame Guilhamon spent the whole evening at the side of the platform, waiting, before exhaustion set in and she was sent away.[53] Paul was only twenty-three; he would be dead before the year was out.

Among the dozens of desperate women was 40-year-old Marie-Hélène Lefaucheux; she was not only the wife of Pierre Lefaucheux ('Gildas'), the regional FFI leader whose arrest in June had led to Rol's promotion, she was also a Resistance leader and a member of the CPL. Early that morning, Madame Lefaucheux heard that prisoners were going to be transported from Fresnes. She had followed the convoy in a motorbike sidecar driven by a friend, after glimpsing the face of her husband in the last bus. After spending much of the day watching prisoners being herded into the cattle wagons, she finally managed to get through the sentries and onto the platform with a food parcel:

A soldier grabbed me by the arm, shouting that he would shoot. I shook myself free and said that it was *ganz egal* [no matter] to me and I hurried along the platform, calling out my husband's name. An officer followed me, uncertain whether to stop me or not. Suddenly a voice replied from one of the wagons: 'Lefaucheux? That's "Gildas" – he's in the next wagon.' I turned to the officer and said, 'I want to give this parcel to my husband.' He hesitated a second and then gestured to a soldier to open the door. I called Pierre's name, gave him the parcel and kissed him. Then I left, without looking at either the officer or the soldier.[54]

At 21:30, in a desperate attempt to stop the deportations, Raoul Nordling went to see Laval at the Hôtel Matignon. Earlier he had been supposed to meet Parodi for the first time, to get Free French agreement for his plans to save the prisoners. But Parodi had not turned up to their Montparnasse rendezvous, so Nordling went empty handed to see Laval. The streets were dark and deserted, and when he got to the Hôtel Matignon, the luxurious building was dimly lit by candles carried by flunkies. Nordling was ushered into Laval's office, which was illuminated by a hurricane lamp, around which huddled Abetz and Laval. The imminent collapse of collaboration was summed up in this scene of desolation. Once again, Nordling denounced the conditions in which the prisoners were being deported, only for Abetz to claim with some glee that he had personally talked to SS General Oberg and from now on 'only' seventy to eighty prisoners would be crammed into each wagon, while the Red Cross would be allowed to give out parcels before the convoy left.

Undeterred, Nordling pressed on and outlined his plan for all political prisoners in the Paris region to be handed over to the Red Cross, stating that in return German prison guards would be allowed to go free. Far overstepping his diplomatic role – and the truth – he stated that he could also speak for 'the French government' in this matter. Laval bridled, pointing out that he was the representative of the French government, but when Nordling made clear he was speaking about de Gaulle's Provisional Government in Algiers, neither Abetz nor Laval batted an eyelid. This was very telling: here they were, the prime minister of France, together with Hitler's diplomatic representative, apparently negotiating with the Free French, and yet nothing could seem more natural. The only sour moment came when Nordling pointed out that Germany might need the goodwill of the Allies. 'So, Monsieur Nordling, you think that Germany has lost the war?' sneered Abetz. 'I think that things are not going very well for your army,' Nordling replied.[55]

Over at Pantin, far from the gilded chandeliers of the Hôtel Matignon, the convoy was eventually completed. Among the prisoners were 168 Allied airmen – American, British, Canadian, Australian and New Zealanders who had been arrested in France.[56] Like the Resistance prisoners, they were classed as 'terrorists', not prisoners of war, because they had been caught trying to escape to Britain. Many of them had been captured in Gestapo stings – they thought they were involved with members of a Resistance escape line, but discovered too late that their contacts were German agents.[57] Also on the train was Alix d'Unienville, a 26-year-old French SOE agent who had been working with Parodi and had been arrested in Paris on D-Day.[58] She had feigned mental illness but the Germans were not fooled and she was sent to Romainville prison. One of her SOE comrades, Eileen Nearne, SPIRITUALIST's radio operator, was also on the train. Other prisoners loaded onto the convoy included Philip Keun, the founder of the JADE-AMICOL intelligence circuit, who would be murdered in Buchenwald in September, and 22-year-old Paul Aribaud, a BCRA radio operator, who had been arrested in Paris in July, and would die in Ellrich concentration camp in January 1945.[59] It is not known how many prisoners were on the convoy, nor how many died in deportation, but at best only one third of those on the train lived to return home.[60]

Some prisoners did not even reach the death camps, as at the last minute the Germans changed their mind over what was to happen to them. André Rondenay, the Free French Military Delegate for the northern zone, had been arrested on 27 July together with his comrade Alain de Beaufort. Thirty-year-old Rondenay had been responsible for organising the campaign of Resistance sabotage that accompanied D-Day; had he evaded capture, he would no doubt have played a vital role in the liberation of Paris. But he had been arrested, tortured and then thrown into the cells at Fresnes.[61] Along with other inmates, Rondenay was herded onto the convoy; then, at the last minute, the Gestapo either worked out who he was or decided they had other plans for him. Rondenay, de Beaufort and three of their comrades were taken out of their wagon and driven off to the north of Paris where, in a small clearing in the forest at Domont, they were murdered by a Gestapo gang led by SS Count Alexander de Kreutz, along with Herbert-Martin Hagen, the Secretary-General of the Paris SS police, and Ernst Heinrichsohn, who normally haunted the Drancy prison camp. After the murders, they returned to Gestapo headquarters on the rue des Saussaies and quaffed champagne in what they proudly called 'an executioners' banquet'.[62]

At some point in the evening, prisoners in the wagons at Pantin heard shouting and the sound of machine-gun fire: a dozen prisoners had managed to escape. But that escape came at a price: one escapee was shot by a guard, while the next day, in a brutal reprisal, the SS took a number of men out of the train, made them dig their own graves and then shot them.[63]

Shortly before midnight, the train lurched and clanged and began to move off. One of the prisoners, the 74-year-old priest Abbé Hénocque, recalled the scene three years later:

> It was completely dark and the heat was suffocating. Our chests were heaving. Air came in only through two tiny openings covered with a grill. What a sad human cargo, reduced to the level of parcels. Torn from our country, taken by the enemy to dens of torture, we understood the full horror of our destiny. Despair froze our hearts. But it takes more than that to crush the French soul. Suddenly, the 'Marseillaise' rang out, vibrant, irresistible, full of hope, a beautiful challenge that was transmitted from wagon to wagon, all down the convoy.[64]

There were some rays of light among the horror. Nineteen-year-old Resistance fighter Madeleine Riffaud had been imprisoned for shooting a German officer in broad daylight three weeks earlier. She had already been sentenced to death, and should have been executed on 5 August, but the Gestapo wanted to torture her some more. Two weeks after the intended date of her execution, Riffaud wrote a poem to convey her experience:

> At rue des Saussaies I heard the sound –
> I swear – of someone playing Bach,
> Accompanied, occasionally drowned,
> By the screams of torture.[65]

As Riffaud stood in the baking-hot wagon at Pantin, word got round that the Red Cross were to be allowed to remove any women who were pregnant, ill or wounded and take them to hospital.[66] To Riffaud's amazement, the other prisoners began helping her and 'Anne-Marie', a 50-year-old Intelligence Service agent, to change their appearance. Clothes were exchanged, hairstyles were altered and then, in a daze, the two women were pushed out onto the platform. Riffaud later said it was like being reborn. Huddled on the platform with over 200 other lucky women, Riffaud and her new comrade eventually saw the train pull away into the darkness in a cloud of steam and smoke, taking with it the women who had saved their lives. As the SS guards were processing the women, who were now in the custody of the Red Cross, Riffaud and Anne-Marie were recognised and were eventually taken back to Fresnes, where they were put back on death row. But at least they were still alive, and not on the train.[67]

*

Earlier in the day the city had felt idyllic, even in the midst of growing military activity. Gabrielle Bonnet, a 37-year-old amateur painter, set up an awning on her balcony and sat in the summer heat, watching the German vehicles in the street below: 'There is an endless stream of cars and lorries, camouflaged with leafy branches, some of them keeping under the shade of the trees to make sure they are hidden. They are moving everything out. Lorries drive by jam-packed with soldiers, coming from the Front no doubt. The soldiers look frightening, their rifles and their machine guns are pointing at the windows in the buildings. The weather is marvellous.'[68] Elsewhere, the ubiquitous parade of bicycles was even more striking than usual. Galtier-Boissière saw an old white-haired lady in a black silk dress, perched on the front pannier of a bicycle, whizzing round the place de la Concorde,[69] while Odette Lainville brewed a whole cultural theory out of the phenomenon:

> Generally, Madame rides behind, side-saddle; sometimes she is jauntily astride the saddle. Some ladies hold tightly onto their man. Others

seem remarkably at ease, and powder their noses or do their hair, for all the world as though they were sitting in a chair. And then there are those who are seated on the rack that goes over the front wheel. They look a bit silly, like a big baby being carted about. Finally, there is the 'sit on the crossbar' brigade, literally in the arms of their happy chauffeur, who is pedalling away with his nose in blonde or brunette hair that is flowing in the wind.[70]

For Robert Brasillach, the fascist author whose pre-war fame had been enhanced by his infamous collaborationist writings, this urban beauty was elegiac, promising the collapse of his world: 'You could feel that everything was at an end. You could measure the catastrophe inch by inch, and yet the weather was marvellous, the women were delicious, and you caught your breath at the most magical sights – the Seine, the Louvre, Notre Dame – the whole while wondering what would become of it all.'[71]

As dusk fell, 37-year-old administrator Roger Trentesaux heard the sound of gunfire. He wrote in his diary that night:

20:00: boulevard Brune, shots fired towards the Porte d'Orleans; I went to look; gunfire everywhere, German patrols firing all over the place, I hurried home; when I'd calmed down, I went out to the waste ground, then the Huns started firing again; 100 m away, on rue Ernst Reyer, a man fell to the ground; I ran home. The shooting got worse, firing at the windows, a German fired at the concierge, Monsieur Jaussaud, to get him to go inside ... Loads of passers-by have taken refuge here, the women are frightened because the Huns keep on firing into the air in our courtyard.[72]

The man Trentesaux saw being shot dead was off-duty policeman Louis Brelivet. A good-looking young man of twenty-seven, with a broad, strong jaw, Brelivet was in his apartment when German troops entered the building to arrest a Jewish family. He tried to stop the Germans, and killed two of them. They responded by machine-gunning him in the face.[73] A 13-year-old boy was also killed in the incident.[74]

As a welcome thunderstorm drenched the city, easing the oppressive heat, Odette Lainville closed her diary on a high note, focusing on what was to come: 'Night falls. Another day has passed, a day that brings us closer to that marvellous liberty, which is already sweeping towards us along our French roads.'[75]

5

Wednesday 16 August: Crimes

André Gillois, the Free French spokesman, broadcasts on the BBC: 'Today the hour of revenge has sounded. Tomorrow it will be the hour of pitiless punishment – punishment for the Gestapo war criminals, punishment for the SS war criminals. We know your names. You are at the top of our list . . . Punishment for those Wehrmacht officers who seek to blame the SS or the Gestapo for things for which they are responsible. For example, is General von Choltitz the military governor of Paris, the absolute master of the city, or is he not? He must have signed the order for the political prisoners to be handed over and murdered. His staff officers are also responsible for this massacre, because they are associated with the order. The leaders of the Wehrmacht, who gave him their authority and thus authorised these crimes, are also war criminals. We have sworn to punish all these criminals, to exact revenge for all crimes, to mete out unforgiving justice. This oath will be upheld.' [1]

Early in the morning, after a slow journey from Pantin, Convoy I-264 came to a halt in a long tunnel about sixty kilometres to the east of Paris. The deportees could see nothing; outside in the darkness there was the sound of jackboots on gravel, accompanied by shouting in German. Even at a standstill, smoke oozed from the engine and soon the fetid air in the wagons mingled with acrid locomotive fumes.[2] The train had stopped in a long tunnel under a hilly ridge near the station of Nanteuil-Saâcy. Word quickly spread down the train that the Resistance had mounted an attack and that everyone would be freed. Sadly for the prisoners, this was not the case. The train had stopped because an Allied bombing raid had destroyed the bridge over the Marne and it was impossible to go any further. After some time there was more clanking and hissing and lurching and the convoy backed out of the tunnel and stopped near a pasture. Over 2000 deportees were ordered out of the stinking wagons and made to stand in the field while the Germans decided what to do next. After an hour or so, the SS guards lined up the men and women, five abreast, and marched them upriver to the next bridge then on to the station at Nanteuil-Saâcy, where another train was to be brought in to take them away. As well as their own meagre affairs, some of the prisoners were given German booty to carry – paintings, cases of wine and champagne – which had been looted from Paris.[3]

As the prisoners were marched through the villages, the inhabitants watched, helpless. Two years later, Virginia d'Albert-Lake recalled the scene: 'Some smiled – tender, sympathetic smiles; others stood immobile with tears in their eyes. We called out to them: "*Bon courage, à bientôt! Vive la France!*" I, too, was blinded by tears. At one place an earnest-looking young fellow suddenly broke from a group of people to take a heavy suitcase from the hand of a weary woman who had not wished to abandon the few things she possessed. The Germans permitted him to stride along beside us.'[4] When the prisoners passed through the village of Méry-sur-Marne, they broke ranks and ran to a water fountain, desperate to slake their thirst. The soldiers blocked their way and hit them with rifle butts. In the confusion, two women prisoners seized their chance and ran. Nicole de Witasse darted into a farmyard and hid in a haystack, but she was dragged out by German guards, who repeatedly smashed her in the face and then took her away. She eventually starved to death in a concentration camp.[5] SOE radio operator Alix d'Unienville was luckier – she ran into a courtyard and disappeared into the shadow of a doorway. Suddenly the door opened and she almost fell into a kitchen; she whirled around and saw a man and a woman sitting there, peeling potatoes. 'Save me!' she said, and grabbed an apron and a peeling knife so she would look like a member of the family. Luckily, the Germans did not come searching for her, and over the next two weeks Alix was passed from house to house until the Americans arrived.[6]

As the stream of prisoners moved down the road, a woman turned up on a bicycle, panting for breath. She was Resistance leader Marie-Hélène Lefaucheux, whose husband was one of the deportees. In Paris she had heard that the train would have to stop at Nanteuil-Saâcy because of the bombed bridge, so in a scene worthy of fiction, she had managed to get a lift to Meaux where she had borrowed a bicycle; she had finally pedalled thirty kilometres to where the prisoners were gathered. After running up and down the shuffling column of men and women, she eventually found her husband, only to be hit in the face with a truncheon by an SS guard. Undeterred, she walked alongside the prisoners for the next few kilometres until a halt was ordered, and another guard allowed her to talk to her husband for a few minutes. Then the march began again and the prisoners moved off to the station.

Marie-Hélène was joined by 23-year-old Claire Girard, who was looking for her brother; together the two women found a hotel room in Saâcy. In the early hours of the next morning, they heard the sound of the re-assembled convoy leaving Nanteuil-Saâcy station, heading eastwards once more.[7] Conditions on the new train were even worse – there were fewer wagons so the prisoners were packed in even more tightly. André Rougeyron recalled: 'Any man who squatted or even bent over slightly was sure to be trampled immediately. We had to remain standing, always standing. Tempers flared, and arguments became frequent, often violent. We were crushing each other; our thirst was unbearable, and some prisoners licked the iron parts of the car to get a sensation of coolness.'[8] As the train progressed relentlessly eastwards, it was tracked by Marie-Hélène and Claire, who had resolved to follow their loved ones as long as they could and, if possible, to free them.

The departure of the convoy from Paris galvanised Raoul Nordling. Diplomacy had failed to prevent the Germans from carrying out their threat to deport thousands of political prisoners, so he decided to take the initiative.[9] In the afternoon, in a bar behind the Opéra, Nordling met Parodi for the first time. Nordling explained his plan to put the prisons in the Paris region under the control of the Red Cross; in return, Parodi, speaking in the name of the Algiers government, said he would allow the remaining German prison guards free passage out of the capital.[10] This included the guards in the Drancy transit camp who had been directly involved in deporting tens of thousands of Jews.

While these negotiations were taking place, the Germans continued to visit their killing ground in the forest at Domont. The day before it had been used to murder Resistance leader André Rondenay and his four comrades; on 16 August the SS, with the support of the Milice, arrested and shot thirteen Resistance fighters from Domont. One of the murdered men was Pierre Alviset, who had joined the Resistance on D-Day.[11] On his twentieth birthday, less than two months before his death, Pierre had written in his diary: 'I am 20 years old. It is a happy age. I want to become a man and an honourable Frenchman.'[12]

*

The Allies continued their movement eastwards, capturing Orleans and Dreux and reaching the centre of Chartres with the help of the local Resistance, allowing a triumphant General Patton to survey the scene, although the city was not yet completely secure.[13] The Allies were now less than 100 km from Paris. To the west, where they were gradually closing the mouth of the Falaise pocket, the very notion of a front line began to dissolve. At one point, two petrol supply columns, one Allied and the other German, swept past each other on a country road, going in opposite directions. In the early hours of the morning, US journalist Thomas Treanor was having a well-earned doze in a French village that was allegedly in Allied hands when a group of German tanks rumbled up and clanked to a halt; Treanor heard a young German soldier calling out: 'I want to sleep!' But after much shouting and squabbling about which way the column should go, the vehicles rumbled off into the night. The next day Treanor found the wreckage of two of the tanks, smoke rising from the blackened hulks.[14]

Meanwhile, General Leclerc was twiddling his thumbs at Argentan. Frustrated at the lack of action, he again pestered Patton, writing a letter reporting that there was no fighting in his sector, and asking whether he could begin gathering his forces for the advance on Paris.

Patton reassured Leclerc that he understood the role that the French troops were to have in the liberation of the capital, but that it was not yet the moment; privately Patton wondered whether Leclerc could be relied on to follow orders.[15]

Allied command was well aware of the situation in Paris. In the morning, Jean Sainteny ('Dragon') of the ALLIANCE spy circuit had ridden through the German lines on the back of a motorcycle driven by his comrade, Bernard de Billy; both were disguised as telephone engineers. MI6 headquarters in London wanted to exfiltrate Sainteny from France, so the leader of ALLIANCE, Marie-Madeleine Fourcade, had spent the previous few days gathering documents for Sainteny to take to the Allies. Sainteny and de Billy arrived at Patton's headquarters near Le Mans in the late afternoon. They passed on the material assembled by Fourcade, together with their own precious observations on the state of German defences, and gave the address of a safe letter-box they had set up behind enemy lines, where material could be picked up by the Allies as they advanced.[16] That evening, de Billy made the return journey, taking back with him 'Lieutenant P', a French spy who worked for the US military intelligence, who had orders to contact the FFI, in order to make a link between the Allies and the Resistance fighters.[17]

As Sainteny left Paris, Chaban was in Le Mans, preparing to return to the capital with bad news. On his way back from London, he had been taken to meet General Gerow, one of Patton's immediate subordinates, just behind the front line of the Allied advance. Gerow told Chaban in no uncertain terms that the Allies had no immediate plans to liberate Paris. Instead, they were going to go around it. The military logic was impeccable – indeed, the Germans were not expecting an all-out assault, but rather some kind of slow siege following encirclement.[18] From a strictly military point of view, the city of Paris had no strategic value, and the 20,000 German soldiers garrisoned there represented no particular threat to the massive Allied armies. However, if the city were to become an Allied responsibility, that could have major consequences for the war. As General Omar Bradley put it some years later: 'I feared that the liberation of Paris might cause our supply line to snap. Each ton that went into that city meant one less for the

Front, and G-5 of Army Group had estimated the Parisians would require an initial 4,000 tons per day. If Paris could pull in its belt and live with the Germans a little longer, each 4,000 tons we saved would mean gasoline enough for a three days' motor march toward the German border.'[19]

Chaban had spent much of his time in London preoccupied by the situation in Warsaw, where the Polish uprising was struggling against massive German forces. He decided that if the Allies would not change their plans and head for Paris quickly, he would have to ensure that the Resistance did not take action until the time was right. Early in the morning, Chaban got on a bicycle and left Allied headquarters at Connerré, just to the north-east of Le Mans. He would have to pedal nearly 200 kilometres to Paris. As 'cover', his luggage rack carried a tennis racket and a pannier containing a chicken and a cauliflower – just the kind of thing your average man would be taking through enemy lines. As an exhausted Chaban pedalled into the capital, very late in the evening, the thunderstorm that had been threatening all day finally broke, soaking him thoroughly.

Earlier in the day, the three members of COMAC, the military leadership of the Resistance, decided to call on the population to rebel against the crumbling edifice of occupation. In the COMAC meeting, General Ely, Chaban's deputy, reiterated the traditional fear of the Free French: premature action could lead to a massacre. Every day this argument was repeated, and every day it had the same motivation: genuine concern for the civilian population but, more fundamentally, a fear that a popular uprising could lead to a rather different outcome from that desired by Algiers. Whatever the case, the Free French felt that the Parisians ought simply to wait to be liberated, either by the Allies or by the Free French.

But in this latest round of the dispute, things shifted as General Ely told the meeting that when he had led the Resistance in Grenoble, he had found that the best reaction to German reprisals was an even more vigorous counter-response. Ely had inadvertently accepted the notion that the Resistance could fight and win, and not merely be passive. Valrimont added to the combative atmosphere by asking London to broadcast a text which indicated that COMAC would not be intimidated by the inhumane treatment of French prisoners by the Germans, and that the Resistance would meet ferocity with ferocity and could even surpass the enemy in barbarity.[20]

For the moment this was mere talk. The Resistance had nowhere near enough weapons to make the kind of aggressive response advocated by Ely and Valrimont. Indeed, earlier that morning, a group of Front National fighters had attempted to take over the Santé prison; they had failed simply because the commanding officer of the guards had brandished a pistol.[21] Nevertheless, the Parisian population outnumbered the German garrison by 200 to 1, and there were now as many striking policemen as there were German soldiers. It was not absurd to suggest that the tables could be turned, in particular if there were weapons to arm those who wanted to fight. In this context, Ely eventually agreed that COMAC should send a message to General Koenig calling for weapons to be sent urgently to the Paris region before the presence of German troops near the drop sites to the east of the capital made it impossible. Ely may have regretted his earlier enthusiasm for the idea that the Resistance should fight. The fact that it took some argument for him to agree to contact Koenig showed once again the ingrained Free French hostility to independent action by the Resistance.

*

Late in the evening, Field Marshal von Kluge had a long conversation with his chief of staff, General Blumentritt. Blumentritt begged von Kluge to convince Berlin to allow the German Western Front commanders to deal with the Allied offensive in any way they saw fit, including retreat: 'The whole apparatus of control is breaking down. Now that the enemy is getting nearer – their probing operations have got as far as Rambouillet – it might become one of great urgency. The communications system will break down all over our area. We must have a free hand, for at Chartres and at Rambouillet strong enemy forces are pressing on and reconnaissance tanks have been reported outside Versailles.'[22] But von Kluge did not ask Berlin for 'a free hand' or anything like it. The best he did was to order the Panzer Lehr Division, which had been able to escape from the Falaise pocket two days earlier, to withdraw from the front in order to recover and prepare for a future offensive.[23] Part of the division crossed the Seine near Fontainebleau, forming a potential defence to the south of Paris, while another group drove through Paris towards the north-east suburbs, where about 1000 fighting men, 20 tanks, four artillery batteries, an anti-aircraft battery, 100 half-tracks and 100 other vehicles were gathered.[24] These were forces that von Choltitz could call upon, if necessary – he had just doubled the number of tanks he had available.

In Berlin, the reality of the Allied offensive in the south of France slowly seeped over Hitler and the High Command, but the outcome was yet another display of incoherence at the very top. In the afternoon, all non-operational units in the south of France were ordered to withdraw to the east of a line running more or less north–south from Orléans to Montpellier. However, within a few hours the Führer finally conceded that the Allied invasion forces represented a substantial threat, and the order was changed, and all units in the south, with the exception of those in Toulon and Marseilles, were ordered to withdraw to the area of Dijon. The Germans were effectively abandoning all but the north-east quarter of France, leaving Paris on the front line.

Inside the capital, the Germans were preparing for a siege. As the evacuation of non-combatant personnel proceeded, von Choltitz finally decided to evacuate the administration in two phases, leaving behind only essential forces to defend the city. In the meantime, all Germans living in hotels or requisitioned accommodation were ordered to gather at the Hôtel Majestic, headquarters of the military administration, which had its defences reinforced.[25] Similar moves were taking place around the Senate building, where the Germans placed motorised guns, protected by anti-tank defences and barbed-wire entanglements.

Von Choltitz also had to decide how to deal with growing unrest from the Resistance. Over the previous couple of days, posters produced by the Front National had appeared all over the city calling for a 'general mobilisation' of all officers and instructing all able-bodied Parisians to join either the FFI or the patriotic militias.[26] The response of the German commander was frankly bizarre: instead of telling his men to rip down the posters or paint over them, he apparently ordered his printers to reproduce the poster, but with a red strip printed diagonally across the middle of the poster, which read 'We are warning you! Think of the fate of Paris' and was signed 'Der Wehrmachtbefehlshaber von Paris' (The Army Commander of Paris). Who pasted up this modified poster is uncertain – it may even have been German troops. Von Choltitz obviously thought this was a great move, as he boasted about it the next day to Field Marshal Model.[27] However, although the modified poster was presumably intended to be threatening, it mainly seems to have aroused perplexity.[28] It could be taken to suggest that the struggle between the Resistance and the Germans might be fought with paper and glue, rather than bullets. And without any clear menace, it could also be dismissed as an empty threat.[29]

With all these signs of retreat and vacillation at the top, at least one German official showed signs of cracking. A leading SS general contacted the Free French in Paris and offered 'a service' of unknown nature, in return for various guarantees. Parodi rejected this proposal, the details of which are still obscure, and was backed by both COMAC and Algiers.[30] Hoping to encourage precisely these kind of doubts among rank-and-file German soldiers, the OSS section in Le Mans prepared leaflets, purporting to be signed by Rommel, which said that the German cause was lost and which advised soldiers to surrender. Copies of the leaflets were taken into Paris by 'an agent', and 9th Tactical Air Command agreed they would also drop the leaflets onto enemy troops.[31] However, despite the low morale of many German troops, there were no reports of mass surrenders.

*

All over Paris, there was traffic madness as Germans and collaborators fled, using whatever means of transport they could commandeer. On the boulevard Saint-Germain, Odette Lainville saw German soldiers requisitioning anything on wheels, stopping the vehicle then telling the driver where to drive it. The pavements were clogged with streams of pedestrians, while the Germans pursued their endless evacuation – hundreds of vehicles rumbled continuously towards the east and apparent safety.[32] On the boulevard Raspail, Andrzej Bobkowski stared in amazement as he saw soldiers loading up a lorry: 'I couldn't take my eyes off the scene; they were running around in shirt-sleeves, panting, covered in sweat, and they are loading up ... bedside tables. What the devil will they do with them all? And then I whispered to myself: "They are fleeing." I was so excited.'[33]

After seeing the unusual sight of a German policeman directing the traffic at the place de l'Opéra, Madame Lainville wrote in her diary: 'Where are we? In Hunland? No: the gentle sky of France is still there above me, above Paris, and the breeze that blows smells of hope.'[34] As a sign of that hope, Odette bought two small brooches that had been quickly put together by some enterprising folk and which bore three flags – French, British and American. Even in the midst of turmoil and uncertainty, there was still a quick franc to be made. 'I bought one for each of the girls,' Odette wrote in her diary, 'but advised them not to wear them until the Allies arrive.'[35]

Many of the Germans were pleased to be leaving Paris. Young Micheline Bood walked past a garage where members of the German transport police were based. The men were completely drunk, very happy, and had been giving away coal to passing Parisians. In her diary, Micheline described the chaotic mess of luggage, cars, lorries and buses that filled the streets, and rejoiced at what it meant: 'For four years, we have been waiting for this moment! ... If we had known it would take four years to come, would we have had the courage to live and to wait? We are all exhausted. But can we be sure that the French people won't forget the shootings of innocent people, the mass arrests, the children burnt with their mothers in churches, the theft, the pillage, the banditry of the Nazi clique? I hope that after all that, we won't say, "They were all right, really!"'[36] Sometimes, the departure was precipitous: Dr Reichl of the Paris command was dining with his French secretary; towards the end of the meal she went to the toilet, but when she returned she found he had left, having been ordered to pack his bags and leave.[37]

As the German occupation of Paris began to collapse, Laval had to finally face reality: his time in government was coming to an end. He summoned his press secretary, Alex Delpeyrou, and had a frank conversation with him. Delpeyrou told him: 'Tomorrow you will be the most unpopular man in France.' Laval took the punch, but then began ranting about how Stalin was preparing to crush the whole of Europe, and that France would face years of misery. He concluded with a typical piece of self-justification – 'The Occupier did not allow me to have my own political positions!' For Laval, everything was the fault of the fascists like Déat, Doriot and the others who, he claimed, had caused more harm to France than the Resistance; he was blameless, his hands had been tied and everyone else was responsible.

Presumably not for the first time, Delpeyrou swallowed this guff and could not hold back his tears as the two men shook hands for the last time.[38] Afterwards, Laval recorded a radio broadcast to the French people giving his analysis of the political and military situation. According to his close colleague, Georges Brécard, Laval seemed as though he was paralysed, his voice dull and low. When he eventually finished, after a number of retakes, 'he stood up without a word and walked into his office with his shoulders hunched and his back bent, as if he foresaw his fate.'[39]

Laval's world really began to disintegrate later that evening, when the scheming around Herriot finally fell apart. At around 23:00, as Laval was eating with his family and a colleague, the telephone rang. There was a silence while Laval listened to the voice at the other end of the line, then he said: 'That's shameful. I'm coming over.' He hung up, turned to his wife and said: 'The Gestapo is at the Hôtel de Ville. They have just arrested Herriot. Abetz gave me his word that Herriot would remain free. I'm going over. I have to be there.'[40]

In the Hôtel de Ville the situation was tense. A German SS officer had turned up at the door of Herriot's apartment stating that he was going to arrest the French politician, but the guards – put there to prevent the Resistance from kidnapping Herriot – refused to let the German in. There was a stand-off while Herriot shouted: 'I always said you people were pigs ... You don't keep your word ... I will not leave like this!'[41] As soon as Laval arrived, he had Ambassador Abetz dragged from his bed and driven over to the Hôtel de Ville to sort things out.[42] Abetz explained that the orders had come from Germany, and that while he had supported Laval's initiative, Himmler was less impressed and had ordered Abetz to abort the whole operation. After several hours of negotiation, and more shouting by Herriot, there was a compromise of sorts: Herriot's arrest was postponed until the following day.[43]

Although many collaborators were preparing to flee with their masters, the weekly anti-Semitic rag *Je Suis Partout* reappeared for the first time since it had been banned weeks earlier for criticising Laval.[44] The collaborationist journalists rejected any suggestion that they would be following the Germans and packing their bags – 'I have not left Paris and I have no intention of leaving,' boasted one. The newspaper proclaimed: 'The next issue of *Je Suis Partout* will be published on Friday 25 August.' There was no 'next issue'.[45]

*

In the morning, in a narrow street just behind the Arc de Triomphe, a group of fifteen young *résistants* gathered together.[46] They were members of two groups – the Jeunes Combattants Chrétiens (JCC – Young Christian Fighters) and the right-wing Organisation Civile et Militaire (OCM). Like all the Resistance groups, they were frustrated by the lack of arms, but a few days earlier they had learnt through a priest, Abbé Borme, that a member of the British Intelligence Service ('Captain Jack') was able to supply them with weapons. Abbé Borme had given the same tip to three other Resistance groups: another OCM section, led by Guy Hémery, and two regional Resistance groups from Chelles, fifteen kilometres to the east of Paris – one FTP, led by 22-year-old Jacques Schlosser, and the other FFI, led by Jean Favé and the 28-year-old Dr Henri Blanchet. All five groups were going to share the treasure.

The pick-up had initially been planned for 15 August, but it had to be postponed until the following day. On the second attempt, things began to go wrong from the outset. The OCM were to provide a lorry that would take the young *résistants* to a garage near Porte Maillot, on the north-western edge of the city, and the weapons would then be transported to a safe house in the eastern suburbs. But the OCM lorry had a puncture, so JCC leader Michelle Boursier, a law student, was sent on her bicycle to Porte Maillot to let Captain Jack know of the delay. The Intelligence Service agent, who was tall and thin with clear blue eyes behind a large pair of glasses, spoke with a slight foreign accent. He reassured Michelle that they would still be able to transport the weapons, gesturing to three lorries parked nearby. Relieved, Michelle pedalled back with the good news, and the rest of the group quickly made their way to Porte Maillot. When they got there, the captain told them to get into the lorries, which started up and then drove for five minutes before stopping unexpectedly. There was a pause, then there were shouts in German: *'Raus! Raus!'* ('Out!') A few of the *résistants* were armed, and there was a brief firefight before the young French men and women bowed to the inevitable. They were caught in a terrible trap.

The Germans herded the *résistants* back into the lorries and drove them off to the Gestapo headquarters on the rue des Saussaies, which was in turmoil as the Germans prepared to evacuate. Suzanne Chocarne, who lived opposite, saw 'two lines of cars and lorries parked on the pavements. In the tight space in the middle of the road there is a traffic jam of vehicles going in the opposite direction ... everywhere there is hoarse and angry shouting.'[47] Micheline Bood, who lived nearby, went down to the Gestapo headquarters out of curiosity. The Germans, like their Milice henchmen, were in a state of frenzy, carting off goods such as champagne and stockings, while at the same time trying to control the traffic and avoid being left behind. She saw a pink-shirted French *milicien* grab a protesting Frenchman by the scruff of the neck and frogmarch him into the Gestapo offices. After a minute the man in the pink shirt came out and crowed: 'He had a revolver. He has been shot.'[48]

The *résistants* caught in the Captain Jack trap were taken through this maelstrom of noise and intimidation into the courtyard of the Gestapo building, where they were interrogated one by one, and made to stand until late into the evening. Michelle Boursier was treated differently – she was beaten, hauled up to the fifth floor and locked in a cell before eventually being released with no explanation. The courtyard was empty. 'What have you done with my comrades?' Michelle asked a German guard. 'We're keeping them,' was the reply.[49]

Shortly after the capture of Michelle's group, the Germans trapped the *résistants* from Chelles and the Hémery group. Both times, things seemed to be going well as the Resistance fighters thought they were being taken on a short drive to pick up the weapons from a German garage on the passage Doisy, a claustrophobic passageway running between two roads in the 16th arrondissement. Then the shocking truth was revealed as German soldiers made them get out at gunpoint, herding them into a cellar where they were held for a while before they too were taken to the rue des Saussaies. While they were in the cellar, a German civilian came over to the prisoners and promised to help them escape by leaving the door open. Every time they were about to take advantage of this unusual generosity, a guard passed and they had to stop. Finally Jean Favé from Chelles managed to escape. While the guards were questioning Dr Blanchet, Favé simply walked out of the cellar. As he later recalled: 'As I left, I heard someone shouting in a foreign language behind me. Two men watched me go by. Further on, a German woman raised her arms. I saluted her, saying that I was on their side. And then I walked out into the street.'[50]

In a final coup, at around 15:00, the Germans trapped a group of FFI fighters from Draveil in exactly the same way as the others, but this time the conclusion was more abrupt. The *résistants* thought they were going to pick up some arms; they clambered into a lorry that took them to the rue Leroux, near the Arc de Triomphe. As the vehicle pulled up, a hail of bullets rang out from all sides, and the seven members of the Draveil group were shot dead. Their bodies were left on the pavement.

In her flat opposite the Gestapo headquarters, Suzanne Chocarne complained that evening of the 'hellish noise of all sorts of material and people being loaded up and driven off – women, men, civilians and soldiers, all mixed up'.[51] Among the human cargo being taken away were the thirty-four Resistance prisoners captured earlier that day. Jean Favé had escaped, while Michelle Boursier had been released, along with two other *résistants* – one because he was a veteran of 1914–18, the other because he had convinced the Germans he was a hapless hitchhiker.[52] Dr Blanchet had been taken to a separate Gestapo office on rue de la Pompe where Friedrich Berger, the Gestapo agent in charge of the operation, shot him in the head. The remaining men were driven off to the nearby woods of the Bois de Boulogne. During the night, while Laval was negotiating with Abetz, while Blumentritt was pleading with von Kluge and while Chaban was pedalling his weary way through the thunderstorm, the sound of machine-gun fire and explosions could be heard from the Bois. The next morning, the park-keepers discovered an awful scene next to a well-known beauty spot, the Cascades ('waterfall'). All the *résistants* were dead, and horribly mutilated – from the position of their bodies it appeared that they had been machine-gunned as they got off the lorries, and were then finished off with grenades. Most were under twenty-five years old; Pierre Bezet, an FFI fighter working with SPIRITUALIST, was eighteen, while the youngest, Jacques Delporte, was just seventeen.[53] In total, forty-two *résistants* were murdered in the operation – thirty-four in the Bois de Boulogne, seven at rue Leroux, and Dr Blanchet, whose body was dumped with those of his comrades.

The next day the bodies from the Bois de Boulogne were taken to a garage where they were cleaned and prepared for burial. Twenty-four-year-old Louis Pauwels helped with the grisly task and wrote about it in his diary:

We scrub their cheeks, their foreheads and their chests, which are covered with mud and blood. And then holes appear, surrounded by a purple halo, while the rest is pale flesh under the ripped shirts that we lift up, under the trousers that we have to tear off. Those who had been hit with grenades have their stomachs ripped out, or their shoulders torn off, or their head smashed up, pouring out the contents. We throw sawdust down before leaning over the bodies, we throw it everywhere so our feet will not be covered in blood and guts.

When they are clean, we realise that we are bathing in the smell of a butchers' shop, in the smell of something fetid, that comes in waves, and we remember the eyes, and the noses and the hands. It is part of us. We realise we are standing over dead men ...

One body has been identified, that of a young doctor and when I turn round, his father is there, a fat red-faced man, on his knees. He raises up the white paper that covers the bodies, he kisses his son's head, which is tilted to one side, he kisses the chest with its holes, he runs his hand through his son's hair and touches behind the hair where the blood has dripped ...

We bring in the coffins, we unscrew the lids, we throw in sawdust and we pick up the bodies by their arms and legs. They seem to come alive in our hands, and it is hard to fit the tallest into the coffins, we have to push on the wrists and the knees, so that everything fits in, so that everything disappears, except in my heart, except in my sleep, except for a second in 10 or 20 years' time, when I will suddenly stop smiling when I am happy.[54]

*

'Captain Jack' was in fact a Gestapo agent whose real name was Guy de Marcheret d'Eu, and the whole thing had been a set-up from beginning to end. Born in Russia in 1914, Marcheret claimed he became a naturalised German in 1942. Together with another Gestapo agent, Karl Rehbein, Marcheret had been trapping Resistance fighters and downed Allied airmen in the Paris region for several weeks. Late in the evening of 11 August, Marcheret's scheming led to the arrest of four *résistants* and seven Allied airmen at a rendezvous in an apartment on the boulevard Sébastopol; all eleven of them were deported on the 15 August convoy from Pantin.[55] Marcheret and Rehbein had been put in contact with the various Resistance groups caught in the trap at Porte Maillot through a well-meaning but naïve *résistant* called Wigen Nercessian, who knew Abbé Borme. Nercessian and Borme both genuinely believed that they had found a much-needed source of weapons and – like the *résistants* themselves – appear to have abandoned elementary security procedures when faced with such an attractive possibility. That was exactly what the Germans had been banking on.

In 1949 Marcheret's case finally came to court. In his defence, he claimed that the Germans had put a 'photo-electric cell' in his brain to control his behaviour; nevertheless, he was convicted and executed.[56] Berger, who ordered the executions and murdered Dr Blanchet, managed to escape to Germany and although he was convicted in his absence was never punished; the case against Rehbein – who continued to be an active Nazi – was dismissed because he was a serving German officer.[57] In 1946, a monument was erected on the site of the massacre at the Bois de Boulogne, and the two oak trees on either side each bear a sign that reads: 'Passer-by: Respect this oak. It carries the traces of the bullets that killed our martyrs.'[58]

6

Thursday 17 August: Twilight

Jean Galtier-Boissière watches the Germans leaving Paris: 'On every street there are dozens, hundreds of lorries, crammed buses, mobile artillery pieces, ambulances full of wounded men on stretchers. The vehicles follow each other, overtake each other, drive in opposite directions. At the Strasbourg-Saint-Denis crossroads and in front of the railway stations, German gendarmes in chain-draped uniforms control the traffic ... On the rue Lafayette shiny sports cars drive by on their way from the luxurious hotels around l'Etoile, carrying splendid monocled generals accompanied by elegantly dressed blondes, looking as though they are off to a fashionable beach. Near the Galeries Lafayette, a bespectacled soldier stands in front of his broken-down lorry, vainly trying to get somebody, anybody, French or German, to tow his vehicle. He smiles at each refusal, without losing either his temper or his confidence. Grenades dangle from his belt.'[1]

At 04:30, as the blood from the bodies in the Bois de Boulogne was soaking into the soil, the French fascist Marcel Déat and his gang fled Paris.[2] As he wrote in his diary: 'We gather together the final packages, of which there are many. With difficulty we all squeeze into the car ... I have my machine gun and my Colt, the chauffeur has my 92 pistol, a *milicien* is with us ... We leave as quickly as we can. Everywhere there are endless convoys.'[3] At the same time, a furious Field Marshal Walter Model turned up at von Choltitz's headquarters in the Hôtel Meurice on the rue de Rivoli. Model had come from Berlin carrying a handwritten order from Hitler giving him command over all German troops in the west, replacing the suspect Field Marshal von Kluge. Model first went to Army Group B headquarters at Saint-Germain-en-Laye, but he found the place deserted except for a drunken doctor. So he continued on to Paris and hauled von Choltitz's aide, Lieutenant von Arnim, from his bed. Von Arnim was ordered to guide the small armoured convoy to von Kluge's headquarters at La Roche-Guyon, so that von Kluge could be relieved of his command and sent back to Berlin where a grim fate awaited him. Von Arnim recalled that the journey through the early morning streets took place in an intimidating silence.[4]

Model had spent most of the war fighting on the Eastern Front and had a reputation for toughness and utter loyalty to Hitler; when he got to La Roche-Guyon, he immediately set about trying to whip the Western Front into shape. One of the first people to attract his bird-like, monocled eye was General Bayerlein, whose Panzer Lehr Division had been withdrawn from the hell of the Falaise pocket because of exhaustion, and ordered to the safe side of Paris. Model was scornful of such behaviour, saying that in the east, divisions 'rested' at the front.[5] A disconsolate Bayerlein was ordered back west along with his tanks and his utterly drained men. Luckily for him, events moved so swiftly that the order was never put into effect.

Model's arrival meant that within the space of a few weeks, all the main German commanders in France had been replaced (twice in the case of the Commander of the Western Armies). The disruption to the German military organisation created an atmosphere of uncertainty that affected the whole line of command. Coupled with the unrealistic and increasingly shrill demands from Berlin, the situation was becoming catastrophic. As Model was throwing his weight about in La Roche-Guyon, German troops in the Falaise pocket were faced with annihilation: 100,000 of them were trapped in an area thirty-five kilometres from east to west by seventeen kilometres north to south. Canadian troops had just captured Falaise, completely destroying the 12th SS Panzer Division combat group that had been delaying them, and were now pushing south together with British units. Troops from the Third US Army were moving north from Argentan, closing the mouth of the 'pocket'. For the Germans the only way out was through a tiny gap that was closing fast. The Field Marshal might have wanted

his men to 'rest' at the front, but the front meant death and destruction. To stay alive, the Germans would have to flee.[6]

*

At 07:00, with the sun already hot in the clear sky, Raoul Nordling's car
drew to a halt and his two German associates, the spies 'Riki' Posch-
Pastor and 'Bobby' Bender, got in. Together with Nordling's nephew
and the head of the French Red Cross, the men were determined to
prevent the remaining political prisoners in the Paris region from being
deported or shot. First, they went to Fresnes prison, in the southern suburbs, where the German commanding officer told Bender he would be
happy to release the prisoners if he were given the order. So Nordling
and his group set off for the Hôtel Meurice in Paris to get a written
order from von Choltitz. While Bender and Posch-Pastor went upstairs
to see von Choltitz, Nordling waited in the foyer. Suddenly, SS General
Carl Oberg stormed through the door. As Nordling later recalled: 'With
a bull's neck and a stiff gait, a monocle stuck on his left eye, he swept up
the staircase to von Choltitz's office. Ten minutes later, he left the building.'[7] Nordling was then called upstairs for his first meeting with the
military commander of Paris.

Five years later, Nordling recalled von Choltitz as a 'fat little man, with
a calm face, looking as though he was indifferent to the debacle which
was beginning to affect the Germans in Paris'.[8] Von Choltitz listened
politely as the Swedish consul explained why the German Army must at
all costs avoid a massacre of prisoners in Paris, which would otherwise
cast a terrible slur on its reputation. Von Choltitz replied by saying that
he was not interested in civilian prisoners; anyone who fired on his
troops would be executed on the spot as a terrorist, but if this was not
the case, he could see no reason not to release all civilians. All that was
required was the relevant paperwork from the German military administration of France and from the SS.

However, the relevant office was about to be evacuated, and the man
whose signature was required, Major Huhm, would be leaving the Hôtel
Majestic at noon. Nordling rushed over to the administrative headquarters to be greeted with the smell of burning paper; it was snowing

ashes as compromising files were destroyed. After some negotiation, Major Huhm agreed to give Nordling and the French Red Cross 'the control, surveillance and responsibility' 'for all political prisoners in Fresnes, Cherche-Midi, la Santé, Villeneuve Saint-Georges, St-Denis, in the hospitals of la Pitié, Val de Grâce, and St-Denis, in the camps at Compiègne, Drancy, Romainville, and in all other places of detention and in all evacuation trains currently *en route*, without exception and whatever their destination'. In return, Nordling agreed to secure the release of five German military prisoners for each French political prisoner.[9] As Nordling later recalled, this final clause was somewhat absurd, as he held no German prisoners, nor was he in any position to ensure that the agreement was enforced.[10]

There was a moment of tension as Huhm discovered that the all-important stamp, without which the document would carry no weight with German underlings, had been packed away deep in a tea chest. It was eventually retrieved, and the document was duly stamped. The final step was to obtain Oberg's approval, so the group drove to the SS head-quarters on boulevard Lannes. During his meeting with von Choltitz, General Oberg had apparently dismissed the question of the prisoners with a terse 'I don't give a damn', before scurrying out of the hotel and returning to his packing.[11] Bender soon returned with the document duly signed by Oberg, but the SS general had added an alarming codicil: 'There are no longer any civilian prisoners in Paris, nor in the region, given that an order for total evacuation was given on 15 August.' Nordling might have his piece of paper, but Oberg was apparently confident that the Swedish diplomat would find that the cupboard was bare.

Oberg was wrong – there were still hundreds of Resistance prisoners in the region, fearful of the fate that might befall them. When Nordling and his group returned to Fresnes in the afternoon to free the first batch of prisoners, one woman initially refused to leave her cell because she was convinced that she was going to be executed. Madeleine Riffaud and her Intelligence Service friend, 'Anne-Marie', who had managed to escape from the Pantin train but were still on death row, heard the cries of joy as prisoners were freed. Eventually they were taken into the courtyard, where Nordling and Red Cross representatives oversaw the transfer. But there were also German officers present, who wanted to keep their hands on the two *résistantes*. The women were so sure that they would be shot at the last minute that they could not express any pleasure, and stayed close to Nordling and the others as they left the prison, lying flat on the floor of the bus that took them away, in case there was an ambush.[12]

At Romainville prison in the north-eastern suburbs, things did not go so smoothly. The SS commander refused to recognise von Choltitz's order, stating that he was under the orders of the SS at Compiègne. Many of the SS guards in the prison were drunk and out of control, but there was nothing Nordling could do. At Compiègne, to the north-east of Paris, it was much the same story – the German prison commander threatened to shoot the delegation on the spot and warned them that the Gestapo and the SS were on their tail. Empty-handed, Nordling and his group returned to Paris, driving on side-roads by the light of the moon, hiding from German patrols and from the waves of Allied bombers that passed overhead.[13] While they were returning home, the Germans at Compiègne dispatched a train full of prisoners – convoy I-265, carrying 1,255 men – to Buchenwald. The youngest person on the train was 15-year-old Serge Tissandier; he was one of the lucky 656 who returned. Of this convoy, 471 men died, while others simply disappeared – only five managed to escape.[14]

The prison at Fontainebleau, fifty kilometres south-east of Paris, had not been included in the paper drawn up by Major Huhm. Fourteen Resistance fighters were taken out of the prison by the Germans; some of the men had been seized the previous day, in a swoop that netted a large number of members of Ceux de la Résistance, including 32-year-old Georges Papillon and 18-year-old Brigitte Servan-Schreiber. Brigitte was severely beaten, then released; on her return to Paris, she showed a horrified comrade the awful bruises that covered her back and her thighs.[15] Papillon was not so lucky; he was among the fourteen prisoners who were taken to a nearby quarry that afternoon and killed. A month earlier, the Germans had executed twenty-two Fontainebleau prisoners in similar circumstances. The bodies of the thirty-six victims from Fontainebleau were discovered only in December 1944; one of them was never identified.[16]

Earlier in the day, Nordling's group had gone to the Drancy transit camp in the north-eastern suburbs. The camp was composed of four-storey prefabricated buildings, built in a massive U-shape that was 200 metres long and 40 metres wide. It was in turmoil. There were no German soldiers to be seen anywhere, and groups of inmates were wandering about in the courtyard, gesticulating and shouting. Nordling was walking into a camp that the Germans had abandoned. In fact, just as Nordling arrived, the SS commander, Alois Brunner, left the camp for the last time. The final words he spoke to an inmate were: 'To hell with the camp.'[17] Brunner, like most of the Germans, was fleeing.

That morning, Brunner carried out his final, cruel wish in Drancy: fifty-one Jews – forty of them political prisoners from Fresnes, including André Amar, the husband of Jacqueline Mesnil-Amar – were made to march from Drancy to the railway station at Bobigny about two kilometres away.[18] They were then loaded into a wagon that had the words '*Juden terroristen*' (Jewish terrorists) chalked on it; this was attached to a small train carrying Luftwaffe men and materiel out of France. Three wagons had been reserved for Brunner: one carried the SS captain and his entourage; another carried German police; the third carried the fifty-one prisoners bound for Buchenwald.[19] The youngest was 12-year-old Georges-André Kohn, who was first subjected to vile Nazi 'experiments' and then murdered just days before Germany surrendered, in May 1945.[20]

Brunner left Drancy at 16:00. Janine Auscher, who had arrived at the camp at the beginning of the month, recalled what happened next, which explains the bewildering scene that greeted Nordling: 'Around 16:30, a shout of triumph runs through the camp: *Take off your stars!* The shock is such that many do not want to believe it. They are frightened it's a trap. Others feverishly rip off the infamous star. Everyone runs into the courtyard, cheering, hugging. *Take off your stars!*'[21]

*

For four years, Radio Paris had oozed Nazi propaganda; now it fell silent, disappearing from the airwaves without a word of explanation as its principal journalists and producers joined the exodus.[22] The offices of Radio Paris were chaotic as typewriters were packed away and compromising documents were burnt. The head of security, extremely drunk, fired his machine gun in the studios. The notorious anti-Semite Charles Lesca, seventy-three years old, collapsed on his luggage, sweating and weeping in despair after being refused refuge in the Spanish embassy. Journalist Pierre Vernier, 'a bit drunk, and very excited', according to his colleague Jean Hérold-Paquis, waved a massive Colt revolver and tried to persuade his friend to go and find machine guns and grenades. Captain Haefs, the German controller of Radio Paris, had managed to buy a number of cars to help everyone escape, but they all turned out to be out of commission. Infuriated, Hérold-Paquis returned home and waited until around 03:00, when a car took him and his family to the headquarters of Doriot's fascist Parti Populaire Français (PPF) on the rue des Pyramides. There the broadcaster made a dramatic entrance with a machine gun at his hip.[23] Later, lorries carried off the collaborators and their families, but even that turned into a farce, as shortly before dawn one of the vehicles first crashed into a wall by the Seine and then ran out of petrol.[24]

The collaborationist print journalists were also fleeing, but they had done their last work the night before, announcing the closure of their newspapers and saying goodbye to their readers in editorials that reeked of self-pity and self-justification. Georges Suarez, the fascist editor of *Aujourd'hui*, was typical: 'I do not deny my ideas, nor do I deny more than four years of common struggle with talented collaborators, devoted employees and workers aware of their duty – at such a time, which is so hard for the editor of a newspaper, their affection is my sole comfort.'[25] Such sentimentality was soon dispelled as the collaborationist mouthpieces were shaken out of their complacency, and made to face the possibility that they would soon experience terrible retribution. In the late afternoon, journalist and self-proclaimed fascist Lucien Rebatet collapsed when he realised that he had been left behind: 'The bastards! I might as well put in a bullet in my head!'[26] He scurried round the hotels trying to find somewhere to stay, but was systematically turned away. Now he was convinced that the fascists' time in power was over.[27] Rebatet bumped into another fascist journalist, Dominique Sordet, who seemed stunned: his chauffeur had just made off with the car and all of Sordet's luggage. 'Everyone has gone mad,' muttered Sordet.[28] Eventually, Rebatet and his wife managed to get on one of the lorries leaving the PPF headquarters. Most of the other passengers were working-class women members of Doriot's party, who looked askance at Rebatet's wife, resplendent in her furs – and on such a hot evening, too.

As Rebatet was waiting for his ticket out of Paris, word came through of a new poster that had been put up on the walls of the city, signed by Rol, 'Commander of Greater Paris': 'Organise yourselves by buildings and by neighbourhood, stun the Huns to grab their arms, free the Paris region – the cradle of France. Avenge your martyred sons and brothers. Avenge the heroes who have fallen for the independence and freedom of the fatherland. Your action will hasten the end of the war. Have as your slogan: "Everyone get a Hun". No mercy for assassins, forward together so that FRANCE WILL LIVE.'[29] This declaration was probably produced by Communist Party members, without Rol's knowledge.[30] Whatever the case, it certainly had the desired effect on the collaborators, leading Rebatet to wonder: 'What the fuck are we doing here?'[31]

The journalists had fled, the print shops and press offices stood empty. Major Schmidtke, commander of the German Propaganda Section, had ordered Lieutenant Eich of the press office to blow up all the newspaper printworks in the capital. But Schmidtke did not hang about to ensure that his orders were carried out, and when Eich and his colleagues left on 17 August the presses were still intact.[32] As a result, over the next few days the men and women who had been producing the underground Resistance newspapers literally walked into the offices left empty by the collaborators and started producing their own publications.[33] For these Parisians, the first whiff of freedom was the smell of printers' ink.

Not every journalist experienced the liberation in quite so romantic a fashion, however. Jean Dutourd, twenty-four years old, was in charge of an armed group that took over the offices of *France-Soir:* 'It is impossible to recall the rest of what happened that day. I can only remember the amazing drinking session that took place. It was one of the rare times in my life when I was completely drunk. I drank white wine, red wine, sparkling wine and Byrrh cassis in alarming quantities. I got so drunk that I collapsed onto the floor of my large office and slept on my back for 10 hours. When I woke up I discovered that someone had stolen my pistol.'[34]

*

Paris began to drift into a strange world where the population could be certain of nothing. There was a massive battle to the west, but no one knew how it was progressing. A desperate, retreating German Army was apparently heading towards the capital, hounded by the forces of liberation, but it was impossible to know if and when it would arrive. The Vichy propaganda machine had fallen silent, while the BBC could not be heard because of a lack of electricity. And even when power was occasionally and briefly restored, there was no reliable news about the state of the battle, as the BBC had stopped giving information on the Allies' progress, apparently for security reasons. Some people were lucky enough to be in the know: Cazaux heard from the Resistance that Paris would not be liberated for several days, and that the first Allied soldiers to enter the city would be from the Leclerc Division.[35] Not everyone who heard this thought it was true: in a discussion with Victor Veau, Pasteur Vallery-Radot expressed his fears that the Americans would arrive first, with neither the Free French nor the Parisian population playing any role in the liberation of the city.[36] Veau retorted that it did not matter, as long as liberation came. PVR, more politically aware and more astute, did not agree.[37]

On the streets, the signs of change were unmistakable. The anti-aircraft guns that had been stationed on the roofs around the Jardin du Luxembourg were lowered into the street, their crews all packed up and ready to leave.[38] Either the Germans thought that the Allies would not be bombarding Paris, or they needed the guns elsewhere. Von Choltitz inspected the strong-points that had been built at key sites around the city, together with one of his staff officers, Herbert Eckelmann. The soldiers who manned these positions did not impress Eckelmann – he described them as 'dear old daddies'.[39] By the evening virtually the whole of the German administration had left the city. All that remained were those soldiers who were to defend the capital.[40]

The sight of the German mass evacuation inevitably drew spectators:

Paul Tuffrau went with his family to watch. In his diary he described the scene at the southern edge of the Jardin du Luxembourg:

> The green cars follow each other in groups of five or six, at short intervals, sometimes driving alongside each other, or going past each other. They are carrying anything and everything, above all non-military material: in one lorry there are two cows, a sheep and a goat; in another a mechanical reaper and yet another bits of agricultural machinery. There are ambulances, family cars, troop transporters full to the gunnels, grey Luftwaffe uniforms or grey-green Wehrmacht uniforms, and then more lorries carrying car tyres, with motorcyclists zooming past.[41]

In general, the parting Germans took this attention in good spirit. After all, they were escaping. One German soldier jeered at gawping passers-by: 'What are you looking at? Haven't you seen enough of us over the last four years?'[42]

Andrzej Bobkowski observed a German convoy of lorries and tanks stationed near Trocadero. The soldiers were unshaven, dirty and ragged; some of them were sleeping under the trees, others just sat with vacant expressions. Down by the river, some German light tanks came to a halt, and oil-smeared soldiers clambered out. As Bobkowski wrote in his diary: 'The crowd looked at them in silence. Down by the water's edge, it was like the Côte d'Azur – Parisians were bathing in the Seine ... I could hear the girls screaming with pleasure, shouting, laughing. And as always, there's a forest of fishing rods and a crowd of anglers. It's an amazing scene, quite idyllic.'[43]

For some of the Germans, evacuation felt cruel: Walter Bargatzky, the army lawyer who had been involved in the 20 July plot but had managed to escape punishment, said goodbye to his wife Camilla, a secretary in the military administration who was being evacuated. The pair had met less than three weeks earlier, and had hurriedly married in the American Cathedral on the avenue Georges V.[44] They might never meet again. Friedrich von Teuchert, another of the junior officers at the heart of the Paris side of the 20 July plot, recalled his departure from the Hôtel Majestic in improbably lyrical terms: 'We were to be packed up and out by three in the afternoon. Then came a surprise. I went to the mess. White linen and silver were on the table. The French staff ordered us a farewell meal. There were six or seven servants, and not one behaved as if we were anything except habitual guests. They said they'd hoped we'd be back. That made a lasting impression.'[45]

If true, von Teuchert's experience was unusual to say the least. Not only were most Parisians overjoyed to see the back of the Germans, in the vast majority of cases the way the occupiers left had none of the gentility apparently seen in the Hôtel Majestic. Opposite the Gestapo headquarters on the rue des Saussaies, Suzanne Chocarne saw the evacuation descend into chaos as the morning progressed and the heat was slowly stoked. Parked vehicles were sprawled everywhere, crammed with cases of champagne and wine, bags of sugar, bulging files and even sheep. Once the Gestapo officers had left, the building was left open for anyone to pillage. First in were Wehrmacht soldiers, followed by a wary crowd that soon grew in courage and began streaming out carrying bottles, boxes and radios and even rolling barrels down the narrow street. Then the German soldiers realised there was money to be made and they began selling stuff from the back of a lorry – silk stockings, sugar, chickens – anything they could get their hands on.[46] Journalist Edmond Dubois recorded the population's reaction: 'How the atmosphere has changed in a matter of hours. Earlier on, there was terror; now the whole neighbourhood is jubilant, stunned by this spontaneous generation of plenty. The champagne corks pop, glasses are filled, drink is poured down throats ... Housewives go home with an unexpected bonus for their next meagre meal. At 16:00, calm returns, and the doors of the building are shut.'[47]

The beginning of the German evacuation cheered the hearts of the Resistance. In his diary, Léo Hamon described his amazement when his secretary told him the news over lunch: 'it all seems so astounding and has such massive implications for us, but we don't have the perspective required to be able to rejoice.'[48] Outside the capital it was the same story: a hurried, massive withdrawal of non-essential forces that looked increasingly like an uncoordinated retreat. Throughout the day, the Luftwaffe evacuated their air base at Villacoublay, six kilometres to the south-west of Paris. Most of the aeroplanes based there had been destroyed by repeated bombing raids on the aerodrome and by dog-fights with the overwhelmingly superior Allied air forces. During the day the surviving air crew and their remaining Focke-Wulf fighters flew off to Beauvais to the north, where they were joined the next day by the ground team. The last German plane left Villacoublay at 20:20; soon afterwards the remaining ground crew blew up the aerodrome build-ings and set fire to the fuel dumps before they too made for Beauvais. Clouds of smoke, coloured red and orange by the flames, billowed up into the sky. Parisians noted the glow in the south; not knowing the cause, they feared the worst.[49] The Luftwaffe occupied Villacoublay in June 1940, when it was hastily evacuated by the fleeing French air force.[50] After four years, the wheel of history had eventually turned. The Germans now had no air bases to the west of Paris; the defence of the capital relied virtually entirely on the dispersed, exhausted and retreat-ing ground forces, and the collection of German soldiers in the city itself.

A brief report from regional FFI intelligence described the German military situation in the Paris region with remarkable accuracy – not only did the report correctly identify the location of the tanks from the Panzer Lehr Division that had moved into the north-east suburbs the day before, but above all it contained a measured conclusion that was guaranteed to warm the hearts of the Resistance: 'General impression: the Germans are not thinking of defending Paris so much as protecting the retreat of their troops from Normandy.'[51]

*

At midday, shortly after SS General Oberg left von Choltitz, Pierre Taittinger, the chairman of the Paris council, was summoned to see the new German master of Paris.[52] Taittinger took with him Bussière, the Prefect of Police, and Bouffet, the Prefect of the Seine. The meeting got off to a worrying start, as von Choltitz fleshed out the threat he had made two days earlier – 'All means, including the most harsh, that can repress disorder, will be utilised . . . Everything will be done to maintain order and to pitilessly repress disorder,' he had said.[53] The German general jabbed a fat finger at a map of Paris and explained that although he did not want the city to become a battlefield, if any of his troops were fired upon he would immediately destroy the area where the shot was fired, killing all the inhabitants.

Thereafter, the discussion became slightly less tense when von Choltitz made it abundantly clear that his main priority was the safety of his men, not holding the city. He seemed to concede that he would not destroy fuel sources within Paris, nor carry out the order to destroy the bridges over the Seine; he even gave Bussière his direct telephone number so the two men could talk in the event of any unforeseen crisis. Before the meeting ended, von Choltitz took his guests onto the sunlit balcony of the Hôtel Meurice, overlooking the rue de Rivoli and beyond it the Jardin des Tuileries, where children were playing. A slight breeze was blowing. As they left, the interpreter heard von Choltitz say in a quiet voice, 'It would be a real pity if such a city were to be destroyed.'[54] The Frenchmen hoped this was a promise, but it could equally have been a threat.

*

The strike wave that had begun a week earlier with the railway workers spread to the postal service as all the post offices closed.[55] Pastor Marc Boegner noted laconically in his diary: 'Postal workers on strike, no letters.'[56] The imprisoned railway workers were released, so Pierre Patin and his colleagues stopped breaking the rail strike on the suburban network – there were now no trains at all. At the same time, Patin was given a Resistance armband carrying the title of the Resistance group he had joined weeks earlier without even knowing its name – 'Ceux de la Libération – Vengeance'.[57] Elsewhere in the city, workers in vital sectors, including those in water distribution and the funeral parlours, went on strike. Whether the Free French wanted it or not, it was beginning to look as if Paris was gripped by a general strike.

In the south Paris suburb of Fontenay-aux-Roses, 72-year-old Paul Léautaud was not happy with what was happening. He was particularly incensed by the police strike, as he wrote in his diary: 'All these policemen should be arrested, locked up and the leaders sacked without any compensation or pension. It wouldn't do any harm if a few dozen were executed. These people aren't citizens. They chose their profession, and they should carry it out irrespective of their political opinions.'[58]

Both the Comité Parisien de la Libération and the Bureau (executive committee) of the Conseil National de la Résistance met to discuss the situation. At the meeting of the CPL, which took place that morning at Ivry in the presence of Colonel Rol, there were only two items on the agenda – drafting a resolution calling for an insurrection, and fixing a date for the uprising.[59] There was a dispute over the date, which ran along familiar lines – there were those who wanted to take action immediately, and those who wanted to wait at all costs. Communist trade union leader André Tollet was in favour of immediately calling the Parisian population to take up arms (the question of where those arms would come from was not discussed).[60] In reply, Léo Hamon, backed by the socialist trade unionist Roger Deniau, won the day by arguing that before making any decision they needed to be clearer about the military situation, and the CNR had to be consulted.[61]

At the CNR Bureau meeting, which took place in the afternoon, the conservative Resistance leaders could sense the situation was slipping out of their control. The meeting began with the all too familiar confrontation – Parodi yet again raised the danger of reprisals and argued for restraint, while the Communist Party representative, Villon, thought it was necessary to act immediately. But the chairman of the CNR, Georges Bidault, raised a third, alarming possibility. It was impossible to stop the existing strikes, he argued, and if the CNR did not wholeheartedly back the movement, then popular support for the CNR and the Resistance organisations might begin to ebb away.[62] In his diary, Léo Hamon put his finger on the problem: the communists had caught the conservative sections of the Resistance in a double bind. The communists were pushing for the official structures of the Resistance to call an insurrection and at the same time they were using their influence in the working class to build that insurrection through strikes.[63] If the CNR opposed the strikes, communist influence would probably increase, as the communists would be seen as the sole voice in favour of action. The Bureau therefore agreed unanimously to extend the strike wave, as a way of building de Gaulle's 'national insurrection'.[64]

In the evening, Parodi sent a four-part message to Algiers, outlining the situation and explaining how he intended to keep control:

> At my request, the CNR [Bureau] will meet daily and will be kept updated of any extension of the strike. In this way I hope to be able to control the situation and gain time. There is a serious danger of bloody reprisals by the Germans ... These events create a tense atmosphere and a worrying situation if liberation is still far off. Unless liberation takes place soon it will be necessary to call for calm and to remind the population that the order for a national uprising which has been given for parts of France is not yet applicable to the Paris region. The population has the duty to remain calm in conditions that are the most difficult it has ever known, and not to undertake any ill-considered action.[65]

To meet this challenging situation, Parodi's team was being reinforced, getting ready to take the reins of power. In the evening of 17 August, Charles Luizet arrived from London ready to become de Gaulle's Prefect of Police once the final vestiges of Vichy had disappeared. With him was Francis-Louis Closon, who was scheduled to be Prefect in the Nord-Pas-de-Calais, but was to remain in the capital and help Parodi until the north of the country was liberated. The original idea had been that Luizet and Parodi would arrive with the Leclerc Division, but Parodi's stream of alarmist messages about the danger of a bloodbath and the strength of the Communist Party had convinced Algiers that he needed help immediately.[66] Despite their relative youth – Luizet was forty years old, Closon was only thirty-four – both men were well suited to the situation. In September 1943, Luizet had been the first prefect of a liberated French department when he took control of Corsica, helping ensure that the Communist Party was fully integrated into local government rather than acting independently. Closon was an experienced Parisian operator who had worked with Parodi's predecessors – including the founder of the CNR, Jean Moulin – and had shown considerable skill at resolving differences between the different Resistance groups.

Hampered by problems with their landing grounds and bad weather, it had taken Luizet and Closon over two weeks to make the journey from London.[67] They finally landed near Avignon on 14 August, and then hired a lorry to take them the 800 km to the capital. They were dropped at the place de la Bastille on the evening of 17 August, and Parodi immediately alerted London of their arrival.[68]

Earlier in the day, in one of its last actions, the Vichy Ministry of Food signed off a report describing the situation in the capital, which was ominous. Supplies of flour coming into the city were at best at 50 per cent of normal; combined with the near-absence of electricity, most bakers were producing far less bread than needed. The flour supplies would run out in four days. The amount of milk arriving in the capital was so low that it was not enough to meet the needs of children less than nine months old. Even worse, the stifling August heat and the collapse of the electricity supply meant that much of the milk was sour. Supplies of concentrated milk were being distributed to children under three years old, but the stocks would be exhausted in a matter of days. If all the German meat stocks were made available, there would be at most nine distributions of the 90g meat ration per person (a rasher of bacon weighs around 45g), while there was only enough pasta in the stores for twelve meals per person.[69] For the moment, there was still enough food to feed the population, and many Parisians still benefited from handouts from relatives living in the countryside, despite the fighting in the west. Nevertheless in only a few days the situation would become critical.

Parisians did not see the report, but the empty shelves and long queues told them that fighting of any duration in the region would produce a humanitarian catastrophe. When food could be found – for example a street-seller hawking salads and radishes from market gardens in the suburbs – it quickly sold out.[70] In his diary that night, 18-year-old Jean-Claude Touche, a devout Catholic, described the situation as he saw it: 'Soon there will be no water. Paris will know famine, a siege, if the Americans don't come on Sunday or Monday ... Holy Mary, please save France!'[71]

On a lighter note, although the restaurants were closed and the theatres were dark due to the power cuts, high-society hairdresser Gervais was still in business, thanks to an unusual power source that he used to dry his customers' hair: cyclists. Less than two weeks later, US photographer Lee Miller described – and photographed – Gervais' ingenuity: 'He has rigged his dryers to stove pipes which pass though a furnace heated by wood debris. The air is blown by fans turned by relay teams of boys riding a stationary tandem bicycle in the basement. They cover 320 kilometres a day and dry half as many heads.'[72]

*

From the outside and with hindsight, the final hours of the Vichy regime were played out like scenes in a farce, with people rushing from room to room in a growing panic, making plans and counter-plans, trying to hide from the inevitable consequences of their own behaviour. To those involved, it was anything but amusing: their lives were at stake. The first act began in the morning, as final, desperate plans were made by sections of the Resistance to save Herriot from the Germans. Yves Cazaux received a phone call inviting him to participate in this final madcap scheme. He agreed, and even warned his wife that they would be expecting 'company', but within ten minutes Herriot – exhausted and bewildered after the rows of the night before – was whisked off to the German embassy, a prisoner of the Germans once more.

In the afternoon, Laval moved centre stage, presiding over a very formal exchange of letters with Ambassador Abetz. Behind the diplomatic niceties there was a tense stand-off as Laval, like Faust, found that payback time had come. In a first letter to Laval, Abetz stated that because of the growing threat of 'internal or external events caused by the war', the French government would be moved to Belfort, not far from the German border. The German government would 'never invite the French government to leave its national territory', wrote Abetz, soothingly. After a brief Cabinet meeting, Laval wrote a reply, politely refusing this 'invitation'. Abetz's response showed the iron hand: it was an 'irrevocable decision of the government of the Reich', he wrote, and if Laval and his ministers refused to leave, 'means of constraint' would inevitably have to be applied. In a final letter, written late in the evening, Laval replied that he would bow to the pressure but that he now ceased to be the head of the French government. He left written instructions for the Prefect of Police and the Prefect of the Seine 'to welcome the Allied military authorities and to represent the French government to them'.[73] Laval's ultimate roll of the dice was that the Allies' mistrust of de Gaulle might yet lead them to rely upon the final vestiges of Vichy in the capital. After a last meal at Matignon with his family, Laval left Paris at around 23:00, taken like a piece of luggage in a German convoy, guarded by the SS.[74] All his ministers except one followed him. And so the curtain fell on four years of delusion and betrayal. The only remnant of the government of collaboration was a confused, vain old man in Vichy. Within three days he, too, would be taken east.

Despite the all-pervading air of collapse and panic, Ambassador Abetz was unbowed, and sneered at Taittinger as he left Paris: 'Do not rejoice too soon or too hastily. We cannot lose the war. We have created terrifying weapons. Do you hear me? Terrifying. The Führer hesitates to use them, because it would be the beginning of the end of the world . . . Yes, we'll be back by Christmas at the latest.'[75]

*

As the evening drew in, Jean Galtier-Boissière leant over his balcony on the boulevard Saint-Michel and watched the evacuation of the German depot below:

Once the last lorry had left, the SS sentries, machine guns at the ready, suddenly moved towards the passers-by who, in a panic, scattered in all directions. From our balcony, the scene was like that Russian photograph of people being fired on at the Winter Palace. Suddenly shots rang out, followed by the sound of machine-gun fire. We ran inside. Bullets whistled by, leaving tracer-lines in the air above the place de la Sorbonne, spitting into walls. Then there were louder explosions. At first I thought these were delayed-action grenades that the Germans had left to cover their retreat, but it must have been a small cannon they used to fire on the Sorbonne chapel. The square is empty. I can't see any bodies. And so to bed, as Pepys said. The gunfire continued for twenty minutes, in a series of spurts.[76]

At around the same time, on the other side of the Seine, there was another shooting incident, in which two Parisians were killed when a German patrol car was apparently shot at on the boulevard Bonne Nouvelle. The soldiers returned fire, and threw grenades and fired incendiary shells into a café and a shop on either side of the boulevard. Both buildings caught fire and the fire brigade was called out; meanwhile a policeman and a nurse began to remove the body of a man lying in the middle of rue Aboukir. As they bent over the corpse, more shots rang out, and both of them threw themselves to the ground; one bullet went right through the nurse's helmet but left her miraculously unscathed. Another body was later found nearby, along with several injured people. Firing continued for some time, with German troops in cars and on foot patrolling the area and firing more or less at random.[77]

As night fell, the German convoys continued to stream out of Paris, but against all the air-raid protection rules they kept their headlights on, and beams swept across the dark rooms of people living by the side of the main roads. Unnerved by the explosions, the sound of shooting and the eerie lights from the street, Yves Cazaux wrote in his diary: 'Are they leaving? We dare not believe it is true. We have been waiting for this moment for so long, dreaming of it, that it's hard to believe it has finally come. But a tightening in the chest, the utter immediacy of the event that is taking place in the night, the awful tension that almost hurts, make it clear that we are indeed living through the longed-for hour.'[78]

At around 22:30 the electricity came back on unexpectedly. All over the city, lights suddenly blazed out of the unshuttered windows, breaking the darkness. Countless radios blared into life, having been left in the 'on' position when the power was cut. On the BBC, Free French spokesman André Gillois was speaking directly to the Parisian population about the importance of strikes as 'an instrument of war'.[79] But instead of encouraging the workers of the Paris region to take action, Gillois forcefully listed all the sectors where workers should *not* go on strike – public services, hospitals, utilities or any part of the food industry. Workers in other sectors should go on strike 'wherever the enemy wants to impose work from which it will benefit'. And even if Gillois argued that workers should stop their workplaces from being destroyed by the Germans, there was no indication of how they should do this.

They were told to organise 'protection squads', but – as usual – there was no mention of weapons.[80] To reinforce the message that these strikes were to be extremely limited, Gillois concluded by saying that striking workers should 'go back to work as soon as possible after the Allies arrive'.[81] And that was it – not a word about fighting the Germans. The question that was on everyone's lips in Paris could not be uttered in London. At a time when much of the public sector was already on strike, when food shortages were threatening the Parisian population, the decisive questions were how people were going to get food and how they were going to get rid of the 20,000 Germans who remained in the city. Whatever the Free French might have wanted, both questions had the same answer: with weapons.

7

Friday 18 August: Waiting

Journalist Pierre Bourdan describes the advance of the Leclerc Division, 200 km from Paris: 'The problem is to hold these men back – they seem to be untouched by fatigue or by the horrors of war. As they pass, the towns and villages that have been liberated by these Frenchmen are covered in flags ... There is only one role now for the enemy, their sole strategic preoccupation is to flee, to escape from the trap, to avoid complete destruction ... In the heart of every Frenchman here there is a name, a goal: Paris, Paris. Will we get there before or after the destruction of the German army? We'll soon see. But for the enemy, hope is dead.'[1]

Traces of the previous night's incidents still littered the Parisian streets. On the boulevard Saint-Michel, the mirrors at the entrance to the Le Latin cinema were starred by bullet-holes; tree branches scattered on the ground showed the violence of the firefight.[2] Shortly after 07:00 Jean Galtier-Boissière walked along the rue Racine where a concierge was throwing pails of water on a bloodstain, then brushing it vigorously. 'One woman was killed here,' explained the concierge, 'and another was killed in front of the tobacconist's.' Further along the street a building had gone up in flames after being fired on. Rumours of the shooting episodes of the previous night grew and became distorted in the re-telling. Yves Cazaux heard that twenty-five people were killed on the boulevard Saint-Germain, while journalist Edmond Dubois was unable to verify any of the reports: 'The overwhelming fact is that we can be sure of nothing, be it strategic, diplomatic or

governmental. We live in a period of "they said" or "it seems that" …
The telephone is the only means of getting precise information from
trusted friends.'[3]

Even the Free French Delegation was not sure what was going on –
Parodi sent Algiers an exaggerated summary of the night's events
('many bloody incidents provoked by excitement of population, nervous German troops, and Gestapo provocations') that reflected rumour
and his habitual fear that the population was about to be massacred.[4]
Although Francis-Louis Closon, newly arrived from Algiers, decided
that the situation was not as grave as the Delegation's earlier messages
suggested, in many parts of the city the tension was very real.[5] At around
09:00 Galtier-Boissière heard gunfire: 'I can see the SS sentries running up the boulevard, machine guns in hand, followed by a sergeant
who is shouting gutturally. They go out of sight, then I see them again,
dragging an unfortunate boy of around 15 years old. They take turns to
slap him about, swearing at him. I don't see them again.'[6] A couple of
hours later, Daniel Boisdon wrote in his diary: 'It is 11 o'clock. As I write
these lines the violent explosions I heard earlier this morning are
carrying on: they are strong enough to make the windows shake.
Aeroplanes fly overhead and the anti-aircraft batteries open up … The
explosions are beginning again, even louder. Paris is getting closer and
closer to the battle.'[7] At Pantin, a German armoured train, which had
been sitting in a siding at the station for several days, fired on passers-by,
wounding a number of them. At the same time, the Germans set fire to
railway wagons in the station and the area was covered in thick black
smoke.[8]

Everyone was jumpy. Although most collaborators had left the previous day, some sections of the Milice were still in Paris, living with
shredded nerves. For them, the liberation of Paris could spell death.
Outside the Lycée Saint-Louis, where members of the Milice had been
billeted, a guard tried to arrest two young men simply because they
had paused briefly in front of the building. For the nervous collaborator the passers-by were guilty of 'spying' on the Milice.[9]

In the eastern suburbs the Free French nightmare of a communist-
led uprising came closer. Early in the morning, the Mairie of Montreuil
was seized by a group of FTP fighters. The tricolour flag was raised in

front of the building and several hundred people gathered to celebrate. At Saint-Mandé a few kilometres away, the tricolour also flew over
the Mairie, even though German vehicles continued to go past the
building.[10] These victories were purely symbolic – the *mairies* had no particular military value – but what they symbolised was very important.
The town halls represented the pre-war republic, the way things were
before the Germans arrived, the way things could be in the future, after
they had gone. For many people they embodied the reality of local
democracy and were the place where people got married and regis-
tered the births of babies and the deaths of loved ones. However, getting
rid of the Germans was more complicated than simply occupying a
building – the *mairies* not only had to be occupied, they had to be held.
In Montreuil, there was a long battle for the Mairie with the Germans
entering the building in the afternoon before finally being driven out
again in the evening.[11]

In the centre of Paris there were also signs of popular unrest. At
10:30 Yves Cazaux heard the 'Marseillaise' being sung from the street
outside his offices at the Hôtel de Ville. He looked out and saw a group
of around 400 Métro workers marching four or five abreast down the
rue de Rivoli, coming to a stop in front of the Hôtel de Ville, shouting
'Bread! Bread!' They were protesting that they had not been paid for
weeks. The strikers, led by Véry, the regional CGT railway union leader
who had been at Villeneuve-Saint-Georges a week earlier, were received
by Pierre Taittinger, the chairman of the Paris council.[12] Taittinger
agreed that the workers would receive an extra month's salary, and
after a brief meeting in front of the Hôtel de Ville the demonstration
dispersed. In the afternoon, Véry organised another meeting for workers at the quai de la Râpée Métro depot, at the end of which the
strikers marched off to the Bourse du Travail, the traditional headquarters of the trade union movement, and took over the office that
had been occupied by the tame Vichy transport union for the last four
years.[13]

The departure of the Vichy government during the night plunged
Paris into a strange parallel political world. Military power was still in the
hands of the Germans, the civil servants were still at their posts, but
there was no police force and there were no ministers. To fill this

vacuum, two meetings took place at the Hôtel de Ville after the striking Métro workers had left. In the oppressive afternoon heat, Pierre Taittinger convened a meeting of the Paris council, together with the Vichy-appointed mayors from the Paris region. Taittinger privately considered that the council was effectively the government of France, though he wisely made no such claim at the meeting. What he did state, however, was that the Germans had accepted that Paris would not be involved in any fighting. This was completely untrue, but the councillors went away reassured, apparently impressed by Taittinger's leadership.[14]

Elsewhere in the Hôtel de Ville the leading civil servants from all the Vichy ministries met in the office of the Prefect of the Seine. The blinds were drawn to keep out the sun, and the windows were open in the vain hope that a breeze would enter. It was hard to hear what was being said, or even to stay awake. Much of the meeting dealt with the dull detail of the departure of Laval and Herriot the night before. Bouffet rejected the suggestion that he should personally contact the Allies or the Free French, saying that a new government would appear 'out of the streets of Paris'. According to one participant, the meeting gave the impression 'of a great desire for inaction and total passivity with regard to the events to come'.[15]

There was also a third meeting to discuss the situation – this involved the secretary-generals of the shadow Free French administration, who were to take over the ministries in Paris. There it was announced that the Germans would leave the city by 21:00, and the Americans would be entering at midnight.[16] When the news got back to Victor Veau, he was so overjoyed that he ordered his manservant to fetch some champagne, and asked for the flags to be brought out of the attic and draped over the building. Thankfully, his entourage managed to dissuade him, arguing that it would be premature.[17] And indeed it was – the Allies still had their advanced headquarters in Le Mans and they had no intention of entering Paris in the coming days. The announcement was completely wrong. If the upper echelons of the Resistance were so out of touch with reality, it was hardly surprising that ordinary Parisians did not know what was going on.

*

The city seemed bizarrely empty of Germans. The German administrative offices were all closed; outside the deserted buildings, chalked signs directed visitors to the Chamber of Deputies, where the last remaining services were being centralised.[18] For four years, the massive café terrace at the Hôtel de Paris on the boulevard de la Madeleine had been reserved for German troops; now it was half-closed, and the only soldiers to be seen there were a few drivers who had stopped their vehicles in front of the café for a quick drink.[19] Although German lorries continued to pass through the capital, they were rarely in convoys, just disordered stragglers. Along the Champs-Elysées, tired, dust-covered soldiers marched disconsolately eastwards.[20]

Faced with the growing realisation that the Germans had truly changed their attitude to the city – it was now used neither for pleasure nor for paper-pushing, but simply for military needs – the rumour mill started to spin out of control. Some said von Choltitz had decided to defend the city street by street, to the last man, while others, following Taittinger, whispered that Paris would be declared an 'open city'.[21] In fact, in a secret memo, the German High Command in the West stated that there was no question of Paris being declared an 'open city' – it could be defended quite adequately against both internal and external threats.[22]

Rank-and-file German soldiers were not so optimistic. Private Walter Dreizner, aged thirty-six, spent the day working on an electrical installation in a command post near the Champs-Elysées. As Dreizner was finishing his job, General Kitzinger turned up in his smart car laden down with baggage, conversed briefly with an officer and then zoomed off. The officer, watching his commander disappear into the distance, said to no one in particular: 'Whoever does not leave Paris tonight will never leave.' Understandably uneasy, Dreizner wrote: 'Paris seemed quiet, the light clothes of the Parisian women cycling still fluttered in the wind. The shops were still open, citizens were still peacefully chatting away in front of their houses. But on the other hand, what did this mean? It was no guarantee. Did this city's history not provide the answer? Were calm and storm not constantly interchanging in this city? At any minute the storm could break, the city's hate could become boundless, its action brutal. Paris is unpredictable.'[23]

*

Field Marshal Model, like his predecessor von Kluge, had taken up his post convinced that imposing strict discipline and organising a determined defence would reverse the German collapse. Model's abrasive approach could be seen as soon as he took over, when he described those who had been on the Western Front – officers and men – as 'cowards' who had been fooled into thinking the Americans were superior.[24] Again like von Kluge, it took Model about twenty-four hours to realise that he was wrong. Model's intention had been to withdraw his men from the closing jaws of the Falaise pocket in an orderly fashion, pulling them back to a north–south line running from near Le Havre, keeping the Seine behind them. But continuous harrying by Allied fighter-bombers, and the complete lack of respite due to the absence of German air cover, meant that any attempt to withdraw would be met with destruction, while the same fate awaited those who stayed. Inevitably, the German troops within the tightening pocket became increasingly alarmed and demoralised as the prospect of encirclement became obvious, and casualties from artillery and air attacks grew by the hour.[25] However, the combined American, Canadian and Polish forces at the open end of the pocket were still too sparse to be able either to push back the troops desperately trying to flee eastwards, or to resist a counter-attack from their rear by the bulk of the Germans forces.[26] There was still a chance for the Germans to escape.

Those sections of the German Army who had already got out of the pocket were still far from safety. The last intact bridge across the Seine downstream of Paris was at Saint-Germain-en-Laye. All the others had been destroyed by Allied bombers or by retreating Germans. Many troops crossed the river in makeshift ferries, but those in charge of heavy equipment had to find a permanent crossing.[27] Massive queues built up at Saint-Germain-en-Laye, which worsened as rumours grew that the bridge was about to be destroyed, and whole convoys turned around and started heading for alternative passages – either upstream, to the south-east, or directly through Paris with its millions of hostile inhabitants.[28]

In and around Paris, the overall situation of the German defences was growing perilous. The western Luftwaffe bases had been withdrawn, while troops in the south of the country who had been ordered north to reinforce the capital were now being diverted – even an armoured division only 100 km from Paris was ordered to change direction. After the war, Lieutenant-Colonel Albert Emmerich of the 1st German Army argued that at this point 'the construction of a cohesive defensive front had become impossible.'[29] Faced with the growing threat from the west, von Choltitz ordered General Aulock and his battle group to defend the approaches to the capital, while General Vierow was to remain in the rear in command of a defence line, in which he was to collect all the various straggling soldiers who had been separated from their units.[30]

Von Choltitz's decision was astute. Throughout the day the Allies had been making a series of probing operations in this area, sometimes with tragic consequences. For example, a US reconnaissance column composed of five vehicles arrived near Crespières, twenty-five kilometres west of Paris. The local FFI decided to send two of its men to help, but they were intercepted by SS troops, who were enraged following the destruction of some of their vehicles by the Americans. In vindictive fury, the Germans executed the two FFI fighters, along with five other local men who happened to be passing.[31] The Americans, obeying instructions, withdrew from the area. Thirty-five kilometres due south, in the early afternoon, a dogfight took place over Rambouillet. Squat US P-47 Thunderbolts, flying to support a US ground operation, were attacked by over a dozen Messerschmitt fighters, and at least one US plane was destroyed. Below, a 200-strong US column consisting of around forty vehicles, including seven Sherman tanks, left Epernon and headed for Rambouillet, ten kilometres to the north-east. Although the Germans were able to repulse the Allied forces, it was obvious that much vaster forces would soon be on their way.[32]

At Choisy-le-Roi the Germans put up posters requisitioning all able-bodied men to dig trenches; those who refused would be severely punished.[33] At Thiais, six kilometres south of Paris, men were simply grabbed off the street and made to start digging trenches that would provide the Germans with an additional defence against an attack from the south.[34] At Versailles and Villacoublay, 88 mm anti-aircraft guns were redeployed to guard the southern approaches to Paris, their long barrels now pointing down the road towards where the Allied tanks would come.[35] Twelve kilometres further south, at Montlhéry, a Panther tank stopped in a narrow road at the junction of the roads leading to Versailles and Orléans, at a potentially strategic point. But the tank was not there to defend the crossroads – it had broken down, right below the windows of a row of houses. After attracting the attention of the whole neighbourhood, the tank was attacked in the night by a group of *résistants* who captured one of the crew before his comrades managed to destroy their vehicle.[36]

Denied armoured reinforcements by Model, von Choltitz was nevertheless able to strengthen his forces following a chance encounter. In the morning, several fifty-ton Tiger tanks arrived in Paris by rail and were taken under the command of General Bayerlein of the Panzer Lehr Division. Later in the day, Bayerlein bumped into von Choltitz on the Champs-Elysées, and when the commander of Paris complained that he did not have sufficient men or weapons to defend the city, Bayerlein seconded the tanks to duty in the capital, where they had an immediate effect.[37] Early in the afternoon, the Germans had surprised everyone by announcing that there would be a curfew beginning at 21:00, and that anyone breaking it would be shot.[38] Ten minutes after the curfew began, two of the new Tiger tanks rumbled up to the Hôtel de Ville and positioned themselves astride the two main east–west thoroughfares – the road running along the banks of the Seine, and the rue de Rivoli which leads down to place de la Concorde. Civil servant Yves Cazaux – who was also a member of a Resistance intelligence group – had been instructed to stay in the Hôtel de Ville for the duration to be ready when Parodi came to take control.[39] Hearing a loud rumbling and clanking, Cazaux fearfully peered out of his office window, worried that street fighting was about to break out. The two behemoths manoeuvred, then clanked off into the twilight, having made exactly the impression that von Choltitz desired.[40]

A few hours earlier, German plans had not gone so well. At around 18:00 a training session at Versailles for soldiers of the Sturm Paris battalion went horribly wrong. The men were being taught to use the new Panzerfaust recoilless anti-tank weapon when an apparently accidental explosion pulverised a thirty-metre stretch of their two-storey barracks, killing 120 of them. A pall of black smoke rose up from the scene as shocked and terrified soldiers ran in all directions. Bodies were still being pulled from the rubble three days later.[41]

As evening fell, a messenger from von Choltitz arrived at Model's headquarters, carrying a clear plan for the defence of Paris. Satisfied that the capital was as well protected as it could be, Model ordered his staff to focus on the defence of the Western Front.[42] The Allies were approaching: towards the end of the day, a US scouting force arrived in Mantes-la-Jolie, an important crossing-point over the Seine, sixty-five kilometres from Paris.[43] In the absence of massive reinforcements, the Germans decided to evacuate Rambouillet during the night, and a new north-west/south-east defensive line was established only twenty-five kilometres from the capital, stretching from Crespières to Limours.[44] The battle for Paris was growing closer and closer.

*

In Le Mans, Colonel Bruce of OSS talked to civilians who had fled the capital. They all told the same story – food and coal were running short, electricity and water supplies were nearly non-existent, while most of the Germans had left.[45] The Allies needed precise information about the state of the Resistance, and the exact positions of the German troops, and that information came from the Resistance itself, which made a series of attempts to pass through the German lines. With the agreement of FFI intelligence, one of the leading Free French agents in Paris, 'Marco' (Captain Guy de Saint-Hilaire), left Paris on a bicycle, carrying reports stuffed into some hollowed-out loaves of bread.[46] At first Marco was preceded by two young girls on bicycles acting as scouts, while behind him pedalled Lucien Le Goff, who had been sent into Paris by Colonel Bruce's OSS group.[47] Marco and Le Goff left the girls behind at Longjumeau, and after passing through the German lines at Etampes in the late afternoon, the two men eventually arrived in the small town of Auneau, halfway to Chartres. The place was in festive mood, as the Germans had left and an American scouting party had arrived, and wine was flowing freely at the local inn.[48] Marco and Le Goff were given some bales of straw to sleep on, and the next morning they headed westwards.

At the same time, Jean Sainteny of the Intelligence Service spy network ALLIANCE was making a habit of dodging through the lines. On 16 August he had managed to reach Le Mans with a precious cargo of documents. On the morning of 18 August, he telephoned Marie-Madeleine Fourcade, the head of ALLIANCE, and to her amazement told her he was back in Paris – US Army intelligence had asked him to return to the capital to find out more about German positions in the region. Fourcade and her comrades spent the day collecting the relevant information, and soon Sainteny was once again heading westwards, riding on the back of Bernard de Billy's motorbike, the pair once again disguised as telephone engineers. After an eventful journey, which saw them escape from German custody, they arrived back in Le Mans later on that evening.[49]

Things did not go so well for a third mission, led by Captain Trutié de Varreux ('Brécy'), who was head of the FFI operations staff.[50] Rol and his Chief of Staff, Roger Cocteau ('Gallois'), had become convinced that the regional FFI needed direct contact with the Allied military command. Exchanges of intelligence were all very useful, but an open channel with the generals in charge had become essential. Brécy was therefore sent westwards, with his orders typed onto a piece of silk sown into the lining of his jacket. Carrying German papers, he travelled south in a butcher's van, following more or less the same route as Marco and Le Goff. But east of Etampes, as the unmarked vehicle passed through the hamlet of Bonvilliers, it was attacked by a US fighter and everyone travelling in it was killed. The attempt to forge a direct link between the FFI and the Allies had ended in bloody failure, the victim of 'friendly fire'.[51]

*

Realising that events were coming to a head, General de Gaulle left Algiers for France. Over the previous days there had been a minor diplomatic spat about whether de Gaulle should travel in his small twin-engine passenger plane, as he desired, or in a massive USAAF Flying Fortress, as the US government preferred.[52] In the end, the giant US bomber followed the Free French aircraft, but the larger aircraft had a mechanical problem that forced both planes to land at Gibraltar.[53] De Gaulle had to wait a while longer before returning home.

*

In the capital the telephones continued to function, but the Germans laid explosive charges in the main Paris telephone exchange on the rue des Archives, which were ready to be detonated.[54] The dedicated telephone lines that ran along the railway lines did not work, however – it was no longer possible to contact stations to the east or the west of Paris, for the wires had been cut. A combination of sabotage, the rail strike and Allied bombing raids meant that vital food supplies were simply not getting through. Ivry station, a major transfer-point for supplies for the Paris region, received no food convoys at all. A trainload of potatoes from the north simply disappeared without trace.[55] And the situation was not going to improve any time soon, as a joint meeting of the illegal railway workers' trade unions decided to call an all-out strike in all areas where the Germans were still present.[56]

Odette Lainville went to the Mairie of the 6th arrondissement and gloomily picked up her ration tickets for a cooked meal, which had been provided by the city council as part of a programme of communal kitchens that was to meet the growing food crisis.[57] At lunchtime, Victor Veau munched his way morosely through the last of the eggs and carrots; there was now nothing left in the house except potatoes and some tins of sardines which he duly ate that evening. On the other hand, the departure of the Germans had led to some of the best white flour being released for the general population, and Veau and his Resistance guests were able to enjoy some fine white bread.[58]

Jacqueline Mesnil-Amar bumped into her husband's cousin, who told her that André was no longer in Fresnes prison and had been transferred to Drancy. Minutes later she heard from her sister that the Germans had left Drancy the night before. The two young women burst into tears and embraced, and Jacqueline's heart leapt with joy and hope. But it did not take long for her to learn the awful truth – André was not among the ex-prisoners who would be making their way home. Along with seven comrades from the Organisation Juive de Combat

(Jewish Fighting Organisation), André had been put on the last train out of Drancy, which had left the previous day. On the telephone, Jacqueline talked to Nadine, one of her friends whose husband was also on the train. Jacqueline's despair flowed onto the pages of her diary:

> Nadine is sure that the Red Cross will stop the train while it is still in France, or that the Resistance will stop it, or that the FFI, in liaison with our Resistance group, will sabotage the track. There will be a miracle operation to free our boys. Because on that train, somewhere in France, there are our loved ones so it must be stopped, no? Alas! What a joke! Now there will be no more trains charging through the night, through France towards Silesia, carrying a cage of human cargo. No more sealed trains travelling through the night. There's just one train left, and you are on it![59]

Despite her heavy heart, Jacqueline still had to look after her daughter Sylvie. The girl was going crazy stuck inside the apartment, so the pair went for a walk. But as they neared Pigalle, German troop carriers screeched to a halt and soldiers blocked off the roads, brandishing their machine guns. Terrified, Jacqueline and Sylvie managed to wriggle to safety and ran down a side-road. That evening Jacqueline sat with her mother in the stifling heat, sewing FFI armbands for the Resistance and listening to the sporadic chatter of machine-gun fire from the place de Clichy.[60]

Although the Germans had fled Drancy, the inmates were still not able to depart. There were gendarmes at the gates and only those with papers in order were allowed to leave. This was a combination of a bureaucratic reflex by the gendarmes and a recognition that ration books and identity papers were needed in the outside world. Furthermore, although Alois Brünner and his vile crew had left the prison camp, German troops were still very much present in Drancy itself and in the rest of the Paris region. There were still trigger-happy patrols and no French person was safe – especially a Jew. In a curious twist of circumstance, Drancy inmate Janine Auscher was allowed to leave the camp with her papers in order, but when she discovered that curfew was about to begin, she decided to return to Drancy to spend a final night in relative safety.[61]

The Pantin train had been trundling slowly through eastern France ever since it had left the Nanteuil-Saâcy station. As it moved, it leaked prisoners. Some escaped through a hole in the floor of one of the wagons, others managed to open a wagon door and dropped, running, onto the side of the track. At Mézy-Moulins, not far from Rheims, local inhabitants took in a number of escaped prisoners, gave them fresh clothes and even dyed their hair to disguise them. At a stop on the route between Rheims and Nancy, a teenage boy rested his hands on the barbed wire that covered one of the windows; the German guard out-side shot him through the hand – the bullet ricocheted up into the ceiling of the wagon but miraculously did not injure anyone else. The guard said that the young man had been trying to rip down the barbed wire, and demanded that he come out and get his wound treated. Reluctantly, the boy got out of the wagon, and was then taken away and shot. The Germans demanded that two volunteers go and bury him; two men were given spades and were taken off to a nearby field. Eventually there was the sound of more machine-gun fire as they were also killed. In total, seven prisoners were murdered, equalling the number that had escaped, and the train continued inexorably on its way to Germany.[62] For three days, Marie-Hélène Lefaucheux had been follow-ing the train as best she could, from village to village. But it was not at all clear that she would be able to help her husband, Pierre, and she was needed back in Paris. Reluctantly, she gave up her bold mission and made her way back to the capital, but she never forgot her husband's plight for an instant, stuck inside a stifling wagon, rattling his way to hell.

Madeleine Riffaud, who had been saved from the train at the last minute, and had then been rescued from Fresnes by Nordling, was made a surprising offer by her fellow escapee, Anne-Marie. Anne-Marie invited Madeleine to join her in her work for British intelligence – much better than working with 'communists', she said. But Madeleine wanted to be with her comrades, so she turned down the invitation. When she found her fellow FFI fighters, they were appalled by her phys-ical state – six weeks in prison had weakened her substantially, and she was sent away to convalesce at Cochin hospital, until the call of the insurrection became too strong.[63]

*

The Resistance began to prepare for the inevitable confrontation with the Germans. Colonel Rol's FFI staff moved their headquarters yet again, this time into the city, to the offices of the water company on the rue de Meaux in the 19th arrondissement, where they had space and easy access to telephones. In the 17th arrondissement posters called for the population to make barricades, to chop down trees to block the main thoroughfares, and to obstruct narrow streets with chicanes. Meanwhile, all over the city the white German road signs written in Gothic script that had littered the capital for four years were taken down by Parisians who were happy to be taking action.[64] More seriously, the twenty men and women of the 'Victoire' armed group, which was affiliated to Ceux de la Résistance, settled into its new barracks – a private school on a wealthy street near the Ecole Militaire (the school's headmaster was Commander Dufresne of the Seine FFI staff). These were not hard-nosed soldiers but ordinary young men and women who wanted to fight to free their country: they had already carried out seventeen sabotage operations and seven attacks on German garages and had sheltered twenty-eight Allied airmen. The group included Fred in his espadrilles, Michel with his heavy boots that hurt his feet, handsome 'Canard' in a pair of shorts that were really short, Edmond with his floppy black hair that he kept flicking out of his eyes, Marianne who was twenty-eight but looked eighteen and had been tortured by the Gestapo, 'Dogue' who wore a thick turtle-neck jumper despite the heat, and the elegant 'Minet' who ostentatiously wore a red, white and blue tie. But although they had determination and style, they did not have many weapons – three Bren machine guns, four Sten guns, five rifles, a few battered old revolvers and about sixty grenades, not even enough to arm each member of the group. Over the next few days, their group would be in the thick of the fighting on the Left Bank. Some of them did not have long to live.[65]

In the late afternoon, the CPL met at Vanves, on the southern border of the capital. Once again the central question was when the insurrection should take place. The delegates from the Communist Party, the CGT trade union and the Front National made it clear that if the CPL did not launch an insurrection, they would go it alone. André Carrel said that the Communist Party had already printed posters calling for an insurrection and they were ready to be pasted on the walls of the capital.[66] Léo Hamon asked Rol the most important question of all: how many weapons did the FFI have? Rol replied that they had around a thousand firearms, to which Hamon responded that this seemed somewhat insufficient as the basis for an insurrection.[67] Rol later explained that the FFI were not looking for a straightforward confrontation with the German Army – 'In such a battle, we would not have been able to win.'[68] Instead, he argued, they wanted to 'submerge the enemy by a large and profound mobilisation of popular forces'. Stripped of the jargon, this meant one thing: not an urban guerrilla struggle, but mass insurrection. Unable to resolve the issue, the CPL decided to refer the question of the timing of the insurrection to the CNR, due to meet immediately afterwards. However, the unexpected announcement of the 21:00 curfew meant that the Bureau meeting was hurriedly cancelled. The eternal questions of when an insurrection would be launched, and who would lead it, were again left hanging in the air.

The next day would be decisive. The Communist Party had already prepared its posters calling for insurrection. That evening, two posters were printed by the trade unions and by the FFI, calling on Parisians to take action. The joint poster from the CGT and the CFTC (the Christian union federation) called for a general strike, while the FFI called for the mobilisation of all able-bodied French men and women, instructing them to join their local patriotic militia. It further instructed all units to arm themselves by whatever means, to attack the enemy and to protect public utilities and services against German sabotage.[69]

In fact, all the Resistance leaders in Paris now accepted this was the right thing to do. After the CPL meeting, Léo Hamon and his Ceux de la Résistance comrade, Pierre Stibbe, agreed that the moment had come for the insurrection.[70] It might have been Rol's determination that swayed them, but it seems more likely that they realised they were faced with an inevitability, and had the choice of leading or following. Better to be in the driver's seat than to allow the communists to take the initiative and the credit. Even Parodi was coming round to this point of view. During the day, members of the Free French Delegation sent extended messages to Algiers, describing conditions in the capital and outlining potential perspectives. Roland Pré set the tone by analysing the agreement between Nordling and the Germans as the expression of a 'profound demoralisation . . . it is the first capitulation by the Nazis.'[71] For Chaban, the situation in Paris was 'very tense' with 'a growing tendency towards a general strike'. 'All the preparatory conditions for an insurrection are in place,' he insisted. And yet again he warned of 'bloody reprisals, upon which the Germans seem to have decided and for which they are prepared'. Chaban repeated the view he had been putting forward over the previous two weeks: 'If the military situation allows it, you must intervene with the Allies to ask for Paris to be occupied rapidly . . . Make an official warning on the BBC to the population in the clearest possible terms to avoid a new Warsaw.'[72]

Parodi had a slightly different approach that, as befitted his post, was more political than military.[73] Mixed in with his usual emphasis on the risks involved and his repeated pleas to General Koenig to hasten the arrival of the Free French troops, Parodi showed an important streak of realism as he outlined his plans. His message – which would not arrive in Algiers for another six days – foresaw 'several days of effervescence' and revealed both the true balance of power in the capital and a real understanding of why the insurrection was not only inevitable but necessary: 'Tonight the CNR will discuss the call for insurrection proposed by the Comité Parisien de Libération. The strikes are continuing and are spreading. The Resistance and much of the Parisian population would be humiliated if the German troops were to leave Paris without the Parisian FFI being involved in an armed struggle.'[74]

Parodi's recognition of the need for the population to be involved in the fighting was similar to de Gaulle's call for workers to strike to help drive out the Germans, or André Gillois' appeal for factory occupations made on the BBC the night before. What was strikingly different was that Parodi seemed to have ceded leadership of the insurrection to the CPL: 'We have agreed with Léandre[75] the following scenario: the Republic will be proclaimed from the Hôtel de Ville and the Provisional Government and General de Gaulle will be acclaimed. In agreement with the terms decided by the CNR for the whole of the country, the insurrection will be led solely by the Comité Parisien de Libération.'

Parodi was making the best of a bad job, dealing with the forces on the ground as best he could. But for the Free French, Parodi's position was infuriating. He had accepted there would be an insurrection, and had even allowed it to be seen as part of the dangerous revolutionary tradition of Paris, in which the Republic would be declared from the Hôtel de Ville, as in 1830, 1848 and 1870. He had agreed that it should be led by the CPL, and by accepting that both the police and the FFI would be involved in seizing the main public buildings, he had gone against the strict instructions that had been sent a few days earlier that had barred the Resistance from this kind of activity.[76] Parodi did not know this – the Free French message had never arrived – and it is not clear what he would or could have done differently. In the August heat, all the forces of the Resistance had accepted that no one was in complete control – not the CPL, not Parodi, not the communists. The mismatch of forces between the Resistance and the Germans was worrying, but the insurrection was inevitable because of the growing tension in the city, and the appetite of rank-and-file *résistants*.

*

One indication of the imminent eruption of unrest was that despite the dangers, the evident fracturing of the occupation was emboldening ordinary people. In her diary, Berthe Auroy described the new atmosphere: 'the occupiers are too busy preparing to leave to spend time harassing us. The time of investigations and raids is over. I can write freely now – they won't come rummaging in my papers. Freedom is beginning to return.'[77] In the afternoon, on the place du Châtelet, a German column of soldiers marched by, three abreast; two young women, pushing their bicycles, paid no attention and simply crossed the road between the front rank of soldiers and the commanding officer, carrying on their conversation. The troops immediately threatened the girls with their machine guns. The officer, not wanting to provoke an incident, signalled the young women to be on their way, and the squad marched over the Seine towards the Latin Quarter.[78]

Lieutenant Heinz Bliss of the German 4th Parachute Artillery Regiment, stationed in Enghien-les-Bains, eight kilometres to the north of Paris, was sent into Paris with a group of men and three lorries to get supplies from near the Arc de Triomphe. When Lieutenant Bliss and his men arrived in the Renault garage, the French workers were having a meeting. The workers angrily told the intruders that there were no working vehicles present and they should leave. Despite having been attacked by the Resistance on their way into Paris, with one man dead and several wounded, Bliss's group did not respond, and once they had found some serviceable equipment they simply went on their way.[79]

Nearby, teenager Micheline Bood got into an argument with a Luftwaffe sergeant over a tin of meat that he had thrown away and which she wanted to take for Darak, her dog. After the man threatened her with his rifle, she told him he was behaving like a peasant, which made him all the more furious. He screamed at her: 'We will never abandon Paris. We would rather reduce the whole place to fire and blood.' Shortly before curfew, Micheline went back, found the tin and Darak got his supper. Just as she returned safely to her apartment, a German car patrol went by; a young soldier pointed his machine gun in her direction and glared. Unperturbed, she glared back at him.[80]

Late in the evening, violent shooting was heard from the Porte des Lilas, and bullets thudded into the walls of the schools around place Anatole France just outside the eastern city boundary. Resistance fighters had seized the Mairie in the suburb of Les Lilas and were now fighting the Germans. Shortly afterwards, the night sky was lit up with immense flames.[81] Flora Groult spent the evening in her apartment with neighbours, talking by the light of a candle. At around 01:00, a friend telephoned to announce that the Allies were at the gates of Paris. Flora wrote in her diary that they were all overjoyed: a bottle of champagne was brought out and they basked in a brief moment of optimism before reality dawned. She wrote: 'We were bursting with emotion and drank in the dark, for the candle went out at this instant. Then we went on hoping for a while and listening, but since nothing happened we went to bed. The last minutes of waiting are always the longest.'[82]

Saturday 19 August:
Insurrection

Journalist Claude Roy writes in his diary: 'The courtyard of the Préfecture is full of men and weapons, always on the move. There are German lorries, cars full of ammunition, vans that have been taken from the enemy. The logistics department finds it hard to get the ammunition the fighters need. One man has a French submachine gun, another has a British weapon, another a light machine gun, while yet another has a German gun. The firefight that is making such a noise outside resounds in the most extraordinary manner around the courtyard, in the corridors and stairwells. Our ears are ringing. In the rare moments of calm, the massive gates open to let ambulances come and go, as the stretcher-bearers wave flags marked with the Red Cross.'[1]

As early morning sunlight poured onto the vast square in front of Notre Dame, several hundred policemen stood in front of the Préfecture de Police, directly opposite the smoke-blackened cathedral. The night before, a group of Resistance policemen had met in Montreuil and had agreed on an audacious plan to occupy the Préfecture. During the night they had contacted hundreds of their comrades of all political persuasions, instructing them to gather on the Ile Saint-Louis at first light and await the orders of the Comité Parisien de la Libération.[2] But the men were impatient, and there was no news from the CPL, so the police Resistance leaders took matters in their own hands and the men streamed into the courtyard of the Préfecture. Yves Bayet, the main organiser of the occupation, clambered onto a car and cried: 'In the name of General de Gaulle and the Provisional Government of the Republic, I take possession of the Préfecture de Police.' There was loud applause, and the 'Marseillaise' was sung. Unknown to the leaders of the Resistance or to the Free French, the Paris insurrection had begun.[3]

By chance, regional FFI leader Colonel Rol was riding past on his bicycle as the 'Marseillaise' rang out, on his way to his new headquarters in the 19th arrondissement. Completely unaware of the plan to occupy the Préfecture and intrigued by the singing, Rol tried to get into the building, but was rebuffed by the guards. Taking his Spanish Civil War colonel's uniform from his bicycle saddlebag, Rol nipped into a nearby garage, got changed and again knocked at the door. The policemen were disciplined, highly sensitive to hierarchies, so this time he was welcomed with a salute and ushered up the stairs to see the people in charge – the Comité de la Libération de la Police. Rol somewhat superfluously handed them a printed copy of an order calling for the occupation of all public buildings, and after some discussion they agreed that the police would remain in civilian clothes with an FFI armband, showing clearly that they were part of the Resistance.[4] With that Rol was whisked off in a car to his headquarters. He never got his bicycle back.[5]

Not far from the Préfecture, both the CPL and the Conseil National de la Résistance were meeting to discuss for one final time whether it was the right moment to launch the insurrection.[6] Everyone agreed that the moment had come, but the meeting was interrupted by the sound of voices singing the 'Marseillaise', followed by gunfire. As the Resistance leaders peered anxiously out of the window, they saw the tricolour flag being raised over the nearby Ministry of Education. The endless backbiting disputes had been overtaken by events. As Léo Hamon noted laconically in his diary: 'The insurrection did not wait for us.'[7]

Following the lead of the Préfecture, the city sprouted flags – on ministries, on town halls, even on Notre Dame itself. For the first time since June 1940, the French flag was flying all over the capital.[8] The whole city could see that the Resistance was now out in the open, brazenly declaring its intention to fight. Virtually absent for over four years, the flag immediately became a powerful symbol of liberation.[9] At 10:00, five tricolour flags were hoisted on the flagpoles around the roof of the Hôtel de Ville, and the assembled crowd sung a tuneless but moving version of the 'Marseillaise'. Shortly afterwards, the nearby Assistance Publique building followed suit.[10] By the end of the morning, the flag was flying over all of the city's twenty *mairies* and over all the ministries. With the approval of Algiers, the Resistance had drawn up careful plans for taking over the levers of government in the capital, but this plan soon fell apart in the unfolding chaos as Resistance groups – both FFI and civil servants – jumped the gun, much to Parodi's annoyance.[11] At the Louvre Museum, the director decided against raising the flag, reminding his colleagues that their main duty was to preserve the treasures that the Louvre contained, not to attract the unwelcome attention of German troops.[12] Ordinary Parisians were less concerned about their safety: on the rue Saint-Louis-en-Ile Paul Tuffrau saw twenty flags, while the narrow rue des Anglais, off the boulevard Saint-Germain, was completely blocked by a huge flag hung from one side to the other.[13] Flora Groult's heart leapt when she saw the French flag on the *mairies* of the 6th and 7th arrondissements.[14] When the flag was raised in the 6th arrondissement, a Resistance fighter deliriously fired his gun, scaring passers-by who 'ran into side-streets, looking for doorways to hide in, like leaves blown by a gust of wind'.[15] Despite such moments of fear, the city was being painted red, white and blue, to the joy of the Parisians.

The poet Camille Vilain described the impact of seeing the flag:

The quai d'Austerlitz is covered with barbed wire roadblocks. A tank is stationed there, its barrel pointing at us. A threatening sentry, machine gun in hand, makes broad gestures to say that no one can pass, not even people who live nearby. I turn round and, suddenly my heart begins beating madly: on the railings around the Jardin des Plantes are two shields marked 'RF' [République Française] surrounded by French flags, just as on Bastille Days in the past. The German soldiers seem not to notice.[16]

In his attic refuge, Albert Grunberg realised that the flags implied he would soon be 'down there' in the street, freed from his self-imposed prison: 'it won't be long now; the red, white and blue flag is flying on all the public buildings, proudly flapping in the wind.'[17]

The Préfecture was both the starting point and the epicentre of the insurrection. Hundreds of *résistants*, journalists and ordinary Parisians headed over to join in. Claude Roy charged through the entrance to the Préfecture on his bicycle, pedalling furiously, his head bent over the handlebars 'like the winner on a stage of the Tour de France'. CPL leader Léo Hamon got there as soon as he could, and made a speech to the assembled policemen saying that the Parisian population, which had often fought with the police in the past, would never forget their patriotic behaviour.[18] Hamon was right: the implications of the police's actions were indeed historic. As a *New Yorker* correspondent put it two weeks later: 'For the first time since Etienne Marcel led a street mob against the royal court in about 1350, the police and the people have been on the same side of the barricades.'[19] When Hamon stopped speaking he got a shock as the men held up their empty revolvers: they had no ammunition. Shortly afterwards the Front National leader in the Préfecture told Hamon that as long as the Germans did not attack in force, the ammunition would hold out until about 05:00 the next morning.[20]

*

With the insurrection growing apace, various minor Vichy figures came out of the woodwork and tried to muscle in on the situation. First, General Brécard, 'Grand Chancellor of the Legion d'Honneur', demanded that the FFI provide him with a guard of honour to enable him to take power until de Gaulle arrived. This ludicrous suggestion – probably made with the support of the remnants of Vichy in an attempt to establish continuity between the collaborationist regime and de Gaulle – was ignored.[21] However, as a precaution, Brécard was confined to his hotel room for the duration of the events.[22] The chairman of the Paris council, Pierre Taittinger, made a last desperate attempt to stop the insurrection and secure his own position by trying to get a poster printed claiming that Paris was an open city, and that any action against the Germans was futile. But the version that finally appeared was reduced to a simple call for calm and a paternalistic injunction to the population 'to listen to the voice of those who are charged with looking after you'.[23] Events at the Préfecture showed that at least part of the Parisian population had decided it could look after itself.

When the flags were raised over the Hôtel de Ville, Taittinger furiously summoned FFI second-in-command Dufresne and insisted that they be taken down immediately, claiming he had just had a telephone call from von Choltitz who threatened to bomb the city and unleash 20,000 SS men on the population. Dufresne replied that the CPL had taken control and that the Vichy council was deposed, then he left Taittinger alone in his office.[24] The Hôtel de Ville was not occupied for the moment, but that was simply because the Resistance had a more pressing task – dealing with the Germans.

As soon as it became apparent that the Préfecture had been occupied, the German command in Paris put the garrison on alert, activating the second level of their security plan. Officers were ordered to 'act without hesitation and to liquidate all important points of resistance' while at the same time ensuring that their troops did not fire needlessly. Above all, 'Calm and order must be restored by any means necessary.'[25] Shortly after these instructions were issued, von Choltitz ordered his aristocratic aide, Lieutenant Dankwart Graf von Arnim, to scout around the Préfecture. Together with three colleagues, von Arnim clambered into a small open-top car and drove through the eerily deserted streets. When they came to the place Saint-Michel, on the Left Bank, there was a sudden burst of firing. One of von Arnim's men was wounded in the arm and chest, and the front tyre of the car was punctured. Von Arnim screamed at the chauffeur 'Drive! Drive! Drive!' and they screeched off down rue Danton, towards the safety of the German garrison in the Senate building. The wounded man died later that day.[26]

Shortly afterwards, a German armoured car fired on the Préfecture from the pont Saint-Michel, accompanied by lorries full of German troops. FFI fighters wearing armbands fired back from the parapets of the quai Saint-Michel, crouched in the entrance to the Métro, or sheltered by the sculpted dragons on either side of the fountain on the place Saint-Michel. One of the *résistants* was shot and fell to the ground; immediately a group of stretcher-bearers appeared, led by a young woman carrying a Red Cross flag, striding proudly across the place Saint-Michel despite the whistling bullets. The wounded – or dead – *résistant* was put onto a stretcher and hurried off into a side-street.[27] A German lorry drove along quai Henri IV on the Ile Saint-Louis, past the apartment occupied by Pablo Picasso, with a sentry draped over its front mudguard, his rifle at the ready.[28] As the lorry tried to cross the place Saint-Michel, the German soldier was shot dead and fell to the ground.[29] In the midst of the gunfire and spilt blood, down by the Seine a solitary angler watched his line bobbing up and down in the current, while a couple of well-muscled young men walked by in their swimming costumes, fresh from a dip in the river.[30]

The *résistants* in the Préfecture who were attacking the passing German vehicles were firing from the office of Inspector David, the leader of police anti-Resistance unit the Brigades Spéciales, who was currently on the run.[31] Journalist Claude Roy was with them as the firing began: 'The windows have been smashed. The ordinary office desk, the blotting paper, the ink-stand and the moleskin armchair are littered with broken glass, chargers, ammunition and weapons. The saccadic chatter of the Sten guns, echoing in the offices and the corridors, makes a deafening racket.'[32] The men were a mixed bunch: 'One of the fighters has put a tricolour armband round his hat. He has a submachine gun, two German grenades stuck into his belt, his trousers tucked into red woollen socks, big shoes, and wears a checked shirt with the sleeves rolled up. He looks like he has stepped out of an American film.'[33]

The occupiers needed food as well as weapons. At lunchtime, they were served corned beef and tomatoes, which left an indelible impression on 9-year-old Michel Barrat, whose father worked for the Prefect of Police: 'I had never eaten anything so good,' he remembered.[34] In the evening, everyone got something to eat, some coffee, and two packets of cigarettes each.[35] Some of the occupiers made their way down to the Prefect's wine cellar and got so drunk that it was apparently decided it would be safer to destroy the whole wine store.[36]

At 15:20 the Préfecture sent out an urgent call for reinforcements to hold off a German attack: a Tiger tank was rumbling around the building. First it fired on the north wing of the Préfecture, causing a minor fire; it then moved round to the eastern side and squatted in front of

Notre Dame, its barrel pointing directly at the narrow entrance to the Préfecture. The tank fired two 90 mm shells, shattering the gate and wounding two men.[37] Inside the building, in the chaos and dust and noise, men rushed to block the entrance with a police bus and sandbags. The tank could easily have pressed home its advantage and smashed through the flimsy obstacles, but to take the building would have required hundreds of hardened infantrymen prepared to fight a bloody battle in the corridors. Without the requisite ground support, the tank turned round and rumbled off, to the relief of the occupiers.[38] At some point during the fighting, 28-year-old policeman André Perrin, who had come from the 20th arrondissement to help, was shot by the Germans and died shortly afterwards.[39] The Hôtel-Dieu hospital, across the road from the Préfecture, was put on a war footing, and a system of triage and treatment was set up in the basement, caring for wounded *résistants*, civilians and soldiers.[40] Shortly afterwards, there was a series of explosions in the courtyards of the Préfecture as the Germans fired a mortar and threw grenades at the building.[41] A final battle took place at around 19:00 when a convoy of six German lorries moved along the quai du Marché neuf. The *résistants* attacked the lorries; one of the vehicles caught fire and crashed into the Hôtel Notre Dame on the corner of the street, setting fire to the building and to another lorry. A massive pall of smoke rose into the sky; FFI fighters jumped into the blazing vehicle and managed to move it; then the fire brigade arrived and by the time night fell the fire was extinguished.[42]

*

All over the city, the day was marked by dramatic incidents as the Germans attempted to regain control. In the morning things were generally calm. Paul Tuffrau described the scene on the Left Bank: 'I walk down the boulevard Saint-Germain towards the pont Sully. Still the usual bustle: pedestrians, cyclists, long queues in front of the bakers' shops. Here and there, passers-by wear tricolours in their hair, dangling from their ears, around the neck or at the waist. German cars and motorcycles with sidecars whizz by.'[43] But the situation soon began to change. In the middle of the afternoon Jean-Paul Sartre and Simone de

Beauvoir saw about twenty German soldiers come out of the Senate and march down the rue de Seine towards the boulevard Saint-Germain. On the boulevard they opened fire indiscriminately – the crowd scattered, two women were hit and fell to the floor. An elderly man found himself trapped outside a shut door; he knocked and knocked, but was shot in the back. As soon as the Germans had left, his body was spirited away by stretcher-bearers, a pool of blood marking the spot where he had fallen. Eventually, the concierge opened the door, peered at the stain on the ground, and went away to fetch a pail of water and a brush. When he returned, a crowd had gathered and people began to berate him: 'You might well want to wash away the blood – you're the reason it was spilt!' The concierge, who had refused to open the door to the trapped man, stared back, expressionless.[44]

Everywhere it was the same story: sporadic outbreaks of fighting, interspersed with periods of apparent calm followed by growing tension. Dozens of people were killed on each side that day.[45] At 11:00 Pastor Marc Boegner was at the Grand Palais exhibition hall when the sound of machine guns and artillery fire came from the place de la Concorde. He scurried to safety as bullets thudded into the building. It is unclear whether this was the Resistance attacking the German Navy headquarters in the Hôtel de Crillon, or jittery German troops firing at passers-by. A German Tiger tank, on its way to the front, broke down near the Arc de Triomphe. Parisians soon surrounded the vehicle, shouting and making threatening gestures; the crew became alarmed and the tank commander ordered the turret to be swivelled round into combat position. The barrel was lowered and swept round menacingly, making the crowd disappear in a flash, like a shoal of fish darting away.[46]

In the afternoon, the twenty-strong Victoire armed group was ordered to help the FFI in the 6th arrondissement, and to move its headquarters from the plush private school by the Ecole Militaire to a seedy hotel on the rue de Seine, which runs from the boulevard Saint-Germain down to the river. As they were settling in, a German armoured car that was parked on the boulevard fired towards their building, damaging the outside of the hotel, killing a young woman and severely wounding a young girl.[47] In the evening there was another burst of machine-gun fire on the boulevard Saint-Germain and one of the Victoire group, Rémy, burst into the hotel, covered in blood. He was unhurt, but Fred Palacio, the young man in espadrilles, lay dead in the street, a bullet through his head.[48]

In the early afternoon, policeman Alexandre Massiani, who had been involved in the occupation of the Préfecture, was near the recently occupied Mairie of the 6th arrondissement when German troops started shooting. Massiani and his comrades threw themselves to the floor, but Alexandre was shot through the neck and died. A couple of hours later, 3-year-old Rose-Marie Massiani was playing at her grandmother's house when someone came in and told the old woman, 'Your son-in-law has been killed.' Rose-Marie can still remember her perplexity – what was a 'son-in-law'?[49] Things were even worse for 5-year-old Daniel Quantin, who was at his home on the first floor of a building on the rue Dauphine. The whole family was looking out of the windows at the events in the street below when a stray bullet hit Daniel's mother, Virginie, and she fell down dead. She was only twenty-eight. Because of the chaos caused by the fighting, and the strike by workers in the funeral services, her body remained in the apartment for the next five days.[50] Bullets were not the only things that could kill: sitting at his first floor window in the 9th arrondissement, Victor Veau saw a young woman knocked off her bicycle by a speeding German car. She died shortly afterwards.[51]

The Germans decided to take pre-emptive action against a police force they now realised was completely out of their control. At around 17:00, a group of SS soldiers smashed their way into a police station near the Gare de Lyon, arresting over a dozen policemen to shouts of 'terrorist police, kaput!' The men were taken to a nearby building, threatened and beaten with rifle-butts, and then driven off to the fort at Vincennes. They were thrown into a large cell, where a sergeant screamed at them in broken French: 'You, no courage, why French police kill German soldiers, why you terrorists?' An officer left them in no doubt as to the fate that awaited them: 'It's too late now, but tomorrow morning you will be shot.'[52]

At lunchtime, 17-year-old Micheline Bood wrote in her diary about the noise of machine guns, the explosions that made the windows rattle, and the bicycles that littered the road as people scattered when they came under fire. Her view of the significance of the events was somewhat particular: 'All this is very *exciting*! I don't think that mum will let me go to the dentist's this afternoon.'[53] Meanwhile, near the Bastille, Pierre Weil and Michel Tagrine, two young Resistance fighters who were only a couple of years older than Micheline, were arrested by the Vichy Milice. There was a vicious firefight and Weil was killed; Tagrine was wounded but managed to escape and rejoin his FFI comrades. Shortly before 17:00, a German armoured car drove down the boulevard de l'Hôpital towards the Gare d'Austerlitz. It fired into the crowd and into nearby buildings, injuring at least two women. Camille Vilain leant out of his window and shouted: 'They're firing on passers-by! Bastards! Bastards!'[54]

In the 18th arrondissement, Berthe Auroy and some of her neighbours began sewing flags – all it took was some sheets, some dye, and a needle and thread. Taking a break from her sewing duties, Berthe bumped into a Jewish neighbour, who was overjoyed because he was no longer wearing the hated yellow star. Some passers-by had told him: 'Tear that thing off straight away, or we'll tear it off for you!'[55] But although some of the worst aspects of the occupation were over, the Germans had still not left. In the afternoon, a German garage on the boulevard des Batignolles, just down the road from Madame Auroy's apartment, was looted. People ran out carrying champagne, tobacco, silk stockings and leather goods. Shortly afterwards German troops arrived and shots were fired from a nearby building. The soldiers replied with sustained machine-gun fire, and at 18:00 a tank arrived and started firing on the building, causing substantial damage.[56] Eighteen-year-old Red Cross volunteer Jean-Claude Touche was sent out to pick up the wounded, but found the battle too intense, as he wrote in his diary: 'We hurry for shelter. The Germans are firing at anything that moves on the boulevard; they control the streets.'[57] After around forty-five minutes of fighting the Germans left, but one of their lorries had broken down on the boulevard. The FFI attacked it, killing two Germans and seizing weapons and fuel.[58]

Most FFI fighters in Paris were ordinary men and – less often – women, who wore civilian clothes and were identified only by a makeshift armband. However, Berthe Auroy found the Mairie of the

17th arrondissement guarded by FFI fighters looking smart in khaki uniforms and helmets, wearing armbands stamped with the Free French cross of Lorraine.[59] In the neighbouring 18th arrondissement, Jacqueline Mesnil-Amar described a more typical situation: the fighters there looked 'rather terrifying, like insurrectionary fighters'. Some wore trousers and vests, others short-sleeved shirts and shorts or old trench-coats; some were bare-chested and blackened with smoke; everyone was wearing different kinds of helmets and armbands.[60]

The situation in the suburbs was just as tense as in the capital. In Montreuil, to the east, the Germans put up posters warning that for every German soldier who was killed, fifty French hostages would be shot in front of the Mairie.[61] Given that the Mairie was by now firmly in the hands of the Resistance, it was not clear how this threat would be carried out, and indeed it never was. At Neuilly on the western side of the city, Resistance fighters seized the Mairie but were soon under fire from a determined German counter-attack commanded by Colonel Jay. After a firefight that led to around a dozen deaths on each side, the Germans smashed their way into the building and seventy *résistants* were taken prisoner. A period of negotiation between Jay and the deposed collaborationist Mayor of Neuilly followed, and all but twenty-one of the prisoners were released, on the spurious basis that they were not fight-ers but air-raid wardens or members of the Red Cross. Turning a blind eye to the subterfuge, Jay said that the released men should return the next day with their papers to prove their non-combatant status. Two days later, the remaining French prisoners were exchanged for German soldiers held by the Resistance.[62] Despite the ferocity of the counter-attack against the Mairie, Jay had not displayed anything like the savage ruthlessness that von Choltitz had ordered his men to show.

There was another sign of the changing balance of power in front of the Hôtel de Ville, where a German soldier threatened the crowd with his gun, and people dived for cover. Yves Cazaux was watching from his office window in the Hôtel de Ville; to his amazement he saw a young woman on a bicycle, her skirt blowing halfway up her thighs, riding by without a thought of the danger inherent in the situation. The German did nothing. 'She knew what was happening,' wrote Cazaux, who felt the young woman's confident, devil-may-care attitude symbolised a fundamental shift in the attitude of the population, 'Right now it is impossible not to feel the weight of the storm that is about to break.'[63]

At the end of the day, the Resistance controlled forty-three out of the eighty neighbourhoods in the city and had clearly gained the initiative.[64] In some neighbourhoods, such as Batignolles, the fighting had begun early in the morning, at the same time as the Préfecture was being occupied, and had carried on throughout the day.[65] The scale of the insurrection understandably alarmed the German troops. Inside the Senate building Quartermaster Wallraf began to feel uncomfortable; shooting had been going on all day, and the common view among the German soldiers there was that they were poorly defended and that a sustained attack by the Resistance would be successful. The commanding officer attempted to rally his troops: 'Believe me – our General, the new Wehrmacht commander, doesn't mess around. When the moment is right, he will use drastic measures. You can count on it, gentlemen!'[66]

*

For those not involved in the fighting, everyday life presented its own challenges. Georges Benoît-Guyod queued at four different bakers before he was finally able to buy a small loaf of ash-coloured bread that looked, smelt and tasted unpleasant and was not even properly cooked.[67] At 06:00, journalist Edmond Dubois went out to buy some ice for his cousin's wedding reception – power cuts meant his refrigerator did not work, and the champagne was disappointingly warm. The city was still calm, but when the small wedding party arrived at the Mairie of the 12th arrondissement at 10:15, the flag was flying. The mayor married the couple in double-quick time and they rode back across the city to Dubois' flat, dodging bullets at the Palais Royal and at place de l'Opéra. The wedding lunch was a frugal affair: tinned vegetables, pâté sandwiches and jam and bread. At least the champagne was cold.[68]

Not all Parisians were happy about what was happening. Daniel Boisdon feared that the communists were behind the seizure of the Préfecture, and that the uprising might lead to the destruction of Notre Dame or the Sainte-Chapelle – the two Gothic marvels situated on either side of the Préfecture. He could not see the military sense in the events, and – in his diary at least – he was scornful about the antics of some of the *résistants*. He got talking to a man who had stopped fighting because he had run out of ammunition: 'His sole weapon was a 6.5 mm Browning pistol, with one charger! In his big hand it looked like a piece of jewellery. And he had used it to fire point blank at a tank. Idiot! Still, I gave him a warm handshake.'[69]

Some Parisians had other preoccupations. Odette Lainville had intended to take Adèle and Suzanne, the two Jewish girls who were hiding in her apartment, back to their mother on the other side of the river. But as Odette and the girls approached the place Saint-Michel they heard the sound of machine-gun fire and saw the crowd scattering to safety, people running half-crouched. A couple of German motorcyclists with sidecars roared by and Odette and the girls dived for cover in a doorway. It was impossible to get through. Returning home, they had to take several long diversions to avoid German patrols or roadblocks. The girls would have to stay with the Lainvilles for at least another day.[70]

*

Because the Paris Resistance did not have sufficient weapons to liberate the city, the success or failure of the insurrection would ultimately be determined by the situation on the Western Front. Things were bleak for the Germans: conditions within the Falaise pocket grew increasingly difficult as Allied troops began to close the opening around Trun; the Third US Army was moving north from Argentan, while the Canadians were moving south from Falaise. Lieutenant-General Elfeldt, commander of the 84th Army Corps which was in the midst of the fighting, later described their situation: 'Concentrated artillery fire and heavy attacks produced more and more casualties. The situation with regard to ammunition, rations and fuel became critical.'[71] Hans Höller of the 21st Panzer Division recalled: 'Ambulances packed with wounded were carbonised. Ammunition exploded, Panzers blazed and horses lay on their backs kicking their legs in their death throes. The same chaos extended in the fields far and wide. Artillery and armour-piercing rounds came from either side into the milling crowd.'[72] Eventually, orders were given to prepare a breakout to safety by attacking the Allies north of Trun that night; cover would be provided by the 2nd SS Panzer Corps, safe on the other side of the Dives river.[73] However, the Panzer Corps had no fuel or ammunition, and Elfeldt discovered that the orders were suicidally impractical because of the density of Allied forces and the nature of the terrain. When he tried to explain this to the field commander, the man was nowhere to be found.[74] Communications were breaking down, increasing the mood of fear and panic among the German troops.

As to what would happen next, von Choltitz correctly expected the Allies to pursue the German Army around the city rather than making their way through it. As he said to a colleague at the end of August: 'I never, never thought that the French or English armies would enter Paris in order to destroy the city. That was the only way I could be able to carry out my task [of defending the city]. I told myself: "If Paris is here, our fellows will go round on the outskirts, close the rear – in this way you may be able to carry out the job."'[75] In the morning, the Allies liberated Mantes, sixty-five kilometres north-west of the capital, and crossed the Seine, creating a bridgehead on the eastern bank; they had made a decisive breakthrough. From the cliffs above the river, General Patton could see the German command post at La Roche-Guyon, which Field Marshal Model had evacuated a few hours earlier. Model's head-quarters were now in Margival, ninety kilometres to the north-east of Paris, a site far from the fighting for the time being.[76]

During the day the Allies attacked at Neauphle, eighteen kilometres west of Versailles, and broke through. The Germans fell back and a new defensive line was established under General von Aulock. His orders were to enable the 5th Panzer Army and the 7th Army, both cur-rently caught up in the hell of the Falaise pocket, to retreat to safety over the Seine. Although this line was armed with a large number of anti-aircraft guns, these were all immobile, dug in to defend the region against air attack. Even worse, most of their crew were young, inexperi-enced men who had not been trained in ground battle.[77] Von Aulock and von Choltitz sought to integrate this line into the communications network that ran between the various German strong-points within the city, but they failed. There was now little prospect of a coordinated defence of the city. The main Luftwaffe air base to the north of the city – Le Bourget – was evacuated, leaving the Germans without any air bases in the region.[78] The German defensive line would not hold for long against the armoured might of the Allied Army that was about to come crashing out of the west, and without air cover the Germans would be picked off.

The chaotic and inadequate nature of the German defences led the Allied High Command to wonder if things could possibly go any better. In a caustic note, an intelligence operative at the Supreme Headquarters of the Allied Expeditionary Forces pondered the impact of the attempt on Hitler's life and asked a surprising question: 'Two things are certain. The enemy has lost the war and the defeat of Seventh Army and Panzer Gruppe West will hasten the end. One thing is uncertain. Would it have been more profitable for the Allies if Hitler's bomb had been a better and bigger one? Or ought the Allies to feel grateful that he has lived to continue his strategic blunders?'[79]

One man with a personal reason to wonder what might have happened if Hitler had been killed was Field Marshal von Kluge, who had been replaced by Model and had been recalled to Berlin. Early in the morning, von Kluge left La Roche-Guyon for Germany and almost certain disgrace and death. In the early afternoon, his chauffeur stopped by a field near Compiègne, eighty kilometres north-east of Paris; von Kluge spread a rug on the ground and took cyanide. His suicide was kept quiet for some time; with his usual warped misperception, Hitler was convinced that von Kluge had been on his way to a rendezvous with Allied troops.[80] In his suicide letter von Kluge stated that Hitler was responsible for the collapse in the west, and pleaded with his Führer to consider surrender: 'If your new weapons have no effect, particularly in the air, you must end the war ... The German people have suffered so unspeakably that it is high time to make an end to this horror.'[81] Von Kluge's appeal went unheeded. The horror would not end for another nine months. Over this period, hundreds of thousands of people would die pointlessly.[82]

*

Raoul Nordling, the Swedish consul in Paris, had saved the lives of hundreds of French prisoners through his negotiations with von Choltitz. On this morning he decided that he could play an even more important role. As Nordling explained to the Swiss diplomat René Naville, he intended to broker an agreement between von Choltitz and the Resistance to save lives and avoid unnecessary destruction. Naville agreed to support him in this so long as it was clear that they were acting purely for humanitarian ends.[83] Shortly after taking this momentous decision, Nordling found himself in the middle of the excitement and chaos of the Préfecture occupation. Unaware that the Resistance had seized the building, Nordling had turned up at the Préfecture hoping to see the Vichy Prefect, Bussière; instead, he had been taken to see Bussière's Free French replacement, Charles Luizet, who was meeting with other Resistance leaders, including Rol.[84] Nordling told the *résistants* that he was willing to play the role of intermediary between the Germans and the Resistance. Luizet ignored the offer and coldly replied that if the Germans massacred defenceless civilians the Resistance would carry out reprisals against German prisoners – including hospitalised men.[85]

If the Resistance was unimpressed by Nordling's proposal, von Choltitz was even less receptive. When Nordling and Naville went to see von Choltitz in the afternoon, the German commander was in a foul mood, shouting that the Resistance were 'scoundrels' and threatening the city with destruction: 'If this goes on, I'll have to use stronger methods. I have orders to destroy the city before we leave.'[86]

Although Nordling was not getting anywhere with either side, other forces were undermining the confidence of the Free French leadership in Paris. In the morning, Parodi endorsed the call for insurrection, and at lunchtime, during a meeting in a safe house near the Eiffel Tower, he agreed that Rol should have complete control over all Resistance forces in the Paris region including the police and the gendarmerie.[87] However, no sooner had Rol left the apartment than a man who described himself as 'the head of the Intelligence Service in Paris' knocked on the door. This was Colonel Ollivier of the MI6 JADE-AMICOL circuit, and he had no compunction in scolding Parodi for his behaviour, even though it was the first time the two men had met: 'You

have launched the insurrection far too soon. You are at the mercy of the
Germans. Several German divisions are retreating and will have to cross
the Seine in or around Paris. You will be unable to resist them. The
Americans will not arrive before Wednesday, and by then you may have
been crushed.'[88]

The vigour of Ollivier's criticism shook the younger man's confidence, and when the spy offered to ask the Allied High Command to
come to Paris as soon as possible, Parodi naturally accepted in a flash.
Shortly afterwards, Parodi met with Chaban and Pré, and the military
delegates both made it clear that they thought the decision to start
fighting was pure folly. Repeating Ollivier's critique, Chaban attacked
Parodi's decision to back the insurrection that morning – it was premature, he said, as the Americans would not be in Paris for at least
another four days, and the Resistance would be crushed by the
Germans. Furthermore, Parodi had disobeyed the orders that Chaban
had brought back from London, which were – as they always had been –
to restrain the insurrection until the Free French arrived. Chaban said
brutally to his comrade: 'When you've done something stupid, you
shouldn't be surprised at the consequences.'[89]

Clearly shaken, Parodi tried to put an end to the debate by saying
that if he had made a mistake, he would regret it for the rest of his life,
but for now the key question was how to regain the initiative in a city
that was buzzing with revolution. He sent an urgent message to General
Koenig, describing the situation in the capital, urging the Allies to move
on Paris as soon as possible, justifying his decision to support the insurrection on political grounds: 'Have asked Colonel IS [Ollivier] to cable
Allied Command requesting immediate Allied occupation Paris. Same
urgent request sent by messenger. I request it again directly from you
now to avoid possible reprisals. Believe mood of population did not
allow delay of insurrection order. Would have caused split between population and Delegation. Present situation dangerous.'[90]

The question of whether it had been the right time to launch the insurrection could be left until later; the Delegation was now faced with the far
more pressing problem of what to do about the Préfecture. Hamon
arrived at the safe house, bringing a desperate appeal for more weapons
and ammunition. The Delegation had neither. When the situation was

explained to General Dassault, the head of the Front National armed groups, he quickly came to the conclusion that the Préfecture would have to be evacuated.[91] After a brief discussion, Parodi drew up an order along these lines, and Hamon left with the fateful message.

In itself, proposing the evacuation of the Préfecture was not a betrayal. Rol's General Order to the FFI, issued that morning, did not make the seizure of public buildings a matter of principle, but rather an objective to be attained 'wherever possible'.[92] Furthermore, despite Hamon's account, the situation inside the Préfecture was unclear. It was later said that policemen brought five tons of weapons and ammunition into the Préfecture during the night of 19–20 August.[93] While this seems unlikely, on 22 August there was an audit of all the weapons inside the Préfecture and the adjoining barracks. The figures reveal a complete hotchpotch – there were 92 automatic weapons (some with little or no ammunition), 111 rifles of varying kinds and nearly 400 handguns. There were no heavy weapons, with the sole exception of a captured German light anti-aircraft gun that had a mere 130 shells – enough for few minutes of combat.[94] FFI leaders Dufresne and Rol subsequently claimed these figures 'spoke for themselves' and indicated the existence of 'important stocks' of weapons and ammunition.[95] However, even if these figures reflected the true state of the Préfecture on the evening of 19 August, the weaponry they represented would not have enabled the men in the building to respond to a sustained attack by the Germans.

Because of the intensity of the fighting, Hamon was unable to get through to the Préfecture, so he telephoned police Resistance leader Fournet and told him that the building must be evacuated to prevent unnecessary bloodshed. Over the previous four days, ingrained respect for authority had enabled the police to obey without question some very unusual orders, such as going on strike or fighting the Germans while wearing civilian clothes. But this was one instruction they would not obey. Fournet replied for all the men present: 'Tell those gentlemen that we will not leave, even if we die here!'[96]

Shortly afterwards, a crucial event changed the course of the insurrection. At around 19:00, Raoul Nordling received a telephone call from someone inside the building, saying that the Germans were preparing a massive attack and that the *résistants* lacked both weapons and ammunition. Nearly seventy years later, it is still unclear who made the call, but its consequences were substantial.[97] Nordling took it as 'a call for help' and decided to activate his plan for a deal between the Resistance and the Germans.[98] The spy Bender was sent to talk with the German command at the Hôtel Meurice, while Nordling telephoned the Préfecture and asked if they would accept a cease-fire if the Germans also agreed. The FFI were not informed about what was going on (Rol learnt of the negotiations only the next morning).[99] Unsurprisingly, the Free French Delegation was heavily involved and even informed Algiers, although the message was not received for another eight days.[100]

According to Nordling, after over an hour of discussion von Choltitz recognised the new French authorities; that is, he recognised Parodi, the official representative of the Free French government, and not the Resistance or the people who were actually doing the fighting. Furthermore, the German commander offered to negotiate with these authorities and to cease all action against occupied buildings and against the FFI, as long as there was no firing against German troops.[101] As a test of the good faith of the Resistance, there would be a thirty-five-minute cease-fire, beginning shortly after 21:00.

After the war, von Choltitz unequivocally and repeatedly stated that he made no cease-fire agreement of any sort; he merely discussed the matter with Nordling in order to come to a *'modus vivendi'*. He even suggested that Bender might have provided Nordling with fake documents indicating that he had made a formal agreement.[102] It seems certain that the 'cease-fire' was in fact nothing more than the informal outcome of a series of discussions between Nordling and von Choltitz. None of the participants recalls having seen any written agreement, and no detailed account of any of the conversations has ever been published. Over a quarter of a century after the events, Parodi wondered whether Nordling had not cleverly told the Germans that the cease-fire was asked for by the Resistance, and vice versa.[103]

Whatever the case, and whatever Bender's exact role and motives, the outcome was that a cease-fire came into operation that evening. Inside the Préfecture, the negotiations had been followed by a small group that included Charles Luizet, Edgard Pisani and Roland Pré – all Free French appointees.[104] Rol might have formal control of all Resistance fighters in the Paris region, but with the help of Nordling and Bender, and with the agreement of Parodi, this informal group – which did not include a single member of the left wing of the Resistance – had managed to divert the course of the insurrection.

As the negotiations concluded, Nordling telephoned the Préfecture to say that if the cease-fire held overnight it might be extended the next day. Léo Hamon realised that there was an advantage to be gained and immediately made plans for his men to occupy the Hôtel de Ville as soon as possible. This would bring the main symbol of Paris's revolutionary past under the control of the non-communist wing of the Resistance, but under the terms of the apparent agreement with von Choltitz, the occupiers would be safe from German attack.[105]

Although Nordling and the Free French were undoubtedly satisfied with the cease-fire, the mood inside the Préfecture was not so good. Claude Roy was in the building when the order to stop firing was given around 21:00: 'Nobody understands. The order is given to cease fire. The men protest. An extraordinary and moving silence falls on the massive building where, throughout the day, the courtyards, the long corridors, the metal staircases have echoed to the noise of cannon fire, the crackling of automatic weapons fire and the harsh snapping of rifles and carbines.'[106]

*

That night there was yet another massive thunderstorm. Mixed in with the sound of thunder there was the dull noise of explosions as the Germans blew up the flour mills by the canal at Pantin, and an important part of the capital's flour stock went up in flames. At around 03:00, Odette Lainville was suddenly woken by a terrible smell of burning. Convinced that her building was on fire, she eventually discovered that the electricity had come back on in the night, and that a pan of precious potatoes had boiled dry.[107]

Two Parisians at different ends of the age spectrum summarised the day's events. Victor Veau, seventy-three-years old, wrote: 'Not far off there is the sound of machine-gun fire. Revolution is in the air, dogs are barking, there is the sound of whistles blowing.'[108] For 17-year-old Micheline Bood, the events promised a great future: 'We don't want to go at walking pace any more, we want to advance by leaps and bounds; there is electricity in the air – everything is going to explode!'[109]

9

Sunday 20 August: Cease-fire

Jean Galtier-Boissière writes in his diary: 'The public seem to be giving marks to the performances of the résistants and applauding their exploits; they also show a mixture of passionate curiosity and an unbelievable lack of thought, interspersed with sudden bursts of fear. At first, passers-by seem naïvely to believe that they are in no danger because they are spectators and not actors; all it takes is for a bullet to whizz by or for a man to fall to the ground for them to realise the risks. Groups of people dissolve, hide in doorways or scatter. In the blink of an eye, the boulevard is empty. Five minutes later, propelled by the demon of curiosity, the passers-by come out again, to risk life and limb once more.'[1]

Léo Hamon stirred in the Préfecture office where he had grabbed a couple of hours' sleep. It was 05:00 and he could just make out the pale form of Roland Pré, clad only in a pair of underpants, stretched out on the floor. The plan was to occupy the Hôtel de Ville at dawn, while the Germans were still obeying the cease-fire, so at 06:00 a small group of men left the Préfecture in the cold, quiet morning and gingerly walked the short distance across the Seine, the streets still damp from the night's thunderstorm. One participant recalled the group 'looked like gangsters' but felt that was appropriate – they were involved in an insurrection, after all.[2] They were led by Hamon and Pré and included Roger Stéphane, who had been wounded in the previous day's fighting and had his arm in a sling. A few days earlier, Hamon's verdict on Stéphane, written in the privacy of his diary, had been vicious: 'an ambitious little queer … unbearable … a nasty little Jew'.[3] Now they were working together, about to seize one of the most important buildings in the capital.

After some confusion – a number of doors in the Hôtel de Ville were locked and the group got lost in the labyrinth of corridors and stairways – they found their way into the offices of the Prefect of the Seine, Bouffet, where they were greeted by a number of civil servants, including Yves Cazaux. There was a long silence as Bouffet took his time coming from his official apartment. Hamon eventually ran out of patience, thumped his fist on the prefect's desk and took possession of the building 'in the name of the Comité Parisien de la Libération and the Provisional Government'. When Bouffet finally arrived, Hamon repeated his declaration.

Bouffet stared at him and asked: 'Who are you?'

'Hamon, member of the CPL,' came the reply.

'Your papers, please,' said the Prefect.

'We've got out of the habit of carrying papers,' said Hamon.

Bouffet was then arrested and the Hôtel de Ville was in the hands of the Resistance.[4] Shortly afterwards, Taittinger was summoned into the prefect's office and Roger Stéphane arrested him. Stéphane made a powerful impression on the collaborator, as Taittinger subsequently recalled: 'I have rarely seen such a disturbing and tormented physiognomy. The head expressed hatred, with its deep-set eyes, its slanting grin that was just the right shape for a cigarette butt, its swarthy complexion. As to the body, it was like a formless and unhealthy maggot. You felt that a well-placed punch would put paid to the Commander in Chief of the troops of the Hôtel de Ville ...'[5]

Whatever Taittinger's feelings, the Resistance was now in command of the building with probably the greatest political symbolism in the city, the building that five times had been the focus of major events – the great revolution of 1789–92, the revolutions of 1830 and 1848, the declaration of the Republic in 1870 and the Paris Commune of 1871. All of the popular images of revolutionary Paris, filtered through art, song and stories, had the Hôtel de Ville at their centre.[6] Now it was at the heart of the Parisian insurrection of 1944.

*

Far off in the west, the German breakout from the rapidly closing Falaise pocket began at first light. It had been planned to take place the previous evening, but there were so many wrecked vehicles lying about that it was impossible to get through in the dark. In early morning fog, thousands of German troops and hundreds of armoured vehicles began to move eastwards.[7] At around 07:00 the Allies unleashed a firestorm of artillery shells on the retreating columns. General Freiherr von Lüttwitz described the situation of his 2nd Panzer Division: 'New pillars of fire arose incessantly into the sky from fuel tanks. Ammunition exploded, driver-less horses rushed about, some severely wounded. The crossing over the Dives bridge was particularly horrible. There, dead men, destroyed vehicles and other equipment were dumped into the Dives, forming a gruesome tangle.'[8] It took most of the German troops at least five hours to reach safety; nearly 4000 men were killed and another 35,000 were wounded or captured in the process.[9] Lieutenant-General Elfeldt commanded a shrinking group of men and tanks that tried to break through near Saint-Lambert-sur-Dives shortly after dawn. Leading from the front, with most of his men wounded, Elfeldt eventually had to acknowledge the overwhelming superiority of the Allies. He made the only sensible choice and surrendered: 'I was compelled, literally after firing the last round, to abandon a struggle which had become senseless,' he wrote.[10]

Visiting the scene a few days later, General Eisenhower was shocked by the scale of the devastation: 'Roads, highways, and fields were so choked with destroyed equipment and with dead men and animals that passage through the area was extremely difficult … It was literally possible to walk for hundreds of yards at a time, stepping on nothing but dead and decaying flesh.'[11] For the Americans, the day was marked by macabre glee, as artillerymen were faced with 'a gunner's dream', firing over and over again into the German ranks.[12] By evening, the Germans had evacuated up to 30,000 men and hundreds of armoured vehicles across the Dives river.[13] However, virtually none of these forces represented intact fighting units. The structure of the Army had broken down, and those thousands of men were shattered, demoralised and exhausted.[14] By refusing to allow his men to make an orderly retreat from a hopeless situation, Hitler had fatally weakened the very armies he was counting upon.[15] These scattered forces now had to cross the

Seine. That was going to prove difficult – the Allies had established a firm bridgehead at Mantes and were already moving men and machines across the river.[16] It looked like the Germans' best choice would be to head for Paris.

*

On opposite sides of the country, the two figureheads of wartime France were journeying in opposite directions. At 08:00, General Charles de Gaulle's plane finally touched down on French soil, after a long journey from Algiers via Gibraltar. De Gaulle would not leave the country again before the whole of France was liberated.[17] Before going on a celebratory visit to Cherbourg, de Gaulle went to see General Eisenhower at his field headquarters. De Gaulle pressed the Allied leader to explain why the Leclerc Division had not been sent towards Paris, as had been agreed before D-Day. Embarrassed, Eisenhower replied that the Allies were going to bypass Paris to avoid damage to the city and the threat of civilian deaths. De Gaulle pointed out that the insurrection had begun and that it was unacceptable to leave the Resistance to fight alone, to which Eisenhower replied that the insurrection had been launched 'too early'. 'Why is it too early?' asked de Gaulle, 'After all, you have crossed the Seine now.' With Eisenhower vaguely promising that the Leclerc Division would be sent to Paris 'soon', de Gaulle took his leave, warning that he was prepared to order Leclerc to move on the capital if the Allies delayed much more.[18]

At the same time as de Gaulle landed in France, Marshal Pétain was being taken from Vichy by the SS. After days of argument, and faced with Pétain's persistent refusal to leave, the Germans' patience finally expired. The old man was removed by force from the Hôtel du Parc, having first been allowed to write a letter of protest to Hitler. In torrential rain, and to the sound of the 'Marseillaise' sung by a handful of hangers-on, a cavalcade of cars and motorcycle outriders headed east, taking Pétain first to Belfort and then to Germany. The poisonous masquerade of Vichy France was over.[19]

*

While these events were taking place, Colonel Rol discovered that a cease-fire had been negotiated behind his back. He immediately alerted COMAC, the military leadership of the Resistance, informing them that Chaban had ordered Colonel de Marguerittes ('Lizé') of the FFI to cease firing.[20] Furious at Chaban's interference in the line of command, Rol ordered the FFI to continue the insurrection and seize control of the city.[21] While Rol was trying to pursue the fighting, an unofficial group composed of Roland Pré and Léo Hamon, accompanied by the socialist Ribière and the communist trade unionist Besse, was in Nordling's office discussing how to prolong the cease-fire.[22] Pré and Hamon were motivated by a mixture of genuine concern about the military position of the insurrection and a determination to keep control of events. Above all, they wanted to keep the city calm until the Allies arrived. The day before, Parodi had given Rol full control of all the Resistance forces in the Paris region, but now de Gaulle's delegate did nothing to ensure that the FFI leader was involved in the cease-fire discussions, or was even told they were taking place. Parodi later claimed that everything was very hurried and that it was impossible to get hold of Rol; it seems far more likely that this was a deliberate move by the Gaullists to create a *fait accompli*.[23]

After less than an hour's discussion, a declaration was agreed that was soon pasted onto walls and broadcast by loudspeaker cars, accompanied by German troops, uniformed policemen wearing FFI armbands, and FFI fighters:[24] 'The German command has promised not to attack the public buildings occupied by French patriots, and to treat prisoners according to the laws of war. As a result, the Provisional Government of the French Republic, the Conseil National de la Résistance and the Comité Parisien de la Libération call on you to stop firing on the Germans until the promised evacuation of Paris.'[25] To sugar the pill, Nordling emphasised that the agreement did not prevent the Resistance from attacking German troops outside the city. What Nordling did not say was that the cease-fire would allow von Choltitz to consolidate his garrison, potentially reinforcing it with elements from the retreating German Army. Nor did Nordling explain when the 'evacuation' was supposed to take place, or under what terms. Amazingly, no one seems to have asked. Furthermore, no German officer was named in the agreement, which merely referred to 'the German command'. The Resistance was being asked to take everything on trust.

Pré urged the other members of the group to accept the agreement there and then, but Hamon said that he did not have the authority, and that the cease-fire would have to be approved by the CPL and the CNR.[26] In parallel, Nordling submitted the agreement to von Choltitz, who insisted on amending it slightly. He was concerned that Berlin might think that he had made some kind of deal with the Resistance, so 'until the promised evacuation' had to be replaced with 'until the total evacuation'.[27] These changes meant that the Resistance was effectively handing von Choltitz peace on the streets of Paris for an indefinite period. What they would gain in return was unclear. As US military historian Martin Blumenson has put it, the cease-fire agreement was 'nebulous'.[28]

The CNR met at 09:00, and all the tensions that had run through the Resistance since D-Day, and even before, came to the surface in a dramatic confrontation.[29] As there was not a quorum for a session of the full CNR, the meeting turned into a sitting of the CNR Bureau. However, even this was not strictly according to the rules, as only four members of the Bureau were present.[30] To add to the confusion, another eight people were in the meeting, and they could speak although they did not have a vote. There were two ordinary members of the CNR as well as six observers: Parodi, Chaban and Pré for the Gaullist Delegation, Hamon for the CPL, and Tollet and General Dassault for the Front National.

The proceedings of the meeting were as confused as its composition. Wild claims were made: Chaban stated that three German divisions were about to pass through Paris and that 200 aeroplanes were ready to bombard the city (neither of these things were true), while Parodi declared that the agreement showed that von Choltitz accepted that the Resistance had liberated the city and CNR President Bidault said that it constituted a capitulation by the Germans (neither of these things were true, either).[31] General Dassault said he could see no problem with the cease-fire, because the FFI could easily harass the enemy outside Paris. He did not seem to appreciate the strategic importance for the Germans of keeping open the route through Paris as part of the retreat from the west.[32] By agreeing to the cease-fire, the Resistance was guaranteeing passage through Paris of the very troops that Chaban said were threatening the city. They were also ignoring a central instruction that de Gaulle had issued eight days earlier: 'Under all circumstances prevent the retreating enemy from withdrawing men and equipment.'[33]

Unsurprisingly, the two communists, Villon and Tollet, were profoundly hostile to the cease-fire, even though it had been negotiated with the naïve support of their comrade Besse. Villon predicted the agreement would undermine the morale of the FFI fighters, but his only alternative was to evacuate those buildings that were at risk of being overrun and then continue the street fighting. The result was inevitable: Villon voted against the cease-fire, while the three other CNR Bureau members voted in favour.[34] For the first time in its history, and at its most crucial moment, the CNR had decided something by a vote – up until this point, all its decisions had been unanimous. Even more importantly, for the first time in its history the Resistance was openly split.

The consequences were immediate. Straight after the CNR meeting, General Dassault explained the situation to the FFI regional command and got a hostile response. All of the staff officers were against the cease-fire, arguing that the enemy's willingness to stop fighting was a sign of weakness; they felt that this was the moment to press home the advantage.[35] And so they simply ignored the decision of the CNR Bureau. While the loudspeaker cars were touring Paris announcing the cease-fire, Rol and Lizé plastered the walls of the city with a declaration in French and German proclaiming that no cease-fire had been agreed upon. This declaration also repeated Luizet's statement to Nordling made the day before: the lives of German prisoners – including wounded men – would be forfeit if there were any further violence against the Parisian population.[36]

When the FFI decision to ignore the cease-fire was explained to the men of the Victoire armed group, they were overjoyed. Commander Dufresne announced the news at his headquarters: 'No cease-fire! More than ever, fight to the death! It is forbidden to obey orders that are not from the FFI staff, who alone command you. You can even fire on the cars that are announcing the cease-fire!' The audience went wild: '*Vive* Dufresne! Three cheers for the commander! He's a tough one!' they shouted.[37]

As the Resistance fighters made clear they would not obey an order they considered to be so profoundly wrong, a furious André Tollet called a poorly attended meeting of the CPL Bureau, at which he described the CNR's support for the cease-fire as 'treason' and had a blazing row with Léo Hamon. Faced with such passion, and with many Bureau members absent, it was decided to postpone any decision regarding the cease-fire until the next day; the CPL's name was therefore taken off the cease-fire declaration before it was published.[38] Then, at 14:30, a full meeting of the CNR took place, its start delayed because Parodi was mysteriously absent – eventually the meeting went ahead without him.[39] Although Bidault wanted the CNR to ratify the Bureau's support for the cease-fire, without Parodi no meaningful decision could be taken, so the meeting simply noted the negotiations and decided to return to the matter the next day.[40] At the most vital moment of the insurrection, the Resistance leadership was unable to do the thing it had spent four years preparing for: lead large numbers of French men and women in a confrontation with the Germans.

Rumours began to spread. René Courtin, the Resistance treasurer, was told by the owner of Parodi's safe house that the Germans were threatening to use flame-throwers against occupied buildings and to set the SS on the city.[41] Colonel Ollivier of the Intelligence Service, still busily involved in matters, told a friend of Victor Veau that three Wehrmacht divisions were heading for Paris and that two SS divisions, trained in street fighting, were coming to subdue the city.[42] Deeply alarmed, Veau's colleague Pasteur Vallery-Radot tried to warn Parodi, but could get through only to his secretary.

The reason for Parodi's absence soon became clear. Claire Chevrillon's job was to encode Parodi's secret messages; in the late afternoon she had a meeting in the small square behind the Bon Marché department store on the Left Bank to pick up the latest batch of signals for coding. Her contact was late, and when she did eventually turn up, she was extremely upset: 'We sat on the park bench stunned,' Chevrillon later recalled.[43] The Germans had arrested Parodi.

*

As planned, at 16:00 the loudspeaker cars left the place Vendôme, manned by German troops and French gendarmes, and drove around Paris announcing the cease-fire.[44] Crowds applauded, relieved that the fighting was apparently over. In the 18th arrondissement, Berthe Auroy heard shouts of joy and saw flags appearing everywhere, while on the Left Bank the deserted anti-aircraft platform near the Jardin du Luxembourg was covered with a gigantic tricolour flag.[45] Micheline Bood heard the loudspeaker car and drew her own conclusions about what it meant for the Germans: 'They must have been furious when they had to sign an armistice with the Resistance fighters ... Paris is less nervous, a gorgeous cool breeze is blowing, and, to sum up, we find ourselves in the pleasant situation of waiting because "something is happening".'[46]

Teacher Jean Guéhenno was less enthusiastic: 'I'm not sure whether or not I'm happy about the armistice that has been signed this afternoon ... A German half-track and a Resistance car met up. The Germans were the first to wave a white flag. Both sides stopped, discussed, then went on their way as the crowd applauded. That applause worries me. The most important point, I think, is that the country can only truly find and express its soul through an honest struggle. And that is not possible in this situation.'[47] Andrzej Bobkowski was openly cynical: 'Bloody marvellous,' he wrote in his diary, 'they fire a few shots, scare the wits out of the Germans and then, after a day, they sign a compromise. Both sides stop shooting, the Parisians can walk about freely, job done. We wait nicely for the Americans to arrive. A real fairy story.'[48]

Shortly after the cease-fire was announced on the Left Bank, Jean-Paul Sartre listened to groups of people arguing in the street about whether it was right or not. Some felt the cease-fire was a sign of German weakness or a German ruse to gain time, others that it was a way of avoiding needless bloodshed, while an old man asked: 'What is there left for us to do if they have signed a cease-fire? Fold our arms, that's all. But liberty isn't something that can be given – you have to take it.' Ironically, the argument was suddenly cut short by gunfire; two women were hit. One of them leant against a tree and blood ran down the trunk.[49]

As the situation was described and passed from person to person, it got distorted. One of those given the wrong end of the stick was Albert

Grunberg, still stuck in his attic hideaway. A neighbour, Madame Oudard, wheezed up six flights of stairs to tell him, in short snatches of breathless speech, that the German commander had capitulated. Perhaps as a result of previous disappointments, Grunberg did not believe her.[50]

About half an hour after the loudspeaker cars had passed down the boulevard Saint-Michel, two German soldiers strolled down the road towards the Seine, rifles at their shoulders. The sight of them provoked a sudden panic among the crowd and people ran down the street away from them. Alarmed, the German soldiers joined in and ran too, unaware that they were the cause of all the agitation. They were so frightened they ran straight to a nearby policeman and demanded to be taken into custody.[51]

At 17:30 in the Hôtel de Ville, the new Free French Prefect of the Seine department, Marcel Flouret, entered his new headquarters, walking up a staircase lined by an honour guard of FFI fighters. When Flouret got to his office he found the tables were covered in ammunition belts and a man was asleep in a chair.[52] An hour later a massive crowd gathered on the rue des Pyramides and invaded the headquarters of Doriot's fascist organisation, the PPF. The whole building was trashed, and the street outside was thick with papers that had been thrown out of the smashed windows. The Germans did nothing. The balance of power had shifted.[53]

In the early evening, the three members of COMAC met and after much discussion issued a long statement on the cease-fire. They understandably expressed annoyance that they and Rol had been sidelined from the discussions, but at the heart of their document was a cogent critique of the arguments used by Parodi, Chaban and the others to justify the agreement with von Choltitz. For example, they examined the claim from the Gaullist Delegation that the Germans were threatening to attack Paris from the air; in reply they pointed out that it was impossible for the Germans to bomb the city without threatening their own troops and blocking the passage through Paris. In the case of the German divisions allegedly heading for the capital to massacre the population, it would be relatively straightforward for the Allies to disrupt and destroy any such troops by bombing them from the air before they arrived. Above all, COMAC argued that the way to liberate the city would involve mobile guerrilla warfare based on the mass of the population, and not a static war of position carried out by small forces holding symbolic buildings. They closed by insisting that if there were to be a cease-fire, it could only be on the basis of the complete surrender of the enemy throughout the country.[54]

COMAC would have been surprised to learn that General de Gaulle shared the final point of their critique. Parodi and Pré had kept Algiers informed of the negotiations but, as usual, most of the messages took days to get through and there was no reply.[55] When de Gaulle finally heard about the cease-fire on 23 August, he said it made 'an unpleasant impression', partly because of his distaste for military compromise and partly due to his suspicions about the involvement of the Intelligence Service.[56] However, irrespective of whether they were manipulated by MI6, Parodi, Pré and Chaban were merely carrying out their orders from General Koenig and the Free French, which were to prevent an uprising in Paris and to ensure the installation of a Free French government. De Gaulle might not have liked what had been done in his name, but it was the logical consequence of this fundamental part of his policy.[57]

*

As the cease-fire was announced on the streets of the capital, Rol summoned his chief of staff, Gallois. There had been a series of contacts between the Resistance and the Allies over the past few days, culminating in the mission of Captain Brécy two days earlier, but there was no indication that the Allies had paid them any attention. (Rol had no idea that Brécy had been killed before he had been able to make contact.)[58] Rol therefore instructed Gallois, who spoke excellent English, to leave Paris immediately, to make his way through the German lines and to contact the Allied High Command. Gallois was to inform the Allies of the cease-fire, emphasising the weakness of the German forces and pleading for arms and ammunition to be immediately parachuted into the capital. A few weeks later, Gallois recalled Rol's closing words: 'As our head of intelligence, you know how weak the German forces are that lie between the Allies and Paris. You must insist that a relief column brushes aside these weak enemy defences and heads for the capital at full speed. Tell them that we are masters of part of the city and of the main buildings, and that they must hurry to take advantage of this situation, and help us.'[59]

By chance Dr Robert Monod, a medical officer with the FFI, had already offered his services for such a mission.[60] As a physician, Monod had a car and fuel, and only two days earlier had encountered an American scouting party far to the south-west of Paris.[61] In the early evening, Gallois and Monod set off, accompanied by a young doctor who spoke German. However, they soon found that it was impossible to get through – following the Allied advance, a new German line had been established and there were roadblocks everywhere.[62] Disheartened, the group had to turn back and eventually spent the night in a small village, trying to sleep on mattresses on the floor, after an evening meal of a few pears – all that their host could offer them. None of the men could sleep, kept awake by the excitement, a terrible thunderstorm and the sound of an aeroplane circling low overhead, as though it were trying to find a drop site for men or equipment.[63]

A few dozen kilometres to the north, Jacqueline Mesnil-Amar could not sleep, either. She was sick with worry about her husband, André, as she confessed in her diary: 'This is the time of night when I ask myself 20 or a 100 times: Where is his train going? Where is it now? Has it passed into the shadows? Is it still in France, this train that the Resistance should be stopping, this train in which he just had to be locked up? Yet another night in which he is taken from me . . .'[64]

The Resistance had not stopped the Drancy train, but the prisoners were not passively awaiting their fate. They had been able to prise free some of the planks on the rear wall of the wagon, and were planning to remove them and then jump from the moving train. Suddenly the train jerked to a halt, there was the sound of running feet and shouting from German guards, then the loud thump of planks of wood being nailed over the very place the prisoners had weakened. They would have to start again.[65]

*

While Gallois and Monod were trying to head westwards to meet the Allies, OSS spy chief Colonel Bruce was making his way eastwards towards Paris, ending up in Rambouillet, sixty kilometres south-west of the capital, on the edge of a hilly forest. Bruce met up with Ernest Hemingway, who was supposedly an embedded journalist with the 4th US Infantry Division but had taken off on his own and had found Rambouillet unoccupied since the Germans pulled back earlier in the day.[66] After surrounding himself with a bunch of local FFI fighters, some gendarmes and a couple of US paratroopers who had gone AWOL, Hemingway had made his headquarters in the Hôtel du Grand Veneur. The scene was chaotic: 'it was like being in Bedlam,' wrote Bruce in his diary. 'Agents were nipping in and out, and everyone, including a stray American woman resident in France, was buttonholing me, asking questions and giving answers at the same time. Newspaper correspondents had sprouted out of the ground, and the world and his wife were eating and uncorking champagne.'[67] Like Hemingway, those journalists had a nose for a story, as well as for alcohol: this was the road to Paris, they thought.

*

In the fort at Vincennes, the policemen who had been arrested at the Gare de Lyon the day before heard the sound of machine-gun fire from the courtyard outside their cell. Eventually they were led outside. 'We found a terrifying sight. The bodies of our comrades were lying on the ground, terribly wounded. Some had their faces ripped off, or their chests stoved in or were dismembered.' The policemen were ordered to dig a mass grave for the eleven dead men, and to carry their bodies, still pouring blood. One of the policemen, Monsieur Sylvestri, was taken away, interrogated, then made to stand on the edge of the mass grave, facing a firing squad. Eye-witnesses reported that Sylvestri was calm and dignified, buttoning up his shirt, smoothing his hair and straightening his tie, before standing to attention and shouting *'Vive la France'* as he was executed. The horror was not over; shortly afterwards there was the sound of more firing, and the policemen were given three more bodies to deal with, while the SS became increasingly aggressive and menacing.

Eventually an officer restored order and the remaining prisoners were taken to their cells. One German reassured the men that they would not be shot, although other soldiers shouted threats outside the cell.[68]

Despite the cease-fire there was fierce fighting in the morning around the place Saint-Michel as the Germans sent armoured vehicles to attack Resistance defences.[69] Around 14:00, Jean-Paul Sartre heard that the Milice were firing from a hotel on rue de Buci on the Left Bank. As he reported it, a group of FFI fighters entered the building and brought out a number of 'Japanese' men who appeared to be the culprits; a relieved and good-humoured crowd gathered and some of the supposed militia-men were grabbed, their trousers were pulled down and they were spanked; when the police van came to take them away they had to hop in as if they were in a sack race.[70] If this incident is true, it raises the question of why the crowd treated them in such a light-hearted way. Not everyone was so benevolent, though, as was shown by what happened when the men were taken to the police station of the 6th arrondissement. One of the 'Japanese' was taken into the courtyard by a member of the Resistance, and shot dead. Following protests, the killer was locked up.[71]

Not far away, on the boulevard Saint-Germain, Georges Benoît-Guyod saw German troops wave down a young woman on a bicycle, who was dressed in trousers and sensible shoes. She ignored their gestures and pedalled furiously; they shouted at her to stop, but she carried on. Shots rang out; she was wounded in the head and careered into a side-road. She was extraordinarily lucky – the bullet had grazed her ear and after some minor repairs from a passing nurse she rode off, without having said a word. Benoît-Guyod concluded that she was a liaison agent for the Resistance.[72]

In the afternoon, FFI fighters on the Left Bank shot at a passing Citroën car and killed three German officers; the bullet-riddled vehicle – which was still working, despite a shattered windscreen – was brought into the courtyard of the hotel where the group was stationed. The seats were covered with blood. Elsewhere in the building, a group of *résistants* were busy pouring petrol into bottles, to use as Molotov cocktails against German vehicles.[73] Nearby, next to the narrow rue de la Huchette, a young FFI fighter clutched his carbine and told stories of the fighting to two wild-looking women.[74] They complimented him saucily and then, their arms around his neck, dragged him off to a nearby bistro 'to get something warm'.[75]

The cease-fire enabled Odette Lainville finally to take the two Jewish girls, Adèle and Suzanne, back to their home in the Marais. It was not straightforward – in the morning they had to turn back because of fighting near the Seine and on the way back home they ran into trouble near Censier-Daubenton. In the late afternoon Odette, her friend Louise and the two girls tried again. This time, although there was no fighting, there were plenty of vehicles with the letters 'FFI' crudely painted on them, bristling with guns. This frightened little Adèle, who had obviously been affected by the morning's events. On the boulevard Henri-IV, on the other side of the river, Odette picked up a spent bullet and gave it to her friend Louise as a souvenir. Even though the girls were glad to be back with their mother, Adèle was still upset from the fright she had received.[76]

The atmosphere grew close as the heat increased and the tension mounted. At about 16:30 a German armoured group consisting of a large tank and four half-tracks drove down the boulevard de l'Hôpital towards the Gare d'Austerlitz and the Jardin des Plantes. About halfway down, opposite the Pitié-Salpêtrière hospital, the tank's turret swivelled round and several bursts of heavy machine-gun fire were sent into the crowd. A young woman went down, her leg smashed; three men found themselves trapped behind a tree for nearly half an hour, unable to move while the fighting continued. Down by the Seine, there was the sound of explosions as grenades were thrown. After about an hour, the loudspeaker cars arrived to announce the cease-fire and the fighting stopped, and Camille Vilain was able to go and see what had happened. It appeared that forty people had been killed in the incident. Vilain saw an FFI car smouldering by the entrance to the Jardin des Plantes and the bus station was burning. A tree had been cut down by the firing, and the gates of the Jardin had been twisted under the impact of the grenade explosions. Where the tricolour flag had flown the day before, making Vilain's heart leap with joy, there was now debris, a huge pool of blood and shattered body parts.[77]

As the fighting ended around the Gate d'Austerlitz there was a ferocious firefight on the Left Bank opposite the northern tip of the Ile de la Cité, downriver from the Préfecture. From the window of his apartment, Yves Cazaux saw a heavily armed SS patrol, backed up by armoured vehicles, attacking an FFI group that had occupied the Monnaie de Paris (Paris Mint). Despite the gunfire, Parisians were lounging on the banks of the Seine and even swimming in the river. After ten minutes, the firing suddenly stopped and then the two cease-fire vehicles drove up, with their white flags.[78] There was more shooting, then the announcement of the cease-fire was made in French and German and the guns immediately fell silent. But as the loudspeaker cars drove off, a grenade was thrown at the people swimming in the Seine, with awful consequences. Within a few minutes, there were ambulances outside the Monnaie picking up the dead and wounded. Cazaux went down to see the damage: the ground was covered with broken glass, spent cartridge cases and pools of blood. A German car was lying upside down next to the nearby Passerelle des Arts footbridge across the Seine, showing the ferocity of the fighting. On his way home, he came across a man and a woman, lying dead in the street. They were passers-by who had been shot by the Germans for no apparent reason.[79]

In the 17th arrondissement it was not just the FFI who were doing the fighting – the population eventually got involved, too. First, there was a day of gunfire in which a number of FFI fighters were killed, including Simone Jaffray, a 29-year-old woman who acted as a liaison agent, and was mortally wounded on the rue Jacquemot.[80] Then, in the early afternoon, two German lorries were seized and used to protect the Mairie by blockading the broad boulevard des Batignolles.[81] This was followed by one of the most spectacular events of the whole insurrection, when an unarmed crowd surrounded a small German R35 tank destroyer. An initial photograph shows about twenty Parisians around the vehicle, but soon the crowd was about 500 strong, and people began to swarm all over the tank. There were a dozen or so German soldiers involved, and a later photograph shows them clinging onto the vehicle as they were overwhelmed by the unarmed Parisians – the vast bulk of the hundreds of people in and around the tank were local residents, not FFI fighters (see Plate 20). In the centre of the photograph, standing atop the vehicle, is Georges Dukson, a 22-year-old from French West Africa (now

Gabon). Sergeant Dukson of the French Army had been taken prisoner in 1940; he managed to escape from a German prison camp, and returned to Paris where he was living in secret.[82] Faced with the overwhelming size of the crowd swarming on and around the vehicle, the Germans eventually simply gave up, without firing a shot. The crowd roared its delight.[83] One of the FFIers climbed onto a car, made a brief speech to the throng, and then the captured tank was driven off to the Mairie, covered in people and flying a massive tricolour, led by Dukson and followed by the joyous crowd.[84]

Around the Mairie of the 17th arrondissement, the excitement began to get out of control, and a woman was accused of collaboration and had her hair shaved off and a swastika daubed on her forehead. A man cried out: 'My concierge is a collaborator, come and arrest her!' Jean-Claude Touche noted: 'This atmosphere disgusts me – it is the lowest form of vengeance.'[85] A couple of hours later, the shaven-headed woman was taken to her home on the rue Tholozé in Montmartre; Berthe Auroy was told that the Resistance had brought back a woman collaborator, whose head had been shaved by a black man. Incredulous, Madame Auroy went onto the street, where she found tufts of hair.[86] Later, the mood darkened further because people in the neighbourhood were advised by the FFI to take down their flags because the Germans were shooting at them.[87] Similar instructions were given elsewhere in the city.[88]

In the 19th arrondissement, German armoured vehicles attacked the FFI headquarters next to the Mairie. Shortly afterwards, FFI fighters Barth and Caplot hurried down to the bottom of the avenue Secretan to pick up a wounded comrade; in turn they were both shot and severely wounded by the Germans. In the early evening, a group of FFI fighters crept out of the hilly Buttes Chaumont park and shot dead the German sentries standing guard over the railway lines. In response, the German garrison at the nearby Villette station launched a ferocious attack, firing on all the surrounding buildings, wounding and killing civilians.[89] There were many other incidents all over the city that day. According to Colonel Rol, 106 Parisians were killed and 357 wounded during the cease-fire.[90]

Some of those deaths happened in the most senseless and haphazard of ways. Daniel Boisdon went to visit the Préfecture, where the revolutionary atmosphere impressed him. He was about to leave for home when suddenly a German vehicle came careering up the rue de la Cité, spraying machine-gun fire. Three women were shot, and Boisdon hurried across the cobbles in front of the Préfecture to help them. One woman was already dead; he cradled another who was riddled with bullets. Blood bloomed on her blouse as he held her.[91]

For young Micheline Bood, this catalogue of danger was strangely thrilling. Her friend Nicole explained how she was nearly injured when the Germans shot at the flags that had been hung out. Micheline wrote in her diary: 'She was sure that I was jealous, and she wasn't wrong, but perhaps I'll have my moment of excitement, too.'[92] Despite the ferocity of the fighting, Micheline still enjoyed her encounters with the German soldiers – as she walked back from Mass that morning there were scores of German troops on the boulevard Malesherbes, pointing their guns. 'Despite this, they smiled at me and looked at me nicely,' she wrote in her diary.[93] She even imagined drawing pictures of the Germans who were billeted in the building opposite: 'One of them eats all the time; another, a redhead, airs his clothes on the window-sill; another plucks his eyebrows and washes his hands all day; a pretentious little blond man writes by candlelight every night and gets dressed up to come to the window.'[94] They were the enemy, but they were also human.

*

In the late afternoon, von Choltitz sat in his office wearing a white uniform. On his desk was a sprawl of papers that had been found in the possession of the three men who were standing in front of him: Alexandre Parodi, Roland Pré and Parodi's close colleague, Emile Laffon.[95] The papers included all the documents that were to be discussed by the CNR, as well as a series of draft declarations, one of which called for insurrection. Two hours earlier, a zealous German sentry had stopped their car. The men had no papers to justify their use of a vehicle, so they were taken in for questioning and were soon in a Gestapo building. To the Germans' amazement, the three men proudly announced that they were leaders of the Resistance, and coolly explained that they had been checking whether the cease-fire was being obeyed, and therefore they could not be arrested. The Gestapo man was not impressed: 'You are terrorists, spies,' he said. 'You should be shot.' In reply, Parodi gave the German his code name – 'Cérat' – and insisted that the officer contact Nordling, who would vouch for them. This must have worked, as not long after the three men were taken to von Choltitz's headquarters at the Hôtel Meurice.[96]

No sooner had they entered von Choltitz's office than Nordling arrived and confirmed that the three Frenchmen were indeed Resistance leaders. Accompanying Nordling were his perpetual companions, Bender and Posch-Pastor; the latter acted as an interpreter.[97] For two tense hours, von Choltitz questioned his captives. The German security officers were jubilant – 'one of the most important arrests we have made recently' said one – but things looked rather different to the German commander, who found himself in an unexpectedly difficult position.[98] Von Choltitz was worried that the communists might gain the upper hand in the struggle for Paris; if Parodi and the others were removed, this might upset the delicate equilibrium that had allowed the cease-fire to be agreed. Although the discussion dragged on, it got nowhere, as Parodi refused any compromise beyond the cease-fire, retreating behind his formal status as a minister in de Gaulle's Cabinet. When von Choltitz offered to provide the population with some of the German food stocks, Parodi rejected the offer, saying: 'The Parisians have been hungry for the last four years; they can put up with starving for another four days.'[99]

Eventually, von Choltitz took an amazing decision: he told the three Frenchmen they could go. He even returned their documents, handing them over to Nordling for safe-keeping. As the men were about to leave, von Choltitz got up, walked to the door and made a final gesture of appeasement. He asked if Parodi was a military man; Parodi said he was. Von Choltitz stuck out his hand: 'Such a gesture is possible between soldiers.' Parodi looked at the outstretched hand and said, 'Under the present circumstances, a French minister cannot shake the hand of a German officer.' And with that he left the room.[100]

*

For the Germans, the day was marked by mounting tension and uncertainty. Private Walter Dreizner and his group of electrical engineers were evacuated from their billet on the rue Cambon and were moved closer to the German command headquarters on the rue de Rivoli. But even that was not safe: Colonel Jay, the newly appointed Battle Commander of Paris, felt uneasy standing near the window of his new office in the Hôtel Meurice in case he was shot by a sniper.[101] During a sortie to carry out essential repairs on a telephone installation, one man in Dreizner's unit was killed, four were wounded and three went missing. A tank was sent to support the group, but it had orders not to fire, so as not to provoke any further incidents with the Resistance. In the evening, Dreizner's unit received instructions not to venture into the east of the city, increasing Dreizner's impression of encirclement, imminent danger and impotence.[102]

Some soldiers simply gave up the fight. At around 15:30, at the bottom of the boulevard Saint-Michel, a German lorry, full of soldiers, was stopped by the FFI. Much to the amazement of passers-by, the unarmed leader of the *résistants* talked with the Germans. Jean Galtier-Boissière recorded the scene in his diary:

> Suddenly, a fat German jumps out of the vehicle and surrenders unexpectedly, handing his submachine gun to one *résistant*, his revolver to another, then his ammunition, and everything else he has. One, two, three, four other soldiers follow his example. But the helmeted soldier with a submachine gun on the roof of the lorry doesn't want to join in and refuses to surrender. A second unarmed *résistant*, very young, decides to convince him, pointing out all the guns that were aimed at him. Eventually, the German climbs down, and hands over his weapons, grumbling.[103]

Had Berlin known the extent to which the Paris garrison lacked the stomach for a fight, it is possible they might have acted differently.[104] But as it was, Hitler sent an order to Field Marshal Model asserting that the key task of Western Command was to hold the line west of Paris, and above all to prevent the Allies from breaking through and heading eastwards. The shattered remnants of the 5th Panzer Army, currently fleeing from Falaise, were to make for the Paris bridges, which were to be held 'under all conditions'. The Seine was to form the new front, and Paris was expendable. Hitler's order put it quite clearly: 'If necessary the fighting in and around Paris will be conducted without regard to the destruction of the city.'[105]

10

Monday 21 August: Conflict

Micheline Bood writes in her diary: 'They say the Allies are not going to enter Paris, because the Resistance is strong enough to take the city on its own. That is really magnificent. From now on, we can hold our heads high and be proud of being French men and women. Our country was betrayed by the likes of Marshal Pétain; we had neither weapons, nor aeroplanes nor tanks and yet we rose up against the enemy in an invincible movement. All that mean-spiritedness can be forgotten. France is still France! Oh, and the lads of the Resistance are so good-looking, fresh-faced and bright and bold. Every one of them is a symbol; today I saw them as though for the first time and they moved me.'[1]

Early in the morning, Resistance fighters gingerly entered the fort at Romainville, on the north-eastern outskirts of Paris, which had served as a German prison. There was an eerie silence. The day before, the fort's last occupants, German Army volunteers from the German occupied area of the Soviet Union, known as 'Georgians', had left the region. As the *résistants* moved through the site, they made a macabre and disturbing discovery. At the foot of a long wall behind the main building lay eleven bodies – ten men and one woman – ripped apart by machine-gun fire. They were all local *résistants* who had been captured by the 'Georgians' and had then been callously murdered before the troops fled. Appalled at what they had found, the *résistants* called in the press, including film-makers, to capture the horror. The whole world had to know.[2]

Later the same day, the female prisoners from Romainville who six days earlier, on 15 August, had been loaded onto the Pantin train finally arrived at their destination: Ravensbrück concentration camp. Few would return. But for some prisoners who had been put on the Drancy train on 17 August, the moment had come to start the long journey home. It was still dark and they were somewhere in France – they had passed through Laon, 120 km north-east of Paris, the previous evening. The journey had been slow and repeatedly disrupted by diversions due to destroyed lines and a Spitfire attack on the train, which had left the locomotive wheezing like a punctured football. Because the prisoners' first escape plan, which had involved breaking through the rear of their wagon, had been foiled a few hours earlier, they turned their attention to the tiny barred ventilation window. After they had cut their way through the first bar with a chisel that had been smuggled aboard, a slender young man pushed his body through the gap and tried to operate the outside lever that would unlock the wagon's sliding door. But the lever was just out of reach, so they had to think again. The window was their only way out. A second bar was removed and now the way was open, for those bold and fit enough to drop from a moving train into utter blackness. The young men went first, disappearing into the driving rain as the train inexorably pulled them all closer to Germany. One of the first to jump was André Amar, Jacqueline Mesnil-Amar's husband. Soon afterwards, brother and sister Philippe and Rose-Marie Kohn leapt into the darkness. As they lay on the stones at the side of the track, Philippe and Rose-Marie could see the red lamp on the last wagon as it disappeared into the darkness. It was carrying the rest of their family, including their 12-year-old brother, Georges-André, into oblivion.[3]

*

On a dull grey Parisian morning, the atmosphere had changed completely from the euphoria of the previous day. In the 18th arrondissement Berthe Auroy wrote in her diary: 'All yesterday's joy has evaporated. Everyone is depressed. No doubt a reaction to yesterday's enthusiasm. The weather is overcast; the flags have been taken down.'[4] In parts of Paris, there was a curious stand-off between the Germans and the Resistance as the cease-fire was partially respected, locally at least. By the Jardin du Luxembourg, a German soldier and a policeman with a Resistance armband both stood on sentry duty, 150 metres apart, paying no attention to each other.[5] Yves Cazaux saw a German patrol passing by a barricade near the Monnaie de Paris; the soldiers stopped, the officer had a few words with the *résistants*, shrugged his shoulders, and the patrol moved off.[6]

Everyone felt exhausted, and those who had supported the cease-fire began to wonder whether they had made the right decision. Early in the morning, Léo Hamon warned Parodi that if they did not renew the fighting there would be a split in the Resistance – the FFI leadership had shown they would act alone if need be. Parodi recognised the danger, but insisted they had to wait another day. First, he saw Rol at the Préfecture, where everyone was preparing for an onslaught from the Germans, even if there was a cease-fire. As one of Parodi's colleagues recalled:

> Its windows were blocked almost to the top with sandbags. Resting on the sandbags were levelled rifles, and above them I saw the tense motionless faces of the Fifis. Inside many other Fifis were standing around in the large courtyard. Carelessly dressed, unshaven, their eyes shining, they were obviously both exhausted and exhilarated. They had hardly slept that night or indeed the previous nights. Perhaps they had also found a supply of wine in the cellars of the Préfecture. To right and left were stacks of rifles, neatly arranged. Fires burned under enormous quarters of meat and smoking pots.[7]

During their discussion, Parodi told Rol that several German armoured columns would soon be crossing Paris. Pointing at a map of the capital, Parodi suggested that the Resistance should allow the Germans safe passage along a number of prescribed routes. Strikingly, only one of these routes involved the Germans crossing the Seine, even though the warnings from Chaban about the supposedly imminent arrival of enemy troops were predicated on the Germans' need to cross the Seine in Paris. This was no longer the case, apparently.[8] Noting that the map showed a mere handful of German defensive positions, Rol dismissed the whole idea curtly: 'There's no going back,' he said, and strode out.[9]

With Rol intransigent, Parodi tried to influence Colonel Lizé, Rol's chief of staff. The previous day, Lizé, like the rest of the Paris FFI leadership, had been strongly opposed to the cease-fire, and even at 10:00 on the morning of 21 August, he sent a message to Rol explaining that the cease-fire was 'being forgotten'.[10] But shortly afterwards, under pressure from Parodi – who strictly speaking had no business interfering in the military line of command – Lizé buckled. As he later put it: 'It took the authority of the [General Delegate], M. Parodi, speaking in the name of General de Gaulle, for me to transmit the order to cease fire.'[11] At 11:45, Lizé issued a cease-fire instruction to all Parisian FFI groupings, 'by order of the Delegated Commissar of the Provisional Government of the French Republic'. The existing barricades would remain but no new barricades were to be constructed, and two routes through Paris would be reserved for German troops, protected by French gendarmes.[12] Parodi had got his way, and so had von Choltitz.

Once again, Parodi appears to have given too much credence to Colonel Ollivier of the Intelligence Service. Two days before, Ollivier had pushed Parodi into accepting the cease-fire, at the same time as the spy 'Bobby' Bender shuttled between Nordling and von Choltitz, tying up the German side of the agreement. Now, at 10:00 on the morning of 21 August, shortly before Parodi met Rol, Ollivier turned up at Victor Veau's apartment with urgent news for Parodi. The Intelligence Service agent stammered that the retreating German Army would cross the Seine in Paris, and that the city would be sacked if the FFI opposed their passage. He went on to say that German parachutists had been dropped at Senlis and were about to encircle the city. It is unclear why the Germans would use parachutists when they controlled Paris and its north-eastern approaches, nor why they would drop them fifty kilometres to the north into a town they already controlled, nor how even a massive parachute drop of men could 'encircle' a capital city.[13] Nevertheless, Veau and his comrades swallowed Ollivier's story and communicated it to Parodi. After being spooked by these tales, Veau and Pasteur Vallery-Radot gave the British spy a Red Cross armband, so he could move about Paris safely. He would put this to good use in the days that followed.[14]

*

With the cease-fire poorly respected, the situation in some parts of the city grew tenser as barricades began to be built. The traditional form of Paris street fighting was re-emerging. Overnight, a barricade went up on the quai des Grands-Augustins, just opposite the Préfecture, made up of two overturned lorries and several burnt-out cars, as well as sandbags, paving stones and the odd kitchen stove.[15] All over the centre of the city, people were building barricades with anything they could get their hands on: food trolleys around the market at Les Halles, massive gold letters from a shop sign reading FASHION on the rue de Rivoli, and everywhere building materials, metal grills from around the bases of Parisian trees and paving stones ripped up from the roads. Everyone was joining in – men, women and children.[16]

One of the men defending a barricade across the boulevard Saint-Germain was Eugène Brahms, a balding cobbler who had lost his right leg in an accident before the war and got about with the aid of a crutch. Despite his handicap, Brahms enthusiastically joined in the fighting – he had been a champion marksman and had lost none of his lethal skill. Shortly after 10:00, a German motorcycle roared up, with two men on the bicycle and a female soldier in the sidecar. First Brahms killed both men, and the motorcycle crashed. Then, as the dazed woman groped for one of her comrade's guns, he calmly shot her dead, too.[17] Cease-fire? What cease-fire?

Brahms was just one of thousands of ordinary Parisians who, for the most part, had done little to oppose the Germans directly during the four years of occupation, but were now in the forefront of fighting to free their city. One of these ordinary fighters, Philippe Barat, described what it was like being involved in armed conflict for the first time: 'During a battle you think of fighting, you think of causing the maximum amount of damage in the ranks of the enemy, you think of – let's say it openly – killing without a worry, without a second thought: it wipes out everything else … During a battle you become bloodthirsty. Why deny it? The most gentle of individuals is transformed and becomes thirsty for the enemy's blood.'[18] In the pressure cooker of the insurrection, people were capable of the most extraordinary behaviour. Pastor Daniel Monod telephoned his colleague Marc Boegner and described how he saw the Germans bringing fifteen unarmed and shirt-sleeved *résistants* into their headquarters. Monod asked how on earth these unarmed young men could fight tanks and armoured cars that were bristling with weapons. Boegner replied laconically: 'That's how revolutions are made.'[19]

In the afternoon the FFI near the Préfecture netted a great catch. A German lorry tried to drive down the boulevard Saint-Michel, and was shot at by FFI fighters; its tyres punctured and its engine riddled with bullets, it ground to a halt. Over a dozen soldiers spilt out, their hands held high – Philippe Barat described the men scornfully as 'old grand-dads who would be better off at home than at war',[20] while for FFI fighter Gilles de Boisgelin they were 'pale, apparently scared by this band of wild civilians running towards them'.[21] To the delight of the *résistants*, the lorry contained a fantastic treasure: a 75 mm anti-tank gun.[22] The artillery piece was quickly manoeuvred into position behind the Saint-Germain barricade and three FFI fighters tried to work out how to fire it. While they were doing this, a Tiger tank, followed by a number of other armoured vehicles, came rumbling down the boule-vard towards them. One of three men, FFI leader Jean Amidieu du Clos, wrote in his diary: 'The gun remained infuriatingly silent; our position became untenable and we hid in nearby houses ... The tanks came within 10 metres of us without seeing the gun, and then went back off up the boulevard Saint-Michel, the Tiger in front. So we ran back to the gun, and began firing on the last tank. We were firing too high and then the gun jammed. We put in a new shell and changed the aim. Suddenly the last tank came to a halt and was covered in smoke. It had taken a direct hit.'[23] Despite this success, the police immediately requi-sitioned the gun for the defence of the Préfecture.[24] This was perhaps just as well – a few minutes later, the tanks returned and peppered the barricade with shells, destroying surrounding trees and nearby kiosks.

During the fighting around the barricade, Gilles de Boisgelin was wounded in the leg; he was quickly taken to the Hôtel-Dieu hospital opposite the Préfecture, where he rapidly went through triage ('Where are you wounded? What's your name? Address? Undress him. Give him an injection. Now send him off to X-ray') and within thirty minutes he was in a cramped hospital ward, surrounded by other patients – police-men, civilians and Germans.[25] The Hôtel-Dieu had been transformed into a field hospital – each patient had their diagnosis and treatment written on a label attached to their wrist, while surgical teams worked six-hour shifts round the clock in four operating theatres. Altogether, about 2000 in the Hôtel-Dieu during the insurrection, many of them medical staff from hospitals on the outskirts of the city where there was less fighting.[26] Film shot at the time shows how some Resistance first-aiders could combine their humanitarian duty with an unswervingly single-minded devotion to the cause of the insurrection. After a German soldier was shot outside the Préfecture, two *résistants* rushed out of the building to him; the first to arrive was a 21-year-old first-aider, Anne Marie Dalmaso. She grabbed the soldier's rifle, grenades and revolver and immediately handed them to her comrade; only then did she help carry the injured German inside the Préfecture, where she tended his wounds.[27]

*

The rank-and-file German soldiers, few of whom were battle-hardened, were beginning to get jittery. A nervous Walter Dreizner was sent – on his own – to carry out some electrical work in the Hôtel Crillon on the place de la Concorde. Although it was only a short walk from his billet, he was still extremely apprehensive, and while he was in the building, the German sentries outside were attacked and fired back, killing a young woman *résistante*. Dreizner noticed how the Parisians had become used to gunfire, scattering when it rang out, but returning to their everyday business as soon as it ceased. This calmness unnerved him even further.[28]

The German troops told each other stories of bad treatment by the Resistance, ratcheting up the tension and the perceived threat repre-sented by the increasingly insurgent city. Quartermaster Robert Wallraf heard a young lieutenant tell how he had been captured by the Resistance and made to stand with his comrades on the parapet of one of the bridges over the Seine. Two of the soldiers took their chance and jumped into the river, and were then shot at repeatedly by the Resistance fighters until they disappeared under the water. The lieu-tenant was taken away and given food and lots of cognac, on condition that he shouted '*Vive de Gaulle*' at each swig. He was eventually freed in a prisoner exchange and told Wallraf: 'I won't let myself be taken prisoner by those people again! Not a chance. I'd rather they shot me!' This fear of the irregular forces of the Resistance – the soldier's traditional fear of a civilian population in arms – grew over the following days. Rank-and-file German soldiers decided that to avoid humiliation, mistreatment and worse, they would surrender only to regular troops; but this fear made it more likely that they would treat the population savagely, which in turn increased the fury of the Parisians.[29]

Not only was the morale of the German troops getting lower by the day, there were squabbles at the very top over where these troops should be deployed. General Kurt von der Chevallerie, commander of the 1st German Army that was holding the line to the south-west of Paris, asked von Choltitz to give him control of the remains of the 17th SS Division and of the Panzer Lehr Division.[30] Von Choltitz turned him down – he had his own plans for the 17th SS Division, while the Panzer Lehr was already heading towards the east – and instead demanded that von der Chevallerie provide the Paris garrison with reinforcements.[31] Predictably, none was forthcoming, and the two men parted on poor terms. A week later, von Choltitz said the 1st Army was 'non-existent', before scornfully describing von der Chevallerie's situation: 'He didn't even have *one* complete Division. He hadn't a Division staff even. All he had was what was left of a battalion from Le Mans, and then there was a lieutenant from Rennes, with one gun. That was the 1st Army!'[32]

There was some good news for von Choltitz: the newly refitted 2nd Paratroop Battalion, composed in part of men who had fled from Falaise, but with all-new weapons and vehicles, became available for the defence of the city, and they were duly deployed north of Versailles. To back them up, artillery was posted on the eastern bank of the Seine, able to fire over the paratroopers and to bombard the bridges at Saint-Germain-en-Laye if necessary.[33] As part of that redeployment, in the early hours of the cold, dark and damp morning, Major Pulkowski led his anti-tank battle group out of the Bois de Boulogne. They were heading for the German headquarters at Saint-Germain-en-Laye, where Pulkowski was to take control of the massive bunker. The Germans were assembling their forces in the region for a counter-attack against the Allied bridgehead at Mantes. The 17th SS Division was ordered to join in, and a column of a dozen armoured vehicles, including Sturmegschütz assault guns (essentially a tank without a mobile turret), was sent across Paris. They encountered small-arms fire from the Resistance at the place de la Concorde, but stayed there for most of the day in relative safety before moving out of the city and heading north-east, away from the front.[34] The presence of the column undoubtedly intimidated sections of the Parisian population, but it had no effect on the growing insurrection. In fact, the movement of the 17th SS Division was an exception – most of the bedraggled and disorganised escapees from the Western Front either went around Paris, in particular to the north and west – or were used to reinforce the defence lines. Despite the alarming predictions of Colonel Ollivier and General Chaban, few of the tens of thousands of retreating German soldiers crossed through the capital, and those who did get through were not the disciplined forces that had been feared.

The movement of the German forces to the north-east of Paris affected Jedburgh Team AUBREY. After several days helping the Parisian Resistance, including giving lectures on sabotage, Guy Marchant and Adrien Chaigneau decided to return to their original mission to support the SPIRITUALIST circuit to the north-east of the capital. The flux of German troops around Paris was making it increasingly difficult for Marchant and Chaigneau to move about, and two of their liaison agents had disappeared.[35] So they got on their bicycles and rode seventy-five kilometres back to base. While they had been away, their radio operator, Sergeant Hooker, had been recovering from mumps. Due to a combination of sickness and the intimidating presence of German radio detector vans in the neighbourhood, only seven routine messages had gone to and fro between AUBREY and London during the ten days that the group had been in the field.[36] But the growing concentration of German troops to the north-east of the city meant that AUBREY and SPIRITUALIST would soon have their hands full.[37]

*

At the end of the morning, a meeting of the Comité Parisien de la Libération was held in a basement near the Bastille.[38] No one knew that Lizé was calling on the FFI to cease fire; this was probably just as well since it would certainly have revived the tensions that had marked the previous day's meeting. As it was, the atmosphere was surprisingly calm, and the genial and moustachioed communist Georges Maranne was able to pull off a remarkable diplomatic coup by proposing that the CPL issue a statement that did not even mention the cease-fire, far less criticise it: 'The struggle continues. It must continue until the enemy has been driven from the Parisian region. More than ever, everyone must join the fight ... Chop down trees, dig anti-tank traps, build barricades. The Allies must be welcomed by a victorious people.'[39] Bizarrely, within only twenty-four hours the split in the Resistance had switched over – the military leadership was divided, with Lizé calling for a cease-fire and Rol opposing it, while the political leadership was united in calling for the insurrection to continue. Confusion on the ground – inherent in any insurrection – had now been compounded by confusion at the top.

Meanwhile, Rol met with COMAC and various Resistance military leaders, along with Chaban and his second-in-command Ely. The meeting took place in Rol's new headquarters, an underground bunker twenty-six metres below place Denfert-Rochereau in the south of the capital. The bunker had been built before the war as a command centre that would function if the city were bombarded. Containing over twenty rooms, including dormitories and a telephone switchboard, with its own generators and air-conditioning, it was exactly what Rol required.[40]

The meeting was tense. None of the men present argued in favour of the cease-fire – not even Chaban – while the right-wing Resistance leaders denounced Parodi's plan to allow the Germans free passage through the capital as 'treason'. When Chaban spoke, he did not respond to any of the criticisms, but confused matters further by proposing that General Dassault, the Front National member who had supported the cease-fire the day before, should be made Military Governor of the capital. This suggestion was seen as irrelevant and was simply ignored. Instead, the three members of COMAC adopted a declaration underlining that, as Parodi had agreed two days before, Rol was in sole

command of all armed forces in Paris, including the police and the gen-
darmes, and that this line of command had to be respected.[41]
Irrespective of Parodi's minor victory with Lizé earlier on, the Free
French Delegation was now on the defensive.[42]

It does not appear that the Free French leadership in London,
Algiers or Normandy was aware of the exact situation in the capital,
although some messages were eventually getting through. That did not
stop de Gaulle, who was in newly liberated Rennes, from writing to
General Eisenhower, repeating the case he had made the day before for
the Allies to turn to Paris. The Free French leader began his letter with
concerns about the state of the food supply to the city, but it was clear
that his real fear was political. Although he wrote about the threat of an
unspecified 'disorder', he really meant the possibility that the Parisian
population, and more specifically the communists, might take power:

> Information that I have received today from Paris makes me think
> that, given the near-total disappearance of the police force and of the
> German Army from Paris, and given the extreme food shortages that
> exist there, serious trouble will occur in the capital in a very short
> space of time. I believe that it is truly necessary for the French and
> Allied forces to occupy Paris as soon as possible, even if this should
> result in fighting and some destruction to the city. If a situation of
> disorder were to develop in Paris, it would subsequently be difficult
> to gain control without serious incidents. This could even threaten
> subsequent military operations.[43]

Eisenhower was unmoved, and gave no response.

*

In the afternoon a series of incidents left dozens of Parisians dead,
underlining that the Germans considered the cease-fire to be a fiction.
On the rue des Morillons near the south-west edge of the city, policeman Philippe Chevrier and two students, Charles Descours and
16-year-old Vincent Finidori, were shot dead. On the rue de Beaune on
the Left Bank, Peter Maroger, riding in an FFI-commandeered car, was

killed during a firefight with German troops. In a building just behind the place Saint-Michel fountain, policeman Joseph Lahuec was collecting arms for the Préfecture when a German soldier shot him dead.[44] At the Gare du Nord, two lads on a scooter, Vincent di Bella and Robert Cabirol, were arrested for giving out Resistance leaflets. They were freed, but were then shot dead as they fled down the rue Maubeuge at the side of the station, the latest victims in a series of over sixty murders by German troops stationed at the Gare du Nord.[45] At around 13:00, a group of three FFI fighters was driving along the boulevard Magenta in a Citroën car. They were heading for Saint-Ouen, a northern suburb of Paris, where they thought they would be able to pick up some weapons. They never made it: as they passed a German checkpoint, the vehicle was machine-gunned and crashed into the shop front on the corner of the boulevard and the rue Saint-Vincent de Paul. Two of the men were killed outright; the third, Edmond Bouchetou, was severely wounded. Photographs of the incident show six bodies scattered on the pavement.[46] Some of these men were FFI fighters from the area, although how they got involved in the firefight is not clear. According to Bouchetou, who survived the incident, the Germans pumped bullets into men who were lying injured on the ground.[47] The shattered car was soon covered with flowers as Parisians paid their respects to those who had been killed.[48] In the bloodiest clash, an SS motorcyclist attacked a Resistance barricade by the square René Viviani, next to what is now the Shakespeare and Company bookshop. Minutes before, the FFI fighters on the barricade had posed for a photograph. After a brief gun battle, eight of the men in the photograph were dead – five policemen from the 5th arrondissement and three civilians.[49]

In the late morning, Micheline Bood went out with her friend Nicole, to take photographs of the fighting. As they wandered near the Gare Saint-Lazare they saw mobile anti-aircraft guns and lorries full of soldiers, weapons at the ready. Each time the Germans passed, the streets emptied in a flash. Micheline and Nicole soon felt 'so excited we couldn't be frightened any more'. At one point, Micheline was hiding barely ten metres from the fighting, readying her camera, when a young man crawled up to her and started giving her advice on photographic technique.[50]

As the day wore on, the Germans began to use heavy weapons in a chaotic series of exchanges. In the late afternoon, Veau and his medical colleagues heard the sound of gunfire from the nearby place Saint-Augustin. As the shooting grew more intense, they looked out of the ground-floor window and saw a dozen German soldiers firing from behind tree trunks. After a while, some tanks moved up towards the square, followed by a heavy machine gun mounted on a car. The car came to a stop outside Veau's building, and the gun barrel was pointed directly at his window. Suddenly a young man ran into the street and was shot dead; a gun fell from his hand. Then a motorcycle ambulance arrived, with the pillion rider carrying a Red Cross flag. They were stopped by three German soldiers, and the pillion rider got off; the German officer took a couple of steps away from him, drew his revolver and shot the young man dead. The motorcycle driver roared off down the boulevard, while the heavy machine gun began to fire. Bullets flew into Veau's apartment, spitting bits of plaster and wood, and everyone dived to the floor. Then the firing ceased and the gun was driven off. A few minutes later a large lorry, with FFI painted in red letters on the side, came thundering along the street and headed towards the place Saint-Augustin. There was the sound of more firing.[51]

Just up the road in the 17th arrondissement the Germans sent tanks to deal with the Resistance; one arrived from the rue des Dames and fired a shell into a building, punching a massive hole in the façade, while another attacked the Ecole Normale on the rue Boursault, also firing on a garage occupied by Resistance fighters, before receiving a hail of machine-gun fire in return and eventually retreating.[52] Once again, the Germans' actions were apparently designed to intimidate but ultimately gave the impression of powerlessness – the destructive power of their weaponry was not fully deployed as there was no infantry to support the tank attack, and the Resistance ended up feeling they had won the confrontation. And in the only way that counted, they had: every time, the Germans pulled back.

At the end of August, the Allies asked von Choltitz why he had first agreed to the cease-fire and then broken it. The German commander explained that he had wanted to save the city from the communists, and that when Parodi did not keep his promise to remove barricades from around the German strongholds, he felt obliged to send in the tanks.[53] Whatever his reasons, all over the city ordinary people were killed by the Germans while the cease-fire was in operation.

*

In the late afternoon, the CNR met in an attempt to resolve the political chaos created by the cease-fire.[54] At one point twenty-two people were crammed into a small airless room partly filled by a piano, not far from Rol's bunker. The cramped conditions, the stifling heat and the deep-seated differences all combined to make for an explosive situation as supporters and opponents of the cease-fire confronted each other.[55] In the front line was the communist Pierre Villon. CNR member Jacques Debû-Bridel recalled: 'with his high forehead, his pointed nose and his steely gaze, Villon, extremely tense with two days' lack of sleep, played the role of prosecutor.'[56] Villon questioned the validity of the previous day's meeting when the CNR Bureau had supported the cease-fire, demanded to know on whose authority the CNR's name had been attached to the declaration and denounced the 'forgery' that had been posted on the walls of Paris in the name of the CNR. To make matters worse, he announced that the Front National was about to publish a poster describing the cease-fire as 'a new manoeuvre by the enemy designed to stab in the back the Parisians who have been fighting heroically against the Hun for 48 hours'.[57] Parodi stood up and said: 'This will mean a split.'[58] The tension in the room grew even stronger.

To calm the atmosphere, Debû-Bridel insisted on the need for unity and underlined the importance of the military situation. This was an invitation for Chaban to give a half-hour explanation of what he called the 'technical' aspects of the insurrection, describing the German forces he claimed were threatening the city, and correctly informing the CNR that the Allies were planning to go around Paris and could not be expected to enter the capital for at least another week. In passing, Chaban described the cease-fire as 'a gentlemen's agreement'.[59] This understandably infuriated his opponents – the Germans had hardly behaved as 'gentlemen' five days earlier at the Cascades in the Bois de Boulogne. This was war, not a game. In reply, Jean de Vogüé, the leader of Ceux de la Résistance and member of COMAC, mocked Chaban's newly acquired rank of General and scornfully attacked the younger man's 'criminal lack of seriousness' in agreeing the cease-fire. De Vogüé's logic was relentless: 'The enemy's morale is broken: he does not want to fight in Paris, but merely save what remains: his proposals show this – they are the product of an enemy who recognises he is defeated ... Any junior officer knows that when the enemy weakens, you must double your attempts to destroy him.'[60]

If that was bad, what followed was worse. Villon went back on the offensive, sneered at the ex-civil servant Chaban ('He should have stuck to his day job') and then described the Military Delegate as 'a coward'.[61] Uproar. Once people had stopped shouting and calling on Villon to withdraw his comment, the communist leader spoke again: 'I do not accuse him of cowardice, but he behaved like a coward.' More uproar. Parodi and Chaban made for the door, Debû-Bridel shouted at Bidault to suspend the session, but the President of the CNR just sat there, stunned.[62] Suddenly, a window smashed; everyone dived for cover. But it was not a bullet – Debû-Bridel had accidentally knocked his chair over and broken the window. As everyone calmed down, fresh air entered the room. Parodi was sobbing.[63]

When the meeting resumed, Villon withdrew his accusation, but did not change one iota of his critique of Chaban and Parodi's position, going point by point through their arguments.[64] It was obvious that if the two Free French delegates pursued the cease-fire any further, the Resistance would be permanently split. It could mean civil war, and it would certainly mean that the Allies would impose AMGOT (Allied Military Government of Occupied Territories) instead of allowing the French to run things, just as Chaban had warned General Koenig less than a week earlier.[65] Under these circumstances, Parodi and Chaban had no choice, and they had to bow to a unanimous CNR resolution calling for the fighting to begin again. However, the two Gaullists posed two conditions: the Front National had to withdraw their defamatory poster, and the fighting should not begin until 16:00 the next day.[66] The unity of the Resistance had been preserved, and Parodi had cleverly gained the extra day he had asked for that morning.

In reality, things were not so simple. As many Parisians could attest, the cease-fire had never really been effective, and even as the CNR was meeting, Rol had ordered Lizé and the FFI to renew the fighting. Rol added that because the SS had been shooting their French prisoners, the Resistance would treat SS prisoners in the same fashion.[67] Relieved by the sudden change in the situation, Lizé sent the order to his men: 'More than ever, fight to the death. Cover Paris with barricades.'[68]

As battle recommenced, Rol asked Chaban and Parodi to provide the Resistance with enough plastic explosives, detonators and fuses to build 'thousands' of anti-tank weapons. It took Chaban two days to transmit the request to the Regional Military Delegate, who viewed the request more seriously than his superior, and immediately sent a message to London asking for a supply drop.[69] There was no response, and no supply drop.

In the absence of any weapons from the Allies, Rol issued instructions for making Molotov cocktails (this involved more than just filling a bottle with petrol) and the leading French physicist Frédéric Joliot-Curie began cooking them up in his laboratories in the Latin Quarter, using petrol, sodium chlorate and sulphuric acid.[70] That night, FFI fighters moved into the upper floors of buildings next to the Saint-Michel barricade, armed with Joliot-Curie's bombs, ready to throw them onto any German vehicles that approached.[71]

Most of the city was now no longer under German control – by the end of the day, the Resistance had liberated sixty-one of the city's eighty neighbourhoods.[72] All of the main government buildings were occupied, with Resistance administrators sleeping in unaccustomed luxury in state apartments, preparing for the arrival of General de Gaulle and the Provisional Government.[73] In the evening, the Resistance radio was finally allowed to broadcast, and the announcer read out two communiqués in the name of the Provisional Government before turning to a programme of music.[74] Parodi was wary of unnecessarily attracting the attention of the Germans, and for the moment refused to allow the radio to transmit a full programme.

Two high-ranking SS officers turned up at von Choltitz's headquarters at the Hôtel Meurice, bearing orders from Himmler to bring back the Bayeux tapestry, which was held nearby in the Louvre. Von Choltitz explained to them that the Louvre was in the hands of the Resistance, but that they could go and get the tapestry if they wanted. They left empty-handed.[75] Meanwhile, Paris Gestapo chief Knochen, who had fled to safety, decided the Gestapo needed its own channel of information about the situation in the capital. So his right-hand man, Nosek, was sent back towards Paris, in a five-vehicle convoy.[76] Something was going on at Gestapo headquarters on rue des Saussaies: Suzanne Chocarne saw five Germans arrive and, after a long discussion with the French policemen who were guarding the building, climb up a ladder and go in through a window. After a while the Germans came out again, each of them carrying a large box, which they loaded onto a lorry. The same procedure was repeated the next day. Whatever was in those boxes, the Germans were keen to get it back, and the policemen were surprisingly compliant.[77] Not all the Paris police seem to have realised that they were supposed to have changed sides.

According to a report written that night by de Vogüé – no doubt still buoyed by his victory at the CNR – there were over 4000 armed FFI fighters in Paris. In contrast, the Germans were estimated to have no more than 6000 'real fighters' in the city (the 14,000 administrators, cooks, translators and others were dismissed by de Vogüé as having 'no fighting value'). The German forces were confined to five or six defensive positions, with a few dozen light and medium tanks patrolling the city but never fully exercising their power and not supported by infantry. 'Feeling insecure, they have abandoned many points without fighting,' wrote de Vogüé. 'As a result, the local balance of power has clearly swung in our favour, even more so considering the growing activity of the population.'[78]

*

At Rambouillet, OSS spy chief David Bruce and Ernest Hemingway found that their entourage of excited journalists evaporated once it became clear that they were not heading for Paris. Bruce was frustrated, as he wrote in his diary: 'It is maddening to be only thirty miles from Paris, to interrogate every hour some Frenchman who has just come from there and who reports that even a very small task force could easily move in, and to know that our Army is being forced to wait – for what reason?'[79] Bruce's perplexity was strengthened by the remarkable speed with which the Allies continued to press northwards and eastwards. They liberated Etampes, fifty kilometres south-west of Paris, and in a deep thrust to the south took the town of Sens, nearly ninety kilometres south-east of the capital. General Patton's glee was palpable in a letter he wrote to his son: 'It worked! We got the bridge at Sens before he [the enemy] blew it. That is worth a week.'[80] Nevertheless, substantial German forces remained west of Paris on the north bank of the Seine around Rouen, blocking the Allies' passage into northern France and Belgium, causing problems for the British troops that were concentrated in this sector. But overall, the map looked as though a flood was surging out of Normandy towards the east, about to sweep round Paris on both sides and carry on towards Germany. Full of self-confidence, General Patton wrote in his diary: 'We have, at this time, the greatest chance to win the war ever presented. If they let me move on with three corps ... we can be in Germany in ten days.'[81]

Bill Downs, a CBS reporter embedded with the Allies, described what it was like being part of this rapid advance: 'You move forward all the time. You eat a lot of cold rations because you're on the move and when you bump into the enemy rearguard the fighting is just as bitter as it was before. And when you take the Nazi-held position you find that there haven't been many Germans because the enemy has retreated, and there isn't much booty and not many prisoners – yet.'[82]

The rapid progress meant that supply lines became stretched. As the Third US Army's After Action Report for 21 August put it: 'Large quantities of clothing, individual equipment, water cans, cleaning and preserving material were requested to be shipped by rail and air. Acute shortage of operating parts for medium and heavy calibre weapons was reported in all corps.'[83]

The closing of the Falaise pocket and the rapid movement of Allied forces eastwards meant that Leclerc's 2e DB had even less reason to hang about in Argentan. However, Patton had rejected Leclerc's repeated requests to move on Paris, while Eisenhower had given de Gaulle the brush-off the day before. The Allies were not going to budge. In the late morning Leclerc's patience finally ran out. In an act of rank insubordination, he ordered Lieutenant-Colonel de Guillebon, together with a small group of about 300 men and fifty vehicles, including ten light tanks, to head towards the capital in a probing operation. Although de Guillebon's orders were simply to reconnoitre the route, it was understood that, should the Allies suddenly make a break for Paris, he was to be with them. Leclerc's instructions were clear: 'You will appreciate that the Allies must not enter Paris without the French Army. That would undermine the national sense of the event. So go as quickly as possible; if any Allied unit enters Paris, I want you to enter with it; I will join you, but, in the meantime, as far as the Allies and the French are concerned, you will act in my place as Military Governor. And of course, if you can enter the city on your own, do not hesitate, just go.'[84] Leclerc wanted to send the whole of the 2e DB on this mission but, as he wrote to de Gaulle that evening, 'Unfortunately, I cannot do the same thing for the bulk of my division because of matters of food and fuels.' But that was not the only reason: Leclerc recognised that he was also constrained by the 'rules of military subordination'.[85] The Leclerc Division was still part of the US Army, no matter how much that might irritate the Free French.

At 12:00 de Guillebon's column left the tiny village of Mortrée, eighty kilometres north of Le Mans, and drove eastwards for the next seven hours, averaging twenty-three kilometres per hour, before bivouacking at Vaubrun, less than thirty kilometres from Rambouillet. Completely unknown to the Allied command, the Free French were catching up with the spearhead of the Allied advance.[86]

*

Early in the morning, Gallois, Dr Monod and their German-speaking comrade, Dominique, left the barn where they had slept overnight and drove due south. Their attempt to get through the German lines to the west had failed, so they decided to try a different route. When they got to Corbeil they met up with the local FFI leader, Commander Georges. The repeated delays had made Gallois very tense, and he was relieved to find himself in the hands of a man who oozed confidence. The problem, Georges explained, was that they had tried to be too cunning. The only way to get through the German lines was by force, he said. To do that, he went on, you needed to be up for it, which in turn meant having a good meal. So he took the three hungry men to a small restaurant in the Essonne valley where they were stuffed full of food and wine. After the meal, they inspected an honour guard of Commander George's FFI fighters, and Gallois made a brief speech. Then Gallois and Commander Georges, accompanied by a *résistant* and a gendarme armed with a submachine gun, got into a baker's van and drove southwest towards Etampes, while Dr Monod and Dominique returned to Paris.

Commander Georges was well known in the region, and in each village he got out of the car to ask about the position of the German troops and have a glass of wine. Finally, in the late afternoon, they learnt that only a German machine-gun post, composed of seven men, stood between them and the US troops a kilometre or so away. Perhaps souped up by all the wine, Commander Georges simply said, 'Let's go. Watch out for the bullets!' And with that the van roared past the surprised Germans without a shot being fired. A few minutes later, Gallois was in the hands of the Americans.

The French envoy was interrogated by a series of Army intelligence officers as they checked out his story. Gallois did not look much like a staff officer – unshaven, exhausted and in rumpled civilian clothes, he felt he resembled a tramp. The most intense interrogation took place in a tent in Third Army headquarters, where Gallois was questioned for over two hours. To his amazement, the intelligence officer had files on all of Gallois' contacts, one of whom had made his way through the lines nearly two weeks earlier. Once the Americans were satisfied that the young Frenchman was who he said he was, at around midnight he was taken into a tent to see 'the general'.

This was the whole point of the mission Rol had given Gallois the day before: to convince the Allied command to send an armoured column to Paris as soon as possible. Gallois did his best, but the general remained unconvinced. The US officer explained that his priority was to get to Germany as soon as possible and destroy the Nazi regime. Nothing – not even the liberation of Paris – would get in the way. 'You chose when to launch the insurrection,' said the American officer bluntly, 'but if you thought you would need us, you should have waited for our instructions.' Gallois was crushed; the American repeated that the Allies could do nothing for Paris at the moment, and that the Frenchman's mission was over. In a final throw of the dice, Gallois asked whether, as a personal favour, he could see General Leclerc. The general went out of the tent for a moment and then returned. 'Are you too tired to make a long journey?' asked the American. 'Not at all,' was Gallois' reply. 'In that case,' said the general, 'get ready for a drive.'

And with that General Patton opened a bottle of champagne and the two men drank and chatted for ten minutes; Gallois still did not know the American's identity. At around 01:30, Gallois climbed into a staff car and disappeared into the night, on his way to see General Leclerc.[87]

*

The ease with which Gallois had passed through the German lines showed the Americans that the German forces to the south and west of Paris were extremely weak. They were not the only ones to make this observation. Early in the morning Daniel Boisdon left his apartment on the boulevard Saint-Germain and pedalled off southwards, with his old army officer's jacket in his rucksack. Hoping he would meet American soldiers, he went prepared to impress them. Boisdon had assumed that what the cease-fire had called the 'total evacuation' by the Germans was imminent, so he was disappointed to note that there were no signs of the Germans leaving. He rode on but could get no further south than Longjumeau, about twelve kilometres from the edge of Paris, where German sentries fired warning shots from their machine guns. When he returned home in the afternoon, he wrote in his diary: 'This zone is still held by the Germans, perhaps not in great numbers, but they remain combative.'[88] That evening a more precise analysis was made by FFI intelligence officers, who concluded: 'The Germans are opposing the American advance with only a thin line of troops. Between this curtain and Paris there is no sign of the presence of any reserve forces.'[89]

Model began to carry out Hitler's order to strengthen the defence of Paris, ordering the remnants of the 5th Panzer Army and 'any able-bodied men' to fall back to the Paris region to reinforce the remnants of the 1st Army.[90] Within a day, all this information, and much more, was available to the Allied Supreme Command through an ULTRA decrypt: one of the decisive breakthroughs of the war was the ability of the Allies to read German messages encoded by the Enigma machines.[91] As a result, the Allies knew exactly what was going on around Paris. Even without ULTRA, however, whatever Model did with his armies was more or less irrelevant, as the decisive factor on the Western Front – and, increasingly, in the whole war – was Allied air supremacy. As General von Badinsky admitted a week later: 'The men have quite lost their nerve. I have seen myself that when an aircraft came over, our men were like frightened rabbits.'[92] Although Model had only been on the Western Front for a few days, he had become acutely aware of this problem, so he sent a telex to General Jodl, Hitler's Chief of Operations Staff, requesting the immediate introduction of a revolutionary secret weapon, the Me 262 jet fighter, in the skies over Paris.[93] Model wanted the Me 262, which could far outpace anything on the Allied side, to provide covering fire for Luftwaffe bombing raids, as German planes were unable to operate in daytime without incurring heavy losses. At the same time, Model asked that the number of classic fighter aircraft in the region be increased to 700.

While awaiting a reply, Model sent a message to Berlin explaining how he was implementing Hitler's orders for Paris. He underlined that the city would need reinforcements if they were to hold the line, and that he was exploring the possibility of a further defensive position to the north-east of the capital. This was not, he emphasised, due to any problems from the Parisians, for he and von Choltitz had taken all necessary measures to stop any trouble in the city. Model said he was confident that the Paris garrison would be able to put down any rebellion.[94] Other German officers were unconvinced that simple repression was the answer: General von der Chevallerie of the 1st Army issued an order warning that the uprising in Paris could threaten German lines with attack from the rear if the population was starving; he therefore insisted that food supplies to the capital should be maintained.[95] His suggestion made no difference.

Shortly before midnight, Model got his answer from Jodl. It was a 'no'. The Me 262 was still being tested and was not yet ready for the front, and there were not enough other types of aircraft in production to increase the number of fighters in the Paris region.[96] Despite this refusal to provide the men and weapons that were needed, Jodl repeated Hitler's order to stem the Allied tide at Paris, whatever the cost.[97] The reality was that Model, von Choltitz and their men were on their own.

*

That evening in Paris, as the heat of the summer day lingered on, Jean Guéhenno described what so many felt: 'Liberty is returning. We don't know where it is, but it is out there all around us in the night. It is coming with the armies. We feel immensely grateful. It is the most profound joy to realise that all that you have thought about people is true. We cannot break our chains alone. But all free men are marching together. They are coming.'[98]

11

Tuesday 22 August: Barricades

At lunchtime, the BBC broadcasts a report from French journalist Daniel Melville 'somewhere in France': 'The advanced American patrols have reached the Seine. We can see the same river that runs through Paris and this renews the strength of the soldiers who have fought non-stop since the breakout at Cotentin. All our weaponry is involved in this massive race. As we pass through towns and villages, we always hear the same question: "Are the Allies in Paris?" For everyone, the coming liberation of the capital will symbolise the liberation of the whole country. This morning, a peasant said to me as he watched massive lorries full of ammunition thunder past his door: "I think the liberation of Paris will affect me even more than the liberation of my own village, because France will once again have a capital."'[1]

For the previous two days, the progress of the Paris insurrection had been disturbed by the cease-fire negotiated by Raoul Nordling and the Free French Delegation. Although the CNR had agreed that the cease-fire would officially end at 16:00 that afternoon, there was a final act to be played out. In the morning, the main representatives of the Resistance met at the Préfecture de Police: the three members of COMAC were there, along with Rol for the FFI and Parodi and Chaban for the Delegation. From the outset, Chaban made clear that the Delegation had changed its position and was prepared to call for the fighting to start immediately, rather than waiting until the late afternoon. He and his colleagues now claimed that the German garrison did *not* in fact have a large number of tanks, that there were only about 3000 combat troops in the city, and that even though the cease-fire was supposed to run until 16:00, the time had come to start fighting again.[2] Trying to reclaim the political high ground, Chaban boldly stated: 'Up until now, I have played the role of a brake; today I have decided to fight. You must realise that I played my role deliberately and tenaciously. Today I say: we must fight.' Jean de Vogüé of COMAC replied acerbically: 'You say you played the role of a brake. Don't worry, you didn't have much effect.'[3]

An order was then issued, written by Rol and signed by Parodi, calling for the immediate renewal of fighting and the building of barricades. The cease-fire was well and truly over, if indeed it ever really existed.

With the whole of the Resistance and the Free French backing an immediate renewal of the fighting, Rol issued posters, declarations and instructions to the FFI and, more importantly, to the whole Parisian population. Calling on Parisians to transform their city into a 'fortified camp', Rol outlined the main elements of guerrilla warfare, emphasising the importance of mobility and that territory should not be held at any cost. He even explained how the city's refuse lorries could be used to attack German blockhouses, by dumping large quantities of rubbish on them, pouring petrol on top, and setting fire to the pile.[4] One FFI poster called for the Parisians to attack German soldiers and seize their arms, ending with the words: 'Everyone get a Hun!'[5] Above all, however, Rol's vision was one of mass involvement of the population in the insurrection through organising the defence of the city in each street and each building. This would allow the best response to the main danger that remained: the firepower of the Germans' tanks. As he explained in a poster: 'The whole Parisian population – men, women and children – must build barricades, chop down trees on all the main thoroughfares. Build barricades on the side-roads and make chicanes. To guarantee your defence against enemy attack, organise yourselves by street and by building. Under these conditions, the Hun will be isolated and surrounded in a few locations, and will no longer be able to carry out reprisals. EVERYONE TO THE BARRICADES.'[6] The vision that the Germans could be defeated if everyone in the city defended their neighbourhoods was not empty rhetoric; faced with a weakened enemy deploying only a few dozen armoured vehicles, hundreds of thousands of Parisians could make it come true.

In many parts of the city, the population needed no encouragement, and men, women and children cheerfully built new barricades to add to those constructed in the previous days. Under the summer sun, plane trees were felled, tarmac was rolled up and the paving stones beneath were pulled up and piled into makeshift barricades.[7] Bernard Pierquin wrote in his diary: 'There are now barricades on each main road: people cut down trees, dig up the paving stones and cover it all with old furniture and scrap metal; everybody in the neighbourhood joins in; it's a big party. My father has taken his weapons out of their hiding place: pistols and revolvers are checked out and cleaned.'[8]

The Germans did little to stop the barricades being built. On rue Soufflot, which leads from the Jardin du Luxembourg up to the Panthéon, three men began to lift up the paving stones to make a new barricade; fifty metres away, at the entrance to the Jardin, the German sentries watched impassively.[9] Although most of the barricades were built by ordinary Parisians, Rol also requisitioned some city council labourers to help out, in return for 'some good red wine'.[10] Immediately, the barricades became part of the urban scenery. Early in the morning, Jean Galtier-Boissière went out to walk his dog, Azor. While Azor went about his business, his owner inspected the barricade on the rue Saint-Jacques.[11]

Over the next three days, more than 600 barricades were erected across the capital, with the joint objective of defending Resistance strongholds and preventing German troop movements.[12] Map 3 shows the barricades scattered like iron filings over the city, but focused on the main thoroughfares. Most were in the working-class areas, especially the north and the east. These were also the sites of the main routes out of the city that would be vital to fleeing German troops. There were notable gaps – only a handful of barricades were built in the rich 16th arrondissement, for example, and none at all in its wealthiest centre. Similarly, the areas around the main German strong-points – the Senate, the rue de Rivoli and the place de la République – were also empty. In the Parisian insurrections of 1830, 1848 and 1871, barricades had played a decisive military and symbolic role. The military situation in

1944 was different, but the power of the barricade as a symbol and as a reminder of the capital's revolutionary past was in everyone's mind.[13] To the discerning eye, the distribution of the barricades across the city corresponded to the class lines that underpinned the conflict between Vichy and the Resistance, while the very presence of the barricades indicated to everyone that these were momentous, historic days.

*

There was a hint that the battle with the Germans could become more violent, as the Resistance tried to procure heavy weapons. FFI fighters from the 17th arrondissement, including Georges Dukson, went to the SOMUA tank factory in the northern suburbs, found a newly produced S35 light tank, and, to the acclamation of the crowd, drove it to the Mairie of the 17th arrondissement.[14] Shortly after 13:00, journalist Claude Roy accompanied Dukson and a group of FFI fighters who marched in single file behind the tank, which now had 'FFI' and a Gaullist cross of Lorraine crudely painted on its sides, as it went out to attack a nest of German soldiers on the boulevard des Batignolles. They were filmed by a newsreel cameraman who was one of the group of cinematographers who followed the insurrection.[15] As the tank manoeuvred near the Citroën garage on the rue de Rome, Dukson was shot in the arm and hastily evacuated.[16] A few minutes later, the Germans waved the white flag, and a dozen troops were captured.[17]

As one FFI fighter was taken away for treatment, another joined the fray: after a few days' convalescence in Cochin hospital, Madeleine Riffaud had more or less recovered from her last-minute escape from the Pantin train, and made her way over to the 19th arrondissement, where she joined the Saint-Just company of the FTP. This was the group that had assassinated Georges Barthélemy, the collaborationist Mayor of Puteaux, six weeks earlier. Riffaud, a slight woman who was just a day short of her twentieth birthday, was promoted to the rank of company captain. The young men she commanded were unimpressed and sneered at 'the little girl', but she soon showed her mettle. The men of the FTP group, including André Calvès, were standing outside the post office, just down the road from the Mairie of the 19th arrondissement.

The police turned up, frogmarching a *milicien* who, they claimed, had been firing from the rooftops and had killed a child. 'Hey, FTP – you can kill this bastard,' they said. Jo, one of the members of the Saint-Just company, looked at the officers and said: 'You cops don't take any risks, do you? You never know, the Germans might end up back in charge.' The police did not reply. The *milicien* threw himself to the floor and begged Madeleine for mercy. She said that she was unable to pardon him – only his victims could that. And so the FTP put him against the post office wall and shot him to the applause of bystanders. Long afterwards, André Calvès said what had happened was 'sad', while Riffaud realised that she should have told the policemen – 'You have arrested him, you should lock him up until he can be tried by a court.' But she failed to say that, and the man was killed.[18]

Riffaud's comrades might have been grudging about her command, but at least she was allowed to fight. Not everyone was so lucky. At lunchtime, Daniel Boisdon went to the Préfecture to sign up. He wore his officer's uniform, but in order not to attract the attention of any passing Germans he also wore an overcoat, despite the summer heat. Sweating profusely, Boisdon was surprised to see quite how informal the insurrection was – many of the men in the Préfecture wore workmen's dungarees, often without a shirt. He was shown into 'Colonel Rol's office' and a man kindly took his phone number and his details and promised to get back in contact with him. They never did. A 60-year-old lawyer with an officer's pretensions, Boisdon was not exactly what the FFI were looking for.[19]

*

Von Choltitz later described the insurrection in Paris as 'a war of nerves' and contrasted the fighting in the capital, where the enemy could strike from anywhere, with the relatively 'normal' conditions around the city where confronting armies did battle.[20] The German troops were unused to dealing with urban guerrilla warfare, and as the days wore on their morale was gradually undermined.[21] Odette Lainville wrote in her diary:

The Huns, prudent, no longer move around the streets on foot or on their own, and they can no longer hang around looking at posters.

They go by in groups, machine guns at the ready, keeping pace with their tanks, and you can feel death hover over their passage: you either hide without attracting attention, or you carry on as though nothing had happened, overcoming your emotion by force of will; in any case, best not to seem as though you are running away, as any sudden movement could be misinterpreted and unleash a hail of bullets.[22]

The reason for the Germans' nervousness was graphically described by Monsieur Reybaz, who watched horrified from his fifth-floor window on the place Saint-Michel as the Resistance attacked a passing German lorry:

> From the first floor the Resistance threw a grenade which blew three Germans to the ground; they lay dead in large pools of blood; one of them, lying on his back, showed a face that was no longer human; bits of brain and other matter had been scattered all around. Two other Germans were shot dead; the one who had been sitting next to the driver and who had been firing with a machine gun was lying to one side, his legs curled up, close to one of the wheels of the lorry. Then the tyre caught fire. The heat was too strong for people to get close and soon the man was burning like a torch.[23]

Troops retreating from the front and passing through Paris found the situation particularly alarming. Quartermaster Wallraf was instructed to leave the Senate building in the Jardin du Luxembourg and cross the Seine to inspect the Hôtel Crillon, where he was due to move his men. As he and his men drove past the Gare d'Orsay (now the Musée d'Orsay) they heard the sound of firing from the place de la Concorde and stopped. Suddenly, a German convoy came charging towards them at full speed. The leading vehicle stopped and an officer got out, shouting furiously. They had come from the front and had been quietly driving across Paris when they had been shot at from all sides. The officer was beside himself with fury at the audacity of the French; when he realised that some of his vehicles were trapped by the gunfire behind him, he ordered his soldiers to turn around and go and rescue their comrades, ignoring Wallraf's pleas to head for the nearest strong-point: 'To hell with your strong-point!' he shouted, 'I want to save my men!'[24]

Things were no easier for the Germans on the other side of the Seine. On the stretch of road between the place Châtelet and the pont Neuf, where all the pet shops now are, an FFI group attacked a small German convoy using grenades and Molotov cocktails, supported by machine-gun fire from the barricade that blocked the pont Neuf. The leading lorry burst into flames, blocking the passage of the two vehicles behind it; the second lorry was also destroyed, while the third was cap-tured along with its precious cargo of two heavy machine guns.[25]

Hundreds of kilometres away, the German public was given a brief glimpse of the situation inside the city, although without any of the awful details. German radio journalist Toni Scheelkopf ventured into the city and broadcast this account of life in Paris back to the Fatherland:

> We knew that the garrisons of the strong-points remaining behind in Paris had to fight in every part of the town in ceaseless skirmishes against the followers of de Gaulle on the one hand, and against the Bolshevist-controlled Resistance on the other. We saw barricades in the side-streets, sand-bags piled high, vehicles driven into one another, pieces of furniture heaped together to form barriers . . . somewhere a machine gun chattered from time to time . . . but we came through unchallenged to the well-defended German strong-points and reached the Champs-Elysées. Here the change which had come over this city was even more noticeable. It was a little after midday. But this street, usually crowded at this time of day with people and vehicles, was empty. On the way from the obelisk to the Arc de Triomphe we counted just over fifty people.[26]

*

Despite von Choltitz's claim that the military situation was clearer outside Paris, this was not exactly true. Coordination of the German effort was becoming increasingly fragmented. Field Marshal Model's

Western Command lost all contact with the 44th Army Corps near Troyes, 180 km to the south-east of Paris. The 48th Infantry Division in the southern suburbs was similarly isolated.[27] Telephone communication with Army Group B in Saint-Cloud collapsed, while links with Paris were 'completely unreliable'.[28] Everyone had to make do with radio messages (which, unknown to the Germans, could be read by the Allies), or telegrams which went via Belgium and took for ever.[29]

To respond to the increasingly difficult situation in and around Paris, Model ordered the 1st Army to defend the capital, in conjunction with those elements of the 48th Infantry Division that could be contacted, while the 6th Parachute Division was instructed to liaise with von Choltitz.[30] Von Choltitz had a poor opinion of the state of what remained of the 1st Army and was not impressed by Model's generosity. He was even less impressed when Model simultaneously ordered the Paris command to release over a dozen Tiger tanks, substantially weakening the garrison.[31] To combat the growing strength of the Allied bridgehead at Mantes to the west of Paris, Model ordered the redeployment of General von Aulock's battle group, which was spread along a thin fifteen-kilometre line on the southern flank of the city.[32] Although von Aulock successfully moved his headquarters to Saint-Cloud, the removal of the anti-aircraft guns turned out to be more complex than expected. They were due to be taken over the Seine at Saint-Germain-en-Laye, but a shortage of vehicles, along with 'badly trained drivers, darkness, overcrowded and clogged roads' meant that a large number of the guns could not be moved.[33] So they remained where they were, pointing down roads that headed westwards. The enemy would be coming on land, not by air.

As well as manoeuvring their forces, the Germans made a concerted attempt to repulse the Allied bridgehead west of Paris. Sustained artillery fire rained down on the US troops while the US 5th Armoured Division was attacked by dozens of German tanks.[34] Throughout the day Luftwaffe planes attacked the bridgehead using rockets. The German fighter-bombers swarmed in bands of thirty to sixty aircraft and then attacked in smaller groups, defended by fighter planes. Although these tactics caused havoc on the ground, destroying several anti-aircraft batteries, the mission was a failure. None of the makeshift bridges was hit, while over a dozen German planes were downed by Allied anti-aircraft fire.[35] Model ordered a night bombing raid, but all the Luftwaffe's heavy bombers had been withdrawn to Belgium and the project was abandoned. There was little the Germans could do to stop the Allied armoured tide.

Despite the situation becoming increasingly desperate, the Germans fought fierce rearguard actions to the south of Paris. In the middle of the forest of Fontainebleau, fifty kilometres from the capital, there was a vicious firefight between elements of the 5th US Infantry Division and the German Security Regiment. By the time the battle ended in the late afternoon, seventy-five Germans were dead and over 200 taken prisoner. The Americans continued to press eastwards towards the Seine snaking south of Paris. Supply problems were still a concern – the Third US Army reported that the overall supply situation remained 'critical' – although the capture of over forty tons of German medical equipment provided some relief.[36]

When Major Quadt of the Parachute Division contacted von Choltitz, as instructed by Model, the German commander of Paris was frank in his assessment: 'The situation in Paris is untenable. All authorities and officials have left the city. The outbreak of a rebellions-movement might take place at any time. Individual shootings are the daily order, individual vehicles are being attacked, looted and their crews taken prisoner. The forces on hand are by far too insufficient to defend the city. All that now matters is to get as much [materiel] and personnel out of Paris as possible, so that it will not fall into the hands of the enemy.'[37]

This defeatist attitude began to permeate everything the Paris garrison did. Later in the day, von Choltitz ordered the combat groups in the city to have 'an intelligent and reasonable attitude' and to be 'self-confident and disciplined' with regard to the Parisians, who were no longer described as 'terrorists' but rather as 'youth on the edge of insurrection or in an active state of insurrection, torn apart by a variety of intellectual and political orientations'. Von Choltitz hoped this approach would enable his men to 'paralyse the enemy' and help 're-establish normal life in Paris, which gives us the only possibility of preserving the routes into and through the city for our fighting troops.'[38] In other words, von Choltitz – like Parodi – was trying to buy time. Not to hold the city for some permanent strategic value, and certainly not to preserve its beauty, but rather to enable the retreating German Army to get to safety. If the German garrison were to engage in full-scale urban warfare with the Resistance, the city would become a lethal trap. Tens of thousands of German troops would find themselves caught between the hammer of the Allied advance and the anvil of the Paris insurrection. Von Choltitz may also have been thinking about saving his own skin: he would undoubtedly prefer to put himself into the hands of the US Army rather than be at the mercy of the Parisians.

FFI intelligence made a sober and accurate analysis of the situation of the German troops in the city, noting that the enemy had concentrated its forces around six centres – the Hôtel Meurice on the rue de Rivoli; the Hôtel Majestic near the Arc de Triomphe; the Ministry of Foreign Affairs on the quai d'Orsay; the parliament building; the Senate and the Jardin du Luxembourg; and the barracks on the place de la République. The FFI estimated that the Germans had around forty armoured vehicles in the immediate Paris region, while there were at most ten German divisions to the south (even this was an overestimate).[39] Despite the repeated claims of Chaban and Parodi, this was very different from the situation in Warsaw, where the full might of the German Army was turned on an insurgent civilian population with devastating effect. Two factors help to explain this difference. Firstly, the Germans in and around Paris were weak and in disarray. The garrison lacked both arms and men, and the Allies had continually smashed the troops fighting on the Western Front. Furthermore, the command structures on the Western Front had been repeatedly shaken up and key personnel replaced, first after the 20 July plot, and then in a series of irrational orders from Hitler to replace officers he thought were defective or untrustworthy. Secondly, the Allies, unlike the Russians outside Warsaw, were advancing at a tremendous rate; this undermined German morale and left little time for clear plans to be developed in a perpetually changing situation. In Warsaw the Germans had a relatively free hand to attack the Resistance for some weeks before the Soviet Army eventually moved against the city.

The situation in Paris was one in which the Germans were vulnerable and lacked confidence, while the Resistance had the support of the whole population and was soon to be reinforced by the Allies.

*

At 14:00, in a moment heavy with symbolism, Parodi chaired a meeting at the French prime minister's official residence, the Hôtel Matignon, which had been seized the day before.[40] In attendance were the secretary-generals, the Free French senior civil servants who had been appointed by Parodi to run each ministry and to prepare for the arrival of de Gaulle and his government. René Courtin, Secretary-General for the Economy, rode to Matignon on his bicycle, and was mightily impressed by the pomp and the power he found there: 'policemen in smart uniforms, machine guns, big rooms, administrative personnel, huge ante-rooms, and a large garden that I had never seen before, with armed guards here, too'.[41] Parodi's decision to hold the meeting at Matignon formed part of the Free French strategy for demonstrating to the Allies that they were in power. The traditional sites of French government were occupied by the Free French, protected by the FFI, and the traditional tasks were being carried out, more or less. For example, despite the fighting outside the Mairie of the 17th arrondissement, a new father, highly irritated by what he called 'all this business', barged his way through the barricades to fulfil his legal obligation to register the birth of his daughter.[42] This attention to the everyday needs of the population underlined the legitimacy of the new power.

Parodi began the meeting at Matignon by describing the swings of opinion over the cease-fire, culminating in the decision to recommence hostilities. Warning his colleagues – as ever – of 'the danger that may be represented by the retreat of German troops to Paris', Parodi ordered the civil servants to evacuate all the ministries to save their lives: their first duty was to protect themselves, he said.[43] Courtin immediately objected – pointing out that they would lose all respect in the eyes of the *résistants* who had seized and were protecting the buildings,. Parodi was unmoved and ordered Courtin to leave his ministry. But Courtin was made of sterner stuff, as he wrote in his diary that night: 'This order could not be carried out – after the spectacular events of Sunday and Monday, it would have looked like we were fleeing.'[44] So Courtin and his team spent an uncomfortable night in their ministry, without any weapons. Outside, German tanks stationed themselves next to the building, but did not attack.[45]

The Germans tolerated this situation for the simple reason that they could do little else. They did not have the men or the firepower to dislodge the representatives of the Provisional Government from the ministry buildings. This did not go unnoticed. In his diary that evening, Jean Guéhenno made an explicit link between the successful seizure of the traditional administrative buildings and the effective loss of control of the city by the Germans: 'The ministries and the *mairies* have been occupied by the FFI. Vichy has disappeared like smoke. The Germans no longer control life in Paris. They hold only the points where they have dug in. There is fighting all around them.'[46]

For many Parisians, the clearest sign of weakening German control was the sudden appearance of the Resistance press. The collaborationist newspapers had disappeared a few days earlier, and the Resistance had taken over the offices. Resistance journalists had then prepared their copy, loyally waiting for Parodi to give them permission to publish.[47] A handful of Resistance newspaper titles, which had been produced in secrecy since the beginning of the occupation, had been authorised to appear publicly for the first time the previous evening – *L'Humanité* had been first on the street with an issue dated 21 August, which was published almost as soon as it was permitted. Other newspapers, like *L'Aube*, a Christian-Democrat paper that had once been edited by Georges Bidault and which ceased publication at the beginning of the occupation, waited until the morning of 22 August.[48] All of these newspapers were printed as single broadsheets sold in the street for a trifling two francs. People crowded round to buy them, even though the news they contained was often out of date or incorrect.

The press reflected the clashes that had taken place over the ceasefire, and the way they treated the story had an effect on the leadership of the insurrection. During the meeting in the Hôtel Matignon that afternoon, Parodi explained that an 'unacceptable' article about Nordling had appeared, for which he had to apologise to his 'friend'.[49]

This was presumably a reference to an article in *L'Humanité* the previous day, which had denounced the activities of 'a "neutral" consular agent who made himself the instrument of the enemy' by negotiating the cease-fire.[50] Other newspapers were more supportive of the Free French. *Défense de la France*, which had been published underground since 1941, followed Parodi's line on the cease-fire, claiming it had been 'asked for by the German authorities ... in order to allow them to evacuate the capital'.[51] *Libération*, which was linked to the Resistance organisation of the same name and had openly appeared for the first time the previous day, claimed erroneously that the Germans had recognised the Free French as the authorities in the city.[52]

While civilians were overjoyed with the new media, and photographs were taken of FFI fighters reading newspapers while lounging against barricades, not everyone was so impressed. Copies of the papers were brought to the Hôtel de Ville, but as Léo Hamon wrote in his diary: 'Later on, they will be called "historic" but there is no time to read them and we really have too much to do.'[53] It was probably just as well that Hamon was so busy. Had he caught sight of *L'Humanité*, he might have burst a blood vessel. In its 22 August issue, the communist paper launched a furious attack on all those who, like Hamon, had supported the cease-fire. Below headlines that read 'DEATH TO THE HUNS AND THE TRAITORS!' and 'DOWN WITH COWARDS AND MANOEUVRERS!', *L'Humanité* made quite clear what the Communist Party thought of those in the Resistance who had engineered the cease-fire: 'Any discussion with the Hun for any other reason than their capitulation without conditions can be nothing other than a betrayal. The Parisians will consider this call to stop fighting against the Hun as a manoeuvre by a desperate enemy.'[54] Despite the agreement to start fighting again, the division in the Resistance caused by the cease-fire ran deep.

*

At 09:30, Rol's envoy to the Allies, Captain Gallois, arrived at General Bradley's headquarters in a small chateau on the outskirts of Laval, after having been driven around 250 km westwards through the night.

Although Patton had promised that Gallois would see Leclerc, the French captain was first taken into a room where several of Bradley's staff officers were sitting around a table, including Major-General Edwin Siebert, Bradley's head of intelligence ('G-2'). While the Americans were all wearing smart uniforms, Gallois' civilian clothes were dirty and creased, and his face was unshaven and strained with fatigue.

With all his remaining passion, Gallois described the situation in Paris and the demoralised state of the Germans, and emphasised the lack of any substantial enemy forces around the capital. He closed by pleading with the US officers to convince the Allied High Command to allow troops to liberate the French capital. Major-General Siebert asked Gallois a single question: 'Do you give me your word as an officer that all this is true?' When Gallois said it was, Siebert simply replied 'Goodbye', and that was that. Gallois was ushered out of the room, none the wiser about what would happen next.[55]

Meanwhile, General Leclerc, bursting with impatience, had left Argentan for Laval to see Bradley and press his case that he should be allowed to move on Paris immediately. As Leclerc was about to board a small plane bound for Laval, he was handed an order from General Gerow, his immediate superior. Gerow was not happy. He had learnt of de Guillebon's unauthorised probing mission and ordered Leclerc to withdraw his men immediately.[56] Leclerc put the order into his pocket, unopened, and took off for Laval. When he got there, Bradley had already left to tell Eisenhower about Gallois' information. The Americans, not the French, were making the decisions about the future of Paris.

As Bradley strode into First Army headquarters to see Eisenhower, he announced he had 'momentous news that demanded instantaneous action'.[57] And indeed, the effect on Eisenhower was immediate. After their meeting, the Supreme Allied Commander wrote: 'It looks now as if we'd be compelled to go into Paris. Bradley and his G-2 think we can and *must* walk in.'[58] Eisenhower's plan was 'to take over from the Resistance Group, reinforce them, and act in such mobile reserve as . . . may be needed'.[59] Bradley transmitted Eisenhower's views in a memo to his officers, explaining that the Leclerc Division would be accompanied by some forces from the US V Corps:

Paris was to be entered only in case the degree of the fighting was such as could be overcome by light forces. In other words, he doesn't want a severe fight to take place in Paris at this time ... It must be emphasised in advance that this advance into Paris must not be by means of heavy fighting because the original plan was to bypass Paris on both sides and pinch it out. We do not want any bombing or artillery fire on the city if it can possibly be avoided ... V Corps will advance without delay on Paris on two routes * take over Paris from the FFI * seize the crossing over the Seine south of the city * establish a bridgehead south-east of Paris.[60]

Rol's gamble had paid off. The Allies were coming. But there were important conditions: first, Eisenhower insisted that they were not to enter Paris until after the cease-fire was due to expire.[61] In other words, it was conceivable that the cease-fire would actually delay the liberation of the city. Furthermore, the Allies would enter the capital only if there was no hard fighting. If the Germans put up strong resistance, the Parisians would be left on their own. And if the Allies did arrive, their intention was clear – they would 'take over Paris from the FFI'.

Eventually, at 18:15, Bradley's plane landed and Leclerc, who had been hanging about since midday when he had arrived and met Gallois, rushed to greet the American commander as he clambered out. Bradley said: 'Ah, Leclerc! Good to see you. I was just about to give you the order to head for Paris.'[62] After briefly introducing Gallois, Leclerc ran to his plane, shouting over his shoulder to Gallois that he would send instructions. In the meantime, Bradley had been whisked off in a staff car, so Gallois was left alone at the airfield. Shortly afterwards he was given a tent and a camp bed; exhausted but elated, he fell asleep, fully dressed, not awakening until the next morning.[63] Leclerc, meanwhile, arrived at his headquarters at Fleuré, south-west of Argentan. He caught sight of his Chief of Operations, Captain Gribius, and called out: 'Gribius! Head straight for Paris!' (*'Gribius! Mouvement immédiat sur Paris!'*)[64] The capital was 200 km away.

While this was going on, de Guillebon's column was continuing its illicit operation in the east. They had been helped earlier in the day by Colonel Bruce of OSS, who had been hanging about in Rambouillet waiting for something to happen. For some time, the precise location of the Leclerc Division had been a mystery. As Bruce wrote in his diary: 'Nobody had been able to tell us exactly where General Leclerc's Second Armoured French Division is located. Like the Scarlet Pimpernel, it is said to have been seen here, there and everywhere.'[65] When Bruce eventually tracked down de Guillebon's group 'in a wheat field beyond Nogent-le-Roi', he gave the Frenchman information about the situation around Rambouillet.[66] Confident that there would be few problems, at around lunchtime de Guillebon sent small armoured groups westwards, towards Rambouillet and Arpajon. For Bruce, this boldness was in stark contrast to the apparent conservatism of the Allied Supreme Command, as he explained in his diary: 'Nobody can understand the present Allied strategy. General Patton's Third American Army has been in a position for several days to take Paris. Two of his Divisions are across the Seine and have moved North. There are no German forces of consequence between us and the capital.'[67]

De Guillebon's men found the population of Rambouillet in the streets, celebrating their liberation, while at Arpajon, only thirty kilometres from Paris, the locals told the Free French soldiers that there was only one anti-aircraft battery and a single German strong-point between them and the capital. In the evening, resting at Arpajon, de Guillebon radioed this information back to the 2e DB headquarters and explained that the next day he would enter Paris from the south. However, he was ordered instead to clear the road to Paris via Versailles, which he knew was heavily defended, and which seemed to offer no advantages over the safer, southern approach to the city. Perplexed, and convinced that his message had not been understood, de Guillebon repeated his signal, but got no response. Frustrated but a man of discipline, de Guillebon decided to wait until 07:00 the next morning, hoping to receive approval from his superiors for what looked like a straightforward move on the capital.[68]

*

In Paris, the collapse of transportation and the disappearance of commerce in the region meant that wheelbarrows were being used to cart flour and wood to the bakers' shops, while only a handful of grocers were open, selling a recently arrived sugar ration.[69] Inevitably, there were long queues and the food that was available soon sold out. As Jean Galtier-Boissière walked up the rue Saint-Jacques shortly after 08:00, he heard the cry 'No more bread!' coming from the *boulangeries*.[70]

Von Choltitz was well aware of the critical state of the food supply, and in the afternoon he received a visit from René Naville, the Swiss legate, and Dr de Morsier of the Red Cross, who that morning had organised a prisoner exchange – fifty wounded German prisoners were exchanged for fifty French prisoners.[71] Now the issue was food. Flour supplies in the city would run out in two days' time, and the two men wanted the German commander to allow 100 lorries to drive to the massive flour silos fifty kilometres to the east of Paris, where over 800 tons of flour was stored. Von Choltitz agreed, but as he then had to get the agreement of all the German authorities and broadcast a message to the Allies, it was more than thirty-six hours before the first vehicles left the capital, flying white flags and with their roofs painted red and blue, the colours of Paris.[72] In the meantime, people continued to go hungry.

Those who ventured out to find food discovered that the renewed fighting posed massive problems. Jean Guéhenno reported sporadic but lethal gunfire: 'German tanks were patrolling. As I was about to cross the boulevard Sébastopol, one of the tanks fired 30 metres in front of me, decapitating a woman, ripping a man's guts out. Strange as it may seem, 50 metres away, in the side-streets, people were sitting on their doorsteps, chatting.'[73] This contrast between armed conflict and everyday affairs was lyrically described by Paul Tuffrau, after walking near the Jardin du Luxembourg: 'This strange life continues: intermittent explosions, some chatter, the sound of a piano playing, windows opening, then children play at marbles or hopscotch, turning their heads or rushing to hide in a doorway for a minute only when firing breaks out.'[74]

A short distance away, the Germans attacked the Mairie of the 5th arrondissement, by the Panthéon, killing several FFI fighters. The sound of the gunfire could be heard some distance away and alarmed Jean Galtier-Boissière.[75] Odette Lainville's husband, Robert, got caught up in a firefight at the Hôtel de Ville: 'German tanks turned up . . . they were soon joined by two lorries and a motorcyclist wearing the field-grey uniform of the Wehrmacht. The hatch of one of the tanks opened and a soldier got out to talk to the motorcyclist; the moment was very tense. Suddenly a shot rang out from the ranks of the Resistance, and the motorcyclist fell to the ground. Then gunfire crackled from everywhere.'[76]

This was only one of a series of confrontations around the Hôtel de Ville that day. In the morning, tanks had fired on the building and had been fruitlessly peppered with small-arms fire, the bullets pinging off the armour. Then, in the early afternoon, Léo Hamon was in his office when more firing broke out. He dived to the floor but carried on his telephone conversation. Shortly afterwards the FFI seized a lorry, killing the driver; according to one report, up to twenty Germans were dead.[77] In the early evening there was yet another firefight and cases of ammunition were bravely – or foolhardily – dragged from a burning lorry by the FFI. When Hamon went to congratulate the people involved, he found they were part of the elite squad stationed in the Hôtel de Ville by Laval a few days earlier to 'protect' Herriot, and had simply switched sides.[78]

The sight of so much apparent unity between the disparate forces of the Resistance led some Parisians to hope that this situation might continue after the war. Odette Lainville wrote in her diary: 'I like to think of all these young people who are today fraternally united by the same love of France; and I dare to hope that (God willing) this magnificent seed of harmony, cast onto a field that has been so thoroughly tilled, will grow beautiful and strong and that no post-war weeds will be able to stifle it . . .'[79] Micheline Bood, much younger, saw events through the prism of her own experience, but had a similar impression: 'It seems that I have got so much older over the last three days. We have experienced so much. I can't remember what happened on Saturday and if I didn't write all the time, I'd be unable to find my way through all this stuff . . . There has never been a time when we have had such an intense life, there has never been a fire that has burnt so brightly. Catholics and Communists are united in the common cause.'[80] However, Micheline's interest in the young FFI fighters was also more worldly, as she explained: 'They are sun-tanned and strong and they look so fierce and wild.'[81]

Flora Groult, who threw packets of cigarettes to the FFIers in the park below her apartment, saw the young men with a bit more distance: 'They are all very young; on the borderline between little boys playing at war and heroes winning it.'[82] For some of those young men, 'playing at war' also involved dying. André Dupont and André Faucher, two cousins aged twenty-two and twenty, were FFI fighters from the 14th arrondissement. Somehow they were both captured by the Germans near the Gare de l'Est, and were then lined up against a wall and shot dead.[83]

*

Youth was the theme of Picasso's latest paintings. In his companion's apartment at the eastern end of the Ile Saint-Louis, Picasso painted two portraits of a young girl, based on his daughter Maya. The watercolours are balanced mid-way between a rich realism and his more well-known, fractured cubist style – in one of the paintings, each side of the girl's face is realistically portrayed, but the two sides do not fit together. The left side looks into the mid-distance, in a classic pose, while the right side stares madly at the viewer.[84]

*

In the early evening, Raoul Nordling and 'Riki' Posch-Pastor went to see von Choltitz, and the German commander impatiently demanded that the Resistance stop fighting. He even suggested that the cease-fire could be renewed, if the Resistance allowed the Germans safe routes out of the city. Nordling recognised that this would be unacceptable to the French – the only person who could convince the Free French to stop fighting was de Gaulle, he argued. When von Choltitz impatiently pointed out that the Free French leader was not in Paris, Nordling suggested that it might be possible to reach him by sending an envoy to the Allies. This gave the German commander an idea, and in a bizarre twist of events, von Choltitz took the unprecedented step of providing Nordling with papers enabling him to go through the German lines in his consular car, to contact de Gaulle and persuade the Resistance to stop the fighting.[85]

But the Swedish consul had an attack of angina and spent the next few days in bed. So his brother Rolf, who did not have any consular responsibility, replaced him on the mission to de Gaulle and the Allies, which was headed by the banker and *résistant* Saint-Phalle.[86] The mission may have been more multi-layered than it first appeared, for the two-car convoy also contained four spies. As well as the inevitable Posch-Pastor and Bender, there was Colonel Ollivier of JADE-AMICOL, masquerading as a doctor with his Red Cross pass, who had managed to inveigle himself onto the mission, while the final member was the banker Jean Laurent, who had been de Gaulle's head of office at the Ministry of War in 1940, and who was now working with the ALLIANCE MI6 intelligence circuit and was in daily contact with Nordling.[87]

The convoy's passage through the southern suburbs did not go unnoticed. Shortly after 20:00, Yves Cazaux telephoned his colleague de Félix at the Préfecture in Versailles. Nothing much was happening, de Félix began telling Cazaux, and then he said: 'Hang on ... just now, in front of my window a car has gone by with a white flag on one side and a Swedish flag on the other, then another vehicle behind it. They are heading towards the American lines.' Perplexed, Cazaux duly noted the conversation in his diary.[88] The mini-convoy headed on into the dark, unaware that Rol had got to the Allies first.[89]

*

As night fell, the weather grew unbearably close. With no street lights and a new moon, the city was utterly dark, increasing the impression of isolation and suspense. Edmond Dubois wrote: 'The atmosphere in the city is extremely unpleasant, the Allies are expected with such impatience that their late arrival is as inexplicable as it is incomprehensible.'[90] On the other side of the Seine, Yves Cazaux felt more or less the same, writing in his diary to the sound of birds roosting on the Ile de la Cité: 'It is so hot and close tonight! After several hours' silence, guerrilla fighting has broken out again here. The FFI troops are much stronger. There are frequent outbreaks of gunfire. Then every now and again there is the loud sound of a tank gun that shakes the windows.'[91] Meanwhile, Victor Veau was depressed again. Even an unexpected evening meal of tinned ham and processed peas had not cheered him up: 'I didn't eat anything. I am too stunned. And to think that this morning I was calm and collected! ... The sound of firing is everywhere ... 22:00 – The night is absolutely black – no moon. The streets are empty and quiet – far off there is the sound of cannon fire.'[92] Edmond Dubois closed the night with some good news. At 21:00 the electricity came on, and he twiddled the dial of his radio. To his amazement, he stumbled across the Resistance radio station. After two days of waiting, the radio had finally been allowed to broadcast more than music.[93] At 22:30 the radio called for the insurrection that had been agreed the previous day: 'The moment has come to finally drive the enemy from the capital. The whole population must rise up, build barricades and boldly take action, to deal a final blow to the invader. The hour of liberation has sounded. French men and women, rise up and join the fight!'[94] Then came the 'Marseillaise'. The call was repeated every fifteen minutes throughout the night, interspersed with other news.[95] Dubois expressed his enthusiasm in his diary: 'Where are they coming from, these radio waves that are directing the liberation of Paris? Excited, breathless announcers sum up the actions of the FFI ... "They need urgent reinforcements in the 11th arrondissement. Comrades, help the struggle ..."'[96] The scratchy voice of the Resistance radio and the intermittent crackle of gunfire became the sound of liberation.

12

Wednesday 23 August:
Destruction

Professor Paul Tuffrau writes in his diary: 'These days are truly extraordinary: the city seems to have been liberated, Resistance newspapers are openly on sale, we can telephone without taking precautions, collaborators are being arrested, the new Prefect of Police and the Secretary-Generals in the various Ministries are giving orders through posters, FFI fighters are openly wearing armbands as they move about the city . . ., there is an electric atmosphere, a mixture of nervous waiting and restrained joy, which fills everyone and everything they do; and yet the Germans are still here, we can hear sudden gunfire and the sound of shooting nearby or further off, unexplained explosions, the noise of isolated bursts of firing.'[1]

At around 03:00, the whole of Paris trembled with a massive explosion.[2] Paul Tuffrau wrote: 'In the middle of the night, the buildings of Paris were shaken by massive gusts of air. Doors and windows shook, tiles fell into courtyards ... The gusts were accompanied by heavy detonations rather than distant rumbling, and by massive flashes to the south. Everyone was woken up.' Camille Vilain went down into the pitch-dark street to see what was happening – 'I have never experienced anything like it in all my career as a soldier and an artilleryman,' he wrote. Micheline Bood's building shook 'like jelly'; everyone from her neighbourhood went onto their balconies in their nightclothes and wondered what had happened. Had the Senate been blown up? Was it an attack by

V1 rockets? Eventually, Micheline returned to bed, only to be awoken again by massive gusts of air from the east, which in the dead of night felt eerie and full of foreboding. As she wrote in her diary: 'It seemed that the dead body of Paris was swinging like a skeleton in the wind. And there was this vast red glow, growing ever larger on the horizon ... It was a *danse macabre*, a world of cataclysm and nightmare.'[3]

In the morning, Micheline's apocalyptic vision was strengthened as the Germans attacked a major Paris landmark. Since the turn of the century, the Grand Palais exhibition hall by the Seine had been a striking feature of the Paris skyline, with its massive art deco vault made of glass and iron. For the last few weeks, the Grand Palais had been hosting the horses and clowns of the Houcke Circus, but now it was the centre of an intense firefight. French policemen stationed next to the Palais apparently fired on a passing German column; the Germans summoned reinforcements from the nearby place de la Concorde, including two Tiger tanks, an armoured car and two unmanned 'Goliath' tanks – squat tracked vehicles about 1.5 metres long and less than sixty centimetres tall, which could carry up to seventy-five kilograms of explosive.[4] They were remote-controlled bombs.

Journalist Claude Roy, who was in the area, had to dive for cover to avoid being hit by gunfire, and saw the two Goliath tanks being manoeuvred around on the lawn in front of the Grand Palais and then sent in. At least one Goliath was blown up, setting fire to the building. Smoke began to pour out of the doors and the roof. It billowed up into the sky and was soon visible from all over the city. From across the Seine, Madame Odette Dedron saw 'an enormous column of thick grey smoke, with pink tinges, rising above the building'.[5] German soldier Walter Dreizner was working on an electrical installation at the Hôtel Meurice; seeing 'an enormous cloud of black smoke', he clambered onto the hotel roof and took a series of photographs of the destruction. From his point of view, the explanation for the destruction was simple: 'The Grand Palais has been occupied by terrorists.'[6]

In the chaos, the circus horses, frightened by the flames and the noise and the overwhelming smell of smoke and gunpowder, were led out of the burning building. One horse – which may have been either from the circus or a passing carthorse – was hit by a stray bullet and collapsed, like a puppet whose strings had been cut.[7] It lay dead on the avenue Montaigne, behind the Grand Palais, where hungry Parisians chopped it into pieces, and soon all that remained was what an eye-witness described as 'a pile of innards and a head with milky staring eyes'.[8] Meanwhile, firemen arrived to try to control the blaze, but they were shot at by the Germans. Among those called to help was young Jean-Claude Touche, who described the scene: 'Huge flames are swelling up inside the building, breaking through the glass vault at various points. The noises of the animals are mixed with the roaring of the flames. We are worried that some FFIers might be dead inside. Shortly afterwards, immense flames burst through the roof. What a blaze. We can hear the sound of explosions from inside.'[9] Nearby, a group of Parisians watched the scene while seated on deckchairs on a grass-covered roundabout on the Champs-Elysées.

Eventually, after some of the *résistants* surrendered, the Germans withdrew with their prisoners and by 13:30 the fire was under control. A few hours later, Edmond Dubois went inside to see the damage: 'The interior is entirely destroyed, but the glass roof and the metal framework have survived. The firemen have carried out a minor miracle. They are in an awful state, tired and dirty. They are black from head to foot, to the extent that, from a distance, I thought they were Negroes.'[10] Shocked at the sight of the smoke billowing up from the Grand Palais, Micheline Bood poured her hatred of the Germans onto the pages of her diary: 'I hate them, I hate them. To think that I believed that they were men. We will never forget. I hope we will be avenged ... Putting Paris to fire and blood! Let our blood pour onto them and their children. They wanted this war, they all wanted it. I swear I will hate them until the end of time.'[11]

*

As the Parisian firemen gained control of the fire, the High Command in Berlin transmitted an order from Hitler reiterating the strategic importance of Paris for his plans. Not only did the city have symbolic value ('Throughout history, the loss of Paris has meant the loss of France'), the Paris region was also an important military location for waging the 'long-distance war against Britain' (the V1 and V2 rocket campaigns)[12]. At the first sign of rebellion, 'the strongest possible measures' were to be taken, including 'blowing up whole city blocks, public executions of ringleaders, and complete evacuation of the affected district'. Finally, Hitler emphasised that he expected Paris to be sacrificed: 'The Seine bridges are to be prepared for demolition. Paris is not to fall into enemy hands other than as a heap of rubble,' he ordered.[13]

Less than a week later, von Choltitz recalled his feelings on reading the message: 'You know, that really made me boil. I was ashamed to face my people.'[14] Deeply disturbed, von Choltitz showed the order to his aide, Colonel Jay. In the late afternoon sunlight, the two men stood on the balcony outside von Choltitz's office on the rue de Rivoli. As Jay later recalled, perhaps through rose-tinted spectacles: 'In front of us the Tuileries lay in sunshine. To our right was the place de la Concorde and to our left the Louvre. The scene merely underlined the madness of this medieval command.'[15]

Shortly after receiving the message from Berlin, von Choltitz telephoned the Chief of Staff of Army Group B, General Speidel. In a sarcastic tone, von Choltitz said he was going to carry out the orders to the letter, destroying major buildings throughout the city. Speidel became alarmed, and it was only when von Choltitz shouted that he was going to demolish the Eiffel Tower to block the surrounding streets that the penny dropped. A relieved Speidel said: 'My thoughts are with you. You know we think exactly the same.' He, too, was convinced that Hitler's order was futile.[16]

Neither von Choltitz, nor Jay, nor Speidel were motivated by any deep-seated love of Paris (von Choltitz had spent a little over a week in the capital) nor were they in principle opposed to the idea of destroying a city (the German commander had done exactly that at Sebastopol two years earlier). They simply did not have the resources to mount any kind of a fight. The Allies were advancing rapidly, and there were no substantial German forces between the front and the French capital. As a result there was nothing von Choltitz could do, except sacrifice his men pointlessly. In his memoirs he claimed: 'The situation in Paris being what it was, I could not successfully oppose the enemy's armoured divisions. All of these orders were mere paper, with no military value whatsoever.'[17] From the very moment he arrived in Paris less than two weeks earlier, von Choltitz had been unconvinced of his mission. Now he was revealing himself to be a defeatist with no spirit for a fight. Hitler's order had been designed to rally the troops and convince his officers to fight to the end, but it was having the opposite effect.

*

Whatever he might have thought in private, in public von Choltitz was determined to bluff the Resistance into submission. The Germans produced a leaflet for the Parisian population that described the Resistance as 'scum' and claimed the fighting had 'stretched the humanitarian sentiments of the German troops to breaking point'. The last section of the leaflet sounded like the threats of a gangster running a protection racket: 'Paris remains for us one of the most beautiful cities in this Europe we are fighting for; we will preserve it from the chaos it has itself created ... It would be easy to leave Paris after blowing up all the depots, all the factories, all the bridges and all the stations, locking up the suburbs as tightly as if they were encircled. Given the lack of food, water and electricity, in less than 24 hours there would be terrible catastrophe!'[18] In a discussion with the Swiss legate, René Naville, von Choltitz threatened that he would deploy '150 Tiger tanks' against the Resistance strongholds and hinted at the possibility of an aerial bombardment before saying, with the leer of a bully, 'I'm sure you agree that it would be quite understandable if a general were to take fright and turn nasty.'[19] The fire at the Grand Palais helped reinforce this atmosphere of menace, and further weaken the resolve of some members of the Resistance. Pasteur Vallery-Radot turned up at Victor Veau's apartment slightly panicked – he feared that following the destruction of the Grand Palais, all public buildings would now be attacked 'by tanks which the Germans had assembled in large numbers in the south'.[20] There were no such tanks. In the same vein the Germans delivered an ultimatum to the *résistants* occupying the Hôtel de Ville: if firing continued, there would be an attack the next morning by forty tanks. Shaken, Léo Hamon consulted fellow-*résistant* Roger Stéphane as to how they should respond, but in the end they decided to do nothing so as not to worry the *résistants* unnecessarily.[21] This was the right decision: there was no attack.

The true balance of forces was revealed in two different events on either side of the city. First, at around 09:30, an old couple stood underneath Victor Veau's window selling Resistance newspapers. Suddenly, a German car screeched up and an officer got out, waving his gun and shouting loudly. 'He grabbed all the newspapers, threw them into the car and then zoomed off. Almost immediately, the newspaper sellers found another stock and were selling again,' Veau noted in his diary.[22] The Germans could not impose their will, even at the simplest level. This was underlined later on in the day, when the Commander of the German barracks at the place de la République sent a polite letter in slightly wonky formal French, addressed to 'Monsieur the Chief of the 11th Arrondissement'. The commander respectfully asked the 'Chief' to remove the barricades that had been erected in the neighbourhood, stating that if this did not occur the commander would find himself obliged to remove them using heavy weapons. His polite conclusion showed the real German position. 'The responsibility of any losses incurred as a result of this action would be entirely yours. As far as the rest is concerned, I am ready to discuss with you as I have already done with the Chiefs or the Mayors of other arrondissements. Please accept, Sir, my most distinguished greetings.'[23] The barricades remained in place and were not attacked. All down the line, the Germans were bluffing.

*

In the darkened corridors of von Choltitz's headquarters at the Hôtel Meurice (power cuts affected the Germans, too), the Swiss legate, René Naville, discussed the possibility of the Germans releasing some of their massive stocks of food. The Germans said they would allow their supplies to be distributed, but only in the 'quieter' parts of the city. When Naville pointed out that the fighting was shifting all over the capital, von Choltitz said he would release the food on condition that the Resistance removed the barricades and ceased shooting at German forces.[24] That was never going to happen.

Gas supplies to the city had been turned off and the electricity cuts not only affected light and power for much of the day, they also made the water supply extremely erratic as they affected the pumping stations. To ease the situation, railway engineer Pierre Patin was asked by his director to convince striking train drivers at the Montrouge depot to move a trainload of coal to a nearby power station. The strikers were unimpressed by the suggestion – some of them said he was a provocateur, and the overwhelming feeling was that any train that moved on the southern section of the line around Paris might be attacked by Allied aircraft. The coal train stayed where it was and the electricity stayed off.[25]

Among those suffering from the lack of water was the collaborationist writer Robert Brasillach, hiding in an attic room just down the road from the German strong-point in the Senate building. With no water, he had nothing to eat but dried noodles and a few tomatoes brought to him by a friend.[26] On the other side of the city, Berthe Auroy weighed her last few potatoes and tried to work out how long they would last, while not far from Brasillach, Yves Cazaux and his young family were reduced to making their own flour. They took turns to grind wheat grains laboriously in the hand-cranked coffee grinder; when they had obtained something like flour, it was carefully sieved and then turned into thick pancakes, which were cooked on a small petrol stove. In addition, the family had hoarded a few tins of sardines and cans of vegetables that were now being slowly consumed.[27]

As food supplies became increasingly scarce, there was a massive opportunity for profiteering. In the plush western suburb of Neuilly, Maurice Toesca saw a concierge selling lettuces and pears for exorbitant sums. But a passing policeman decided to impose a bit of on-the-spot price control and rationing, and ordered the woman to drop her prices and to sell only one kilo of pears to each buyer.[28] In the 17th arrondissement, people queuing to buy radishes and salad from a cart were shot at by a passing German motorcycle crew; one badly injured girl had to have her leg amputated.[29]

Daniel Boisdon took three hours to make the round trip from his home near the rue des Ecoles in the 5th arrondissement across the boulevard Saint-Michel to the place Saint-Sulpice – a distance of around three kilometres. He had to duck for cover nearly a dozen times. As he wrote in his diary:

> German tanks were prowling around the Senate, firing everywhere. Machine gunners, hiding down by the Odéon theatre, were shooting from behind the columns, all along the rue Racine, where a man was shot dead just as I was about to cross. I waited until it was quiet and then ran over to the other side. Everywhere there were stretcher-bearers taking the wounded away. The sight of deserted Parisian streets, covered in all kinds of debris, with these groups of four or five men running along them, generally preceded by one or two nurses waving Red Cross flags, will remain one of the most striking images of these truly glorious days.[30]

Not all parts of the city were equally affected by the fighting, as shown by the provisional figures for dead and wounded which the police drew up that day.[31] Approximately the same number of French policemen and German soldiers had been killed in the first four days of the insurrection (sixty-two and sixty-eight, respectively). The vast bulk of casualties were among the civilian population, which presumably included non-uniformed Resistance fighters: 483 dead and nearly 1200 wounded. Most of these tragic incidents were in the working-class areas: strikingly, no one had even been wounded in the wealthy 16th arrondissement.

*

Throughout the day there was fighting in many neighbourhoods, especially in the less well-off areas.[32] In the 19th and 20th arrondissements, there was a dramatic incident involving three German trains. At around 08:00, news arrived at FFI headquarters that the Germans were moving trains along the inner Paris railway line, from Bercy in the south up to the Gare de l'Est. As one train emerged from the tunnel at Belleville-Villette station, the local Resistance stopped it and removed the driver. In so doing, they blocked the tunnel, trapping a second train which was just behind – FFI fighters surrounded the other end of the tunnel at

Ménilmontant station to prevent it from reversing out. After more than five hours waiting in the stifling dark under the hill, the German troops eventually surrendered. Over thirty prisoners were taken, along with the contents of the trains, which apart from guns, ammunition and flour also included central-heating radiators, electric batteries and swastika pennants. Hundreds of Parisians streamed out to watch what was happening, crowding onto bridges and peering through railings.[33]

Unknown to the FFI fighters at Ménilmontant, there was a third German train, further north on the line, waiting in a tunnel between Belleville and a deep cutting that runs through the eastern edge of the Buttes Chaumont park. Young Madeleine Riffaud and three of her FTP comrades from the 19th arrondissement, including 16-year-old Max, heard that the train would shortly be emerging from the tunnel. They grabbed whatever weaponry they could find – two machine guns, grenades, Molotov cocktails and some flares – and sped off in a car to the bridge where the railway passes under the rue Manin. As the train puffed out of the tunnel around 150 metres away, sentries on the engine started firing at the four *résistants* on the bridge, who responded by raining their rag-bag set of explosive devices onto the locomotive as it passed beneath them. Alarmed, the Germans put the engine into reverse and chugged back into the safety of the tunnel, which was blocked at the Belleville end by FFI fighters. There was a brief stand-off, during which the Resistance managed to uncouple the locomotive and drive it out of the tunnel, leaving the wagon-loads of Germans isolated in the dark. After a while, dozens of men surrendered and a trainload of valuable food was captured.[34]

Despite such successes, the Resistance was still fighting with one arm tied behind its back. The lack of arms and ammunition was becoming a major impediment to defending whole neighbourhoods from marauding German tanks. The FFI therefore sent the Allies yet another desperate plea for a supply drop. There was no response.[35] The need for decent weaponry was made amply clear by events in the 17th arrondissement, where German tanks prowled around all afternoon, firing into buildings. Jean-Claude Touche wrote in his diary: '16:00. The tanks are still firing violently from the place Villiers onto the boulevard des Batignolles and the rue Boursault. What fireworks! ... 17:14:

Another round of cannon fire from the tank, which makes an incredible noise. Again the sound of machine guns. The tank isn't on the place Villiers any more, but it is still firing. I can see people running along the rooftops. Despite the noise, we can still hear the sound of cannon fire in the distance. It must be coming from the front.'[36] The fighting eventually calmed down after a young FFIer on the rue de Courcelles threw a Molotov cocktail at one of the tanks, severely injuring a German officer and leading to the capture of two soldiers. At 19:35, Jean-Claude wrote:

> Everything is quiet. I take a trip round the neighbourhood. The place Villiers, on the Batignolles side, has been severely damaged. Virtually all the windows are broken. There is a shell hole in the road, which is covered with bits of masonry. In front of the Monceau 'Uni' shop, three burnt-out German lorries lie on their sides. One of them is still ablaze. The firemen are trying to put it out ... Another lorry lies empty on the rue Larribe, its tyres punctured. Yet another lies upside down, its wheels in the air, in the middle of the rue de Constantinople. The boulevard des Batignolles looks like it has been hit by a hurricane.[37]

Similar tank attacks took place on the avenue des Gobelins in the 13th arrondissement, while near the Hôtel de Ville a fire-bomb attack by a young *résistant* called Michel Aubry destroyed a Panther tank; the crew, unable to put out the fire, fled and left their vehicle to burn.[38]

At around 19:00, Yves Cazaux heard the sound of fighting from the Latin Quarter. He telephoned his cousin, who told him there was a major battle taking place – German tanks were firing on two buildings, which were severely damaged. Dr Monin, in his apartment on the boulevard Saint-Michel, saw it all from his window: 'Great emotion: the tanks have come back and have taken up position in front of us and are firing at the Saint-Michel barricade. The shop windows are smashed. In our bedroom a window pane breaks; another is pierced by a bullet which buries itself in the back wall, and by another which goes through the open door leading onto the landing. It lasts about 20 minutes, then the tanks retreat and relative calm follows the noise of firing.'[39] Then a case of munitions exploded like so many fireworks. Cazaux, safe in his apartment about 150 metres away, could hear the crowd shouting 'Bravo!'[40]

The poet Camille Vilain saw everyone from his neighbourhood help build a barricade by the boulevard Saint-Marcel:

> What an extraordinary sight – it is as though we are reliving the heroic days of 1848. The whole neighbourhood is here: men, women and children, and for two hours, everyone is working like crazy. Determined men in shirt-sleeves rip up the paving stones, women and children form a human chain to pass the stones along. The barricade is built with great enthusiasm. I can see local shopkeepers, officer workers, labourers, the boss of a biscuit factory, women of all classes. I join in, too – my wife looks after the stones.[41]

On the barricades and in the ferocious street fighting, the rousing slogans of *L'Humanité* were being realised on the streets of the capital: 'All of Paris to the barricades! . . . Attack is the best form of defence. Harass the enemy! Not a single Hun should leave insurgent Paris alive.'[42]

*

In the heart of the insurrection, the new Paris was being forged, as many people began to ponder what would happen after the Germans had left. The Comité de Libération at the Préfecture gave the order for all policemen to put their uniforms back on, ready to maintain law and order and to defend 'republican institutions'. In other words, to make sure that there would be no communist uprising.[43] Assuming that the communists did not take power, the whole economy of the country, and of Paris as the economic and political centre of France, was about to make a major lurch. After liberation, the new France would clearly be trading primarily with the Allies rather than with the Germans. The banks were keen to adapt to this coming shift in the economy, and to make contact with the newly installed secretary-generals in the ministries. Robert Labbé, head of the Worms Bank, went to see René Courtin in the newly liberated Ministry of the Economy, to plead for financial support for coal-importers, who would have to gain new contacts in the UK to replace their previous clients in occupied Europe. As Courtin acidly observed in his diary: 'The Germanophile gang is replaced by the friends of England.'[44]

For the first time in nearly two years, Albert Grunberg came down from his attic hideaway and moved into his old apartment, which had remained empty all that time. His legs trembling with emotion, Grunberg opened the windows. Blinded by the sunlight, he peered out; neighbours at windows in the buildings opposite waved in greeting. In the evening, he even ventured out into the street and drank a cup of coffee in a nearby bar. A new life had begun for him.[45]

For Robert Brasillach, trapped in his own hideaway a mere kilometre away, the approaching world was frightening. The same friend who brought him the tomatoes told him that there had been a wave of arrests and that 300,000 people would be thrown into prisons and camps. Brasillach, no doubt feeling the noose around his neck, concluded that 'they' would 'try to make out that the greatest industrialists, the greatest artists and the greatest writers were traitors'.[46]

In Marie-Thérèse Walter's apartment on the Ile Saint-Louis, Pablo Picasso turned his dark eyes onto a reproduction of Poussin's *The Triumph of Pan*. Painted in 1636, this joyous canvas shows a woodland scene in which a tangled set of naked satyrs riotously cavort with some scantily clad nymphs, accompanied by Pan and a couple of goats. Picasso took his pen and began to interpret Poussin's classical creation in his own way, transforming and distorting the bodies into a fluid, writhing mass.[47] This sketch, which he would pursue and develop into a painting over the next few days, marked a decisive change in his work, heralding a new focus on reinterpreting the great works of art history.[48]

All over the city, the Resistance media became increasingly visible. In a few days, Resistance newspapers had become a feature of life in the capital and a major source of information. The cameramen who had filmed the tumultuous events met in an office on the Champs-Elysées and viewed the first rushes as the film came back from processing.[49] Within days they would produce a thirty-minute newsreel showing the whole world what had happened during the liberation of Paris. Meanwhile, the Resistance radio station began transmitting in earnest, interviewing CNR leader Georges Bidault and broadcasting directly from the streets. As the radio car drove to meet Bidault, complete with a gendarme in uniform for protection, they were stopped by a German patrol who wanted proof that they were indeed acting for the Gaullist Provisional Government. Nonplussed, the gendarme took out the Resistance armband that he had been hiding in his pocket and put it on. Satisfied, the Germans let the group go on their way. In the topsy-turvy situation that had engulfed the city, what would once have been a guarantee of arrest, or even execution, now secured free passage.

The radio team gathered in the back room of a small café near place de la République, where presenter Pierre Crénesse interviewed Bidault, who looked dapper with a spotted tie and a pocket handkerchief. It was more of a speech than an interview, with Bidault praising the unity and courage of the French people, emphasising the importance of General de Gaulle and underlining the pioneer role of the Resistance, which had fought long before D-Day, 'instead of waiting'. But what made Bidault's broadcast so memorable was that despite his opening proclamation that 'Paris is liberated', the sound of gunfire in the background made it clear that the battle was not yet over: 'In the working-class neighbourhood where I am speaking from, you can hear the sound of enemy cannons and of French rifles, which alternate virtually without interruption, but confidence and determination are not on the side of the heavy weapons. Now is the time to fight.'[50]

Not everyone agreed. Some people were so suspicious of the events taking place in the city that they claimed the gunshots in the background of Bidault's broadcast were a sound effect added in the studio.[51] Polish exile Andrzej Bobkowski was scornful of a barricade he inspected – 'If a butterfly sat on it the whole thing would collapse in an instant,' he thought.[52] Edith Thomas overheard a pharmacist saying to a customer: 'What do you expect? They fire at the Germans, so the Germans defend themselves. And now they're building barricades! What a mess.' In her diary, Thomas concluded bitterly: 'I have the strong impression that most of the population, while not hostile to the Resistance, would have preferred that the liberation of Paris had been carried out by the Americans. No problems, get on with life. Paris is like a whore who waits with its legs spread.'[53]

On the telephone, Jean Guéhenno had an argument with his friend 'B', which summed up two strikingly different attitudes to the insurrection. B said that the fighting was pointless, merely a way for Parisians to convince themselves that they were playing a role in their impending liberation, which was really the work of the Allies. The price of this game was being paid in lives, said B. In his diary, Guéhenno was less cynical, and less critical:

> Perhaps a people needs such illusions ... We know that the storming of the Bastille was not the Revolution, but the Bastille had to be stormed for the idea of the Revolution to live for centuries in the French popular imagination ... 'B' points out that the current street fighting does not involve the masses, but only a fighting minority. That's true; but there can be no doubt that this minority has in some way been delegated in this role by the majority, and that it represents the best elements of the population.[54]

That was certainly the view expressed in the editorial in the Resistance newspaper *Combat*, which had adopted the banner 'From Resistance to Revolution': 'The Paris that is fighting this evening wants to command tomorrow. Not for the sake of power, but for justice; not for the sake of politics, but for morality; not for the sake of dominating the country, but for its greatness.'[55]

Nowhere was that turnaround in fortunes more clearly expressed than in the faces of captured German soldiers. Journalist Claude Roy visited a group of fifty German prisoners who were being held in a primary school. Overall, they were happy – *'Pour nous, guerre finie!'* said one ('For us, war over') – but they had the vacant air typical of all captured soldiers, and were particularly surprised to have been captured by the ordinary people they had previously passed every day in the street. The soldiers had never imagined the fury behind the stony faces of the Parisians.[56]

*

At 22:15, von Choltitz had a telephone conversation with Army Group B in which he explained that the situation in the capital was spiralling out of control. Von Choltitz's superiors were well aware of this – General

Blumentritt, Model's chief of staff, had been unable to get into the city because of the barricades. Von Choltitz explained that it was no longer possible to get supplies to the various strong-points around the city – indeed, no supplies were arriving in the city at all – and there was shooting everywhere. It was 'no longer feasible' to carry out Hitler's order for savage reprisals against the Resistance, he said, and it was equally impossible to destroy the bridges over the Seine as the German troops did not have access to them. Furthermore, he argued, any attempt to carry out this order would probably outrage the population and push them even further into the arms of the Resistance. Motivated by a mixture of loyalty and a determination to cover his back when faced with the inevitability of failure, von Choltitz insisted that this information be transmitted to Berlin.[57]

During the night, Model had a series of exchanges with his counterpart in Berlin, General Jodl.[58] Model emphasised that the situation in Paris was evolving so quickly that Hitler's orders could soon be outdated, to the extent that Berlin might have to brace itself for 'things turning out differently from what was expected'. In reply, Jodl simply stonewalled and said that the priority was to hold Paris. Slightly exasperated, Model responded that he wanted clear orders about how to defend Paris since this was impossible with the forces available. There were not enough explosives to blow up the bridges. Model did not understand Hitler's obsession with Paris and did not have the means to ensure that the Führer's orders were carried out.

Hitler's only gesture towards providing the Paris garrison with weapons had been made nine days earlier, when he ordered one of his new weapons – a mobile 38 cm assault mortar (effectively a large mortar on a tank chassis) – to be transported from Germany to 'help in the defence of Paris'.[59] The first three of these weapons had just trundled off the production line; the other two were sent to Warsaw, where they were used against the uprising. The Paris-bound weapon got lost somewhere along the way, and despite Hitler asking after its whereabouts 'several times a day', it never arrived.[60]

In such a confused military situation, the German commanders in the Paris region were increasingly at odds with each other. In the evening, the Luftwaffe chief of staff in France told von Choltitz that

Paris was to be bombed. Given that bombing raids were notoriously imprecise, and that the Allies had complete daytime air supremacy, the only option would be an inaccurate night-time raid which would undoubtedly lead to the deaths of many German soldiers. Von Choltitz stated that unless it could be guaranteed that his men would not be victims of 'friendly fire', he would have to withdraw them from the city – exactly what Hitler had told him not to do. The Luftwaffe's plans were shelved.[61]

A more violent verbal confrontation occurred when Field Marshal Model sent a blistering message to the commander of the 5th Panzer Regiment, complaining that the German counter-attack against the Allied bridgehead at Mantes had failed due to 'insufficient forces and inadequate fighting spirit', and blaming the 'neglect' shown by the commanders.[62] Less than an hour later, he received a stinging reply from General Sepp Dietrich, commander of the 1st SS Panzer Korps. Dietrich demanded to be relieved of his command and for Hitler to be informed. 'I am not a schoolboy who can be pushed around,' he spat.[63] But no matter how much his feathers were ruffled, Dietrich remained in command, and the Allies retained control of the bridgehead at Mantes, pouring men and machines eastwards towards Paris and the north of France while the Germans gradually retreated.

The Gestapo reconnaissance group that had been dispatched to the capital two days earlier to provide clandestine radio updates finally reached the Paris suburbs. But the leader of the eleven-man group, SS Captain Roland Nosek, considered that the situation was too dangerous and decided they would go no further. After a brief peek at the Porte de Vincennes and the Porte de Montreuil on the eastern edge of the city, the group scuttled off to the relative safety of Meaux to the east, before eventually running for cover on 28 August.[64]

*

At lunchtime, incredulous Parisians heard the Free French announce on the BBC that Paris had been liberated the day before: 'Yesterday, 22 August, after four days of fighting, the enemy was beaten everywhere. Patriots occupied all public buildings. The representatives of Vichy were arrested or were on the run. Thus the people of Paris took a determining role in the liberation of the capital.'[65] This carefully worded statement did not in fact say that the city was liberated, but rather that the Germans were 'beaten everywhere'. Nevertheless, the overall impression was clear and within minutes, the BBC Home Service announced in unambiguous terms 'Paris is free!' The 'news' flashed around the Western world and soon bells were ringing in celebration from Manchester to Quebec, and from London to New York. President Roosevelt issued a statement describing Paris as 'a precious symbol of that civilization which it was the aim of Hitler and his armed hordes to destroy', going on to 'rejoice with the gallant French people at the liberation of their capital'.[66] In London, the War Cabinet ordered a thanksgiving service to be celebrated in St Paul's Cathedral, while the Foreign Secretary, Antony Eden, stated: 'Every citizen of every free country has no doubt been moved by the news about Paris.' The Lord Mayor of London sent a telegram to General Koenig congratulating him on this 'supreme moment of victory', proclaiming that 'a world without Paris is inconceivable', while de Gaulle received a similar telegram from King George.[67] All around the world, people were delighted. The *New York Times* reported that 'Leading designers of women's clothing who have been independent of Paris leadership for the last four years were overjoyed . . . by the liberation of the great French city,' while department stores set up special displays in their windows, on the theme 'Paris is Free'.[68] Even Berlin was taken in by the news, telephoning Paris to ask for further information, only to be reassured that the Germans were still in control.[69]

French people outside of the capital were equally enthusiastic. In Lyons, still occupied by the Nazis, 20-year-old Denise Domenach wrote in her diary: 'Paris is free. As soon as anyone opens their mouth, they say these three words. We can't get over hearing them. The FFI have taken Paris. My father went to the cellar to fetch a good bottle of wine to celebrate the event . . . Paris is liberated, and by a curious ricochet, it is as though we are, too.'[70] In the tiny Belgian village of Wegnez, also still occupied by the Germans, Monsieur Baiverlin heard the news on the BBC and just sat there, tears running down his face and saying to himself: 'Paris is a beautiful city, a great city.' In Brussels, a housewife baked a special cake in celebration, with the words 'Long Live the Allies' on the top, while her 11-year-old son saw a neighbour weeping at the news and was struck by the realisation that 'old people cry too'.[71]

The bizarre announcement was no accident; it was carefully planned in London by Georges Boris of the Free French, although it is still not clear what exactly he hoped to achieve. For Jean-Louis Crémieux-Brilhac, who was one of the first people Boris consulted about the stunt, the intention was to underline the important role of the FFI in liberating the capital; Marcel Bleustein-Blanchet, who sanctioned the whole thing, felt it was a way of intimidating the Germans.[72] For General de Gaulle – who appears to have taken it in remarkably good spirits – the aim was to encourage the Americans to overcome their doubts about the need to liberate the capital.[73] None of these explanations seem particularly convincing, and the affair remains mysterious. Strictly speaking, it was the BBC newsroom that had over-interpreted the Free French broadcast, and the next day SHAEF would issue a categorical denial that Paris had been liberated. Predictably, this did not get anything like the same coverage.[74]

In Paris, journalist Edmond Dubois imagined the excitement and agitation that must have been gripping newsrooms all round the world, and then wondered how the Parisians were reacting.[75] We know, for all over the city, people were busy expressing their feelings in their diaries. They were not happy. With heavy understatement, Marc Boegner wrote: 'As much as we feel free again, we find all this a trifle premature.'[76] Berthe Auroy was bemused and assumed she had missed something: 'I clearly don't understand anything at all,' she wrote.[77] A friend of Micheline Bood's was 'furious': 'They are saying on the BBC that the bells are ringing to celebrate the liberation of Paris. But we know they aren't!'[78] Odette Lainville was simply scornful: 'Does London not know that our sons are still fighting, with such difficulty and against such odds, against the loathsome Hun?'[79] Victor Veau was curt, describing the announcement as 'madness, or stupidity, or politics'.[80] Paul Tuffrau underlined the uncertainty the report created: 'Listening to the news and at the same time hearing the sound of gunfire and the rumbling of artillery, one is stupefied. Can we believe the other news items?'[81] Jean Guéhenno, meanwhile, was incandescent: 'What do these lies mean?

248Who do they serve? The truth is far more important. Paris has rejected German control, it has given itself new free institutions and the price of this self-affirmation is being paid, every minute, in blood.'[82] Jean-Paul Sartre managed to combine irony and political insight:

> We listened to the broadcast, a friend and I, lying flat on the floor because a burst of firing had broken out around the building. As a result, we couldn't help thinking that for the Parisian population this announcement was somewhat surprising and even untimely. Paris was liberated, but it was impossible to leave the building; barricades blocked the rue de Seine where I live; a German tank squatted on the pont des Tuileries, pointing its gun barrel towards the Left Bank. However, shortly afterwards we thought about it and decided that if they announced that Paris was liberated, then it must mean that the Allied Command had decided to enter the city. Tomorrow they will be here.[83]

Sartre was right. They were on their way.

*

Shortly before midnight the previous evening, tank driver Gaston Eve and his comrades of the Leclerc Division, camped near Argentan, heard they were to head towards Paris the next morning. Enthusiasm and excitement swept through the division's camps. Eve's crew slept for a few hours around their Sherman tank, named *Montmirail* (a battle won by Napoleon), and then moved off in the early morning as part of a massive column, the tanks so close to each other that the crews' faces were blackened with diesel fumes. The crew of *Montmirail* soon noticed there was a smell of burning – the Sherman's tracks were covered in rubber that heated up as they drove over tarmac. Whenever possible the crews either stopped to throw water over the tracks, or drove through streams and puddles.[84]

Putting the 2e DB on the road was no easy matter. With over 16,000 men and more than 4000 vehicles (including 200 tanks), the column would stretch over 100 km, even if the vehicles were tightly packed. To make matters easier, the division headed eastwards along two parallel routes. In one of the vehicles was Gallois, the FFI officer whose information had helped persuade the Americans to change their plans and head for Paris. Early in the afternoon he had been given an American uniform and US Army dog-tags, supplied with a jeep and a driver, and told to head for the route the Leclerc column was taking. As he recalled a few weeks later:

> Pretty quickly we overtook the rearmost elements of the Leclerc Division and soon we were driving among the tanks and cars of the 2e DB. It was an extraordinary spectacle. Across fields, down roads, the Leclerc Division was charging towards Paris. The tanks were covered with flowers: the turrets were draped with daisy chains, the crews were cheering. We tore through a region that had been severely hit, where everything was marked by the fighting that had taken place a week earlier. Bodies and twisted metal littered the roads and the nearby fields; at some crossroads, destroyed German tanks were piled up to the treetops. Through these ruins, the 2e DB was rushing to the capital, singing enthusiastically, driving at 70 km per hour.[85]

The French soldiers may have revelled in their welcome, but Leclerc was criticised by the Americans for allegedly spending too long fraternising with the local populations. As General Bradley wrote later: 'The French 2d Armoured stumbled reluctantly through a Gallic wall as townsfolk along the line of march slowed the French advance with wine and celebration. Although I could not censure them, neither could I wait for them to dance their way to Paris.'[86]

In his memoirs, Bradley claimed that he decided to send US troops towards Paris because Leclerc's progress was so slow. In fact, the order given the previous day had clearly stated that the Leclerc Division was to be accompanied on its advance on Paris by the 4th US Infantry Corps, the 102nd Cavalry Group and the shadowy 'T-Force' (Target Force): a group of Allied intelligence operatives whose aim was to secure any enemy information – military, political or security-related – that could help the Allies.[87] After a successful 'pilot' during the liberation of Rome in June, T-Force was set up on 20 August, with Paris as its first objective.

A group of 115 Allied intelligence and counter-intelligence operatives was hastily assembled in Le Mans, and they too joined the column on the road to Paris.[88]

In the middle of the night, as the men and women of the Leclerc Division were trying to snatch some sleep by their vehicles, Rolf Nordling and his group of spies managed to get through the German lines in the first phase of their mission from von Choltitz to de Gaulle. There had been a tricky moment when they were nearly arrested on the outskirts of Versailles, escaping only because Bender was able to negotiate with the local German commander. Having seen the group safely across the lines, Bender then returned to Paris.[89] In the morning, Rolf Nordling and the four spies were taken by plane to see Patton, while Leclerc's tanks were revving their engines.[90] In his diary, General Patton described the arrival of the Rolf Nordling delegation in terms that contrast with his comradely (though unhelpful) attitude to Gallois thirty-six hours earlier: 'The brother of the Swedish Consul in Paris, a man named Ralf [sic] Nordling, and a group of other French individuals from Paris were in camp with a proposition. I immediately thought that they might be asking for a surrender [on the part of Germany] ... It turned out that these people simply wanted to get a suspension of hostilities in order to save Paris, and probably save some Germans. I sent them to Bradley.'[91]

There were probably two reasons for Patton's dismissive attitude. Firstly, the group brought no new information beyond that provided by Gallois the previous day – indeed, they were repeating the stories of a massive German troop presence that the Allies now knew were untrue. More importantly, unlike Gallois, who simply called on the Allies to send their troops as soon as possible, the delegation wanted the Allies to declare Paris an 'open city', thereby precluding a battle for the capital.[92] Nothing could have irritated the warrior Patton more. The mission was too late and its participants severely misjudged the outlook of the Allied leaders.

The sight of the Leclerc Division rumbling along the roads from Normandy impressed OSS agent Colonel Bruce, who described in his diary how he 'passed miles of tanks, trucks etc. of the Second Armoured Division ... these Frenchmen look extremely tough and fit'.[93] At the same time, Colonel de Guillebon's scouting group was heading back in the opposite direction from its bivouac at Arpajon, south of the capital. Because of a communications failure, de Guillebon had not received the news that the division was heading for Paris, and had dutifully followed orders and headed back to Rambouillet, where he arrived at about 09:00. As his group left Arpajon, they were taunted by passers-by who shouted: 'Where are you going? Are you leaving us? What about Paris?'[94] As soon as they arrived in Rambouillet, the group sent out two reconnaissance probes north-east towards Versailles, as they had been ordered. Colonel Bruce warned them that they could expect substantial opposition in that direction, and he was right. As one of the groups approached the outskirts of Versailles, a German tank shell hit the lead vehicle, an M8 Howitzer self-propelled gun named Le Sanglier (Wild Boar).[95] Three of the five crew members were killed. One of the survivors, gunner André Perry, recalled what happened:

I fired three shells at the German tanks. There were three shocks and then a fourth one, which was extremely violent. As I opened my mouth to ask the young gun-loader what was happening, he collapsed on top of me. At the same time, everything burst into flames and my comrades began to moan or scream. We had been hit. At the time I felt no pain, but there was blood running down my face and into my mouth. Despite my shouts and my exhortations, the gun-loader did not move from the turret. I grabbed him and pushed him out towards our comrades, who were behind the vehicle. Then I dived back in to try and get the driver and the radio operator. Because of the flames and exploding ammunition, I couldn't get to them. It felt like I was in hell; suffocating, and with my clothes on fire, I managed to get out. As I collapsed outside my eyes fell on a road sign that read: Paris, 36 km.[96]

General Leclerc arrived in Rambouillet at 13:00, and was immediately surrounded by a gaggle of American journalists. Colonel Bruce wrote in his diary: 'The correspondents are furious with Leclerc because he will not tell them his plans. He, in turn, is angry with them and with reason, for they are looking for a story and he is trying to make plans to capture Paris.'[97] In the late afternoon, General de Gaulle arrived in Rambouillet, having travelled from Le Mans, overtaking the Leclerc Division column as he went, acclaimed by the crowds of excited French men and women along the way. During a brief meeting, de Gaulle approved Leclerc's plans for taking the capital, and closed with words that gave some hint of the turmoil of emotion and excitement that must have been churning beneath his notoriously glacial manner: 'You are very lucky.'[98]

Leclerc's plan involved two lines of attack – one from the west using troops based at Rambouillet, the other from the south. Among the groups chosen for the more southerly route was one commanded by a stocky 36-year-old, Captain Raymond Dronne, and which included young Gaston Eve. They managed to get as far as Limours before bivouacking as a massive thunderstorm broke over their heads.[99] They did not care about the appalling weather: that night, Free French tanks were less than twenty-five kilometres from the capital.[100]

*

As night fell, Edmond Dubois reflected on the day's events and ultimately gave his approval to the BBC's strange claim that the city was already free:

> In front of my windows, to the south-east, there is another extremely violent thunderstorm. The sound of cannon fire is drowned by this celestial racket. In the flashes of lightning, I can make out Paris, which has been proclaimed as liberated, huddled in its isolation and ignorance, fearing the worst, fighting on the barricades, without transport, light, or food, a Paris streaming with rain, a Paris turned in on itself, a Paris desperately waiting for the Allies. And yet, tonight, listening to the radio or reading the newspaper, the farmer in Texas, the Swiss mountain dweller, the fisherman in Madagascar, the shopkeeper in Saigon or the notary in Carpentras will feel their heart beating joyously as they whisper 'Paris is liberated'.[101]

13

Thursday 24 August, Day:
Battle

Matthew Halton, an embedded Canadian correspondent, broadcasts from the Paris suburbs: 'Wherever we drive, in the areas west and south-west of the capital, people shout: "Look, they are going to Paris!" But then we run into pockets of resistance here or there and are forced to turn back. It's clear that we are seeing the disintegration of the German Army – but we never know when we are going to be shot at. There are still some units of the German Army, fanatical men of the SS or armoured divisions, who are willing to fight to the last man. They are moving here and there all over this area, trying to coalesce into strong fighting forces . . . The people everywhere are tense with emotion. Their love of freedom is so very deep, and a nightmare is lifting from their lives; and history races down the roads towards Paris.'[1]

At 06:30, radio technician Pierre Schaeffer was woken by the sound of a familiar voice coming from the radio set. It was his colleague Bertrand d'Astorg on the early morning shift at the Resistance radio station. Without any experience in front of the microphone, and without a script, Bertrand was speaking to Paris as though to a friend: 'The studio is asleep,' murmured d'Astorg. 'My colleagues are all in bed and I don't really know what I am doing. Day is breaking. In the distance I can hear bursts of machine-gun fire. Fighting has already broken out again around some of the barricades. The studio smells of stale cigarette smoke . . .'[2] Outside, it was raining heavily and the streets were wet. The gunfire d'Astorg could hear on the clammy early morning air turned out to be an isolated incident, as the bad weather seemed to dampen everyone's spirits.[3] A few hours later, Professor Victor Veau wrote in his diary: 'It is raining. There is no one in the streets, there is no sound of firing.'[4] At lunchtime, 18-year-old Jean-Claude Touche noted: 'Rainy morning; up until 13:00, nothing to report.'[5] Meanwhile, Yves Cazaux received a telephone call from his superior in the Resistance, ordering him to help set up a counter-intelligence service in Paris. With that he stopped writing his diary; being part of history was understandably more important than recording it.[6]

With no fighting to report on, journalist Claude Roy spent the morning at the Hôtel-Dieu, the hospital just opposite the Préfecture de Police. Medical students and stretcher-bearers were working around the clock to tend the wounded on both sides. At lunchtime, Georges Bidault made an official visit; after giving a brief speech to the medical staff and touring the wards full of injured French people, he then went into the German ward and spoke magnanimously to the wounded troops: 'German soldiers! I am the leader of the French Resistance, and I have come to wish you a good recovery. Let us meet again in the future, once Europe and Germany have both been liberated.'[7] Outside, one of Marc Boegner's friends saw a young woman selling tricolour bouquets of flowers. 'What's going on?' he asked. 'Today we will become French once more,' she replied.[8]

The tension returned as the day wore on and the rain eased. The German troops in the barracks on the place de la République made repeated forays towards the barricades in the 11th arrondissement and fired artillery rounds at Resistance forces on the rue du Faubourg du Temple and the boulevard Voltaire. The Faubourg du Temple barricade was briefly overrun by the Germans but the Resistance managed to regain the lost ground after fierce fighting with grenades and Molotov cocktails.[9] At the square du Temple, a two-car German patrol shot at a group of *résistants* who fired back, killing an officer, wounding two soldiers and destroying one of the vehicles. Six soldiers fled the second car and took refuge in a building overlooking the square; for nearly three hours there was an intense firefight that lasted until a German armoured car came and rescued the soldiers.[10]

There were also violent confrontations in the southern part of the

1. Marshal Pétain addresses the crowd at the Hôtel de Ville, April 1944.

2. The Champs-Elysées, June 1944.

3. Micheline Bood, 1944.

4. Odette Lainville.

5. Private Walter Dreizner, 1944.

6. Jean-Claude Touche, 1944.

7. 'Chaban' – General Jacques Delmas, 1945.

8. Colonel 'Rol', 1944.

9. Raoul Nordling, consul of Sweden, 1944.

10. General Dietrich von Choltitz, 1944.

11. The 'Rochambelles' medical group about to embark for France, August 1944.

12. Jedburgh Team AUBREY about to leave for France, August 1944.
L to R: US airman, WAAF, Hooker, Chaigneau, Marchant (hidden),
US airman.

13. The liberation of the Mairie of the 17th arrondissement, Batignolles, Paris; 19 August.

14. Resistance fighters inside the Préfecture de Police.

15. FFI fighters. The car contains at least one captured German soldier.

16. FFI fighters inside the Hôtel de Ville; the figure in the background appears to be Léo Hamon.

17. Building a barricade.

18. FFI fighters at the Hôtel de Ville. The man second from the right is wearing a policeman's badge.

19. Resistance fighters in Batignolles with a captured German tank.

20. The crowd at Batignolles swamps a small German tank destroyer, 20 August.
Inset: Georges Dukson atop the vehicle.

21. The courtyard of the Préfecture de Police. The lorry is towing the German anti-tank gun that was captured on 21 August.

22. The front page of *Franc-Tireur*, 23 August.

23. General Leclerc (second from left) orders Captain Dronne (left) to head for Paris, 24 August. On the far right is Lieutenant-Colonel de la Horie.

24. The tanks of the Dronne column arrive at the Hôtel de Ville and are lit up by flares, 24 August.

25. On the morning of 25 August, Captain Dronne consults a map of Paris with a Resistance fighter, on the place de l'Hôtel de Ville.

26. FFI fighters in Paris, 25 August. The woman is Simone Segouin; she had come from Chartres to help liberate the capital.

27. A soldier of the
2e DB greets a child
in Paris, 25 August.

28. General
Leclerc (centre)
in his command
car, avenue de
Maine, 25 August.
Slightly hidden
behind Leclerc is
Chaban.

29. German prisoners shot dead at the Arc de Triomphe, 25 August. The soldier on the left is Jacques Desbordes.

30. German prisoners stream out of the Hôtel Meurice, 25 August.

31. Gare Montparnasse, 25 August. L to R: de Chevigné, de Gaulle, Leclerc, Juin, Chaban, Rol.

32. Arc de Triomphe, 26 August. L to R: Bidault, de Gaulle, Parodi, Dukson.

33. Crowds at the place de la Concorde, 26 August.

34. Parisians shelter from the firing at the place de la Concorde, 26 August.

35. Picasso and Lee Miller in Picasso's studio, August 1944.

36. Parisians on the Champs-Elysées, 26 August.

city. At 17:00, there was heavy fighting around the Cambronne Métro station, and a number of FFI fighters were killed, included 37-year-old Charles Mainini, shot while trying to help a wounded comrade.[11] The 300 or so Germans holed up in the Senate were defended by twelve tanks, including four large Panthers – some of which were apparently used in a battle with the FFI around the rue de Grenelle. Swiss journalist Edmond Dubois reported: 'From a doorway that is miraculously sheltering me from this battle, I can see the tanks in action around 100 metres away. The tremendous noise of shells being fired echoes around the narrow street where I am, while the blast fills the street and smacks into your face. It gives an amazing impression of force and power; there is the overwhelming smell of gunpowder. Despite all this, a housewife trots up and asks me if the corner shop is open.'[12] A kilometre or so away there was a fierce firefight on the southern edge of the Jardin du Luxembourg. Earlier in the day, the Germans had destroyed their blockhouse in the neighbourhood. They were focusing all their resources on a handful of strong-points; they knew the decisive battle was about to begin.

Just down the road, Albert Grunberg saw the FFI take on two large tanks on the rue des Ecoles. His building shook as shells were fired. Despite being terrified, he decided to go and join the FFI. On his way to the local headquarters, he stopped to call in on some neighbours, only to find that the FFI were interrogating his friend, who had been denounced as a collaborator in an anonymous letter. Grunberg managed to convince the FFI to release his friend, partly by pointing out the deranged stupidity of the accusatory letter.[13] Then the FFI turned their attention to Grunberg and asked him for his papers. He had none. Or rather, as he readily admitted, his papers were fake. 'That's all right,' said the FFI leader breezily, 'ours are fake, too.' Grunberg and his friend were soon given FFI armbands, but not guns. There were not enough to go round.[14]

There was intense fighting in the northern quarters as the Germans tried to escape in convoys along the main roads heading eastwards, or sought vainly to flee from the Gare de l'Est or the Gare du Nord, where there were no trains. By the end of the afternoon, the FFI had taken control of the stations and had captured prisoners and heavy machine guns.[15] In the 20th arrondissement, on the eastern edge of the city, 28-year-old Henri Louvigny was part of an FFI group harassing German troop lorries leaving the city. The Germans threw grenades at their attackers; Henri tried to throw one back, but it blew up in his hand and he was killed.[16] On the other side of the city there was fighting in the well-to-do area near Victor Veau's apartment, with the rattle of Resistance rifle fire alternating with the sound of German grenades and tank shells.[17] The lack of coffins meant that funeral services had to be postponed, and temporary morgues were set up.[18] First-aider Jean-Claude Touche was sent to one of these morgues, in a concert hall on the rue de la Boétie. It affected the young man deeply: 'There were six bodies, each covered with a sheet, except one which has not yet been identified – it had no papers and was horribly disfigured. The head was split open so you could see the brains, and there was a big hole in the stomach.'[19]

At around the same time, three of the gendarmes who were held by the SS at Vincennes were freed in a prisoner exchange.[20] The remaining men, together with another thirty or so prisoners, were eventually allowed to leave later in the evening, as the SS evacuated the fort.[21]

*

The rumours that the Allies were about to reach Paris were becoming increasingly precise and believable. Charles Lacretelle read in *Combat* that 'an Allied column of about 30,000 men and 300 tanks has occupied Arpajon and is marching towards Paris.'[22] Paul Tuffrau saw a duplicated poster on the window of the closed Métro station at Saint-Placide, near the Jardin du Luxembourg, which declared that the Leclerc Division was at Arpajon, together with two US divisions from New Orleans, who spoke French![23] FFI headquarters were equally confident, but then again their information was more accurate: they had sent out two scouts – one to the south, the other to the west. Both scouts talked to local Resistance fighters who had been in direct contact with Allied troops, confirming that the German forces were relatively sparse. FFI intelligence correctly concluded that 'the divisions of General Leclerc are coming into Paris on the road from Orléans.'[24] This was verified as the day went on, and in the late afternoon the FFI staff learnt that the Allies were advancing in an arc across the southern suburbs that passed through Antony, Fresnes, Orly and le Petit-Clamart.[25]

The Allied advance was not straightforward. In the morning, Gallois finally met up with General Leclerc near Longjumeau, which was now in Free French hands. The Germans were defending tenaciously and already two of the 2e DB's tanks had been destroyed. Leclerc spoke tersely to Gallois: 'Your information was wrong. We are encountering a well-organised defence.' Gallois felt responsible, but the real issue was not so much the strength of the German troops as their location: many of the makeshift anti-tank weapons were in urban sites. These positions commanded the main approach roads to the capital; the surrounding civilian population made it impossible for the French to use artillery or aerial bombardment to eliminate the gun batteries.[26] As a result, progress was slower than anyone expected, including General de Gaulle, who had sent a top-secret telegram to the government in Algiers announcing that he would be in Paris that evening.[27]

Leclerc deployed his men in three task forces. The main attack on the capital was to come from the south, under Colonel Billotte, protected on its eastern flank by the 4th US Infantry. Another group, commanded by Colonel de Langlade, was to approach from the southwest. The third task force was to distract the Germans and head for Versailles and then the western part of the capital. Photographs of the 2e DB's advance through Longjumeau that morning show a drizzly day, with groups of residents standing outside their doors or leaning from their windows while an eclectic group of tanks, half-tracks, jeeps and even amphibious vehicles drive down cobbled streets slick with rain, draped with sodden tricolour flags.[28]

In the morning, the new Paris Prefect of Police, Luizet, telephoned the Longjumeau gendarmerie and talked to one of Leclerc's staff officers. Luizet urged the division to make haste, as the Préfecture was running out of ammunition.[29] Chaban also got a message to Leclerc, via Lieutenant Petit-Leroy who managed to pass through the sparse enemy lines and get to Longjumeau. Petit-Leroy told Leclerc that Hitler had given the order to destroy the city, and described the situation of the Resistance as dire, emphasising how few weapons they had. He then claimed that 'the Communist Party and its allies are determined to seize the initiative and set up a "Paris Commune" – a kind of revolutionary government.'[30] How they were to do this with so few weapons was not explained. Unable to change the situation immediately, Leclerc dictated a letter to von Choltitz in which the German general was told he would be held personally responsible if Paris was destroyed. Petit-Leroy was to take the message back to Paris and ensure it was communicated to von Choltitz. But the message did not get through: on his return to the city, Petit-Leroy was killed by a German patrol.[31]

Despite the proximity of the Allies – in fact, precisely because liberation was apparently so close – the tensions between the Free French Delegation and the Resistance leadership became acute. The jostling for position could only continue for a matter of hours, and those hours might be decisive for the future of France. Far from Paris, General Koenig, the nominal head of the FFI and the newly appointed Military Governor of the capital, was well aware of the stakes, and tried to reassert Gaullist control over the police force ahead of the arrival of the Leclerc Division. At 10:55, Chaban received this message from Koenig: 'Due to imminent arrival in Paris of Allied troops and members of Provisional Government, essential to put all police forces under direction of Prefect. Police elements fighting in ranks of FFI must be immediately put at disposition of Prefect. Will advise Prefect directly. In friendship. See you soon. Koenig.'[32]

Luizet immediately put the order into effect; policemen were withdrawn to the Préfecture and neither arms nor men were sent to the barricades in the south of the city despite urgent requests from Colonel Lizé and de Vogüé. This triggered yet another row at a meeting of COMAC that morning, although Chaban quickly defused the matter by suggesting that only one third of the police should be transferred to Luizet's command. Koenig apparently feared that the Resistance was planning to seize power, and wanted to regain control over the police and strengthen the Prefect's hand. Chaban had no such worries – indeed, he argued that the FFI should be at the forefront of the welcoming party for the Leclerc Division.[33] Chaban's approach was more astute because he was convinced that neither the Resistance nor the Communist Party would try to take power. But he showed his hand too much when he informally suggested that the three Vs – Valrimont, de Vogüé and Villon – should all be given the rank of general in the Free French Army, as part of the incorporation of COMAC into the Ministry of War. This rather transparent attempt to buy support was politely rejected.[34]

*

In the early afternoon, certain that liberation was close, Parodi summoned all the secretary-generals to the Préfecture de Police so they would be there to welcome 'the General'. René Courtin, Secretary-General for the Economy, dashed across town, unsure whether he was going to meet Leclerc or de Gaulle. When he got to the Préfecture he was amazed by the bustle: 'German lorries, FFIers, guards in uniform. The whole of the Delegation is there, as well as most of the Secretary-Generals and Chaban.'[35] But the General did not arrive, and as Courtin noted wearily, 'the day wore on, broken only by the sound of machine-gun fire.' Meanwhile, on the other side of the Seine, the members of the Conseil National de la Résistance and the Comité Parisien de la Libération turned up at the Hôtel de Ville, also to wait for the General. They, too, were unsure which general they should expect.[36]

For four years, the Resistance and the Free French had held contrasting views about the fight against the Nazis and the collaborators. Although they were united by the desire to drive out the Germans, each side had its own aims, objectives and methods. With their military/administrative approach, the Gaullists were more focused, but for most of the war they had also been weaker – they were completely dependent on the Allies. The Resistance may have had forces on the ground, but their views were varied and sometimes incoherent, although the one thing that united them in their opposition to Nazi Germany was their recognition of Charles de Gaulle as figurehead. Now, as the moment of victory beckoned, that political division took a clear geographical form, as the two forces were separated by only a few hundred metres and the waters of the Seine. The Free French, who represented the unfolding Gaullist state, naturally felt at home with the most visible representation of state power and order in the city – the police. For Parodi and Chaban, the Préfecture was the perfect place to welcome the liberating forces of the Free French Army and stamp the seal of Gaullist authority on the new France. The CNR and the Resistance, with all their varied and contradictory views, were expressions of the self-sacrificing, popular and insurrectionary movement that had seen tens of thousands die in fighting across the country, and which had reached its paroxysm in the Paris insurrection. For the Resistance, the Hôtel de Ville, with its powerful, centuries-old revolutionary tradition that resonated in the minds of all Parisians – indeed, the minds of all French citizens – was the natural place to be.

Because the Resistance radio was controlled by the Ministry of Information, not by the Resistance, the radio station dispatched a mobile studio to the Préfecture de Police, not the Hôtel de Ville. All afternoon, those Parisians lucky enough to have electricity heard a series of Free French figures present their view of the events of the previous ten days, not so much rewriting history as writing it as it took place. Without a trace of irony, Parodi (who remained anonymous) praised the Parisian population for its enthusiastic participation in the insurrection, and claimed that through the uprising the city had proved itself 'worthy of General de Gaulle'. Then there were two speeches emphasising the role of the police – Luizet claimed that the population and the police would be forever bound in mutual respect, while the new head of the municipal police, Bayet, explained how the police had launched the occupation of the Préfecture to be in the vanguard of the fighting. Pisani (Luizet's chief of staff) brazenly justified his support for the cease-fire, simultaneously arguing that it was a success because the Germans acknowledged the Resistance as the government in the city, and that it had merely been a ruse to gain time. Well-informed listeners must have been surprised by the enthusiasm these men proclaimed for the insurrection they had done so much to restrain.[37]

*

In the afternoon the rain stopped, and the weather became unbearable. Sitting at his window, Victor Veau noted: 'The road is quiet and utterly deserted – it is very hot.'[38] The close atmosphere added to the growing tension. Berthe Auroy heard so much shouting in the street that she thought the Americans had arrived. She raced down the stairs only to find that the excitement was caused by a case of head-shaving.[39] Paranoid rumours – not necessarily unjustified – began to run rife. Paul Tuffrau's neighbours heard that the Germans had mined the nearby Senate building and were about to blow it up. Similar announcements were made later in the evening by the air-raid wardens.[40] In the evening, FFI headquarters heard that the Germans were preparing to destroy the main telephone exchange on the rue des Archives, but were prevented from doing so by a German communist soldier who was in contact with the Resistance.[41] Odette Lainville expressed a widespread feeling of unease when she wrote in her diary: 'It feels like we are sitting on a volcano! Were the Huns not moving around in the sewers last night? What were they doing down there? Have they planted explosives?'[42]

As the final moment approached, Rol ordered the FFI to prevent acts of pillage, which were becoming widespread. Anyone caught pillaging was to be immediately executed and a sign reading 'pillager' was to be hung on the corpse.[43] As the tension grew, there was the potential for tragic mistakes. Daniel Boisdon and his family were having lunch when there was a knock at the door. When his daughter answered, a man pushed a revolver under her nose and barged his way in, a grenade in his left hand. Behind him there was another man with a submachine gun, a string of grenades at his belt. Horrified, Boisdon stared at them with his coffee cup in his hand. The men were chasing someone who had been firing from Boisdon's building over the last few days, and they had gone up the wrong staircase. Although they laughed off their mistake, they nevertheless cast a quick eye over the apartment, including lifting up the sheet that protected the bath full of precious drinking water, before leaving sheepishly.[44]

Not far away, Pablo Picasso began work on a watercolour and gouache version of the ink drawing of Poussin's *The Triumph of Pan* that he had made the previous day. He sang loudly as he worked, drowning out the sounds of gunfire that rattled the windows of the Ile Saint-Louis apartment. Despite its classical theme, the exuberant painting was clearly inspired by the events taking place in the street below, and by the tension and excitement that everyone felt.[45] Poussin's mountainous backdrop was transformed into an urban setting of grey walls and square shapes, like those of the tomato plant paintings of two weeks earlier. Picasso amplified the main colour notes in Poussin's original (pink, flesh and blue) to red, white and blue, the colours of the tricolour flag. A group of characters that in Poussin's rural version were a putto and a satyr helping a drunken Pan to his feet were transformed into a figure wearing a red revolutionary cap, protecting a man who was helping a stricken comrade.[46] The war had decisively got into Picasso's art, transforming his work. Through the power of his unique vision, it had also transformed a 300-year-old masterpiece.

A few days later, Picasso was visited by Squadron-Leader John Pudney, the RAF intelligence officer and poet. Picasso told the young man that he had created his version of Poussin's painting as 'an exercise, a self-discipline, a healthy fascination'.[47] But above all, Picasso underlined the significance of the date the work had been started – the prelude to liberation. That liberation was clearly signified in the background to the painting, where Poussin's pale twilight had become a radiant sunrise.

*

The German defences west of Paris were crumbling. A planned air attack against the Allied bridgehead at Mantes did not take place because the requisite support from the Parachute Regiment failed to materialise. In fact, the regiment did not hear of the order until the morning – the staff officer carrying the instruction was ambushed by Resistance fighters during the night and got lost, then his vehicle broke down and he had to wait until daybreak before proceeding.[48] In the mid-afternoon, General von Aulock gathered commanders from all the combat zones around Paris to discuss the situation. He decided to destroy the bridges over the Seine at Colombes and Bezons north-west of Paris, but had neither the men nor the equipment he needed.[49] In the late afternoon, German troops began to pull out of Versailles, but they were harassed by the Resistance and by the advancing Allies, and fighting continued into the night.[50] As an indication of how German commanders in the field saw the coming battle, von Aulock moved his battle group headquarters from Saint-Germain-en-Laye on the western side of the city to Le Bourget on the northern flank. The secondary line of defence that General Model had wanted to create to the north and east of Paris was beginning to become a reality.

As the German retreat became increasingly disorganised, they left behind vital supplies. The substantial stock of torpedo warheads in the tunnel under the hill at Saint-Cloud was initially intended to destroy the Paris bridges; now it was supposed to be either removed or destroyed. In a brief message, Admiral Kracke reported that because of the growing insurgency, it was 'almost impossible' for him to transport the torpedo heads from Saint-Cloud. The army was welcome to take the explosives, he said, but he thought it 'doubtful' that it would be able to do the job, either. And with that he fled Paris.[51] The torpedoes were neither removed nor detonated – Colonel Kurt Hesse, one of von Aulock's officers, left Saint-Cloud in the middle of the night without carrying out an order to destroy the torpedoes.[52]

Von Choltitz knew little of this – he was cut off from the southern defences, and could not even contact the strong-points around the city by telephone.[53] Von Aulock had warned him that a massive Allied attack was expected in the morning, but the German commander of Paris did not know what was happening at the front. It was therefore hardly surprising that dissent began to appear in the German ranks. The previous day, one of von Choltitz's staff officers had argued that the Germans should leave the city, as they would be unable to resist the Allied onslaught. Furious at this challenge to his authority, von Choltitz called a meeting of all his senior officers, and gave them their final orders. To leave the city would be to lose their honour, he said, and anyway it would be impossible to organise an orderly retreat.[54] Instead, he expected his men to do the 'honourable' thing and fight on.

Not all Germans saw things this way. Walter Dreizner was ready to roll; his bags were packed and the order in which his unit's vehicles would leave the city had been decided. 'The only thing missing is our marching orders,' he wrote impatiently in his diary.[55] Quartermaster Robert Wallraf was equally unenthusiastic about making a stand. Together with the rest of the administration, he had moved from the Senate building and was now on the other side of the Seine, hunkered down in the Hôtel Crillon on the place de la Concorde, listening to the sound of gunfire coming from the Champs-Elysées. Eckelmann, the head of the German administration, came into the hotel and told his men that von Choltitz was infuriated that the Resistance newspapers were openly on sale, and that the city's walls were covered with declarations. Von Choltitz's annoyance was quite understandable. *L'Humanité* intimidated the German troops with screaming headlines: 'EVERYONE GET A HUN! CONSOLIDATE THE BARRICADES! UNION IN BATTLE! FIGHT LIKE LIONS. ARM YOURSELVES BY DISARMING THE ENEMY. TO ARMS! TO ARMS! TO ARMS!'[56] The Préfecture adopted a slightly different approach as it produced hundreds of posters printed in German: 'German soldiers, surrender! Your leaders have already surrendered.'[57] If no other solution could be found, said Eckelmann, then tanks would have to be sent to destroy the newspaper printworks around the rue Réaumur. 'No one should think they will be able to escape from defending Paris,' said Eckelmann, ominously. However, not all the tasks were frightening or dangerous: Wallraf was simply told to listen to the Resistance radio station in case he learnt something important.[58]

*

To the south of the capital, Allied progress was slow as the scattered German defences held out. South of Versailles, Free French Sherman tanks were destroyed by German anti-tank guns at Toussus le Noble and at Buc, while there was a fierce firefight in the aptly named forest of l'Homme Mort (the Dead Man), where a German 88 mm anti-aircraft gun was holding up progress. A Sherman tank piloted by Jean Zagrodzki managed to destroy the gun with two shells. Zagrodzki's tank – named after his brother, who had been killed in Normandy two weeks earlier – then proceeded north until it approached the main road to Versailles. At 14:00 the tank came to a halt, and suddenly the whole forest exploded as armour-piercing shells and grenades crashed onto the machine over and over again. A camouflaged German motorised anti-aircraft gun was no more than twenty metres away and was firing at almost point-blank range. The Sherman fired back and began to reverse but it became stuck against a tree stump; the motors overheated and the tank stopped moving. It was a sitting duck. Over forty shells hit the vehicle, and as the crew leapt out, Jean Zagrodzki was killed outright along with two of his comrades. The German gun was soon destroyed by Free French reinforcements, who reduced the enemy weapon to a heap of twisted metal and either killed or captured its crew.[59]

US journalist John MacVane was with Leclerc during the fighting near Fresnes, a couple of kilometres east of Antony. A small German anti-tank weapon was positioned in a drain and was firing from pavement level, making it impossible for a French Sherman tank to lower its barrel sufficiently to destroy it. The tank was hit several times, without too much damage, before a group of French infantrymen approached the drain and threw in grenades, ending the German resistance. Meanwhile, the local population was enthusiastic, as MacVane recalled: 'The people of the suburb were so happy that they seemed incapable of staying out of the way of the battle. They could not comprehend that their homes and their streets were the front line.'[60] Veteran journalist Ernie Pyle had observed this behaviour by French locals a number of times: 'You would have tense soldiers crouching in ditches and firing from behind low walls. And in the middle of it you would have this Frenchman, in faded blue overall and beret and with a nearly burned-up cigarette in his mouth, come striding down the middle of the road.'[61]

Sometimes the locals were rather too enthusiastic. The 'Rochambelle' ambulance group drove into Arpajon as night was falling; a girl jumped onto the running-board of Suzanne Torrès' ambulance, stuck her head through the window into the dark cabin and said to Torrès, 'Kiss me!' Suzanne gave her a peck on the cheek. 'Not like that,' said the girl in a husky voice. 'Happy to oblige,' replied Torrès, 'but I'm a woman.' The girl let out a shriek and jumped to the ground.[62]

The presence of German 88 mm cannons along the road from Longjumeau meant that the Free French task force advanced in fits and starts. Eventually a substantial traffic jam built up, as hundreds of vehicles began to block the main route and the side-roads, unable to advance until the Germans had been dealt with. At one point Colonel Bruce of OSS, along with Hemingway and his rag-tag band of fighters, was forced to wait by a munitions dump that began exploding after a tank shell hit it. Bruce was alarmed: 'The crackle of small arms ammunition, tracer bullets, and the heavy roar of larger stuff exploding was not only annoying but quite dangerous, as missiles were whizzing by in every direction. We finally passed within a few yards of the edge of the dump, and I for one found this part of the journey terrifying.'[63] As they crawled towards the capital, they were repeatedly mobbed by the population, kissed and given fruit, flowers and drink. Bruce wrote in his diary: 'We yelled ourselves hoarse, shouting "Vive la France" as we passed through the crowds. Everyone thrust drinks at us that they had been hoarding for this occasion. The combination was enough to wreck one's constitution. In the course of the afternoon we had beer, cider, white and red Bordeaux, white and red Burgundy, champagne, rum, whiskey, cognac, Armagnac and Calvados.'[64] The joyous advance came to a halt about a mile from Paris, as the tanks found themselves engaged in a hard battle with some Germans sheltered in a factory building. With the Eiffel Tower literally in sight, they could do nothing but wait.

RAF intelligence officer and poet John Pudney was also caught up in the advance:

Late that evening we followed French armoured columns through a lush suburban countryside south of Paris. 'If you see a place without the flags out,' we were told, 'you'll know that you're getting the wrong side of the line.' Down the road a bunch of Luftwaffe ground staff came marching in bare feet over the cobbles. A boy in a fireman's helmet of shining brass flourished a revolver and gave them 'left, right, left, right' in ever-increasing tempo. He explained that he was sixteen years old, that he had captured the Germans with two school friends, that he was now in a hurry to get home because his mother didn't know he was out. We stopped and, in the shadows of a wooded defile, found the overnight headquarters of General Leclerc. Fires burned; there were barricades in the village; the FFI, youthful in their bandoliers, accompanied by tricolour-decked vivandières, fraternised with the tough, joyful troops Leclerc brought out of Africa. The master race, hobbling by, was booed. It was the Revolution again . . .[65]

Thursday 24 August, Evening: Arrival

A journalist for Franc-Tireur, one of the main Resistance newspapers, writes: 'As we approach the capital, the atmosphere becomes utterly extraordinary. As the capital gets closer, the soldiers can no longer hide their joy, which they express by clumsy, large childlike gestures that are so moving. They blow kisses, and with the backs of their rough hands they dry cheeks that are wet with tears. They are surprised, and somewhat embarrassed, by the marvellous privilege they have been given by destiny. Rising up on the horizon before them they can see the beautiful indented profile of the city, the sky still pink from the last glimmer of the sun.'[1]

In the late afternoon, General Leclerc was stuck in the centre of Antony, frustrated by the lack of movement. He knew that the US commanders were becoming impatient – General Barton of the 4th Infantry Division had just been ordered 'to force a way into the city as rapidly as possible.'[2] This impatience was understandable, but any implied criticism of the 2e DB's progress was unfair. A British intelligence report noted that 'the French Armoured Division is moving into Paris ... Those enemy elements ... in the way ... have been very roughly handled indeed.'[3] The price that had been paid by the 2e DB that day was not small: 71 dead and 225 wounded, with the loss of 35 armoured vehicles.[4]

Nevertheless, under pressure from General Gerow to continue his advance that night and perhaps fearful that the US might enter the city first, Leclerc took decisive action.[5] A small Piper reconnaissance aircraft was sent towards Paris, hopping over the rooftops. The plane's crew – pilot Captain Jean Callet and observer Lieutenant Etienne Mantout – were told to drop a message into the courtyard of the Préfecture de Police, which was much more difficult than it sounded. As the plane approached the building, Callet pitched the nose down and the plane plunged into a steep dive. At the last moment, Callet pulled out of the dive and Mantout threw down a small weighted bag containing the message, then the plane turned back home, dodging flak and bullets.[6] Mantout did not quite reach his target – the bag with its bright gold streamer fell just outside the Préfecture, on the corner of the quai du Marché Neuf. Scribbled on an official US Army telegram form, the message was simple: 'General Leclerc says: Hold on, we're coming.'[7]

To back up that promise, Leclerc found Captain Dronne, whose 9th Company of Mechanised Infantry was heading south, away from Paris, to avoid the traffic jam that was building up. 'What the hell are you doing, Dronne?' snapped Leclerc. 'Heading south, sir,' replied Dronne, 'I was given an order, sir.' 'You should never obey a stupid order,' said Leclerc.[8] And with that the stocky captain was instructed to assemble a column rapidly: 'Quickly, get whatever forces you can ... Head straight for Paris. Go by whatever route you want. Tell the Parisians and the Resistance not to lose their nerve, and that tomorrow the whole Division will be in Paris.'[9]

The 9th Company – some parts of which were still far south of Antony, stuck in the giant traffic jam – was nicknamed 'La Nueve' ('Nine' in Spanish) because 146 of its 160 members were either of Spanish origin or were Spanish exiles. Most of them were communists or anarchists who had fought in the Civil War, and they were allowed to wear the Spanish Republican flag on their Free French uniform. In a very public declaration of their origins, five of the vehicles in La Nueve were named after Spanish Civil War battles or leaders.[10] To complement his half-tracks, Dronne requisitioned three Sherman tanks – *Romilly*, *Champaubert* and Gaston Eve's *Montmirail*. In the gathering twilight, the twenty-two vehicles and 150 men set off for the capital at around 20:00, with Dronne's jeep leading the column.[11] Taking side roads, and avoiding the Germans' makeshift but effective anti-tank weapons, they moved rapidly northwards without meeting any opposition. Dronne decided they would head for the Hôtel de Ville because, as he later put it, 'it was the heart of the capital and the symbol of Parisian and national liberties.'[12]

*

All through the day, Parisians had heard that the Leclerc Division was coming to the capital. Now it appeared to be true. The progress of the Dronne column was feverishly followed in the newly created newsrooms of the Resistance newspapers and broadcast by the radio station. Telephone calls came in from contacts in the southern suburbs, heightening the journalists' greatest fear – that they might miss the most momentous event in the city's history. Shortly after 18:00, journalist René Dunan and a couple of his colleagues piled into a car and went off to find the Leclerc Division, zigzagging past the barricades, driving alongside crowds of men, women and children who all seemed to be heading in the same direction.[13]

In less than an hour Dronne and his men were at the place d'Italie in southern Paris, by which point the crowd was so dense that the vehicles could barely move. René Dunan and his colleagues found themselves caught up in the mêlée: 'About 30 metres away I can see a tank, immobile, covered in people. In an effort to hold on, people are grasping each other, limbs are intertwined, heads close together. The crowd around the tank wave their arms, scream their lungs out, use any means they can to show their elation … The young soldiers, in khaki uniforms, their American helmets tipped back on their heads, their faces tanned, deep rings around their eyes, are stunned and astonished by the welcome.'[14] One of those soldiers was the driver of *Montmirail*, Gaston Eve:

We were being kissed on our faces and on our berets as so many people were totally overwhelmed by the madness of the moment. Our blackened faces were soon smeared with lipstick. People were giving us bottles of wine and these were put away in the tank safely. We gave away packets of biscuits, little bits of our survival rations of chocolate and of course we returned the kisses being given us and hugged the people we were fighting for ... To open up a path through the crowd the Lieutenant decided to give some blasts of the siren while advancing very gently. I started to tell those on and around the tank that they must get off and those round about started pushing and shouting 'Get off!' That proved effective and we started to see clear ahead of us. We departed behind *Romilly* very slowly because the way through was very narrow. Everybody was shouting I don't know what and waving us goodbye with their hands. We responded and waved away like gladiators going into the arena. What a moment for a soldier to have lived. Such moments live on in the soul ever more, believe me![15]

Shortly before 21:00, Camille Vilain was standing on sentry duty by 'his' barricade near the Jardin des Plantes when he saw a crowd rushing down the boulevard de l'Hôpital. Vilain turned, expecting to see a German armoured car. Instead, in the fading light, what he saw amazed him:

Coming down the boulevard de l'Hôpital, swept along by a tornado of applause, are the first armoured vehicles of the Leclerc column, covered in flags and young FFI fighters. They have French names written on their steel flanks. The enthusiasm is indescribable. People are singing, dancing, jumping up and down, shouting, screaming. Every time a vehicle goes by, the noise doubles in intensity. We form a human chain to stop the crowd from being knocked down by the tanks, whose path they are blocking. Women are perched on the top of some of the tanks, looking joyful. They are here! They are here![16]

Guided by a young motorcycle rider, the twenty-two vehicles in the Dronne column crossed the Seine by the Gare d'Austerlitz and then followed the right bank of the river westwards, until they arrived at the place de l'Hôtel de Ville as night fell. The three tanks backed up to the building and parked with their guns facing onto the square, defending this key symbol of Republican France. The time was 21:22 and the Leclerc Division had arrived in the heart of Paris.

*

Claude Roy had been waiting in the Hôtel de Ville, finding the situation unbearably tense and thinking of his comrades in exile or in prison. Also waiting was a young woman from Alsace, a region that had been annexed by the Germans in 1940. Her name was Jeanne Borchert, and she had turned up in traditional Alsatian costume – a red skirt, a white blouse with a black apron, and a large black head-dress. Clutching a French flag, Jeanne hung around the Hôtel de Ville all day, waiting for the Free French Army to arrive. Inside the building, in the large office of the Prefect of the Seine, a bust of 'Marianne' – the symbol of the Republic – had been dug out of a cupboard and perched on a trolley, and the leaders of the insurrection sat impatiently. Every now and then the telephone would ring and news would come through of the progress of the Leclerc Division. Above the fireplace there was a badly reproduced photograph of de Gaulle with a tricolour ribbon across it, while the open windows were filled with sandbags and bristled with machine guns pointing onto the square in front of the building. In the courtyard, FFI fighters cobbled together Allied flags.

In the early evening, everyone went to the refectory to eat pasta and bread.[17] Suddenly, Bidault stood up, called for silence and announced that French tanks were in Paris and had crossed the Seine. There was chaos as some people clambered onto the tables and began to sing the 'Marseillaise', while others rushed for the doors. Outside, the three tanks of the Dronne column had just arrived and were bathed in eerie light as flares were set off in celebration.[18] Monsieur Lecomte, a hospital administrator, was in the Hôtel de Ville with the *résistants*. He wrote: 'I hadn't seen the tanks arrive, so their sudden appearance was like magic. A crowd seemed to appear from nowhere, covering the square, and the high windows of the Prefect's office were lit up like they have not been for five years, illuminating the night.'[19] Soon there were hundreds of Parisians on the square, singing and dancing.

Dronne was almost carried up to the Prefect's office, where he was welcomed by Georges Bidault, in the name of the 'soldiers without uniform' who had been fighting in France.[20] As Bidault moved to embrace him, Dronne protested: 'But I'm so dirty, so filthy – it's been such a long drive!' Suddenly a burst of machine-gun fire crashed into the room.

Everyone dived to the floor, then someone managed to turn the lights off. The Germans were still in the city, and they could still kill.[21]

Shortly before Dronne arrived, radio journalist Pierre Crénesse, who had spent the whole day producing the broadcast from the Préfecture, walked over to the Hôtel de Ville to check the radio set-up for what he thought would be a momentous day. As he arrived in front of the Hôtel de Ville, he was amazed to see Dronne's tanks. He rushed into the building, grabbed a telephone and called the studio, demanding to be patched through, live to air.[22] Breathless with excitement and exhaustion, Crénesse gave an improvised report that lasted over five minutes and which captured the meaning of the moment:

> Tomorrow morning will be the dawn of a new day for the capital. Tomorrow morning, Paris will be liberated, Paris will have finally rediscovered its true face. Four years of struggle, four years that have been, for many people, years of prison, years of pain, of torture and, for many more, a slow death in the Nazi concentration camps, murder; but that's all over ... For several hours, here in the centre of Paris, in the Cité, we have been living unforgettable moments. At the Préfecture, my comrades have explained to you that they are waiting for the commanding officers of the Leclerc Division and the American and French authorities. Similarly, at the Hôtel de Ville the Conseil National de la Résistance has been meeting for several hours. They are awaiting the French authorities. Meetings will take place, meetings which will be extremely symbolic, either there or in the Préfecture de Police – we don't yet know where.[23]

Crénesse then handed the phone over to Bidault, who made a brief speech underlining that Germany was still not beaten, and urging the whole of France to support the Allies. Then Rol spoke – he had arrived at the Hôtel de Ville a few minutes earlier. He emphasised that 'the capital has largely been liberated thanks to the guerrilla tactics carried out by the FFI,' before closing with an appeal that could have been made by de Gaulle: 'Open the road to Paris for the Allied armies, hunt down and destroy the remnants of the German divisions, link up with the Leclerc Division in a common victory – that is the mission that is

being accomplished by the FFI of the Ile-de-France and of Paris, sim-
mering with a sacred hatred and patriotism.'[24]

As they were broadcasting, the great bell of Notre Dame, which had
been silent throughout the occupation, began to toll in celebration –
Charles Luizet had ordered a dozen policemen to the cathedral to ring
it.[25] From the radio studio, Pierre Schaeffer called on all the churches
of the city to join in and ring their bells, too. And all over Paris, the
noise of bells rang out.[26]

In the tumult, two policemen turned up at the Hôtel de Ville and
summoned Dronne to the Préfecture. The Gaullist Delegation could
easily have made the trip over the Seine, but they clearly wanted to
regain the media initiative from the Resistance, and highlight their
presence at the Préfecture, with all that it symbolised in terms of the re-
establishment of the state. Once Dronne had walked the few hundred
metres across the Seine, Parodi was shoved in front of the radio microphone: 'I have in front of me a French captain who is the first to arrive
in Paris. His face is red, he is grubby and he needs a shave, and yet I
want to embrace him!'[27] When the interview was over, Luizet asked
Dronne if there was anything he needed; the soldier replied simply: 'A
bath'. After a brief ablution in the relative luxury of Luizet's official
apartment, Dronne – clean and not quite so tired – took his leave and
returned to the Hôtel de Ville. He spread his sleeping bag on the pavement next to his jeep and went to sleep, to the sound of his Spanish
comrades singing republican songs.[28]

*

A few minutes after Dronne arrived at the Hôtel de Ville, Colonel
Massu's column, accompanied by a group of Americans led by Captain
Peterson of the 102nd Cavalry Group, had reached the pont de Sèvres,
only two kilometres away from the south-western edge of Paris.[29] A
journalist from *Franc-Tireur* described the situation in an article published the next day:

It all happened in a flash. First the place was empty then, without
warning, the bridge was full of tanks, real tanks, and not simply young

men armed with rifles and revolvers. The lads of Leclerc's army are
here. The tanks are covered with young girls, with women who are
hugging these first uniformed men of the French Army. They get
down from their tanks. They move among the crowd which presses
around them to hail them, to thank them for being there. I push my
way through the madding crowd, a crowd that is crying for joy, and
which can do nothing other than cry its joy.[30]

All of a sudden, the electricity came on and the streets were flooded
with light, the river below the bridge flashing as the reflections danced
in the water.[31]

Colonel de Langlade was with Massu's column, and he ordered a group
of tanks to cross the Seine and to wait on the other side of the river.
Having set up his headquarters in a café on the western bank of the Seine,
near the massive Renault factory situated in the middle of the river on the
Ile Séguin, de Langlade repeatedly tried to contact Leclerc's headquarters
to explain their position. It was impossible to get through on the radio.
The men at the headquarters of the 2e DB were equally frustrated: a Free
French intelligence report glumly concluded that 'for all practical purposes, liaison between the columns no longer exists.'[32] De Langlade was,
however, able to get through to his mother, by simply picking up the telephone in the café and dialling her number. It was the first time he had
spoken to her in five years. He said he would be with her on the following
afternoon, and that under no circumstances should she go outside.[33]

Shortly afterwards, Lieutenant Lorrain Cruse turned up at de
Langlade's headquarters with news of the situation in the city. Although
Cruse was an FFI officer, he was one of Chaban's men and liaised with
Nordling at the Swedish consulate; he was also in continual contact with
the spy Bender.[34] Although it was clear from Cruse's description that there
were few if any German troops between Sèvres and the centre of the city,
any advance would require passing by the Bois de Boulogne where,
Bender had claimed, an SS regiment was stationed.[35] The issue was finally
resolved when de Langlade discovered that the tanks were nearly out of
fuel, and the refuelling convoy had yet to arrive. They would have to wait.[36]

*

In the Hôtel Meurice, von Choltitz and his closest advisors, including his secretary, Fraulein Grün, were taking a last supper together. They were morosely drinking champagne and drawing parallels with the Saint Bartholomew's Day massacre, which had taken place in Paris exactly 372 years earlier, on 24 August 1572, and in which thousands of French Huguenots were killed.[37] Then they heard the bells ring out.

'So, they are here!' said Colonel Jay to von Choltitz.[38]

Von Choltitz went into his office, picked up the telephone and spoke to Speidel and Model. He held the telephone out of the window, into the night that was full of the sound of bells ringing.

'Can you hear that?' he asked.

'Yes, I can hear bells,' Speidel replied.

'That's right,' said von Choltitz, 'the Franco-American Army has entered Paris.'

'Ah,' said Speidel.

After a short silence, von Choltitz asked for orders. Speidel and Model had none to give him.

'In that case, my dear Speidel,' sighed von Choltitz, 'there remains nothing for me to do except to bid you adieu. Take care of my wife, and of my children.'

'We will do that, General,' said Speidel, 'we promise you.'[39]

And with that, von Choltitz's group went to bed. Von Arnim took his father's old suitcase, which had accompanied him throughout his military career, and packed away his few precious affairs. He slipped a Bible and a copy of *Conversations with Goethe* into his trouser pocket, then lay down on the bed in his small attic bedroom.[40]

Just down the road, on the edge of the place de la Concorde, Major Roskothen, a military lawyer who had served as a judge and had sentenced many Resistance fighters to death, was taking what he assumed would be his last meal at the Hôtel Crillon. Wearing his best uniform with its white jacket, he drank a bottle of champagne and recalled the good times he had experienced in Paris.[41] Then, after leaving a large tip for the waitress, he went up to his room and packed his possessions into a small rucksack, ready for whatever the next day might bring. He left a box of cigars on the table, together with a note in English and French that read 'Please help yourself.' He undressed, lay naked on his bed because of the heat, and fell into a deep sleep.[42]

Walter Dreizner had drawn the short straw. While the others were in bed, he was on lookout duty, sitting on top of his building in the 'dark, humid summer evening'. Squinting into the gloom, he tried to make out signs of movement on the street below. Every now and again there were explosions in the darkness. Then everything changed:

> All the bells of Paris are ringing. They send their eerie call into the dark summer night. It goes chillingly down your spine. If only you could turn them off. Yet the sounds pitilessly press themselves against your ear ... Heavily, eerily, the bells send their call out into the dark night like the verdict of a higher court ... The voice of history, the voice of the nation, sounds from the heart of the city, from the Ile de la Cité ... Seconds of silence hang over Paris. And then the spell is broken: thousands and thousands of voices cry out. The hurricane of voices does not stop. At one stroke, the sky above eastern Paris becomes lighter and lighter. The excited population is setting off fireworks. Paris is in joyous delirium. Paris is in its element.[43]

*

At exactly the same time, about two kilometres away, Victor Veau peered out of his window, but it was too dark to see anything in the street below. Then: '*Bells*. Shouting. Applause in the street ... Dogs bark, frightened by the noise. Machine guns fire, no one pays them any attention ... We all shout "*Vive de Gaulle*".'[44] Micheline Bood had been feeling poorly all day, but now showed her usual enthusiasm as she wrote in her diary: 'Paris is literally in revolution, the Allies are arriving right now, the radio says they are at La Muette and at the Hôtel de Ville.'[45] Marc Boegner wrote: 'The bells are ringing and guns are firing all around us. I feel overcome with emotion and my heart is leaping with joy.'[46] In Montmartre, Pierre Patin heard the announcement of the arrival of the Dronne column and went down into the street to celebrate: 'The whole city was in darkness – even the air-raid safe street lights were off – but a car was parked in the rue

Steinkerque, just below Sacré-Coeur, and its headlights were shining up onto the church, which was the first and only monument in the city to be lit up.'[47] Simone de Beauvoir recalled: 'I had dinner – two potatoes – that evening ... Some cyclists going past shouted out that the Leclerc Division had just reached the place de l'Hôtel de Ville. We pushed down to the carrefour Montparnasse; people were gathering from all quarters. The guns fired, all the bells of Paris began to peal, and every house was lit up. Someone kindled a bonfire in the middle of the road; we all joined hands and danced around it, singing.'[48] Jean-Claude Touche wrote in his diary: 'We are crying for joy. The explosions continue. On the balcony, you can hear the bells from all over Paris ringing out. And it's not the radio any more. It is real. It's so moving. We hurriedly get back inside because someone is firing a machine gun in the street below. The explosions continue. The sky is still all aflame.'[49] Deep in Rol's bunker underneath Denfert-Rochereau, there was an outbreak of joy that did not amuse the stern Colonel Rol. His wife, Cécile, who acted as his secretary, later recalled: 'When we heard that Dronne had arrived, all the women went a bit giddy and had a pillow fight to celebrate. It just happened, and we had a great time. It didn't last long – maybe 10 minutes. But the next day, when Henri heard about it, when people said, "Ah! If only you'd seen Madame Rol!" he had a real go at me! "A colonel's wife does not have pillow fights," he said.'[50]

Jean Guéhenno wrote the final words in the diary he had kept since 1940: 'In the night, all the bells of all the churches rang out, drowning the sound of cannon fire. Liberty and France are beginning again.'[51] Jacqueline Mesnil-Amar also heard the bells, and her heart rejoiced, too, but not for long. Her thoughts were never far from her husband, who as far as she knew was still on a train to hell: 'I cry for my missing loved one. He is so far away, where is he going so late in the night? Has he eaten? Has he slept? What is he thinking? Does he know that tonight all the bells in the city are ringing, and do they know – he and his comrades – the marvellous news that Paris is free? Do they know that they *must* live, because the world will be free again?'[52]

*

Late that night, Model sent a message to Berlin, which he requested should be passed on to Hitler. 'Given the evolution of the situation,' he began – not knowing quite how bad the situation actually was – 'I draw the following conclusions.' He wanted the remaining troops west of Paris to be brought to safety, forming a new defensive line to the east of the city, which he had been preparing for days. Although he did accept that 'the question of Paris is urgent', Model's only solution was to bring in additional forces over the next couple of days, but he warned that they could be overwhelmed by the Allies.[53] Despite his loyalty to Hitler, Model was clearly not prepared to hold onto the French capital at all costs, focusing instead on more pressing military issues. None of the Germans – perhaps not even Hitler – really thought Paris was of such importance that it had to be destroyed.[54]

To the west of Paris, fighting continued chaotically in the darkness. US Captain Dale Helm heard a shot and a scream on the edges of his unit's position on the northern bank of the Seine. Running to find out what had happened, in the darkness he tripped over a dying soldier who had collapsed over one of the unit's machine guns. Feeling for the helmet, Helm realised with relief it was not one of his men, but a German soldier. Nearby, one of Helm's comrades, Robinson, was slumped against a wall, sobbing. He had been guarding the gun when he heard footsteps; he challenged a shadowy figure, who nevertheless continued to advance. Robinson fired his gun and the German dropped like a stone. 'I killed him. I didn't know what I was doing. I was too scared,' said the distraught young man. In his diary that night, Helm recorded the event and concluded: 'It did no good to point out to Robinson that killing an enemy was nothing to worry about. Try as we did to calm him, our efforts were in vain and he had to be evacuated to the medics.'[55]

Meanwhile, somewhere in the southern suburbs, ambulance driver Suzanne Torrès turned nurse and spent the night tending two young soldiers, one a badly burnt Frenchman, the other a severely wounded German. To both she whispered words of comfort which she barely believed.[56] Even in Paris, there was still fighting. A group of German parachutists found their passage eastwards blocked by Massu's column at the pont de Sèvres. They launched an attack and most of them managed to get past the French troops, but dozens were killed or captured.[57] De Langlade recalled that when dawn came 'the last 500 metres of the Versailles road on the approach to the pont de Sèvres were covered in vehicles and dead bodies.'[58]

All through the night, the Resistance radio continued broadcasting an improvised programme led by Pierre Schaeffer. Announcements were read out and orders were given, appeals were made for FFI fighters to go to the aid of the Mairie in the 11th arrondissement, which was being attacked by the Germans and where the ammunition was running out.[59] At midnight, Schaeffer announced that the German artillery batteries at Longchamp were firing on the city and that shells had fallen in the 15th arrondissement.[60] At one point the programme was broadcast in English, in the hope that British or American listeners – or military commanders – would hear. As Bertrand d'Astorg was announcing the arrival of the Leclerc Division in English, the studio door opened and he was handed an urgent message to read out – this time in German: '*Achtung!* This is the staff of Colonel Rol, commander of the FFI in the Ile-de-France. We have learnt that the German commander in Colombes is going to shoot 10 French hostages. If he carries out his plan, we will shoot 10 German Army soldiers, 10 members of the SS and 10 German women auxiliaries.'[61]

The battle for Paris was not over yet.

15

Friday 25 August, Day:
Endgame

*Bernard Pierquin writes in his diary: 'August 25th was without doubt the
most amazing and extraordinary day that I have ever experienced.'*[1]

It was cold in the early morning mist as the soldiers of the 2e DB left
their bivouacs and climbed into their vehicles shortly before dawn.[2] But
within a couple of hours the sun had come up in the summer sky and
the day turned into one of the hottest and most beautiful of the year.
The German forces that had hampered the advance of the 2e DB and
the 4th US Infantry the day before had either been destroyed or melted
away, and by mid-morning each of the southern routes into the centre
of Paris was a metal river of tanks, half-tracks, lorries and jeeps, while the
sides of the roads were lined with thousands of cheering people.[3]

Jean Galtier-Boissière rushed down to see the Leclerc Division passing in front of his door: 'On the rue Saint-Jacques, there was an
unforgettable sight: an excited crowd surrounded the French tanks,
which were covered in flags and bouquets. On each tank, on each
armoured car, next to each khaki-clad, red-capped soldier, there were
girls, women, kids, and armband-wearing "Fifis". The people on either
side applauded, blew kisses, shook hands and shouted to the victors
their joy in liberation!'[4]

One of those in the crowd was Edith Thomas. Although she shared the
joy, her feelings were mixed. As she wrote the next day in a newspaper
article: '"Bravo! Bravo!" shouts the crowd. This time, I start to cry. I cry for

all those who should be here, standing in the front row, but are not here. What do the people in the camps know of our joy? I think of all those who have died.'[5] The *Manchester Guardian* correspondent also watched the vehicles roll by: 'it was for most of the French soldiers their first sight of Paris since their mobilisation four or five years ago. As the tanks crashed by, many of them wrote notes, rolled them up, and threw them into the crowd. I picked one up. It was a message to anyone who found it to tell the parents of the writer who lived in such and such a street that André was safe.'[6] One of those notes was written by Sergeant Jean Vandal, and it was taken to his mother's house by a generous passer-by: 'Dear Mum. I am here – see you soon. Kisses to everyone, Jean.'[7]

Squadron-Leader John Pudney was driving in the Leclerc column:

As the sun came through the mist and there was more confidence in the light, more people gathered with more flags. They threw flowers and flags: they threw themselves. They clung to the car: they tried to climb on top. The FFI youth leapt upon the mudguards. While they screamed the words 'Royal Air Force' and sang the 'Marseillaise' and 'Tipperary', we managed to keep moving, juggernaut fashion. The only time we stopped we had to be dug out by twenty gendarmes. Suddenly I recognised boulevard Montparnasse over the heads of the crowd. We were at Gare Montparnasse! Gunfire, cheers, whistles, shots, tears, kisses, champagne, poured in at the driving window, through the roof. 'We have waited so long ... Thank you for coming ... RAF, RAF, RAF ... I am English ... My brother went to join the Royal Air Force ... Kiss me, please ... You must drink this: I kept it for the first Englishman I met ...' That pillow fight of goodwill begins my Paris memory.[8]

*

The arrival of the 2e DB meant that the final phase of the liberation of Paris would be determined by an army, not by the Resistance or by the population. As a result, the political forces that had created the conditions for freedom found themselves completely sidelined. Throughout the day, the members of the Conseil National de la Résistance and the

Comité Parisien de la Libération sat in the Hôtel de Ville. They waited. Long stretches of boredom were interspersed with brief peaks of excitement as they heard that de Gaulle was about to arrive, and then he did not.[9] In the morning, the CNR and the CPL issued a declaration in the name of 'the French nation' that praised 'our uniformed and our non-uniformed soldiers, who have met up at the crossroads of a city where everyone has risen up'. Empty of anything except rhetoric, the declaration made no mention of de Gaulle even though it was also signed by Parodi in the name of the Provisional Government.[10] This declaration turned out to be the swan song of both the CNR and the CPL. The embryonic state apparatus controlled by Parodi and Luizet was now fused with the armed might of the 2e DB – everything that the Free French needed to take control of the capital was now in place. The CNR and the CPL could have done nothing to oppose this even if they had possessed the political will, which they did not. Despite its long underground struggle, the Resistance had not created any alternative forms of civil power and its military forces were weak. Above all, it was not a united force that politically wished to stem the rising tide of the Free French. Although the Resistance had forced the Allies' hand by launching the insurrection and obliging them to enter Paris, the Gaullists would come out triumphant, and the Resistance would soon disappear as a force, to become part of French mythology. But first, Paris had to be liberated.

For many Parisians, it was still a normal Friday, or as normal as it could be in a city that had been in the throes of insurrection for a week. Many of the city's schools were providing childcare and participated in the amazing events that were taking place.[11] In the 11th arrondissement, primary school children made tricolour rosettes to celebrate; at 09:00, the headmaster of the boys' school on the rue Keller climbed onto the first-storey roof above the entrance and put a tricolour flag into the empty grey metal flag-holder, which has the letters R and F (République Française) on either side. The pupils stood neatly in a row and sang the first verse of the 'Marseillaise' in piping voices, while a crowd of parents, teachers and onlookers joined in the rousing and bloodthirsty chorus, so appropriate for a day of liberation:

Aux armes, citoyens!	To arms, citizens!
Formez vos bataillons!	Form your battalions!
Marchons, marchons!	March, march!
Qu'un sang impur	Let impure blood
abreuve nos sillons![12]	water our fields!

*

The enemy had not gone away. There were still thousands of German soldiers in the city, protected by dozens of armoured vehicles. But they were no longer patrolling the streets; they had retreated into their strong-points. The insidious web of control, domination and repression that the Nazis had spun over the city for four years had evaporated, its remnants congealing into a handful of minor fortresses at the Ecole Militaire and the Senate building in the southern part of the city; the Hôtel Majestic near the place de l'Etoile, the Hôtel Meurice on the rue de Rivoli, and the place de la République in the northern half; along with outposts at the Opéra, the rue des Archives and the Porte de Clignancourt. Inside the walls that both protected and imprisoned them, the Germans were waiting for the inevitable onslaught from an overwhelming enemy. The 2e DB and the 4th US Infantry had targeted the German strong-points with hundreds of armoured vehicles and tens of thousands of battle-hardened, well-armed men. Furthermore, the FFI and the Parisian population had now lost all fear, and were prepared to risk their lives to free their city. The looming battle could have only one outcome; the only question was the price that would be paid in blood and destruction.

Leclerc's plan was to attack in separate but coordinated movements. The focus would be on four areas: the Hôtel Majestic, the Ecole Militaire and the Senate building in the south, and above all the complex of buildings around the place de la Concorde that housed the German headquarters centred on the Hôtel Meurice, where von Choltitz and his staff had been putting their affairs in order, waiting for the inevitable. During the night, the German commander arranged for seventy female army auxiliaries in the building to be put under the protection of the Red Cross. At 06:00 the women were driven away from the

Hôtel Meurice in two Red Cross lorries and taken to the Hôtel Bristol, to howls of protest from people in the neighbourhood, including young Micheline Bood, who watched the whole thing from her balcony in her nightdress.[13] Then, in the early morning light, von Choltitz and Colonel Jay went out on an inspection tour. As Jay recalled:

> Anyone who has spent even a few summer days in Paris knows what it looks like on such a morning. Von Choltitz went with me through the Tuileries in order to inspect our so-called positions. There were groups of soldiers moving around, armed with machine guns, crouched behind sandbags or other defences, shooting at FFI fighters, who replied from the other side of the Seine. On the opposite bank of the river we could see tanks driving up and down – our snipers took shots at them, but without any effect.[14]

The two men then returned to the Hôtel Meurice, where von Choltitz went up to his office and wrote some letters. Then it was time for lunch, and everyone went to the hotel dining room, overlooking the rue de Rivoli, and had their usual meal of rations, with red wine.[15] In a nod to the situation outside, the tables were pushed into the middle of the room, away from the windows, as bullets whistled by and fragments of masonry flew into the room. 'In all other respects,' recalled von Arnim, 'it was the same setting, the same waiter, the same food.'[16] In the nearby Hôtel Mont Thabor, Walter Dreizner and his comrades were desperately hoping that the vehicles massed around the hotel would be used for their escape, but they were not. As he glumly wrote shortly afterwards, 'We stayed in Paris.'[17] Dreizner and his comrades also had lunch, which was unusually copious and varied; their quartermaster must have realised that this would probably be the final meal he would serve up in Paris.

Meanwhile, an attempt to relieve the German garrison was being made from the north-east. During the night, a section of the Panzer Lehr Division had been ordered to fight its way into the centre of the city. Commanded by Captain Hennecke, a small battle group composed of tanks and infantrymen left Le Bourget in the morning, but soon found its advance bogged down by the barricades and by sustained attack from *résistants*. The open-topped troop carriers were particularly vulnerable to Molotov cocktails hurled from windows, and by the early afternoon the operation had been called off.[18] A schoolteacher in the north-east suburb of Pantin described the situation: 'A German column of about 60 vehicles, including 10 tanks, moves towards Paris; it drives along the side of the school towards the Porte de la Villette. Half an hour later, it turns up again, heading back to Le Bourget. There is gun-fire; some bullets hit the front of the school.'[19]

Dr Hans Herrmann, who was the surgeon with the group, wrote about the failed operation in his diary: 'We were involved in heavy street fighting in Paris which meant a lot of work for me. Street fighting is always the worst. We were fired upon from windows and we could never see the enemy ... I stood on the running board with a carbine under my arms, driving through the streets to treat the wounded. The feeling was strange. One would hear a round whistle through the air and not know from where it came.'[20] The Paris garrison's last hope of reinforce-ments – a hope von Choltitz did not even know existed – had collapsed. The Germans in Paris were on their own.

*

The first fighting of the day involved Captain Dronne and the men of La Nueve. In the morning they were sent from the Hôtel de Ville to seize the nearby central telephone exchange on the rue des Archives, to prevent the Germans from destroying it. The telephone system had continued to function throughout the insurrection, giving the Resistance an enormous advantage and helping the Parisians cope with the uncertainty and the lack of reliable information that had charac-terised the previous ten days. To allow the Germans to sabotage the telephone network as freedom was about to dawn would be a disaster. Dronne split his men into two groups and sent them along the rue des Archives and the rue du Temple, both of which stretch north-east from the Hôtel de Ville. The group advancing up the rue des Archives joined with a local FFI section and soon cleared out the telephone exchange and took a few dozen prisoners.[21] All that remained was the task of dealing with 100 kilos of explosive charges that had been laid in the building.[22] Meanwhile, on the rue du Temple, Warrant Officer Caron climbed out of his tank to help a group of FFI fighters moving towards the place de la République, where an SS regiment was based. A German machine-gun nest hidden in the entrance to the Temple Métro station shot him dead, along with three FFI fighters.[23] Although the telephone exchange had fallen without much resistance, the strong-points would prove more costly.

Soldiers of the 4th US Infantry commanded by General Barton also entered the city. The first US soldier into Paris was Captain William Buenzle. Desperate to win a bet, Buenzle drove his armoured troop car at full tilt right to the centre of the city. At 07:30 Buenzle radioed his headquarters: 'I am at Notre Dame.' 'How do you know?' they asked. 'Dammit,' he replied, 'I am looking right up at Notre Dame!'[24] Most of the US advance was more sedate. Keeping to the east of the main advance of the 2e DB, Barton's soldiers swept through the southern suburbs and into the eastern parts of the city, taking the Bastille and then moving towards Nation and the German barracks at Vincennes. They were cheered at every step. Hard-boiled war correspondent Ernie Pyle wrote: 'Gradually we entered the suburbs and soon into the midst of Paris itself and a pandemonium of surely the greatest mass joy that has ever happened ... Everybody, even beautiful girls, insisted on kissing you on both cheeks. Somehow I got started kissing babies that were held up by their parents, and for a while I looked like a baby-kissing politician going down the street. The fact that I hadn't shaved for days, and was grey-bearded as well as bald-headed, made no difference.'[25] As the US troops passed through the southern suburb of Orly, a child was held out to a soldier in a lorry. The child said, 'Daddy dead in war.' The soldier took the child, kissed it, and explained that he too had a baby. As one observer wrote: 'All around us, eyes shone with tears.'[26]

*

At around 09:30, General Leclerc arrived at the Porte d'Orléans – the main southern entrance to the city – accompanied by Chaban, who had been summoned to help guide the 2e DB vehicles.[27] Leclerc's aides were concerned about sniper fire from Germans and die-hard collaborators, so the Free French general transferred to an armoured scout car. It made no difference: heedless of the danger, Leclerc stood upright in the open-topped vehicle as they drove up the avenue that now bears his name, passing first by place Denfert-Rochereau and then on to the Gare Montparnasse, where Leclerc set up his headquarters.[28]

Leclerc's aides were right to be worried about snipers – shortly after 11:00, two soldiers of the 2e DB were shot dead near the Ecole Militaire.[29] There were dozens of similar incidents all over the city, giving rise to a widespread fear about '*les tireurs des toîts*' – the snipers on the rooftops. At least some of these *tireurs* were in fact members of the Resistance sent up to look for snipers. For example, at the beginning of the afternoon, Bernard Pierquin's concierge told him there were snipers on the roof; wearing his FFI armband, Bernard climbed on top of the building. He found no Nazis, but the FFI fighters below shot at him, thinking he was a sniper.[30]

Two left-wing activists, members of the Front National who had sheltered Allied airmen, were victims of mistaken identity, with dreadful consequences. Max and Madeleine Goa were on the balcony of their apartment on the avenue d'Italie when shots rang out. The crowd below pointed up at them and a group of people, convinced that they had discovered the culprits, charged up the stairs and barged into the couple's apartment. The pair were manhandled down the stairs by what was turning into a lynch mob and, on the avenue, Max fell under the tracks of a passing tank, either thrown there by the mob, or stumbling by accident. Madeleine, having seen her husband killed before her eyes, was accused of being a sniper. Her nightmare soon grew even worse: she was taken away by a rogue FFI group who locked her up in their 'prison' at the Institut Dentaire in the 13th arrondissement, where she was subject to terrible abuse and gradually lost her mind.[31]

Odette Lainville and her husband Robert had direct experience of the firing when they went down to the boulevard Raspail to join the crowds. Odette had brought some flowers from her balcony, and she threw them on top of a tank. Along with the rest of the crowd, she shouted at the top of her voice: '*Vive la France! Vive de Gaulle! Vivent les Alliés!*' All of a sudden, over the noise of the cheering crowd and the rumbling engines, shots rang out. Everyone ran for shelter, people flattened themselves against the wall; Odette crouched down while her husband protected her. The tanks swivelled their barrels up to the windows where the shots had come from. Eventually the firing ceased – had those shots really been fired in anger? – and the tanks rumbled past once more. Odette and Robert returned home, where, to Odette's amazement, Robert began to cry. The last time she had seen her husband so upset was at the outbreak of World War I. 'I feel overwhelmed,' he said, 'it has stirred up all those feelings of love for our country that are deep inside me.' Odette took him in her arms and comforted him.[32]

As Odette and Robert were finishing their lunch, there was a knock at the door. A 12-year-old boy was standing there, breathless, clutching a note. It was from Odette's nephew, Bob, who was a soldier with the 2e DB: 'Am on boulevard Montparnasse, your son is well, and Nelly too. Come quickly.' After giving the young lad a glass of wine and a couple of biscuits as a reward, they dashed off to find Bob, who gave them news of their two children who were with the Free French (Jean was fighting in Italy, Nelly was an airborne nurse). While they were talking there was more shooting, and everyone dashed for shelter; soon the firing died down and the crowd returned to the street, thronging round the tanks and half-tracks. Odette spent the rest of the afternoon with Bob, shaking hands with US generals, talking to US soldiers and greeting Bob's comrades, walking in the sun-filled streets until her feet were aching in her wooden-soled shoes.[33]

On the other side of the city, crowds gathered in the place Beauvau, where the Ministry of the Interior was now draped with massive flags and banners. Someone found a set of German flags inside the building and brought them out into the street, where they were burnt as girls danced around in a ring, singing the 'Marseillaise'. Micheline Bood was watching: 'I will never, ever, forget the sight, even if I live to be 100 years old. It was as though we were burning Hitler.'[34]

*

Colonel Billotte of the 2e DB was given the order to move on the heart of the German occupation of Paris – von Choltitz's headquarters at the Hôtel Meurice. Billotte had set up his headquarters in the billiard room of the Préfecture de Police; after a brief discussion with Parodi and Chaban, it was agreed that Billotte would first demand von Choltitz's surrender.[35] No one else was consulted about how the city was to be formally liberated: from the very beginning of the final day of the German occupation, the Free French ignored the Resistance completely.

Billotte's ultimatum letter gave von Choltitz thirty minutes to surrender and closed with a threat: 'Should you decide to continue a combat that has no military justification, I will pursue that fight until your complete extermination.'[36] Colonel Billotte signed himself 'General Billotte', perhaps to impress von Choltitz.[37] To get the letter to the German commander, the services of the Swedish consul would be needed, so Lieutenant-Colonel de la Horie was ordered to take the letter to Raoul Nordling at the Swedish consulate on the rue d'Anjou. Eighteen-year-old Jean-Claude Touche saw two French armoured cars driving up the rue d'Anjou, which was draped with French, American and English flags, as well as a huge banner that stretched across the rue de Rome which read: 'Welcome'.[38] The vehicles, which were soon surrounded by an enthusiastic crowd, carried de la Horie and 30-year-old Gisèle Hasseler, who had been Chaban's secretary and was now acting as a liaison officer and unofficial guide to Paris.[39]

Inside the consulate, de la Horie gave the letter to Nordling, who was up and about again after his angina attack. Nordling, accompanied by the omnipresent 'Bobby' Bender, left for the Hôtel Meurice but could get only about halfway down the rue de Rivoli before being stopped by German gunfire. Sheltering in the arcades that line the northern side of the street, they proceeded on foot until they got to the rue Saint-Honoré, where they were stopped by German guards. The troops were unimpressed by Nordling's credentials, and it took a great deal of persuasion before their officer agreed to telephone von Choltitz and tell him that the Swedish consul wanted to deliver a letter from the Free French. Lieutenant von Arnim, the German commander's 25-year-old Ordnance Officer, was sent down to say that there was no question of the letter being accepted.[40] Shortly afterwards, Billotte ordered his men to attack the Hôtel Meurice. Nordling's final attempt to negotiate a peaceful end to the German occupation of Paris had failed.[41]

*

On the other side of the Seine, two separate columns of the 2e DB were headed for the German strong-point at the Ecole Militaire. In the late morning, Bernard Pierquin saw the Leclerc Division tanks attacking while Parisians milled around and soldiers shouted at them to take cover: 'They might as well have saved their breath,' wrote Bernard in his diary; 'men, women and children were running around the tanks without a care, completely unaware of the danger ... Every now and again, someone would fall – wounded or killed. But it didn't seem to matter; the party went on. The weather was marvellous, the sun was glorious, and the buildings were covered with flags (I have never seen so many flags in Paris) and, at the end of the day, the Germans were not fighting with much determination and surrendered quite easily.'[42]

Pierquin might have felt the Germans were not putting up much of a fight, but it did not look that way to those who were involved. As the battle raged to take the Ministry of Foreign Affairs on the edge of les Invalides, two tanks – *Quimper* and *Saint-Cyr* – were firing on a German bunker when an anti-tank shell hit the *Quimper* and it burst into flames. The crew, alive but badly burnt, fled the tank shortly before an explosion dramatically blew off the turret. After the fighting was over, someone painted on the side of the hulk: 'Three French soldiers died here'.[43] In fact, no soldiers died in the tank, but four men were killed in the fighting on that stretch of road.[44] One of them was Lieutenant Jean Bureau of the *Saint-Cyr*, who was advancing on foot by the side of his vehicle when he was shot dead; an hour earlier Bureau had telephoned his father to say he would soon be home.[45] Also involved in the fighting were FFI fighters from near Orléans who had come to help drive out the Germans. After making their way along the left bank of the Seine, the Resistance fighters found themselves underneath the pont Alexandre III, the bridge that spans the river between les Invalides and the Grand Palais. They were then ordered to join in the fight to take the ministry. As the building went up in flames, several of the men were killed or seriously wounded.[46]

Less than two weeks earlier, 18-year-old Michel Varin de Brunelière had joined the Leclerc Division along with his twin brother, Paul, as the 2e DB passed through Alençon. In his identity photograph, Michel has an upturned collar, slicked-back thick hair and a serious mouth. He was involved in the fighting to take the Eiffel Tower, where the Germans had installed machine-gun posts at each corner of the first stage. Crouched on the bridge that crosses the Seine at the foot of the tower, Michel found time to write to his sister Renée: 'There is fighting all around me ... Paul is at the other end of the bridge. The machine guns are crackling, we're in the middle of a firefight, it's astonishing. We have had an amazing welcome from the Parisians, it's enough to make you cry. There are Germans all around me. But Paris will soon be ours ...' Shortly afterwards, the tricolour was hoisted atop the Eiffel Tower. Michel did not have much time to appreciate it, as his group was soon sent across the Seine to attack the Chambre des Deputés. About an hour after writing to his sister, Michel was shot through the head. He died in hospital that night.[47] A few dozen metres away from where Michel was shot, Sergeant Jean Vandal of the 2e DB, who had got a message to his mother announcing his imminent arrival, was severely wounded. He also died in hospital.[48]

*

About 500 Germans were stationed in the network of buildings that housed the Luftwaffe headquarters in Paris, and which was centred on the Jardin du Luxembourg. The buildings were defended by seven tanks (including four Panthers), three armoured flame-throwers and a number of armoured cars.[49] Alongside the 2e DB, FFI fighters led by Colonel Fabien were heavily involved in the fight to contain and then destroy the German strong-point.[50] Paul Tuffrau, who lived nearby, chatted to a couple of them and found them to be 'polite young folk, looking awkward in their helmets, as though they were embarrassed by their rifles'.[51] By the early afternoon the situation had grown tense as fighting broke out along the southern stretch of the boulevard Saint-Michel. Attempts by the FFI to deal with the German bunkers located at each corner of the Jardin proved costly: Paul Tuffrau heard shouting from a foolhardy group of spectators on the western edge of the park:

'There you go. They got him.'

'Who? A Hun?'

'No, a Frenchman. Killed stone dead.'

Shortly afterwards, an ambulance turned up with stretcher-bearers standing on the running boards, waving Red Cross flags.[52] They took away the body of 31-year-old Jean Lavaud, an FFI fighter from Fontenay-aux-Roses.[53] Lavaud was just one of dozens of people killed in the neighbourhood that day.

*

At 12:00, Colonel de Langlade's column crossed the bridge at pont de Sèvres and streamed through the Porte Saint-Cloud, the south-east entrance into the city. Like all the other Allied soldiers, they were fêted by the population, kissed repeatedly by the women, and generally made slow progress because of the crowds. Colonel Bruce of OSS, who was with them, wrote in his diary: 'Kissing and shouting were general and indiscriminate. It was a wonderfully sunny day and a wonderful scene. The women were dressed in their best clothes, and all wore somewhere the tricolour – on their blouses, in their hair, and even as earrings.'[54] As the column entered Paris, the 2e DB artillery regiment led by Commander Mirambeau fired salvo after salvo of shells onto the German artillery batteries to the west, ensuring that there would be no counter-attack.[55] By the early afternoon, de Langlade's group had made it to the place de l'Etoile, where they were greeted by thousands of Parisians. De Langlade positioned tanks facing down each of the major avenues that radiate out from the Arc de Triomphe and then set up his headquarters next to the monument. His target was the German administrative centre at the Hôtel Majestic, just down the avenue Kléber, where the Germans had built a massive concrete bunker. Shells fired by two of de Langlade's Shermans destroyed three German tanks and several vehicles stationed outside the hotel, while a Free French infantry anti-tank unit took out a small Panzerjäger tank by the avenue d'Iéna. Within minutes, the Germans in the Majestic were surrounded and had no significant defences.[56]

As smoke from the burning vehicles poured into the sky, a bare-headed, balding German officer appeared waving a white flag. Frightened by the baying crowd – the Parisians seemed completely heedless that they were in a battle zone – the German attempted to negotiate surrender conditions. De Langlade replied curtly that there was only one condition – either they surrendered within thirty minutes or they would all be killed. The officer returned to the Majestic, accompanied by Colonel Massu, a number of soldiers and even a film crew. Shortly afterwards around 350 Germans marched out of the bunker.[57] The first German strong-point had fallen.

Even so, the fighting in the neighbourhood was not over. As the Germans were leaving the bunker, their hands held high, one of them threw an incendiary grenade at the French troops, injuring two men.[58] A few minutes later, at the place de l'Etoile, there was a similar incident, with even more tragic consequences. Infantryman Jacques Desbordes was crouching behind a tree at the end of the avenue de Wagram when German prisoners marched around the Arc de Triomphe, escorted by a group of 2e DB soldiers, including Colonel de Langlade.[59] Suddenly, a smoke grenade exploded, enveloping everyone in acrid, stinging fumes. In the chaos, a machine gun began firing into the grey cloud and Desbordes joined in without realising it: 'To my surprise, the sharp recoil of my rifle told me that I was firing – I couldn't hear my shots because of the amazing racket. Slowly, the smoke cleared, the machine gun stopped firing and I got up ... The machine gunner crawled forwards on my right to see what had happened. I'll never forget his words, spoken with an accent from Bab el-Oued in Algiers: "Bummer. What a mess."'[60] Seven German soldiers lay dead or severely wounded under the bright sun. Miraculously, de Langlade and the other French soldiers were all unhurt. According to Desbordes, although stretcher-bearers took away some of the Germans, the most severely wounded were shot through the head. Desbordes felt the whole incident was a catastrophic accident – the grenade had gone off by mistake, and the 2e DB had fired in a mixture of panic and a justified reaction to prisoners who were apparently trying to escape.[61] Whatever the case, seven men were needlessly dead.[62]

Marc Boegner witnessed a final awful incident near the Arc de Triomphe. Boegner had spent all afternoon with the massive crowd, watching the tanks of the de Langlade column chugging up the avenue Victor Hugo. In his apartment that night, Boegner recorded what he saw next: 'On the place de l'Etoile we see prisoners being taken away.

There are four soldiers, barefoot, their tunics unbuttoned, their hands behind their heads. They are taken into the middle of the place, facing down the Champs-Elysées. People scurry round, photographing them. Then something terrible happens! Because one of them had killed a French officer when they had said they were surrendering, they are all shot dead, straight away, on the corner of the avenue de Wagram.'[63]

This brutal killing was filmed, but the footage was not included in the newsreel that was soon shown around the world.[64] According to the unbroadcast commentary, the four men were 'Georgians' who had been firing on the crowd from surrounding rooftops and had killed a woman and a child. The film shows that the man who mowed down the 'Georgians' with a spray of machine-gun fire was a 2e DB soldier.[65] Why he killed the four men is not known.

*

The Hôtel Meurice and the neighbouring administrative buildings on the rue de Rivoli were protected by at least seven tanks, including five Panthers, which were stationed in and around the Jardin des Tuileries.[66] They were the major military problem the 2e DB had to face, but they proved remarkably easy to deal with. Intimidating though they might be, tanks are not at their most effective in urban warfare – they require the support of determined infantrymen and light armoured vehicles, and the Germans had neither.

Shortly before 14:00, Colonel Billotte launched two groups of tanks and infantrymen westwards from the Hôtel de Ville towards the Hôtel Meurice, one group on either side of the Tuileries. When a group of Shermans entered the Tuileries, they began a ferocious firefight and soon all the German tanks were destroyed or abandoned and their crews were either killed or captured. Columns of thick black smoke climbed skywards, marking the destruction.

Meanwhile, 2e DB soldiers, accompanied by FFI fighters, crept up the rue de Rivoli followed by five Shermans. Unlike in the other battles in Paris, there were no joyous civilians to get in the way. The street was empty and the air was filled with exhaust fumes, dust, the smell of cordite and the sound of gunfire. After some of the French soldiers were killed, the tanks moved to the front of the column, smashing through the flimsy anti-tank defences the Germans had set up in the road, and destroying a small tank at the corner of the rue d'Alger, right next to the Hôtel Meurice. Flame-throwers devastated German vehicles in streets adjacent to the rue de Rivoli, adding to the stench of chaos. But the final part of the advance was not entirely straightforward: the crew of the ill-named Sherman *Mort de l'Homme* were extremely imprudent – they had left the turret hatch open. A German soldier in one of the hotels at the side of the rue de Rivoli threw a grenade into the tank; it exploded, seriously burning the crew.

In one of the few offensive manoeuvres made by the Germans, a Panther moved out of the Tuileries and onto the place de la Concorde, from where it fired at the de Langlade group up at the place de l'Etoile, missing the Free French tanks but hitting the façade of the Arc de Triomphe. When the shell smashed into the edifice, Colonel Bruce of the OSS was on top of the Arc, where he had been invited by a group of veterans who had draped a massive French tricolour over the front of the monument.[67] In his diary, Bruce laconically noted the mixture of the beautiful and the terrifying: 'The view was breathtaking. One saw the golden dome of the Invalides, the green roof of the Madeleine, Sacré-Coeur, and other familiar landmarks. Tanks were firing in various streets. Part of the Arc was under fire from snipers. A shell from a German 88 nicked one of its sides.'[68]

After the Panther had fired its shell, one of the Shermans near the Arc de Triomphe turned its gun down to the gates of the Tuileries where the enemy tank was squatting. The gunner, Robert Mady, was ordered to open fire, range 1500 metres. But some rote school-learning from his childhood told him that the Champs-Elysées was 1880 metres long, so he ignored orders and set the range to 1800 metres.[69] He hit the Panther with two shots that damaged but did not destroy it. At the same time, another Sherman, which was much closer, fired a shell into the left flank of the Panther and smoke began to pour from the vehicle. Finally, one of the Sherman tanks from the rue de Rivoli, commanded by 23-year-old Sergeant Bizien, turned onto the place de la Concorde and found itself track to track with the Panther. Bizien's tank rammed the stricken vehicle and fired at point-blank range. The Panther burst into flames and its crew fled into the Tuileries.[70] A minute later Bizien was dead, shot through the head.

By this point the infantrymen of the 2e DB had made their way into the ground floor of the Hôtel Meurice, throwing smoke grenades and firing their machine guns.[71] In the rooms directly above, von Choltitz was flooded with indecision, so Colonel Jay seized the initiative. The young officer graphically summarised their situation – hopeless – and proposed that the fighting against the FFI should continue, but that if regular troops attacked, then everyone would surrender. Von Choltitz agreed.[72] This revealed the classic military fear of being captured by undisciplined civilians, but above all it showed how isolated the German Paris command had become: they did not even know who was attacking them. A few minutes later, Lieutenant Karcher of the 2e DB burst into the room and told von Choltitz that he was now a prisoner. Then Lieutenant-Colonel de la Horie entered and demanded that the German commander order his men to stop fighting. Von Choltitz agreed. It was all over. The last German commander of Paris was taken out of the back entrance of the Hôtel Meurice and was driven off to the Préfecture de Police, to sign his surrender.[73] The second, decisive, German strong-point had fallen.

*

A few hundred metres to the north, by the Opéra, another column of 2e DB soldiers made short work of the Kommandantur, which had housed a large part of the German administration. After shells were fired and a vehicle was destroyed, filling the area with choking smoke, the few hundred Germans surrendered. Within minutes the men and vehicles of the 2e DB were swamped by celebrating Parisians. Lieutenant Bachy recalled: 'All of a sudden there were over a thousand people there – I don't know where they came from – surrounding each soldier, joyously celebrating our presence, such that the Section Leader could not gather his men together, or indeed give any order at all.'[74] Spanish exile Victoria Kent wrote in her diary: 'We clap our hands and hold them out to our liberators. We would like to do more. We would like to put the tanks on our shoulders and take them through Paris, from the north to

the south, from the east to the west, but all we can do is smile and hold
out our hands.'[75] By 14:45 German prisoners were streaming out of the
place de l'Opéra, marching in the sunlight to the Mairie of the 9th
arrondissement, where they were held in a makeshift prison.[76]

Not far away, a retired French air force pilot invited Colonel Bruce
and his colleagues for a drink. After a short walk, wrote Bruce, 'we
found a most beautiful apartment, with very fine furniture and Chinese
porcelains, his lovely wife and a magnum of iced champagne.' When
they returned to their vehicle, they discovered a retired French lieutenant-colonel plying Ernest Hemingway and his crew with champagne,
which was brought out in hampers by the officer's manservant.[77] Among
the crowd of people gathered round the Sherman tanks at the Arc de
Triomphe was Micheline Bood, dressed in red, white and blue clothes
and with red, white and blue ribbons in her hair. As she wrote in her
diary that night: 'It's crazy: little girls, young women, young people
climbed onto the tanks, even dogs wearing tricolour bows. The cheeks
of the French soldiers are covered in lipstick; the men are magnificent,
bronzed and burnished by the sun.'[78] Micheline's decision not to join in
the kissing – 'I think the soldiers must have been fed up with it' – might
have been wise, as not all the encounters with the liberators went well.
Micheline's friend, Huguette, was in tears because her father had found
her kissing a soldier, and had slapped her. People consoled the poor
girl, and a soldier gave her some chewing gum to cheer her up.[79]

Despite the joy at the Arc de Triomphe, at the other end of the
Champs-Elysées, the fighting continued around the place de la
Concorde, in particular in front of the Navy Ministry and the Hôtel
Crillon, where many of the high-ranking officers had their apartments.
A German bazooka unit in the Crillon fired on the Free French tanks;
in reply a shell hit one of the building's decorative columns, which dramatically collapsed onto German vehicles below.[80] A US journalist
described the situation on the radio: 'From where I am speaking to
you I can hear the explosions of shells and the spatter of machine guns:
Boche machine guns, machine guns of the regular army, and the
machine guns of the FFI. The Germans set fire to the Navy Ministry and
the Hôtel Crillon and the sky is ablaze in the direction of Neuilly and
Vincennes. These are the last jerks of the beast receiving the mortal

blow.'[81] Inside the Hôtel Crillon, Quartermaster Wallraf observed the situation: 'An Allied tank . . . tried to cross the place de la Concorde. A group of foot soldiers followed it, covered by the tank. From the fourth floor, our machine gun fired at the group of infantrymen; the men rapidly turned back, but one of them leapt into the air and fell on his back onto the floor, where he remained, immobile. His comrades came to get him.'[82]

Young stretcher-bearer Jean-Claude Touche had been instructed by his mother not to leave their apartment, but on the pretext of going to play cards with a local priest, he made his way to the local Red Cross post. Together with a 29-year-old nurse, Madeleine Brinet, he was ordered to the place de la Concorde. As the two first-aiders ran across the rue de Rivoli to tend to a wounded soldier, they were cut down by machine-gun fire from the windows of the Navy Ministry. Madeleine was killed instantly; Jean-Claude was badly wounded and died in hospital four days later.[83]

Wallraf later explained why the fighting went on so long – they simply did not believe that von Choltitz had surrendered: 'A general who, only a short time ago, said he would shoot anyone who tried to get out of defending Paris, such a man could not have surrendered at the first shot, leaving others to carry on fighting!' It took von Choltitz's personal signature to convince the Germans to lay down their arms.[84]

The battle of Paris was won, but it was not yet over. The Germans were still dug in at the Ecole Militaire, the Senate and at place de la République. There was still fighting to be done, and lives to be lost. After more than four years under the Nazis, Paris would soon be free. But at a price.

16

Friday 25 August, Evening: Triumph

US war correspondent Ernie Pyle writes: 'I had thought that for me there could never again be any elation in war. But I had reckoned without the liberation of Paris – I had reckoned without remembering that I might be a part of that richly historic day. We were in Paris on the first day – one of the great days of all time.'[1]

General von Choltitz was led into Billotte's headquarters in the light-filled billiard room at the rear of the Préfecture de Police. The German commander had a stunned air, his face was puffy, and his monocle stared blankly from his right eye. Von Choltitz's nemesis, General Leclerc, was gaunt and utterly focused. The Frenchman stared like a hawk at his defeated enemy and then spoke in German: 'I am General Leclerc. Are you General Choltitz? Please sit down.'[2]

The room was crowded – Chaban, four French commanders, a 2e DB translator and one of von Choltitz's aides were all there in a space dominated by the large billiard table. The room soon became even busier: first when a small table was brought in so that the surrender document could be signed, and then when Valrimont and Rol entered. Valrimont had initially been in the adjoining room; realising the importance of what was taking place, he had asked Luizet if he and Rol could be allowed in as representatives of the Resistance. Luizet, who as Prefect of Police was nominally in charge of proceedings, recognised that their presence could help smooth over the remaining differences with the

Resistance, so he persuaded Leclerc and Chaban to accept this in-cursion into military protocol, and the two men were ushered in. Valrimont, wearing an ill-fitting suit and a tie with pastel stripes, was the only civilian in the room.[3]

When everyone was ready, the 2e DB translator, Captain Betz, read the surrender terms to von Choltitz. The German commander appeared to become unwell and went pale, sweating heavily. As the translator began to read through the terms a second time, Valrimont – who certainly did not lack courage – spoke up and said that Rol should also sign the surrender document. Leclerc, slightly bemused, pointed out that he was signing as 'Commander of the French Forces in Paris', and that Rol was therefore represented by him. With that, two copies of the document were signed by Leclerc and von Choltitz, one of which was retained by the German general. The first stage of the German surrender was over.

Von Choltitz was then driven the short distance to Leclerc's head-quarters in the Gare Montparnasse. Photographs show Leclerc and Chaban standing up in front; von Choltitz, slumped over, is seated behind, while Rol and Valrimont stand up at the back; the streets are lined with cheering, jeering Parisians, delighted to scream their joy and howl their contempt at the defeated occupier.

The station was eerily empty and quiet, a striking contrast to the noise outside. There were no trains, and the building was deserted apart from Leclerc's staff and a handful of railway employees.[4] Von Choltitz was taken to an office and told to sign orders instructing his men to surren-der, which were to be taken to each of the remaining German strong-points around the city.[5] The German officer's demeanour was striking: 'He seemed completely vacant, as if in a dream; his face was livid and he seemed to be completely stunned by events.'[6]

Meanwhile, Valrimont again suggested that Rol should sign the sur-render document. Chaban supported him and Leclerc finally agreed, although he remained nonplussed – he was perhaps not up to speed on the tensions that existed between the Resistance and the Free French. Leclerc's copy of the surrender was therefore amended in handwriting, with Rol's name appearing before that of Leclerc.[7] The most significant aspect of the document, however, was that both Rol and Leclerc signed

in the name of the French Provisional Government, not as representatives of the Allies. This was a Free French triumph, and the signatures
signified that Paris was under the control of de Gaulle's Provisional
Government. The final battle in the four-year conflict between the Free
French and the Allies over de Gaulle's significance and the future government of the country had been resolved at the stroke of a pen.[8]

Questioned by Leclerc's staff officers, von Choltitz insisted that he
had not ordered any buildings or bridges in Paris to be mined, nor
were there any booby-traps.[9] This was basically true. Although there
were large quantities of explosives in some of the strong-points, these
were simply stocks that the Germans did not want to fall into enemy
hands. The only charges that were to be used for sabotage purposes
were those at the telephone exchanges on the rue des Archives and the
rue Saint-Amand, and a 500 kg mine under the Pont Saint-Cloud.[10] All
the rumours about the Germans preparing to destroy the city were just
that – rumours. Nothing had been done to carry out Hitler's momentous order of two days earlier, which had concluded: 'Paris is not to fall
into enemy hands other than as a heap of rubble.'[11]

Shortly afterwards, de Gaulle arrived at the station along with a
couple of dozen aides and hangers-on, including the Free French delegate to the Liberated Territories, André Le Troquer, plump and wearing
a large homburg hat. For the last two days, the Free French leader had
exerted no influence on how events unfolded in the capital; now he was
at the centre of affairs. De Gaulle was shown to a table at the end of one
of the platforms, where he sat down and read the surrender document.
Film shows him surrounded by various members of his staff, together
with an FFI fighter in classic pose – white shirt, pullover, baggy trousers
and Sten gun at the ready. Rol, standing at ease, looked almost girlish as
he nervously swung his body from side to side. Throughout all this,
Chaban stood to attention in front of the table, ramrod-stiff like a keen
recruit, face to face with his leader for the first time. De Gaulle stu-
diously ignored the young man in front of him and carried on reading.
The Free French leader became visibly annoyed, and he called over
Leclerc, asking him why Rol had also signed – von Choltitz had not surrendered to Rol, Rol had a subordinate rank to Leclerc, and yet his
signature appeared first, snapped de Gaulle.[12] Leclerc smiled and

brushed aside the question. Mollified, or simply realising that the issue was ultimately irrelevant, de Gaulle took off his glasses and stood up. Leclerc then stepped in and gestured to Chaban, still standing to attention: 'Sir, do you know General Chaban?' De Gaulle jabbed a cigarette in his mouth, and stared at Chaban ferociously. Chaban thought he could read the emotions flowing through his leader's mind as he realised that this young man – twenty-nine years old but barely looking twenty, according to Chaban himself – had been given such massive responsibilities. Incredulity, surprise and even anger apparently swept over de Gaulle's face, recalled Chaban: 'Then the statue moved. I was given a strong handshake – double strength – while the voice pronounced three words against which all awards and honours paled: "*C'est bien, Chaban.*"'[13]

De Gaulle was then introduced to Rol, who was wearing his distinctly non-regulation uniform and black beret from the Spanish Civil War. Whatever annoyance de Gaulle might have felt about Rol's involvement in the surrender, he congratulated the FFI leader and shook hands with him.[14] De Gaulle even talked to Valrimont, although the two men were both prickly, and the brief exchange was primarily a verbal joust.[15] As de Gaulle left, he spoke to a French radio journalist and gave a fair summary of what had happened: 'The German general commanding the Paris region has surrendered to General Leclerc and the commander of the Forces Françaises de l'Intérieur.'[16]

*

Despite the surrender of the German commander, fighting continued around all the remaining German strong-points. Probably the most destructive battle was at the Ecole Militaire, where the 2e DB launched a frontal attack, moving down from the Eiffel Tower in three columns. Despite important damage to the Ecole, the Germans held on. The decisive moment came when a sustained grenade attack on the northern corner of the building enabled the 2e DB infantry, supported by FFI fighters, to pour inside. After some fierce fighting, hundreds of Germans surrendered, leaving fifty dead and many more wounded. Even today, the scars of the battle remain – there are pockmarked walls and huge chunks missing from the masonry around the windows.[17]

Other strong-points surrendered only when given the order. Colonel Jay, along with two of von Choltitz's other senior aides, was driven to the Gare Montparnasse, where he was handed the order for the remaining outposts to surrender. Jay was sent with two 2e DB soldiers, accompanied by a 2e DB tank, to the place de la République where the imposing barracks was protected by two 75 mm cannons, six 37 mm guns, and an armoured car.[18] FFI fighters from Madeleine Riffaud's Saint-Just group, together with two FTP units commanded by 25-year-old medical student Commander Darcourt, had attacked the barracks early in the morning, and fighting had continued sporadically, without any help from the 2e DB.[19] Over a dozen *résistants*, stretcher-bearers and passers-by were killed or fatally wounded in the fighting, as shown by the plaques that can be seen on the walls of the surrounding streets.[20] One of the last casualties was 22-year-old Michel Tagrine, who had been wounded at the Bastille on 19 August, and had just been promoted to the rank of lieutenant. Despite his injury, Michel had insisted on returning to the fighting, but was killed by a bullet in the head as the final attack was launched.[21] When Colonel Jay arrived, he was given a white tea-towel tied to a stick, and strode out into the square as the bullets whizzed by. Inside the barracks, the local commander and his aides were not impressed by von Choltitz's order, but eventually had to bow to reality and the threat of complete annihilation. Five hundred German soldiers surrendered.[22]

The place de la République was not the only place where the FFI had fought alone. Earlier in the day, Victor Veau had seen dozens of Germans marching down the rue de Miromesnil, guarded by just five FFI men, only one of whom had a gun.[23] The FFI also took the barracks at Clignancourt, on the northern edge of the city, and held down the German headquarters in Neuilly, to the west.[24] However, although the FFI at Neuilly were able to prevent the Germans from escaping, they were unable to take the two buildings where the enemy were holed up. In the early afternoon, two 2e DB armoured groups arrived, destroying German half-tracks and motorised anti-tank guns, littering the street with twisted metal and smouldering rubber. Eventually, one of von Choltitz's officers turned up with the order to cease fire, and around 800 German prisoners surrendered. Three men of the 2e DB were killed, along with a number of FFI fighters.[25]

FFI actions continued in the suburbs, too. At Joinville-le-Pont, five kilometres south-east of Paris, on the edge of a huge loop in the Marne, a dozen German soldiers turned up from the east with instructions to destroy the bridge over the river. While they were trying to get access to the underground chamber where the explosive charges had supposedly been laid, they were fired upon by local FFI fighters. The Germans called for reinforcements, and scores of soldiers launched a firefight that lasted all afternoon. Eventually, one of von Choltitz's officers arrived with the cease-fire order and the Germans surrendered. Around a dozen FFI fighters and residents of Joinville had been killed in the operation.[26]

The most determined German resistance came around the Jardin du Luxembourg and the Senate. By the late afternoon, tanks from the 2e DB destroyed the German bunkers, and infantrymen and FFI fighters entered the gardens. The German defences were slowly reduced with the help of a 4th US Infantry bazooka unit, and the tanks in the Jardin were destroyed; a Panther in front of the Odéon theatre was hit by three shells fired by a 2e DB Sherman. German snipers in the Senate clock tower were dealt with when two tanks fired on the building, demolishing part of the tower. At around 17:30, a German officer was sent into the Senate, accompanied by two French soldiers, carrying von Choltitz's order to surrender. After discussions that lasted forty minutes, a German officer came out marching 'like a robot', waving a white flag, and that was the end. The swastika flag that had flown over the Senate for four years was hauled down and replaced by a French tricolour.[27]

The Jardin du Luxembourg was littered with shattered concrete and machines – abandoned or destroyed tanks, lorries and armoured cars.[28] The Senate courtyard was a complete mess, full of burnt-out vehicles and the detritus of a defeated army. Inside, it was even worse. A reporter for *Défense de la France* described the scene:

> Everywhere, in the never-ending linked galleries and salons, in the great Conference Room, in the library, among the trampled maps, the scattered dossiers, the magazines and books ripped apart as though by a tornado, on desks and under furniture, there are dishes full of mouldy food, half-finished glasses of kummel liqueur, broken crockery,

ripped clothes, bottles of champagne and yet more bottles of champagne! Throughout the building, an indescribable mess covers the furniture, which is coated with thick dust from the bombardment.[29]

As German prisoners filed out of the Senate, three abreast, their hands on their heads, the tanks of the 2e DB returned to their stations. For Gaston Eve and his comrades of the *Montmirail*, this meant taking up a position on the boulevard Saint-Michel, opposite the Sorbonne. While Gaston was showing a boy and a young woman around his tank, there was a burst of gunfire and he sheltered them with his body. When it was time for the girl to go home, Gaston lent her his helmet. Her name was Odette Lampin, and she returned the helmet the next morning. They were married in October 1945.[30]

On the other side of the Seine, Jacqueline Mesnil-Amar powdered her nose, put on some lipstick and a clean dress and rode her bicycle all over the north of the city. As she wrote in her diary that evening: 'What sudden lightness of being throughout the city; people are singing, running, everyone is in the street, setting up dances at every crossroads – we will dance tonight. There are flags everywhere, made of bits of old cloth, poorly sewn together, hurriedly dyed, tricolours and Allied flags, draping the windows. Banners painted on wallpaper stretch across the streets from one building to another, shining and shaking in the air, dancing in the blue sky.'[31] But Jacqueline's thoughts were never far from her husband, André:

Why aren't you here on this unforgettable night, under this beautiful sky, why aren't you in these streets, on your bicycle, by my side or here on this balcony? . . . I call to you, I call to you again from the depths of my sadness and my joy . . . I call to you from partying Paris, where innocent people will be able to live, where children will be able to grow up, where those who have done no harm will be able to sleep at night, in this extraordinary union which will not last, in the beauty of this evening, which you would have loved so much . . . You who are so far away, I call to you as never before.[32]

*

As the German prisoners streamed out of the hotels on the rue de Rivoli, they felt the full fury of a Parisian population that had lived under the Nazis for four years. In his diary, Walter Dreizner described how people threw water and even a bicycle at the German soldiers, while a man burst from the crowd and thumped a soldier to the floor. When they reached the top of the rue de Rivoli, they were hit by a gale of hatred and the soldiers began to fear for their lives:

> A flood of abuse swept over us. These curses came from so many throats that they numbed our ears. They turned into a battle cry: from all sides the masses pressed against us with calls of 'Hang them!', 'Murderers!', 'Band of pigs!', 'Band of murderers!', 'Thieves!' and 'Down with the Huns!' They hit us, pushed us and spat at us. They were completely out of control. Wild beasts had been unleashed upon us and we were their victims, victims who could not defend them- selves and were not even allowed to do so. This meant death, a tortuous death. The Parisians were in their element. In the midst of this unbelievable screeching we were pushed, hit and forced to the Palais Royale opposite the Louvre. The tall iron railings around the Palais offered us some protection. We could breathe. I felt as if I were in a cage, but a cage where the beasts were outside, pushing up against the iron bars.[33]

Sometimes, the Germans fought back. As the prisoners filed out of the Hôtel Crillon, the headmaster of the boys' school on the nearby rue Cambon observed the chaotic scene: 'I arrived at the Concorde just as they were bringing the German flag out of the Navy Ministry, and were hoisting the French flag. Hundreds of German officers and soldiers were coming out of the Crillon, being screamed at by the crowd. They jostled each other to get into the lorry quickly. Sitting next to the driver there was a German officer who was white with anger; when the lorry started off he thumped one of the women in the crowd.'[34] The Germans were stunned by their capture. In Montparnasse station, Captain Gallois saw what he felt to be one of the most striking signs of the German defeat: '40 high-ranking German officers, covered with medals and rib- bons, were gathered together on a main-line platform. There were no

seats, so they sat on the platform like a string of onions, their feet touch-
ing the rails; every now and again one of them would get up and walk to
the water fountain to drink from a soldier's beaker.'[35] Writer Léon
Werth, who had recently arrived in Paris, saw the captured soldiers of
the Senate garrison sitting down in tightly packed rows, dejected. Their
plight prevented Werth from truly rejoicing: 'The humiliation of these
men makes me suffer. It is necessary, it is according to the principles of
justice. I approve of it, it satisfies me, it calms me and yet I cannot
rejoice in it. Is this feeling so complicated, so difficult to understand?
When I tell people this, they say, "But you are forgetting what they have
done, the killings, the torture ..." I forget nothing. But a man who is
humiliated, his humiliation is in me.'[36] German soldiers who managed
to escape from the collapse of the garrison reported their treatment by
Parisians to their comrades in the surrounding region, reinforcing the
atmosphere of threat created by the insurgent population. Dr
Herrmann of the Panzer Lehr Division wrote in his diary: 'The German
prisoners were abused, spat upon, flogged and treated as they were in
1918, perhaps even worse.'[37]

And there was worse. Lieutenant von Arnim was in the line of soldiers
marching up the rue de Rivoli, their hands held high. He later recalled:

> There was screaming, threats, fists were shaken. The accompanying
> guards found it difficult to protect us – and themselves. Over and again
> one of us was knocked down by someone in the crowd and was tram-
> pled upon. Just in front of me on the march was a friend of mine, Dr
> Kayser von Hagen, a highly educated and sensitive Francophile.
> Suddenly a shirt-sleeved, bearded giant of a man leapt out of the
> crowd, put a gun to Dr Kayser von Hagen's head and pulled the trigger.
> I stumbled over his fallen body, hauled myself up and staggered on.[38]

*

Even before the guns fell silent, the political manoeuvring had begun.
A few days earlier, Parodi had invited the CNR to be present at the
Préfecture to welcome General de Gaulle when he eventually arrived in
Paris. CNR President Bidault turned down the invitation – he felt that

de Gaulle should come to the Resistance, not the other way round, and that the Republic should be declared from the Hôtel de Ville, as in the revolutions of the nineteenth century, and as Parodi had agreed a week earlier.[39] Bidault's intransigence led to an impasse. Both sides realised the historic significance of the moment they were about to live through, and both sides were determined to shape events to produce the outcome they desired. Only one side could win.

Once he was in the city, de Gaulle made his intentions clear. After leaving the Gare Montparnasse and briefly embracing his son, who was fighting with the 2e DB, he headed for the Ministry of War on the rue Saint Dominique, which had been his office until June 1940. This appeared very humble – after all, his only official position was that of Minister of War. However, behind this false modesty lay a clear-eyed political project. De Gaulle's view was that Pétain, Vichy and everything that went with them were a mere aberration. France – the Republic – had continued to exist, in London, in the shape of the Free French. The occupation was nothing more than a four-year interlude, and now things could return to normal. There would be no declaration of the Republic, and most certainly no revolution.

De Gaulle rarely made matters easy for his friends and supporters. Over the previous tumultuous weeks, Parodi had done his utmost to carry out de Gaulle's instructions and to ensure that the Resistance did nothing that would block the General's pathway to power. Parodi was loyal to the point of self-abnegation, and had operated without support or instructions for most of the insurrection. Now, at the crucial moment, he had no idea of de Gaulle's whereabouts. When he did eventually track the General down to the Ministry of War, Parodi was given the brush-off – 'We will arrange an audience for you', said an aide over the telephone. Parodi had to insist quite forcefully before he was finally allowed to meet the man to whom he had devoted the last four years of his life. For a first meeting, it was not auspicious. The atmosphere was tense, as Parodi argued that de Gaulle had to go to the Préfecture and the Hôtel de Ville to meet with the men and women who had risked their lives to liberate the city.[40] Eventually, de Gaulle bowed to political necessity and acceded to Parodi's wishes. But before he left the building, the Free French leader told Parodi and Luizet that he would hold a triumphal march through Paris the next day. Significantly, this was not discussed with any representatives of the Resistance. What was to be de Gaulle's apotheosis was decided by him alone, without any reference to the people who had enabled him to take power.

At 19:00 de Gaulle got into an open-top ministerial car and was driven to the Préfecture, with Parodi seated at his right hand. They were accompanied by police motorcycle outriders and a Resistance film crew who captured the vehicle slaloming through the gaps in the barricades to cries of joy from startled *résistants*.[41] At the Préfecture de Gaulle was welcomed with a fanfare from the police band, and was presented with bouquets by two young women.[42] After quickly saluting Luizet's staff, de Gaulle walked the short distance over the river to the Hôtel de Ville.[43]

*

Radio journalist Pierre Crénesse had spent the whole day at the Hôtel de Ville, waiting for de Gaulle to arrive. He had interviewed anyone he could get hold of – infantrymen, tank drivers and, that classic journalistic last resort, other journalists. But his patience paid off and he was there, ready with his microphone, when de Gaulle finally strode up the great staircase inside the building. Crénesse got his scoop and provided a running commentary on the event, broadcasting the historic moments to the city and the world.[44]

Inside a chandelier-lit salon, de Gaulle was greeted with enthusiasm by the crowd – for virtually everyone there it was the first time they had set eyes on their leader.[45] The walls of the room had been splintered by gunfire, there were holes in the windows and bullets had starred the mirrors. The air was already stifling from the late afternoon August heat and the packed crowd; when the spotlights were turned on for the newsreel cameras, the temperature rose even more. In this hot, buzzing atmosphere, Georges Maranne, the communist President of the CPL, read a speech in which he welcomed de Gaulle and generously put the General at the centre of the amazing events that everyone had just lived through, even at the price of historical accuracy: 'On 19 August you ordered a national insurrection. Paris obeyed, magnificently. It was

liberated by the Forces Françaises de l'Intérieur and by its whole population. But it owes that liberation to you. And it thanks you for it.'[46]

In reply, de Gaulle led the crowd in a rousing verse of the
'Marseillaise', and then Georges Bidault spoke, in the name of the CNR.
This was the first time that de Gaulle and Bidault had met, and it was
not a good start.[47] Like Maranne, Bidault praised de Gaulle: 'Today, the
uniformed Resistance and the non-uniformed Resistance are united
around the man who, from Day One, said "No" . . . Like the General, the
French people have never surrendered. For four years they fought with
empty hands. Today they are triumphant.' But Bidault then went on to
pay a moving tribute to his comrades who had been tortured, and to
those who had died in battle or in prison. He singled out 'the first president of the Conseil National, our leader, our friend who has
disappeared, Max, whose real name we cannot pronounce because
there is still the hope that we will see him again. On this day of triumph,
I evoke his memory with pride and tenderness.'[48] 'Max' – Jean Moulin –
had in fact been killed by the Nazis nearly fifteen months earlier.

Then it was de Gaulle's turn to speak. Microphones were thrust in
front of him, and with Bidault and Parodi standing by his side, de Gaulle
launched into one of the most significant speeches of his life. It was
improvised, spoken in a voice that was so familiar to everyone who
heard, whether they were present in the room or hunched round their
radio set.[49] While Maranne and Bidault had both been generous about
de Gaulle, the General did not return the compliment. There was not
one mention of the Resistance, nor was there any recognition of the terrible sacrifices that had been made over the last four years. In the
opening section of his speech, which has become part of French culture, de Gaulle made a moving and telling description of his view of the
liberation of the capital: 'Paris! Paris humiliated! Paris broken! Paris
martyrised! But now Paris liberated! Liberated by herself, by her own
people with the help of the armies of France, with the support and aid
of France as a whole, of fighting France, of the only France, of the true
France, of eternal France.'[50] Although de Gaulle went on to underline
the need for national unity in pursuit of the war, and the importance
of universal suffrage as a way of uniting the nation, it was his mystical
invocation of 'eternal France' that predominated.[51] And who had

represented 'the true France' for all those years? The question did not
need to be asked.

After another burst of the 'Marseillaise', Bidault asked de Gaulle
privately whether he would now declare the Republic. De Gaulle's reply
was glacial, and summed up his whole political thinking: 'The Republic
has never ceased to exist ... Vichy was always, and remains, null and
void. I am President of the government of the Republic. Why should I
proclaim it?'[52] And with that de Gaulle went into the offices of the
Prefect of the Seine, overlooking the packed square in front of the
Hôtel de Ville. When he appeared at an open window, there was a huge
shout from the crowd. Before anyone could stop him, he leapt onto the
window-sill and, holding precariously onto the window frame, waved to
the thousands of people below.[53] After soaking up the adulation, de
Gaulle climbed back through the window and returned to the Ministry
of War, where he spent the night before what was to be the most
momentous day of his life.

As soon as de Gaulle had left the building, the CNR met.[54] The
Resistance leaders were aghast.[55] They expected that the political roles
they had been developing in the years of clandestinity would finally be
recognised, but de Gaulle had shown he was intent on creating a different reality, one in which he – not the Resistance – represented the
continuity of 'France'. Far from being simply a military leader and a
figurehead for Resistance, de Gaulle was determined to play a major
role in the politics of post-war France. Outmanoeuvred and deflated,
the best the CNR could do was to instruct Bidault to express their
disappointment to de Gaulle and to ask him to reconsider his decision
not to declare the Republic. But de Gaulle was not a man who changed
his mind, and it was even less likely than usual that he would do so on
this occasion.[56] For all their years of underground experience and
despite their political intelligence, the CNR had been bested by a man
they had dismissed as a mere general.

While the members of the CNR were politicking in the Hôtel de
Ville, the soldiers retired for a victors' banquet at Les Invalides.
General Koenig and General Leclerc invited Colonel de Boissieu and
Colonel de Langlade of the 2e DB, along with Chaban, Lizé of the FFI
and some of Koenig's staff, to a meal served by smartly dressed waiters

and obsequious ushers, who presumably had been equally subservient to their collaborationist masters. The soldiers wore their dirty battle fatigues, except for Chaban, who cut an odd figure in his pristine uniform. He also stood out because of his youth – de Langlade was stunned when he heard the smart young man addressed as 'General'. But here, too, there was politicking. During the meal, Chaban recounted the insurrection, lingering over the details of the cease-fire and the role of the Communist Party. At the end, Koenig said: 'We have narrowly avoided another Paris Commune.'[57] For some leaders of the Free French, the meaning of the liberation of Paris was clear: a decisive political victory had been won.

*

Most people in Paris that evening did not care about politics. They were simply elated to be free. As dusk fell and the stars came out in the clear sky, Victor Veau went to the place de l'Etoile: 'What an amazing scene – I am glad to have seen it before I die. ... A huge, joyous crowd surrounds thousands of tanks and other vehicles. People are shouting and clapping. The soldiers – all French – invite people onto their tanks and explain how they work.'[58] The place de l'Opéra was still a heaving mass of joyful bodies, full of people shouting their joy. Caught in the maelstrom were Colonel Bruce of OSS and Ernest Hemingway, trying to make their way to Hemingway's pre-war watering-hole at the Café de la Paix. As Bruce recorded in his diary, they could not get through, so 'after kissing several thousand men, woman and babies, and losing a carbine by theft' they 'escaped to the Ritz', which was deserted, and where they and their men were served fifty martinis and 'a superb dinner'.[59]

Odette Lainville sat at her desk and wrote a poem which concluded:

> Oh, those soldiers, tanned and bronzed by battle!
> Oh, those laughing eyes of our boys!
> Oh, those French soldiers ... French ... Can it be true?
> Then so many Americans, like happy children.
> And our dear British boys ... my heart almost fails me ...
> – And Paris, our own dear Paris, swept clean of Germans![60]

There were magical moments. At 19:00, two tiny Free French Piper air-craft audaciously touched down on the avenue de la Grande Armée, which extends north-west from the place de l'Etoile towards the sub-urbs.[61] Amazed and enchanted, the crowds gathered round the fragile machines that had suddenly come down to the ground.

On the Left Bank, Daniel Boisdon felt a great sense of satisfaction as the light slowly faded on an extraordinary day:

> To the west, at the end of the boulevard Saint-Germain, the sun, which had already set, painted the clouds pink in a pale blue sky. A great calm fell on the destruction, the felled trees, the ripped-up paving stones, the broken glass, the barricades still bristling with rifles and machine guns. The streets were full of people out strolling. There was no overwhelming excitement . . . Every now and again, a group of noisy young people passed by. In the lorries of the Leclerc Division, stationed along the sides of the road, the men talked quietly or slept, exhausted. As I returned home, there was a small procession. It was headed by hospital staff, wearing white coats and waving Red Cross flags as if they were in a battle, then there were the local firemen, and two or three thousand people passed by, arm-in-arm, right across the boulevard, singing the 'Marseillaise'.[62]

*

It was not all joy and celebration. In the newly liberated Ministry of Health by the Arc de Triomphe, Bernard Pierquin threw himself to the floor as machine-gun fire shattered the windows. The shots were fired from some of the 2e DB tanks stationed nearby, following rumours that there were snipers in the building. Although Bernard was unhurt, three people in the building were severely wounded.[63] On the other side of the river a group of American soldiers – including one woman – were visiting the 6th arrondissement police station, just behind the church at Saint-Germain. There was a burst of machine-gun fire and at least two people on the rue Bonaparte fell dead. The killers – Germans or mem-bers of the Milice – were never found.[64]

There were yet more incidents of head-shaving, as ordinary citizens turned on women suspected of 'horizontal collaboration' with the Germans. While it was generally men who did the shaving, in the southern suburb of Orly a group of women demanded that 'the Germans' girlfriends' should have their heads shaved – six 'culprits' were found and punished.[65] In her diary, Flora Groult showed some sympathy with the victims:

> Women who have 'sinned' with the Germans are having their heads shaved, their foreheads marked with swastikas and being paraded through the streets naked to the waist ... Our neighbour has been enlisted for this business and he came home last night as proud as a hero. I do not think I would have the strength to be the instrument of destiny and the razor of punishment. *'La chair est triste, hélas!'* [The flesh is sad, alas!] when it makes you pay so cruelly for your pleasure. I hope I do not meet any of the women. I could neither hate them nor be sorry for them.[66]

Railway engineer Pierre Patin was at an impromptu street party in the 18th arrondissement, where hundreds of people were dancing to the music of a clarinet and an accordion. Three slightly drunken men turned up, manhandling a terrified woman, whom they claimed had slept with Germans. She should be shot, they said. Patin, who was wearing his FFI armband, convinced the men to hand her over to the local FFI, and ensured that she would soon be released. That night, as he lay in bed with the sound of music and revelry coming through his windows, he reflected that although he might not have killed anybody during the insurrection, he had perhaps saved someone's life, which was probably better.[67]

In his attic hideaway near the Senate building, collaborationist author Robert Brasillach felt less positive about things, realising that 'it was the end'. He heard the sound of gunfire die away, and one of his neighbours announced loudly in the courtyard that the Germans were surrendering. Finally, he heard the strains of the 'Marseillaise'. Scornful of the struggle to drive the Germans out of Paris, Brasillach juggled with his feelings but soon resorted to his default emotion – self-pity:

I was now totally isolated from other people. I found their joy to be naïve, stained with lies ... And yet, these naïve people were happy, and they were my people. I was not involved in their joy as I should have been ... Why should I not also go down into the street, why should I not also fly a flag? I should have been happy like the passer-by who kissed a soldier of the Leclerc Division, dressed in an American uniform, or who acclaimed the first tanks. But I remained there, alone and unjustly punished.[68]

At 20:00, Field Marshal Model, who still did not know that von Choltitz had surrendered, noted the failure of the small relief column that had advanced from Le Bourget. To regain the initiative, he ordered that on 27 August a new attempt to reach the centre of Paris should be made using new forces massed on the eastern side of the city.[69] Model even planned a propaganda march of German troops through Paris 'just to show the French that we still have some Divisions left'.[70] Recognising that it would be hard to hold the region around the capital, the German commander also made further preparations to strengthen the line east of Paris, instructing the 5th Panzer Army to disengage from the Allied bridgehead at Mantes and set up a new defensive line from the Oise river to the capital, following the overnight withdrawal of the 6th Parachute Division.[71] However, as Colonel Frank of the 5th Panzer later admitted, 'this represented hardly more than a screen of outposts'.[72] More decisively, Model ordered 'all available Luftwaffe forces' to prepare for a night attack to the south of Paris, to take place the following evening.[73]

While Model continued to fight, von Choltitz prepared for a life in captivity. Taken into custody by the Americans (Gallois reported they were 'very interested' in the German general), von Choltitz was questioned the next day by Colonel Dickson.[74] The German officer claimed that the arrival of the Allies 'saved Paris from going up in smoke' and that 'the internecine war between the French surpassed all his expectations ... he was damn glad to get rid of the job of policing both Paris and the Frenchmen, both of which he apparently detests'. Dickson concluded that that German commander 'realised quite a while ago that the job of trying to defend the city was hopeless and that he had taken no great steps to try to do so'.[75] Within a couple of days, von Choltitz was settled in the prison camp at Trent Park on the outskirts of London, where his garrulous and boastful conversations with the other prisoners were secretly recorded, providing the Allies with valuable insights into German morale.[76]

*

At 22:00, the US Army T-Force convoy finally arrived in Paris after a long drive through the southern suburbs.[77] Its role was to immediately secure any potential intelligence sources, including documents and individuals. After setting up base in the Petit Palais, next to the burnt-out hulk of the Grand Palais, T-Force sent out its first search teams shortly after midnight. Although they had a measure of success in securing some buildings, it soon became apparent to the T-Force commanders that 'the local Police Station would be a good source of information'.[78] The crack Allied counter-intelligence group had no idea about the situation in Paris. They had assumed they would be in complete control of the city, and that they alone knew who and what needed to be secured. It turned out that the French were doing quite well on their own, and T-Force found that most of their targets were already under French control. Over the next two days, T-Force arrested a mere eleven people out of their 514 'personality targets'.[79]

*

The victorious soldiers of the Leclerc Division spent the night camped in the Jardin des Plantes in the centre of Paris, along with the Rochambelle ambulance group.[80] People chatted to them through the park gates, and later on in the evening there was an improvised ball on the rue Geoffroy-St-Hilaire, which runs down the side of the Jardin, and the soldiers joined in.[81] That was not all they got up to. Suzanne Torrès recalled: 'From all around there were stifled sighs and ticklish giggles. Many Parisian women were too charitable to let our lads spend their first night in the capital alone.'[82] For others, however, life went on as though nothing had happened. Marc Boegner wrote in his diary:

'General de Gaulle is at the Hôtel de Ville. In the building opposite, the old lady who lives on the first floor is playing her usual evening game of patience.'[83]

But for one person, life began again. Late in the evening, Jacqueline Mesnil-Amar finally learnt that her husband André had escaped from the train taking him to Germany. He was in Fontenay-sous-Bois, five kilometres east of Paris, waiting to walk the final stage; three other escapees had already managed to get back home to Paris that night. 'I run, I have wings. I believe!' an overjoyed Jacqueline wrote in her diary at midnight. 'They will be here tomorrow.'[84]

André was safe, and would soon be with his family again, but the two dozen people who did not jump from the Drancy train met a very different fate. That evening, as Paris was dancing and celebrating, the last convoy from Drancy pulled into Weimar station. The men were sent on to Buchenwald; the five women went to Birkenau. Fewer than half of the prisoners survived the next nine months of horror, before the final collapse of the Nazi regime and the liberation of the camps.[85]

17

Saturday 26 August:
Celebration

On the Blue Network radio station, US reporter Herbert Clarke describes the amazing atmosphere in the capital: 'I can't stay at my typewriter, I can't stay off my balcony away from the spectacle of all the delight that's outside. Words can't describe Paris today. You need music for it. Some tune that is a cross between the spine-tingling "Marseillaise" and the rollicking roll of "Turkey in the Straw", and the rhythm of the Brazilian samba. [1]

It was cold and misty again as day broke. Paris was hungover.[2] A tousle-headed, bleary eyed woman emerged from the turret of a Leclerc Division tank; the place de la Concorde was littered with debris and still smelt of burning metal and rubber, while on the Left Bank the streets were covered with shattered masonry, splintered glass, broken branches and the wreckage of German vehicles. Gradually, the day took shape. Odette Lainville cycled down to Montparnasse to find her nephew Bob and his comrades, and was given an amazing gift – a cup of real coffee. The Ritz hotel had no coffee, so Colonel David Bruce of OSS had to make do with a bottle of Chablis to accompany his breakfast omelette. At Pré-Saint-Gervais, just outside the north-eastern walls of the capital, sixty-five young pupils from the boys' school, accompanied by five teachers, began to march towards the centre of Paris, waving French and Allied flags and singing as they went.[3] They were just some of the hundreds of thousands of people who began to pour into the city centre for the hastily organised victory parade that was to mark the liberation of the city, and which de Gaulle had decreed the previous evening. As the morning wore on, the mood of the city became 'relaxed but vibrant, slightly tipsy, happy and still feverish', as Paul Tuffrau put it in his diary.[4] News of the parade was spread by word of mouth, by the Resistance radio station and by the Resistance press, which was unanimous in its enthusiasm. Even *L'Humanité* trumpeted on its front page in massive capital letters: 'AT 15:00, FROM THE ARC DE TRIOMPHE TO NOTRE DAME, THE PEOPLE WILL UNANIMOUSLY ACCLAIM GENERAL DE GAULLE'.[5]

The parade very nearly had to be cancelled due to a furious row between the Free French and the Americans. De Gaulle understandably felt that the 2e DB should be at the heart of the parade, and invited General Gerow and his staff, along with two dozen representatives of the US Army, to join in.[6] Gerow was not impressed. The American general considered himself to be in command of the city; he was also, as everyone accepted, Leclerc's commanding officer. That morning, Gerow sent Leclerc a furious note: 'You are operating under my direct command and will not accept orders from any other source. I understand you have been directed by General de Gaulle to parade your troops this afternoon at 1400 hours. You will disregard those orders and continue on the present mission assigned you of clearing up all resistance in Paris and environs within your zone of action.'[7] After some squabbling – de Gaulle allegedly said to the Americans: 'I have given you Leclerc; surely I can have him back for a moment?' – it was agreed that while some sections of the Leclerc Division would go on the parade, the rest would move northwards towards Aubervilliers and Saint-Denis to deal with the German forces there.[8] Paris might be liberated, but it was by no means secure, and the Germans remained a formidable and determined enemy. Although a handful of American and British officers took part in the parade, the bulk of the American troops were nowhere to be seen. The parade was very much a French event, and deliberately so. De Gaulle wanted to use the parade to demonstrate and cement his importance and to show that French unity and power had been restored. In this he succeeded completely.[9]

*

From the late morning onwards, the men and machines of the 2e DB began to assemble along the five-kilometre route from the Champs-Elysées to Notre Dame. Amid the noise of manoeuvring armoured vehicles and the jostling crowds, Captain Gallois managed to track down General Leclerc. They had not spoken since Leclerc had ordered Dronne to head for Paris two days earlier. The general greeted the younger man laconically: 'Ah!' he said. 'There you are. Well, that didn't go too badly.'[10]

Around fifty half-track armoured vehicles were parked in a neat line across the whole width of the place de l'Etoile, facing down the Champs-Elysées, leaving a gap in the centre through which de Gaulle and the rest of the cortège would pass. Shortly before 15:00, de Gaulle arrived. After reviewing the troops, he went to the Tomb of the Unknown Soldier, directly underneath the Arc de Triomphe. Flanked by North African soldiers in fine red fezzes, the Free French leader laid a wreath of pink gladioli wrapped in a tricolour ribbon. There was a continuous clack-clack from the press cameras – the photographers seemed to be the only people who were not carried away by the immensity of the moment. Standing just behind de Gaulle was Georges Dukson, the FFI fighter from Gabon who had been wounded at Batignolles a few days earlier and had been dubbed 'The Lion of the 17th' by the press.[11] His arm still in a sling, Dukson, along with other notable fighters, had apparently been invited to the ceremony.[12] De Gaulle took time out to complain to COMAC hardman Jean de Vogüé that a group of FFI fighters were not standing precisely in line.[13] But the FFI men were perfect examples of discipline compared to the joyous chaos that reigned behind the massive circle of policemen and firemen stationed around the circumference of the place de l'Etoile. Crowds of people were shouting and cheering; there were British, American and French radio cars, with reporters standing on top of them shouting 'Go ahead' into their microphones; there was even a woman in Alsatian traditional costume – surely it must have been Jeanne Borchert again.[14]

Ignoring the crowd, de Gaulle turned to face down the Champs-Elysées. Accompanying him, slightly behind, were key members of the government – Parodi, Luizet, Flouret, Le Troquer, and two leaders of the Free French armed forces, General Leclerc and General Koenig.

Georges Bidault, the President of the CNR, was in the front row, while on de Gaulle's right were CNR members who, strikingly, represented political parties rather than Resistance organisations. Behind them came de Vogüé and Valrimont of COMAC, along with members of the CPL, led by the communist André Tollet.[15] The CPL delegation included Léo Hamon, his enjoyment of the day spoilt by the boot nails that poked through into his feet – his battered shoes needed re-soling.[16] Hamon walked alongside Marie-Hélène Lefaucheux, who wore black clothes and hat. Above the noise of the crowd Hamon told her that he was thinking of her husband who had been deported on the Pantin train. Visibly moved, Madame Lefaucheux explained she felt the parade was like a film without one of the main actors.[17] Most of these names and faces are now forgotten, and even at the time, few of them were known to the public. The crowds were not cheering the men of the Provisional Government, they were not cheering the anonymous leaders of the Resistance, they were cheering the idea and the reality of liberation, and the presence of the one man they had all heard of – General Charles de Gaulle.

De Gaulle – taller than any of the others, his height exaggerated by his military cap or kepi – wore a modest dress uniform, with no medals or ribbons except a small Free French cross of Lorraine. In contrast, the Prefect of the Seine, Flouret, had ribbons galore on his smart new uniform, while Le Troquer, wearing a bow tie and carrying his homburg hat in a gloved hand, looked as self-important as ever. Parodi and Bidault were frankly shabby – pale and gaunt, wearing ill-fitting suits, their threadbare appearance revealing the reality of four years of life underground during the occupation. Photo-hungry press photographers pushed their way to the front, jostling each other and the Free French leaders, desperate to get 'the' picture of de Gaulle and his comrades framed by the massive arch, with the vast billowing folds of the tricolour flag filling the sky.[18] As a grim-faced de Gaulle set out past the cheering crowds, he was preceded by four clanking Sherman tanks that clouded the air with their stinking exhaust, and by a gaggle of motorcycle outriders and jeeps, some of them weighed down by newsreel camera crews.

And so Charles de Gaulle walked into history for a second time.[19] The first occasion had been four years earlier, on 18 June 1940, when he had entered a BBC studio in London to make his first broadcast to France. Now, in the heart of the French capital, at the Tomb of the Unknown Soldier – a location of the greatest significance for a military man – de Gaulle reached the end of that long road. In so doing, he began another phase in his life and that of France, one heralded by the well-prepared printed banners that had been handed out to the crowd, reading: '*Vive de Gaulle*', '*Vive la République*', '*De Gaulle au pouvoir*' ('All power to de Gaulle').[20] As Valrimont commented acidly: 'The Free French Delegation had done its work well.'[21]

*

Initially irritated by the noise and the disorder, de Gaulle softened as he realised the scale of the event. Even today, it is hard to grasp the sheer numbers of people who were there – it must have been the largest gathering in the history of France. As de Gaulle wrote in his memoirs twelve years later, describing the vast crowds lining the Champs-Elysées: 'Ah! It is the sea.' Bernard Pierquin, watching from the windows of the Ministry of Health on the place de l'Etoile, had a similar impression and wrote in his diary: 'our great General looked so small in the middle of this sea of humanity'.[22] Elsewhere in the same building, Victor Veau was not so lucky. The old surgeon had been brought to the ministry in an FFI car and was initially pleased with the vantage-point that had been found for him – a comfortable armchair on a large and airy first-floor balcony. But what with the trees and the crowds and the half-tracks lined up in front of the Arc de Triomphe, he could see nothing.[23]

The crowds were immense – over twenty deep on either side of the road, all the way from the Arc de Triomphe to the Hôtel de Ville.[24] Children were carried on shoulders, or were pushed to the front where they could see and would be safe.[25] Odette Lainville took a folding chair and gingerly balanced at the back of the crowd, just about able to see between people's heads. One woman had brought along a home-made periscope consisting of a mirror fixed on a stick, while a little old lady turned up with a stepladder.[26] All along the route, the buildings were covered with people, thronging at the windows, standing precariously on shop fronts, gathered in clumps on the roofs, clinging onto the chimneys.[27] Micheline Bood ended up sitting on a lorry at the end of the avenue de Marigny, with a fantastic view. She was completely swept up in the adoration of the General: 'I can understand that people become fanatical about him, that you could die for him. He is a super-man. The crowd was literally going crazy.'[28] Journalist Claude Roy was less impressed, and captured de Gaulle's strange, slightly diffident manner as he marched down the Champs-Elysées in the heat and the dust, under the bright August sun: 'It was as though his arms were made of wood. He moved his hands in a funny little way to thank every-one, as if to say yes, there you are, good people, thank you.'[29]

Unable to get onto the place de la Concorde because of the crowds, Paul Tuffrau went into the Tuileries and stood on one of the metal chairs he found there, so gaining an excellent view of the parade.[30] On the packed pavement just below him was Berthe Auroy.[31] Colonel Bruce of the OSS was unable to find any vantage point at all: 'The crowds were so great that I could see little of it,' he wrote glumly in his diary, so he wandered off to one of his old haunts in a smart part of town.[32] On the rue de Rivoli, Benoîte and Flora Groult stood on a friend's car in order to get a better view. Gradually, more and more people joined them until suddenly the car collapsed 'like a broken toy'.[33] Daniel Boisdon climbed on top of a 2e DB tank that was in front of the entrance to the Tuileries, facing up the Champs-Elysées. It brought back memories of the 14 July parade in 1919, when he had watched the French Army march down the avenue, led by three marshals on horseback, one of whom was Pétain.[34]

Despite the tanks that opened the parade, despite the uniforms that dominated the official cortège, and despite the omnipresence of the armoured vehicles of the 2e DB all along the route, this was not a mili-tary event. Marc Boegner, slightly amazed, wrote in his diary: 'It was nothing like an official parade. At the forefront was the Paris of the bar-ricades, wearing its fighting clothes with rifle, machine gun and revolver.'[35] For Simone de Beauvoir, it was 'a magnificent, if chaotic, popular carnival show'.[36]

Among the besuited politicians and the smart officers at the front of the official cortège, one man stood out alongside de Gaulle, although he barely came up to the General's shoulder: Georges Dukson, who appears to have been the only black man on the parade. Dukson's presence was noted by one observer in terms that were neither politically correct, nor entirely accurate: 'An FFI escort of honour surrounds General de Gaulle; we can see a big black devil, his arm in a sling, who played an important role in the fighting in the 17th arrondissement, having killed several Germans and been involved in the capture of a tank.'[37] Paul Tuffrau saw him, too: 'Everyone applauded a surprising black man, who wore an enormous tricolour scarf covered in ribbons and waved to everyone.'[38] From her position at the western end of the rue de Rivoli, Berthe Auroy saw 'a negro, running along the road, bizarrely dressed, covered with tricolour scarves. He smiled at the crowd and waved, getting a terrific response.'[39]

Behind the governmental contingent there were groups of FFI fighters marching in a more or less coordinated fashion and carrying home-made placards – 'The Red Army on the barricades of Clichy' read one. Then came dozens of jeeps creaking under piles of passengers, and even a lorry festooned with flags and carrying a big banner reading 'Liberation', accompanied by people holding placards marking the main dates in French history.[40] And all the time, there were the cheering, yelling, shouting crowds.

*

The afternoon was extremely hot and sunny, and the fevered, slightly dream-like atmosphere was reinforced by two Piper Cub aeroplanes circling above the demonstration, repeatedly swooping dangerously low over the crowd. They carried US newsreel crews who filmed the amazing event, providing an additional spectacle for the population.[41] When the parade reached the place de la Concorde, the scale of the event was almost overwhelming. There were tens of thousands of people, hanging from the massive ornamental lampposts, climbing all over the huge statues, perched on the shiny tanks of the 2e DB and on the blistered wreck of the Panther tank that had been destroyed the previous day. Having arrived at the end of his walkabout, de Gaulle was almost submerged by the crowd, which pressed around him, and a way was forced through to an open-top car. With Parodi seated at de Gaulle's side, the car weaved through the milling thousands on the place de la Concorde and then drove down the rue de Rivoli, the pavements thick with people, heading towards the Hôtel de Ville, where tens of thousands more Parisians awaited him.[42] Berthe Auroy was disappointed – all she saw of de Gaulle was a quick flash of a kepi as the car zoomed past. 'It's not very nice of the General not to take the time to salute the crowd,' she complained to the person next to her.[43] For journalist Ernie Pyle there was no reason to be critical: 'the kissing and shouting and autographing and applauding were almost overwhelming. The pandemonium of a free and loveable Paris reigned again. It was wonderful to be there … it was already hard to believe that there ever had been a war; even harder to realize there still was a war.'[44]

But as de Gaulle left the place de la Concorde, everyone soon realised that the war was indeed still going on. All of a sudden, there was the sound of gunshots, apparently coming from the Hôtel Crillon. Along with the rest of the vast crowd by the place de la Concorde, Paul Tuffrau dived to the floor; a young girl and her mother were on top of his legs; by his neck a woman sobbed with fear. The men of the Leclerc Division fired back, first with rifles then with heavy machine guns, shooting at the windows of the Crillon and the Navy Ministry. On the other side of the Tuileries, too, the crowd was cowering, and Tuffrau saw a woman, covered in blood, being carried away on a stretcher.[45] A few metres away, Berthe Auroy flattened herself against the wall of the Tuileries. Children around her cried, 'Mummy, I'm frightened!' Berthe managed to get into the gardens and then ran towards the Louvre, crouching from tree to tree, occasionally diving to the floor when the shooting became intense.[46]

Jean Galtier-Boissière was in the Tuileries when the firing broke out and the crowd panicked: 'We were all lying face-down on the grass. Women were shaking with fright, children were crying. I got up and could clearly see machine-gun fire coming from three windows of the Pavillon de Marsan [the north-west corner of the Louvre], sweeping across the rue de Rivoli and the terrace of the Tuileries.'[47] When FFI fighters opened fire on the Pavillon, fighters on the other side of the river, near the Gare d'Orsay, joined in the shooting. FFIers near

Galtier-Boissière, thinking they were under attack, fired back at their comrades. It was chaos.

The confusion was captured by BBC reporter Robert Dunnet who was on the place de la Concorde as the firing broke out, and carried on broadcasting throughout:

> ... there's been some shooting broken out from the – one of the buildings – I think it's in the neighbourhood of the Hôtel Crillon, just following the passage of General de Gaulle, and there's smoke now rising from the building and the people – there's a great crowd – has broken out [*confusion, voices – French and English*] ... the tanks are firing back – the tanks massed in the square are firing back at the hotel, and I'm standing looking just straight across at it – smoke – smoke rising, and whoever opened up on the crowd from the hotel is [*several voices speaking in French*] ... [*sound of gunfire*] ... It's rather difficult to place where all the fire is coming from. I certainly can hear bullets going past at the moment – that peculiar whistling noise they make – and still these men with the Red Cross flags stand up on this balustrade, right out in the open, holding up their flags and waving, smiling – 'People, just take it quite easy, it's all going to be all right.'[48]

Eventually, the firing ceased and calm returned, although many people were injured. The event might have been put down to overexcited FFIers and the widespread fear of '*les tireurs des toîts*', except that at the same time there was another outbreak of shooting, higher up the Champs-Elysées. A cheery-looking bald man in his mid-sixties was walking his dog on the grass when there was a burst of firing and the crowd rushed for shelter in the Marigny theatre, sweeping him along with them. As he cowered inside the theatre foyer, a dead woman was brought in and laid down beside him. The man was P. G. Wodehouse, who was living in the nearby Hôtel Bristol. As he later told a friend: 'It was all very exciting, but no good to me from a writing point of view.'[49] Watching from his window, Swiss journalist Edmond Dubois saw a woman collapse, blood pouring from her neck.[50] As the firing became more intense, the crowd became completely panic-stricken, and Dubois' apartment building was soon full of passers-by sheltering from the gunfire.[51] As soon as the shooting started, Micheline Bood hurried to her nearby home, furious that the day had been ruined by the snipers. She stomped up to the very top of her building and stuck her head out of the window, convinced that the firing was coming from next door. To her shock, she found herself face to face with a young man armed with a revolver – and wearing an FFI armband. He had been sent up to deal with the source of the shooting, but found nobody.[52]

It was not only the French who were trigger-happy. The T-Force head-quarters at the Petit Palais was hit by gunfire from a US armoured car, which opened fire with its heavy machine gun because the gunner saw 'a gun barrel pushed out from behind the curtains'. Six people were wounded, including three members of T-Force. The commander of the armoured car was immediately relieved of his duties.[53] Worried that many people could be hurt if the soldiers began to shoot indiscriminately, Colonel O'Brien of the US Army ran along the ranks of his men, ordering them to hold their fire until it became clear who was doing the shooting.[54] It never did become clear.

The outbreak of firing at the Champs-Elysées and at the place de la Concorde was dramatic enough, but what occurred at Notre Dame was even more spectacular. The end-point of the parade was due to be a celebratory Mass in the great Gothic cathedral. Parodi had made the arrangements, and had decided that the Archbishop of Paris, Cardinal Suhard, would not be involved. The Archbishop's conciliatory attitude towards Vichy – including welcoming Pétain in April, and celebrating the funeral Mass for Henriot in July – had not been forgotten by the Resistance.[55] As soon as de Gaulle arrived in front of the cathedral, shots rang out and the soldiers began to fire back, aiming up at the bell towers. The whole thing was recorded by the BBC journalist Robert Reid, whose microphone was briefly but dramatically disconnected in the panic.[56] Eventually Leclerc and the other officers managed to restore order – there was no clear source of gunfire – and the Mass went ahead, without the organ or any lights, as there was no electricity.

The ceremony had barely begun when there was another outbreak of firing, inside the tall vault of the cathedral itself. Yet again, the origin of the firing was unclear. The noise became unbearable as returning machine-gun fire from FFI and 2e DB men echoed round the stone walls.[57] People dived for cover, spilling chairs in the process.[58] Robert Reid reported: 'Some of the snipers had actually got on to the roof of the cathedral. There was an awful din going on the whole time. Just by me, one man was hit in the neck, but I will say this for the Parisian crowd, there was no real panic inside the cathedral at all; they simply took reasonable precautions. Round every pillar you'd see people sheltering, women with little children cuddled in their arms.'[59] Despite the noise and chaos, de Gaulle stood there, unmoved. Eventually, yet again, the firing stopped and order was restored. The mass was cut short and de Gaulle emerged into the bright sunlight, to cries of '*Vive de Gaulle*', 'God save de Gaulle' and 'Holy Virgin, save de Gaulle'.[60] At the same time, there were also outbreaks of gunfire at the place des Pyramides, on the rue de Rivoli and in front of the Hôtel de Ville.[61] Each incident followed the same sequence: a small number of shots led to massive responses from the FFI and the men of the 2e DB, while the civilian population dived for cover and then eventually – once the firing had stopped and the wounded had been taken away – returned to the festivities.

According to the correspondent of the *Manchester Guardian*, a German sniper in civilian clothes was captured by the FFI on a nearby roof.[62] This 'German' may have been one of a number of junior doctors from the Hôtel-Dieu hospital, who were watching de Gaulle's arrival at the cathedral from the hospital roof, and were arrested on suspicion of being snipers.[63] Robert Reid reported that four 'snipers' in grey flannel trousers and white singlets had been arrested inside the cathedral – 'They've got their hands above their heads, and they look very obvious Germans,' he broadcast.[64] Wild rumours circulated – Micheline Bood heard that a family of six had been arrested for carrying out some of the shooting (the 65-year-old grandmother had directed the firing, she was told).[65] In fact, there is no firm evidence of a single arrest for sniping anywhere in Paris that day. One man was arrested, however: Jean Mansuy, one of the *miliciens* who had murdered Georges Mandel in July. He was recognised at the Hôtel de Ville by a *résistant* he had tortured. The next day, Mansuy was shot dead 'while trying to escape'.[66] Whatever the cause of the gunfire at Notre Dame, 120 people were treated for their injuries – bullet wounds, bruises and the effects of being trampled – in the hours after the incident.[67]

The official government line – probably not too far from the truth – was that 'an accidental shot led to a brief burst of gunfire.'[68] At the time, de Gaulle described the firing as 'boastful nonsense' and in a letter to his wife, who was still in Algiers, put the whole incident into context: 'There are many armed people here, who, excited by days of fighting, will fire at the roofs for no reason. The first shot then unleashes a hail of gunfire. It won't last . . . Please send me clean clothes and a pair of slippers.'[69] Years later, de Gaulle changed his mind and suggested that the whole thing had been a communist plot designed to weaken his power.[70] There is no evidence for this.

Whatever the case, there was a widespread conviction that German agents were lurking on the rooftops and taking pot-shots, and people tried to root them out – even Colonel Henderson of the British Intelligence Service spent that evening crawling around on the rooftops, 'chasing three snipers with machine guns who . . . finally evaded him'.[71] In some cases, it was clearly a fuss about nothing. For example, a flag had been fixed on the bell-tower of Saint-Odile church in the 17th arrondissement; during the night the flag was blown about until it rolled around the pole, and in the dim light it looked like a rifle barrel. Local FFI fighters peppered the bell-tower with rifle fire before someone was sent up to deal with the 'sniper' and discovered that there was no one there.[72] Fireman René Bertel was less lucky – he was sent up the steeple of the Saint-Léon church in the 15th arrondissement and was shot dead, although it is not clear by whom.[73]

*

Despite the gunfire, the parade had been a tremendous success, and had shown everyone – the Free French, the Resistance and the Allies – the depth of popular support for de Gaulle. For Pasteur Vallery-Radot, marching behind the General, it seemed as though his life had reached its pinnacle. He went to the empty Ministry of Health, near the place de l'Etoile, and, overcome with emotion, collapsed into a chair and through his sobs declared: 'This is my destiny. I would like to die tonight.'[74]

Others had more of an appetite for the new politics that would shape liberated France. The CNR – its feathers ruffled from de Gaulle's failure to consult with them over the parade – again discussed de Gaulle's refusal to declare the Republic. After a long debate, in which many people argued that the CNR should be the nucleus of a future Constituent Assembly, it was agreed that de Gaulle should be invited to the next session of the CNR (he never came). Tellingly, for the first time the minutes of the CNR meeting contained the true names of the participants, and not their Resistance code names.[75] Although the whiff of cordite had barely faded away, ordinary politics was beginning to reassert itself.

Down the rue de Rivoli, in the northern wing of the Louvre, the leading civil servants at the Ministry of Finance met to discuss monetary policy. There was a clash between the 'Parisians' – those who had remained in France throughout the occupation and wanted to see an increase in salaries in order to kick-start the economy – and the 'Algerians', the Free French who had been part of the Algiers think-tanks and wanted to impose a rapid deflationist policy by cutting state spending. The debate that would characterise much of the post-war history of capitalism – France included – was beginning as soon as the capital was liberated. Although the debate had the same fundamental political lines as today – the left wanted to use the state, the right wanted to reduce its power – it was superimposed on the radically different wartime experiences of the Free French and the Resistance.[76]

That evening Parodi held a dinner at a swish dining club, the Cercle Interallié, to which all the secretary-generals and their spouses were invited. The menu was less swish, however, because of the food shortage: as one guest reported, it included soup ('quite good'), roast beef ('mediocre but plentiful'), a few potatoes, good wine, champagne and tinned fruit. During the dinner conversation, Parodi expressed his fear that severe political conflicts were on the horizon, as de Gaulle brought over his ministerial apparatus from Algiers, replacing the Resistance structures that had been built up during the occupation and the secretary-generals who had taken office during the insurrection.[77] In fact, matters were moving even more quickly than Parodi realised. It would be less than twenty-four hours before his prediction came to pass.

Finally, far from Paris, decisions were being taken about the future of France. As de Gaulle led the parade down the Champs-Elysées, the Provisional Assembly in Algiers was shaping the country's future, as it finally adopted an order that set out the crime of *indignité nationale* (impugning the national honour).[78] This was a minor version of treason that covered 'direct or indirect aid to Germany and its allies, or deliberate damage to the unity of the French national or to the Liberty and Equality of Frenchmen and women'. As well as the obvious people who were part of the collaborationist state or political groups, the new law was aimed at the authors of 'articles, brochures, books, or lectures in favour of the enemy, of collaboration with the enemy, or of racism and totalitarian doctrines'. The penalties ranged from being deprived of all civic rights to restrictions on where the guilty could live.[79]

One man who would have reason to fear the settling of accounts with Vichy was collaborationist writer Robert Brasillach. In the late afternoon, Resistance fighters climbed onto the roof of the building where he was hiding, looking for snipers. When they kicked their way into the flat next door, Brasillach began to panic and decided to find somewhere else to stay. Slipping out of the building, and having removed his glasses in a half-hearted attempt to disguise himself, Brasillach made his way to the hotel room of a friend, who scared him even more with blood-curdling tales of the arrest of an acquaintance. In the end, Brasillach decided he would be better off back in his hideaway, so he returned to the building, only to be accosted by the building manager, who wanted to know who he was and where he lived. Brasillach managed to spin a story of sub-letting someone's apartment, and he was allowed back to safety.[80]

*

In the southern suburbs, two contrasting events took place. A grim discovery was made at Bagneux cemetery: a couple, Robert and Pauline Vermandel, both in their fifties, were found dead, shot through the head. A piece of paper pinned to one of the bodies explained that they were members of Déat's fascist party and that their whole family had been collaborators. The end of the note read: 'Following a trial, they have been executed on orders. Signed: The FFI Commissar of Security.'[81] There was no such rank in the FFI, and no trial had taken place. This extra-judicial killing of two fascists indicated that habits learnt in the Resistance would not disappear overnight.

Not far away, at Chevilly-Larue, just to the north-east of Fresnes, a local lad, wearing the uniform of the 2e DB, turned up at the school. The headmaster of the school, Monsieur Godfroy, described the young man's welcome: 'He explains how he risked his life crossing the Pyrenees, then got through Spain. He describes his time in Morocco, where he joined the famous Leclerc Division, then in England, then his arrival in Normandy, the stupendous battle, the bloody fighting in which his cousin was killed at his side. He is straightforward, quiet, and not at all boastful. He is resolute like all his comrades. This 22-year-old tank commander is my son.'[82]

*

The advance of the Third US Army to the south-east of Paris was so rapid that its supply lines were stretched to breaking point. The army needed 450,000 gallons of fuel each day; only 315,000 were received.[83] By the end of the day, the Allies had reached Troyes, while Allied aircraft bombed Field Marshal Model's new headquarters near Rheims 100 km to the north, destroying important parts of the command post. The German retreat was in disarray: communication with the retreating Army Group G, which was being chased up the Rhône Valley by the joint US and Free French forces that had landed on 15 August, was sporadic at best.[84] During the fighting to the east of Paris, communication with the 17th SS Panzer Grenadier Division collapsed, while the 48th Infantry Division was dispersed and most of its signalling equipment was captured.[85] The Germans were fighting blind.

The Allies were not making major advances to the north of the capital. The 5th Panzer Army had been able to hold its position at the Seine near Rouen, despite the Allied advance to the south. However, as the Allies streamed across the Seine upriver, the 5th Panzer Army's position became untenable and virtually the whole army pulled back eastwards, leaving only a small group to defend the Seine near Elbeuf.

At the Seine bridgehead at Mantes, the battered and exhausted men of the 1st SS Panzer Corps, who had been holding back the Allies and were hoping to withdraw, were ordered to cover the retreating 5th Panzer Army, which was endangered by Allied attacks that threatened to break through and surround them.[86]

To the north-east of the city, the German 47th Infantry Division was ordered to take up an east–west line at Le Bourget to stop the Allies from breaking out of the capital.[87] In the morning, as part of the agreement with General Gerow, Leclerc sent two probing missions out to the north and north-east of Paris. While the group that headed north through Saint-Denis met no serious opposition beyond occasional bouts of mortar fire, the other group ran into the German troops at Le Bourget. The machine-gunner on one of the jeeps, Le Burel, was killed by a burst of gunfire that ripped his throat out and covered his comrade Louis Rabier with blood. Rabier set the dead man on the floor, then – in his own words – he turned into a robot. He picked up a machine gun, screamed 'Revenge! Revenge!' and started firing pell-mell at the German position. 'I fired so much that in the end the shots were going off on their own,' he later recalled.[88] He eventually came to his senses and ran for cover, zigzagging to avoid enemy fire. It turned out that they had bumped into a large column of German infantry and were substantially outnumbered, so they rapidly retreated back to Saint-Denis.[89]

It seems that the Germans were emboldened to move in daylight due to the relative lack of Allied air cover that day.[90] The Germans were reinforced by the von Aulock Division, a makeshift group composed mainly of clerks and orderlies, with no artillery, although they did have light tanks. Troops from the combined unit were spread out all over the region north-east of Paris, with their headquarters at Moussy-le-Vieux, twelve kilometres away from the village of Saint-Pathus where Jedburgh Team AUBREY was based.[91] These German troops were involved in a particularly bloody incident, as the men of AUBREY – Marchant, Hooker and Chaigneau – put on their uniforms and joined forces with hundreds of FFI fighters who had been summoned to the nearby village of Oissery by Major Armand ('Spiritualist') and local FFI leader Charles Hildevert.

The reason why these men converged on Oissery is uncertain, but a contemporary account suggests they were to be reinforcements for an imminent Allied parachute attack behind German lines.[92] One participant later stated they were to secure the nearby landing ground in preparation for a major supply drop.[93] Whatever the case, the men were instructed to make their way to the small village but not to use their weapons on the way: 'Do not open fire, even on isolated German soldiers', read their orders.[94] London apparently urged that the operation should be postponed because of delays on the ground, but Captain Marchant decided they should go ahead nonetheless, as changing the plans would only cause confusion.[95] The men were supposed to leave their rallying points in the north-east suburbs early in the morning of 25 August, but for some reason their departure was delayed by twenty-four hours.[96] Nothing went quite according to plan, as one of the groups captured a number of German vehicles and prisoners en route, while other units were delayed or never left. Those who did make it to the rendezvous – a sugar-beet processing plant at Oissery – were given weapons, including four Bren machine guns and five Piat anti-tank weapons. But two of the machine guns were still covered in their protective grease and had to be cleaned, while only the three Jedburgh men knew how to fire the Piats, and had to instruct the FFI fighters. A makeshift field hospital was set up at the processing plant, and wounded FFI fighters and German soldiers were left there with some nurses, while the rest of the group gathered on a low-lying road by the side of a small lake on the south-eastern outskirts of Oissery.[97]

As soon as the men arrived at the lake, they came under sustained fire from a German light tank and an unknown number of soldiers. After an hour of fighting, two more tanks turned up and began shelling the Resistance position. A number of Frenchmen were killed and wounded, including one inexperienced man who had his jaw broken while using the Piat anti-tank weapon. By 12:30 it became clear that the German firepower was overwhelming, and the order was given to disperse. This proved easier said than done – Marchant found his escape blocked by German troops and had to hide in the lake, where he remained for nearly nine hours while the surface was repeatedly raked with machine-gun fire. Meanwhile, Captain Chaigneau and a nurse crawled along the small stream that snakes south-east from the lake, with Sergeant Hooker and Major Armand about thirty metres behind them. Suddenly there was a massive explosion and Hooker heard the nurse screaming; Chaigneau was dead. A German tank was stationed just the other side of the stream, and Hooker and Armand had to stay where they were for three hours. The enemy vehicle was so close that Hooker could hear the crew speaking and could even make out the sound of the Morse code being broadcast by the tank radio operator. Eventually, they made their way to a safe house and were picked up by advancing American troops; Hooker was sent to Paris, while Armand was dispatched to London for debriefing by SOE. On 30 August, Hooker returned to pick up Marchant, who had escaped from the lake during the night, and both men were brought back to Britain.

Over 100 Frenchmen were killed in the fighting at Oissery, including FFI leader Hildevert. Another sixty-five were taken prisoner; many were deported and never seen again. The sugar-beet processing factory was completely destroyed, and over twenty badly burnt bodies were found in the ashes. On his return to the UK, Marchant wrote: 'The Germans shot everyone, all the prisoners and the wounded, even a nurse, and burned the corpses.'[98] Of the French men and women who died as a result of what happened at Oissery, either in the fighting or in the concentration camps, the oldest was aged fifty-eight, while the youngest was 16-year-old Yves Goussard, a young black man from Martinique. Yves was captured at Oissery, was deported and eventually died in Bergen-Belsen of typhus, at the same time, in the same place and of the same cause as another, more renowned teenage victim of Nazism: Anne Frank.[99] Whole families were destroyed by the battle – Charles Hildevert's two sons, Georges (nineteen) and Roger (twenty-one) died alongside their father in the fighting at the lake.[100] The one-sided combat had involved French men and women from all over the north-eastern suburbs. They had come from their homes early in the morning, and over 150 of them never returned, caught up in an operation that remains obscure.

*

That night, the shocked and grieving villagers of Oissery and Saint-Pathus heard the sound of aeroplanes flying overhead. Some thought that this was the promised weapons drop arriving too late. But the air-craft were German planes from bases in Holland and Germany and they were heading for Paris, as ordered the day before by Field Marshal Model.[101] With Paris still celebrating, there was no air-raid warning, no time to get to the shelters. Berthe Auroy, still in her nightdress, huddled in her cellar as the bombs fell on her neighbourhood, hitting the nearby Bichat hospital.[102] When the attack finished, Berthe returned to her apartment and saw an apocalyptic vision: 'The Paris sky is on fire. Whole neighbourhoods are burning, sending gigantic flames shooting skywards. The northern suburbs are all lit up. I don't dare go back to sleep.'[103] Near the Jardin du Luxembourg, Paul Tuffrau initially thought the aircraft were Allied planes, but soon realised they were not. Peeking through the shutters of his apartment, Tuffrau saw red flares floating down to the east, accompanied by terrible detonations.[104] Not far away, Odette Lainville and her husband Robert hid in the cellar, then when the explosions stopped the couple emerged into the courtyard, where it was as bright as day, although the sky was a horrific bright red – 'faerie-like and awful', wrote Odette in her diary.[105]

Poet Camille Vilain was an air-raid warden near the Jardin des Plantes, out in the open and directly beneath the bombs. Once he had herded the inhabitants of his building into the nearest shelter, Camille took up his warden's post on the boulevard Saint-Marcel and watched hell descend on earth. To the north, a cascade of bombs hit the Halle aux Vins, the massive wine and spirits warehouse by the Seine; to the south, the flour mills at the Moulins de Paris were also destroyed. In both cases, the consequences were catastrophic. The spirits in the Halle aux Vins combusted dramatically, while at the Moulins de Paris the par-ticles of flour formed an inflammable aerosol, and the air burned. At 01:00 Camille climbed up to the roof to watch blazes that threatened to spread and set the whole south-east part of the city alight: 'The specta-cle is nightmarish. Inside the building, it is as bright as day. The flames are easily leaping hundreds of metres into the sky. Suddenly a particu-larly massive jet of fire spurts up incredibly high, and rolls and roils almost to where we are standing. We can hear the roar of the flames quite clearly.'[106] In the Jardin des Plantes, women fled from the warm arms of the soldiers of the 2e DB, while the smell of burning alcohol filled the air, and the frightened animals in the zoo roared their fear.[107] Venturing out into the street, Daniel Boisdon saw a sight to rival the images of Saint Paul's in the London Blitz from earlier in the war: 'I have never seen anything more amazing than the silhouette of the cathedral, floating in a black sky above a blood-red River Seine.'[108]

Over 200 people were killed and nearly 900 injured in the bombing.[109] To give a name to just one of the victims, Colette Roy, a pupil at the primary school on the rue des Pyrenées, was killed by shrapnel.[110] Among the shattered buildings and wrecked homes there were also minor but distressing losses. Monsieur Lecomte, a hospital administrator and amateur entomologist, was utterly distraught at the destruction of his thirty-year-old insect collection when his study was smashed by a German bomb. As he wrote in his diary, this was 'the greatest entomological catastrophe of my life, which far surpasses everything that I have suffered, everything that I have had to endure ... My whole life has been destroyed ... Can it be true? Can such an awful event be possible?'[111] More gravely, in a striking symbol, some of the hundreds of German bombs dropped on Paris that night destroyed the warehouses at Austerlitz that had housed the Jewish prisoners and the Parisian part of *Möbel Aktion*.[112] It seemed as though the Germans were trying to cover their traces.

18

27 August–31 December: Restoration

On 28 August, Colonel David Bruce of OSS writes in his diary: 'Already, the Liberation of Paris seems almost like a dream. I have never imagined a scene that was, all in all, so dramatic, so moving, and so beautiful and picturesque . . . The frenzied joy of the crowds is impossible to describe. Yet during it all, there was an element of danger that added an almost sinister flavour to the feast . . . It is fitting that it was Leclerc's Armoured French Division that occupied the city and joined the French Resistance Forces, who had for some days been battling there, in cleansing it of the enemy. It is true that the Resistance people, ill-organized and unused to weapons, are a dangerous nuisance in some respects. Yet it is they who, throughout France, have raised the standard of revolt.'[1]

The German garrison in Paris had surrendered, but other German troops were only a few kilometres away and they still posed a threat to the French capital. On the morning of 27 August, five armoured columns of the Leclerc Division spread out to the north and north-east of Paris and soon met German defences. There was a series of encounters and German tanks and armoured vehicles were destroyed – the enemy forces were relatively weak, acting primarily as a buffer between the Allied spearhead and the main retreating German divisions. The hardest fighting took place around the airport at Le Bourget, which had been evacuated by the Luftwaffe eight days earlier.[2] According to a reporter from the *Daily Mail*: 'The desperation and hopelessness of German resistance is typified by the battle for Le Bourget aerodrome. For six hours German troops fought fanatically ... The enemy had three defence lines, but no heavy armour or artillery and they were butchered by the French tanks.'[3] By 18:00 the battle was over and, at the end of an operation that was personally commanded by Leclerc, Le Bourget was in French hands for the first time in over four years.[4] Among the men of the 2e DB who lost their lives that day were 18-year-old Yves Mairesse-Lebrun, the gunner on one of the armoured cars, and Sub-Lieutenant Pity, killed aboard his Sherman, just after he had shot a brave German who had climbed onto the back of the vehicle and tried to throw a grenade into the turret.[5] One of the men fighting at Le Bourget was Odette Lainville's nephew, Bob. Although he survived, many of his friends were killed, including one of the officers who had celebrated the liberation with Odette, four days earlier.[6] Thanks to the Allied advance to the south and the north-east of Paris, there was no longer any direct threat to the capital.

As the Germans continued their retreat to their frontiers, they began to ask why they had lost control of Paris so easily. On 28 August, Field Marshal Model began a court martial investigation of von Choltitz, because he had 'not lived up to expectations'. The collapse of the Paris garrison was clearly a surprise to Model, and he wondered whether the explanation for von Choltitz's 'weakness of will and determination' might lie in his having been wounded or threatened, or even whether he had been the victim of 'an enemy chemical agent'.[7] Nothing came of these proceedings – over the next eight months the German High Command had more pressing matters to deal with. After the end of the war, the leading Nazi Hermann Göring was questioned about this period:

Q: How important a part did Paris play in your defence scheme?

A: I don't know anything about the importance of holding Paris. At that time I was ill and confined to bed.

Q: Did General von Choltitz receive authority to surrender the city?

A: One thing I do know: General von Choltitz had no authority to hand Paris over to the FFI.[8]

So rapid was the Allied advance and so headlong was the German retreat that within a week most of France was liberated, with the exception of the north-eastern corner of the country closest to Germany and some isolated Atlantic ports. That did not mean that the capital was safe, however. At the beginning of October, V1 and V2 rockets were launched from Germany against the Paris region, destroying buildings and killing dozens of people.[9] A month later, an abandoned German ammunition train at Vitry-sur-Seine exploded, leaving thirty-one dead, ninety-seven wounded and dozens of buildings severely damaged.[10] The capital felt one final spasm of fear in December, when the faint-hearted were momentarily shaken by an audacious but short-lived German counter-attack in the far-off Ardennes – 'the Battle of the Bulge'. But by the end of the year the Germans were once again retreating, and the final phase of the war had begun.

*

As the military security of the capital was assured, de Gaulle moved to consolidate his political and military dominance over a chaotic situation. Although his personal popularity was not in doubt, there was no central authority in the city, no government, no reliable way in which 'order' – a key word in de Gaulle's vocabulary – could be imposed. Throughout the insurrection, the Parisian Resistance and its armed groups had repeatedly shown that they could not be expected to do the General's bidding without question. According to Eisenhower, on 27 August de Gaulle asked him 'for the temporary loan of two US divisions to use, as he said, as a show of force and to establish his position firmly'.[11] Eisenhower was unable to comply, but he did agree that on 29 August the 28th US Infantry Division and the 5th Armoured Division – neither of which had been involved in the fighting to liberate the capital – would march through the city. De Gaulle later denied that any such conversation took place, and insisted that the US parade had nothing to do with a show of strength.[12] Perhaps, but it certainly did not do any harm: marching twenty abreast, the infantry were smart and disciplined; the new tanks and field artillery that followed them were a perfect expression of overwhelming Allied military might, leaving the crowds amazed, exactly as might have been hoped.[13] The parade could not have been a greater contrast to the joyous mess of the French affair three days earlier. Saluted from a podium by de Gaulle and General Bradley, the soldiers – all white – marched straight through the city and off to the north and east to fight the Germans.[14] De Gaulle's later description accurately sums up what he was doing, and why: 'Despite its wounds, our country would soon find itself on the road of national recovery. On condition that it was governed, which meant removing any power that was parallel to my own. The iron was hot, so I struck it.'[15]

De Gaulle's first move against this 'parallel power' was political. On 27 August, he summoned all the secretary-generals who had been running the ministries since the beginning of the insurrection. He asked each in turn what his previous job had been and, most often, brusquely advised them to prepare to return to their pre-war occupation. All of those involved were shocked by the General's cold demeanour, by the lack of even a word of thanks or recognition of their work during the years of occupation.[16] Despite their loyalty, despite the fact that they had occupied the ministries at no small risk to themselves in order to give a semblance of continuity, and despite many of them having worked underground for years, the secretary-generals were suspect in de Gaulle's eyes. Unlike the politicians and civil servants in Algiers, whom de Gaulle had tamed, the Parisians were an unknown quantity. And although the Allies accepted his role as head of the government, that might easily change. To secure Allied acceptance of the Free French as the government of France, de Gaulle needed to show that the new regime in Paris was essentially the same as the one that had operated in Algiers, with the same personnel and the same politics.[17]

General Leclerc shared de Gaulle's view, as he showed in a highly critical private letter to his commander, describing the situation he had found in the capital: 'The leaders of Paris, even those appointed by your government, are ... extremely timid. This, I think, is the one of the cruxes of the problem. It is not my business, but having seen certain things, I felt I had to tell you. You will not find your task easy, Sir.'[18]

Even more important than dealing with the civilian administration was finding a way of getting control of the thousands of *résistants* in the city who were still armed – de Gaulle could not expect the US to continue marching their men through the capital. In over half the country, the Resistance had taken over as the Germans fled, sometimes without a shot being fired; Paris was just one example where people had acquired a taste for action and could glimpse the potential and the excitement of running the world in a different way. The usual mainstay of order, the police force, was nearly useless: its members were either hopelessly compromised by their collaborationist past or they were basking in the glow of popular approval following their turncoat change earlier in the month, and could not be relied upon to move against the very people who were cheering them in the streets.

The first metaphorical shot in a battle that would last two months was fired on 28 August, when de Gaulle ordered that the FFI should be incorporated into the Free French Army, while the FFI staff should be dissolved. This provoked an immediate row with the Resistance who wanted to retain this parallel military power, and led COMAC leader Pierre Villon to refuse to join the new government, which was formed on 9 September.[19] Nevertheless, many Parisian FFI fighters joined the 2e DB before it left the Paris region, and the men and women of the FFI soon either returned to civilian life or fused with the army. Leclerc was not particularly impressed by the FFI fighters – he told de Gaulle that 10 per cent were 'really brave, real fighters', 30 per cent would follow the best soldiers, while the remainder were 'useless or even detrimental' to military activity.[20] Among the FFI volunteers from the Paris region who were accepted into the army were Colonel Fabien and his group, including André Calvès. They were attached to the Third US Army and left for the front in early September (Fabien was killed in an accident at the end of the year). Madeleine Riffaud wanted to join up with her comrades, but she was told that no matter what she had done during the insurrection, there was no place for her in the army, although whether this was because of her politics or her gender was not clear. Madeleine was demobilised; a year later she was awarded the Croix de Guerre.[21]

To explain his controversial decision to dissolve the FFI, de Gaulle made a radio broadcast on 29 August, the same day that US soldiers were marching down the Champs Elysées. The speech contained his first public recognition of the role of the Resistance in liberating the capital, as he saluted the 'brave people who for a long period actively organised resistance to the oppressor', before recognising that the 'irresistible offensive' of the Allied armies had made it possible to liberate the capital.[22] This was mere window-dressing. The decisive part of the speech came at the end, where after a lot of rhetoric about 'The nation' and its '2000-year history', de Gaulle made clear what he intended to do: 'the French people have decided, by instinct and by reason, to meet the two conditions without which nothing great can be achieved: order and passion. Republican order, under the only valid authority, that of the state; concentrated passion, which makes it possible to build the structure of renewal legally and fraternally. That is the meaning of the red-blooded celebrations in our towns and villages, finally purged of the enemy. That is the sound of the great voice of liberated Paris.'[23]

*

Foreign journalists visiting Paris shortly after the liberation were struck by the joy they found on the streets of the capital. The *New Yorker* correspondent A. J. Liebling reported: 'For the first time in my life and probably the last, I have lived for a week in a great city where everybody is happy.'[24] Embedded war photographer and fashion journalist Lee Miller, newly arrived from the Normandy front and furious to have missed the liberation, was struck by something else – the smell of Paris had changed: 'It used to be a combination of patchouli, urinals and the burnt castor oil which wreathed the passing motorcycles,' she wrote. 'Now it is air and perfume wafting across a square or street. All the soldiers noticed the scent and, asked what they thought of Paris, became starry-eyed. They said, "It's the most beautiful place in the world and the people smell so wonderful."'[25]

On Sunday 3 September the whole city seemed to turn out just to have fun. Ordinary Parisian Monsieur Lasalle wrote:

There is joy in the air. The boulevards and the Champs-Elysées are back to their bustling selves. Different types of Allied aeroplane fly over the capital endlessly. There are still flags at the windows and rosettes on the chests of the men and in the hair of the women. Americans, Canadians, Englishmen and soldiers of the Leclerc

Division fraternise with the population. There is still no gas, no electricity, no Métro. It doesn't matter! This is the first relaxed Sunday of the Liberation. Paris has been given back to us. Paris is coming back to life.[26]

That day there were massive crowds in Clichy and Batignolles as Parisian women and soldiers mingled in a way that would have been unthinkable during the occupation. Lee Miller cast a professional eye over the way the women were dressed:

Everywhere in the streets were the dazzling girls, cycling, crawling up tank turrets. Their silhouette was very queer and fascinating to me after utility and austerity England. Full floating skirts, tiny waist-lines. They were top-heavy with built up pompadour front hair-does and waving tresses; weighted to the ground with clumsy, fancy thick-soled wedge shoes. The entire gait of the French woman has changed with her footwear. Instead of the bouncing buttocks and mincing steps of 'pre-war' there is a hot-foot long stride, picking up the whole foot at once.[27]

Prudish Berthe Auroy was slightly shocked by the behaviour of the young women: 'The girls proudly display themselves on American lorries, in the arms or on the knees of these warriors, who must think that what they have heard is true – Parisian girls are easy. Of course it was inevitable that the youth should get carried away in the joy of the Liberation, but I would have liked a bit more discretion, and a bit less vulgarity.'[28]

Berthe would not have approved of Benoîte and Flora Groult, who were heavily involved in entertaining the Allied troops. In September, the two sisters were invited to a Franco-Allied party full of girls and soldiers, and they both had a whale of a time: 'We danced; we laughed; we drank coffee with thick milk, deliciously over-sugared, ate doughnuts dripping with butter and felt admitted, without complicated examination, into a little universe without problems.'[29] Benoîte's relations with the soldiers were frank and open ('No hypocrisy, no nonsense. Yes means yes; no is okay, and one leaves it at that,' she wrote in her diary). She was particularly taken with an American officer called Rudi, who had 'a delicious back with tremendous freckles ... His back smells of the prairie, the West and childhood. His chest is a discreet savannah ... his legs are hairy from top to bottom on every side and of an unexpected strength.'[30] In October, when Rudi returned after a week's absence, the two of them sat in the bus from the airport scarcely saying a word, with the same thoughts going round and round in their heads: 'Do you want me? I want you. How I want you. We want each other.'[31]

Even the less worldly Parisian women appreciated the presence of the Allied troops. On 31 August, teenager Micheline Bood wrote in her diary: 'Oh, I forgot to say that there are Americans in the Rothschild apartment opposite, instead of Germans. There was a bunch of them, sitting on top of a wall like birds. I have just begun to realise that THEY ARE HERE ... and to feel happy.'[32]

For Pablo Picasso, the sudden influx of Allied soldiers restored his celebrity status, as intellectuals enlisted in the Allied armies took advantage of their passage through Paris to see one of the great figures of the twentieth century.[33] This eventually became wearing – 'Paris was liberated, but I was under siege,' Picasso said later.[34] His old friend Lee Miller was welcome, however, as she wrote at the time: 'Picasso and I fell into each other's arms and between laughter and tears and having my bottom pinched and my hair mussed we exchanged news about friends and their work, incoherently, and looked at new pictures which were dated on all the battle of Paris days ... Afterward I ate one of the tomatoes from the flower pot vine which was his favourite model. It was a bit mouldy but I liked the idea of eating a work of art.'[35]

One of Picasso's first visitors was John Pudney, RAF intelligence officer and poet, who wrote in the pages of the *New Statesman*: 'When the firing died down and one wept less often at the singing of the "Marseillaise" and less champagne was forced across one's altogether willing palate in the name of liberation, I went down to see Pablo Picasso.'[36] In Picasso's apartment, Pudney noted the tomato plant, and looked on as Picasso showed him a selection of French art magazines from the occupation: 'He has quietly collected the Nazi and collaborationist periodicals in which his work has been attacked. His quick remarkable hands turned over the pages that reproduced his work. *Picasso the Jew ... the decadent Pablo Picasso ... the obscene pornographer ...*

went the captions. "And now, at least, that is at an end," he said.'[37] Except it was not at end, not entirely. In October, at the Palais de Tokyo, Picasso exhibited a selection of the work he had produced during the occupation. Protestors complaining about the art disrupted the opening and the building had to be evacuated by the police; two weeks later, reactionary students demonstrated in front of his studio on the quai des Grands-Augustins, although whether they were complaining about his art or his recent decision to join the Communist Party was not clear.[38] Picasso's art retained its power, strengthened by the convulsive and transformative experience of the liberation.

*

Although it took months for life to return to a semblance of normality, the elation of the liberation was relatively quickly replaced by the mundane problems caused by the continuation of the war. No matter what it must have felt like in Paris and beyond, the liberation of the French capital did not mark the end of the war.[39] By mid-September the Métro had re-opened, albeit with a severely reduced service, but all theatres, cinemas and music halls remained closed.[40] However, the flourishing Resistance press gave people plenty to read – there were seventeen daily newspapers and twenty-one weeklies in the capital.[41] For most people, the biggest problem was getting enough food. On 2 September, Victor Veau noted that his household still could not buy butter or vegetables, but they were happy to get a tin of '*singe*' ('monkey' – slang for corned beef) from the butcher. This was the first time in two weeks they had been able to eat something other than their dwindling larder stock.[42] At the beginning of September, Berthe Auroy had to queue for three hours to buy six tomatoes. When some American soldiers gave her a bar of chocolate, she went into raptures: 'Heavens! What amazing chocolate! Melting, vanilla-scented and delicious!'[43] In the continued absence of rail or postal connections to the capital, many Parisians were beginning to find life very difficult; when partial services were restored in mid-October, it was a massive relief.[44]

Throughout the autumn, power supplies remained problematic. By the beginning of October, the electricity was on for forty-five minutes per day, with gas available for an hour at lunchtime. As the weather grew cold and the nights drew in, the lack of heat and light made life increasingly oppressive.[45] Unemployment continued to bite as the companies that had worked for the Germans ceased functioning. Even the benign presence of Allied troops did not make up for the loss of business with the Nazis – a mere 10,000 labourers in the Paris region were employed by the Allied military.[46] Many families who had been ripped apart by war now had no prospect of being reunited in the near future. Paradoxically, the departure of the Germans meant that there would be no more deals between the government and the Germans to bring the prisoners home. The number of men affected was substantial: on 31 October, veteran *résistant* Henri Frenay, now the Minister for Prisoners of War, announced that 2,355,000 French men and women were still held hostage in Germany; this included around 1 million POWs, 750,000 young people on labour conscription and 600,000 people who had been deported.[47] None of these hostages – around 8 per cent of the adult population – would be able to return home before the end of the war. Some would have had no home to return to – hundreds of Parisians were either homeless from the various Allied and German bombing raids, or were too fearful to return to their homes. They slept in the Métro in sordid conditions, in corridors that stank of urine.[48]

The occupation continued to give up its terrible secrets, even while ordinary life went on. On the morning of 27 August, Paul Tuffrau was walking past the Jardin du Luxembourg when he heard from a guard that nine recently buried bodies had been found in the gardens that morning. The victims – all policemen – had been shot, and they all bore awful marks of torture. Even after four years of occupation and the tumultuous events of the liberation, Tuffrau found it hard to believe the horror.[49] Not far away, little girls played at shop in a burnt-out building near the smashed remains of the Halle aux Vins, while boys played at war on a barricade on the nearby rue Montagne-Sainte-Geneviève.[50]

*

An important element of the short-lived power struggle that took place between the Free French and the disparate forces of the Resistance involved what to do with the remnants of the Vichy regime. On 27 August, 70-year-old economist Charles Rist gave an optimistic view in his diary:

> What's most surprising is the way that everything to do with Vichy has simply vanished, totally and without a murmur ... That mishmash of pietistic cant, of blimpish stupidity and the cynical scheming of ambitious politicians and embittered nobodies, that whole despicable, stinking attempt to wheedle a few baubles of power from the enemy – the power that France had always refused to give to them when it was free; all that has gone, blasted away by a tremendous hurricane of common sense and faith in the future.[51]

But Vichy had not truly disappeared. There were many former collaborators still in the Paris region, hoping they would be able to avoid the gaze of the victorious Resistance and an enraged population. Long before the liberation of Paris, the Free French government had been preparing *l'épuration* – the purge.[52] In the first few weeks after the liberation, the legal system was not yet functioning – the three new courts that were supposed to deal with crimes committed during the occupation were not established until 4 October – while the police seemed completely uninterested in dealing with the crimes of collaboration.[53] Because there was no legal framework to deal with the crimes (real or imaginary) of the accused, the population took matters into their own hands (this period was later known as *l'épuration sauvage* – 'the lawless purge').[54] Within days of the liberation, thousands of collaborators – real or suspected – were arrested by the Parisian FFI and were herded into the Vel' d'Hiv', where over 4000 Jews had been held before being deported, in 1942.[55] Conditions in the massive arena soon deteriorated – according to the FFI Medical Inspector, Dr Duhamel, there were only ten toilets and seven washbasins between more than 2500 inmates; Pierre Taittinger recalled that the queue for the toilets lasted more than two hours.[56] After a few days, the prisoners were moved to Drancy prison camp, in the same Paris buses that had transported Resistance prisoners and Jews during the occupation.

Dr Duhamel was barely more satisfied by the conditions in Drancy –

there were clear signs of physical mistreatment of prisoners, vermin-ridden mattresses, poor food, no cutlery or utensils, while the primitive sanitary conditions led to cases of dysentery. Duhamel concluded that the situation 'lowers us to the same level as that of the occupiers whom we criticised so much'.[57] Within a week, conditions improved substantially, although Taittinger was still appalled by the people who were holding him, who he claimed were 'Spaniards from the International Brigades, communists, or even people who tortured Jews'.[58] Opinions about the situation in Drancy differed. For Marc Boegner, the very existence of the camp was a 'scandal', whereas for Yves Cazaux, the only thing that was scandalous was that some people were apparently able to buy their way out of prison.[59] Whatever the case, the bigger collaborationist fish were imprisoned in Fresnes: nearly 900 ministers, admirals, bankers and journalists.[60] By the middle of September, de Gaulle claimed that there had been around 6000 arrests in Paris. There were massive problems with the system for dealing with those accused of collaboration, as the Prefect of the Seine highlighted: 'On the one hand people have been arrested who should not have been, either because they are innocent or because they are small fry who have committed minor crimes. On the other hand, notorious collaborators and Vichy supporters remain in their jobs or have begun work again without being disturbed in the slightest.'[61]

It was not only French collaborators who were being hunted. Attempts were made to identify those Germans responsible for the most brutal and savage aspects of the occupation. On 11 October a photograph was discovered of the Gestapo staff at rue des Saussaies – a kind of obscene team photograph. The Resistance press immediately published the photograph and set about putting names to faces, preparing the ground for future trials for war crimes.[62]

When the legal system eventually laid its hands on some of the individuals who symbolised either collaboration or repression, the guilty sometimes paid a heavy price for their terrible betrayal. At the end of October, Boèro and Néroni, who had been involved in the murder of Georges Mandel four months earlier, were sentenced to death and subsequently executed.[63] On 14 September, Brasillach walked to the Préfecture and handed himself in.[64] In January 1945 he was tried for treason and found guilty. He was executed on 6 February 1945, despite a petition from a number of well-known writers and *résistants* calling for clemency.[65] Whatever some leading intellectuals thought about the disproportionate nature of the punishment, most of the population was in favour of Brasillach's execution.[66] This feeling was even stronger when it came to Laval and Pétain, both of whom were brought back from Germany and tried in Paris by the newly created court, the Haute Cour, in the second half of 1945. Pétain was found guilty of treason and sentenced to death; de Gaulle commuted his sentence to life imprisonment in recognition of his service during World War I and he died in prison in 1951, aged ninety-five. Unsurprisingly, Laval was also found guilty and sentenced to death. On the morning that the sentence was due to be carried out, the Prefect of Police, Charles Luizet, and his advisor, Edgard Pisani, went to Laval's cell. The prisoner was lying inert, having swallowed a cyanide pill. The prison doctors then intervened, pumping Laval's stomach to save his life, so that he could then be killed. A few hours later Laval was strapped to a post and executed by a firing squad.[67] Despite these two examples, in general the *épuration* did not lead to a wave of blood-letting among the political leaders of occupied France: of the 108 cases dealt with by the Haute Cour, forty-two cases were dropped, while eight men were sentenced to death, only three of whom were eventually executed.

One of the most contradictory cases dealt with during the *épuration* was that of the Paris police force. The police had joined the Resistance just in time to save their honour, and now enjoyed an unusually positive relationship with the Parisian population. Nevertheless, it was obvious that some sections of the police had collaborated with gusto, playing an essential role in the deportation of Jews and in the persecution of the Resistance. Within a week of the liberation, 700 policemen out of around 20,000 were suspended. Over the next sixteen months the cases of nearly 4000 men were examined by one of the Commissions d'Epuration that were set up nationally and regionally to deal with collaborators in various professions and businesses.[68] Of those 4000 policemen, 400 were tried, twenty were sentenced to death and seven were executed. These cases were not distributed evenly among the different ranks: the vast majority of the senior officers were sacked, while only a minority of the lower ranks were purged.[69] Above all, the men of the hated Brigades Spéciales, which had specialised in 'anti-terrorist' work, were severely dealt with. The most notorious member of the Brigades, Inspector Fernand David, was arrested on 12 October, condemned to death and executed on 5 May 1945. David's colleague René Hénocque fled Paris and managed to escape justice; he died in Brussels in 1996.[70] Of the 235 policemen working for the Brigades Spéciales, 186 were purged, the vast majority of them sacked without a pension. But within a couple of years, some were quietly allowed back. They had skills the new regime required.[71]

In the frenzy of liberation, terrible injustices occurred. To modern eyes, some of the worst instances appear to have been the head-shaving of women, although this gradually died out in September as the chaos receded.[72] Few people subsequently admitted to feeling positive about these punishments. For example, in late August, Paul Tuffrau was caught up in one incident, when a crowd gathered and howled abuse at two women, who were stripped half naked and had their hair hacked off. Suddenly, a woman burst through the crowd and began slapping the elder of the two women. Tuffrau held the attacker back and the victim pleaded with him to help her. Tuffrau, ill at ease, said he would stop the young woman from being hit, but nothing more. He rode off on his bicycle feeling very uncomfortable.[73]

In the 18th arrondissement, the fear of rooftop snipers nearly got out of hand. In separate incidents, two teachers were each accused of firing from their windows on the crowd, and were taken away by the FFI. Both men were shocked not only by the accusations – which were clearly false – but also by the youth and indiscipline of the FFIers, in particular by a young woman, Lise, who had 'bare legs, short shorts, wild hair, and a revolver in her hand'.[74] One of the men, Monsieur Weill, was merely manhandled and then prevented from sleeping in his apartment for a few days; the other – a headmaster – was subjected to a crowd baying for his blood ('We're taking him to the Mairie'; 'Don't bother! Kill him here!'), got thumped in the face by a passer-by and was then held prisoner, before the FFI accepted that there was no evidence against him.[75]

The two men were lucky; had they been in the south of the city, they

might not have survived. At the Institut Dentaire in the 13th arrondissement, where weeks earlier Colonel Fabien had briefly stationed some of
his men, there was an unofficial 'prison' run by a rogue FFI group.[76]
The Institut Dentaire was part of a shadowy network of unauthorised
prisons scattered around the Paris region.[77] One of the first victims was
Madame Albertini, the wife of fascist leader Georges Albertini; she had
been arrested by FFI fighters on 25 August, separated from her young
baby and beaten in order to discover where her husband was.[78] After a
couple of days, she was transferred to the Institut Dentaire, where over
200 people were held. Some were collaborators, others were deluded or
had simply been in the wrong place at the wrong time. None of them
received anything like a trial. In conditions that were shockingly remi-
niscent of the German camps, prisoners were beaten, terrorised and
sometimes killed, while a piece of doggerel written on a blackboard
claimed the prisoners were facing 'workers' justice', and concluded
with the lines: 'For most of those who are here / only death will free
them from their fear.'[79]

Over the next few weeks, dozens of bodies were found around Paris,
some tagged with labels identifying them as fascist collaborators, but
more – twenty-eight in all – were found in the Seine with bullet wounds
to the head. Each corpse was weighted with a paving stone, attached by
rope to the victim's neck. In total, the gang at the Institut Dentaire murdered thirty-six people, including the Vermandels – the fascist couple
whose bodies had been found at Bagneux on 26 August. A court later
concluded that had the victims been tried, some of them might have
been condemned to death, but at least they would have had a trial; however, thirteen of the victims were clearly not guilty of any crimes linked
with the occupation.[80] One of those murdered was Madeleine Goa, a
member of the communist-influenced Front National, who had been
arrested on 25 August when the crowd lynched her *résistant* husband,
Max, who was suspected with no evidence of firing on the 2e DB. During
her days at the Institut, Madeleine gradually went mad. A placard was
placed on her dumped corpse claiming that she was a traitor. A few
days later, the local FTP put a notice on the door of the dead couple's
apartment setting the record straight and claiming that those who had
falsely denounced the pair would be punished.[81]

The police eventually took an interest in the murders after the Institut had been closed down on the orders of FFI leader Lizé and the killing had ceased, in the middle of September.[82] Identifying the culprits proved difficult, because many of them were known only by their code names, and although there were trials in 1946 and 1948 none of them ended in a conviction. The main culprit turned out to be a member of the Communist Party, René Sentuc, who had been imprisoned as a *résistant* during the occupation and masterminded a mass prison escape in 1944. After a long court case in the 1950s, during which Sentuc's lawyers insisted that he had been following the orders of Colonel Fabien, Sentuc was acquitted on the grounds that there was a 'reasonable possibility' that these terrible acts were carried out in order to liberate the country.[83]

Although the Institut Dentaire was an awful aberration, it showed that in the chaos of the liberation, unscrupulous or deranged people could take advantage of the situation to settle scores. This extended to political disputes, too. Some sections of the Communist Party arrested Trotskyists; communist leader Georges Maranne intervened and ordered that they should be freed.[84] Twenty-two-year-old Mathieu Bucholz, a member of a tiny Trotskyist group, had no such luck. On 11 September he was discussing politics with a group of Communist Party youth in the 20th arrondissement, when a group of communist militants burst into the room and took Mathieu away; his body was later found in the Seine, riddled with bullets.[85]

In an article in *Action* newspaper, Resistance leader Pascal Copeau put the violence into context, underlining the responsibility of the leaders of the Free French and of the Resistance, recalling all those broadcasts on the BBC calling for murder and assassination, or the bloodthirsty declarations from the Resistance:

For four awful years, the best French people learnt to kill, to assassinate, to sabotage, sometimes to steal, and always to avoid being caught by what they were told was the law ... Will we soon dare imagine where we would be if these outlaws had not existed, if these nice boys had not become killers? And who taught these good Frenchmen to kill? Who gave them orders to murder? Who else but you, General, unless it was you, Maurice Schumann, the radiophonic 'Passionaria', or you, Georges Bidault, the President of the Conseil National de la Résistance.[86]

As might be expected, ordinary criminals also used the chaos of liberation to commit crimes: men wearing FFI armbands robbed Princess Gagarine of 500,000 francs in cash and 2 million francs worth of jewellery, while 'US Military Policemen' stole nearly 2 million francs from a bar owner.[87] These 'false *résistants*' paled into insignificance beside the case of an FFI doctor who was arrested in October. He was Dr Petiot, a serial killer who had been murdering people in Paris from 1942 onwards. The police had been hunting for Petiot since the beginning of the year, following the shocking discovery of a torture chamber full of dismembered bodies in the basement of his Parisian house. At the time, many Parisians suspected that Petiot was an invention of the Gestapo, but he was only too horribly real. Petiot's trial, in March 1946, was a confusing affair, with the prosecution stating that Petiot had killed twenty-seven people, while he claimed to have killed sixty-three – but all his victims were German soldiers or collaborators, he said, and he had always acted under orders from the Resistance. Petiot's stories were not believed, and he was executed in May 1946.[88]

Meanwhile the sordid link between collaboration and criminality became clear with the arrest of Pierre Bonny and Henri Lafont, two underworld figures who had worked for the Gestapo and had tracked down *résistants* and tortured them. Together with seven other members of their gang, Bonny and Lafont were found guilty and executed on 27 December.[89]

Petty crime also flourished, dragging in some very real *résistants*. In the days after the liberation, Georges Dukson, the young FFI fighter from West Africa, became a minor celebrity. His picture was in the papers after the 26 August celebrations, and he was stopped in the street for his autograph and was soon hob-nobbing with famous actresses. But he was gradually seduced by the possibility of getting easy money by dealing on the black market; arrested by an FFI group, Dukson was shot in the thigh while trying to escape. Taken to hospital, Dukson died on the operating table. 'The Lion of the 17th' had perished ignominiously and was soon forgotten, like the vast majority of Resistance fighters.

*

One of the most striking features of the *épuration* in Paris was that so many people seemed to escape its attentions – in particular those who had business dealings with the Germans. At the end of September, Galtier-Boissière sat at the terrace of a bar, where he overheard two fat well-dressed men discussing a forthcoming government inquiry into the money that some people had made during the war. 'We had a quiet life for four years!' said one. 'Now the trouble is going to begin,' said the other.[90] They need not have worried. The economic *épuration* was largely toothless.[91] The banks mostly avoided punishment, even though they had been up to their necks in German cash throughout the occupation. Although the four main banks were nationalised at the end of 1945, this was part of French post-war economic planning rather than a punishment for collaboration, and all the shareholders were generously compensated. Few of the leading figures in the world of banking were punished for their behaviour during the occupation, while only a third of the cases brought against Parisian construction companies led to any kind of punishment, and most of those affected the smaller firms.[92] In the autumn, the centre-right politician Max André was optimistic: 'A decisive struggle is taking place between businessmen and the members of the Resistance. These businessmen must understand that the Resistance did not only have the aim of ridding France of the invader, but also of cleansing the country.'[93] But in general, the businessmen won.

There were two major exceptions, with consequences for the post-war history of Paris and its region. The Renault car company, with its massive Billancourt factory on an island in the Seine just downstream of Paris, was put under state control.[94] This meant that both Renault workers and the general public viewed the company as at least partly 'theirs'; this attitude contributed both to the industrial disputes that punctuated the post-war decades, and to buoyant sales. The boss of the company, Louis Renault, was charged with collaboration and died in Fresnes prison in October 1944. Renault remained under state control until 1996, shortly after the closure of the Billancourt plant.

The other focus for retribution was the Paris Métro company, which had slavishly ensured that collaboration in the capital went smoothly, creating a dedicated police service in the Métro to stop people defacing German posters, and setting aside vehicles for use by the German troops in the period following D-Day. Following a proposal by Léo Hamon at one of the last meetings of the CPL, the Métro company was taken under state control, although the wealthy shareholders, who had happily trousered the profits from the company's collaborationist activities, were all generously compensated.[95] The resultant organisation – the RATP – still runs the Paris Métro and many other urban transport systems around the world.

With the Germans gone and the collaborationist factory managers either arrested or having fled, workers in the engineering factories of the Paris region – in particular the aeronautical industry – stepped into the void and carried out their own economic *épuration*. A number of factory committees sprang up and took control of workplaces across the Paris region, organising supplies and production, showing a glimmer of what could have emerged from the chaos of the collapse of the occupation. But as August turned into September, it became clear that there would be no second Paris Commune. The Communist Party – the main force within the working class – did not encourage the creation of factory committees, while the mass of the population were either unaware of the possibility of taking control of their workplace, or were simply uninterested in the prospect. With Communist Party and FTP leader Charles Tillon as Minister for Air, the government was ideally positioned to ride out the minor wave of occupations that continued until the end of the year, and in 1945 the committees were given a neutered, legal form, in the shape of the Comités d'entreprise which still play an important role in the running of French companies.[96]

The failure of the *épuration* to deal with most cases of economic collaboration, coupled with the impression that the new regime did not seem to represent much of a change compared with the pre-war Third Republic, led many people to become disillusioned. In 1945 the Trotskyist Fourth International furiously complained about the outcome

of the 'so-called "insurrection" in which so many young workers sacrificed themselves'.[97] While such a criticism might be expected from
revolutionaries, at the end of the 1950s René Hostache, a historian who
was highly sympathetic to de Gaulle, recognised that 'the collapse of
Vichy provided an important opportunity to thoroughly renew the political and social regime in France, but it was passed over. Even today, many
people are still bitter about this aborted revolution.'[98]

During September and October, the tension increased between the
government and the Parisian Resistance. With the FFI effectively fused
with the Free French Army, de Gaulle's desire to remove any vestige of
a 'parallel power' was focused on disbanding the remaining armed
groups – now known as the Gardes Patriotiques – and on rendering the
CPL powerless.[99] This was not simply de Gaulle's view – the government included two Communist Party ministers (Charles Tillon and
François Billoux) as well as Georges Bidault, and they all went along
with the policy, despite the sometimes half-hearted opposition of both
the Resistance organisations (the CNR and CPL) and the Communist
Party. Eventually, on 28 October, the Council of Ministers ordered the
Gardes to be disbanded: 'The Council of Ministers pays homage to the
service that these groups gave during the insurrectional period. But the
insurrectional period is over. It is now solely the responsibility of the
government and its representatives to ensure administrative and police
powers, following the laws of the Republic.'[100]

Although there were protests from the CNR and some of the Resistance
newspapers, there was no real opposition to the dissolution of the final
armed vestige of the insurrection, and the Paris police were able to regain
their position of undisputed power. There were some minor hiccoughs –
on 2 November the police stopped a Gardes Patriotiques van containing
a ton of ammunition, while Commander Gerl of the Gardes refused to
hand over his weapons to the Police Commissioner of the 13th arrondissement, saying he was determined 'to retain them by any means necessary
to save the nation and ourselves'.[101] On the whole, however, the relative
ease with which the Resistance gave up its arms and any semblance of
political power showed that the Paris insurrection was finally over.[102]

*

For many people, the liberation of Paris was the high point of their lives, and it was hard to imagine that anything could surpass those moments. On 15 September, Jean Galtier-Boissière went for a drink at Aux Deux Magots with 'Z', a friend whom he had not seen since the beginning of the war. During their conversation, Z revealed that throughout the occupation he had been hiding in Paris, working for the Resistance. For four years it had been as though he had been living in the pages of a thriller. In the early autumn sunshine, Z turned to his friend and asked wistfully: 'What the hell am I going to do now?'[103]

Two people who had probably had enough of adventure were Marie-Hélène and Pierre Lefaucheux. Pierre was deported to Buchenwald on the 15 August train from Pantin; Marie-Hélène had been a member of the CPL throughout the insurrection. On 27 August Marie-Hélène decided her work in Paris was over, and recommenced her audacious attempt to rescue her husband from the clutches of the Nazis. Driving in a car borrowed from the Red Cross, she travelled eastwards and was soon in the midst of the Allied advance and then, in the early evening, she was behind the German lines. Her rapid and trouble-free progress gives some indication of the total collapse of the German front, as soldiers fled from the onrushing Allied armies. In Nancy, Marie-Hélène met Molinari, the Italian boss of a road-haulage company. One of Molinari's close friends – an Italian anti-fascist – had been deported to Buchenwald. Molinari put Lefaucheux in contact with von Else, a Gestapo man in Nancy who had previously helped get a parcel to Molinari's friend. She could hardly believe her luck.

On 29 August, Hélène met the Gestapo agent – 'a young man, thin, with dark eyes and glasses, who looked slow and stupid' – and pleaded with him to provide her with papers so she could visit her husband in Germany. Amazingly, von Else first issued an order releasing both Pierre and Molinari's friend into the custody of the Nancy Gestapo, and then, two days later, agreed to accompany Lefaucheux and Molinari all the way to Buchenwald, to ensure that the order was carried out. Von Else was not politically sympathetic, nor did he want a bribe, but Molinari's promise of a car and petrol to enable the German and his family to escape the imminent collapse of the occupation of France could not have been unwelcome.

Caught up in the chaos of the fleeing German Army, the ill-matched trio – Molinari, Marie-Hélène and von Else – drove along the motorway past Mannheim and Frankfurt, which to Marie-Hélène's gratification were badly damaged by Allied bombing raids. Late in the morning of 3 September, they arrived at the outskirts of Buchenwald. Parts of the camp were smouldering, having been hit by Allied bombs during a raid on a nearby factory a few days earlier.[104] For four hours Marie-Hélène waited by the barbed wire fence, wracked with impatience and anxiety, imagining all the awful possibilities – perhaps Pierre was already dead, shot by the Germans or killed in the bombing raid. Eventually, von Else came out of the camp, accompanied by 'a tall, thin tramp' with a shaved head. It was Pierre. He got into the car, Marie-Hélène simply asked, 'Hello, how are you?' and they drove off. By 04:00 the next morning they were in Metz, where they parted company with their Gestapo saviour.

Word of Pierre Lefaucheux's amazing escape soon got around. René Courtin wrote in his diary: 'Clearly, his wife is one of the most remarkable people in the Resistance ... The story is even more amazing than I could have imagined and shows that to the fearless, nothing is impossible.'[105] Once they were back in Paris, on 5 September, Marie Hélène telephoned Claire Girard, the young woman she had met at Antheuil-Saâcy station less than three weeks earlier, to announce her joyous news. Claire's mother answered the phone; Claire was dead. She had been executed in the tiny village of Courdimanche to the north-west of Paris on 27 August, the day Marie-Hélène left the city.[106]

Epilogue

Mythification

> *Howard C. Rice, an American academic in Paris, writes in January 1945: 'In France, more than in any other country, the popular imagination transforms the present into history with extraordinary rapidity. Events and collective experiences are miraculously crystallised into symbolic dates and emotion-laden myths. Already "La Libération" is such a myth ... it would seem that French thinking must, in order to face the future, first review and digest the recent past.'*[1]

As soon as the battle of Paris ended, the battle for history began. Keenly aware that those days of August represented a dramatic new page in the history of the city, and a decisive moment in the liberation of France, participants in and observers of the events began to assemble their views, to impose their vision of what had happened. The tumultuous history of France plays a key role in the country's culture, and the rapidity with which this major event was examined, re-examined and turned into urban, cultural and intellectual artefacts is quite remarkable. Almost immediately, the battles of the liberation wrote themselves onto the face of Paris. Within six weeks, the names of eighteen Parisian streets were changed to commemorate those who died in the insurrection, or who were Resistance fighters.[2] The Lycée Rollin in the 9th arrondissement was renamed 'Lycée Jacques Decour' after a teacher who had been shot for giving out leaflets to German troops in 1942.[3] Plaques were placed on the walls of buildings to commemorate the dead, replacing the informal tributes that had appeared in the immediate aftermath of the insurrection. There are hundreds of these plaques scattered around the main sites where fighting took place, many still garlanded with flowers on the anniversary of the death they commemorate.[4] Equally emotive but less obvious are the scars of battle that have been left unrepaired on the main public buildings – the Préfecture, the Ecole Militaire, the buildings around the Jardin du Luxembourg, the walls of the Tuileries, and elsewhere.

The images of the liberation – the sun, the cheering crowds, the gallant FFI fighters, the bronzed men of the 2e DB – became fixed in the popular imagination through a series of books and magazines and also by a major exhibition of photographs which ran from November to December 1944.[5] For children there were comics describing the battles in and around Paris, and printed cardboard sheets featuring cut-out figures (de Gaulle, FFI fighters, Leclerc Division soldiers) that could be displayed against an appropriate backdrop (the Arc de Triomphe, a barricade, a Parisian street). A flood of diaries and memoirs was published, culminating in Adrien Dansette's 1946 *Histoire de la libération de Paris*, a remarkable piece of contemporary history that is still valuable today. The French Government got involved, producing a photo-filled English-language booklet describing the insurrection. The booklet was widely circulated, even among the US armed forces.[6] Over the next six decades, the torrent continued, backed up by special issues of magazines, TV programmes and, most recently, DVDs, often driven by the rhythm of anniversaries.

In October 1944, the Provisional Government set up the Commission pour l'Histoire de l'Occupation et de la Libération de la France, to gather material – documents, artefacts and eye-witness accounts – dealing with the war years in France, and including a major section on the liberation of Paris.[7] This material was eventually placed in the Archives Nationales; much later it was digitised and is now available on the Internet.[8] 1994 saw the creation in Paris of a single-site pair of museums, one devoted to the Leclerc Division and the liberation, the other to Jean Moulin, the rather clumsily titled Musée du Général Leclerc de Hauteclocque et de la Libération de Paris – Musée Jean Moulin. Displays and exhibitions in the city have recently reinforced this systematic memorialisation of the liberation, most recently an exhibit at the Hôtel de Ville based on an appeal for hitherto unseen documents

from Parisians themselves.[9] In 1994, during the fiftieth anniversary celebrations, there was a massive open-air *son et lumière* piece of theatre,
stretching over four kilometres and with hundreds of participants and
period vehicles, finishing in front of the Hôtel de Ville.

Probably the most influential portrayal of the liberation was the documentary film *La Libération de Paris*, made during the insurrection by
cineastes from the Comité de Libération du Cinéma Français, which was
hastily edited in the days following the German surrender and was first
shown in Paris on 29 August.[10] Over the next few months, over half the
adult population of the capital would see the film, as would hundreds of
thousands of spectators all over the world. Thirty-two minutes long, the
film portrays the insurrection with amazing power. Through the spoken
commentary and the choice of shots, the city becomes a living being,
the central participant. Like the best documentaries, the film gives the
viewer the overwhelming impression of actually being there, of seeing
it like it was. But, like any film, it is constructed – some sequences were
included, others were omitted; they were assembled in a particular
order, to tell a particular story.[11] As the film-makers were creating the
documentary – choosing which scenes to record, and then choosing
which scenes to include – they avoided controversial issues. There is no
reference to the cease-fire; the Allies are reduced to a walk-on role in
the shape of an American soldier with a charmingly comic French
accent; there is no footage of the shootings at Concorde or Notre
Dame, nor any scenes of head-shaving. Some events that were filmed –
such as the killing of the four German soldiers by the Arc de Triomphe
on 25 August – were not included in the documentary, but have since
resurfaced; others, such as the cease-fire being announced, have disappeared without trace.[12]

The film-makers – many of whom were communists – deliberately
chose not to make any reference to the role of the PCF or any other
grouping (even the FFI are mentioned only in passing). Instead they
presented a vision of the insurrection that put the city and its population at the heart of events – the city as a whole appears to have
liberated itself.[13] This vision of national unity – irrespective of class –
and the absence of the Allies chimed completely with de Gaulle's conception.[14] In the popular imagination of France, these images – the

barricade-building, the urban warfare, the joyous sun-filled parade down the Champs-Elysées – came to represent not only the liberation of Paris, but the liberation of France as a whole, even though they bore little relation to what occurred in the vast majority of towns and cities. This was not simply because of the fantastic nature of the events, and the skill of the film-makers, but because this view merged with deep historical currents in France, in which Parisian insurrections so often played a vital role.[15] Those previous insurrections had shaped the psychogeography of the capital; the events of August 1944 added a new layer to the palimpsest of Paris, putting new images into the minds of the population, providing new locations to act as historical markers and indicators of past struggles.[16]

*

In the months and years after the liberation, there were explicit attempts to deal with the main historical controversies that remained – the role of the communists, the meaning of the cease-fire and the motivations of von Choltitz. In 1944 de Gaulle apparently thought that the communists had wanted to seize power – at least that is what he told Marc Boegner on 21 September – and during the Cold War it became widely accepted that the communists were thwarted in their ambitions by the arrival of the Allies and the 2e DB.[17] Such views, widely expressed at the time on both the right and the left, were based partly on recent historical experience – the closing stages of World War I saw the Russian revolution of 1917, followed by a wave of revolutionary events in Europe, including the German revolution of 1918–19. In the case of France in 1944, neither a full-blown workers' revolution nor a communist coup was on the cards.

Although the Communist Party undoubtedly, and legitimately, wished to increase its influence (for the next four decades it received more votes in parliamentary elections than any other party), there is no evidence that it was preparing a coup. Above all, Moscow did not support such a policy, and the French communists were entirely wedded to the policies of the Soviet Union. There are no signs that the Communist Party was truly doing any of the things necessary for a revolution or even a coup (stockpiling weapons, creating alternative forms of power, mobil-ising tens of thousands of people to this end). The bulk of the population had no spontaneous appetite for taking power; exhausted after four years of occupation and steeped in the idea of national liber-ation, not social revolution, they were more than happy to see the back of the Germans and to cheer de Gaulle. Although many people had been involved in the fighting, they had not been organised into any con-sistent form of what de Gaulle called a 'parallel power'. 1944 would not be 1917.

The issue of the cease-fire, and the role of the Free French Delegation in Paris in promoting it, was raised within weeks of the lib-eration by the left-wing Parisian press.[18] There was even an attempt by the CPL to set up a commission to investigate the cease-fire. The com-mission summoned Parodi and Bidault to give evidence in October 1944, but both men declined to appear. Parodi said the whole business seemed 'extremely inopportune' given that the war was still continuing, while Bidault pointed out that he was now Minister of Foreign Affairs answerable only to the government.[19] In the end, the commission appears to have lasted only a morning, and the question was referred to the CPL Bureau where it disappeared, although it continued to re-surface in magazines and on television over the subsequent decades, whenever the story of the liberation was told.[20]

Most strikingly, the role of von Choltitz gradually came to the fore, primarily through the efforts of von Choltitz himself. Within days of the liberation, the Allies were interrogating him in London. The official transcript records sarcastically that the one-time German commander of Paris 'launched into a long and dramatic story about his noble efforts to save the civilian population of Paris from destruction at the hands of the Communists'.[21] Von Choltitz was released from Allied custody in 1947, at least partly on the initiative of Parodi, who clearly did not bear any grudges.[22] Shortly afterwards, the German officer began to present his side of events, first in a series of articles in *Le Figaro* in 1949 (these pro-voked a blistering response from the Resistance press, in particular *Franc-Tireur*),[23] then in two sets of memoirs, published in Germany in 1950 and 1951. The focus of this flurry of activity was summarised in the title of a series of articles in *Le Figaro*: 'Why I did not destroy Paris in

1944'.[24] Von Choltitz's explanation was that he wanted to preserve the city; he never mentioned that he did not have the means to destroy it.

Von Choltitz's version got international attention with the publication in 1965 of the bestseller *Is Paris Burning?* by Larry Collins and Dominique Lapierre, which in 1966 was turned into a major feature film of the same name, with an all-star cast.[25] The striking title is a reference to a telegram that Hitler allegedly sent to Paris, although von Choltitz never actually saw a message containing this phrase, and did not even hear about it until 'later'.[26] In fact, there is no evidence that Hitler ever sent such a telegram – the dramatic phrase is probably an invention.[27] The focus of both book and film was on von Choltitz as the 'saviour' of Paris who had disobeyed Hitler's orders, and on Nordling, who had negotiated the cease-fire and persuaded the German commander not to destroy the city. As might be expected from a book written during the Cold War, the underlying message was that the cease-fire and the arrival of the Allies helped stop an imminent communist takeover.[28]

Von Choltitz's role was much less dramatic than that presented in either the book or the film. Although he was apparently disillusioned by the military situation before he took up his brief two-week command of Paris, the decisive factor that determined his behaviour was the fact that the High Command did not send him the troops and materiel needed to defend the city against the massive Allied onslaught. He could have gone to a Wagnerian end, with the Hôtel Meurice crashing down around him in flames, but the attractiveness of that fate was undermined by his lack of faith in Hitler, and his conviction that the war in the west was lost, which in turn was underlined by the lack of military force available to him. Von Choltitz did not have the means to destroy Paris – the bridges were not mined, the buildings were not riddled with dynamite, and neither the Luftwaffe nor the Wehrmacht could provide the massive killer blow that Hitler required in his order of 23 August; they were overwhelmed by Allied air superiority and they were hellbent on retreating. The air-raid of 26 August, while horribly destructive, was a mere pin-prick given the size of the city. Von Choltitz did not disobey his orders – he was completely unable to implement them. Who knows what he would have done had he been provided with the means?

Von Choltitz was not the 'saviour' of Paris, he was merely its final, weak, German commander.[29]

Ultimately, the liberation of Paris was not about von Choltitz, nor about Nordling, nor even about de Gaulle. It was about the ordinary people of Paris who rose up against the Germans and made it impossible for the Allies to pursue their intended policy of skirting round the city. The population did not liberate the city single-handed, but their courage and sacrifice changed the situation, while the advance of the Allied armies not only gave the population the confidence that overwhelming force would soon be on their side, but also forced the surrender of the German garrison. In its final phase, the liberation of Paris was a joint operation between the Resistance, the Leclerc Division and the Americans. Each of those forces lost hundreds of lives, and similar numbers of Parisians were killed by stray gunfire or by German shells. The number of German dead and wounded is unknown. The exact number of people killed during the liberation of Paris is unclear, but there were thousands of victims – mainly FFI fighters and Parisians, while the 2e DB lost more men during the fighting for Paris than in any previous phase of the war.[30] Those dead – only some of whom are commemorated on the walls of the capital – were the price the city paid to be free.

There are many versions of what the liberation of Paris meant. For de Gaulle and the Free French, it was the climax of four years of lonely opposition to Vichy, finally giving them the opportunity to govern. For the collaborators, it was the end of a dream, and for some, the end of their lives. For the men and women of the Resistance, it was the culmination of all their sacrifice and courage; in a savage twist of history, their victory meant their immediate disappearance as a political force. For the Allies, who wanted to go around Paris, the relative ease with which the city fell was a pleasant surprise, and provided a powerful symbol of the imminent collapse of the Nazi regime. For the Germans who survived the fighting, it was a chance to escape the horrors of the war and to begin cleansing their lives and their country of the stain of Nazism. For the bulk of the Parisian population it was the chance to be free. For everyone, everywhere in the world, the message of the liberation of Paris contained all these things, and something more – inspiration. In

1944 the British Government French-language publication *Cadran*[31] put it well: 'All the war news fades when faced with the liberation of Paris. For the whole world, Paris is a symbol of civilisation and of liberty: the first echo of victory could be heard in the bells of Notre Dame ... By liberating themselves, the Parisians showed the world that the soul of a people is invincible, stronger than the most powerful war machine.'

Bibliography

MULTIMEDIA

DVD-ROM:
La Libération de l'Ile de France (AERI, 2004).

DVD:
Documentaries
D-Day to Berlin (George Stevens, 1998).
Eté 44: La Libération (Patrick Rotman, 2004).
La Libération de Paris (Mairie de Paris, 2004).
La Mémoire Courte (Henri Torrent, 1963).
Les Témoins de la Libération de Paris (Jorge Amat, 2004).
The Eye of Vichy (Claude Chabrol, 1993).
Vingt ans en août 1944 (Jorge Amat, 2004).
Fiction
Is Paris Burning? (René Clément, 1967).
The Train (John Frankenheimer, 1964).

WEB SOURCES

***La Libération de Paris* (film, 1944)**
archive.org/details/LaLiberationdeParis1944

***Paris XIe Août 1944* (unedited film, 1944)**
www.dailymotion.com/video/x8867e_paris-xie-aout-1944_webcam

BBC broadcast, 26 August 1944
tinyurl.com/cdjjtdh

Resistance radio broadcasts, 22–26 August 1944
www.youtube.com/watch?v=2P6un2OzJCA
www.youtube.com/watch?v=YnwCdydurZE
www.youtube.com/watch?v=g5ul1jfO4B8
www.youtube.com/watch?v=U-znY-9D-Uw
www.youtube.com/watch?v=om0G2_oVbr4

Other websites
www.liberation-de-paris.gilles-primout.fr
www.gastoneve.org.uk

Links to all these sources can be found at elevendaysinaugust.com

[All URLs accessed July 2012]

ARCHIVES

**US National Archives Foreign Military Studies
(Microfiche Publication M1035)**

A-956	'Employment of the 6 Para Div in N. France 44' by Major-General von Heyking (1 January 1946).
A-967	'Northern France' by Major-General von Boineburg (6 April 1946).
A-968	Annex to report of 18 April 1946 by Generalleutnant Elfeldt (n.d.).

US National Archives, Administrative History Collection ETOUSA

ADM 72A	'Circular 131' (29 July 1945).

After Action Report
(available at http://cgsc.contentdm.oclc.org/cdm/compoundobject/collection/
p4013coll8/id/2212/rec/14 [accessed July 2012])

Third US Army, 1 August 1944–9 May 1945. Vol. 1. The Operations.

Archives Nationales, Paris

AN 72AJ/42/IV/1	'Journal de Léo Hamon: L'Insurrection de Paris' (n.d.).
AN 72AJ/42/IV/3	'L'Insurrection parisienne 17–25 Août 1944. Extrait des souvenirs inédits de Léo Hamon' (n.d).
AN 72AJ/45/I/5a	'Procès-verbal de la séance du COMAC du 14 août 1944' (n.d.).
AN 72AJ/45/I/6M	'Copie d'un mémorandum établi pour le CNR (août 1944)' by de Vogüé (n.d.).
AN 72AJ/45/I/6N	'Copie d'un compte rendu d'une réunion Comac CNR' by de Vogüé (21 August 1944).
AN 72AJ/45/I/6O	'Copie d'un rapport de M. GALLOIS communiqué par de Vogüé' (n.d.).
AN 72AJ/49/III/31	'Procès-verbal de la séance du COMAC du 16 août 1944'.

AN 72AJ/49/III/32	'Programme d'Action de la Résistance' (17 August 1944).
AN 72AJ/54/II/10	'7ème Synthèse, 2ème Bureau EMN FFI' (19 August 1944).
AN 72AJ/57/III/4	'Rapport d'Edmond Coattrieux' (3 November 1944).
AN 72AJ/58/VIII/1	'Additif au témoignage de Mr. Fournet alias Anthoine' (27 June 1946).
AN 72AJ/59/IV/2	'Historique du réseau Marco' (n.d.).
AN 72AJ/61/I/1	'Itinéraire du Général de Gaulle dans Paris les 25 et 26 août' by Henri Michel (July 1964).
AN 72AJ/61/I/4b	Letter from Boucher to Comité de Libération de la Police (18 August 1944).
AN 72AJ/61/I/9	'Opérations et historique du 2e regiment "Armor" du 10 Août au 31 Août 1944' (n.d.).
AN 72AJ/61/I/10	'Compte rendu de la semaine insurrectionnelle de Paris – Groupe Cartier' (n.d.).
AN 72AJ/61/I/13	Agreement between Nordling and Major Huhm regarding prisoners (17 August 1944).
AN 72AJ/61/I/14	'La Libération de Paris vue de la Plaine Monceau, par A. Lasalle, 32 rue de Chezelles, Paris 17e' (n.d.).
AN 72AJ/61/I/17	'Compte rendu de la mission du commandant Gallois (Roger Cocteau) auprès du général Bradley' (August–September 1944).
AN 72AJ/61/I/21	'Rapport sur les fusillés de la cascade du Bois de Boulogne' (n.d.).
AN 72AJ/61/I/22	*La Voix de Paris* (19–20 August 1945).
AN 72AJ/61/II/1	Notes on the liberation by Monsieur Lecomte (n.d.).
AN 72AJ/61/II/2	Letter from General Koenig to Adrien Dansette (14 April 1967).
AN 72AJ/61/II/3	'Compte-rendu de la réunion des Secrétaires Généraux, tenue le 22 Août 1944, à 14 heures, à l'Hôtel Matignon, sous la Présidence du Ministre Délégué Général aux Territoires Occupés' (22 August 1944).
AN 72AJ/61/II/8	'Erlebnisbericht über der Eückmarsch des Stabes des Chefs der Militärverwaltung aus Frankreich' (n.d.).
AN 72AJ/61/III/1	'Mémoires du Général de Marguerittes' (February 1945).
AN 72AJ/62/I/4, pp. 1–8	'Récit des 20 rescapés du Fort des Vincennes du 19 au 24 août 1944' (n.d.).
AN 72AJ/62/I/4, pp. 9–12	'Relation des faits qui se sont passés depuis notre arrestation le 19 août 1944, jusqu'au 24

	août pendant notre internement au fort de Vincennes' by Juvenal Guillet (27 August 1944).
AN 72AJ/62/I/6	'Rapport de Monsieur Poirier 15.2.45'.
AN 72AJ/62/I/7	'Capture des trains de Belleville-Villette (mardi 22 août 1944)' by Charles Bour (4 July 1946).
AN 72AJ/62/I/8	'La guerre vue d'une fenêtre de la rue des Saussaies, en face de la Gestapo par Suzanne Chocarne' (n.d.).
AN 72AJ/62/I/10	'Notes sur la libération de Paris vue de l'Avenue de Suffren, (112 ter)' by Mme Odette Dedron (n.d.).
AN 72AJ/62/I/15	'A ma fenêtre en attendant les libérateurs' by Dr Monin, 46 boulevard Saint Michel (n.d.).
AN 72AJ/62/I/16	'Récit de ce que j'ai fait, vu et entendu pendant la libération de Paris' by Henri Rebière (November 1944).
AN 72AJ/62/I/23, pp. 26–7	'Itineraire choisi sur la demande du Commissaire Délégué du Gouvernement Provisoire de la République Française aux colonnes allemandes traversant Paris' by Colonel Lisey [*sic*] (n.d.).
AN 72AJ/62/II/2	'Comment les Allemands ont quitté Paris' by Victor Veau (n.d.).
AN 72AJ/62/II/4	'Tract émanant du commandant de la Wehrmacht du Grand Paris, trouvé sur les Champs-Élysées. 26 août 1944'.
AN 72AJ/62/III/3	'La Lutte pour la Mairie du XVIIe' (no author, n.d.).
AN 72AJ/62/III/4	'Fragments d'un Journal écrit pendant la Libération de Paris, par M. Boisdon, avocat à Bourges résidant alors 37 Boulevard Saint German (Ve)' (n.d.).
AN 72AJ/62/IV/1, pp. 4–5	'Témoignage du Directeur de l'Ecole des garçons, rue Campon' (15 September 1944).
AN 72AJ/62/IV/1, pp. 6–8	'La semaine de Libération dans le 2è Arrondissement' (23 September 1944).
AN 72AJ/62/IV/1, pp. 36–42	'Rapport sur les évènements qui se sont déroulés dans le 11e arrondissement et sur la vie scolaire pendant la semaine de la libération' (n.d.).
AN 72AJ/62/IV/1, pp. 49–51	'Rapport sur les évènements de fin août 1944 dans le Ecoles de Garçons du XIIIème arrondissement' (1 October 1944).
AN 72AJ/62/IV/1, pp. 75–6	'Report du Directeur de l'Ecole des Garçons, 18 rue Ste Isaure' (12 September 1944).
AN 72AJ/62/IV/1, pp. 88–90	Report by Monsieur Weill, Instituteur at the Ecole des Garçons, 4 rue Erckmann-Chatrian (15 September 1944).

AN 72AJ/62/IV/1, pp. 97–103   'L'école et la Libération de Paris' by the headmaster of the boys' school, 55 rue de la Chapelle (19 September 1944).

AN 72AJ/62/IV/1, pp. 104–105   'A Paris pendant la semaine du 9 au 26 août dans le 20e Arrondissement' (20 September 1944).

AN 72AJ/62/IV/2, pp. 56–61   'Les journées de la Libération dans la commune de Cheilly-Larue' by M. Godfroy (19 September 1944).

AN 72AJ/62/IV/2, pp. 62–5   'Commune de Cheilly-Larue. Les journées de la Libération' by Mme Godfroy (n.d.).

AN 72AJ/62/IV/2, pp. 68–78   'Les journées de la Libération à Choisy-le-Roi' by Mme Proskawiec (21 September 1944).

AN 72AJ/62/IV/2, pp. 103–28   'Libération de Fresnes' (n.d.).

AN 72AJ/62/IV/2, p. 142   'Ville de Joinville-le-Pont: Rapport sur la libération' (n.d.).

AN 72AJ/62/IV/2, pp. 143–6   'La bataille de la libération au Pont de Joinville – 25 août 1944' by Mlle Michaelis (n.d.).

AN 72AJ/62/IV/2, pp. 181–2   'Journées de la Libération – Rapport' (19 September 1944).

AN 72AJ/62/IV/2, pp. 183–5   Letter from the headmaster of the Collège Moderne et Téchnique, Pantin (16 September 1944).

AN 72AJ/62/IV/2, pp. 186–8   'Les écoles de Pantin pendant la période qui a précédé la Libération' (October 1944).

AN 72AJ/62/IV/2, pp. 189–91   'Bataille de la Libération au Pavillons-s/-Bois' (16 September 1944).

AN 72AJ/62/IV/2, pp. 196–9   'Les journées de fin août 1944 au Pré-Saint-Gervais' (n.d.).

AN 72AJ/62/IV/2, pp. 236–7   'Journées de la Libération à Saint-Mandé' by La Directrice de l'E. M. St Mandé (22 September 1944).

AN 72AJ/62/IV/2, pp. 257–60   'Commune de Thiais: Rapport sur les évènements du fin Août 1944' by the headmaster (15 September 1944).

AN 72AJ/62/V/5, p. 11   Letter from Jacques Romazzotti of the Paris municipal council (18 August 1944).

AN 72AJ/62/VII/3   Articles from *Le Franc-Tireur* (October 1949).

AN 72AJ/67/IV/18   'Témoignage de M. Pierre Lefaucheux' (20 January 1951) and 'L'évasion de Mr. Lefaucheux' by Mme Lefaucheux (August 1945).

AN 72AJ/71/VI/2a, pp. 2–5   'Mon activité dans la Résistance' by Max Barioux (n.d.).

AN 72AJ/71/VI/2a, p. 33   'Historique du reseau Goëlette' by Paul Kinderfreund (2 March 1950).

AN 72AJ/71/VI/2b   Opinion poll reports from Service de Sondages
                              et Statistiques (July 1944).

AN 72AJ/71/IX/5   'Témoignage de Charles Le Nevez' (23–27 June
                              1946).

AN 72AJ/71/IX/7   'Compte rendu de l'activité résistante durant
                              l'occupation allemande du Commissaire de
                              Police Délégué Raymond Levasseur' (n.d.).

AN 72AJ/71/IX/17   'Témoignage de Mr. Le Rousès' (15 May 1946).

AN 72AJ/71/IX/19   'Témoignage de Jean Le Jossec' (21 May 1946).

AN 72AJ/74/III/10   'Note relative à l'étude des "rapports journaliers
                              des gares de la région Ouest de la SNCF" pour la
                              période du 1er juillet au 6 septembre 1944'
                              (n.d.).

AN 72AJ/231/I/13   'Telegrammes du COMIDAC pour la Résistance
                              intérieure' (20 August 1944).

AN 72AJ/231/II/8   'Témoignage de M. Hessel' (n.d.).

AN 72AJ/232/III/5   'Compte-rendu de la mission PATHFINDER' by
                              Marcel (Vincent Saubestre) (4 September
                              1944).

AN 72AJ/234/VI/23   'Lettre d'Y. Morandat à d'Astier' (9 August
                              1944).

AN 72AJ/234/VI/24   'Lettre d'Y. Morandat à d'Astier' (15 August
                              1944).

AN 72AJ/234/VIII/3   'Témoignage de M. Closon' (5 January 1950).

AN 72AJ/234/IX/22   'Memorandum sur les problèmes de la région
                              parisienne' by Closon (28 July 1944).

AN 72AJ/235/I   Coded telegrams.

AN 72AJ/235/II   Telegrams from France ('France Arrivée').

AN 72AJ/235/II/165   No. 21, 31 July 1944, d'Orente.

AN 72AJ/235/II/170–3   Nos. 25–28, 1 August 1944, Secnord d'Arnolphe,
                              'Résultats simili Gallup'.

AN 72AJ/235/II/178–9   Nos. 34 and 35, 1 August 1944, Secnord de
                              Belladone, 'Rôle du COMAC'.

AN 72AJ/235/II/190–1   Nos. 46 and 47, 3 August 1944, Secnord de
                              Belladone, 'Problèmes que soulèvera la libéra-
                              tion de Paris'.

AN 72AJ/235/II/212   No. 65, 6 August 1944, Secnord de Belladone,
                              'Problème prise de pouvoir Paris = reglé'.

AN 72AJ/235/II/224   No. 80, 7 August 1944, Secnord de Belladone,
                              'Opérations prisons politiques'.

AN 72AJ/235/II/245   No. 95, 9 August 1944, Secnord de Belladone,
                              'ALGEBRE signale aucun câble reçu depuis
                              2.8.44'.

AN 72AJ/235/II/250   Unnumbered, undated and unsourced message
                              (received 15 August 1944), 'Massacres de pris-
                              onniers politiques'.

AN 72AJ/235/II/252   No. 1, 11 August 1944, Secnord de Délégation, 'Préparatifs militaires allemands aux environs de Paris'.

AN 72AJ/235/II/253–4   Nos. 3 and 4, 11 August 1944, Secnord de Belladone, 'Pour Merlin et le Comidac. Délégué Général demande instructions et définit. ses Pouv.'.

AN 72AJ/235/II/266–7   Nos. 16 and 17, 11 August 1944, Secnord de Belladone, 'Tractations PETAIN LAVAL avec les Américains etc.'.

AN 72AJ/235/II/284   No. 33, 14 August 1944, Secnord de Belladone, 'Massacres des prisonniers – Attaque des prisons'.

AN 72AJ/235/II/289   No. 45, 15 August 1944, Secnord de Belladone, 'Affaire HERRIOT-LAVAL'.

AN 72AJ/235/II/290   No. 46, 15 August 1944, Secnord de Belladone, 'Grève de la Police'.

AN 72AJ/235/II/291   No. 47, 15 August 1944, Secnord de Belladone, 'Pour le COMIDAC, Situation à Paris'.

AN 72AJ/235/II/299   No. 52, 17 August 1944, Secnord de Belladone, 'Situation à Paris – Grèves. – (I)'.

AN 72AJ/235/II/300   No. 53, 17 August 1944, Secnord de Belladone, 'Situation à Paris – Grèves. – (II)'.

AN 72AJ/235/II/301   No. 54, 17 August 1944, Secnord de Belladone, 'Situation à Paris – Grèves. – (III)'.

AN 72AJ/235/II/302   No. 55, 17 August 1944, Secnord de Belladone,'Situation à Paris – Grèves. – (IV)'.

AN 72AJ/235/II/303   No. 56, 17 August 1944, Secnord de Belladone, 'Arrivée à Paris de JUBEOL et PARAFFINE'.

AN 72AJ/235/II/306   No. 59, 18 August 1944, Secnord de Belladone, 'Situation à Paris – (I).'

AN 72AJ/235/II/307   No. 60, 18 August 1944, Secnord de Belladone, 'Situation à Paris – (II).'

AN 72AJ/235/II/308   No. 61, 18 August 1944, Secnord de Belladone, 'Situation à Paris – (III)'.

AN 72AJ/235/II/309   No. 62, 18 August 1944, Secnord de Belladone, 'Situation à Paris – (IV)'.

AN 72AJ/235/II/310   No. 63, 18 August 1944, Secnord de Belladone, 'Situation à Paris – (V)'.

AN 72AJ/235/II/311   No. 64, 18 August 1944, Secnord de Belladone, 'Situation à Paris – (VI)'.

AN 72AJ/235/II/313   No. 64, 18 August 1944, Secnord de Délégation, 'Affaire Herriot-Laval – (IV)'.

AN 72AJ/235/II/322   No. 87, 23 August 1944, Secnord de Belladone, 'Situation de Paraffine'.

AN 72AJ/235/II/333   No. 62, 18 August 1944, Secnord d'Oronte, 'Accord avec les Allemands'.

AN 72AJ/235/III/449	No. 41, 30 June 1944, à Secnord pour Quartus, 'Nomination d'ARC au grade de Général de Brigade'.
AN 72AJ/235/III/491	No. 10, 27 July 1944, à Secnord, 'Liste des nominations de la lune d'août'.
AN 72AJ/235/III/494	No. 17, 29 July 1944, à Secnord pour Belladone, 'Massacres de détenus – Création de groupes armés'.
AN 72AJ/235/III/503	No. 76, 17 August 1944, à Secnord pour Belladone, 'Intrigues Pétain–Laval–Américains – (II)'.
AN 72AJ/235/III/504	No. 77, 17 August 1944, à Secnord pour Belladone, 'Intrigues Pétain–Laval–Américains – (III)'.
AN 72AJ/236/I	'Registres de télégrammes. France: arrivée et départ'.
AN 72AJ/236/I/5/44	Undated and unnumbered message (received 13 June 1944) from Secnord to Algiers.
AN 72AJ/237/I/7	'Notice biographique du colonel André Rondenay, redigée par M. Tuffrau' (n.d.).
AN 72AJ/237/II/2a/36	No. 39, 3 July 1944, from Polygone.
AN 72AJ/247/I/2	'Ordonnance du 26 août 1944'.

Archives de la RATP   'Poste de Commandement nº 2 place Denfert-Rocherau'.

US National Archives Foreign Military Studies (Microfiche Publication M1035)

B-015	'Defense of Paris' by Freiherr von Boineburg (May 1946).
B-034	'OKW War Diary (1 Apr–8 Dec 44)' by Major Percy E. Schramm (n.d.).
B-176	'Campaign of Northern France, 26 August to 34 September 1944' by Alfred Zerbel (6 October 1950).
B-308	'OB West, Atlantic Wall to Siegfred line, a study in command' by Generalleutnant Bodo Zimmerman (October 46).
B-546	'Supplementary Report: Northern France Campaign (Aug 26–Sept 4)' by Generalmajor Carl Wahle (n.d.).
B-611	'Defense of Paris (Summer 1944)' by Professor Kurt Hesse (11 March 1947).
B-728	'The battles of the 1.Armee in France from 11 Aug to 15 Sep 1944' by Oberst Albert Emmerich (22 September 1946).
B-729	'Report on the Fighting of the Fifth Panzer

Army from 24 August to 4 September 1944' by Oberst Paul Frank (18 November 1947).

B-741 'Actions of the 352nd Infantry Division during the Battle in Northern France (1 August–10 September 1944)' by Oberstleutnant Fritz Ziegelmann (22 December 1947).

Bibliothèque de l'Académie Médicale, Paris
BAM VV 'Comment les Allemands ont quitté Paris' by Victor Veau (n.d.).

Bibliothèque de Documentation Internationale et Contemporaine, Nanterre
BDIC FΔ rés 844/03/9 'Histoire de la résistance dans le secteur nord-est' by Louis Marcou (July 1946).

US National Archives Foreign Military Studies (Microfiche Publication M1035)
ETHINT 1 'From the invasion to the Siegfried line' by General der Artillerie Walter Warlimont (20 July 1945).

ETHINT 5 'The 20 July 1944 Attempt. Was von Kluge a Traitor?' by General der Artillerie Walter Warlimont (3 August 1945).

ETHINT 30 'An interview with Reichsmarschall Hermann Goering' (21 July 1945).

ETHINT 59 'An interview with Genmaj Rudolf Frhr von Gersdorff. Reactions to the Newspaper Article on Patton and the Third Army' (16 May 1946).

ETHINT 63 'An interview with Genmaj Otto Remer: The 20 July 44 Plot' (15 August 1945).

ETHINT 67 'An interview with Genlt Fritz Bayerlein. Critique of Normandy breakthrough. Pz Lehr Div from St Lo to the Ruhr' (7–9 August 1945).

Musée du General Leclerc – Musée Jean Moulin, Paris
ML 90/43 Front National leaflet calling for a general strike (n.d.).

ML 99/211 'Août 1944: Libération de Paris' by Gabrielle Bonnet (n.d.).

ML Arc Cables from Arc (Chaban) 19–25 August 1944.
ML Chaban 'Lettre du Général Chaban Delmas au Général Koenig, 15 Août 1944'.

ML EMFFI 'Compte-rendu EMFFI sur les émission du 23 et 24 août et le communiqué SHAEF du 24 août 1944'.

ML Vigne   'Le Chef d'escadron Vigne, Commandant le
                                   S/Secteur Nord 2, à Monsieur le Commandant
                                   du Secteur Nord (n.d.).

UK National Archives, Kew
NA CAB/65/42/26   War Cabinet Minutes, 1944.
NA GRGG 180   'Report on information obtained from Senior
                                   Officer PW on 25/26 Aug 44' (WO208/4363).
NA GRGG 181(C)   'Preliminary report on information obtained
                                   from CS/211 – General der Infanterie Dietrich
                                   von CHOLTITZ, Commandant of PARIS, cap-
                                   tured PARIS 25 Aug 44' (WO208/4363).
NA GRGG 182   'Report on information obtained from Senior
                                   Officer PW on 27/28 Aug 44' (WO208/4363).
NA GRGG 183   'Report on information obtained from Senior
                                   Office PW on 29 Aug 44' (WO208/4363).
NA GRGG 184   'Report on information obtained from Senior
                                   Officer PW on 30 Aug 44' (WO208/4363).
NA HS 9/739/6   'Ivar (sic) Alfred HOOKER, aka THALER –
                                   born 27.11.1923' – SOE personnel file.
NA HS 9/1223/5   'RACHELINE, Lazare' – SOE personnel file.
NA HS 9/1498/2   'Alix D'UNIENVILLE, aka MYRTIL, aka MICHEL,
                                   aka Aline DAVELAN, aka FACHANYERT' –
                                   SOE personnel file (closed until 1 January 2019).
NA KV/2/3550   'Papers regarding P. G. Wodehouse'.
NA WO 373/98   'The London Omnibus list for gallant and dis-
                                   tinguished services in the field'.
NA WO 373/153   'Recommendations for honours and awards
                                   for gallant and distinguished service (Various
                                   awards).'

King's College, London
OSS War Diary

PRINTED SOURCES

Abel, Jean-Pierre (pseudonym of René Chateau) (1947), *L'Age de Caïn: Premier témoignage sur les dessous de la libération de Paris* (Paris: Editions Nouvelles).

Abetz, Otto (1953), *Histoire d'une politique franco-allemande, 1930–1950: Mémoires d'un ambassadeur* (Paris: Stock).

Adler-Bress, Marcelle (1955), 'Von Choltitz a-t-il changé d'avis?', *Revue d'histoire de la Deuxième Guerre mondiale* 19:116.

Alary, Eric, Vergez-Chaignon, Bénédicte & Gauvin, Gilles (2006), *Les Français au quotidien 1939–1949* (Paris: Perrin).

Albertelli, Sebastien (2010a), 'RONDENAY, André (1913–1944)' in François

Broche, Georges Caïtucoli & Jean-François Muracciole (eds), *Dictionnaire de la France libre* (Paris: Robert Laffont), p. 1277.

Albertelli, Sebastien (2010b), 'RACHLINE, Lazare (1913–1944)' in François Broche, Georges Caïtucoli & Jean-François Muracciole (eds), *Dictionnaire de la France libre* (Paris: Robert Laffont), pp. 1215–1216.

Amouroux, Henri (1988), *La grande histoire de Français sous l'occupation. Joies et douleurs du peuple libéré 6 juin–1 septembre 1944* (Paris: Laffont).

ANACR (n.d.), 'Le Dernier convoi: témoignages', *Les Cahiers de la Résistance Seine-et-Marnaise*, 1.

ANACR (2005), *1940–1945: La Résistance dans le 19e arrondissement de Paris* (Pantin: Le Temps des Cérises).

Andrieu, Claire (1997), 'Les résistantes, perspectives de recherche' in Antoine Prost (ed), *La Résistance, une histoire sociale* (Paris: L'Atelier), pp. 69–96.

Andrieu, Claire (2004), 'Le CNR et les logiques de l'insurrection résistante' in Fondation Charles de Gaulle (ed), *De Gaulle et la Libération* (Brussels: Editions Complexe), pp. 69–126.

Anonymous (n.d.), *L'Insurrection parisienne. 19 août–1944–26 août* (n.p.: Parti Communiste Français).

Anonymous (1944), *Paris Libéré* (Paris: Flammarion).

Anonymous (1945), *La Libération de Paris* (Paris: OLB).

Anonymous (1964), *La Libération de Paris* (Paris: Denoël).

Anonymous (ed) (1965), *Pages d'Histoire 1939–1945: Les Policiers français dans la Résistance* (Paris: CNPACR).

Anonymous (1978), *Facsimile de La Vérité clandestine (1940–1944)* (Paris: EDI).

Anonymous (2004), *Paris Occupé, Paris Libéré* (Paris: Arcadia).

Aron, Robert (1959), *Histoire de la Liberation de la France, juin 1944–mai 1945* (Paris: Arthème Fayard).

Aron, Robert (1967), *Histoire de l'épuration. 1. De l'indulgence aux massacre, novembre 1942–septembre 1944* (Paris: Fayard).

Aron, Robert (1969), *Histoire de l'épuration. 2. Des prisons clandestines aux tribunaux d'exception, septembre 1944–juin 1949* (Paris: Fayard).

Audiat, Pierre (1946), *Paris pendant la guerre* (Paris: Hachette).

Auroy, Berthe (2008), *Jours de guerre. Ma vie sous l'Occupation* (Paris: Bayard).

Aury, Bernard (1945), *La Délivrance de Paris: 19–26 août 1944* (Paris: Arthaud).

Babelay, Jean-Louis (1945), *Un An* (Paris: Raymond Schall).

Bachelier, Christian (1996), *La SNCF sous l'Occupation Allemande 1940–1944* (Paris: SNCF) (available at www.ahicf.com/ww2/rapport/av-propos.htm [accessed June 2012]).

Ballarin, Adriano (2010), 'Quand la mort réunit des destins qui se voulaient différents', *Vivre à Crespières* 8:5.

Baker, Carlos (1972), *Ernest Hemingway* (Harmondsworth: Penguin).

Barat, Philippe (1945), *Pavés sanglants* (Paris: Armand Fleury).

Barcia, Robert (alias Hardy) (2003), *La Véritable histoire de Lutte ouvrière* (Paris: Denoël).

Bardoux, Jacques (1958), *La Délivrance de Paris: Séances secrètes et négociations clandestines* (Paris: Arthème Fayard).

Bargatzky, Walter (1969), 'The last round – in Paris' in Hans-Adolf Jacobsen (ed), *Germans Against Hitler: July 20, 1944* (Bonn: Presse-und Informationsamt) pp. 156–60.

Barozzi, Jacques (1980), *La Libération de Paris* (Rennes: Ouest-France).

Barr, Alfred H. (1945), 'Picasso 1940–1944: A digest with notes', *The Bulletin of the Museum of Modern Art* 12(3):2–9.

Barr, Alfred H. (1946), *Picasso: Fifty Years of His Art* (New York: The Museum of Modern Art).

Beevor, Antony (2009), *D-Day* (London: Penguin).

Beevor, Antony & Cooper, Artemis (2004), *Paris After the Liberation 1944–1949* (London: Penguin).

Benoît-Guyod, Georges (1962), *L'Invasion de Paris* (Paris: Les éditions du Scorpion).

Bergot, Erwan (1980), *La 2ème D.B.* (Paris: Presses de la Cité).

Berlière, Jean-Marc (1994) 'La police parisienne change de camp', *L'Histoire* 179:18–22.

Berlière, Jean-Marc (1996), 'L'Epuration de la police parisienne', *Vingtième Siècle. Revue d'Histoire* 49:63–81.

Berlière, Jean-Marc (2001), *Policiers français sous l'Occupation* (Paris: Perrin).

Berlière, Jean-Marc & Liaigre, Franck (2007), *Liquider les traîtres: La face cachée du PCF 1941–1943* (Paris: Laffont).

Berlière, Jean-Marc & Liaigre, Franck (2012), *Ainsi finissent les salauds: Séquestrations et exécutions clandestines dans Paris libéré* (Paris: Laffont).

Bernert, Philippe (1975), *Roger Wybot et la Bataille pour la DST* (Paris: Presses de la Cité).

Berthonnet, Arnaud (2003), 'L'Histoire d'une épuration: L'industrie du bâtiment et des travaux publics en région parisienne (1944–1949)', *Guerres mondiales et conflits contemporains* 212:75–104.

Bidault, Suzanne (1973), *Souvenirs de guerre et d'occupation* (Paris: La Table ronde).

Billotte, Pierre (1972), *Le Temps des armes* (Paris: Plon).

Bleustein-Blanchet, Marcel (1984), *Les Ondes de la Liberté 1934–1984* (Paris: Lattès).

Blond, Georges (2005), '2 400 hommes et femmes ont franchi la Marne à pied', *Le Parisien* 16 August 2005.

Blumenson, Martin (1961), *Breakout and Pursuit* (Washington: Centre of Military History).

Blumenson, Martin (1996), *The Patton Papers 1940–1945* (New York: Da Capo).

Blumenson, Martin (1998), 'Politics and the military in the Liberation of Paris', *Parameters* Summer 1998, pp. 4–14.

Blumenson, Martin (2000), *The Duel for France 1944* (n.p.: Da Capo).

Bobkowski, Andrzej (1991), *En Guerre et en paix: Journal 1940–1944* (Montricher, Switzerland: Editions Noir et Blanc).

Boegner, Philippe (1992), *Carnets du Pasteur Boegner, 1940–1945* (Paris: Fayard).

Bood, Micheline (1974), *Les Années doubles. Journal d'une lycéenne sous l'Occupation* (Paris: Laffont).

Boudard, Alphonse (1977), *Les combattants du petit bonheur* (Paris: La Table ronde).

Bourdan, Pierre (1945), *Carnet de retour avec la Division Leclerc* (Paris: Editions Pierre Trémois).

Bourderon, Roger (2004), *Rol-Tanguy* (Paris: Tallandier).

Bourderon, Roger (2006), 'Francs-tireurs et partisans français' in François Marcot, Bruno Leroux & Christine Levisse-Touzé (eds), *Dictionnaire Historique de la Résistance* (Paris: Laffont), pp. 188–90.

Bourdrel, Philippe (1988), *L'Epuration sauvage* (Paris: Perrin).

Bourget, Pierre (1979), *Paris 1940–1944* (Paris: Plon).

Bourget, Pierre (1984), *Paris, année 44: Occupation, libération, épuration* (Paris: Plon).

Bourget, Pierre (1994), 'La Trève' in Christine Levisse-Touze (ed), *Paris 1944: Les Enjeux de la Libération* (Paris: Albin Michel), pp. 243–57.

Bourget, Pierre & Lacretelle, Charles (1959), *Sur les murs de Paris 1940–1944* (Paris: Hachette).

Bourget, Pierre & Lacretelle, Charles (1980), *Sur les murs de Paris et de France 1939–1945* (Paris: Hachette).

Bradley, Omar N. (1951), *A Soldier's Story of the Allied Campaigns from Tunis to the Elbe* (London: Eyre & Spottiswoode).

Braibant, Charles (1945), *La Guerre à Paris (8 novembre 1942–27 août 1944)* (Paris: Corréa).

Brasillach, Robert (1955), *Journal d'un homme occupé* (Paris: Les Sept Couleurs).

Brassaï (1999), *Conversations with Picasso* (London: University of Chicago Press).

Brassié, Anne (1987), *Robert Brasillach, ou Encore un instant de bonheur* (Paris: Robert Laffont).

Breton, Philippe (ed) (1964), *La Libération de Paris* (Paris: Denoël).

Brissaud, André (1965), *La Dernière année de Vichy 1943–1944* (Paris: Presses Pocket).

Broué, Pierre (1995), 'Raoul, militant trotskyste', *Cahiers Léon Trotsky* 56:5–186.

Brown, Antony Cave (1988), *The Secret Servant: The Life of Sir Stewart Menzies, Churchill's Spymaster* (London: Michael Joseph).

Buffetaut, Yves (2004), 'Campagne de Normandie (4): Les Alliés franchissent la Seine', *Armes Militaria Magazine* Hors-série 55.

Burton, Richard D. E. (2001), *Blood in the City: Violence and Revolution in Paris 1789–1945* (London: Cornell University Press).

Buton, Philippe (1993), *Les Lendemains qui déchantent: Le Parti communiste français à la libération* (Paris: Presses de la Fondation nationale des sciences politiques).

Buton, Philippe (1994), 'Les premières décisions du pouvoir' in Christine Levisse-Touzé (ed), *Paris 1944: Les Enjeux de la Libération* (Paris: Albin Michel), pp. 390–402.

Calvès, André (1984), *Sans bottes ni médailles. Un trotskyste breton dans la guerre* (Montreuil: La Brèche).

Campaux, S. (ed) (1945), *La Libération de Paris (19–26 août 1944). Récits de combattants et de témoins réunis par S. Campaux* (Paris: Payot).

Carell, Paul (1962), *Invasion – They're Coming!* (London: Harrap).

Carrière, Bruno (1994), 'Août 1994: Paris, les cheminots et la libération', *La Vie du Rail* 2458 (24–30 August 1994), pp. 20–6.

Castetbon, Philippe (2004), *Ici est tombé: Paroles sur la Libération de Paris* (Paris: Editions Tirésias).

Cazaux, Yves (1975), *Journal secret de la Libération* (Paris: Albin Michel).

Césaire, Frédérique (2006), *L'affaire Petiot* (Paris: de Vecchi).

Chaban-Delmas, Jacques (1975), *L'Ardeur* (Paris: Stock).

Chaigneau, Jean-François (1981), *Le Dernier wagon* (Paris: Julliard).

Chamberlain, Peter & Doyle, Evelyn (1999), *Encyclopaedia of German Tanks of World War Two* (London: Weidenfeld & Nicolson).

Chamberlin, William Henry (1965), 'How Paris was spared', *Modern Age* 9:419–20.

Chevandier, Christian (2002), *Cheminots en grève ou la construction d'une identité (1848–2001)* (Paris: Maisonneuve & Larose).

Chevandier, Christian (2008), 'Cesser d'obéir et maintenir un ordre: les policiers parisiens en août 1944' in André Loez & Nicolas Mariot (eds), *Obéir, désobéir* (Paris: La Découverte), pp. 280–92.

Chevrillon, Claire (1995), *Code Name Christiane Clouet: A Woman in the French Resistance* (College Station: Texas A&M University Press).

Childers, Thomas (2004), *In the Shadows of War* (New York: Owl).

Christienne, Odette & Plancard, Frédéric (n.d.), *Le Régiment de Sapeurs-Pompiers de Paris 1938–1944*, vol. 2 (Paris: Mairie de Paris).

Ciechanowski, Jan. M. (1974), *The Warsaw Rising of 1944* (Cambridge: Cambridge University Press).

Cleveland-Peck, Patricia (2000), 'The Sussex network', *History Today* 50(9):4–5.

Closon, Francis-Louis (1974), *Le Temps des passions: De Jean Moulin à la Libération 1943–1944* (Paris: Presses de la Cité).

Cobb, Matthew (2009a), *The Resistance: The French Fight Against the Nazis* (London: Simon & Schuster).

Cobb, Matthew (2009b), 'The lost lion of Paris: the extraordinary story of George Dukson', *Independent* 12 August 2009 (available at tinyurl.com/dukson [accessed June 2012]).

Cogniot, Georges; Duclos, Jacques; Gillot, Auguste; Rol-Tanguy, Henri; Tollet, André; Villon, Pierre & Willard, Germaine (1974), 'La Liberation de Paris: Table ronde', *Cahiers d'Histoire de l'Institut Maurice Thorez* 8–9:192–221.

Cointet, Jean-Paul (2001), *Paris 40–44* (Paris: Perrin).

Collins, Larry & Lapierre, Dominique (1965), *Is Paris Burning?* (New York: Simon & Schuster).

Conte, Arthur (1984), *Août 1944: La Libération* (Paris: Carrere-Michel Lafon).

Corbin, Alain & Mayeur, Jean-Marie (eds) (1997), *La Barricade: Actes du colloque organisé les 17, 18 et 19 mai 1995* (Paris: Publications de la Sorbonne).

Cordier, Daniel (1999), *Jean Moulin: La République des catacombes* (Paris: Gallimard).

Courdesses, Colonel Maurice (1994), 'Les combats de la 2e division blindée dans Paris' in Christine Levisse-Touze (ed), *Paris 1944: Les Enjeux de la Libération* (Paris: Albin Michel) pp. 299–315.

Courtin, René (1994), *De la Clandestinité au pouvoir. Journal de la libération de Paris* (Paris: Editions de Paris).

Craipeau, Yvan (1978), *La Libération confisquée* (Paris: Savelli/Syros).

Crang, Jeremy A. (2007), 'General de Gaulle under sniper fire in Notre Dame cathedral, 26 August 1944: Robert Reid's BBC commentary', *Historical Journal of Film, Radio and Television* 27:391–406.

Crémieux, Francis (1971), *La Vérité sur la libération de Paris* (Paris: Belfond).

Crémieux-Brilhac, Jean-Louis (ed) (1976), *Ici Londres ... Les Voix de la Liberté. Tome V. La Bataille de France: 9 mai 1944–31 août 1944* (Paris: La Documentation Française).

Crémieux-Brilhac, Jean-Louis (2001), *La France Libre: De l'appel du 18 juin à la libération*, vols 1 & 2 (Paris: Gallimard).

Crémieux-Brilhac, Jean-Louis (2010), *Georges Boris: Trente ans d'influence. Blum, de Gaulle, Mendès-France* (Paris: Gallimard).

Crénesse, Pierre (1944), *La Libération des ondes* (Paris: Berger-Levrault).

Culmann, Henri (1985), *A Paris sous Vichy: Témoignage et souvenirs* (Paris: Editions La Bruyère).

Cumberlege, Geoffrey (1946), *War Report* (London: Oxford University Press).

Cumont, Jacques (1991), *Les Volontaires de Neuilly-sur-Marne du 'groupe Hildevert' et le réseau 'Spiritualist'* (Le Mée-sur-Seine: Editions Ammattéis).

Daix, Pierre (1994), *Picasso: Life and Art* (London: Thames & Hudson).

Dalisson, Rémi (2002), 'La propagande de Vichy. Mythes fondateurs, relecture nationaliste et contestation en France de 1940 à 1944', *Guerres mondiales et conflits contemporains* 207:5–32.

Dansette, Adrien (1946), *Histoire de la libération de Paris* (Paris: Arthème Fayard).

Dansette, Adrien (1966), 'Von Choltitz, "Sauveur de Paris"?', *Le Monde* 9 November 1966.

Darrobers, Martin (1989), 'La Libération. De la mémoire à l'histoire. Compte rendu d'un colloque sur les pouvoirs à la Libération', *Matériaux pour l'histoire de notre temps* 17:67–9.

d'Astier, Emmanuel (1965), *De la chute à la libération de Paris. 25 août 1944* (Paris: Gallimard).

Davies, Norman (2004), *Rising '44* (London: Pan Macmillan).

de Beauvoir, Simone (1965), *The Prime of Life* (Harmondsworth: Penguin).

de Boissieu, Alain (1981), *Pour combattre avec de Gaulle, 1940–1946* (Paris: Plon).

de Boissieu, Alain (1994), 'La participation de la 2e DB à la libération de Paris', *Espoir* 96:93.

Debono, Emmanuel (2004), 'Le film *La Libération de Paris*: Histoire, enjeux, analyse', *La Lettre de la Fondation de la Résistance* 37:7–9.

de Chézal, Bertrand (1945), *A travers les batailles pour Paris, août 1944. Bonneval–Chartres–Paris* (Paris: Plon).

Debû-Bridel, Jacques (1978), *De Gaulle et le CNR* (Paris: France-Empire).

de Gaulle, Charles (1956), *Mémoires de guerre: L'Unité 1942–1944* (Paris: Plon).

de Gaulle, Charles (1962), *Mémoires de guerre: L'Unité 1942–1944* (Paris: Plon).

de Gaulle, Charles (1970), *Discours et messages. 1: Pendant la guerre juin 1940–janvier 1946* (Paris: Plon).

de Gaulle, Charles (1983), *Lettres, notes et carnets: juin 1943–mai 1945* (Paris: Plon).

de Langlade, Paul (1964), *En suivant Leclerc. D'Alger à Berchtesgaden* (Paris: Robert Laffont).

Delarue, Jacques (1964), *The History of the Gestapo* (London: MacDonald).

Delattre, Lucas (2006), *A Spy at the Heart of the Third Reich: The Extraordinary Story of Fritz Kolbe, America's Most Important Spy in World War II* (London: Grove/Atlantic).

Denis, Henri (1963), *Le Comité parisien de la Libération* (Paris: PUF).

Denoyelle, Françoise (2006), 'Walter Dreizner, un amateur sous influence: Des télécommunications à la photographie', *Francia* 33:85–94.

de Saint-Pierre, C. (pseudonym of Odette Lainville) (1945), *Des ténèbres à l'aube. Journal d'une française (Paris, 10 août–10 septembre 1944)* (Paris: Arthaud).

de Saint-Pierre, C. (pseudonym of Odette Lainville) (1951), *A Travers la tourmente: Poèmes 1939–1945* (Paris: La Revue Moderne).

Desfeuilles, André (1945), *Le Consul Général de Suède, Raoul Nordling et la Libération de Paris (août 1944) (Extrait du Bulletin Historique du Royal-Suédois)* (Paris: Institut Tessin).

de Thézy, Marie & Gunther, Thomas Michael (eds) (1994), *Images de la Libération de Paris* (Paris: Paris Musées).

Domenach-Lallich, Denise (2001), *Une jeune fille libre: Journal (1939–1944)* (Lyons: Les Arènes).

Dresden, Major D. W. (1946), *Le Chemin de Paris: Journal d'un officier américain* (Paris: Editions du Myrte).

Dreyfus, Jean-Marc & Gensburger, Sarah (2003), *Des camps dans Paris: Austerlitz, Lévitan, Bassano; juillet 1943–août 1944* (Paris: Fayard).

Drieu La Rochelle, Pierre (1992), *Journal 1939–1945* (Paris: Gallimard).

Dronne, Raymond (1970), *La Libération de Paris* (Paris: Presses de la Cité).

Dubois, Edmond (1944), *Vu pendant la Libération de Paris. Journal d'un témoin* (Lausanne: Payot).

Dubois, Edmond (1946), *Paris sans lumière. 1939–1945: Témoignages* (Lausanne: Payot).

Duchemin, Gérard (2011), 'Paul Aribaud: un résistant, une vie brisée', *Le Doralien* 10:8.

Duclos, Jacques (1970), *Mémoires. 3: Dans la Bataille clandestine. Deuxième partie 1943–1945* (Paris: Fayard).

Dunan, René (1945), *'Ceux' de Paris: Août 1944* (Geneva: Editions du Milieu du Monde).

Dupuy, Ferdinand (1945), *La Libération de Paris vue d'un commissariat de police* (Paris: Librairies-Imprimeries réunies).

Durand, Paul (1968), *La SNCF pendant la guerre: sa résistance à l'occupant* (Paris: PUF).

Dutourd, Jean (1983), *Le Demi-solde* (Paris: Folio).

Echenberg, Myron (1985), '"Morts pour la France"; The African soldier in France during the Second World War', *Journal of African History* 26:363–80.

Eisenhower, Dwight D. (1948), *Crusade in Europe* (London: Heinemann).

Eismann, Gaël (2010), *Hôtel Majestic: Ordre et sécurité en France occupée (1940–1944)* (Paris: Tallandier).

Elgey, Georgette (1993), *Histoire de la IVe république: La République des illusions 1945–1951* (Paris: Fayard).

Elkins, Aaron (2002), *Turncoat* (New York: E-Rights/E-Reads).

Fabre-Luce, Alfred (1947), *Journal de la France* (Paris: Diffusion du Livre).

Favreau, Bertrand (1996), *Georges Mandel, ou la passion de la République 1884–1944* (Paris: Fayard).

Felstiner, Mary (1987), 'Commandant of Drancy: Alois Brunner and the Jews of France', *Holocaust and Genocide Studies* 2:21–47.

Fenby, Jonathan (2010), *The General: Charles de Gaulle and the France He Saved* (London: Simon & Schuster).

Féron, Yvonne (1945), *Délivrance de Paris* (Paris: Hachette).

Fish, Colonel Robert M. (ed) (1990), *Memories of the 801st/492nd Bombardment Group 'Carpetbaggers'* (n.p.: 801st/492nd Bombardment Group Association).

Fitzgerald, Michael C. (1996), 'A triangle of ambitions: art, politics and family during the postwar years with Françoise Gilot' in William Rubin (ed), *Picasso and Portraiture: Representation and Transformation* (London: Thames & Hudson), pp. 296–335.

Florentin, Eddy (1997), *Quand les Alliés bombardaient la France* (Paris: Perrin).

Fonde, Jean Julien (1969), *J'ai vu une meute de loups . . .* (Paris: Fernand Nathan).

Fontaine, Thomas (2005), *Les oubliés de Romainville: Un camp allemand en France (1940–1944)* (Paris: Tallandier).

Foot, M. R. D. (1965), 'Paris saved', *Times Literary Supplement* 30 September 1965.

Foot, M. R. D. (2004), *SOE in France* (London: Whitehall History Publishing).

Footitt, Hilary & Simmonds, John (1988), *France 1943–1945* (Leicester: Leicester University Press).

Fourcade, Marie-Madeleine (1972), *L'Arche de Noë* (Geneva: Crémille).

Fourcade, Marie-Madeleine (1973), *Noah's Ark* (London: Allen Unwin).

Fournier, Laurent & Eymard, Alain (2009), *La 2e DB dans la Libération de Paris et de la région parisienne. Tome I: De Trappes à l'Hôtel de Ville* (Paris: Histoire & Collections).

Fournier, Laurent & Eymard, Alain (2010), *La 2e DB dans la Libération de Paris et de la région parisienne. Tome II: De l'hôtel 'Majestic' au Bourget* (Paris: Histoire & Collections).

Funk, Arthur F. (1994), 'Les services secrets alliés et la libération de Paris, renseignement et action' in Christine Levisse-Touze (ed), *Paris 1944: Les Enjeux de la Libération* (Paris: Albin Michel), pp. 226–37.

Galassi, Susan Grace (1996), *Picasso's Variations on the Masters: Confrontations with the Past* (New York: Harry N. Abrams).

Galtier-Boissière, Jean (1944), *Mon journal pendant l'Occupation* (Paris: La Jeune Parque).

Gensburger, Sarah (2005), 'Essai de sociologie de la mémoire: le cas du souvenir des camps annexes de Drancy dans Paris', *Genèses* 61:47–69.

Gerbier, Guy (2007), 'Les câbles souterrains à grande distance de 1919 à 1939', *Les Cahiers de la FNARH*, 103:21–31.

Gilot, Françoise (1964), *Life with Picasso* (New York: Signet).

Giolitto, Pierre (2002), *Histoire de la Milice* (Paris: Perrin).

Girard, Claire (1954), *Lettres de Claire Girard. Fusillée par les Allemands le 27 août 1944* (Paris: Lescaret).

Glass, Charles (2009), *Americans in Paris: Life and Death Under Nazi Occupation 1940–44* (London: Harper).

Gobille, Boris (1997), 'La mémoire à demi-mots. Analyses d'une commémoration impossible', *Genèses* 28:95–110.

Goglin, Jean-Louis & Roux, Pierre (2004), *Souffrance et liberté: Une géographie parisienne des années noires (1940–1944)* (Paris: Paris Musées).

Golson, Eric B. (2012), 'Did Swedish ball-bearings keep the Second World War going? Re-evaluating neutral Sweden's role', *Scandinavian Economic History Review* 60:165–82.

Granet, Marie (ed) (1961), *Le Journal 'Défense de la France'* (Paris: PUF).

Granet, Marie (1964), *Ceux de la Résistance (1940–1944)* (Paris: Editions de Minuit).

Gratias, Louis (1945), *Barricades* (Paris: Editions Occident).

Greiner, Helmuth & Schramm, Percy Ernst (1982), *Kriegstagebuch des Oberkommandos der Wehrmacht (Wehrmachtführungsstab). Band IV: 1. Januar 1944–22 Mai 1945* (Munich: Bernard & Graefe Verlag).

Groth, John (1945), 'Picasso at work, August 1944', *The Bulletin of the Museum of Modern Art*, 12(3):10–11.

Groult, Benoîte & Groult, Flora (1965), *Diary in Duo* (London: Barrie and Rockliff).

Grunberg, Albert (2001), *Journal d'un coiffeur juif à Paris sous l'Occupation* (Paris: L'Atelier).

Guéhenno, Jean (2002), *Journal des années noires* (Paris: Gallimard).

Hamon, Léo (1991), *Vivre ses choix* (Paris: Robert Laffont).

Hazan, Eric (2010), *The Invention of Paris: A History in Footsteps* (London: Verso).

Hazard, Jean (1998), 'Hommage au personnel hospitalier lors des combats de la Libération de Paris du 19 au 27 août 1944', *Histoire des Sciences Médicales* 32:389–98.

Helm, Dale (1996), *From Foxhole to Freedom: The Word War II European Journal of Captain H. Dale Helm of Indiana* (Indianapolis: Guild Press).

Hénocque, Abbé G. (1947), *Les Antres de la Bête ... Fresnes, Buchenwald, Dachau* (Paris: Durassié).

Hérold-Paquis, Jean (1948), *Des illusions ... désillusions!* (Paris: Bourgoin).

Hervé, Pierre (1945), *La Libération trahie* (Paris: Grasset).

Hewitt, Nicholas (2007), 'Non-conformism, "insolence" and reaction: Jean Galtier-Boissière's Le Crapouillot', *Journal of European Studies* 37:277–94.

Hinsley, F. H. (1988), *British Intelligence in the Second World War: Its Influence on Strategy and Operations*, vol. 3, pt II (London: HMSO).

Hoffmann, Peter (1970), *The History of the German Resistance 1933–1945* (London: MacDonald and Jane's).

Hoffmann, Stanley (1968), 'Collaborationism in France during World War II', *The Journal of Modern History* 40:375–95.

Holman, Valerie (2005), 'Carefully concealed connections: The Ministry of Information and British publishing, 1939–1946', *Book History* 8:197–226.

Hostache, René (1958), *Le Conseil National de la Résistance: Les Institutions de la clandestinité* (Paris: Presses Universitaires de France).

Houssin, Monique (2004), *Résistantes et résistants en Seine-Saint-Denis: Un nom, une rue, une histoire* (Paris: Les Editions de l'Atelier).

Institut Hoover (ed) (1958), *La Vie de La France sous l'Occupation* (Stanford: Hoover Institution on War, Revolution and Peace).

Jackson, Julian (2001), *France: The Dark Years 1940–1944* (Oxford: Oxford University Press).

Jacobs, Bruce (n.d.), *On to Paris!* (Washington DC: HSM & NG).

Jacobsen, Hans-Adolf (1969), *Germans Against Hitler, July 20, 1944* (Bonn: Presse- und Informationsamt).

Jasper, Willi (1995), *Hôtel Lutétia* (Paris: Editions Michalon).

Jauffret, Jean-Charles (1994), 'Les combats de la 2e DB au nord de Paris' in Christine Levisse-Touzé (ed), *Paris 1944: Les Enjeux de la Libération* (Paris: Albin Michel) pp. 344–50.

Jay, H. (n.d.), *Erinnerungen an den II.Weltkrieg* (n.p.: no publisher).

Jeffery, Keith (2010), *MI6: The History of the Secret Intelligence Service 1909–1949* (London: Bloomsbury).

Kaplan, Alice (2000), *The Collaborator: The Trial and Execution of Robert Brasillach* (London: University of Chicago Press).

Kaspi, André (1994), 'Les Etats-Unis et la libération de Paris' in Christine Levisse-Touzé (ed), *Paris 1944: Les Enjeux de la Libération* (Paris: Albin Michel), pp. 41–8.

Kaufmann, Dorothy (2004), *Edith Thomas: A Passion for Resistance* (London: Cornell University Press).

Kent, Victoria (1947), *Quatre ans à Paris* (Paris: Le Livre du Jour).

Kershaw, Ian (2011), *The End: Hitler's Germany 1944–45* (London: Allen Lane).

King, David (2012), *Death in the City of Light* (London: Hachette).

Kinnis, Arthur G., & Booker, Stanley (1999), *168 Jump into Hell: A True Story of Betrayed Allied Airmen* (n.p.: Kinnis).

Kitson, Simon (1995), 'The police in the Liberation of Paris' in H. R. Kedward & Nancy Wood (eds), *The Liberation of Paris: Image and Event* (Oxford: Berg), pp. 43–56.

Klarsfeld, Serge (1996), *French Children of the Holocaust: A Memorial* (London: New York University Press).

Kriegel-Valrimont, Maurice (1964), *La Libération: Les Archives du COMAC (mai–août 1944)* (Paris: Editions de Minuit).

Krivopisco, Guy & Porrin, Axel (2004), *Les Fusillés de la Cascade du bois de Boulogne 16 août 1944* (Paris: Mairie de Paris).

Laborie, Pierre (1994), 'Les manifestations du 26 août' in Christine Levisse-Touzé (ed), *Paris 1944: Les Enjeux de la Libération* (Paris: Albin Michel), pp. 377–89.

Lacroix-Riz, Annie (1986), 'Les grandes banques françaises de la collaboration à l'épuration: la non-épuration bancaire 1944–50', *Revue d'histoire de la Deuxième Guerre mondiale* 142:81–101.

Lambauer, Barbara (2001), *Otto Abetz et les Français, ou l'envers de la collaboration* (Paris: Fayard).

Langlois, Suzanne (1997), 'Images that matter: The French Resistance in Film, 1944–1946', *French History* 11:461–90.

Langlois, Suzanne (1998), 'Would the Allies arrive in time? The liberation of Paris on ABC', *Journal of Popular Film & Television* 26:34–41.

Lankford, Nelson D. (ed) (1991), *OSS Against the Reich. The World War II Diaries of Colonel David K. E. Bruce* (Kent, Ohio: Kent State University Press).

Laval, Pierre (1948), *The Unpublished Diary of Pierre Laval* (London: Falcon).

Léautaud, Paul (1946), *Journal littéraire. XVI Juillet 1944–Août 1946* (Paris: Mercure de France).

Lecoeur, Auguste (1963), *Le Partisan* (Paris: Flammarion).

Lefranc, S. (1965), 'A mon ami R ...' in Anonymous (ed), *Pages d'histoire 1939–1945: Les Policiers français dans la Résistance* (Paris: CNPACR), pp. 107–117.

Le Mée, Isabelle-Cécile (2004), 'Des photographes dans la Libération' in Anonymous (ed), *Regards sur la Libération de Paris* (Monum: Paris), pp.7–11.

Levisse-Touzé, Christine (ed) (1994a), *Paris 1944: Les Enjeux de la Libération* (Paris: Albin Michel).

Levisse-Touzé, Christine (1994b), 'Le Comité parisien de libération' in Christine Levisse-Touzé (ed), *Paris 1944: Les Enjeux de la Libération* (Paris: Albin Michel) pp. 201–217.

Levisse-Touzé, Christine (2007), 'Les Espagnols dans la Résistance intérieure et dans l'armée de la libération' in Roger Bourderon (ed), *La Guerre d'Espagne: L'Histoire, les lendemains de la mémoire* (Paris: Tallandier), pp. 161–75.

Lévy, Jean (1992), *Le dossier Georges Albertini: Intelligence avec l'ennemi* (Paris: L'Harmattan).

Lewis, S. J. (1991), *Jedburgh Team Operations in Support of the 12th Army Group, August 1944* (Fort Leavenworth, Kansas: Combat Studies Institute).

Liebling, A. J. (1944) 'Letter from Paris', *The New Yorker* 9 September 1944.

Lindeperg, Syvlie (1993), 'La Résistance rejouée: Usages gaullistes du cinéma', *Politix* 24:134–52.

Litoff, Judy Barrett (ed) (2006), *An American Heroine in the French Resistance: The Diary and Memoir of Virginia d'Albert-Lake* (New York: Fordham University Press).

Longden, Sean (2009), *T-Force: The Forgotten Heroes of 1945* (London: Constable).

Lorain, Pierre (1983), *Clandestine Operations* (New York: Macmillan).

Lottmann, Herbert (1992), *The Fall of Paris: June 1940* (London: Sinclair-Stevenson).

Lowe, Keith (2012), *Savage Continent: Europe in the Aftermath of World War II* (London: Viking).

Luneau, Aurélie (2005), *Radio Londres (1940–1944): Les voix de la liberté* (Paris: Perrin).

Lyon, Harold C. (1948), *Operations of 'T' Force, 12th Army Group, in the Liberation and Intelligence Exploitation of Paris, France, 25 August–6 September 1944* (Fort Beuning, Georgia: Academic Department, The Infantry School).

MacVane, John (1979), *On the Air in World War II* (New York: Morrow).

Mahuzier, Albert (1961), *Camera sous la botte* (Paris: Le Livre Contemporain).

Marc, N. (pseudonym of Nicolas Marcoux, a.k.a. Spoulber) (1945), 'L'Impérialisme français en quête de grandeur', *Quatrième Internationale* 20–21:5–13.

Martens, Stefan & Nagel, Friedrich-Rudolf (2006), 'Walter Dreizner: Ein deutscher Soldat erlebt die Befreiung von Paris im August 1944', *Militärgeschichtliche Zeitschrift* 65:505–44.

Massiet, Raymond (1945), *La Préparation de l'insurrection et la bataille de Paris* (Paris: Payot).

Massu, Suzanne (1969), *Quand j'étais Rochambelle. De New York à Berchtesgaden* (Paris: Grasset).

Matot, Bernard (2010), *La Guerre des cancres: Un lycée au coeur de la Résistance et de la collaboration* (Paris: Perrin).

Maudru, Pierre (1944), *Les Six glorieuses de Paris* (Paris: Société Parisienne d'Edition).

Méadel, Cécile (2000), 'Pauses musicales ou les éclatants silences de Radio-Paris' in Myriam Chimènes (ed), *La Vie musicale sous Vichy* (Brussels: Editions Complexe), pp. 235–52.

Merlat, Odette (1947), 'La Commission d'histoire de l'occupation et de la Libération de la France', *Revue Historique* 1:70–8.

Mesnil-Amar, Jacqueline (2009), *Ceux qui ne dormaient pas. Journal, 1944–1946* (Paris: Stock).

Mesquida, Evelyn (2011), *La Nueve 24 août 1944: Ces républicains espagnols qui ont libéré Paris* (Paris: Le Cherche Midi).

Michel, Henri (1980), *La Libération de Paris* (Brussels: Editions Complexe).

Middlebrook, Martin and Everitt, Chriss (1985), *The Bomber Command War Diaries: An Operational Reference Book, 1939–1945* (Harmondsworth: Viking).

Minguet, Simonne (1997), *Mes années Caudron: Une usine autogérée à la Libération* (Paris: Syllepse).

Mitcham, Jr., Samuel W. (2007), *Retreat to the Reich: The German Defeat in France, 1944* (Mechanicsburg, Pennsylvania: Stackpole).

Model, Hansgeorg & Bradley, Dermot (1991), *Generalfeldmarschall Walter Model (1891–1945). Dokumentation eines Soldatenlebens* (Osnabrück: Biblio Verlag).

Molden, Fritz (1979), *Exploding Star: A Young Austrian Against Hitler* (New York: William Morrow).

Moore, William Mortimer (2011), *Free France's Lion: The Life of Philippe Leclerc, de Gaulle's Greatest General* (Newbury: Casemate).

Monniot, S. (1965), 'La Préfecture de Police dans la résistance et libération de Paris' in Anonymous (ed), *Pages d'Histoire 1939–1945: Les Policiers français dans la Résistance* (Paris: CNPACR), pp. 79–101.

Monod, Robert (1947), *Les Heures décisives de la libération de Paris* (9–26 août 1944) (Paris: Gilbert).

Muggeridge, Malcolm (1973), *Chronicles of Wasted Time: The Infernal Grove*, vol. 2 (London: Collins).

Müller, K. J. (1994), 'Le développement des opérations du groupe d'armées B fin juillet–fin août 1944' in Christine Levisse-Touzé (ed), *Paris 1944: Les Enjeux de la Libération* (Paris: Albin Michel), pp. 102–25.

Nash, Steven A. (1998), 'Introduction: Picasso, War, and Art' in Steven A. Nash & Robert Rosenblum (eds), *Picasso and the War Years 1937–1945* (London: Thames & Hudson), pp. 13–37.

Navarre, Henri (1978), *Le Service de renseignements 1871–1944* (Paris: Plon).

Naville, René (1950a), 'Il y a six ans: Paris était libéré', *Journal de Genève* 22 August 1950.

Naville, René (1950c), 'La discussion d'un "modus vivendi" entre von Choltitz et la Résistance', *Journal de Genève* 24 August 1950.

Naville, René (1950d), 'La famine menace la capitale', *Journal de Genève* 25 August 1950.

Naville, René (1950e), 'La situation s'aggrave', *Journal de Genève* 26 August 1950.

Naville, René (1950f), 'La journée des barricades', *Journal de Genève* 29 August 1950.

Neiberg, Michael (2012), *The Blood of Free Men: The Liberation of Paris, 1944* (New York: Basic Books).

Neitzel, Sönke (2007), *Tapping Hitler's Generals: Transcripts of Secret Conversations, 1942–45* (Barnsley: Frontline).

Newman, Victoria Beck (1999), '"The Triumph of Pan": Picasso and the Liberation', *Zeitschrift für Kunstgeschichte* 62:106–22.

Noguères, Henri & Degliame-Fouché, Marcel (1981), *Histoire de la Résistance en France. Juin 1944–mai 1945*, vol. 5 (Paris: Laffont).

Nordling, Raoul (2002), *Sauver Paris: Mémoires du consul de Suède (1905–1944)* (Brussels: Editions Complexe).

Novick, P. (1968), *The Resistance Versus Vichy: The Purge of Collaborators in Liberated France* (London: Chatto & Windus).

Ouzoulias, Albert (1972), *Les Bataillons de la jeunesse* (Paris: Editions Sociales).

Paillat, Claude (1991), *Dossiers secrets de la France contemporaine. Le monde sans la France: 1944–1945*, vol. 8 (Paris: Laffont).

Paillat, Claude & Boulnois, Francis (1989), *Dossiers secrets de la France contemporaine. La France dans la guerre américaine, 8 nov. 1942–6 juin 1944*, vol. 7 (Paris: Laffont).

Pasteur Vallery-Radot, Louis (1966), *Mémoires d'un non-conformiste 1886–1966* (Paris: Grasset).

Patin, Pierre (1994), *Rails et pavés. Paris, août 44: récit d'événements vécus* (Paris: La Pensée universelle).

Pauwels, Louis (2004), *Un jour je me souviendrai de tout* (Paris: Editions du Rocher).

Péan, Pierre (1994), *Une jeunesse française: François Mitterrand 1934–1947* (Paris: Fayard).

Penrose, Roland (1962), *Picasso: His Life and Work* (New York: Schocken).

Penrose, Antony (ed) (2005), *Lee Miller's War* (London: Thames & Hudson).

Perrin, Nigel (2008), *Spirit of Resistance: The Life of SOE Agent Harry Peulevé DSO MC* (Barnsley: Pen & Sword).

Persico, Joseph (1979), *Piercing the Reich* (London: Michael Joseph).

Petersen, Neal H. (ed) (1996), *From Hitler's Doorstep: The Wartime Intelligence Reports of Allen Dulles, 1942–1945* (University Park, Pennsylvania: Pennsylvania University Press).

Pierquin, Bernard (1983), *Journal d'un étudiant parisien sous l'occupation (1939–1945)* (n.p.: no publisher).

Piketty, Guillaume (ed) (2009), *Francais en Résistance: Carnets de guerre, correspondances, journaux personnels* (Paris: Robert Laffont).

Piketty, Guillaume (2011), *Résister: Les archives intimes des combattants de l'ombre* (Paris: Textuel).

Pisani, Edgard (1974), *Le Général indivis* (Paris: Albin Michel).

Pogue, Forrest C. (1954), *The Supreme Command* (Washington: Office of the Chief of Military History, Department of the Army).

Pryce-Jones, David (1981), *Paris in the Third Reich: A History of the German Occupation, 1940–1944* (London: HarperCollins).

Pudney, John (1944a), 'Picasso – a glimpse in sunlight', *The New Statesman and Nation* 16 September 1944, pp. 182–3.

Pudney, John (1944b), 'A Paris diary', *The New Statesman and Nation* 23 September 1944, p. 197.

Pyle, Ernie (1944), *Brave Men* (New York: Grosset & Dunlap).

Quellien, Jean (2005), 'La répression nazie en Basse-Normandie après le débarquement' in *La Répression en France à l'été 1944: Actes du Colloque organisé par la Fondation de la Résistance et la Ville de Saint-Amand-Montrond à Saint-Amand-Montrond, le mercedri 8 juin 2005* (available at www.fondationresistance.org/documents/ee/Doc00004-006.pdf [accessed June 2012]).

Ragueneau, Philippe & Florentin, Eddy (eds) (1994), *Paris libéré: Ils étaient là!* (Paris: France-Empire).

Rainat, Max (2004), *Comme une grande fête* (Paris: Editions Tirésias).

Rajsfus, Maurice (1996), *Drancy: Un camp de concentration très ordinaire* (Paris: Le Cherche Midi).

Rajsfus, Maurice (2004), *La Libération inconnue: A chacun sa résistance* (Paris: Le Cherche Midi).

Ratcliffe, Sophie (ed) (2011), *P. G. Wodehouse: A Life in Letters* (London: Hutchinson).

Rayssac, Michel (2008), 'Août 1944: le train d'Aulnay-sous-Bois', *Historail* 4:30–3.

Rebatet, Lucien (1976), *Les Mémoires d'un fasciste. II 1941–1947* (Paris: Pauvert).

Rémy, Jean-Michel (1994), 'Les braves gens, les gens braves', *Icare* 148:134–6.

Renoult, Bruno & West, James (2008), *1944 Guerre en Ile de France. Défense du Grand Paris*, vol 3 (n.p.: no publisher).

Renoult, Bruno & West, James (2009), *1944 Guerre en Ile de France. Combats pour Paris*, vol. 4 (n.p.: no publisher).

Renoult, Bruno & West, James (2010), *1944 Guerre en Ile de France. La Chute du Grand Paris*, vol. 5 (n.p.: no publisher).

Rice, Howard C. (1945), 'Post-Liberation publishing in France: A survey of recent French books', *The French Review* 18:327–33.

Riffaud, Madeleine (1994), *On l'appelait Rainer* (Paris: Julliard).

Rist, Charles (1983), *Une Saison gâtée: Journal de la Guerre et de l'Occupation* (Paris: Fayard).

Ritgen, Helmut (1995), *The Western Front 1944: Memoirs of a Panzer Lehr Officer* (Winnipeg: J. J. Fedorowicz).

Rocheteau, Jean (2004), 'Paris Libéré! 19–27 août 1944', *Batailles* Hors-Série 2.

Rol-Tanguy, Colonel & Bourderon, Roger (1994), *Libération de Paris. Les Cent documents* (Paris: Pluriel).

Roskothen, Ernst (1977), *Gross-Paris: Place de la Concorde 1941–1944* (Bad Dürrheim: no publisher).

Rougeyron, André (1996), *Agents for Escape: Inside the French Resistance 1939–1945* (London: Louisiana State University Press).

Roulet, Christiane (2004), 'Commemoration 60ème anniversaire 1944 Villeneuve-St-Georges' *CGT IHS Cheminots Les Cahiers de L'Institut* 24:22–3.

Roussel, Eric (2002), *De Gaulle I: 1890–1945* (Paris: Perrin).

Roy, Claude (1944), *Les Yeux ouverts dans Paris insurgé* (Paris: Julliard).

Rudolph, Luc (ed) (2010), *Au coeur de la Préfecture de Police: de la Résistance à la Libération – 2ème partie, La préfecture de police: Une résistance oubliée 1940–1944* (Paris: Préfecture de Paris).

Scheck, Raffael (2010), 'French colonial soldiers in German prisoner-of-war camps (1940–1945), *French History* 24:420–46.

Schramm, Percy Ernst (1982), *Kriegstagebuch des Oberkommandos der Wehrmacht (Wehrmachtführungsstab) Band IV: 1 Januar 1944–22 Mai 1945* (Munich: Bernard & Graefe).

Schrijvers, Peter (2009), *Liberators: The Allies and Belgian Society 1944–1945* (Cambridge: Cambridge University Press).

Seaman, Mark (1997), *Bravest of the Brave: The True Story of Wing Commander 'Tommy' Yeo-Thomas – SOE Secret Agent – Codename 'The White Rabbit'* (London: O'Mara).

Sebald, W. G. (2001), *Austerlitz* (London: Hamish Hamilton).

Seth, Ronald (1963), *Petiot: Victim of Chance* (London: Hutchinson).

Shulman, Milton (1986), *Defeat in the West* (London: Secker & Warburg).

Silverstone, Lou & Drucker, Mort (1967), 'Is Paris Boring?', *Mad* 113.

Simmonet, Alain (2010), 'Temps de guerre à Domont', *Châteaubriant* 235:12.

Sonneville, Pierre (1968), *Les Combattants de la liberté: Ils n'étaient pas dix mille* (Paris: La Table ronde).

Speer, Albert (1970), *Inside the Third Reich: Memoirs* (London: Weidenfeld & Nicolson).

Speidel, Hans (1971), *Invasion 1944: Rommel and the Normandy Campaign* (Westport: Greenwood Press).

Sproat, Iain (1981), *Wodehouse at War* (London: Milner).

Sproat, Iain (1999), 'In all innocence', *Times Literary Supplement* 29 October 1999.

Steinhardt, Frederick P. (2008), *Panzer Lehr Division 1944–45* (Solihull: Helion).

Stéphane, Roger (2004), *Fin d'une jeunesse* (Paris: La Table ronde).

Studer, Sébastien (2003), *L'Engagement résistant d'Alexandre Parodi (1940–1944)* Unpublished Ph.D. thesis. Ecole des Chartes, Paris.

Suttill, Francis J. & Foot, M. R. D. (2011), 'SOE's "Prosper" disaster of 1943', *Intelligence and National Security* 26:99–105.

Sylvan, William C., Smith, Francis G. & Greenwood, John T. (ed) (2008), *Normandy to Victory: The War Diary of General Courtney H. Hodges and the First US Army* (Lexington, Kentucky: University Press of Kentucky).

Taittinger, Pierre (1948), . . . *Et Paris ne fut pas détruit* (Paris: L'Elan).

Thérive, André (1948), *L'Envers du décor* (Paris: La Clé d'or).

Thomas, Edith (1995), *Pages de Journal 1939–1944* (Paris: Viviane Hamy).

Thomas, Martin (2003), 'The colonial policies of the Mouvement Républicain Populaire 1944–1945: From reform to reaction', *English Historical Review* 118: 380–411.

Thornton, Willis (1963), *The Liberation of Paris* (London: Hart-Davis).

Tillon, Charles (1972), *Les FTP: La Guérilla en France* (Geneva: Editions de Crémille).

Tillon, Charles (1977), *On chantait rouge* (Paris: Laffont).

Toesca, Maurice (1975), *Cinq ans de patience (1939–1945)* (Paris: Emile-Paul).

Tombs, Robert (1995), 'From revolution to resistance: August 1944 in historical context' in La Résistance et les Français: Villes, centres et logiques de décision, *Supplément au Bulletin de l'IHTP* 61:47–58.

Touche, Firmin (1946), *Mon fils Jean-Claude* (Paris: Bloud & Gay).

Tournoux, Raymond (1982), *Le Royaume d'Otto. France 1939–1945: Ceux qui ont choisi l'Allemagne* (Paris: Flammarion).

Tuffrau, Paul (2002), *De la 'drôle de guerre' à la Libération de Paris: Lettres et Carnets* (Paris: Imago).

Umbreit, Hans (1994), 'La libération de Paris et la grande stratégie du IIIe Reich' in Christine Levisse-Touzé (ed), *Paris 1944: Les Enjeux de la Libération* (Paris: Albin Michel), pp. 326–43.

Valland, Rose (1997), *Le Front de l'art: Défense des collections françaises, 1939–1945* (Paris: Réunion des Musées Nationaux).

Vaughan, Hal (2004), *Doctor to the Resistance: The Heroic True Story of an American Surgeon and his Family in Occupied Paris* (Dulles, Virginia: Brassey's).

Vergez-Chaignon, Bénédicte (2010), *Histoire de l'épuration* (Paris: Larousse).

Verity, Hugh (2000), *We Landed by Moonlight: The Secret RAF Landings in France 1940–1944* (Manchester: Crécy).

Vilain, Camille (1945), *Quand le canon tonnait aux Gobelins. Journal d'un Parisien pendant la Semaine Héroique (Août 1944)* (Paris: Meyer-Ruelle).

Villate, R. (1958), 'La bataille de Paris vue du P.C. Ile-de-France', *Revue d'histoire de la Deuxième Guerre mondiale* 30:58–78.

Villon, Pierre (1984), *Résistant de la première heure* (Paris: Editions Sociales).

Vinen, Richard (2006), *The Unfree French: Life under the Occupation* (London: Allen Lane).

Virgili, Fabrice (2000), *La France 'virile': Des femmes tondues à la Libération* (Paris: Payot).

von Arnim, Dankwart Graf (1995), *Als Brandenburg noch Mark hiess* (Munich: Goldmann).

von Choltitz, General (1949), 'Pourquoi, en 1944, je n'ai pas détruit Paris', *Le Figaro* 6–17 October 1949.

von Choltitz, General (1969), *De Sébastopol à Paris (Un soldat parmi des soldats)* (Paris: J'ai lu).

von Gaertringen, Frierich Frieherr Hiller, (1995), 'Sie sollten jetzt schweigen, Herr Präsident' – Oberstleutnant d. R. Cäsar von Hofacker' in von zur

Mühlen, Bengt & Bauer, Frank (eds), *Der 20 Juli 1944 in Paris: Verlauf – Hauptbeteiligte – Augenzeugen* (Berlin-Kleinmachnow: Chronos), pp. 41–60.

von Senger und Etterlin, F. M. (1969), German Tanks of World War II: The Complete Illustrated History of German Armoured Fighting Vehicles 1926–1945 (London: Arms and Armour).

von zur Mühlen, Bengt & Bauer, Frank (eds) (1995), *Der 20 Juli 1944 in Paris: Verlauf – Hauptbeteiligte – Augenzeugen* (Berlin-Kleinmachnow: Chronos).

Warlimont, Walter (1964), *Inside Hitler's Headquarters 1939–1945* (London: Wedenfeld & Nicolson).

Watts, Don (2009), 'Eavesdropping on the *Wehrmacht*: What Germany's generals *really* thought about Hitler and his war', *Intelligence and National Security* 24:876–93.

Werth, Léon (2007) *Déposition. Journal de guerre 1940–1944* (Paris: Points).

Whitney, Peter D. (1944), 'Picasso is safe', *San Francisco Chronicle* 3 September 1944, p. 3.

Wieviorka, Olivier (1994), 'La Résistance intérieure et la libération de Paris' in Christine Levisse-Touzé (ed), *Paris 1944: Les Enjeux de la Libération* (Paris: Albin Michel) pp. 137–51.

Wieviorka, Olivier (2007), *Histoire du débarquement en Normandie* (Paris: Seuil).

Winock, Michel (1994), 'Fallait-il fusiller Brasillach?', *L'Histoire* 179, July–August 1994, pp. 62–8.

Wodehouse, P. G. (1953), *Performing Flea: A Self-Portrait in Letters* (London: Herbert Jenkins).

Zaloga, Steven J. (2008), *Liberation of Paris 1944: Patton's Race for the Seine* (Botley: Osprey).

Zaloga, Steven J. (2009), *Operation Dragoon 1944: France's Other D-Day* (Botley: Osprey).

Zervos, Christian (1963), *Pablo Picasso, Oeuvres de 1944 à 1946*, vol. 14 (Paris: Editions Cahiers d'Art).

Zvenigorodsky, Odile (1994), 'Paris et son métro' in Philippe Buton & Jean-Marc Guillon (eds), *Les Pouvoirs en France à la Libération* (Paris: Belin), pp. 269–80.

Acknowledgements

A couple of clarifications: first, I am not related to Professor Richard Cobb, the historian of France, although in a bizarre coincidence my father was called Richard and Professor Cobb had a son called Matthew. Second, as those of you who search for me on the Internet will discover, writing history is not my day job. Since I published *The Resistance: The French Fight Against the Nazis* in 2009, I have been touched by the generosity of the community of French historians in the UK, who welcomed this outsider and have been both kind and supportive. My thanks go to all of them. In particular, Julian Jackson and Rod Kedward have turned out to be as insightful and kind hearted as their writings suggest, and their encouragement helped give me the confidence to write this book. My Manchester colleague Jean-Marc Dreyfus focused my mind on the grim aspects of the pillaging of the Parisian Jews by the Germans, while Simon Kitson helped me try and unravel the story of what happened to the tricolour after June 1940. I hope that my discussions with the historian of art Victoria Beck Newman will lead to a joint project on the work of Pablo Picasso during this period.

My publisher, Mike Jones, and my agent, Peter Tallack, helped me set up this story and gave me the opportunity to turn a vague idea into something much more precise and detailed. Katherine Stanton, my copy-editor, showed me how to cut down some particularly baggy material and make it much more nimble. She also scrutinised the manuscript and picked up so many of my mistakes. I am also especially grateful to my readers, who have spent a vast amount of time going through the manuscript, encouraging me or suggesting useful rewrites: Dr Ludivine Broch of Birkbeck College whose knowledge of the railways in the occupation is unparalleled, Jerry Coyne whose help I have bought by guest-blogging at whyevolutionistrue.com, Martin Empson who helped me emphasise class issues, Professor John Merriman of Yale University who encouraged me to explore the social geography of Paris, and Christina Purcell who helped me make things clearer. I am particularly indebted to my friend Barbara Mellor, who picked nits, bravely volunteered to help check the proofs, came up with some great translations and has been an enthusiastic partner in working on the Lainville family. A special mention goes to David Drake, who is writing a book on Paris during World War II (*Paris at War: 1939–1944*), that will provide the back-story to much of what I have written about here. David was a tremendous help, exchanging sources, sharing frustrations about the exact nature of various aspects of the Vichy regime and helping me declutter my prose. He even sent me a CD, *Jazz sous l'Occupation*, which makes an ideal audio accompaniment to reading and writing on this period. The book would be much the poorer without his help. I would also like to acknowledge the kindness of Hélène Steinberg and the late Bill Ford, who welcomed me to Paris in 1984 and first showed me the traces of the liberation on the walls of their city. Bill would have loved arguing with me about this book.

Jean-Louis Crémieux-Brilhac answered my questions generously and patiently, and expressed his immense personal frustration at being stuck in London during the liberation of Paris. Comrade Ben Lewis translated many of the German texts I used, thereby enabling me to get an essential insight into what was happening in Paris. My colleague Reinmar Hager also helped by responding rapidly to e-mails when I was uncertain about how exactly to translate a particular passage from German. Sébastien Studer generously sent me a pdf of his excellent unpublished thesis on Alexandre Parodi. I am especially thankful to Gilles Primout, an amateur historian who has created an excellent website on the liberation of Paris, full of eye-witness accounts and useful detail. It is highly recommended to anyone who can read French: liberation-de-paris.gilles-primout.fr/ [accessed July 2012].

Librarians around the world have helped in all sorts of ways, and my thanks go to the staff at the John Rylands University Library of Manchester, the UK National Archives, the US National Archives and Records Administration, the Courtauld Institute of Art, the Liddell Hart Centre for Military Archives at King's College London, and the Musée du Général Leclerc de Hauteclocque et de la Libération de Paris –

Musée Jean Moulin. The following people all generously sent me information and documents: Cathleen Pearl and Amelia Meyer of the National Guard Memorial Museum; Francine Bouré of the Musée des Beaux-Arts, Rheims; Lisa Saltzman of Bryn Mawr College; Barbara Seddik of the Office de Tourisme de la Ferté; and Mary Laura Kludy of the Virginian Military Institute Archives. Above all, I am grateful to the bemused member of staff at the Archives Nationales in Paris who, when I asked to see a particular document, replied in an amused voice, *'Mais Monsieur, pourquoi? Tous les documents sont sur notre site Internet!'*

While I was writing this book, Tina was writing up her Ph.D., so we were a two-book household, not something I recommend. Despite this, Lauren and Evie seem to have survived and even flourished. My gratitude goes to all three of them – without their forbearance, support and love, none of this would have been possible.

Notes

INTRODUCTION

1 Lottmann (1992), p. 319.

2 It was over twenty years after the end of the occupation before a satisfactory attempt was made to come up with a typology of the forces of collaboration (Hoffmann, 1968). Hoffmann distinguished between collaboration with Germany for reasons of state (*'collaboration d'état'*), and collaborationism with the Nazis, which could be based on ideology or mere realpolitik. Over the four years of the occupation, this nauseating kaleidoscope of reaction shifted and changed its pattern as individuals moved between the various types and sub-types delineated by Hoffmann – it was, as he admits, 'infernally complicated'. It is even more complicated to discern exactly how decisions were taken, and who – Vichy or the Germans – had effective control of which area of policy or administration in which area of the country. While it is undoubtedly the case that the Germans were in ultimate control, they were not interested in deciding everything in occupied France – that was precisely why they used Pétain, Laval and the rest of their gang.

3 The Gaullist forces went through several different name changes during the war; I have preferred to use their first, widely known name, 'the Free French', even though strictly speaking this is an anachronism for the period covered here.

4 The shooting of German soldiers in the Paris region was largely the work of the Communist Party, which had something to prove: for the first year of the occupation it did not call for resistance because the Soviet Union – the source of its political inspiration and outlook – was then in an alliance with Germany. Only after Hitler attacked the USSR in June 1941 did the communists change their line and become an important component of the Paris Resistance. Their influence grew when they began shooting German soldiers, a campaign that attracted the admiration of some Parisians, but which had catastrophic consequences. The Germans responded by taking hundreds of French people hostage – many of them communists – and executing them in retaliation for the few dozen Germans who were shot by the communist fighters. The Germans eventually wiped out most of the armed groups in Paris and the Communist Party changed its tactics – no German soldiers were killed in the Paris region during the first six months of 1944. Cobb (2009a).

5 For the collapse of the SOE circuit ('PROSPER') see Cobb (2009a), pp. 195–7 and 363–5, and Suttill & Foot (2011). There was a US-backed sabotage mission early in 1944, when the US Office of Strategic Services (OSS – the forerunner of the CIA) sent a group called VARLIN into Paris 'to work with the CGT in directing sabotage and psychological warfare among French laborers being deported to Germany' (OSS War Diary 3:208). VARLIN was part of the Labor Desk project that involved sending German communists into Nazi Germany (Persico, 1979). VARLIN sabotaged the SKF ball-bearing factory at Ivry, a massive art deco tomb-like building, setting fire to 6000 litres of petrol, destroying vital electrical equipment and damaging key parts of the production line (Granet 1961, p. 264). But that was more or less the end of their activity – they had no radio operator and spent much of the period up until mid-August without contact or instructions. Shortly before the Paris insurrection broke out, members of SOE and the Resistance who could have played a vital role in the fighting were deported to Buchenwald concentration camp from the Gare de l'Est. The deportees included Stéphane Hessel, 'Tommy' Yeo-Thomas, Maurice Southgate, Harry Peulevé, Noor Inayat Khan and Violette Szabo (Seaman, 1997). Perrin (2008) includes a list of many of the prisoners, drawn up by Yeo-Thomas (pp. 138–9). Stéphane Hessel's account of this part of his wartime experience states that the train left the Gare du Nord (AN 72AJ/231/II/8, p. 12).

6 One set of voices is largely absent – that of those ultra-conservative supporters of Pétain, the 'ordinary collaborators'. The views of those Parisians, who must have numbered tens of thousands, have left little trace in the historical record. If they wrote diaries – and scores of them must have done so – their writings have not surfaced in the archives, nor have they been published. Families may well be keeping them hidden, out of embarrassment or shame. This is frustrating in that the irrational fears of the passive Pétain supporters, who were so important in providing the occupation with some kind of social base, were part of the political tapestry of Paris during the liberation.

7 Each year around 15 August, the Parisian swifts leave on their long southward migration. Their evocative cries would have been absent from most of the period described here.

PRELUDE

1 Pierquin (1983), pp. 119–120.
2 Florentin (1997), pp. 293–6; Middlebrook & Everitt (1985), p. 496.
3 Guéhenno (2002), p. 405.
4 Auroy (2008), pp. 296–7.
5 Grunberg's remarkable diary was recently discovered (Grunberg, 2001). Grunberg's apartment is next to the L'Harmattan bookshop, well known to Parisian book-buyers.
6 All distances and orientations are approximate, and are given as the crow flies. Distances to and from Paris are given to the edge of the city.

7 Grunberg (2001), p. 299.
8 Fabre-Luce (1947), p. 607.
9 AN 72AJ/62/IV/1, p. 75
10 Florentin (1997), p. 296.
11 Pétain's speech at the Hôtel de Ville can be seen in Claude Chabrol's documentary *The Eye of Vichy* (1993). The approximate figure of 10,000 is obtained by a sampling head-count of a photograph of the crowd (see Plate 1). If those on the rue de Rivoli and the avenue Victoria, also visible on the photograph, are added, at most around 15,000 people appear to have attended. This corresponds with the estimate made at the time by Maurice Toesca, the principal private secretary of the Prefect of Police. Shortly afterwards, Marcel Déat claimed that a million Parisians had fêted Pétain (see *The Eye of Vichy*).
12 Cointet (2001), p. 269.
13 Grunberg (2001), p. 300.

CHAPTER 1

1 Groult & Groult (1965), pp. 293–4.
2 Cordier (1999), p. 272; Crémieux-Brilhac (2010), p. 275.
3 Mahuzier (1961); see the plate opposite p. 209.
4 Mahuzier (1961), pp. 158–68. The 21-minute documentary was eventually released in 1945 under the title 'Réseau X', and was presented in competition at the first Cannes Film Festival in 1946. It is available in the Gaumont archives under reference EXTMAH 4500ATFDOC00016 (www.gaumontpathearchives.com). Because of the progress of the Allied invasion, the three men could not escape from France; they remained in Paris until it was liberated.
5 The British Foreign Secretary, Anthony Eden, ruled that although de Gaulle should be treated with utmost courtesy, he would not be allowed to hold any public meetings or to gather crowds in the street (Amouroux, 1988, p. 547).
6 The warmth expressed by the traditionally reserved population of Normandy moved de Gaulle's aide, Hettier de Boislambert, who was from the region: 'Our walk in Bayeux took on a triumphal air. Everyone knew the General was there, everyone wanted to acclaim him, to see him, to touch him. As a Normandy man, I was amazed by this enthusiasm, which was more typical of the south of the country.' Amouroux (1988), p. 551, n. 2.
7 Chaban's promotion was announced in a message on 30 June 1944. AN 72AJ/235/III/449.
8 Cobb (2009a).
9 Crémieux-Brilhac (2001), p. 1255.
10 Two months earlier he had written: 'the liberation of the country must be the work of the French people, led by the fighters of the Resistance, grouped together in the FFI. This liberation must be obtained by a country-wide insurrection.' (Granet, 1964, p. 159). See also the undated Projet de manifeste de 'Ceux de la Résistance' in Granet (1964), pp. 271–3. In apparently

authoritative contemporary and modern sources, de Vogüé's name is spelt in various ways – Vogüé, Vogüe and Vogué. I have adopted de Vogüé.

11 Massiet (1945), p. 85. In April 1944, the FFI in the Paris region claimed only 155 of its men were armed (Rol-Tanguy & Bourderon, 1994, p. 76).

12 Lefaucheux was a leader of the right-wing Resistance group, l'Organisation Civile et Militaire (OCM). Political leaders could also be leaders of the umbrella armed group, the FFI.

13 'Rol' was the name of one of Tanguy's International Brigade comrades who was killed in fighting in the Sierra Caballes (Roy, 1944, p. 114).

14 Even though no more than 25 per cent of the Communist Party armed group FTP fighters were card-carrying communists, the organisation still followed the Communist Party lead (Tillon, 1972, p. 241; Granet, 1964, p. 220, n. 5). Full details of FFI composition are given in Massiet (1945), pp. 72–85. See Buton (1993), p. 125, for details of FTP. Bourderon (2006), p. 190, points out that claims about the size of the FTP are 'unverifiable'. The FTP was officially known as the Franc-Tireurs et Partisans Français, but was more widely known by its three-letter initials.

15 All details of FFI structure from Massiet (1945), pp. 24–5.

16 The Socialist Party had secretly decided to oppose the slogan of a 'national insurrection' because it might play into the hands of the communists (AN 72AJ/236/I/5/44).

17 The building is now the headquarters of the Socialist Party. The reports given by the policemen are partially reproduced in Bourget (1984). On 22 September 1944 Charles Gonard ('Morlot') published a description in the Resistance newspaper *Action* (Kriegel-Valrimont, 1964, pp. 239–43); many years later he provided a second account (Noguères & Degliame-Fouché, 1981, pp. 187–90). There are insignificant differences of detail between the two versions (for example, in one version Madame Henriot is completely silent, in the other she screamed). It has been stated that the Resistance men were dressed in Milice uniforms (e.g. Cobb, 2009a, p. 281). This was not the case (Noguères & Degliame-Fouché, 1981, p. 189). *Mea culpa.*

18 Although it has been claimed that COMAC gave citations to the men involved in the operation (Crémieux-Brilhac, 1976, p. 78), this was not officialised after the war as Henriot's assassination was seen as a political act rather than a military one (Amouroux, 1988, p. 420, n. 1). Despite a campaign by the Milice to find those responsible and the promise of a 20 million-franc reward, only one of the sixteen men involved was caught. Betrayed by a friend, petty thief and part-time *résistant* Pierre Desmoulins was lured into a trap and was shot by the police (Bourget, 1984, pp. 133–7).

19 Henriot broadcast each day at 12:40 and again at 19:40. In the period 7 February–3 April, Henriot made eighty broadcasts; together with repeats he appeared ninety-five times in a mere fifty-six days. Crémieux-Brilhac (1976), p. 54. Henriot gained a misplaced reputation for straight-talking. In fact, his speeches were no different from the rest of collaborationist propaganda – as well as pouring bile on the Allies, the Resistance and the Free French, he repeated the usual fetid fascist fantasies; one of his regular targets was 'the

diabolical plot of the plutocrats of the City of London and the Judeo-Bolsheviks of Eastern Europe' (Crémieux-Brilhac, 2001, p. 1066). A report to the Free French in Algiers admitted that 'his broadcasts provoke admiration or anger, but never indifference' (Crémieux-Brilhac, 2001, p. 1066). Jean Guéhenno described Henriot's tone in his diary: 'In Henriot, Vichy, hypocrisy and treason found their voice; a solid, sneering, nasal voice.' (Guéhenno, 2002, p. 421.)

20 Grunberg (2001), p. 318. Henriot's final broadcast, made the night before he was assassinated, was prophetic: 'Am I expected to be impressed by the threats of … machine-gun bullets that have already killed so many of my friends and comrades? If I was going to be affected by this kind of talk, I would have kept quiet long ago. Insult me, pour your self-proclaimed outrage on my head. I will not reply. If there is to be blood between us, it is you that will have spilt it.' (Bourget, 1984, p. 119.) COMAC had floated the project of kidnapping Henriot earlier in the year, with the subsequent support of the CNR. (Debû-Bridel, 1978, pp. 69–73.) Marcel Degliame-Fouché, who was in overall charge of the operation, claimed that he first had the idea of 'neutralising' Henriot, in 1942, on overhearing conversations in a train following one of Henriot's early broadcasts. The first request for help from London was made in January 1944 (Noguères & Degliame-Fouché, 1981, p. 187). In May 1944, Jean-Louis Crémieux-Brilhac heard the head of the British Special Operations Executive (SOE) French Section, Maurice Buckmaster, discussing Henriot with two Free French Intelligence Service members: 'Kidnap him, and I'll sort out the transport to London,' said Buckmaster (Crémieux-Brilhac, 2001, p. 1066).

21 Luneau (2005), p. 278. Laval's lachrymose commentary can be found in Bourget (1984), p. 127, together with the responses of various collaborationists.

22 Rebatet (1976), p. 172.

23 Amouroux (1988), p. 421, presents an analysis of the extensive mail interceptions carried out by Vichy. Of 10,528 letters that were intercepted between 29 June and 4 July 1944 in the Aude département in the south-east Pyrenees, only 287 (2.7 per cent) mentioned Henriot's assassination – the overwhelming majority of these (271) were sympathetic to Henriot. The Aude may not have been typical of France, and, given it was known that Vichy intercepted the post, it might have been unwise to express support for Henriot's assassination.

24 Grunberg (2001), p. 318. Similar views were expressed by a range of people. Jacques Bardoux, a minor collaborationist politician, wrote in his diary that most of the people he talked to were less affected than he had expected, while his newspaper seller merely said, 'That's one less snake!' Bardoux (1958), p. 280. Charles Braibant wrote: 'Philippe Henriot had a striking eloquence and did a great deal of harm. The patriots who killed him have rendered a huge service to the country. He got what he deserved.' Braibant (1945), p. 501. Two policemen were overheard talking in the Métro: 'That's one down – it's the beginning,' said one; his colleague replied, 'It was nicely

done – it must have been one of us who did it.' (Bourget, 1984, pp. 128–9.) The nosy eavesdropper was Max Knipping, head of Vichy's fascist Milice in the northern zone, who zealously took down their police numbers and sent the information to the Prefect of Police, demanding disciplinary action. According to Monniot (1965), p. 83, a policeman named Poulain killed Henriot; see Bourget (1984), pp. 137–9 for an examination of this unlikely claim.

25 Grunberg (2001), p. 318. Speaking on the BBC, Jean-Jacques Mayoux said, 'We refuse to hide our joy at his expiration' (Crémieux-Brilhac, 1976, p. 78). According to Goebbels, 'It is not France that is in mourning, but the whole of Europe, to which Henriot had devoted the whole of his life in his struggle for liberty.' (Giolitto, 2002, p. 319.) Jean Guéhenno acerbically remarked over a month later: 'Every evening, the German propaganda machine resuscitates Henriot . . . Every evening, at 10:15 precisely, he is called from beyond the grave and made to sound off one of his old broadcasts and to remind us of our European duties. He is a servile ghost . . . but if German propaganda is reduced to mobilising ghosts, that's a good thing. However, *Je suis partout* [a collaborationist newspaper] is worried: apparently the discs are wearing out incredibly quickly, and unless there's some technical breakthrough, this "great voice that saves France" will, in a very short time, be silenced forever.' Guéhenno (2002), p. 427.

26 There was a series of squabbles over the organisation of the funeral, between the Germans and French fascists on the one hand and the Paris municipal and police collaborators on the other; these were indicative of the growing stresses within the forces of collaboration. See Bourget (1984), pp. 129–33 for an exhaustive account. Although collaborationists queued up to pay their respects to Henriot at the Hôtel de Ville, not everyone was so enthusiastic. Police psychiatrist Dr Michel Laurent – or Laurent Michel; accounts vary – saw a grief-stricken old lady crying in the queue. Unable to restrain himself, the doctor hissed at her, 'Don't forget he was a well-known traitor!' A few minutes later he was arrested by the Milice, having been denounced by the old lady. For two days Dr Laurent was questioned, beaten, threatened with a gun at his temple, stripped and stabbed with scissors.

27 Including in Lyons, Toulouse, Grenoble and Mâcon. Two weeks earlier, the Milice had murdered the left-wing one-time Minister of Education, Jean Zay (Giolitto, 2002, pp. 331–8).

28 Favreau (1996), pp. 471–9 and Giolitto (2002), pp. 338–52, describe Mandel's final days. For accounts of the post-liberation trials of his murderers and those implicated, see Giolitto (2002), pp. 356–9 and Favreau (1996), pp. 484–93.

29 Favreau (1996), p. 476.

30 Cobb (2009a), pp. 79–87.

31 Calvès (1984), pp. 98–9. Yves Cazaux recorded the assassination of Barthélemy in his diary, simply noting that the dead man had pursued 'the closest collaboration with the Occupant' (Cazaux, 1975, p. 61).

32 Cazaux (1975), p. 64.

33 Martens & Nagel (2006), p. 517.

34 Cazaux (1975), p. 62. Denis (1963), pp. 92–3, claims that the government changed its mind at the last minute and that 14 July was not in fact a holiday. This seems to be based on a misreading of the CPL minutes of 18 July (Denis, 1963, p. 214); the last-minute decision was to make the day a holiday.

35 Auroy (2008), pp. 312–315. The week before, the Comité Parisien de la Libération (CPL) had seriously discussed the possibility of evacuating all women and children from the city, due to the severe food shortages, even though no one could say where the hundreds of thousands of evacuees would go. Although the discussion was inconclusive (broadly speaking the right-wing members were for evacuation, the left-wing members were against), the very fact that the CPL took seriously such a far-fetched proposal indicates the extremity of the situation. See the minutes of the thirtieth meeting of the CPL, 7 July 1944, in Denis (1963), pp. 211–213.

36 The assassination of Barthélemy and the attack on two German soldiers at Thiais appear to have been the result of this instruction. The CPL was following the lead of the national Resistance leadership, which had called for 'A 14 July of struggle'. For the CNR's decision and its call, see Debû-Bridel (1978), pp. 141–2 and pp. 266–8. See also Noguères & Degliame-Fouché (1981), pp. 259–60. The CPL resolution is reproduced in Denis (1963), pp. 167–9. At the end of July 'Colonel Fabien' (Pierre Georges), a 25-year-old veteran of the Spanish Civil War and of the armed struggle against the Germans, wrote a letter to his comrades in the Communist Party's armed wing, the Franc-Tireurs et Partisans (FTP), calling for revenge attacks following the execution of three of their young comrades:

> In the past few days in various places, and notably in Montrouge, the Huns have shot young Frenchmen. In such cases we must go onto the street in large numbers; everyone should be involved in the action. Everyone – from the whole military committee to the local patriotic militia – needs to join in. Each FTP fighter must be motivated by a sacred hatred of the Hun, the members of the Milice, the assassins of Oradour and of a thousand other towns. We must respond to each blow from the enemy. As in 1941–1942, we will fight terror with terror. Two eyes for an eye … It is easy to grab two, three, four or five Huns, take them to the place where they shot our people and then kill them like dogs. Any members of the military committees who do not organise such a response to any assassinations of our people will be considered to be cowards. (Ouzoulias, 1972, pp. 419–420.)

The three dead men were Marcel Laurent, Robert Degert and Claude Guy. There is a plaque to their memory at 107 rue Maurice Arnoux, Montrouge, at the edge of what is now a sports ground.

37 Debû-Bridel (1978), pp. 269–71.

38 Cazaux (1975), p. 65; Denis (1963), p. 214; Ouzoulias (1972), pp. 398–400.

39 At the CPL meeting of 18 July, the Front National representative stated that 100,000 people were involved (Denis, 1963, p. 214). The main historian of the liberation of Paris, Adrien Dansette, who was generally not sympathetic

to communist claims, puts the figure at 100–150,000 (Dansette, 1946, p. 154). These figures are impossible to verify; we can only conclude that there were many demonstrations, each with dozens or hundreds of participants. On the other hand, not everyone saw the demonstrations; Edith Thomas was on the place du Panthéon and was disappointed to find herself alone, apart from three urchins who sold her some tricolour bouquets of wilting flowers (Thomas, 1995, p. 202).

40 Grunberg (2001), p. 323. This is in fact his entry for 15 July. On 14 July (presumably earlier in the day) he wrote: 'Once more, a sad 14 July this year. No, we won't be dancing in the streets of Paris this 14 July.'

41 At the CPL meeting of 18 July, the President, communist trade unionist André Tollet, reported that 'in general, the police behaved well'. Denis (1963), p. 214.

42 Ouzoulias (1972), p. 398; Debû-Bridel (1978), p. 143.

43 See Kitson (1995).

44 Ouzoulias (1972), p. 399. The street in the 10th arrondissement where Yves Toudic was killed now bears his name.

45 The varying figures for the number of arrested railway workers are discussed in Chevandier (2002), p. 208, n. 113. An undated (end-July 1944?) report from the Union des Syndicats ouvriers de la région parisienne gives the figure of seven arrests (Cogniot et al. 1974, p. 73), while a letter from the Laval government to the Germans, written on 13 August 1944, requested the liberation of fifty-two railway workers in the Paris region (Bachelier, 1996, section 7-3-8).

46 Michel Germa, who was a teenager at the time, recalled: 'When the Germans opened fire, Michel Dermont threw me to the ground and we escaped by running through the nearby gardens, before eventually finding our comrades at the normal meeting place.' See www.lalande2.com/articles.php?lng=fr&pg=571#twenty-five [accessed January 2011].

47 The following material is based on the account of local union and resistance activity written in an undated (end-July 1944?) report from the Union des Syndicats ouvriers de la région parisienne (Cogniot et al., 1974).

48 Letter from the Laval government to the Germans (13 August 1944) (Bachelier, 1996, section 7-3-8).

49 Bourget (1984) devotes a whole chapter to the incident and possible explanations (pp. 145–72). He includes a list of the twenty-eight victims, most of them petty criminals, several of whom were still on remand awaiting trial.

50 Picasso's amazing wartime production ranged from classic images of Paris, through portraits of his lovers, to the famous *Bull's Head* composed of a bicycle saddle and handlebars (Nash, 1998).

51 Barr (1946), p. 223.

52 Warlimont (1964), p. 440. In August 1945 Warlimont recalled the events as follows: 'About 1250, there suddenly occurred a terrific explosion which seemed to cover the whole room in dust, smoke and fire, and throw everything in all directions. When I got up, after a short period of unconsciousness, I saw that Hitler was being led backwards through the door, supported by

several attendants. He did not seem to have been seriously hurt.' ETHINT 5, p. 2.

53 The plotters were not against the extermination of the Jews, they did not want to change the fascist policies that had governed their country for the last eleven years; they wanted to kill Hitler, they wanted to stop the war in the West and they wanted Germany to join forces with the Allies and turn all its strength against the USSR. As early as May 1944, the conspiracy had outlined these views to the USA, although the Allies played no part in the plot (Hoffmann, 1970, pp. 746–9). The Parisian plotters had also talked to the ALLIANCE British intelligence circuit in the French capital, asking to be put in contact with the Free French (Fourcade, 1973, pp. 326–7).

54 For a dramatic first-hand account of events in Berlin, see the 15 August 1945 interview with Major-General Otto Remer, who was involved in putting down the putsch. ETHINT 63.

55 Bargatzky (1969), p. 157. All of the key figures in the German Army command structures in France were directly or indirectly involved: General Carl-Heinrich von Stülpnagel, the military commander of occupied France; Lieutenant-General Wilhelm von Boineburg, military commander of Paris; and the commander of Army Group B in France, Field Marshal Erwin Rommel, who was severely wounded on 17 July and played no part in events. On 15 July, Rommel sent Hitler a message that described the situation on the Western Front in the most graphic terms and concluded: 'The troops are fighting heroically everywhere, but the unequal contest is drawing to an end. I must beg you to draw the conclusions without delay.' (Speidel, 1971, p. 116.) In the original draft, Rommel spoke of 'political conclusions'. Rommel never fully recovered from his wounds, and finally committed suicide in October 1944.

56 Von Boineburg, guided by a recently updated map of the location of SS and SD (Nazi Intelligence Service) forces, ordered raids on the SS and SD headquarters on avenue Foch and on the various SS barracks around Paris. The operation did not begin until later in the evening in order to ensure that as many of the SS troops as possible were back in their barracks. An execution range was prepared at the Ecole Militaire.

57 Bargatzky (1969), p. 157.

58 Bood (1974), p. 306.

59 Bourget (1984), p. 195. Stragglers who were out on the streets or in bars were attracted by alarm sirens and then rounded up. The troops were carted off to prison at Fresnes or at Saint-Denis, while the top brass were locked up in cells in the basement of the Hotel Raphael. Hoffmann (1970), p. 475; Bargatzky (1969), p. 159.

60 Oberg's crony, SS Colonel Helmut Knochen, was hauled out of a Parisian nightclub into the warm evening air and the welcoming arms of his comrades-turned-captors (Hoffmann, 1970, p. 475).

61 Matters were further complicated because von Kluge had just taken on the additional post of Commander of Army Group B after Rommel had been wounded. During his meeting with Hitler when he had been given his new

assignment, von Kluge had been convinced by the Nazi leader's infectious mania that the situation on the Western Front was in fact far better than those on the ground imagined. It took no more than a few hours at the front for von Kluge to accept that Rommel had been right: the Allies would break through in a matter of weeks if not days. This striking proof – if further proof had been needed – of Hitler's crazed incompetence should have emboldened the man who was in charge of the whole Western Front. Instead it seemed to encourage his indecisiveness.

62 Hoffmann (1970), pp. 470–8.

63 Gaertringen (1995); Jacobsen (1969), 'Synchronoptical Table' in supplementary pocket. According to Hoffmann (1970), these words were uttered over the telephone by another conspirator, General Ludwig Beck, who was in Berlin (Hoffman, 1970, p. 472). See the photographs of the Army Group B headquarters and of the room where von Kluge, von Stülpnagel and Hofacker met, in Mühlen and Bauer (1995), opposite p. 81.

64 Watts (2009), n. 14.

65 Already the Luftwaffe and the Navy leaders in the French capital were putting pressure on von Boineburg's men to free their SS comrades. Neither of these men had any substantial troop forces to hand (Bourget, 1984, pp. 187 and 189).

66 Speidel (1971), p. 122.

67 Bourget (1984), p. 186. After the war, von Boineburg said bitterly: 'The failure of the enterprise was due to the indecision of Field Marshal v. Kluge.' (A-967 pp. 2–3.) It is not clear what von Boineburg thought would have happened had von Kluge been more decisive and had the Paris 'enterprise' succeeded.

68 Bargatzky (1969), p. 159.

69 After the war, a British major questioned Abetz as to why the Parisian SS did not immediately arrest the conspirators and did not carry out a thorough investigation into the Parisian events. Abetz's explanation was that the different services in the Parisian garrison had grown used to working together against the unreasonable demands of Berlin (Abetz, 1953, p. 323). For Lieutenant Karl Wand, who was directly involved in arresting the SS and SD (Nazi Intelligence Service) troops, the SS and SD leaders did not wish to attract the attention of the SS Commander in Berlin, Himmler, who would no doubt have wished to know why his crack troops in Paris meekly allowed themselves to be arrested without a fight (Bourget, 1984, p. 193). This was also the view of von Boineburg (Bourget, 1984, p. 201).

70 Bourget (1984), p. 196.

71 AN 72AJ/234/IX/22.

72 That day, Rondenay and de Beaufort had a series of meetings with military leaders. First, Rondenay met with the regional Military Delegate for Paris, Pierre Sonneville ('Equilateral'), to discuss a hare-brained plan to cut off all supplies of water, electricity and gas to the capital (this was dismissed as threatening the civilian population rather than the Germans) (Sonneville, 1968, pp. 338–9). Then Rondenay had two meetings in the west of Paris. It

was between these two rendezvous that the arrests occurred: first Rondenay met his equivalent in the southern zone, Maurice Bourgès-Maunoury ('Polygone'), while the meeting that never happened was to be with Chaban himself (AN 72AJ/237/II/2a/36). Sonneville suggests that Chaban was present when he and Rondenay discussed the crazy sabotage plan. This would raise the question of why Chaban and Rondenay were also to meet later on the same day. It is possible that Sonneville was mistaken and that the discussion with Chaban took place at another time.

73 Albertelli (2010a) and www.ordredelaliberation.fr/fr_compagnon/855.html [Accessed May 2011]. Rondenay was replaced by Lorrain Cruse.

74 Felstiner (1987).

75 Felstiner (1987), p. 35.

76 These figures are taken from a letter written in July 1944 by Georges Edinger, Président Générale of the UGIF, reproduced in Rajsfus (1996), p. 350. Dreyfus & Gensburger (2003), p. 245, write of 350 children being arrested.

77 Klarsfeld (1996).

CHAPTER 2

1 Bourdan (1945), p. 9.

2 Massu (1969), p. 125. After the war, Torrès married Jacques Massu of the 2e DB.

3 Cobb (2009a). The 2e DB was composed of nine regiments split across three tactical groups, each group named after their commanding colonel.

4 Moore (2011).

5 For the role of colonial troops in the Free French army see Echenberg (1985) and Scheck (2010).

6 This was known as *le serment de Koufra* – 'the Kufra Oath'.

7 On 30 December 1943, de Gaulle met with Eisenhower and discussed the future invasion of France and the apparent opposition of the British to the presence of Free French 'indigenous troops' in Free French infantry divisions were they to be in Britain prior to the invasion; on the other hand, said de Gaulle, 'our armoured divisions are made up principally of French elements' (de Gaulle, 1956, p. 675). Shortly afterwards Bedell Smith wrote a memo marked 'Confidential' in which he discussed which Free French division should be involved in the liberation of Paris: 'It is more desirable that the division mentioned above consist of white personnel. This would indicate the Second Armoured Division, which with only one fourth native personnel, is the only French division operationally available that could be made one hundred per cent white.' Bedell Smith went on to argue that if it was not possible to use a racially cleansed version of the 2e DB, then it would be necessary to 'create a force, from scratch, composed of white troops'. Two weeks earlier, Bedell Smith's predecessor, General Frederick Morgan, had written a note summarising a discussion with Churchill's Chief of Staff, General Hastings Ismay, showing they were on the same

wavelength when it came to deciding which Free French troops should be
allowed to liberate Paris: 'General Ismay and I have emphasised to Colonel
de Chevigné [the Free French Chief of Staff] that we would accept only
with great reluctance anything but troops from France proper. He quite
understood ... I have told Colonel de Chevigné that his chances of getting
what he wants will be vastly improved if he can produce a white infantry
division.' All quotes from Wieviorka (2007), pp. 364–5. The first clear
description of a process of racial cleansing in the 2e DB was made during
a conference held in February 1994 in Paris. General Jean Compagnon,
who had been a member of the Leclerc Division, made what he called an
'anecdotal clarification': 'the British wanted as few "indigenous" troops as
possible. I don't know why – furthermore there were only white soldiers!
This was clearly set out in a note dated 28 January 1944, written by General
Bedell Smith on Eisenhower's orders.' (Levisse-Toussé, 1994a, p. 96.) The
first serious examination of the question was carried out by Wieviorka
(2007), who unearthed the archival sources quoted here. This discovery
was immediately picked up by the *Independent* (31 January 2007). Over two
years later, in 2009, the BBC website announced that: 'Papers unearthed by
the BBC reveal that British and American commanders ensured that the
liberation of Paris on 25 August 1944 was seen as a "whites only" victory.'
(news.bbc.co.uk/1/hi/world/europe/7984436.stm [accessed July 2012].)
These were the same papers that had been published in Wieviorka's book in
French in 2007, and in an English translation in June 2008, and to which
General Compagnon had referred in 1994.

8 Levisse-Touzé (2007); Mesquida (2011).
9 Free French units participating in the 15 August 1944 landings on the
   Mediterranean coast included both black and Arab soldiers. Either the question of race was not considered by the Allies, or if it was, it was thought that
   it was less of an issue in the south.
10 Beevor (2009), p. 376.
11 Boegner (1992), p. 276.
12 Beevor (2009), p. 433.
13 Lankford (1991), pp. 145–6 and 154. These people were all members of a
   SUSSEX group (see chapter 3).
14 Blumenson (2000), p. 11. Oddly enough, in some photographs von Choltitz
   bears a striking resemblance to the British comic Les Dawson.
15 NA GRGG 183, pp. 6 and 13.
16 Neitzel (2007) p. 94. After his capture on 25 August 1944, von Choltitz was
   held at the Combined Services Detailed Interrogation Centre at Trent Park,
   north of London (the building is now the site of Middlesex University),
   together with over sixty German generals and other high-ranking POWs.
   Unbeknownst to the inmates, a wing of British intelligence, MI19, secretly
   recorded their discussions. Verbatim transcriptions were made in German,
   and English summaries, together with translations of some of the conversations (which accounts for their sometimes odd English), were circulated to
   various British intelligence organisations. These documents are now held

at the National Archives in Kew. Translations of some of the German
transcripts have been published (Neitzel, 2007); however, many of the documents have hitherto been unexploited, and are reproduced here for the
first time.

17 NA GRGG 183, p. 4.

18 Hitler said: 'It is your business to see that all people unfit for combat and all
those not prepared to fight are evacuated from the town immediately. That
all those who are fit for combat are armed.' NA GRGG 183, p. 5. Von
Choltitz's appointment was just one example of the bewildering series of
changes that the German High Command made to its front-line commanders, generally at the instigation of Hitler, who insisted on micro-managing
military matters, as a result of both his deluded self-confidence in his strategic and man-management abilities and his increasing paranoia and distrust
of the military high-ups, which was not entirely unjustified. As Goering later
put it: 'When serious reverses hit us, the Führer often changed commanders.' ETHINT 30, p. 6.

19 Von Choltitz (1969), pp. 206–208.

20 Neitzel (2007), p. 192. Original emphasis.

21 Neitzel (2007), pp. 255–8.

22 NA GRGG 184, p. 6.

23 NA GRGG 183, p. 2, recorded on 29 August 1944, shortly before von
Choltitz's arrival at the POW camp.

24 NA GRGG 182, p. 5. This comment was made by General von Broich, who
was also responsible for the unflattering schoolboy memories cited above.

25 NA GRGG 181(C), p. 1.

26 Mitcham (2007), p. 121.

27 NA GRGG 180, p. 3.

28 Warlimont (1964), p. 449.

29 Kriegel-Valrimont (1964), p. 166. Rol went on to complain that Allied
weapons were nonetheless getting through to forces that were backed by
Free French intelligence and MI6.

30 The communications delays meant that it would have been days if not weeks
before a call from the Delegation led to containers falling into a field in the
Paris region. Earlier that day, Chaban's deputy, Colonel Ely ('Algebre'), sent
a desperate plea from Paris to General Koenig, complaining that they had
received no messages for a week. In fact, things were even worse than Ely
thought: the file copy of the message is marked 'received 16.8.44' – a week
after it was transmitted (AN 72AJ/235/II/245).

31 Footitt & Simmonds (1988), p. 116. The footnotes for this chapter of Footitt
& Simmonds are mixed up; the correct source for this quote is in note 12.

32 Amazingly, the Civilian Delegation also suffered from Chaban's stinginess
with weapons. At the end of July, Parodi's second-in-command, Roland Pré,
sent a cable to Free French intelligence reminding them that the members
of the Civilian Delegation needed weapons to defend themselves: 'Despite
repeated requests, for four months we have found it impossible to obtain a
single weapon from the Military Delegate.' AN 72AJ/235/II/165.

33 Parodi's pseudonyms included 'Cérat', 'Quartus' and 'Belladone'. There is no biography of Parodi. Apart from Parodi's own brief published accounts, the main source for his life at this period is an unpublished Ph.D. thesis (Studer, 2003).

34 The three other members of the CPL were from non-communist Resistance organisations (Libération-Nord, Ceux de la Résistance and l'Organisation Civile et Militaire).

35 AN 72AJ/235/II/178-9.

36 AN 72AJ/235/II/190-1.

37 Denis (1963), p. 95. Somewhat prosaically for a meeting of people planning to seize power, the meeting began with 'corrections to the minutes' as each committee member sought to ensure that their precise positions were preserved for posterity. For example, the representative of the Libération-Nord Resistance group insisted that the minute of the previous meeting that read 'The representative of Libération would have preferred that we did not associate all the Germans with these crimes' should be replaced by 'The representative of Libération would have preferred that we did not associate all of the German people with these crimes' (Denis, 1963, p. 220). Much of what followed was taken up with reproaches and counter-reproaches about various minor political and organisational issues, generally along a line that divided the Communist Party and the Front National from the others. The key point of debate was whether the new Prefect of the Seine département (which included Paris) should have been appointed by the Free French, rather than by the CPL. This thorny organisational issue, which combined both local and global politics, was eventually resolved with great diplomacy at the following meeting when the newly appointed Prefect, Marcel Flouret, made clear that he considered himself to be merely the acting Prefect until the dispute was settled after the liberation (Denis, 1963, p. 225). See Denis (1963), pp. 66–70 for an exhaustive account.

38 AN 72AJ/235/II/212.

39 Wieviorka (1994), p. 143.

40 Many of the coded cables sent from London to Algiers can be found in AN 72AJ/235/I and are of passing interest, if perplexing to all but amateur code-breakers. The ledger containing references to all the telegrams received by the Ministry of the Interior in Algiers can be found at AN 72AJ/236/I/7. For example, on 10 August 1944, the Ministry received nineteen messages from Secnord (the northern zone secretariat), dated from 31 July to 4 August; the next day another eighteen messages from this period arrived. One message from Paris, sent on 3 August, arrived on the 15th, while one message sent on 8 August finally trundled into Algiers on 25 August, as Paris was being liberated. Details of the three Parisian radio sets – Pleyel Violet, Montparnasse Black and Apollo Black – and their three equivalents in the suburbs, together with information about how the radios were used, are given in Collins & Lapierre (1965), pp. 94–5, although they provide no sources.

41 AN 72AJ/235/II/245. Parodi was still complaining about communications being down on 14 August, in the hearing of Victor Veau. BAM VV, 14.8.

42 Jackson (2001), p. 561. Studer (2003) demonstrates that Parodi never received this message, and that Parodi learned of it only after the war.

43 Rol-Tanguy & Bourderon (1994), p. 162.

44 de Gaulle (1970), pp. 437–8. The broadcast caused a great deal of consternation among the Free French in London and, even more so, at the highest level of Allied command – SHAEF was horrified by the section dealing with the workplaces and immediately made it known that it was completely opposed to the call for a general strike (Crémieux-Brilhac, 2010, p. 294).

45 AN 72AJ/234/VI/23.

46 Chaban's visit to London was approved by Algiers at the end of July, and communicated to Paris on 27 July 1944, before the communications breakdown (AN 72AJ/235/III/491). Chaban-Delmas (1975), p. 102 describes the trip in frustratingly brief detail, without giving any explanation of why a visit was necessary rather than correspondence. In a 1964 radio interview, Chaban-Delmas said: 'Faced with the evident insufficiency of our means of communication ... I left for London at the end of July.' (Crémieux, 1971, p. 13.) Note that Chaban-Delmas situates his visit a week earlier than it in fact took place. See also the interview with Chaban-Delmas in Ragueneau & Florentin (1994), p. 187.

47 Verity (2000), p. 209; AN 72AJ/235/III/491.

48 AN 72AJ/235/II/250. This unnumbered cable is not dated, nor is there a record of who sent it to whom. It arrived in Algiers on 15 August 1944; assuming it took the same time to go through the meanders of the Free French communication system as other messages, it was probably sent from Paris about a week earlier.

49 Ciechanowski (1974), p. 266.

50 Davies (2004).

51 See for example the diary entry for 5 August in Cazaux (1975), p. 110, and the articles in *The Times* from 2, 4, and 7–9 August 1944.

52 Wieviorka (1994), p. 143.

53 Bobkowski (1991), p. 600.

54 Alary et al. (2006), p. 536.

55 The report, drawn up by Dr Jean-Marie Musy, is reproduced in Taittinger (1948), pp. 118–26.

56 It is often stated that Picasso painted these pictures in the apartment of his lover, Marie-Thérèse Walter, on the boulevard Henri IV (e.g. Daix, 1994, p. 273). However, there is no direct evidence for this, and the reason generally given – he wanted to be with Walter and their daughter, Maya, during the fighting – is based on a misreading of the chronology: there was no fighting in Paris when the tomato-plant canvases were painted. Less than three weeks later, visitors to Picasso's studio remarked on the tomato plant on the window-sill and made the link with the paintings: 'There were a number of drawings of the pot of growing tomatoes which stood in the window, and at least two paintings clung round those same tomatoes as a central theme' (Pudney, 1944a). Of course, Picasso could have had tomato plants in both places, or he might have just moved the plant.

57 For images of these nine pictures see Zervos (1963) or the Online Picasso Project (picasso.shsu.edu). The paintings were all 72 x 93 cm. Most of these paintings are in private collections and have not been seen in public for decades. In 2006 the 10 August painting sold at Sotheby's for nearly $14 million.

58 Cazaux (1975), p. 113.

59 Von Choltitz (1969), p. 210. Technically, the two men did not have equivalent positions. Von Boineburg had been the military commander of Greater Paris, whereas von Choltitz was the commander of the Wehrmacht in Greater Paris. Von Choltitz's title gave him command over all German troops, which von Boineberg did not have and found frustrating (B-015, p. 6). Robert Wallraf, the quartermaster of the German troops who were stationed in the Senate building, later wrote his memoirs, *Paris en danger de mort. Souvenirs.* These are cited by Bourget (1984), who unfortunately gives no source for this document. Wallraf reports the discussions between von Boineburg and von Choltitz in some detail, allegedly on the basis of information provided by von Boineburg. Unable to consult the original source, and uncertain as to how Wallraf obtained his information or even when his memoirs were written, I have limited my citations of Wallraf to events he observed directly. Despite von Boineburg's involvement in the 20 July plot, he was not troubled at the time by Berlin, and when he was eventually summoned by a military tribunal investigating the collapse of the Paris garrison, his appearance was delayed until he was overrun by the Americans. Milton Shulman, who was a Canadian intelligence officer and interviewed von Boineburg immediately after the war, wrote that the German 'must have been born with a horseshoe in his mouth and four-leaf clovers clutched in each tiny paw' (Shulman, 1986, p. 189).

60 AN 72AJ/61/II/8.

61 Mesnil-Amar (2009), p. 73.

62 Cazaux (1975), p. 125.

63 The German general later described this as 'a show parade' (von Choltitz, 1969, p. 212).

64 Bourget (1984), pp. 211–212. It has been said that it took place on 14 August (Müller, 1994, p. 103); however, the account of *L'Oeuvre* and Cazaux's diary make it clear that this was not the case. Collins & Lapierre (1965) cite the account of a participant, Sergeant Werner Nix (p. 57). Strikingly, of all the Parisian diaries I have consulted, only Cazaux makes any reference to this event – if it was intended to inspire fear in people, it failed singularly.

65 After the war, Colonel Kurt Hesse, who commanded Feldkommandatur (military administrative headquarters) Paris at Saint-Cloud in summer 1944, interviewed all the key members of the German command in Paris for the Historical Division of the US Army. Hesse concluded that Vierow 'was excellently familiar with the conditions in the Western and Southern area of Paris ... and ... had taken up with great energy the strengthening of the defence of Paris in the sector assigned to him, had to give up his place as

senior officer although he was willing to unconditionally put himself under the command of General von Choltitz.' B-611, p. 14.

66 B-611, p. 13.

67 Zaloga (2008), p. 27.

68 Their deployment in the valleys to the south-west of Paris provoked the concern of the Free French Military Delegation, who sent an urgent message warning the Allies about this development (AN 72AJ/235/II/252).

69 B-611, p. 17. One notable addition in May had been the arrival of a battalion of translators who were stationed at Saint-Cloud, but it was reported that they 'did not show much fighting spirit'.

70 B-015.

71 B-015, p. 4.

72 Cobb (2009a).

73 B-611, p. 2.

74 B-611, p. 3.

75 B-728, p. 7. This was by Lieutenant-Colonel Albert Emmerich.

76 AN 72AJ/62/III/4. For a flavour of Boisdon's subsequent career (he was an MP after the war), see Thomas (2003).

77 Cazaux (1975), p. 120.

78 Tuffrau (2002), p. 72.

79 Tillon (1977), pp. 388–9.

80 Rol-Tanguy & Bourderon (1994), p. 166. Tillon's letter did contain an oblique instruction – Rol was to put forward proposals for FFI action 'after having discussed with our friends'. This was presumably a reference to either the Communist Party (PCF) or the communist leadership of the FTP, but in both cases there is no evidence that Rol ever had such discussions, and he subsequently consistently rejected any suggestion that he had done so (see for example Bourderon, 2004, pp. 354–60).

81 This point is made sharply by Rol in a commentary section of his collection of 100 documents relating to the liberation of Paris (Rol-Tanguy & Bourderon, 1994, p. 175). Tillon's 10 August document does not appear among them; it is not even mentioned by Communist Party leader Jacques Duclos in his memoirs (Duclos, 1970). One possible explanation is that Tillon was expelled from the Communist Party in 1953 and, in some respects, his dissidence began in August 1944. Only the first two, relatively anodyne, paragraphs are quoted by Tillon's ex-comrade, Albert Ouzoulias (Ouzoulias, 1972, pp. 422–3).

CHAPTER 3

1 Boegner (1992), p. 277.

2 According to police figures, by 09:15 1,200 workers were on strike, and by 09:45 a further 600 had downed tools. Chevandier (2002); Carrière (1994).

3 *La Vérité* 18 August 1944, in Anonymous (1978). The brief report is headed '*Jeudi 9 août*'; as Chevandier (2002), p. 210, n. 115 points out, this should read '*Jeudi 10 août*'.

4 Carrière (1994), p. 22.

5 The CGT had produced an illegal leaflet which had been given out a few days earlier, reminding workers about their arrested comrades and giving a rousing call to action: 'To respond to the Nazi threats, set up patriotic militias, involving all workers who want to see their country liberated. Sabotage, sabotage anything that could be useful to the Huns who are starving the people; stop the movement of military supply trains. Forward for action, for a strike, for a national uprising that will liberate France' (Roulet, 2004, p. 22). Before the strike began, on 4 August, Captain Robert Vitasse, of the SPIRITUALIST circuit set up by the SOE, organised an attack on the Villeneuve-Saint-Georges marshalling yards. Vitasse and his men blew up the water towers and a 35-ton crane, and drove a 48-ton locomotive into the turntable, blocking the locomotive roundhouse for nearly a week – *L'Humanité* 10 August 1994; Cumont (1991), pp. 70–5. Cumont reproduces notes made shortly after the attack; the date 3–4 August has been replaced by 4–5 August.

6 Carrière (1994), p. 22.

7 'Rapport de Véry' 14 August 1944, in Cogniot et al. (1974), pp. 80–2. Véry's real name was Maurice Sentuc.

8 Durand (1968), p. 546; Carrière (1994), p. 23.

9 Cazaux (1975), p. 122.

10 Details in this paragraph taken from *La Vérité* 18 August 1944 (Anonymous, 1978); Carrière (1994); Chevandier (2002), p. 211; AN 72AJ/74/III/10; AN 72AJ/61/I/9. This last report dates the hostage-taking at Noisy to 10 August, which I have assumed to be a mistake. On 11 August, Yves Cazaux wrote in his diary that a number of railway workers were executed at Noisy-le-Sec (Cazaux, 1975, p. 124). I have found no other mention of this. Carrière (1994) p. 23 suggests that there may have been some kind of complicity between management and the strikers, in order to protect the hostages; he argues that SNCF reports may have underplayed the strength of the strike in order not to antagonise the Germans.

11 Patin (1994), p. 28.

12 Cogniot et al. (1974), p. 81.

13 Cogniot et al. (1974), p. 83.

14 Chevandier (2002), p. 212.

15 Laval's letter read: 'After three days of strike action in the Paris region, the situation shows that the railway workers truly want to go back to work, but they are literally terrorised by elements of the Resistance and in particular by the communists. The government considers that the return of the 52 prisoners would be a powerful argument in favour of a return to work in the workshops and depots.' Bachelier (1996), section 7-3-8.

16 Bachelier (1996), section 7-3-8. The chronology of events is not entirely clear; it may have been that the hostages were freed before the government sent its letter, following the intervention of the Minister of Transport.

17 Chevandier (2002), p. 213.

18 Chevandier (2002), pp. 213–214.

19 Pierquin (1983), p. 130.
20 SKF was able to make money out of both sides in the war – the company produced 60 per cent of the ball-bearings used by the German military machine, and over 30 per cent of British ball-bearings (Golson, 2012).
21 Desfeuilles (1945); Nordling (2002). The name of the prisoner was Jacques Merleau-Ponty; he was married to one of Nordling's nieces (Nordling, 2002, p. 83, n. 11). The issue of the prisoners had already been raised with Nordling, in a discussion with Parodi's emissary, the 44-year-old banker Count Alexandre de Saint-Phalle. A week earlier Emmanuel d'Astier in Algiers had sent a message to Parodi, calling for the creation of armed groups that could attack the main French prisons and free the Resistance prisoners (AN 72AJ/235/III/494). Parodi replied saying he would do all he could, but he needed arms; he also expressed his habitual fears about the dangers of reprisals were the Resistance to take action (AN 72AJ/235/II/224). This version of events, in which discussions with the Resistance first alerted Nordling to the potential threat to prisoners, is not given by Nordling in his near-contemporaneous account (Desfeuilles, 1945) or his later memoirs (Nordling, 2002). However, it is supported by a message from Parodi to London sent on 14 August 1944 (AN 72AJ/235/II/284) and by the description of the First Secretary of the Swiss legation in Paris, René Naville, who was involved in Nordling's work and published a series of articles in the *Journal de Genève* in 1950 (Naville, 1950a–f). Various aspects of Nordling's memoirs appear to be confused – there are repeated contradictions in the details of what happened between his 1945 version, his undated memoirs (published in 2002), and the recollections of René Naville. For example, in 1945, less than a year after the events, Nordling stated that the Caen massacre had taken place at the beginning of August, and its proximity played an important role in his motivations (Desfeuilles, 1945, p. 6). In fact it took place on D-Day, two months earlier (Quellien, 2005).
22 Molden (1979), pp. 121 and 123. According to Molden, Posch-Pastor was 'an elegant young man ... He wore a moustache and had an amiable and very Austrian air. There was a hint of arrogance around the mouth, perhaps, but the eyes had a smile in them.' Fritz Molden was an Austrian anti-fascist who later worked for OSS, and became friends with Posch-Pastor in Paris in 1942. Posch-Pastor's full name was Erich Posch-Pastor von Camperfeld. Collins & Lapierre (1965) report that of the hundreds of participants that they contacted, only Posch-Pastor refused to comment on his role in the events of August 1944. It has been suggested that he deserted from the German Army in July 1944 (Collins & Lapierre, 1965, p. 190). De Gaulle described 'Poch-Pastor' [*sic*] as 'von Choltitz's aide and an Allied agent' (de Gaulle, 1956, p. 303), but von Choltitz insisted that he only ever met 'von Posch-Pastor' [*sic*] twice, each time in the company of Nordling (von Choltitz, 1969, p. 232). Collins & Lapierre (1965), p. 190 and Vaughan (2004), pp. 102–5, state that Posch-Pastor was a member of the GOELETTE circuit, under the name Etienne Paul Provost (or 'Pruvost' according to Vaughan), and helped transmit plans of V1 launching sites via Dr Sumner Jackson, a doctor at the

American Hospital in Neuilly (Vaughan, 2004, pp. 104–105). GOELETTE was controlled by Free French intelligence (BCRA), not by MI6, so Posch-Pastor may have been involved in several layers of clandestine activity (AN 72AJ/71/VI/2a, p. 33).

23 There is a photograph of Bender in Collins & Lapierre (1965) (his first name is variously spelt Emil or Emile).

24 Nordling (2002), pp. 87–9. Nordling states that he also met with the Swiss Legate in Paris, René Naville, during this period. According to Naville (1950a), they did not meet until 13 August.

25 The first time Nordling raised the issue on the telephone, he was fobbed off by an aide, who said the embassy had no power in the matter, and that the question would have to be referred to Berlin, where Himmler would have the final say. A discouraged Nordling handed over a letter to Abetz outlining the diplomatic consequences for Germany's reputation were the prisoners to be treated badly. This was hardly the kind of thing to worry a Nazi, but it was probably all the neutral diplomat could do.

26 Nordling (2002), p. 90. There is no mention of Nordling and the prisoners in Abetz's memoirs (Abetz, 1953), or in a recent study of the German ambassador's role (Lambauer, 2001). The university professor was the head of the Ecole Normale Supérieure.

27 Naville (1950a).

28 AN 72AJ/235/II/284.

29 Kriegel-Valrimont (1964) p. 78; AN 72AJ/45/I/5A, p. 8.

30 Bardoux (1958), p. 334. Bardoux's self-serving diary contains an extremely detailed account of these futile manoeuvres, and inadvertently shows the extent to which the collaborationist politicians were out of touch with political and military reality, as well as being fatally compromised on the moral plane.

31 For complex ideological reasons relating to the political position of the capital, Paris did not have a mayor from 1794 to 1977, apart from during the revolutions of 1848 and 1870–1. The current system began in 1977, with the election of Jacques Chirac.

32 A week earlier, the Vichy government had banned the anti-Semitic newspaper *Je Suis Partout* because of its abusive attacks on Laval.

33 Bourget (1984), p. 217.

34 Brissaud (1965), pp. 234–8.

35 Institut Hoover (1958), p. 1071. The idea was apparently floated in a conversation with Georges Bidault, who allegedly supported it, but thought that Laval would never agree.

36 Brissaud (1965), pp. 242–3. Although Dulles' reports to OSS headquarters about his conversations with Enfière do not contain any such statement (Petersen, 1996, p. 334) that does not mean that he did not say such a thing. The long-standing antipathy felt by the US administration towards de Gaulle and the Free French, and the profound illusions the US had held for much of the war about Vichy coming over to the Allied side, all suggest that the US might indeed have favoured such a transitional government. The assumption that the US would be open to Laval's scheme was widespread on both

sides of the political and military divide. De Gaulle believed it after the war – he gives a detailed account of these manoeuvres in his war memoirs (de Gaulle, 1956, p. 290). The fascist collaborator Marcel Déat was certain that Laval intended to do a deal with the Americans, and he in turn became determined to scupper it, by whatever means necessary – see the letter by the collaborationist Georges Albertini in Institut Hoover (1958), p. 1294. For a discussion of these events from the US point of view, see Glass (2009).

37 Institut Hoover (1958), p. 1040.

38 Details from Taittinger (1948), pp. 153–4 and Cazaux (1975), p. 129. Cazaux's contemporaneous diary entry gives the time of Herriot's arrival as 08:30, but confirms the dressing-gown detail.

39 Auphan carried a letter containing Pétain's instructions; he was to find a solution 'in order to avoid a civil war and to reconcile all French men and women of good faith', but above all to ensure that 'the principle of legitimacy that I represent should be safeguarded' (Dansette, 1946, pp. 109–110). The very idea that de Gaulle, or the Resistance, would ever consider that Vichy represented any kind of legitimacy indicates either that the old man's advisors were completely deluded, or that they were telling him what he wanted to hear. Furthermore, talk of 'avoiding a civil war' was hard to take seriously from the man who had allowed the fascist Milice to wage a *de facto* civil war against the Resistance.

40 Dansette (1946), pp. 109–110. This message was allegedly sent with the help of a senior member of the Resistance. There is no trace of Auphan's message to Algiers in the archive of cables sent from France (AN 72AJ/235/II). On 15 August, Parodi cabled Algiers and simply stated, 'Both Laval and Pétain's entourage are trying to enter into contact with the Delegation' (AN 72AJ/235/II/290). De Gaulle received the letter after the liberation of Paris, viewing it with as much scorn as could be expected (de Gaulle, 1956, pp. 319–21).

41 AN 72AJ/235/II/253–4, AN 72AJ/235/II/266–7.

42 AN 72AJ/235/III/503–4.

43 Drieu La Rochelle (1992), p. 416.

44 Drieu La Rochelle (1992), p. 421; he describes his day in a later diary entry for 15 October.

45 Her diary was initially published under the pseudonym C. de Saint-Pierre (1945). The diary was begun on 10 August, but the entries for the first two days were written on 12 August (de Saint-Pierre, 1945, p. 9).

46 de Saint-Pierre (1945), p. 11.

47 Kent (1947), pp. 195–7.

48 de Saint-Pierre (1945), p. 16.

49 de Saint-Pierre (1951), p. 77.

50 Lewis (1991).

51 On the handwritten cover page of Hooker's SOE personnel file (NA HS 9/739/6), his first name appears to be 'Ivar', and this is the name that is given in the National Archives index. Subsequent pages of the file make clear that he was in fact called Ivor.

52 OSS War Diary 4:768.

53 OSS War Diary 4:772.

54 SUSSEX involved dropping small teams of British, French and US agents behind German lines to collect intelligence and guide parachute drops to the Resistance (Lorain, 1983, pp. 97–9). By D-Day there were seventeen SUSSEX groups, including one in Vincennes to the south-east of Paris. 'The presence of teams in Paris constituted a great risk ... Most of the material passed through Paris. It was carried by truck from the dropping field. The greatest complications were found in despatching men and material from Paris to their various destinations.' OSS War Diary 3:144. The two cafés were at 8 rue Tournefort, just behind the Pantheon, and at 5 rue du Faubourg-Montmartre in the 9th arrondissement. The rue Tournefort café was owned by Madame Andrée Goubillon and in 1944 sheltered a total of twenty-one SUSSEX agents and their equipment, also serving as a 'letter box' for Allied communications (Cleveland-Peck, 2000, p. 5). After the war, the café was renamed Le Café du Réseau Sussex; it is now a restaurant and there is a plaque on the building commemorating Madame Goubillon's activity. OSS War Diary 3:236 reproduces her citation for the US Medal for Merit. Madame Goubillon's name is heavily redacted in the archive, indicating that such matters were still sensitive when it was released. The rue du Faubourg-Montmartre café was run by Marguerite Kiel. It is still there, but there is no indication of its historic role. Madame Kiel sheltered thirteen agents and their equipment, including radios and weapons, in the period up to August 1944. Madame Kiel's name in the OSS War Diary (3:236) is too heavily redacted to read, beyond the fact that her first name began with 'M'; Funk (1994), p. 228 and p. 235, n. 6, provides the details (see also AN 72 AJ/232/III/5, p. 9 and Jeffery, 2010, p. 651). Kiel was also awarded the Medal for Merit. After the war, Kenneth Cohen of MI6, joint founder of the SUSSEX missions, wrote a piece of doggerel which ridiculed the process by which the UK Foreign Office awarded medals to these women. Although Jeanette Guyot (a French officer, who was part of SUSSEX) was given an OBE, Goubillon and Kiel were given the lesser award of a British Empire Medal, because MI6 had not provided evidence that they had sufficient social standing to deserve an OBE:

> How do you feel
> About Marguerite Kiel?
> Can Andrée Goubillon
> Dance the cotillion?
> At what social summit
> Stands Mlle Jeanette?
> Their assets, their accents, their undies laid bare,
> Then, only then can we apportion the share:
> B.E.M.s may be spared for intelligence chores
> But O.B.E.s are reserved for the silkiest drawers. (Jeffery, 2010, p. 651)

55 The fullest description of JADE-AMICOL can be found in Paillat & Boulnois

(1989), pp. 611–49. See also Funk (1994), p. 227. Keun was captured by the Germans in June 1944. Jeffery (2010) does not mention Ollivier; he does mention the circuit and Keun in passing, but not his fate (p. 530).

56 Fourcade was in fact her married name after the war; her name at the time was Méric. Her memoirs have been published in English, but in a truncated translation – Fourcade (1972 and 1973). With around 5000 agents, ALLIANCE provided invaluable information on the situation inside France, including detailed descriptions of the German V-weapons. For a copy of one of the ALLIANCE reports on the V2, see Brown (1988), pp. 782–3.

57 Verity (2000), p. 208.

58 Fourcade (1973), pp. 329–45. This is a substantially truncated translation; see Fourcade (1972), pp. 252–81.

59 Fourcade (1972), pp. 280–1.

60 Verity (2000), p. 206.

61 Rajsfus (1996); Dreyfus & Gensburger (2003), p. 242. Gensburger (2005) examines how the Parisian camps were 'forgotten' after the war. It has been suggested – for example in W. G. Sebald's work *Austerlitz* (Sebald, 2001, pp. 401–3) that the Austerlitz camp was located on the site of what is now the Bibliothèque nationale de France. This is not the case; the two warehouses were much closer to the Métro line at boulevard Vincent Auriol. The location is now the site of an apartment block. See for example blog.bnf.fr/lecteurs/index.php/2010/08/02/la-bnf-a-lemplacement-dun-ancien-camp-nazi/ [accessed July 2012].

62 This was the story that was subsequently dramatised in the film *The Train* (1964), directed by John Frankenheimer. The cases of artworks had been prepared by Rose Valland, a conservator at the Musée du Jeu de Paume. For full details, see Rayssac (2008).

63 On 5 August, the internees from Bassano were returned to Drancy, where they waited for the next convoy to be assembled. On 12 August, both Lévitan and Austerlitz were shut down in those dramatic early morning raids. Even so, *Möbel Aktion* continued: later on the same day, a whole Jewish-owned building on the rue Erlanger in the 16th arrondissement was ransacked. A car and two lorries were required to carry off the contents. Dreyfus & Gensburger (2003), p. 243.

64 Dreyfus & Gensburger (2003), p. 257.

65 de Saint-Pierre (1945), p. 23.

66 de Saint-Pierre (1945), p. 24.

67 Massu (1969), pp. 138–40; Bergot (1980), p. 96.

68 de Boissieu (1981), p. 244.

69 Blumenson (1998).

70 Speidel (1971), p. 135. Von Choltitz (1969), p. 121 recalled there were two meetings, on 13 and 15 August. Lieutenant-General Bodo Zimmerman states there was one meeting 'On 14 or 15 Aug 44' (B-308, p. 142), and gives some details (e.g. with regard to the destruction of bridges) that were not known on 14 August, but were on 15 August, which is when von Choltitz recalls they

were discussed. I have assumed that there were two meetings, on 14 and 15 August.

71 B-308, pp. 143–4.

72 B-308, p. 144.

73 Message from Abetz to Grand, 14 August 1944. Obtained by OSS spy 'George Wood' (Fritz Kolbe) in Berlin, and transmitted from Berne by Allen Dulles on 18 August 1944 (Petersen, 1996, pp. 371–2). For the amazing work of Fritz Kolbe, see Delattre (2006).

74 BAM VV, 14.8.

75 For the resolution, plus Valrimont's satisfied summary, see Kriegel-Valrimont (1964), pp. 170–1.

76 Wieviorka (1994), p. 143.

77 For discussions of the role of the police in the Resistance, see Anonymous (1965), Chevandier (2008), Kitson (1995) and Rudolph (2010).

78 Lefranc (1965), p. 109. The suburbs were Saint-Denis, Courbevoie and Asnières. Lefranc gives a slightly different version of this story in Breton (1964), pp. 36–41. The transcription of Emile Hennequin's telegram in Dupuy (1945) suggests there were only two police stations involved (p. 4). Dansette (1946) states that only Asnières and Saint-Denis were disarmed, and provides an unsourced description of the events in Saint-Denis, suggesting that it was indeed all a misunderstanding by a local German patrol (p. 156).

79 Dansette (1946), p. 156.

80 BAM VV, 13.8. Veau's diary was originally written 'hour by hour on small pieces of paper'; the fair copy in the Bibliothèque de l'Académie de Medicine (BAM) in Paris contains transcriptions of these entries, interspersed with clearly identified subsequent clarifications. There is a typewritten version of the diary in the Archives Nationales (AN 72AJ/62/II/2), but it is not clear which parts are contemporaneous and which are subsequent additions. I have therefore referred to the BAM version. Yves Cazaux heard of the police action but in the early evening could see no evidence of it – there seemed to be just as many uniformed policemen guarding public buildings. By this stage, the protest was over (Cazaux, 1975, p. 128).

81 Dupuy (1945), p. 4.

82 Institut Hoover (1958), p. 615.

83 Rol also sensed that the stakes were getting higher by the hour. He contacted the Front National leader in charge of work with the gendarmes in the Paris region, and the two men agreed that they would argue for gendarmes to go on strike by refusing to carry out duties in uniform, and if possible, to join the FFI, taking their arms and equipment with them. Bourderon (2004), p. 364. The '*Note de Service*' containing these orders is reproduced in Crémieux (1971), pp. 147–8.

84 After agreeing to the strike, they had talked to Henri Ribière, of their parent Resistance organisation, Libération-Nord. Ribière was less than enthusiastic about the proposed strike: like Parodi, Chaban and many of the non-

communist leaders of the Resistance, he was paralysed by the prospect of reprisals. Ribière was also concerned that this was an initiative that came from the Front National, and that his men might thereby be caught up in a communist manoeuvre. Details that follow are from Bourderon (2004), Dansette (1946) and Lefranc (1965).

85 Dupuy (1945), p. 5. Ironically, this chimed with the view from the other side of the barricades: the collaborationist Prefect of Police, Amédée Bussière, had got wind of the threatened action and had written to every Paris policeman explaining the risks they ran if they went on strike.

86 Lefranc (1965), p. 111 reproduces a copy of a document that purports to be the original strike 'order'. However, this document, dated 13 August, is signed by all three organisations and contains the precise address where the meeting of the Front National took place the previous day. The date/signature combination is simply wrong, while the inclusion of the address seems impossible. The same text – but without the address or date – is given in Dansette (1946), p. 480, together with the FFI declaration (pp. 479–80). For a discussion of the significance of the strike 'order' (*'ordre de grève'*) rather than a strike call (*'mot d'ordre de grève'*) see Chevandier (2008). Monniot (1965) suggests the meeting of the three Resistance groups took place on the 13th, but this is clearly an error.

87 Dansette (1946), pp. 479–80.

88 Denis (1963), p. 174.

89 Kriegel-Valrimont (1964), p. 178; Bourderon (2004), p. 364. For Dufresne's own account of his arguments with Colonel Lizé of the FFI, see Massiet (1945), pp. 62–4.

90 Mesnil-Amar (2009), pp. 78–9.

CHAPTER 4

1 Cumberlege (1946), pp. 185–6.

2 All details from Mitcham (2007), pp. 161–76 and Zaloga (2009).

3 The road gives stupendous views of the surrounding countryside; the villages are beautiful and welcoming. It is one of my favourite parts of the world.

4 Warlimont (1964), p. 451.

5 After Action Report, p. 33; Renoult & West (2008), pp. 102–104.

6 Blumenson (1998).

7 Cazaux (1975), p. 130.

8 Boegner (1992), p. 279.

9 AN 72AJ/71/IX/17, p. 3; AN 72AJ/62/I/6, p. 1.

10 Cazaux (1975), p. 131.

11 Tuffrau (2002), p. 73.

12 AN 72AJ/71/IX/17, p. 3.

13 The strike figures are given in AN 72 AJ/71/IX/5, p.5.

14 All details from Dupuy (1945), pp. 5–7.

15 This is the telling title of an article by the historian of the French police,

Jean-Marc Berlière (1994). For analyses of the strike, see Chevandier (2008) and Kitson (1995).

16 AN 72AJ/235/II/291.
17 See transcripts of conversations between General Bridoux and Laval in Institut Hoover (1958), pp. 1700–1701.
18 Dansette (1946), p. 108; Institut Hoover (1958), p. 1075.
19 AN 72AJ/235/II/289.
20 Rol-Tanguy & Bourderon (1994), p. 191.
21 Bourderon (2004), p. 367.
22 Tillon (1977), p. 390; Tillon (1972), p. 234, n. 1.
23 Amouroux (1988), p. 624.
24 AN 72AJ/234/VI/24, p. 3.
25 ML C-K.
26 Reproduction of article from *Paris-Soir* (15 August 1944), in ANACR (n.d.), p. 2. In *Aujourd'hui* (15 August 1944), the headline read: 'An appeal to Parisians to maintain order and food supplies. Any attempt at insurrection will be brutally repressed' (see reproduction in Conte, 1984, p. 16).
27 Cazaux (1975), pp. 131–2.
28 Bourget (1984), p. 213; von Choltitz (1969), p. 219.
29 Von Choltitz (1969), p. 212.
30 B-308, p. 143.
31 NA GRGG 183, p. 3.
32 For an intriguing but inconclusive examination of whether von Kluge was really in contact with the Allies, see Brown (1988), pp. 609–610. When asked whether he thought von Kluge was a traitor, Goering evaded the question (ETHINT 30, p. 6).
33 Carell (1962), p. 259. According to Speidel (1971), p. 134, this episode took place on 12 August. However, Walter Warlimont, who was present in Rastenburg at the time, places it on 15 August (Warlimont, 1964, p. 450).
34 Cazaux (1975), p. 132.
35 AN 72AJ/234/VI/24, p. 1.
36 Grunberg (2001), p. 335.
37 Boegner (1992), pp. 279–80.
38 Pastor Marc Boegner, who was in touch with all the goings-on in the highest circles of what remained of the French government, wrote in his diary on 16 August: 'With the full knowledge of the Germans, officers of the Intelligence Service and American Officers are negotiating with Laval and others.' (Boegner, 1992, p. 280.) This rumour was repeated by the usually reliable Adrien Dansette in his history of the liberation of Paris: '[Laval] even negotiated with the Americans. On either 15 or 16 August, he met with two American emissaries. He outlined his twin projects – one with Pétain, the other without ... he asked them to let General Eisenhower know his proposals.' (Dansette, 1946, p. 112). There is no evidence for such a meeting. Most tellingly, in Laval's self-serving 'diary' (Laval, 1948), written while he was in prison, Laval made no mention of any such meeting. If it had indeed occurred he surely would have described it.

39 Galtier-Boissière (1944), p. 251. For more on Galtier-Boissière and his scurrilous magazine, *Le Crapouillot*, see Hewitt (2007).

40 Flora Groult, Benoîte's sister, wrote in her diary: 'In the clear sky there is a continuous, low background noise. Papa says it is gunfire twenty miles away.' Groult & Groult (1965), p. 298.

41 Tournoux (1982), p. 317.

42 Armand's real name was René Dumont, or more precisely René Dumont-Guillemet (Cumont, 1991, p. 37). But see also his post-war recommendation for a Distinguished Service Order, where his name is given as 'Dumont-Guillement' (NA WO 373/98).

43 OSS War Diary, 3:769.

44 OSS War Diary, 3:774.

45 Galtier-Boissière (1944), p. 251.

46 BAM VV, 15.8.

47 See for example, Tuffrau (2002), p. 73; Vilain (1945), p. 6; AN 72AJ/62/III/4, p. 10.

48 All quotes from Mesnil-Amar (2009), diary entry for 15 August, pp. 80–2. Mesnil-Amar's pet name for her daughter was, confusingly, 'Sylvio'.

49 Rougeyron (1996), p. 122.

50 The carefully folded note got to its destination. It is reproduced as Plate 9 in Litoff (2006). For Virginia d'Albert-Lake's description of being taken from Romainville, and the role of the bus driver in delivering her note and several others, see Litoff (2006), pp. 142–4.

51 OSS War Diary 3:232. At the time the War Diary was written, in 1945, it was thought that Clément was still alive.

52 Houssin (2004), p. 260.

53 Bachelier (1996), section 7-3-12.

54 AN 72AJ/67/IV/18, p. 10.

55 Nordling (2002), pp. 94–5.

56 Kinnis & Booker (1999), Childers (2004).

57 The stories of many of these 168 men are gathered in Kinnis & Booker (1999), and have recently been the subject of a documentary film, *Lost Airmen of Buchenwald* (2011). See also chapter 5.

58 Alix d'Unienville (a.k.a. 'Myrtil') is still alive, so her SOE personnel file (NA HS 9/1498/2) is closed until 2019. The details of her activity can be found in Rémy (1994). Sadly, her family tells me she is not well enough to be interviewed.

59 Paillat & Boulnois (1989), p. 618, n. 13; Duchemin (2011).

60 For example, in 1951 Pierre Lefaucheux stated that he was one of 1468 male deportees, of whom only 34 returned (AN 72AJ/67/IV/18, p. 7). Krivopisco & Porrin (2004) reproduce a 1965 claim from a survivor of the convoy that there were 2080 male deportees, of whom only 27 survived (p. 12). Blond (2005) claims that there were a total of 2400 deportees, of whom less than 800 survived. More details can be found at www.bddm.org [accessed July 2012] which suggests that there were 1654 men and 543 women on the train, of whom 48 per cent either died in deportation or disappeared. Thirty-eight per cent (838 deportees) returned from the camps;

the fate of 14 per cent is unknown. Only six people escaped, and five were freed by the Germans.

61 For details of Rondenay's life, see AN 72AJ/237/I/7. It was Rondenay who found Pierre Lefaucheux on the train so that Marie-Hélène could speak to him.

62 Albertelli (2010a) mistakenly suggests they were killed at Pantin. There is a monument at the Domont site, on the road that is now called la route des Fusillés, commemorating all those who were murdered there (see chapter 5). Hagen and Heinrichsohn, who were both heavily involved in the deportation of Jews from France, were each tried *in absentia* by French courts in the 1950s and were sentenced to life imprisonment and death, respectively. In 1979 they were finally tracked down and tried by a German court, and sentenced to twelve and six years in prison, respectively. For a powerful account of the trial, see Pryce-Jones (1981) pp. 269–72. The details of the 'executioners' banquet' are taken from the French indictment of Heinrichsohn in 1956 (Pryce-Jones, 1981, p. 271).

63 Rougeyron (1996), pp. 122–3. When shouts of protest against the shootings came from some of the wagons, the prisoners from those wagons were made to strip and had to spend the rest of the journey naked.

64 Hénocque (1947), p. 39.

65 Riffaud (1994), p. 129.

66 It is not clear why the Germans had this change of heart, but Raoul Nordling's repeated attempts to see Abetz in the previous days may have been responsible.

67 All details from Riffaud (1994), pp. 113–115. There was another successful operation to free prisoners this day: in the late afternoon, a group of armed *résistants* arrived at the Hôtel-Dieu hospital by Notre Dame cathedral and barged their way into one of the wards on the fifth floor of the building, where they took away a number of patients who were members of the Resistance and were being treated there under German guard (Cazaux, 1975, p. 137).

68 ML 99/211, p. 2.

69 Galtier-Boissière (1944), p. 251.

70 de Saint-Pierre (1945), p. 27.

71 Pryce-Jones (1981), p. 197.

72 Trentesaux's unpublished diary is available on Gilles Primout's excellent website: www.liberation-de-paris.gilles-primout.fr/tfrancoise.htm [accessed May 2011].

73 Castetbon (2004), p. 48.

74 Cazaux (1975), p. 133.

75 de Saint-Pierre (1945), p. 27.

CHAPTER 5

1 Crémieux-Brilhac (1976), p. 176.

2 See Virginia d'Albert-Lake's memoir of this phase of the journey, written in

1946; Litoff (2006), pp. 146–7. To ease the tension while the train was trapped in the tunnel, one of the women in d'Albert-Lake's wagon told a series of shockingly filthy jokes. See also the graphic descriptions of the Allied prisoners, in Kinnis & Booker (1999), and those of the *résistants* in ANACR (n.d.).

3 Goglin & Roux (2004), p. 148.

4 Litoff (2006), p. 148.

5 Litoff (2006), p. 148. Rémy (1994) gives her name as 'Vitasse'; ANACR (n.d.), which reproduces Alix's account from Rémy, gives 'Witasse'.

6 Rémy (1994). The full account of Alix d'Unienville's time in the villages of the Marne is fascinating. After the war, she went on to become an air hostess (this was highly unusual and glamorous at the time) and wrote a very successful book about her new career. For many eye-witness accounts of how the population supported and responded to the prisoners, see ANACR (n.d.).

7 Details of Madame Lefaucheux from AN 72AJ/67/IV/18, pp. 10–11. Bachelier (1996), section 7-3-12 suggests that Nordling was following the convoy and tried to convince the Germans to release the prisoners at Nanteuil-Saâcy. There is no evidence from Nordling's account that this happened – he described receiving a phone call from the Red Cross letting him know that the train was stopped at Nanteuil-Saâcy and resolved to take action first thing the next morning (Nordling, 2002, p. 97).

8 Rougeyron (1996), p. 124. Details of the arrival in the tunnel and the transfer to the new train are from Rougeyron's account. There is now a plaque at Nanteuil-Saâcy station commemorating the event, and a ceremony is held there each year on 16 August.

9 Nordling (2002), p. 97.

10 Nordling (2002), p. 96.

11 Simmonet (2010).

12 Commemorative plaque on the outside of Collège Pierre Alviset, rue Monge, Paris.

13 After Action Report, p. 33; B-741, p. 9; Blumenson (1996), p. 513. On 17 August, Colonel Bruce of OSS was unable to get to the centre of Chartres because of German snipers (Lankford, 1991, pp. 152–3).

14 Cumberlege (1946), pp. 188–9.

15 Blumenson (1998). Curiously, there is no mention of this in the entry for 16 August in Blumenson (1996), pp. 521–4.

16 Fourcade (1972), vol. 2, pp. 285–7.

17 This is an extrapolation on my part. On 18 August, the head of regional FFI intelligence, L'Arcouest, wrote to Rol explaining that two unnamed agents had been sent by motorbike to Le Mans; the motorcyclist was then ordered by the Allies to bring back 'Lieutenant P' (Rol-Tanguy & Bourderon, 1994, p. 182). Although it is possible that this mission was entirely separate from that of Sainteny and de Billy, involving two different men, the proximity in time and place, and the fact that both missions used motorcycles, makes it more likely that they were in fact the same mission. In his description of these events, Rol refers to a liaison officer from the FFI in Brittany, a

Lieutenant Mallet, who arrived on 16 August (Rol-Tanguy & Bourderon, 1994, p. 196). Lieutenant P and Lieutenant Mallet could be the same person, but the situation is complicated by the presence of another man moving between Le Mans and Paris at this time, 'Le Goff' (see chapter 7). There may have been one, two or three such agents.

18 B-728, p. 3.

19 Bradley (1951), pp. 386–7.

20 Kriegel-Valrimont (1964), p. 182; see also AN 72AJ/49/III/31, p. 6. The text was allegedly a quote from Prussian military theorist Carl von Clausewitz and read: 'It is generally believed that, by treating prisoners in a barbaric fashion, the enemy will destroy our courage. What a pointless idea! We can decide to meet barbarity with barbarity, and ferocity with ferocity. It would be easy for us to surpass the enemy and to bring them back into reasonable, human limits.' I have been unable to identify this alleged quote from von Clausewitz; I presume it is incorrect or there is a confusion in the minutes of the COMAC meeting.

21 AN 72 AJ/62/I/6, p. 1; Dansette (1946), p. 160.

22 Schramm (1982), p. 201.

23 'Lehr' was a term shared by a number of German divisions and referred to the original training function of these units (Steinhardt, 2008, p. 16).

24 ETHINT 67, p. 18. See also Steinhardt (2008), pp. 152–3.

25 AN 72AJ/61/II/8.

26 Although these posters carried the French flag and were headlined in the name of the Republic, the 'French Army', and the FFI, they were signed by the (unnamed) 'Chief of Staff' of the FTP. They were certainly not issued by the Free French. The Germans appear to have been unaware of the tensions and contradictions that existed between the various wings of the Resistance and the Free French in Algiers – if they had known, they would surely have sought to exploit them.

27 von Choltitz (1969), pp. 221–2.

28 Yves Cazaux saw one of the posters and wrote in his diary: 'Intrigued, I ran my finger and nail over the edges, where you should have felt the raised edge of the paper. Nothing – I felt nothing. The poster has a false sticker printed on it.' (Cazaux, 1975, p. 137). Similarly, Henri Rebière was surprised to see that the posters had not been destroyed, but instead had a sticker on them: 'A passerby pointed out to me that the strip was not a sticker, but had been directly printed onto the poster.' (AN 72AJ/62/I/16, p. 1.) Rebière concluded that the fact that the sticker was apparently printed on the whole poster indicated that the poster was the work of German provocateurs and therefore dismissed the Resistance appeal as well (AN 72AJ/62/I/16, p. 2).

29 Crémieux-Brilhac (1976), opp. p. 176, has a photograph of one of these posters, carrying the red strip added by the Germans, which clearly looks like a sticker rather than part of the poster itself. At its meeting on 16 August COMAC also discussed the issue: 'It is significant that, on the posters calling for mobilisation, they have stuck red strips threatening reprisals.'

(AN72AJ/49/III/31, p. 7.) It is possible that the Germans used both stickers and specially printed posters in this strange campaign.

30 AN 72AJ/49/III/31, p. 2. It is not known who the officer was, nor what 'service' he proposed.

31 Lankford (1991), p. 152. According to the diary of Colonel Bruce of OSS, some of the leaflets were hidden in the spare tyre of a 'wood-burning seventon truck' which was driven towards Paris, but broke down as it crossed the German lines (Lankford, 1991, p. 154).

32 AN 72AJ/61/I/14, p. 1.

33 Bobkowski (1991), p. 605.

34 de Saint-Pierre (1945), p. 29.

35 de Saint-Pierre (1945), p. 28.

36 Bood (1974), p. 314.

37 Boegner (1992), p. 281.

38 Institut Hoover (1958), p. 682.

39 Institut Hoover (1958), p. 1194.

40 Institut Hoover (1958), p. 1041.

41 Dansette (1946), p. 113.

42 Institut Hoover (1958), pp. 1075–6.

43 Dansette (1946), pp. 114–115. Himmler had been alerted by Déat, who was determined to stop Laval's scheme.

44 AN 72AJ/62/I/6, p. 2.

45 Galtier-Boissière (1944), pp. 252–3.

46 The description that follows is based on Bourget (1984), Krivopisco & Porrin (2004) and an anonymous, undated (internal evidence suggests 1946–8), archival account of the events, focusing on the experience of the group led by Michelle Boursier (AN 72AJ/61/I/21). This archival account is the basis of a dossier by Adam Rayski which is available online: clioweb.free.fr/dossiers/39-45/rayski/cascade.htm [Accessed May 2011]. There is also a good summary of events in Ouzoulias (1972), pp. 420–2. The fullest account is in Bourget (1984), pp. 281–307. However, although Bourget uses a great deal of detailed archival evidence (in particular from the trials of those involved), his presentation of events is extremely convoluted. Krivopisco & Porrin (2004) present a much clearer account, although lacking in detail. For the sake of clarity, I have not referred to the role of Rehbein, a.k.a. 'Charles', a.k.a. 'Porel', who also claimed to be an Intelligence Service agent, or to that of his partner, Lydia Tscherwiska ('Katherine'). Sabine Zatlin ('Jeanne') who had been the headmistress at the Izieu Jewish refuge that was raided by Klaus Barbie in April 1944 (Cobb, 2009a, p. 208) was also involved in the affair, inadvertently helping to introduce the Gestapo agents to the *résistants* (Krivopisco & Porrin, 2004, p. 5).

47 AN 72AJ/62/I/8, p. 1.

48 Bood (1974), pp. 313–314.

49 AN 72AJ/61/I/21, p. 8.

50 Bourget (1984), p. 294. Because of the unlikely circumstances of Favé's

escape, he was suspected of complicity, arrested in 1945 and imprisoned for three years. The case was eventually dismissed (Bourget, 1984, p. 298, n. 2).

51 AN 72AJ/62/I/8, p. 1.

52 Bourget (1984), p. 298.

53 Krivopisco & Porrin (2004), pp. 14–15. It is sometimes said that those killed were 'adolescents'; although many were in their early twenties, the eldest victim of the massacre at the Cascades was Luigi Vannini, aged forty-five.

54 Pauwels (2004), pp. 117–118.

55 AN 72AJ/71/IX/7, p. 6. For an account of the experience of USAAF bomber pilot Roy Allen, who met 'Captain Jack', was arrested in the 11 August raid on the boulevard Sébastopol and was deported to Buchenwald on 15 August, see Childers (2004), pp. 198–249. I found Childers' work hard to use as it is impossible to distinguish fact from imagination; he admits: 'in telling the story, I have relied on literary devices more commonly associated with fiction' (p. 421). Masquerading as an Intelligence Service officer seems to have been a widespread Gestapo technique. André Amar, Jacqueline Mesnil-Amar's husband, was arrested following a similar ploy by the Germans (Chaigneau, 1981, p. 160). Dufresne (Massiet, 1945, pp. 58–60) describes his encounters with a 'Marquis de Wiet', a corpulent man who claimed to be an Intelligence Service agent and offered to supply the FFI staff officer with hundreds of machine guns. Dufresne smelt a rat and did not go through with the contact; de Wiet turned out to be a Gestapo agent.

56 Bourget (1984), pp. 300–301.

57 Bourget (1984), p. 299; Krivopisco & Porrin (2004), pp. 32–3.

58 In 1949, a commemorative plaque was placed at 65 rue Chardon-Lagache, where the bodies of all those killed were gathered on 17 August. It stated that they had been 'shot by order of General von Choltitz'. In 1966 it was replaced by a version that read 'shot on the orders of the Gestapo'. There are conflicting accounts of this change: Krivopisco & Porrin (2004), p. 34 state that it was made 'on the sole instructions of the Prefect of the Seine, Maurice Papon' (despite his elevated post-war position, Papon had been a notorious collaborator in Bordeaux; he was finally convicted for his involvement of the deportation of the Jews in 1998). This contains at least a minor error: Papon was never Prefect of the Seine, rather he was the Prefect of Police in Paris (1958–67). More seriously, Bourget (1984), p. 303 shows that von Choltitz himself took the initiative to get the inscription altered in 1963, and that the Prefect of the Seine, the socialist Raymond Haas-Picard, who was in post 1963–6, made the decision. There is no evidence that von Choltitz directly and specifically ordered the killings. However, although the general order to shoot 'terrorists' had been adopted before von Choltitz's arrival, he had clearly upped the stakes with his declarations on 15 August: 'All means, including the most harsh, that can repress disorder, will be utilised ... Everything will be done to maintain order and to pitilessly repress disorder.' (Cazaux, 1975, pp. 131–2.)

CHAPTER 6

1 Galtier-Boissière (1944), pp. 253–4.
2 Institut Hoover (1958), p. 1295.
3 Tournoux (1982), p. 318.
4 All details from von Arnim (1995), pp. 241–2.
5 ETHINT 67, p. 18. See also Carell (1962), p. 259, and Speidel (1971), p. 137. Speidel – who greeted Model at La Roche-Guyon – states that Model arrived on the afternoon of 16 August.
6 Details from Speidel (1971), p. 137 and Carell (1962), pp. 259–60.
7 Nordling (2002), p. 100.
8 AN 72AJ/62/VIII/3, p. 2.
9 AN 72AJ/61/I/13. Note that the Santé prison was not under German control.
10 Nordling (2002), p. 101.
11 All details from AN 72AJ/62/VIII/3; Nordling (2002), pp. 100–101; von Choltitz (1969), pp. 229–30. The accounts are reasonably concordant.
12 Nordling (2002), p. 104; Riffaud (1994), pp. 115–116.
13 Nordling (2002), p. 105–106.
14 Details of the convoy from www.bddm.org [accessed July 2012]. See also Nordling (2002), p. 109.
15 AN 72AJ/42/IV/3, p. 4.
16 Noguères & Degliame-Fouché (1981), p. 465.
17 Felstiner (1987), p. 37. Brunner had left earlier in the day, but had unexpectedly returned to collect something he had forgotten. It is not known what this was. Nordling (2002), p. 105; Rajsfus (1996), p. 357.
18 Rajsfus (1996), p. 357.
19 For a novelised account of this journey, based on eye-witness accounts and reproducing some archival material, see Chaigneau (1981). The details of the train and of those who escaped are taken from this source.
20 Bachelier (1996), section 7-3-12.
21 Rajsfus (1996), p. 358.
22 Only those whose electricity supply escaped the power cuts would have immediately noticed this. There were no transistor radios, so wireless sets relied either on mains electricity or – for the lucky few – massive accumulator batteries. For a discussion of the way that music was used as part of the Radio Paris propaganda broadcasts, see Méadel (2000).
23 Rebatet (1976), p. 186.
24 All details, including the unflattering portraits, from Hérold-Paquis (1948), pp. 19–21.
25 Cazaux (1975), pp. 138–9.
26 *Le Parisien Libéré* 22 August 1944. Rebatet was the author of the article attacking Laval that had led *Je Suis Partout* to be banned by Vichy (AN 72AJ/54/II/10, p. 15).
27 Rebatet (1976), p. 186.
28 Rebatet (1976), p. 186.

29 Rol-Tanguy & Bourderon (1994), p. 181.
30 The first Rol knew about this declaration was when he saw it posted on a wall. He did not sign it, and he certainly did not write it. It was full of exaggerations and inaccuracies (Rol was not 'Commander of Greater Paris'; 'hundreds' of prisoners had not been shot at Fresnes; the Germans were not taking hostages in each neighbourhood; the Germans were not putting about the rumour that Paris would be declared an open city; and so on), and the brutal call to 'get a Hun' had not hitherto been seen in Resistance statements. The tone and the manner of publication suggest strongly that this was produced by the Communist Party leaders of the FTP – Ouzoulias and/or Tillon – with the assumption that their comrade would agree. This probably explains why Rol seems to have been remarkably incurious about where it came from – several decades later he said that he agreed with its thrust, so he assumed responsibility for it. See Bourderon (2004), pp. 372–5 for a discussion of the affair.
31 Rebatet (1976), p. 187. The original French was '*Qu'est-ce qu'on fout là?*'
32 Pryce-Jones (1981), p. 248.
33 See Dunan (1945) for a description of what it was like creating a newspaper from scratch in the days that followed.
34 This is taken from Dutourd's self-deprecating, amusing and probably unreliable memoir written in 1964 (Dutourd, 1983, pp. 11–12).
35 Cazaux (1975), p. 144.
36 Pasteur Vallery-Radot (1966), p. 279.
37 BAM VV, 17.8.
38 Tuffrau (2002), p. 76 describes the scene, which he witnessed.
39 Pryce-Jones (1981), p. 256.
40 AN 72AJ/61/II/8.
41 Tuffrau (2002), p. 77. On 15 August, writer André Thérive recorded in his diary that he had seen a car carrying 'three young men in beachwear – orange or red trousers – bearded and with long hair like Bohemians; their luggage included skis (despite the heat) and a live bear in a cage'. He insisted 'I have not made this up' and 'in the future I'll be accused of lying or of having had a fantastic dream' (Thérive, 1948, pp. 212–213). What should we make of this account – is it true, or not? How could we know?
42 Galtier-Boissière (1944), p. 254.
43 Bobkowski (1991), p. 606.
44 Pryce-Jones (1981), p. 242.
45 Pryce-Jones (1981), p. 243.
46 AN 72AJ/62/I/8, pp. 1–2.
47 Dubois (1944), pp. 41–2. Similar scenes were played out outside the offices of the Sicherheitsdienst (security police) on avenue Foch, while on the place de la Concorde, food was thrown to passing soldiers from the Navy stores (Martens & Nagel, 2006, pp. 519–520).
48 AN 72AJ/42/IV/3, p. 3.
49 For example, Cazaux (1975), p. 144.
50 Renoult & West (2008), p. 143.

51 Rol-Tanguy & Bourderon (1994), p. 181.
52 The participants have left three accounts of this meeting: Taittinger's self-serving memoir, which contains extensive and unlikely verbatim accounts (Taittinger, 1948, pp. 160–9); von Choltitz's version, which is only a paragraph long (von Choltitz, 1969, pp. 227–8); and the diary of Maurice Toesca (Toesca, 1975, pp. 321–4). They are generally concordant.
53 Cazaux (1975), pp. 131–2.
54 Toesca (1975), p. 323.
55 Dubois (1944), p. 41.
56 Boegner (1992), p. 281.
57 Patin (1994), pp. 37–8.
58 Léautaud (1946), p. 37.
59 Denis (1963) reproduces the minutes of most of the CPL meetings. The meeting of 17 August is not among them, but according to Noguères & Degliame-Fouché (1981), p. 463, the minutes consist of no more than two sentences.
60 Rol later claimed that the question of arms was discussed at this meeting (Rol-Tanguy & Bourderon, 1994, p. 194). Hamon's apparently contemporaneous diary (AN 72AJ/42/IV/3, p. 5) suggests that this discussion in fact occurred on 18 August (see chapter 7).
61 Dansette (1946), p. 163; Denis (1963), p. 97; AN 72AJ/42/IV/3, p. 2. Dansette (1946) p. 163 claims that COMAC also met on 17 August; the date was in fact 16 August (see chapter 5).
62 Frustratingly, there are no records of this meeting of the CNR Bureau in the Archives Nationales in Paris, or in the various works dealing with the history of the CNR, beyond the brief account in Dansette (1946), pp. 163–4.
63 AN 72AJ/42/IV/3, p. 3.
64 See Parodi's brief summary of the meeting in his message to Algiers, AN 72AJ/235/II/300. The meeting also put the finishing touches to a CNR Action Programme (AN 72AJ/49/III/32) that called for extensive nationalisations and social reforms and ordered the FFI immediately to launch attacks on the Germans. Most importantly, the programme publicly complained about the lack of arms and called on the Free French to do everything possible to remedy the situation. It had no effect. Although adopted on 17 August, the Action Programme had gone through a very long gestation, traces of which remained. For example, the CNR called on the FFI to cooperate with the Allies 'in case of Allied landings'. At Champigny in the south-western suburbs, Albert Ouzoulias called a meeting of all the local FTP leaders, ordering them to seize vehicles, adapt them for battle, and prepare for the insurrection (Ouzoulias, 1972, p. 424).
65 Messages 52–5 of 17 August 1944, AN 72AJ/235/II/299–302.
66 Dansette (1946), p. 167.
67 A colourful account of the journey can be found in Closon (1974), p. 213–26.
68 AN 72AJ/235/II/303.

69 Institut Hoover (1958), pp. 296–7.

70 AN 72AJ/61/I/14, p. 2.

71 Touche (1946), pp. 84–5.

72 Penrose (2005), p. 71. This page also shows Miller's photograph of the cyclists, together with their bicycle. A few days later, Colonel Rol's headquarters was moved into a bunker that had emergency power generated by bicycles (see chapter 10, n. 40). The power-generating cyclists in the French animated film _Les Triplettes de Belleville_ (2003) were not entirely fictional.

73 All these letters are reproduced in Dansette (1946), pp. 466–9. The respective part of the letter to Bouffet and Bussière reads:

> The government has been constrained by the Occupation Authority to leave Paris, and the strongest protests that I made to the German Ambassador have had no effect. I therefore instruct the Prefect of the Seine and the Prefect of Police, each in their relevant fields, to take all appropriate dispositions in order to ensure public order, food supplies, transport and, more generally, to deal with all the questions that affect the material and moral life of the Parisian population to which I remain so attached. I also entrust you to welcome the Allied military authorities and to represent the French government to them.

74 Laval's daughter, Josée de Chambrun, has written her own very personal account of this last day. Institut Hoover (1958), pp. 1078–81.

75 Taittinger (1948), p. 159.

76 Galtier-Boissière (1944), pp. 253–4.

77 Bourget (1984) pp. 272–3. This account is based on contemporary reports by emergency workers.

78 Cazaux (1975), p. 144.

79 Crémieux-Brilhac (1976), p. 180.

80 The chronic lack of weapons was revealed when the regional FFI drew up a plan for protecting the ten key power stations in the Paris region. The idea was to protect each site with 100 _résistants_, who would stop any attempt by the Germans to sabotage the installation. The FFI estimated that for each site they would need three machine guns, three pistols and fifty grenades. In reality, this level of armament would do nothing to prevent German troops from doing their worst, but as the FFI admitted, they could not supply even such a meagre level of weaponry (Massiet, 1945, p. 119).

81 This formulation was agreed after an argument between Georges Boris in London and de Gaulle's office in Algiers. De Gaulle's initial instruction to Paris workers read: 'Return to work immediately and in an orderly fashion as soon as the Allies arrive' (Crémieux-Brilhac, 2010, p. 297). Boris was concerned that de Gaulle's formulation gave the impression that the Free French feared the working class and that they wanted to stop any strike movements as soon as possible. (Both of these 'impressions' were basically true.) Boris felt that calling for an 'immediate and orderly' return to work seemed condescending and reactionary – the population would quite naturally end up taking a few days off in the explosion of joy that would follow

liberation. De Gaulle's response to this criticism is not known, but the next day Algiers adopted Boris's more vague formulation – 'Return to work as soon as the Allied forces arrive'. Jean-Louis Crémieux-Brilhac, Boris's friend, comrade and biographer, points out that Boris is mentioned only once in the three volumes of de Gaulle's war memoirs, and suggests that this was a consequence of de Gaulle's irritation at this criticism (Crémieux-Brilhac, 2010, p. 298). This was partly a storm in a teacup, but it also revealed a very important truth: the Free French were extremely concerned about workers going on strike, no matter how useful that might be in military terms, because they feared the strikers would not go back to work. And that was not at all the kind of liberated France that de Gaulle wanted to see.

CHAPTER 7

1 Crémieux-Brilhac (1976), p. 184.
2 Tuffrau (2002), p. 79. Daniel Boisdon also walked down the boulevard Saint-Michel, and noticed that a cinema and nearby several shops were riddled with bullet-holes. He was told that a convoy had shot at the passers-by and people coming out of the cinema, and that a woman had been killed. AN 72AJ/62/III/4, p. 17.
3 Cazaux (1975), p. 148; Dubois (1944), p. 47.
4 The full message reads:

> More details Paris situation: many bloody incidents provoked by excitement of population, nervous German troops, and Gestapo provocations. Sporadic shooting last night, notably Place Odéon, Place Médicis, in front of the Gare du Nord, Boulevard de la Chapelle, Boulevard Barbès. Place de la République SS fired machine-guns, anti-aircraft guns. Shots fired at German troops on Boulevard Bonne Nouvelle; latter burned house . . . and café . . . All those trying to flee were machine-gunned. Number of other victims rue Saint-Denis and Faubourg Saint-Denis. Rue Rivoli this morning, for no reason, German truck opened fire killing woman. (Chevrillon, 1995, p. 158.)

Chevrillon was one of Parodi's coders; against all the rules, she kept some key messages, which she reproduced in her memoirs. Some of these messages (including this one) are not present in the Archives Nationales collection AN 72AJ/235/II.
5 AN 72AJ/234/VIII/3, p. 11.
6 Galtier-Boissière (1944), p. 257.
7 AN 72AJ/62/III/4, p. 17. Victor Veau reported hearing explosions at the same time (BAM VV, 18.8).
8 AN 72AJ/62/IV/2, p. 183, AN 72AJ/62/IV/2, p. 186.
9 Benoît-Guyod (1962), p. 285.
10 AN 72AJ/62/IV/2/p. 236.
11 Bourget & Lacretelle (1980), pp. 188–90; Ouzoulias (1972), p. 425;

L'Humanité 23 August 2004. The latter article reproduces the account of Georges Valbon, who was aged twenty when he participated in the events. He recalled that two German Tiger tanks were sent against the Mairie. The events are celebrated in a mural painting by Charles Fouqueray in the council chamber of the Mairie de Montreuil. Some of the portraits used by Fouqueray for his composition are taken from photographs of the insurrection in Paris rather than Montreuil.

12 Cazaux (1975), p. 147. Taittinger discussed the situation with a delegation of the strikers (Taittinger, 1948, p. 182). According to a CGT internal report of the demonstration (presumably written by Véry – reproduced as Annexe VIII in Cogniot et al., 1974, p. 237) there were 5–6000 people present. Parodi sent a message to London describing the demonstration: 'Towards noon in front of Hotel de Ville, demonstration by postal clerks on strike, marching, singing Marseillaise, Internationale, carrying French, English, American flags.' (Chevrillon, 1995, p. 158). The CGT report made no mention of the 'Internationale' being sung.

13 Cogniot et al. (1974), p. 237.

14 Taittinger (1948), pp. 182–3.

15 Culmann (1985), p. 281.

16 BAM VV, 18.8. Senator Jacques Bardoux, who was continually and ineffectually active in the background throughout August 1944, trying to find a political solution that would give pride of place to the Senate, wrote in his diary that he met with a number of senators and 'the "political delegate" of de Gaulle' (Bardoux, 1958, p. 348). Parodi was de Gaulle's political delegate, but I can find no corroboration of his presence, and the issues discussed – primarily the exchange of letters between Abetz and Laval of the previous evening – do not seem likely to have interested him.

17 BAM VV, 18.8. One of Yves Cazaux's contacts at the Préfecture at Versailles told him that in the morning Free French army officers, part of Allied staff headquarters, came to discuss with the Versailles civil servants the state of food supplies in the locality (Cazaux, 1975, p. 146). While this may have been true, it seems highly unlikely – the 2e DB was still 150 km from Versailles. The key point is that Cazaux believed it to be true.

18 Dubois (1944), p. 48.

19 Dubois (1944), p. 49.

20 Pierquin (1983), p. 131.

21 Dubois (1944), p. 50; Boegner (1992), pp. 281–2.

22 Greiner & Schramm (1982), p. 347.

23 Martens & Nagel (2006), pp. 519–520.

24 ETHINT 67.

25 A-968, p. 14.

26 Ritgen (1995), p. 128; Beevor (2009), p. 469. Beevor (2009) highlights the difficulty of knowing exactly what was happening inside the pocket, in particular because of the exaggerated claims of the USAAF and RAF, which claimed 'preposterously high' rates of destruction of German vehicles (p. 466).

27 Buffetaut (2004), pp. 12–17, reproduces photographs of German troops using ferries, canoes and even a home-made raft to get across the river. Strikingly, no vehicle heavier than a small lorry can be seen.

28 Renoult & West (2008), pp. 163–4.

29 B-728, p. 5.

30 A photograph and transcription of this order are in Renoult & West (2008), p. 150.

31 Ballarin (2010). The FFI fighters were Christian Pouillard and Maurice Cayen. Ballarin lists only five men; the plaque on the side of the RN 307 gives the names of eight men.

32 Renoult & West (2008), pp. 163–6.

33 AN 72AJ/62/IV/2/p. 69.

34 AN 72AJ/62/IV/2/p. 257.

35 Renoult & West (2008), p. 158.

36 Renoult & West (2008), p. 172. This source includes an impressive photograph of the tank blocking the street.

37 ETHINT 67; Bayerlein describes the 'six' tanks as having been part of the 12th SS Panzer Division 'Hitler Youth'. However, this group was still trapped in the Falaise pocket on 18 August. For Renoult & West (2008), p. 174, there were a dozen Tiger 2 tanks from 503rd Heavy Panzer Battalion, commanded by Captain Walter Scherf. Despite the discrepancies in the details, I have assumed these two events are one and the same. According to Chef d'escadron Vigne of the FFI sous-secteur Nord 2, in the evening of 18 August, the Resistance attacked and destroyed a Tiger tank on the quai des Célestins (ML Vigne). I have seen no other reference to this event.

38 Cazaux (1975), p. 148.

39 Cazaux (1975), p. 151.

40 Cazaux (1975), p. 150. For details of the Tiger tank, see von Senger und Etterlin (1969) pp. 68–73.

41 B-015, p. 16; B-611, p. 16. Pictures of the devastation caused by the explosion can be seen in Renoult & West (2008), p. 160. The exact cause is not known; it has been suggested that the explosion was not due to the Panzerfaust demonstration, but rather because of the accidental detonation of a lorry-load of explosives (Renoult & West, 2008, p. 159).

42 Model & Bradley (1991), p. 249.

43 Blumenson (1996), p. 518.

44 B-741, p. 9.

45 Lankford (1991), p. 154.

46 Navarre (1978), p. 299.

47 Navarre (1978), p. 299; AN 72AJ/59/IV/2, p. 80. Le Goff might have been the 'Lieutenant P' who was brought back from Le Mans by Bernard de Billy on his motorbike on 16 August, but the exact identity of the men is confused (see chapter 5 note 17). In de Saint-Hilaire's detailed account of the adventure (Navarre, 1978, pp. 298–301), Le Goff is presented as his 'bodyguard'. The documents carried by de Saint-Hilaire were presumably those referred to by the head of FFI regional intelligence, L'Arcouest, in his letter

Notes to pages 133–136

to Rol-Tanguy dated 18 August 1944, although as L'Arcouest refers to a '*motorcyclist de Bourgoin*' (Rol-Tanguy & Bourderon, 1994, p. 182) this may indicate a different mission. One of the documents, relating to a detailed description of the German tanks in the Paris regions, is reproduced in Rol-Tanguy & Bourderon (1994), p. 183. For an account of the Kléber-Marco circuit's work by de Saint-Hilaire, including this expedition, see www.aassdn.org/xlde11532.htm [Accessed July 2011].

48 An amateur film of Auneau shot at the time by Jacques Dagron shows US soldiers carrying vast bouquets of flowers, and the corks popping on many bottles of champagne. See memoire.ciclic.fr/1394-avant-programme-liberation-a-auneau [accessed June 2011]. All other details from Navarre (1978), pp. 298–9.

49 Fourcade (1972), vol. 2, pp. 287–9. The story is somewhat unbelievable (which does not make it untrue): they were stopped by a German patrol who searched their luggage, but thankfully did not look inside the neatly folded pair of grey trousers which contained the precious documents. Nevertheless, the soldiers were suspicious and took the two men off to a nearby house where they were locked up in a desultory fashion – the Germans were not too concerned with their prisoners, leaving them alone in the house, with the motorbike at the front door, so they apparently simply walked out and got back on the bike.

50 Villate (1958), p. 61.

51 Bourderon (2004), p. 378. The aircraft may have been part of the group that was engaged in the dogfight over Rambouillet, only twenty-five kilometres away. There is a monument at the side of the D837 just north of Bonvilliers to mark the site.

52 de Gaulle (1983), p. 295.

53 de Boissieu (1994).

54 Because of the postal strike, municipal workers had to be paid in cash rather than by bank transfer. This was announced in a duplicated letter from Jacques Romazzotti, the chief accountant of the council (AN 72AJ/62/V/5, p. 11). It seems surprising that people were habitually paid by bank transfer at this time; this may have applied only to certain sectors of the workforce.

55 Durand (1968), pp. 549–50.

56 Chevandier (2002), p. 214.

57 de Saint-Pierre (1945), p. 42.

58 BAM VV, 18.8.

59 Mesnil-Amar (2009), p. 106. This entry is dated 19 August, but a number of the events she refers to (the liberation of Drancy the day before, the announcement of a curfew) make it clear that the entry was written on 18 August. Similarly, the entry for 18 August describes scenes of German departure *en masse* and has her pedalling, carefree, around Paris in the late evening, when there would have been a curfew, but there would not have been on 17 August. I have therefore used the appropriate historical date for each entry, rather than that given in this version of her diary.

60 Mesnil-Amar (2009), p. 106–107.

61 Rajsfus (1996), p. 358. Rajsfus suggests that the failure to allow everyone just to leave was 'extremely revealing of the stupid and sordid behaviour of the French gendarmes, even after the departure of the Germans' (Rajsfus, 1996, p. 358, n. 7).

62 ANACR (n.d.), pp. 28–34.

63 Riffaud (1994), p. 134.

64 AN 72AJ/61/I/14, p. 2.

65 Barat (1945), pp. 31–3.

66 Dansette (1946), p. 164, n. 2.

67 AN 72AJ/42/IV/3, p. 5; Noguères & Degliame-Fouché (1981), p. 470. Dansette (1946) says the discussion at the CPL involved 'a violent debate' (p. 164). However, Hamon's unpublished diary, which was written at the time (Hamon, 1991, p. 180), says that Rol 'replied very loyally to my question' (AN 72AJ/42/IV/3, p. 5), which suggests the discussion was relatively calm. The figure of 1000 weapons is taken from the entry for 18 August in Léo Hamon's unpublished diary, which was apparently written that evening. It is often said that Rol claimed they had 600 weapons (e.g. Dansette, 1946, p. 166; Bourderon, 2004, p. 376); I have been unable to find an original source for this. Dansette (1946) presents the exchange as though from the minutes, although these have never been published nor have I been able to find them in any archives. Denis (1963), the only book on the activity of the CPL, provides no further information (see p. 99) and seems to base its account on Dansette. Hamon later also recalled the figure of 600 (Noguères & Degliame-Fouché, 1981, p. 470); he even did so in his memoirs, which were partly based on his diary (Hamon, 1991, p. 185). In an interview, André Tollet also recalled Rol talking of 600 weapons, although he added: 'That was more or less the figure. He wasn't too sure himself.' (Crémieux, 1971, p. 50.) (Note that Tollet also recalled the meeting as taking place on 17 August.) In the absence of any more precise source than Dansette (1946) for the figure of 600, I have followed the only contemporary figure I can find, that of 1000, contained in Hamon's diary. It seems unlikely that Hamon would not recall the precise figure when he wrote his diary. It can be assumed that 1000 would be an upper estimate for a figure that was essentially unknowable with any degree of precision. The description by Collins & Lapierre (1965) pp. 96–7 of this meeting does not correspond to any of the contemporaneous accounts, and appears fanciful.

68 Cogniot et al. (1974), p. 196. This 'round table' discussion by Communist Party militants recalling their activity during the liberation of Paris should be read critically, but there is no reason to doubt Rol-Tanguy's memory on this point.

69 I have been unable to find a copy of the CGT-CFTC poster. The description of it is taken from Dansette (1946), p. 164. The FFI and Communist Party posters are reproduced in Dansette (1946), pp. 480–2. Dansette states that these posters were actually put up on 18 August, and considers that it is 'remarkable' that the CPL did not discuss them at its meeting on the

afternoon of that day (Dansette, 1946, p. 164). In fact, there is no evidence that they were actually published on 18 August; the earliest reference to the communist poster is in an entry by Paul Tuffrau from lunchtime on 19 August (Tuffrau, 2002, p. 81). Rol-Tanguy makes clear that although he wrote his declaration on 18 August, it was not pasted up until the night of 18–19 August (Rol-Tanguy & Bourderon, 1994, p. 195). This is also reported by Duclos (1970), p. 201. According to Dansette, Carrel alluded to the fact that the communist poster was 'ready' but 'no doubt he did not know that at that very moment it was being posted on the walls of Paris' (Dansette, 1946, p. 164, n. 2); it seems most likely that Carrel was telling the truth.

70 AN 72AJ/42/IV/3, p. 6.

71 AN 72AJ/235/II/333.

72 Dansette (1946), p. 483. There is a partial and occasionally inaccurate translation of this message in Collins & Lapierre (1965), p. 95.

73 AN 72AJ/235/II/306–11. The fourth part of the message was partially garbled, rendering the name of a person or a group unreadable (AN 72AJ/235/II/309).

74 AN 72AJ/235/II/306–8.

75 It is not clear who this refers to. 'Léandre' was the pseudonym of Roger Herlaut, a policeman who was a member of the Communist Party (Rudolph, 2010 p. 66) but it seems more likely that Parodi is referring to a Resistance leader, perhaps Georges Bidault.

76 AN 72AJ/235/II/305.

77 Auroy (2008), p. 316.

78 Galtier-Boissière (1944), p. 257.

79 Renoult & West (2008), p. 157.

80 Bood (1974), p. 316.

81 AN 72AJ/62/IV/2, p. 196.

82 Groult & Groult (1965), p. 300.

CHAPTER 8

1 Roy (1944), p. 18.

2 AN 72AJ/61/I/4b and AN 72AJ/71/IX/19, p. 2. The occupation of the Préfecture was decided the night before in Montreuil (AN 72AJ/71/IX/5, p. 6); the man behind it was Yves Bayet ('Boucher'), who was in charge of Resistance work in the police, and was a leading member of Honneur de la Police, which was linked to the Socialist Party (AN 72AJ/58/VIII/1, p. 2). One of those involved, Charles Le Nevez, who was a leader of the Police et Patrie group linked to the right-wing OCM, later claimed that unsuccessful attempts were made to prevent Police et Patrie from being involved in the morning's events (AN 72AJ/71/IX/5, p. 7). It has been claimed that the operation had in fact begun nearly two hours earlier, when a few dozen policemen took over the key command points of the Préfecture – see the list of the number of men needed to take over the Préfecture reproduced in

Anonymous (1965), p. 119. This version of events is also presented in d'Astier (1965), p. 185, and it may be true, but there is no contemporary evidence.

3 Campaux (1945), pp. 27–8.

4 Bourderon (2004), p. 385. Rol claimed that some sections of the police had been ordered to end their strike (Crémieux, 1971, p. 37; Bourderon, 2004, p. 385). Although the only evidence for this comes from Rol, he reported this at the time, as shown by an initial draft of his end-of-day report (Bourderon, 2004, p. 393). It is not known who gave this order or why, but it was clearly stopped by Rol's intervention, and the police remained in civilian clothes.

5 Crémieux (1971), pp. 37–8.

6 In fact it was the *bureaux* – the small executive committees – of the two committees that met. The meeting took place at 41 rue de Bellechasse, off the boulevard Saint-Germain; there is a plaque marking the site. It is generally claimed that the CNR and the CPL met in separate rooms (e.g. Noguères & Degliame-Fouché, 1981, p. 471). This is partially true; Léo Hamon's diary makes it clear that the two committees briefly met to recognise their fundamental agreement on support for the insurrection before going to separate rooms to draw up their respective declarations (AN 72AJ/42/IV/3, p. 6).

7 AN 72AJ/42/IV/3, p. 6. For the CPL declaration see Denis (1963), pp. 99–100.

8 Campaux (1945), p. 68.

9 The exact status of the tricolour flag under the occupation is complex; although it disappeared from the occupied zone, it was officially used in a number of regions and was also often part of the iconography of the Vichy regime (Dalisson, 2002; Vinen, 2006, p. 96). One exception to the disappearance of the tricolour from Paris was the Ministry of the Interior on place Beauvau; from early 1943 the tricolour had flown from this building, following the request of the Vichy ambassador to the occupying forces, de Brinon (Dubois, 1944, p. 60). Furthermore, when Pétain visited Paris in April 1944, the tricolour flew from the Hôtel de Ville for the first time. This can be seen on the contemporary newsreel (see *The Eye of Vichy*, 1993). On 1 July 1944 at a Milice swearing-in ceremony in the Ecole Militaire, attended by SS chief Oberg, there was a massive tricolour flag (see photographs LAP-27248 and HRL-524039 at www.parisenimages.fr [accessed July 2012]). Despite these exceptions, the power of the unofficial appearance of the flag in Paris on 19 August 1944 is undeniable.

10 Cazaux (1975), pp. 152–3.

11 Footitt & Simmonds (1988), pp. 127–8. For Parodi's complaint, which was expressed the following day, see Courtin (1994), p. 30.

12 Valland (1997), pp. 202–203. In fact, many of those treasures had already been stolen by the Germans, or were in safe storage, ready to be shifted to Germany.

13 Tuffrau (2002), p. 81.

14 Groult & Groult (1965), p. 300.

15 Tuffrau (2002), pp. 80–1.

16 Vilain (1945), p. 19.

17 Grunberg (2001), p. 340.

18 AN 72AJ/42/IV/3, p. 7.

19 Liebling (1944), p. 44.

20 AN 72AJ/42/IV/3, p. 9. They also needed cigarettes and wine, Hamon was told.

21 Brécard's letter is reproduced in Massiet (1945), p. 126. For a discussion of the significance of this manoeuvre for Vichy, see Bourget (1984), pp. 324–5.

22 Bourget (1984), p. 325.

23 Taittinger's original draft and the printed version are both reproduced in Taittinger (1948), pp. 190–1. Taittinger claimed that 'the Resistance' insisted that the section relating to Paris being an 'open city' be removed because they wanted to provoke a conflict and did not want the Germans to leave peacefully (Taittinger, 1948, p. 188).

24 Massiet (1945), pp. 127–8. See Taittinger (1948), pp. 184–5 for an alternative, less detailed, account.

25 Bourget (1984), pp. 317–318. For a slightly different French translation, which changes nothing in terms of the content, see Kriegel-Valrimont (1964), p. 192: 'The commanders of the tactical groups must act without pity in their zone and liquidate all important points of resistance.'

26 von Arnim (1995), pp. 243–4.

27 Campaux (1945), p. 68.

28 Tuffrau (2002), p. 82.

29 Campaux (1945), p. 69.

30 Campaux (1945), p. 44; Thomas (1995), p. 209.

31 Roy (1944), pp. 21–2. For David's fate, see chapter 18.

32 Roy (1944), p. 21.

33 Roy (1944), p. 24.

34 At the time, corned beef was nicknamed 'singe' ('monkey'); Monsieur Barrat also recalled: 'Ever since I have loved "singe", especially with tomato sauce. But it never tastes as good as on 19 August 1944!' See adminet.tv/barrat/liberation.html [accessed July 2012].

35 Roy (1944), p. 22.

36 This was testified by Lambolley, one of the leaders of Police et Patrie, in a 1948 court case brought by Hennequin, Director of the Paris Municipal Police, who claimed that the wine cellar had been pillaged. Berlière & Liaigre (2007), p. 453, n. 405.

37 Maudru (1944), p. 84. The entrance to the Préfecture still bears the scars of the fighting.

38 Campaux (1945), p. 28.

39 www.plaques-commemoratives.org/plaques/ile-de-france/plaque.2006-09-29.0385352623/view [accessed July 2012].

40 Hazard (1998), p. 390.

41 Roy (1944), p. 21; Fournier & Eymard (2009), pp. 17–18. There are a number of photographs of these incidents, some of which can be timed precisely because of the presence of clocks in the images.

42 For a dramatic photograph of this, taken by someone who lived nearby, see the cover of Aury (1945). In his end-of-day report, Rol claimed that a German tank was destroyed at the place Saint-Michel (Rol-Tanguy & Bourderon, 1994, p. 204). There is no corroborating evidence for this, although Odette Lainville's husband Robert telephoned from the Préfecture and told her that the Resistance had just destroyed two tanks (de Saint-Pierre, 1945, p. 52). It seems most likely that the destroyed lorry became a tank in the re-telling; this can be taken as an indication of the confusion and lack of reliable information that predominated. Surprisingly, Rol-Tanguy & Bourderon (1994) uncritically repeat this claim (p. 219).

43 Tuffrau (2002), p. 81.

44 Sartre's report is reproduced in Campaux (1945), p. 122. The same story was also told by Simone de Beauvoir, who was with Sartre (de Beauvoir, 1965, p. 593).

45 There are no accurate sources for the number of dead and wounded. Amouroux (1988), p. 650, n. 2, claims that on the first day of the insurrection 125 French people were killed and 479 were wounded; 40 Germans were killed and 70 wounded. However, there is no source given, so it is impossible to verify these figures.

46 Levisse-Touzé (1994a), p. 275.

47 A drawing of the building can be see in Maudru (1944), opposite p. 174. It looks pretty similar today.

48 All details from Barat (1945), pp. 42–4. There is a plaque to the memory of Fred Palacio, aged twenty-one, at the junction of the boulevard Saint-Germain and the rue de Buci. FFI commander Dufresne was 'deeply moved' by Palacio's death (Massiet, 1945, p. 134).

49 Castetbon (2004), p. 174. Alexandre Massiani was killed near the statue of Corneille that is on the northern side of the Panthéon (the Germans had removed the statue; it has since been replaced). There is a plaque on the base of the urn in front of the Panthéon to commemorate his death.

50 www.liberation-de-paris.gilles-primout.fr/tquantin.htm [accessed July 2012].

51 BAM VV, 19.8.

52 AN 72AJ/62/I/4, pp. 1–8 and AN 72AJ/62/I/4, pp. 9–12.

53 Bood (1974), p. 317. 'Exciting' is in English in the text.

54 Vilain (1945), p. 9.

55 Auroy (2008), pp. 318–319.

56 AN 72AJ/61/I/14, p. 3.

57 Touche (1946), p. 90. The precise timing of Jean-Claude's detailed, but brief, account of the fighting does not coincide with those of the other eye-witnesses cited here, but the overall description is similar.

58 AN 72AJ/62/III/3, p. 1.

59 Auroy (2008), pp. 318–319.

60 Mesnil-Amar (2009), p. 109.

61 Bourget & Lacretelle (1959), p. 189.

62 Jay (n.d.), pp. 67–70; Dansette (1946), pp. 184–5. In his memoir, written

in 1970, Jay stated that Dansette 'describes the course of events [in Neuilly] correctly' (Jay, n.d., p. 68).

63 Cazaux (1975), p. 157. In Chapter 7 of his *History of the Russian Revolution*, Leon Trotsky underlined a similarly symbolic moment, in which a protester ducked under the horse of a Cossack, confident that it was safe: 'The revolution does not choose its paths: it made its first steps toward victory under the belly of a Cossack's horse.'

64 Massiet (1945), p. 133. Each of the twenty arrondissements was divided up into four *quartiers* (literally, quarters) or neighbourhoods.

65 Touche (1946), p. 88.

66 Bourget (1984), pp. 321–2.

67 Benoît-Guyod (1962), p. 19.

68 Dubois (1944), pp. 54–5.

69 AN 72AJ/62/III/4, p. 20.

70 de Saint-Pierre (1945), p. 46.

71 A-968, p. 14.

72 Beevor (2009), p. 468.

73 Carell (1962), p. 262.

74 A-968, pp. 14–15.

75 NA GRGG 183, p. 6.

76 Renoult & West (2008), p. 182.

77 B-741, p. 10.

78 Renoult & West (2008), p. 199.

79 Hinsley (1988), p. 368.

80 On 31 August Hitler recorded a rambling conversation about von Kluge's suicide, in which he complained bitterly that he had given von Kluge extra medals and money, and stated that he was convinced that the field marshal was about to go over to the Allies: 'It's like a western thriller ... If it became known that Field Marshal Kluge was planning to lead the entire army in the West to surrender and himself wanted to go over to the enemy, that might perhaps not lead to a breakdown of morale of the German people but it would at least make them despise their Army, So now I'd rather keep my mouth shut about it. We have merely told the generals that he committed suicide. He did commit suicide ... Actually he was waiting for the English patrol which ... they missed each other.' Warlimont (1964), pp. 454–5.

81 Speidel (1971), p. 138.

82 See Kershaw (2011) for a chilling study of why the Germans did not surrender.

83 Naville (1950c).

84 Nordling (2002), pp. 111–112.

85 See Rol's end-of-day report reproduced in Rol-Tanguy & Bourderon (1994), pp. 203–204. Several decades later, Rol recalled that when he found out who Nordling was, he brusquely dismissed him by saying 'he had no reason to be there' (e.g. Crémieux, 1971, p. 38; Bourderon, 2004, p. 386). In his memoirs, Nordling did not mention meeting Rol at all (Nordling, 2002, p. 112). Rol's contemporaneous account simply states that Nordling was present.

86 Nordling (2002), pp. 114–115. In contrast, Swiss consul René Naville reported that whenever he saw von Choltitz during this period, the German commander was always calm and good humoured (Naville, 1950c). Nordling later recalled that von Choltitz's tone had softened as Nordling suggested how bad it would look if the German commander went down in history as the man who destroyed Paris with all its beautiful buildings (Nordling, 2002, p. 116). However, there is nothing in von Choltitz's memoirs or in Nordling's 1946 account of these events to support this version.

87 The two men adopted an order that mobilised all able-bodied men aged eighteen to fifty years old, through which Parodi effectively ceded command to Rol (Rol-Tanguy & Bourderon, 1994, p. 198). By the end of the afternoon an order to this effect was pasted up all over the city. For details of the publication of the order, see Bourderon (2004), p. 388. Rol then returned briefly to the Préfecture where he met the three members of COMAC – Villon, Valrimont and de Vogüé – before returning to his headquarters in the south of the city; by the evening, however, he and his staff had decided to move once again, this time into a safe underground bunker below place Denfert-Rocherau, which had been built before the war to house the military defence of Paris in the event of an air attack (Bourderon, 2004, pp. 392–3).

88 Dansette (1946), pp. 191–2. Thirty years after the events, Parodi gave a briefer description of Ollivier's intervention which, while less alarming in its detail, conveyed the same tone (Crémieux, 1971, p. 47); see also Studer (2003), p. 497.

89 AN 72AJ/42/IV/3, p. 10; Noguères & Degliame-Fouché (1981), p. 476. Earlier that day, Chaban had sent a message to London urging the Free French to demand 'a rapid occupation of Paris. If this is impossible it is necessary first to tell us what you want us to do, and second to warn the population clearly on the BBC in order to avoid a new Warsaw.' (ML Arc.)

90 Chevrillon (1995), pp. 158–9. It is not clear who the 'messenger' sent on 19 August was. Because there is no copy in the 'messages received' file, nor any trace in the register in the Archives Nationales (AN 72AJ/236/I), it is not known when this message arrived in Algiers, if ever. The conspiratorially minded might be excited by the fact that the final pages of the register have been cut out (AN 72AJ/236/I, p. 44).

91 It is striking that just as Rol had not previously met Parodi, this was the first time that Hamon had met Chaban.

92 Rol-Tanguy & Bourderon (1994), p. 197. Interestingly, Rol-Tanguy previously summarised this part of the order as stating that buildings should be occupied 'without holding on whatever the cost' (Anonymous, 1964, p. 61), which is not the same thing. This latter interpretation was accepted by Noguères & Degliame-Fouché (1981) in their discussion of the events of 19 August (pp. 475 and 478). The following day, 20 August, Villon told the CNR that the aim of the insurrection was not to seize buildings, but to harm the enemy (Dansette, 1946, p. 492).

93 This was claimed by *résistant* and policeman Henri Buisson (Rol-Tanguy & Bourderon, 1994, p. 219).

94 All details from Massiet (1945), pp. 147–9.

95 Massiet (1945), p. 147 and Rol-Tanguy & Bourderon (1994), p. 220, respectively.

96 Campaux (1945), p. 29. According to Campaux, it was 'the CNR' that telephoned and ordered the evacuation.

97 The clearest account of this mysterious and, at this distance, undoubtedly unresolvable enigma is to be found in Bourget (1994). Bourget had previously alleged that the person who made the call was the Vichy Prefect of Police, Bussière, who was under arrest (Bourget, 1984, pp. 319–320). In his later analysis Bourget rejects this hypothesis but does not provide another name.

98 Nordling (2002), p. 117.

99 Rol-Tanguy & Bourderon (1994), pp. 220–1.

100 Bourget (1994), p. 246. Roland Pré, who was involved in the negotiations (AN 72AJ/42/IV/3, p. 13) sent the following message to Algiers: 'The Préfecture de Police has been attacked by the Germans since this afternoon. This evening, the German military command threatened to bomb the neighbourhood, then, via the intermediary of the Swedish consul, proposed to stop the attack on the Préfecture, to treat prisoners as soldiers, and to allow the fire brigade to move freely. This proposition is currently being applied, with no end in sight.' (Bourget, 1994, p. 246).

101 Nordling (2002), p. 118.

102 von Choltitz (1969), p. 232 and von Choltitz's account published in *Le Figaro* 10 October 1950. In his memoirs, von Choltitz wrote of the cease-fire: 'I would like to underline the fact that I had no contact with the enemy, that no formal cease-fire was agreed and that I made no agreement of any kind. Furthermore, I had no knowledge, at least officially, of the change that had taken place at the head of the Hôtel de Ville and the other administrations, changes that the French considered as the first steps towards liberation. To sum up, I did nothing more than create a modus vivendi which followed the orders that I had received' (von Choltitz, 1969, p. 232). Von Choltitz also claimed that he had no personal recollection of Bender, and that his aide insisted that he only ever met Bender in the company of Nordling (von Choltitz, 1969, p. 232). In his first description of the cease-fire after the war, Nordling did not refer to anything more than a verbal agreement between himself and von Choltitz (Desfeuilles, 1945, p. 14). For an account of negotiations from within the Préfecture, see Hamon's diary, AN 72AJ/42/IV/3, p. 12.

103 Crémieux (1971), p. 80.

104 Dansette (1946), p. 208.

105 AN 72AJ/42/IV/3, p. 13.

106 Roy (1944), p. 22.

107 de Saint-Pierre (1945), p. 53.

108 BAM VV, 19.8. Professor Veau's friend, Pasteur Vallery-Radot (PVR), shamelessly stole these words when he published his own diary (Pasteur Vallery-Radot, 1966, p. 280). PVR explained that he used Veau's diary to

establish the exact times of events (Pasteur Vallery-Radot, 1966, p. 278, n. 1),
but did not declare that he copied whole sections.
109 Bood (1974), p. 317.

CHAPTER 9

1 Galtier-Boissière (1944), p. 261.
2 Campaux (1945), p. 109. The detail in the rest of this paragraph is from
Hamon's diary: AN 72AJ/42/IV/3, p. 14.
3 AN 72AJ/42/IV/1, p. 209.
4 This description is based on the contemporary accounts by two of the participants – Hamon (AN 72AJ/42/IV/3, pp. 14–16) and Cazaux (1975), pp.
158–60.
5 Taittinger (1948), p. 209. Stéphane, arm in sling, can be seen briefly in
footage of the occupation of the Préfecture in *La Libération de Paris*, at 07:00.
He looks quite debonair.
6 Burton (2001), pp. 90–117.
7 First Lieutenant Graf of the 902nd Regiment recalled: 'The panzers
advanced, followed on a wide front by SPWs [half-tracked armoured vehi-
cles], then numerous vehicles, artillery, trucks. The infantry marched on the
side for security. Enemy tanks and anti-tank guns then opened fire against
our panzers. An armoured duel ensued. Nervously the column sought protection in the hedges ... Then we learned that we were being fired upon
from all sides. Where is the enemy? Who is the enemy?' (Ritgen, 1995, p.
130). For an account of the breakout from the German point of view,
emphasising the bravery of the German Army, see Carell (1962), pp. 262–8.
8 Ritgen (1995), p. 129.
9 Ritgen (1995), p. 129. After the war, Major General Rudolf von Gersdorff
wrote: 'The loss of all the German war diaries makes it very difficult to give
an accurate figure of the German forces which were thus saved from annihilation. Estimates vary between 20,000 and 30,000 men.' (ETHINT 59, p.
5.) Carell (1962) claims that 50,000 Germans broke out, 10,000 were killed
and 40,000 were captured (p. 268).
10 A-968, p. 16.
11 Eisenhower (1948), p. 306.
12 Beevor (2009), p. 471. For the 1500 Polish troops on Mont Ormel, things
were not quite so straightforward: with little fuel and less ammunition, they
were attacked from the east by German forces seeking to relieve the pressure
on their comrades, and had to fight valiantly to survive.
13 Beevor (2009), p. 478. Beevor argues that the Germans were able to get so
many men to safety because Field Marshal Montgomery had been unable to
close the Falaise gap rapidly with British troops alone but had refused
American help. The Germans appear to have been aware of this. After the
war, Major General Rudolf von Gersdorff described the surprising ease with
which his group was able to break out:

> As commander of a task force which had been formed ad hoc, I succeeded in breaking through weak enemy opposition during the early morning of 20 Aug 44 at St Lambert. Subsequently, individual combat teams repeatedly succeeded in breaking through at exactly the same spot ... At the time we were unable to understand why this 'hole' was [not] closed, although we knew that the British-American boundary ran through this area. This had been one of the reasons why the breakthrough was undertaken at this point. (ETHINT 59, p. 5.)

14 German military historian K. J. Müller has stated: 'According to the War Diaries and the archives of Army Group B, the escapees from the Falaise pocket no longer formed coherent units. They were a mass of disorganised soldiers.' (Levisse-Touzé, 1994a, p. 181.)

15 Umbreit (1994), p. 334.

16 Zaloga (2009), p. 42.

17 Roussel (2002).

18 de Gaulle (1956), p. 296.

19 Brissaud (1965), pp. 282–95. Film of Pétain's desultory departure can be seen in *La Mémoire Courte* (1963).

20 Rol-Tanguy & Bourderon (1994), p. 215. For Rol's account, see Rol-Tanguy & Bourderon (1994), p. 223. There is no description of this in Lizé's memoirs (AN 72AJ/61/III/1).

21 Rol-Tanguy & Bourderon (1994), pp. 215–216.

22 The description of the discussions is based on the only contemporary eye-witness account, Léo Hamon's diary (AN 72AJ/42/IV/3, pp. 16–18). Dansette (1946) provides a detailed account, though with no sources. De Saint-Phalle, who had acted as an intermediary between Parodi and Nordling, was apparently also present (Dansette, 1946, p. 215). A cruel view would be that Besse was there as a stooge, and that he played his part.

23 For Parodi's half-hearted justification, see Crémieux (1971), p. 81; Rol's response can be found in Rol-Tanguy & Bourderon (1994), p. 221.

24 During the negotiations with Nordling, which took place in the Swedish consulate on rue d'Anjou in the 8th arrondissement, Hamon initially argued that the only possible agreement would be one that involved the Germans surrendering to the Resistance, and refused to have any direct contact with them. Nordling – an experienced diplomat – pointed out that Hamon's preconditions were unreasonable, and that it would be clear to everyone that the Resistance was victorious because they held the public buildings and the Germans had made a deal with them. During these discussions, Nordling was repeatedly interrupted by telephone calls from the Resistance, telling him about attacks by German troops, or the appearance of threatening concentrations of German men and machines. Each time, Nordling telephoned von Choltitz and asked him to intervene in order to stop the fighting (AN 72AJ/42/IV/3, p. 18). Pierre Taittinger claimed that he was also involved in the negotiations: even though he was under arrest, he said he was allowed to telephone Nordling and participate in the discussions

(Taittinger, 1948, p. 212). There is no mention of this in either Nordling's or Hamon's accounts.

25 AN 72AJ/42/IV/3, p. 17.

26 AN 72AJ/42/IV/3, pp. 17–18.

27 Nordling (2002), p. 124. Von Choltitz also insisted that an appeal for the population to remain calm should be added to the end. According to Nordling, these changes were communicated to the Préfecture de Police at around lunchtime, and it was agreed they should be included (p. 124). It is not clear who agreed to this, or whether it was ever brought to the attention of any of the *résistants* who had negotiated the cease-fire. For the final version see Dansette (1946), p. 495.

28 Blumenson (1961), p. 597. Although the cease-fire has been the subject of many partisan discussions (for a recent polemical account, see Rajsfus, 2004, pp. 224–43), it has never been the focus of any academic study, although Studer (2003) provides a brief account.

29 Hamon rightly pointed out in his diary that it was amazing that in the middle of an insurrection, the organisation that was supposed to be in charge was not meeting. The preliminary views of the members of the CPL he was able to contact were predictable – the right-wing OCM supported the cease-fire, while the communists would not say one way or another (AN 72AJ/42/IV/3, p. 18). The minutes of the morning meeting of the CNR are reproduced in Dansette (1946), pp. 488–91. The only eye-witness account of the meeting is in Hamon's diary (AN 72AJ/42/IV/3, pp. 18–19). Collins & Lapierre (1965) give a confused description of a series of meetings in the Préfecture at which the Free French warned that there would be bloody reprisals. According to Collins & Lapierre, Lorrain Cruse overheard Chaban warning Rol that the price of the insurrection would be 200,000 dead; Rol allegedly replied: 'Paris is worth 200,000 dead' (p. 145). This claim, which has no other basis, and strikingly was never made by Chaban, was vigorously denied by Rol (Crémieux, 1971, pp. 134–6).

30 They were Bidault, Villon, Avinin (from the Franc-Tireur Resistance group) and Bloch-Masquart (OCM). *Le Monde* 25 August 1945, p. 3.

31 Dansette (1946), pp. 489 and 491.

32 Dansette (1946), p. 490. The point about the importance for the Germans of keeping an open passage through Paris was made forcefully by General de Marguerittes ('Lizé') in his unpublished memoirs (AN 72AJ/61/III/1, p. 273).

33 de Gaulle (1983), p. 289. This is pointed out by Andrieu (2004), p. 89.

34 Dansette (1946), p. 491.

35 AN 72AJ/61/I/17, p. 11.

36 Rol-Tanguy & Bourderon (1994), pp. 224–5. They also ordered their men to stop the loudspeaker cars 'by force if necessary'.

37 Barat (1945), p. 48.

38 Denis (1963), p. 108; AN 72AJ/42/IV/3, p. 20. One of the reasons for this delay was that Marie-Hélène Lefaucheux, who had just arrived back from eastern France after following the 15 August Pantin train that was carrying her husband to Germany, wanted further information.

39 Extracts from the minutes of this second meeting are given in Dansette (1946), pp. 491–5. An eye-witness account is in Debû-Bridel (1978), pp. 158–9.

40 Hamon thought the CNR decision was 'bizarre' (AN 72AJ/42/IV/3, p. 21). In fact, it showed that Hamon, Parodi and Chaban did not represent the whole of the Resistance.

41 Courtin (1994), p. 31. Courtin heard that the SS tanks from Vincennes would be set on the city; there was no Waffen SS Panzer group at Vincennes – the tanks there were part of the 5th Security Regiment (Renoult & West, 2009, p. 9).

42 BAM, VV 20.8. Veau describes the source, who was a friend of Père Chaillet, as 'a French colonel, in contact with the Intelligence Service, who is working with Nordling'. I have assumed that this refers to Ollivier/Arnould. On the Left Bank, Georges Benoît-Guyod also heard the story about the two divisions from the south (Benoît-Guyod, 1962, pp. 292–3). This may have been based on the fact that troops from the south had been scheduled to arrive in Paris, although they had in fact been diverted; see chapter 7 and B-728, p. 5.

43 Chevrillon (1995), pp. 160–1. Chevrillon's contact was the actress Jeanne Boitel. Security was so tight that Chevrillon had never met Parodi (p. 163).

44 Nordling (2002), p. 125–7. Nordling himself had to explain to the French policemen what they were to do. At this stage Nordling thought the Resistance was entirely behind the agreement. It took some time for the police loudspeaker cars to arrive from the 13th arrondissement. For a photograph of one of these vehicles at the place de l'Etoile, surrounded by onlookers, see Rocheteau (2004), p. 13.

45 Auroy (2008), p. 302; Tuffrau (2002), p. 89.

46 Bood (1974), p. 320.

47 Guéhenno (2002), p. 434.

48 Bobkowski (1991), p. 609.

49 Campaux (1945), p. 124.

50 Grunberg (2001), p. 341. Madame Oudard's confusion may have been partly due to the vagueness of the terms of the cease-fire, which merely referred to 'the German command'. A similar effect was noted on the boulevard Saint-Michel, when people heard the term and deduced that 'Hitler has demanded an armistice!' (Galtier-Boissière, 1944, p. 264).

51 Galtier-Boissière (1944), p. 264.

52 Campaux (1945), p. 36. For an account of the scene a few hours earlier, see Georges le Fèvre's report in Campaux (1945), pp. 61–2.

53 See the message to the Préfecture in Campaux (1945), p. 230. Photographer Robert Doisneau captured the aftermath (see de Thézy & Gunther, 1994, p. 17), while the event itself, showing several hundred people, can be seen in Anonymous (1944), p. 39.

54 The document is reproduced in Kriegel-Valrimont (1964), pp. 197–200.

55 Allied pilots flying over the city had seen pillars of smoke and explosions, but were unsure whether these were due to Resistance actions or the Germans blowing up their depots (Crémieux-Brilhac, 1976, p. 191).

56 de Gaulle (1956), p. 301.

57 Rajsfus (2004), pp. 224–43. However, Parodi and Chaban had overlooked a key part of de Gaulle's 12 August instruction to the Parisian population: 'in all cases, prevent the retreating enemy from withdrawing his men and materiel.'

58 See chapter 7. The fate of the Brécy mission was unclear for months and even years after the liberation of Paris; in his memoir, written in 1947, Dr Robert Monod hoped that Brécy might still be alive (Monod, 1947, p. 52, n. 1).

59 AN 72AJ/61/I/17, p. 13. Gallois' extensive account of his mission was written in August/September 1944. Sections of it are reproduced in Monod (1947). Collins & Lapierre (1965), following Monod, state that Rol did not ask for the Allies to turn to Paris and that this was later decided by Gallois; Gallois' near-contemporaneous account indicates that this is incorrect.

60 For Monod's contact with Parodi a week earlier, see Monod (1947), pp. 21–3.

61 Monod (1947), pp. 36–7. It turned out that Monod and Cocteau already knew each other through their Resistance work, as 'Prospero' and 'Gallois', respectively.

62 For details of the establishment of this line see B-741, p. 10.

63 AN 72AJ/61/I/17, pp. 17–18; Monod (1947), pp. 55–6. According to Monod, they slept on sofas, not mattresses.

64 Mesnil-Amar (2009), p. 112. See chapter 7, note 59 regarding dating in Mesnil-Amar's diary.

65 Chaigneau (1981), pp. 182–5.

66 Baker (1972), p. 621.

67 Lankford (1991), p. 161.

68 AN 72AJ/62/I/4, pp. 1–8 and AN 72AJ/62/I/4, pp. 9–12. Some sections of these two accounts (the second of which is undated and unsigned) are near-identical.

69 Campaux (1945), p. 30.

70 Campaux (1945), p. 124. On 24 August, Paul Tuffrau described a rumour he had heard about 'Japanese' men on a road near boulevard Saint-Germain who 'ran like monkeys along the guttering and shot at passers-by' (Tuffrau, 2002, p. 99).

71 Dupuy (1945), pp. 21–2. Dupuy was a policeman in the 6th arrondissement; he reports that the policeman who arrested the *résistant*, Monsieur Nicolas, was in turn arrested for disrespect to a member of the Resistance, and was released twenty-four hours later after protests from his comrades (Dupuy, 1945, p. 22).

72 Benoît-Guyod (1962), pp. 289–90.

73 Campaux (1945), p. 110.

74 G.-Jean Reybaz, the author of the diary that is the source for this anecdote, described the women as looking like '*pétroleuses*' (Campaux, 1945, p. 71). These were the revolutionary women of the 1871 Paris Commune who captured the bourgeois imagination by their (undeserved) reputation for setting fire to buildings, allegedly while in a state of *déshabillée*.

75 Campaux (1945), p. 71.

76 de Saint-Pierre (1945), pp. 58–9.

77 All details in this paragraph taken from Vilain (1945), pp. 10–12.

78 In his order to FFI troops that afternoon, Rol pointed out that: 'The white flag is flown by troops that wish to surrender.' (Rol-Tanguy & Bourderon, 1994, p. 218).

79 All the material in this paragraph is from Cazaux (1975), pp. 162–3. Cazaux states that the two dead people he found were on the corner of the rue de Verneuil and the rue de Bellechase (p. 164); however, the two streets do not have a junction.

80 Simone Jaffray died of her wounds shortly afterwards; there is a plaque to her memory at 18 rue Jacquemot.

81 See the photographs taken by Camille Rapp, reproduced in Fournier & Eymard (2009), p. 24.

82 Echenberg (1985), p. 373. The only source for Dukson's life is Dunan (1945). Many African POWs were held in labour camps in north-eastern France, and used various subterfuges to escape. An estimated 5000 Africans were living in Paris during the occupation (Echenberg, 2005; Scheck, 2010).

83 A photograph apparently showing this can be seen in Anonymous (1944), p. 32.

84 The vehicle was a Panzerkampfwagen R35, a small tank destroyer armed with a 4.7 cm cannon, based on the French R35 light tank (Fournier & Eymard, 2009, p. 24–5). Fournier & Eymard, 2009, p. 25 shows a blurred photograph of the tank surrounded by about a dozen people; the photograph of the seizure of the tank, much clearer and presumably taken afterwards, can be seen in Plate 20 – Dukson is in the middle of this image, on top of the tank. Another photograph on the same page shows the same vehicle being driven along the streets accompanied by a large crowd; Dukson is leading the tank, walking backwards with his back to the camera. Rocheteau dates this event to 25 August; however, this is clearly wrong, as Dukson is not wearing a sling, so the photographs must have been taken before the afternoon of August 22, when he was shot (see chapter 11). Fournier & Eymard state that the event took place on 21 August, but provide no evidence. On 20 August Jean-Claude Touche was an eye-witness to the seizure of what he described as a *'camion'* (lorry), which in all other respects was identical to the events seen in the photographs; I have therefore included it in this chapter (Touche, 1946, pp. 92–5). He makes no reference to a black man.

85 Touche (1946), pp. 92–5.

86 Auroy (2009), p. 324. The editors of Berthe Auroy's diaries note 'there is no certainty that these incidents were true' (p. 324). This seems excessively cautious on their part – it is quite conceivable that the black man was Georges Dukson or another black *résistant*. There is no suggestion of racism in Madame Auroy's account; indeed she suggests that black people were particularly likely to be denounced by collaborators during the occupation. According to Dubois (1944), on 22 August 'scalps' were put on the railings outside the Mairie of the 17th arrondissement (p. 72).

87 AN 72AJ/61/I/14, p. 3.

88 See Benoît-Guyod (1962), p. 292 for instructions with regard to the Left Bank.

89 ANACR (2005), p. 283.

90 Crémieux (1971), pp. 90–1. It is unclear where Rol got this information; furthermore, he claims that only five Germans were killed in the same period, which seems a rather low figure. This latter figure coincides with that given by Dufresne (Massiet, 1945, p. 147, n. 1). Dufresne does not give a source, either, and his other figures are different from those provided by Rol.

91 AN 72AJ/62/III/4, pp. 11–12. High-ranking Vichy civil servant Henri Culmann had a similar experience in the late afternoon. He had been having a drink with friends on their balcony on the rue Soufflot, which leads from the Jardin du Luxembourg up to the Pantheon. After the loud-speaker cars had gone by, all was quiet and he began to make his way home, only to bump into a German tank, squatting on the boulevard Saint-Michel:

> ... the machine gun on the tank lowered itself in our direction and, from about 15 metres away, let loose a hail of fire ... Everyone ran, screaming and falling. I tripped over someone and, in a comical moment, just managed to avoid a dog turd on the pavement as I fell. Myself and one other person got up. Five bodies lay on the ground, trying to raise themselves, bleeding. I looked down at my trousers – no trace of blood or turd. We dragged the wounded people out of the line of fire of the tank and into a hotel foyer on the rue Le Goff ... I tied my tie round the thigh of a young girl who was bleeding like a stuck pig and ran to a telephone to call for help. (Culmann, 1985, pp. 297–8.)

92 Bood (1974), p. 321.

93 Bood (1974), p. 320.

94 Bood (1974), p. 321.

95 There are four main versions of this incident, all of which have been used here; three by participants (Nordling, 2002, pp. 129–32; von Choltitz, 1969, pp. 233–6; and Parodi in Crémieux, 1971, pp. 83–60) and the most detailed version, provided by Dansette (1946), pp. 226–33. A critical analysis can be found in Bourget (1984), pp. 330–2, while a typically lush account is given by Collins & Lapierre (1965), pp. 147–50.

96 The detail here is based on Dansette (1946), pp. 226–9. This is a deliberately compressed version: in fact, the three men had initially been taken to the Hôtel Meurice, but von Choltitz was absent; they were then taken away to a Gestapo building on the edge of Paris, before being returned to the German headquarters after von Choltitz became aware that they had been arrested.

97 Nordling (2002), p. 129, implies that Posch-Pastor was already in the room, and does not mention Bender. In his account, von Choltitz says: 'Nordling arrived soon afterwards, accompanied by two men I did not know – I assumed they were interpreters.' (Von Choltitz, 1969, p. 234.) Dansette (1946), p. 229 states that Bender and Posch-Pastor arrived with Nordling. Parodi repeatedly had the impression that his words were not being precisely translated by Posch-Pastor (Crémieux, 1971, p. 85); according to Nordling,

Posch-Pastor 'did all he could to moderate Parodi's responses so as not to irritate the General' (Nordling, 2002, p. 130).

98 Nordling (2002), p, 131. According to Dansette, a Gestapo officer said as the men were leaving: 'That's the most important arrest of my career. It's a dirty trick to let them go!' (Dansette, 1946, p. 233).

99 Nordling (2002), p. 131.

100 Crémieux (1971), p. 86; Dansette (1946), p. 233. The men were followed by two Gestapo agents, but came to no harm. Nordling returned most of the papers to Parodi, keeping a few for form's sake. Earlier in the day, de Gaulle's Minister of the Interior, veteran *résistant* Emmanuel d'Astier, had sent a message to Parodi showing the confidence that the Free French had in their delegate: 'You alone have the authority to decide all the arrangements for the seizure of power in Paris and to set up any provisional administrative structures.' (AN 72AJ/231/I/13, p. 2.) It is not known if Parodi received this message.

101 Jay (n.d.), p. 70.

102 Martens & Nagel (2006), p. 522.

103 Galtier-Boissière (1944), pp. 262–3.

104 Herbert Eckelmann recalled that 'Speer' came to visit Paris on 20 August (Pryce-Jones, 1981, p. 298). It has understandably been assumed that this was Albert Speer, Hitler's Industry Minister (e.g. Renoult & West, 2009, p. 10). However, there is no mention of any such visit in Speer's memoirs (Speer, 1970), suggesting either that Eckelmann was mistaken, or that he was referring to a different Speer.

105 B-034, p. 368; Blumenson (1961), p. 598.

CHAPTER 10

1 Bood (1974), p. 323.

2 Fontaine (2005), pp. 130–2. Footage of the awful scene at Romainville is included at 12:00 in *La Libération de Paris* (1944).

3 Chaigneau (1981), pp. 188–94. Only their father would return, a broken man.

4 Auroy (2008), p. 325.

5 Courtin (1994), p. 34.

6 Cazaux (1975), p. 167.

7 Chevrillon (1995), p. 163. The eye-witness was Claire Chevrillon, who was told to go to the Préfecture and code Parodi's messages. But she forgot to take her code books, so she was ordered to go to what is now place du Président Mithouard and await instructions. In the subsequent turmoil it seems she was forgotten, as she waited there for a couple of days before finally joining in the fighting. The scene inside the Préfecture, pretty much as Chevrillon described it, including the steaming cooking pots, can be seen at around 8:30 in *La Libération de Paris* (1944).

8 Parodi's agreed routes were later announced by Colonel Lizé (Massiet, 1945,

pp. 144–5); see also AN 72AJ/62/I/23, pp. 26–7. One route stayed on the north bank of the Seine, from la Défense, via the '*grands boulévards*' to République and thence to Nation and Vincennes. The other began on the south bank, from the porte d'Italie, crossing the Seine at the pont National, and then went to Vincennes.

9 Rol gave slightly different versions of this: Bourderon (2004), pp. 410–11; Crémieux (1971), pp. 89–90 and Rol-Tanguy & Bourderon (1994), pp. 243–4. The exact words Rol recalls using were '*C'est joué*'. Parodi never gave his version of these events.

10 Rol-Tanguy & Bourderon (1994), p. 243. The full text of Lize's message is not given; it is not even mentioned in Massiet (1945), pp. 144–6, which is an otherwise complete set of Lize's communications on 21 August.

11 AN 72AJ/61/III/1, pp. 274–5.

12 Massiet (1945), pp. 144–6. For the next five hours, Lizé issued a series of instructions along these lines, ordering his troops not to attack German forces unless they were hostile or were holding prisoners. Parodi's title was not in fact 'Delegated Commissar of the Provisional Government'; he was the General Delegate.

13 The nonsensical story about the Senlis parachutists was heard two days later by Yves Cazaux (Cazaux, 1975, p. 176).

14 All information in this paragraph from BAM VV, 21.8. Veau and Pasteur Vallery-Radot do not seem to have considered that giving Ollivier a Red Cross armband was in any way inappropriate. The next evening, Professor Veau noted with surprise that the BBC said nothing about Senlis (BAM VV, 22.8).

15 Barat (1945), p. 67.

16 Roy (1944), p. 25.

17 Brahms' story is told in Dunan (1945), pp. 171–93. There is a photograph of Brahms in the Préfecture courtyard, next to a captured 'PAK 40' 75 mm gun (see note 22 below), in Gratias (1945), no page number, caption: '*La maison de l'ordre . . .*'.

18 Barat (1945), p. 69.

19 Boegner (1992), p. 287. Monod had allowed Claire Chevrillon to hide the codes for Parodi's messages in the organ pipes of his church on rue Roquépine (Chevrillon, 1995, p. 126).

20 Barat (1945), p. 71.

21 Campaux (1945), p. 111.

22 Barat (1945), p. 72. See Plate 21. Identified as a PAK 40 75 mm gun in Fournier & Eymard (2009), p. 29. There are photographs of the captured gun in Gratias (1945) (no page number, caption: '*Le canon de la Préfecture de Police*') and in Barozzi (1980), p. 90. A drawing of the gun being towed off by the police to the Préfecture is in Maudru (1944), opposite p. 62. The gun can be seen being manoeuvred at the Préfecture at 10:48 in *La Libération de Paris* (1944).

23 Campaux (1945), p. 103.

24 Campaux (1945), p. 103.

25 Campaux (1945), p. 112. De Boisgelin's diary stops at this point. A photograph of the busy courtyard of the Hôtel-Dieu can be found in Rocheteau (2004), p. 26.

26 Hazard (1998), p. 391.

27 Later on, Anne Marie was wounded in the hand, and after the liberation was fêted as 'Anita the Amazon' (see the photograph by René Zuber, taken on 21 August, in Anonymous, 2004, p. 27). Anna was a member of the Equipes nationales, a volunteer group set up by Vichy that provided first-aid during bombing raids. Footage of this incident can be seen at 16:00 in *La Libération de Paris* (1944).

28 Martens & Nagel (2006), p. 522.

29 Walraff wrote: 'Many stories like this were circulating. Of course, they strengthened our determination to defend ourselves against the Resistance and to stop fighting only when regular, disciplined troops attacked our strongholds.' Bourget (1984), pp. 338–9.

30 Renoult & West (2009), p. 31.

31 von Choltitz (1969), p. 238.

32 NA GRGG 183, p. 6. This estimation was largely correct; according to the German military historian K. J. Müller, the 1st Army 'was made up of two or three poorly combative divisions, very weak as far as vehicles and armour were concerned' (Lévisse-Touzé, 1994a, p. 180). In the original transcript of von Choltitz's conversation, each of the military titles is given in inverted commas.

33 A-956, p. 10.

34 Renoult & West (2009), p. 53; Massiet (1945), p. 159.

35 The Team AUBREY 'Report Upon Return from the Field' describes these two people as 'cousins' (OSS War Diary 3:774). I have interpreted this to mean liaison agents.

36 The messages are summarised in OSS War Diary 3:770–7; Hooker's account of the period he was separated from the rest of the team is given in OSS War Diary 3:779–82.

37 All information from OSS War Diary 3:771–4.

38 AN 72AJ/42/IV/3, p. 22; Denis (1963), p. 109.

39 Denis (1963), p. 110. For Hamon's later description of his attitude at this meeting, see Crémieux (1971), p. 93.

40 For the plans of the bunker, see Archives de la RATP. A version of the plan is given in Bourderon (2004), pp. 420-1. The generators were diesel-powered, with additional bicycle power if necessary; Rol was grateful that they never had to use the bikes (Bouderon, 2004, pp. 419–20). When Rol was first taken down the concrete steps leading to the bunker, he was touched to see that the air-conditioning system had been built by the engineering factory where he had worked before the war (Bourderon, 2004, p. 419). Although the rooms still exist, it is not possible to visit them; they are apparently empty, full only of ghosts. The short stretch of the place Denfert-Rocherau that contains the entrance to the bunker is now named avenue du Colonel Henri Rol-Tanguy. A photograph of Rol-Tanguy in the

bunker can be found in Kriegel-Valrimont (1964), opposite p. 224 and de
Thézy & Gunther (1994), p. 30. A newsreel including footage of the facil-
ity, shown in November 1944 but containing scenes apparently filmed
during the insurrection, can be seen at www.ina.fr/histoire-et-conflits/sec-
onde-guerre-mondiale/video/AFE86002885/l-armee-nouvelle-les-ffi-pc-du-
colonel-rol.fr.html [accessed July 2012].

41 Kriegel-Valrimont (1964), pp. 202–205. See also Rol's account in Bourderon
(2004), p. 411. After the war, Rol-Tanguy was always extremely generous in
his description of Chaban's behaviour during the insurrection. This incident
was no exception. Rol-Tanguy said: 'During this meeting, Chaban seemed
somewhat embarrassed, avoiding answering questions, no doubt caught
between the need to obey his orders and his awareness of the reality of the
situation, in particular because he was so attached to the importance of the
unity of the Resistance.' (Bourderon, 2004, p. 411.) Chaban never gave his
version of this meeting.

42 In a series of messages to London on 21 August, Chaban explained what had
been happening in the capital and underlined the dangerous position the
Free French found themselves in, as the population and the Resistance
seemed to have gained the upper hand, with the support of an important
section of the population:

> The Bank of France and the major department stores are on strike and
> have the same demands and the same strike-leaders as in 1936 ... We
> could not stop the movement, so the leadership of the Resistance called
> for an insurrection ... the German general in command of Paris pro-
> posed a cease-fire, allowing the FFI to remain in the occupied buildings
> and recognising the FFI as regular soldiers. QUARTUS [Parodi] and
> myself were able to obtain a vote in favour of this ... It remains vital that
> the Allies arrive quickly as there are severe risks that the agreement will be
> broken. The agreement represents a major victory for the Resistance as it
> avoids the destruction of the city and any massacre of the population.
> (ML-Arc.)

43 de Gaulle (1956), pp. 702–703.

44 Castetbon (2004) contains photographs of these victims and the plaques
commemorating their lives, along with moving interviews with their surviving relatives. Lahuec's wife, 26-year-old Lucienne, was in the countryside with
her three small sons, and did not learn of his death until September.

45 There are over sixty plaques in the area, many of which are shown here:
www.liberation-de-paris.gilles-primout.fr/emagenta.htm [accessed July
2012].

46 Anonymous (2004), p. 70. This version of the photograph has been heavily
retouched, and it is difficult to know whether some details (for example the
revolver that a German soldier standing near the dead bodies appears to be
holding in his hand) are original.

47 All details from Ouzoulias (1972), pp. 447–8. Bouchetou and his two comrades, Yvan Penetier-Eldarof and Guy Brulé, had just participated in the

liberation of the Communist Party headquarters on the rue Pelletier (it had been occupied by the Milice). Their mission was to find more weapons in order to be able to defend the building from the Germans.

48 Anonymous (2004), p. 71. A total of seven people are commemorated on the plaque at the site; the names of five of the dead remain unknown.

49 A photograph of men on the barricade, and of the plaque that was subsequently erected on the railings of the square René Viviani, can be seen in Anonymous (1945), no page number, caption: '*De ces FFI qui montent la garde, sept d'entre eux trouveront la mort quelques instants plus tard*'. According to the plaque erected at the time there were only two civilians killed; the current plaque identifies three dead.

50 Bood (1974), pp. 323–4.

51 All details from BAM VV, 21.8. Bood (1974) pp. 325–6 also describes the events. Micheline and her friend Nicole went outside, promising Micheline's mother they would go no further than the entrance to their building. But as soon as they were downstairs, they hurried over to where they heard firing from the boulevard Haussmann. To Micheline's disappointment, the armoured vehicle had left, but she did see the lorry go careering past. Marc Boegner and journalist Edmond Dubois heard of the incident, too (Boegner, 1992, p. 286; Dubois, 1944, p. 68).

52 AN 72AJ/62/III/3, p. 3; Bood (1974), p. 324. There are many photographs of the dramatic damage to the building; see for example Rocheteau (2004), p. 14, which also includes a contemporary photograph of the site, for comparison.

53 NA GRGG 181(C), p. 4.

54 According to Dansette (1946), p. 241, the meeting took place at 18:00; Jacques Debû-Bridel, who was a participant, recalled it taking place at 14:00 (Debû-Bridel, 1978, p. 160). The minutes of the meeting state that it began at 17:00 (Dansette, 1946, p. 499) – I have assumed this timing to be correct. The building was at 8 avenue du Parc Montsouris (now avenue René Coty) (Kriegel-Valrimont, 1964, p. 205). It has since been demolished.

55 Debû-Bridel (1978), pp. 160–4, provides an eye-witness account.

56 Debû-Bridel (1978), p. 161.

57 The text of this poster is reproduced in Dansette (1946), p. 499.

58 Debû-Bridel (1978), p. 162. The minutes say flatly: 'The General Delegate observed that in that case, there would be a split.' (Dansette, 1946, p. 501.)

59 See the summary of Chaban's contribution in the minutes of the meeting; Dansette (1946), pp. 501–503, and Dansette's account (Dansette, 1946, pp. 243–5). 'Gentleman's agreement' was the term used, in English (Dansette, 1946, p. 244). Nearly thirty years later, Chaban was still arguing that the cease-fire was justified in part because the Germans had '110 or 120 bombers at Le Bourget aerodrome, their bomb-bays full, with massive reserves in the hangars' (Crémieux, 1971, p. 99). Le Bourget had in fact been evacuated by the Luftwaffe two days earlier and had been bombarded by the Allies. For a measured analysis of Chaban's various inexactitudes, see Rol-Tanguy & Bourderon (1994), p. 247.

60 This is de Vogüé's summary of his intervention, written immediately afterwards. AN 72AJ/45/I/6N, p. 2 (see also Kriegel-Valrimont, 1964, pp. 205–7).
   De Vogüé reiterated these attacks on Chaban – and worse – in a memorandum for the CNR written the next day (AN 72AJ/45/I/6M).

61 Dansette (1946), p. 246.

62 Debû-Bridel (1978), p. 164.

63 This detail is recalled by de Vogüé in his document written that evening (AN
   72AJ/45/I/6N, p. 1) and by Kriegel-Valrimont (1964), p. 207. There is no
   mention of it in Debû-Bridel (1978) or Dansette (1946).

64 Dansette (1946), pp. 503–504.

65 Dansette (1946), p. 249.

66 Dansette (1946), pp. 250 and 504.

67 Rol-Tanguy & Bourderon (1994), pp. 235–6.

68 Rol-Tanguy & Bourderon (1994), p. 246.

69 Rol-Tanguy & Bourderon (1994), p. 236.

70 Rol-Tanguy & Bourderon (1994), p. 237; Audiat (1946), p. 315. A photograph of a man at a barricade together with a series of these paper-wrapped
   Molotov cocktails can be seen in Anonymous (1944), p. 51.

71 Campaux (1945), p. 104.

72 Massiet (1945), p. 161.

73 René Courtin spent the night in the luxury of the Ministry of the Economy,
   but slept badly as a result of the heat and the sound of explosions (Courtin,
   1994, p. 33). The day before, Parodi had written a note to all the secretary-
   generals of the various ministries, upbraiding them for showing themselves
   too early. 'I have it from a reliable source that the Allied troops could be
   delayed for longer than we expected. I am trying to speed things up, but I
   cannot be sure I will obtain the desired result. In these conditions, if you
   have already occupied your ministry, please do not show your presence,
   and immediately put yourself in a safe place.' (BAM VV, 20.8.) Among the
   secretary-generals was 'Morland', who took control of the Ministry for
   Prisoners of War – 'Morland' was the code name of the young François
   Mitterrand (Péan, 1994, pp. 437–40). Footitt & Simmonds (1988) suggest
   that an SOE agent was parachuted in to seize the Ministry of the Interior on
   place Beauvau (pp. 128 and 135). This is based on a misreading of M.R.D
   Foot's 1966 work *SOE in France* – see Foot (2004), p. 502, n. 80, which states
   that Racheline (his name should apparently be spelt 'Rachline' – Piketty,
   2009, pp. 1095–7; Albertelli, 2010b), an 'old friend' of SOE, took over the
   Ministry of the Interior for the Free French. As a Free French agent, Lazare
   Rachline had worked with the 'RF' section of SOE which was devoted to
   work with the Free French, but his arrival in France was entirely part of the
   Gaullist strategy – he was acting as a secretary-general when he took over the
   ministry. He was not parachuted into Paris, as might be implied, but into the
   Ain maquis (Piketty, 2009, p. 1097; Albertelli, 2010b). His SOE personnel
   file (which also gives his name as 'Racheline') is at NA HS 9/1223/5, but
   contains little of interest, and nothing on the liberation of Paris – one of the
   War Office's main preoccupations with Rachline after the war was whether

he was of sufficient social standing and wealth to be worthy of an OBE. Although Rachline left some documentary traces of his Resistance activity, they do not cover the liberation of Paris (Piketty, 2009).

74 Crénesse (1944), p. 16.

75 von Choltitz (1969), p. 238. For more extensive versions of the same story, recalled earlier, see NA GRGG 184, pp. 3–4 (conversations recorded on 30 August 1944) and von Choltitz (1949), 12 October 1949. Also leaving Paris – for the second time – was the German ambassador, Otto Abetz. His convoy, which had left the capital the day before, had been blocked by Resistance activity around Meaux. He returned to the capital and finally left on the evening of 21 August. During his trial for war crimes in 1949, Abetz implied that during this period he had persuaded von Choltitz not to destroy the city. There is no evidence for this (Lambauer, 2001, pp. 639–40).

76 Delarue (1964), p. 355. The convoy included a radio car; the personnel was composed of five Germans and five collaborators.

77 AN 72AJ/62/I/8, pp. 2–3. The scene on 22 August was also reported by Dubois (1944), p. 73.

78 AN 72AJ/45/I/6M.

79 Lankford (1991), pp. 163–4.

80 Blumenson (1996), p. 523.

81 Blumenson (1996), p. 523.

82 Cumberlege (1946), pp. 181–2. Downs' report continues: 'But there are mines, hundreds of them ... And there are plenty of the S mines – the nasty anti-personnel type that jumps into the air before it explodes and then hurls bits of steel and ball bearings to kill or wound anything living within a hundred feet radius.'

83 After Action Report, p. 40.

84 Fournier & Eymard (2009), p. 30.

85 Blumenson (1961), p. 601. For Leclerc's letter, see de Gaulle (1956), p. 704.

86 Fournier & Eymard (2009), p. 30.

87 All details in the above paragraphs are taken from Gallois' detailed account of his trip, written 'a few days after the Liberation of Paris' (AN 72AJ/61/I/17, pp. 19–27). There is no reason to doubt Gallois' account of his meeting with Patton, but it is striking that Patton makes no mention of this encounter in his diaries or letters (Blumenson, 1996, pp. 523–5 covers this period). For the first part of this day, see also Monod (1947), pp. 59–62. Neither Gallois nor Monod explained what happened to their translator, 'Dominique'. I have assumed he returned to Paris with Monod.

88 AN 72AJ/62/III/4, p. 29.

89 Rol-Tanguy & Bourderon (1994), p. 240.

90 Model & Bradley (1991), p. 252.

91 Hinsley (1988), p. 370.

92 NA GRGG 182, p. 2.

93 Model & Bradley (1991), p. 254.

94 Model & Bradley (1991), pp. 256–7.

95 There is a photograph of this order in Renoult & West (2009), p. 32.
96 Model & Bradley (1991), pp. 254–5.
97 Blumenson (1961), p. 597.
98 Guéhenno (2002), p. 435.

CHAPTER 11

1 Crémieux-Brilhac (1976), p. 198. This story was filed on 19 August.
2 Some of this information came from Rol. The weight given by the Free French to this is explained by Parodi in Crémieux (1971), p. 102.
3 Kriegel-Valrimont (1964), pp. 208–209.
4 These documents can be found in Rol-Tanguy & Bourderon (1994), pp. 249–53. It is not clear if the refuse lorry tactic was ever used.
5 This slogan had first been used five days earlier in an FFI declaration that was not written by Rol (see chapter 6). Not only did Rol not write this poster either, it was not even signed by him, but rather by the non-existent 'Commandant du Grand Paris des FFI'. As with the 17 August declaration, this was presumably the work of some of Rol's more enthusiastic Communist Party comrades (Bourderon, 2004, p. 730, n. 176).
6 Rol-Tanguy & Bourderon (1994), p. 250.
7 See for example the newsreel film *La Liberation de Paris* (2004), or the many photographs of the barricades, such as those in Gratias (1945).
8 Pierquin (1983), p. 131.
9 Galtier-Boissière (1944), pp. 267–8.
10 Villate (1958), p. 73, n. 1.
11 Galtier-Boissière (1944), pp. 267–8.
12 Levisse-Touzé (1994b), p. 215. German ambassador Otto Abetz later claimed that many of the barricades were built in the same places as those that were set up in the great revolutionary moments of Paris's past – 1830, 1848 and 1871 (Abetz, 1953, p. 327). There is an element of truth in this, but only an element. Despite the massive redevelopment of Paris with broad boulevards after the 1848 revolution – designed precisely to limit the efficacy of barricades in case of street fighting – the fundamental geography of Paris remained, so in 1944 there were barricades along the main boulevards and at the main points entering the city (see Map 3). But the geography of the insurrection, as defined by its sociology and its objectives, had changed. For example, in both 1830 and 1848 the streets of the quartier Saint-Merri, near where the Pompidou Centre now sits, were covered in scores of barricades, often in the same place in the two revolutions (Corbin & Mayeur, 1997, plate 1). Many of these barricades had little apparent strategic value – for example, in both 1840 and 1848 there were four barricades in a short fifty-metre stretch of the narrow rue Quincampoix, where I once lived. However, in 1944, there were no barricades on this street, and few in the surrounding area (Map 3; Dansette, 1946; Barozzi, 1980, pp. 44–5).

13 As Rol put it many years later:

> ... the barricades appeared in the collective imagination and conscience
> for the first time since the Commune. The ideological reference to popu-
> lar revolts of the distant past functioned because the barricades
> corresponded to current pressing preoccupations. Paris never lifts up its
> paving stones without an overwhelming reason. Whatever the case, our
> approach paid off, at least in the poorer neighbourhoods, where there
> were far more barricades than in the richer neighbourhoods in the west of
> Paris. And that relates both to the historic weight of the barricades and to
> the immediate political fears felt by sections of the population.
> (Bourderon, 2004, p. 437.)

A different view was given by Polish exile Andrzej Bobkowski, who was
viciously cynical in the pages of his diary. He sneered at the fact that in
many parts of Paris there were no barricades and, not inaccurately, predicted how Gallic pride would be boosted by an insurrection which he saw as
a fraud, punctuating his entry with cock-crows to mock the French before
concluding in amazement: 'And the whole world wets itself with admiration
for eternally heroic and rebellious France!' (Bobkowski, 1991, pp. 601–611.)
For a brilliant discussion of the role of barricades in 1944 and in previous
Paris insurrections, see Tombs (1995).

14 AN 72AJ/62/III/3, p. 2. Footage of Dukson and his comrades atop the captured SOMUA tank can be seen at 14:15 in *La Libération de Paris* (1944),
followed shortly by film of the tank manoeuvring. For a more dramatic –
and almost certainly fictitious – version of Dukson's involvement, including
a drawing of him leaping onto the tank to capture it, see Dunan (1945), pp.
260–1. It seems probable that the relatively simple removal of the SOMUA
tank from the factory has been mixed up with the dramatic mass seizure of
the R35 tank destroyer, which took place in Batignolles the previous day (see
chapter 10). For a faintly racist description of 'the Jaguar' (presumably
Dukson) by one of the film-makers involved in the insurrection, see Maudru
(1944), pp. 167–9 (the fact that jaguars are not found in Africa is not lost on
Maudru). For more on Dukson see chapter 10 and Cobb (2009b); he can be
seen with a group of captured German soldiers at 06:35 in *La Libération de
Paris* (1944). SOMUA stood for Société d'Outillage Mécanique et d'Usinage
Artillerie; the company made machine tools, artillery, tanks, agricultural
equipment and buses.

15 His name was Georges Méjat; see Roy (1944), pp. 29–31. For a discussion of
the role of the film-makers, see Langlois (1998). See also chapter 19. The
Parisian professional photographers were also organised in a collective and
allocated different zones of the city to photograph in order to cover as many
neighbourhoods as possible. This, together with the many amateur photographers who recorded events, accounts for the phenomenal photographic
coverage of the liberaqtion (Le Mée, 2004).

16 This scene can be seen at 15:18 in *La Libération de Paris* (1944).

17 Roy (1944), pp. 29–31.

18 All details from Riffaud (1994), pp. 134–8 and Calvès (1984), p. 102.
19 AN 72AJ/62/III/4, pp. 16–17.
20 von Choltitz (1949), 11 October 1949.
21 Walter Dreizner wrote that the mood of the garrison was marked by 'the utmost nervousness' – Martens & Nagel (2006), p. 522.
22 de Saint-Pierre (1945), p. 64.
23 Campaux (1945), pp. 76–7.
24 Bourget (1984), p. 347.
25 AN 72/AJ/61/I/10, p. 2.
26 Shulman (1986), p. 191.
27 B-728, p. 3; B-741, p. 11.
28 B-308, p. 158.
29 B-308, p. 158.
30 See the facsimile in Model & Bradley (1991), p. 258. Müller (1994) p. 107, citing the same source, claims the order was dictated on the evening of 21 August; however, the facsimile shows that the date was 22 August 1944. The order also instructed Army Group G – which was withdrawing from southern France – to link up with the 19th Army and form a line through Dijon and Dole, defending the Germans' southern flank. The 15th Panzer Division was to move eastwards to the region of Troyes, while General Bayerlein was put in command of the Panzer Lehr Division.
31 Model & Bradley (1991), pp. 259–60. The tanks had been taken under von Choltitz's command a few days earlier when they had passed through Paris, heading for the front. Walter Dreizner noted the telephone call from Model (Martens & Nagel, 2006, p. 523); von Choltitz (1969), p. 212 describes the event but does not give a precise date. According to Dreizner, the tanks ran out of fuel at Saint-Germain and had to be destroyed.
32 B-611, pp. 17–18; the author of this document, Professor Kurt Hesse, said that von Aulock had 'tactically little training but was energetic and filled with ambition' (p. 14).
33 A-956, p. 13.
34 Renoult & West (2009), pp. 90–2; After Action Report, p. 40.
35 Renoult & West (2009), pp. 82–4; Zaloga (2008), p. 46.
36 After Action Report, p. 40. For a map of the US advance to the Seine south of Paris, see Zaloga (2008), pp. 52–3.
37 A-956, p. 12.
38 All quotes in this and previous paragraph from Bourget (1984), p. 348. A slightly different French translation of von Choltitz's General Order No. 3 can be found in Rol-Tanguy & Bourderon (1994), p. 268. There is no archival source for this document.
39 All details in Rol-Tanguy & Bourderon (1994), pp. 256 and 263–4.
40 AN 72AJ/61/II/3. Morandat and his secretary (she was also his fiancée), Claire, had simply walked into Matignon and taken over; the staff welcomed him and carried on as though this was a normal change of minister. There is a flowery account of this in Collins & Lapierre (1965), pp. 156–62.
41 Courtin (1994), p. 35.

42 Roy (1944), p. 28.

43 The text of Parodi's circular detailing his instructions was copied by Professor Veau, to whom it was provided by Pasteur Vallery-Radot who was Secretary-General for Health. See BAM VV, 22.8; the document is also reproduced in Bourget (1984), p. 346.

44 Courtin (1994), p. 37.

45 Courtin (1994), p. 38.

46 Guéhenno (2002), p. 436.

47 Dunan (1945) describes the difficulties experienced by journalists in trying to get their newspapers published.

48 See the facsimile in Conte (1984).

49 Courtin (1994), p. 37.

50 *L'Humanité* 21 August 1944. The article read:

> Through the intermediary of a 'neutral' consular agent who made himself the instrument of the enemy, the Germans proposed an armistice to the FFI. The German commander made this proposal to allow the passage through Paris of three German divisions that were retreating faced with the Allied troops. Some people, who were ready to sell French dignity cheaply, accepted this discussion ... We must not allow ourselves to be taken in by manoeuvres by the Germans or by certain enemies of the people.

51 Granet (1961), p. 270. For a facsimile of p. 1 of this issue, see Conte (1984).

52 Conte (1984).

53 AN 72AJ/42/IV/3, pp. 25–6.

54 *L'Humanité* 22 August 1944.

55 AN 72AJ/61/I/17, pp. 27–8; Blumenson (1961), p. 603. According to Mary Laura Kludy, Virginia Military Institute (VMI) Archives and Records Management Assistant, there is no trace of this in any of General Kibler's papers at the VMI.

56 A French translation of this order is given in Dansette (1946), p. 509. A few hours later de Gaulle sent Leclerc a letter supporting Leclerc's decision to send the de Guillebon column, and reporting that Eisenhower had promised that the 2e DB would be sent to Paris (Dansette, 1946, p. 510).

57 Blumenson (1961), p. 607.

58 Pogue (1954), pp. 240–1. Pogue's account is confused; the content of Eisenhower's note shows it must have been written after Bradley and Siebert saw Gallois. According to Pogue, the note was scribbled on a letter de Gaulle had sent Eisenhower the previous day following their stormy discussion on 20 August (see chapter 9).

59 Blumenson (1961), p. 606.

60 Jacobs (n.d.), pp. 27–8, quoting a Memorandum of Information from the Commanding General, 12th Army Group. Blumenson (1961), p. 607, cites parts of this as a memo from Bradley to General Hodges, dictated on 22 August. A full French translation of this document, dated 23 August, can be found in Dansette (1946), pp. 510–511. The memo orders the dispatch of

the 2nd Armoured Division (Leclerc), a US infantry division from V Corps, a reconnaissance group and 'T' force (see chapter 12).

61 Jacobs (n.d.), pp. 27–8. The memo states that the Resistance envoy had said that the cease-fire was due to expire on Wednesday afternoon; Eisenhower therefore ordered that 'no advance must be made into Paris until after the expiration of the Armistice'. As it happens, the only Allied force in a position to reach the capital immediately after this time was the de Guillebon column, the location of which was unknown to Allied command. None of this is described in Eisenhower's memoirs (Eisenhower, 1948). Blumenson (1961) suggests that in order to ensure that the Allies arrived at the same time as the Germans withdrew and the cease-fire expired, 'an intelligence officer of the "'Economic Branch' of the US Service" was dispatched to confirm with Choltitz the "arrangement" that was to save the city from damage' (p. 604). This is yet another version of the rumour that the US were negotiating with von Choltitz, which swirled round Paris from mid-August onwards. However, there is no contemporary evidence that there was such an envoy, or that he negotiated with the German commander.

62 Bergot (1980), p. 107.

63 AN 72AJ/61/I/17, pp. 29–31. According to Gallois, in their brief conversation Bradley said that an important decision had been taken, and three men would have to carry the responsibility for it: Bradley, who had made the decision; Leclerc, who had to carry it out; and Gallois, who had supplied the information upon which the decision was based. None of this seems to have left any impression on Bradley. In his account of the liberation of Paris, published seven years later, Bradley does not mention Gallois at all, and instead suggests the key role was played by Rolf Nordling's mission (see below), despite the fact that the decision to turn to Paris had been taken before Nordling and his colleagues had left Paris (Bradley, 1951, pp. 390–2). Blumenson (1961) (chapter 29, note 53) notes this 'incorrect time sequence' in Bradley's account. Furthermore, in Bradley's version of events, the decision to liberate Paris was taken by him alone; Eisenhower is not even mentioned. Kaspi (1994) argues that the decision to move on Paris had already been taken by Eisenhower before Gallois was able to discuss with Bradley and his staff and that, as a result, Gallois' mission was irrelevant. However, as shown above, this was not the case. Following his discussion with de Gaulle, Eisenhower realised that it might be necessary to turn to Paris earlier than necessary; his meeting with Bradley (who was armed with the information from Gallois) convinced him of this.

64 Bergot (1980), p. 107; Dronne (1970), p. 266.

65 Lankford (1991), p. 167.

66 Lankford (1991), p. 167.

67 Lankford (1991), p. 167.

68 Fournier & Eymard (2009), pp. 30–1.

69 Dubois (1944), p. 69.

70 Galtier-Boissière (1944), p. 268.

71 Hazard (1998), p. 393.

72 Naville (1950d).
73 Guéhenno (2002), p. 436.
74 Tuffrau (2002), p. 91.
75 Galtier-Boissière (1944), p. 270.
76 de Saint-Pierre (1945), p. 69.
77 Cazaux (1975), p. 173.
78 AN 72AJ/42/IV/3, pp. 24–5.
79 de Saint-Pierre (1945), p. 67.
80 Bood (1974), p. 328.
81 Bood (1974), p. 328.
82 Groult & Groult (1965), p. 302.
83 Gratias (1945).
84 Barr (1946), p. 242; Daix (1994), p. 273.
85 von Choltitz (1949), 13 October 1949; von Choltitz (1969), pp. 244–5.
86 Nordling (2002), p. 137.
87 Nordling (2002), pp. 137–8 and 143–4. Nordling writes of 'Doctor Arnoux who, for certain reasons, could get his companions rapidly through Allied lines' (p. 143). He describes 'Arnoux' as 'a well-known French doctor ... who as a Health Service inspector could move about quite freely' (p. 133). Like Collins & Lapierre (1965), p. 189, I have taken this to be Colonel Arnould ('Ollivier'), who was not a physician and who was travelling with the Red Cross papers supplied by Victor Veau and Pasteur Vallery-Radot (see chapter 10). It seems probable that Nordling either did not realise he had been duped, or later confused 'Arnoux' with Dr Monod, who initially accompanied Gallois and did indeed work for the health service (see chapter 9). Jean Laurent's link with Marie-Madeleine Fourcade and Nordling is described in Fourcade (1972), vol. 2, p. 286. Laurent lent de Gaulle the keys to his London apartment in June 1940, the day before de Gaulle left France. But Laurent would not accompany the General across the Channel and this still rankled the Free French leader (as too, no doubt, did Laurent's contacts with the MI6-run ALLIANCE circuit). De Gaulle describes the arrival of the delegation, although he omits the name of Arnould/Ollivier; he may not have seen him (de Gaulle, 1956, p. 303).
88 Cazaux (1975), p. 174.
89 Various websites (e.g. Wikipedia) suggest that on 22 August, Pierre Favreau, a physician who worked for the Parisian fire service (Sapeurs-Pompiers), also went through the German lines to contact the Allies. I have found no supporting evidence for this claim; in particular, there is no mention of this in the detailed account of the resistance activity of the Parisian Sapeurs-Pompiers (Christienne & Plancard, n.d.).
90 Dubois (1944), p. 74. One of the mythical events that shroud the liberation of Paris supposedly took place this night. According to Collins & Lapierre (1965), p. 183, General Koenig ordered weapons to be parachuted into Paris that night under the name of 'Operation Beggar', but cancelled the mission at the last minute. This claim has no sources. It seems probable that this story is based on a garbled version of a message from Koenig to de Gaulle, sent late

in the evening of 22 August, in which Koenig transmitted a demand from the FFI for a supply drop in Paris, including anti-tank weapons; Koenig did not comment on this request (for the text of this message, see de Gaulle, 1956, pp. 705–706). There is a great deal that is unbelievable about the story as told by Collins & Lapierre, not least the idea that the Free French were able to order any arms drops anywhere – that was the sole prerogative of the British and the Americans. According to Collins & Lapierre, the mission was due to be carried out by the 'Carpetbagger Squadron', and Koenig's contact was the commander, Lieutenant-Colonel Bob Sullivan. I have found no evidence for this. There is no trace of this or any similar operation, planned or carried out, in the collection of memories of members of the 801st/492nd Bombardment Group (the 'Carpetbaggers') (Fish, 1990). In 1967, General Koenig was questioned about this incident by the historian Adrien Dansette. On the basis of his own knowledge and that of his staff officer, General Lajeune, Koenig stated that 'there were no parachute drops planned for Paris at this time, nor, of course, were any carried out' (AN 72AJ/61/II/2, p. 4). That would appear to close the matter.

91 Cazaux (1975), pp. 174–5.
92 BAM VV, 22.8.
93 The Free French Delegation was still worried about the safety of the radio team as they could theoretically be located and attacked by the Germans. See the account of sound engineer Pierre Schaeffer in Campaux (1945), pp. 137–40. For the position of the Provisional Secretary-General for Information see AN 72AJ/61/II/3, and Courtin (1994), p. 37.
94 Crénesse (1944), p. 17.
95 Crénesse (1944), p. 17.
96 Dubois (1944), p. 73.

CHAPTER 12

1 Tuffrau (2002), pp. 97–8.
2 Virtually every diary I have consulted mentions this event. While these extra-ordinary noises were waking people, the Saint-Michel barricade was attacked by a group of SS soldiers. In the pitch black there was chaotic hand-to-hand fighting, grenades were thrown and it was not clear who was the enemy. Eventually the FFI fighters were able to repel the Germans, killing at least four with bursts of machine-gun fire (Barat, 1945, pp. 78–80; Massiet, 1945, pp. 169–70). Dufresne was wounded by grenade shrapnel during this incident; Barat led the FFI counter-attack.
3 Tuffrau (2002), p. 9; Vilain (1945), p.16; Bood (1974), p. 329.
4 D'Astier (1965), p. 204; Chamberlain & Doyle (1999).
5 AN 72AJ/62/1/10, p. 3. Footage of the fire can be seen at 12:30 in *La Libération de Paris* (1944).
6 Martens & Nagel (2006), p. 523. One of Dreizner's photographs of the fire at the Grand Palais is reproduced in this source.

7 Roy (1944) pp. 34–5; AN 72AJ/62/1/10, p. 3.

8 Dubois (1944), p. 77.

9 Touche (1946), p. 97.

10 Dubois (1944), p. 77.

11 Bood (1974), pp. 329–30. Not everyone had such affection for the building. The satirist Galtier-Boissière reassured a friend distraught at the architectural vandalism: 'It's no great loss', he said (Galtier-Boissière, 1944, p. 272).

12 On 29 August 1944, von Choltitz was secretly recorded saying: 'Adolf Hitler also wrote in his order concerning Paris that I must understand that I also had to defend the launching ramps of the reprisal [V] weapons.' NA GRGG 183, p. 10.

13 A facsimile of this document is reproduced at www.choltitz.de/bilder-seiten/redentexte/truemmerfeldbefehl.htm [accessed November 2011] with a reference of OKW/WFSt/Up (H) Nr. 772989/44 (23.8.1944, 11.00 Uhr). There is a surprising lack of clarity over the exact content of this order, and even the dates on which it was transmitted and received. An ENIGMA decrypt is summarised in Hinsley (1988), pp. 371–2, note †, and is described as 'an order by Hitler at 0900 on 23 August'. A French translation of the order is given in Jasper (1995), p. 338, but no source is given (Jasper cites Schramm (1982), but the order is not mentioned there); Jasper states the order was received on 22 August. Warlimont (1964), p. 636, n. 9 reproduces the final two sentences of the order, claims to have seen an archival source (not given) and records it as having been sent on 23 August. Speidel, who was Chief of Staff of Army Group B, also states that the order was sent on 23 August (Speidel, 1971, p. 143), although he reproduces a clause that is not given in the facsimile: the bridges were to be destroyed 'even if residential areas and artistic monuments are destroyed thereby'. According to von Choltitz the order was received on 22 August (von Choltitz, 1949; von Choltitz, 1969, p. 239). Von Choltitz (1969) gives a different, less conditional, version of the final sentence, and also adds a further phrase, which is not present in any other source (italics indicate the new material): 'Paris *is to be transformed* into a pile of rubble. *The Commanding General must defend the city to the last man and, if necessary, will die in the ruins.*' To add to the confusion, Müller (1994), p. 107, states that the order was received on 22 August but was dated 21 August; however, his only source is von Choltitz (1969). Given the date on the facsimile, the decrypt cited by Hinsley (1988) and the recollections of Warlimont and Speidel, I conclude that the order was transmitted and received on 23 August.

14 NA GRGG 183, p. 6. Although the order was addressed to Model as the German Commander in the West, von Choltitz received a copy. See von Choltitz (1969), p. 241 and Speidel (1971), p. 143 for some of the details of how the message got to Paris.

15 von Choltitz (1969), p. 239; Jay (n.d.), p. 72. Jay also says that the order was received on 23 August. This discussion would have taken place in the late afternoon, by which time the fire at the Grand Palais had been put out. Had the discussion taken place a few hours earlier, the black smoke pouring

from the shattered roof of the Grand Palais would literally have cast von
Choltitz and Jay's conversation in a different light.

16 von Choltitz (1969), pp. 240–1; Speidel (1971), pp. 143–4. This version of
the conversation is different from that von Choltitz gave less than a week
later in a secretly recorded conversation with General von Thoma when
he was a POW, although both versions reveal a caustic von Choltitz and a
complicit Speidel. According to von Choltitz's earlier recollection, the conversation went thus:

> I have no guns, I have no HE [high explosives?], I have only that poisoned
> arrow, rifle '98', and yesterday morning at the changing of the guard I saw
> one MG [machine gun?] still firing, but how I am to set fire to the Louvre
> with that, or raze the Chambre des Deputés to the ground, I don't know ...
> I said: 'Speidel, you have got a "Feldmarschall" here, what does he say to
> it?' 'Nothing at all, he can't say anything either.' ... I said: 'Speidel, you
> give me five thousand men scattered over a city of five million inhabi-
> tants, defended by knife rests. As for food – I have ten cases of tinned
> pork.' (NA GRGG 183, p. 7.)

17 von Choltitz (1969), p. 240.
18 AN 72AJ/62/II/4. This copy is marked 'Champs Elysées, 26 août 1944'; this
must refer to when it was found. A copy of the leaflet is also reproduced in
Renoult & West (2009), p. 127, where it is dated 23 August. According to
Thornton (1963), p. 175, this leaflet was dropped on the capital by a German
plane on the night of 22–23 August. Thornton supplies a full translation.
19 Naville (1950e). According to Nordling (who was not present), von Choltitz
complained to Nordling's colleague, Forssius, that the French were breaking
his windows by firing at the Hôtel Meurice, before concluding, philosophi-
cally: 'Paris is like a beautiful woman: if she slaps you, you don't respond'
(Nordling, 2002, pp. 141–2). Naville, who was involved in these discussions
with von Choltitz, makes no reference to any such comment.
20 BAM VV, 23.8.
21 AN 72AJ/42/IV/3, pp. 26–7.
22 BAM VV, 23.8.
23 Campaux (1945), pp. 246–7.
24 Naville (1950e).
25 Patin (1994), pp. 73–7.
26 Brasillach (1955), pp. 288–9.
27 Auroy (2008), pp. 328–9; Cazaux (1975), p. 178.
28 Toesca (1975), p. 331.
29 AN 72AJ/61/I/14, pp. 4–5.
30 AN 72AJ/62/III/4, pp. 40–1.
31 Bourget (1984), pp. 352–3.
32 There is no space to detail all the fighting that took place; Massiet (1945) pp.
175–9 summarises much of the action.
33 Photographs of the train at Menilmontant can be seen in Barozzi (1980), pp.
80–1. There is a plaque to mark the event at the junction of the rue de

Ménilmontant and the rue Sorbier, where the road passes over the now-disused sunken railway.

34 Riffaud (1994), pp. 138–9. In this source, Riffaud does not give a date for the attack. For her eye-witness account see *Vingt ans en août 1944* (2004) on the DVD *Héros de la Résistance*. Noguères & Degliame-Fouché (1981), p. 533 state that it took place on 24 August; the plaque that commemorates the event on the bridge over the railway lines says it took place on 22 August; Bourget (1984), p. 354, dates the event as 23 August, upon the basis of another account by Riffaud and, above all, the messages sent to the Préfecture de Police. The exact number of prisoners, the content of the train, and even the number of trains, also differ from account to account.

35 Massiet (1945) p. 174. This was one of over sixty messages sent by the FFI, if the numbering system is to be believed.

36 Touche (1946), p. 99. During the fighting in the 17th arrondissement, Henri Molinier, who was in charge of his Trotskyist group's military activities, was killed by a German shell (Craipeau, 1978, p. 40).

37 AN 72AJ/61/I/14, pp. 4–5; AN 72AJ/62/III/3, p. 2; Vilain (1945), p. 18; Touche (1946), pp. 99–100.

38 Pictures of the tank and a description of the attack can be seen in Fournier & Eymard (2009), p. 21.

39 AN 72AJ/62/I/15, p. 3.

40 Cazaux (1975), p. 178.

41 Vilain (1945), pp. 18–19.

42 *L'Humanité* 23 August 1944. There were also plenty of Parisians who would not live. On the extremely narrow rue de Beauce, just south of the Mairie of the 3rd Arrondissement, 21-year-old Antoine Luitaud, a good-looking young man with horn-rim glasses and slicked-back hair, ran into a bar to hide from a German patrol. The Germans machine-gunned the room and Antoine was shot dead, a bullet through the eye (Castetbon, 2004, pp. 148–53). There is a plaque on the wall where the café used to be, 9 rue de Beauce. FTP fighter Henri Périer who was forty-two years old was in a car with a group of comrades, on the rue Nationale, near the overground Métro in the 13th arrondissement. Their car was attacked by German soldiers and Henri was killed. It was several days before his family – his son, his daughter and his wife – learnt that he was dead (Castetbon, 2004, pp. 180–5). Although there is a plaque on the wall at 182 rue Nationale, the neighbourhood has been completely transformed since the war, with the exception of the overground Métro lines.

43 Both statements are in Dupuy (1945), pp. 33–4.

44 Courtin (1994), p. 39.

45 Grunberg (2002), pp. 347–8.

46 Brasillach (1955), p. 290; Brassié (1987), p. 304.

47 For Picasso's sketch, the whereabouts of which are unknown, see Zervos (1963), p. 22. There are two versions of Poussin's painting. The original is now in the National Gallery in London and appears to be the version Picasso used. A copy (also by Poussin) was in the Louvre (Penrose, 1962, p. 313) before

being lent to the Musée des Beaux Arts in Rheims from 1949 until 1961. According to Françoise Bouré of the Musée des Beaux Arts, it is now back in Paris. The London version can be seen at www.nationalgallery.org.uk/paintings/nicolas-poussin-the-triumph-of-pan [accessed July 2012].

48 Galassi (1996).

49 Roy (1944), p. 32.

50 Bidault continued: 'Soon, the Allies will be in Paris, welcomed by a victorious Parisian population. General de Gaulle and the Provisional Government of the French Republic will be received by the Conseil National de la Résistance, and, after so much pain and sadness, we will rebuild, with joy and pride, a great people that is strong, independent and just. *Vive la France!*' (Crénesse, 1944, pp. 18–20). Pierre Audiat was enthused by the sounds of the Resistance radio: 'Its broadcasts were marked by the sounds of explosions and gunfire, and nothing was more striking than hearing the speeches of Resistance leaders against a backdrop improvised by the sound of battle' (Audiat, 1946, p. 318).

51 Radio technician Pierre Schaeffer wrote later: 'The sound of gunfire punctuated his sentences, breaking the silences, forming a magnificent counterpoint to his words. People thought we'd faked it. That was pretty annoying.' (Campaux, 1945, p. 139).

52 Bobkowski (1991), p. 612.

53 Thomas (1995), p. 213. Thomas tempered her view later that day, writing a poem, 'Paris is fighting', which expresses precisely the opposite sentiments (Thomas, 1995, pp. 214–215). There is a translation by Kaufmann (2004), p. 115:

> Paris is no longer a tart with makeup
> Who waits for her client in a doorway
> Paris is no longer a whore
> Who opens her legs
> Paris is fighting

The poem concludes (my translation):

> Paris is fighting
> To the sound of the song of the poplar trees
> And under the blue wings of pigeons in flight
> Tanks against the fists
> Tanks against the bare chests
> Tanks against the will
> Of these men who have risen up from the paving-stones
> Shouting
> Liberty
> – Oh death which will end this wild life
> Oh death which will not end our freedom.

54 Guéhenno (2002), pp. 436–7.

55 de Saint Pierre (1945), p. 84.

56 Roy (1944), pp. 37–8.

57 Model & Bradley (1991), p. 262.

58 Model & Bradley (1991), p. 264; Müller (1994), p. 110.

59 Warlimont (1964), p. 636, n. 9, ETHINT 1, p. 43. This shows that despite the suggestion by Collins & Lapierre (1965), pp. 58–9, Hitler intended the mortar to be used primarily against the Allied armies, not against the Resistance or the population of Paris.

60 Warlimont (1964), p. 636, n. 9; Schramm (1982), p. 349; ETHINT 1, p. 43; Crémieux (1971), pp. 183–4. Collins & Lapierre (1965) describe (pp. 58–9 – see also the photograph after p. 128) what they claim was the weapon Hitler wanted to deploy in Paris – the massive 'Karl' siege mortar, which fired 54 or 60 cm shells (von Senger und Etterlin, 1969, plates 247 and 248). This is wrong. According to Warlimont in 1945 (Crémieux, 1971, pp. 183–4) the weapon Hitler commanded to the French capital was not the Karl, but a 38 cm Sturmtiger mortar, and it was to be used to defend the city. At the time of the Paris insurrection there were only three production models of the Sturmtiger in existence, two of which were being used in Warsaw. According to Collins & Lapierre (1965), pp. 200 and 221, the siege mortar was stuck on the railway line at Soissons, 100 km north-east of Paris. There is no evidence for this (Warlimont recalled it was 'lost somewhere in Germany' – ETHINT 1, p. 43), but whatever the case, neither the Sturmtiger nor the Karl was used in France.

61 von Choltitz (1969), p. 246. This is the only source for this story.

62 Model & Bradley (1991), p. 261.

63 Model & Bradley (1991), p. 262.

64 Delarue (1964), pp. 355–6.

65 Crémieux-Brilhac (2010), p. 300.

66 *New York Times* 25 August 1944.

67 NA CAB/65/42/26, p. 292; Crémieux-Brilhac (1976), pp. 202–204; the telegram is reproduced in de Gaulle (1956), p. 708.

68 *New York Times* 24 August 1944.

69 Nordling (2002), p. 136. Von Choltitz (1949, 1969) makes no reference to this conversation, which may be imaginary.

70 Domenach-Lallich (2001), pp. 146–7.

71 Schrijvers (2009), p. 44.

72 Dansette (1946), p. 331; Crémieux-Brilhac (2010), pp. 300–301; Bleustein-Blanchet (1984), pp. 269–73. Collins & Lapierre (1965), p. 204, suggests that the 'monumental hoax' was perpetrated by Colonel André Vernon of the FFI in London. There is no evidence for this, and I can find no reference to a Colonel Vernon. Neiberg (2012), p 204, suggests that a mistranslation by an 'overeager BBC reporter' of 'Cité' – the island where the Préfecture is situated – was at the origin of the event. But the Parisians heard the announcement in French on the Free French BBC programmes and would have been in no doubt – the only reference to 'Cité' is in 'l'Ile de la Cité'. Whatever the case, the remainder of the French statement, cited above, was clearly designed to deceive.

73 de Gaulle (1956), p. 303.
74 The *New York Times* published a brief article blaming the announcement on an 'error in translation' (*New York Times* 25 August 1944). Koenig's staff in London tried to straighten out the mess and work out exactly what had happened; they too noted that the Boris statement did not actually say that Paris had been liberated, and that this was an interpretation by the BBC (ML EMFFI).
75 Dubois (1944), p. 76.
76 Boegner (1992), pp. 290–1.
77 Auroy (2008), p. 329. This entry was written in the morning of 24 August.
78 Bood (1974), p. 331.
79 de Saint-Pierre (1945), p. 82.
80 BAM VV, 23.8.
81 Tuffrau (2002), p. 98. This entry was written in the morning of 24 August.
82 Guéhenno (2002), p. 437. This entry was written in the morning of 24 August.
83 Campaux (1945), p. 130. Simone de Beauvoir gives a far briefer account of the same event; Sartre's friend would appear to have been the playwright Armand Salacrou (de Beauvoir, 1965, p. 596).
84 www.gastoneve.org.uk/paris.html [accessed November 2011].
85 AN 72AJ/61/I/17, p. 33.
86 Bradley (1951), p. 392.
87 See Jacobs (n.d.), pp. 27–8 and chapter 11.
88 Lyon (1948), pp. 14–17; Longden (2009), p. 33.
89 Collins & Lapierre (1965), p. 192. Nordling (2002), pp. 144–6 has a similar description of the passage through the lines, but makes no mention of Bender leaving the group and returning to Paris. However, Nordling later reports that Bender was in Paris on the evening of 24 August, and played a vital role in negotiating the surrender of von Choltitz the next day, so he must have left Rolf Nordling's group at some point (pp. 151–3).
90 Nordling (2002), pp. 143–7. No source is given for Nordling's account (he was not present); presumably his brother told him what happened.
91 Blumenson (1996), p. 525.
92 Beevor (2009), p. 494 reproduces the notes taken by Major General Gilbert Cook during the conversation with Patton.
93 Lankford (1991), p. 170.
94 Dansette (1946), pp. 341–2; Fournier & Eymard (2009), p. 34.
95 Lankford (1991), p. 168; Fournier & Eymard (2009), p. 32 – this page and the following include maps, quotes and pictures of the incident. The area where the event took place has been completely redeveloped; the road is a dual carriageway and the surrounding area is typical of the soulless outskirts of many French towns – chain restaurants, advertising hoardings and builders' merchants.
96 Fournier & Eymard (2009), p. 32. Paul Rondeau, the radio operator, was killed outright; driver Louis Rink and Moïse Jardin, the loader, were severely wounded and died the next day.

97 A colourful account of the scene is given in Beevor & Cooper (2004), pp. 42–3. See also Lankford (1991), p. 169. Bruce and Ernest Hemingway, who was still hanging about Rambouillet, were questioned by Leclerc and asked to pass on their intelligence to the 2e DB intelligence officer. According to Hemingway, Leclerc closed their discussion by saying, 'Buzz off, you unspeakables' (Baker, 1972, p. 629); Bruce's description of the encounter does not contain any intimation of such hostility.

98 de Gaulle (1956), pp. 302–303.

99 Dronne (1970), p. 267.

100 For striking descriptions of the chaotic progress of the Leclerc column, see the various personal accounts in Fournier & Eymard (2009), pp. 34–6.

101 Dubois (1944), pp. 79–80.

CHAPTER 13

1 Cumberlege (1946), pp. 189–90.

2 Campaux (1945), p. 139.

3 AN 72AJ/62/III/4, p. 41.

4 BAM VV, 24.8.

5 Touche (1946), p. 100.

6 Cazaux (1975), p. 181. Cazaux's Free French counter-intelligence contact, Colonel Gérar-Dubot, later received the OBE from the British (NA WO 373/153, p. 897).

7 Roy (1944), p. 41.

8 Boegner (1992), p. 291.

9 Breton (1964), p. 150.

10 ML Vigne, p. 5.

11 Castetbon (2004), pp. 158–61.

12 Dubois (1944), p. 81.

13 The letter read in part: 'You will soon join your Hun friends, along with your yid of a wife.'

14 Grunberg (2001), pp. 348–9.

15 Campaux (1945), pp. 143–4.

16 Castetbon (2004), pp. 142–5.

17 AN 72AJ/61/I/14, p. 5.

18 Boegner (1992), p. 292.

19 Touche (1946), p. 101.

20 AN 72AJ/62/I/4, p. 12.

21 AN 72AJ/62/I/4, p. 8.

22 Bourget (1984), p. 365.

23 Tuffrau (2002), p. 98.

24 Massiet (1945), pp. 182–3.

25 Massiet (1945), p. 185.

26 A few weeks later, Gallois wrote that Leclerc did not yet have his artillery with him. The price of the mad race towards Paris by the tanks and armoured

vehicles was that the slow-moving artillery batteries were still some way behind, while the foul weather prevented the use of either spotter planes or air strikes (AN 72AJ/61/I/17, pp. 35–6).

27 de Gaulle (1970), p. 296.

28 Fournier & Eymard (2009), pp. 61–73.

29 de Boissieu (1981), pp. 249–50. To prove that he was who he said he was, Luizet pointed out that he and Leclerc had been in the same year at the military academy at Saint Cyr, and they had neighbouring beds in the dormitory.

30 de Boissieu (1981), p. 251. De Boissieu heard Petit-Leroy's conversation with Leclerc, and wrote these words down that evening in the Division's log book. In his memoirs, de Boissieu drew attention to this fact and justified his quotation in these terms: 'I am therefore quite certain that these are the exact words that were used' (de Boissieu, 1981, p. 252). It seems unlikely that this part of the message came from Chaban, who had a more nuanced and realistic view of the role – potential and actual – of the Communist Party.

31 de Boissieu (1981), p. 252. De Boissieu claimed that the letter was found on Petit-Leroy's body and was communicated to the German Parisian command, and that this was stated in von Choltitz's memoirs. Von Choltitz wrote: 'In the afternoon I was asked on the telephone if I would be prepared to accept a letter from the enemy forces which would call on me to surrender the city. I declined this offer, stating that it was not my habit to exchange letters with enemy generals before the end of the fighting.' (Von Choltitz, 1969, pp. 248–9.) This may refer to the letter carried by Petit-Leroy.

32 Kriegel-Valrimont (1964), p. 218.

33 Kriegel-Valrimont (1964), pp. 218–220.

34 Kriegel-Valrimont (1964), p. 219. According to Kriegel-Valrimont, Chaban's suggestion was dismissed by de Vogüé, who insisted that COMAC should maintain its status as a Resistance organisation.

35 Courtin (1994), p. 41. Courtin was referring to the Préfecture de Police opposite Notre Dame, and not the Préfecture de la Seine, in the offices of which worked Yves Cazaux, and which were situated in the Hôtel de Ville. According to Victor Veau, in the early evening 'the Secretary-Generals have been summoned to the Hôtel de Ville to receive a group of soldiers from Leclerc's army which will arrive in the evening.' (BAM VV, 24.8.) It seems that Veau got his wires crossed on this occasion.

36 AN 72AJ/42/IV/3, p. 27.

37 Crénesse (1944), pp. 21–7.

38 BAM VV, 24.8.

39 Auroy (2008), p. 330.

40 Tuffrau (2002), pp. 100–1.

41 Massiet (1945), pp. 193–4.

42 de Saint-Pierre (1945), p. 85.

43 Rol-Tanguy & Bourderon (1994), pp. 277–8. There is no record of this penalty having been put into practice.

44 AN 72AJ/62/III/4, p. 43.

45 Zervos (1963), p. 23; Penrose (1962), p. 313; Nash (1998), pp. 36–7; Newman (1999). The painting was in Picasso's personal collection until his death; its current location is unknown. A lithograph was made of the painting in the 1950s and can be seen, for example, at the National Gallery of Australia and on its website, under the title *La Bacchanale* (cs.nga.gov.au/Detail.cfm?IRN=115972 [accessed July 2012]). There is a photograph of Picasso with the painting, shortly after the liberation, in Barr (1945), p. 9. The painting was begun in Marie-Thérèse Walter's apartment on the Ile Saint-Louis, and completed on 28 August in Picasso's studio on the rue des Grands-Augustins (Galassi, 1996, p. 94). Historians of art have conflicting views as to where the work was created: Penrose (1962) is unclear; Newman (1999) considers it was painted in the Ile Saint-Louis apartment (p. 110), Gilot (1964) is ambiguous, but may imply she thought it was painted in the Saint-Louis apartment (p. 55).

46 Newman (1999) provides a perceptive description of the painting, although her political analysis is not shared by all scholars (e.g. Fitzgerald, 1996). Galassi (1996), pp. 94–6, focuses on its relation to Poussin's original and its place in the major shift in Picasso's artistic orientation that occurred in the post-war years. Picasso's friend and biographer, Roland Penrose, described the painting in these terms: 'Its spirit of ritualistic abandon in an Arcadian setting was in keeping with his optimistic mood. Retaining the essentials of the composition and the movement of the ring of dancers, he reinterpreted the figures with freedom and gave the colour a gaiety which makes Poussin's revellers look demure.' Penrose (1962), p. 313. Also shown in the painting were Picasso's lover, Françoise Gilot, a nude dancing figure reaching out to a drunken Pan, and a stylised self-portrait in which Picasso offered a basket of red fruit (tomatoes?) to another dancing figure. Daix (1994), p. 273; Newman (1999).

47 Pudney (1944a), p. 183.

48 A-956, p. 15.

49 Renoult & West (2009), p. 166.

50 Renoult & West (2009), pp. 164 and 180.

51 Krancke's message is reproduced in Renoult & West (2009), p. 186.

52 It is not clear when they were actually destroyed, or how many warheads there were. In 1967, General Koenig promised Adrien Dansette that he would provide an official wartime report of what was done with the torpedoes, but there is no indication that he did this (AN 72AJ/61/II/2).

53 von Choltitz (1969), p. 248.

54 von Choltitz (1969), pp. 246–7; Jay (n.d.), p. 76.

55 Martens & Nagel (2006), p. 523.

56 *L'Humanité* 24 August 1944.

57 Campaux (1945), p. 250.

58 Bourget (1984), p. 367.

59 Fournier & Eymard (2009), pp. 44–9. This includes maps and many striking photographs of the aftermath.

60 All information in this paragraph from MacVane (1979), pp. 284–5.

61 Pyle (1944), p. 315.

62 Massu (1969), p. 146.

63 Lankford (1991), p. 171.
64 Lankford (1991), p. 171.
65 Pudney (1944b). A *vivandière* is a camp-follower, authorised to supply the troops with food and drink.

CHAPTER 14

1 Féron (1945), p. 48.
2 Blumenson (1961), p. 614.
3 Blumenson (1961), p. 614.
4 de Boissieu (1981), p. 249, n. 1.
5 Blumenson (1961), p. 614.
6 The slow-flying Piper Cub was extremely vulnerable to enemy fire. In the late afternoon another Cub was shot down over Versailles; the pilot survived, but the observer was killed (Renoult & West, 2009, p. 163).
7 For Callet's account, see Fournier & Eymard (2009), pp. 90–3; Noguères & Delgiame-Fouché (1981), p. 538. Dufresne claims that he personally received this message, through his chief of the southern sector, who got it via 'a carrier pigeon' (Massiet, 1945, p. 188 – this also includes a reproduction of the message). There is a plaque commemorating the event on the wall of the Préfecture de Police, on the corner of the quai du Marché Neuf.
8 Dronne (1970), p. 280.
9 Dronne (1970), pp. 280–1. Amazingly, the scene in Antony when Leclerc instructed Dronne to head for Paris, and the moment that the column headed off, were all captured on film by local residents – see Fournier & Eymard (2009), pp. 127–9. See also Plate 23.
10 Levisse-Touzé (2007); Mesquida (2011), pp. 117–18. Four half-tracks were named after civil war battles – Santander, Guadalajara, Teruel, Brunete – and one was named after a Republican leader, Admiral Buiza (Fournier & Eymard, 2009, pp. 128–9). As a compromise, one 2e DB half-track was called 'Les Pingouins' ('The Penguins'), because its original name – 'Durruti', after a Spanish anarchist leader – was rejected by the Spanish communist soldiers (Levisse-Touzé, 2007, p. 173).
11 Dronne's command jeep was originally called 'Mort Aux Cons' ('Death To Twats'). Leclerc was not impressed and initially ordered Dronne to remove the slogan before resigning himself to asking: 'Why do you want to kill them all?' The original jeep was destroyed in Normandy, and Dronne could not recall whether he had had the name painted onto its replacement. However, he pointed out that even if it had been on the front of the vehicle, it would not have been visible as the windscreen was folded down, covering the area where the words would have been written (Dronne, 1970, p. 283).
12 Dronne (1970), p. 282.
13 Dunan (1945), pp. 272–3.
14 Dunan (1945), pp. 275–6.
15 www.gastoneve.org.uk/paris.html [accessed July 2012].

16 Vilain (1945), pp. 20–1.
17 They were allegedly served by women whose heads had been shaved because of 'horizontal collaboration' (Breton, 1964, p. 154).
18 All information in this paragraph from Roy (1944), pp. 44–8. Roy was an eyewitness. According to Gallois, Dronne radioed Leclerc: 'Am at Préfecture. What should I do?' 'Stay there,' replied Leclerc. AN 72AJ/61/I/17, p. 37. This can only be hearsay, as Gallois was not present.
19 AN 72AJ/61/II/1.
20 Breton (1964), p. 155.
21 The next day, Claude Roy, who was present, wrote in *Front National* that Dronne was slightly wounded in the fighting (Féron, 1945, p. 53). Dronne does not describe this.
22 A filmed reconstruction of this can be seen at www.ina.fr/video/ CAB94080058/liberation-de-paris.fr.html [accessed July 2012].
23 Crénesse (1944), pp. 29–30. He continued:

> These soldiers of the Leclerc Division and their comrades of the FFI on the place de Hôtel de Ville, machine guns over their shoulders, automatic weapons in their arms, revolvers in their hands, renewing an old acquaintance, seemed to me to symbolise the resurrection of France, the union of the fighting external armies and those of the Interior who have been hunting the Hun for the last five days and who have already liberated the main public buildings in the city, and taken the main strategic points in the city. The vanguard of the Allied army of liberation tells us that, in a few hours, the bulk of the British, American and French troops will be on this place de l'Hôtel de Ville, right in the middle of Paris, and that we will able to hail them, and the last Huns will have been chased from the capital!

24 Crénesse (1944), pp. 33–4.
25 Campaux (1945), p. 254.
26 The radio broadcast of the bells can be heard at: www.youtube.com/ watch?v=dyKtQyIAzJU [accessed July 2012].
27 Dronne (1970) p. 285; Courtin (1994), p. 42.
28 Dronne (1970), p. 285; Mesquida (2011), p. 161.
29 Jacobs (n.d.), p. 35. Jacobs reproduces Peterson's claim to have gone into Paris on the night of 24 August and to have met with Colonel 'Maginetti' (more likely, Minjonnet), Chief of Staff of the 2e DB, at the Arc de Triomphe. This seems extremely unlikely; there are no records of any 2e DB presence at the Arc de Triomphe at this time, Minjonnet's column was stuck at Clamart, south-west of Paris, until the following morning, and there is no corroborating evidence of Peterson's story.
30 Féron (1945), pp. 42–3.
31 Féron (1945), p. 43.
32 de Langlade (1964), pp. 210–11; Blumenson (1961) p. 615.
33 de Langlade (1964), p. 214. The whole area – including the bridge – has been completely redeveloped in one of the less prepossessing pieces of French urban architecture. There is no trace of de Langlade's café.

34 Nordling (2002), pp. 139–40; the footnote by Fabrice Virigili gives 'Lorrain Cruze'. Like Chaban, Lorrain Cruse – not Cruze – ('Lelorrain') (1915–1989) was an inspector of finances. Cruse took over after the arrest of Rondenay at the end of July.

35 There are contradictory versions of this moment. According to Nordling (2002), p. 151, 'Lorrain Cruze' telephoned the consulate from de Langlade's headquarters at 'Saint-Cloud'. 'Cruze' said that the Colonel wanted to enter Paris by going through Billancourt and the Bois de Boulogne; Bender, who was in the consulate, advised against it, citing the presence of the SS regiment in the Bois de Boulogne. De Langlade (1964) recalls that 'Lorrain-Cruze' encouraged him to head into Paris because there would be no oppposition, and the only thing that prevented him from being the first into the city was the lack of fuel (pp. 212–213). According to Collins & Lapierre (1965), pp. 241–2, Bender met Lorrain Cruse at Nordling's bedside in the consulate and told the Frenchman how the 2e DB could enter Paris without encountering opposition. Cruse then disappeared on his bicycle with the news. De Langlade later discovered that Cruse was a close relative by marriage (de Langlade, 1964, p. 218).

36 de Langlade (1964), pp. 212–13. In these memoirs – allegedly written in the 1940s (p. 9) – de Langlade states that the head of the refuelling convoy had fallen asleep about 500 metres away. He also claims, somewhat bitterly, that a deliberate 'political' decision had been made by Leclerc to favour the Billotte and Dio columns: 'Obeying political reasons, which had to dominate sentimental reasons, the General considered it right and necessary that the Billotte and Dio columns should be the first to enter Paris.' de Langlade (1964), p. 211. He gives no indication of what these 'political reasons' might be.

37 von Arnim (1995), pp. 248–9.

38 Jay (n.d.), p. 76. According to Collins & Lapierre (1965), pp. 253–4, the group sat down to a meal of asparagus in hollandaise sauce, followed by pâté de foie gras and profiteroles with chocolate. Jay was scornful of this description: 'Journalistic claptrap!' (Jay, n.d., p. 76.)

39 von Choltitz (1969), pp. 249–50.

40 von Arnim (1995), p. 249.

41 Cobb, 2009a, pp. 57–8. Those who were sentenced by Roskothen include the men and women of the Musée de l'Homme group; amazingly, the survivors of this group do not appear to have thought ill of Roskothen.

42 Roskothen (1977), pp. 303–304.

43 Martens & Nagel (2006), p. 524.

44 BAM VV, 24.8.

45 Bood (1974), p. 333.

46 Boegner (1992), p. 292.

47 Patin (1994), p. 84.

48 de Beauvoir (1965), p. 596.

49 Touche (1946), pp. 103–104.

50 Bourderon (2004), p. 450.

51 Guéhenno (2002), p. 438.
52 Mesnil-Amar (2009), p. 127.
53 Model & Bradley (1991), pp. 265–6.
54 Questioned by the Americans after the war, Hitler's aide, General Warlimont, was unable fully to explain Hitler's apparent obsession with holding Paris:

> Q: What was Hitler's object in holding on to Paris? Prestige value?
> A: His object in holding on to Paris was not so much prestige as to prevent your getting the routes leading north from Paris and a fear that you would push north before it was possible to evacuate the coastline between the Seine and the Somme. Thus, the retention of Paris was to some degree militarily justifiable. Hitler believed your main effort would be directed against Paris and retaining Paris would in itself influence your drive along the whole Seine front. (ETHINT 1, pp. 42–3.)

55 Helm (1996), pp. 19–20.
56 Massu (1969), p. 148.
57 Renoult & West (2009), pp. 198–200.
58 de Langlade (1964), p. 214.
59 Touche (1946), pp. 103–104.
60 Boegner (1992), p. 293.
61 Crénesse (1945), p. 38. This was also recorded by Marc Boegner (Boegner, 1992, pp. 293–4).

CHAPTER 15

1 Pierquin (1983), p. 133.
2 Fournier & Aymard (2009), pp. 146–7 provide both photographs and war diaries. A major problem in establishing a precise chronology of events is caused by the fact that the Germans had imposed Berlin time on the city (GMT +1 hour), while the Allies operated on London time (GMT -1 hour). Combatants on either side and civilian observers could be referring to either of these times.
3 Fournier & Aymard (2009), pp. 149–82 provide an amazingly detailed set of amateur photographs of the entry of the 2e DB into the capital.
4 Galtier-Boissière (1944), pp. 275–6.
5 Thomas (1995), p. 218.
6 *Manchester Guardian* 28 August 1944.
7 Castetbon (2004), p. 206.
8 Pudney (1944b). An audio file of a BBC broadcast by Robert Reid can be heard at news.bbc.co.uk/player/nol/newsid_6540000/newsid_6546500/6546557.stm [accessed July 2012]. For more on Reid and his activity in Paris, see Crang (2007).
9 AN 72AJ/42/IV/3, pp. 28–30.
10 The declaration is reproduced in Dansette (1946), p. 512 and Breton (1964), p. 181.

11 See for example the description of the boys' school on the rue Doussoubs in the 2nd arrondissement, AN 72AJ/62/IV/1, p. 7; or the boys' schools in the 13th arrondissment, AN 72AJ/62/IV/1, p. 49.

12 AN 72AJ/62/IV/1, p. 41. In Pré-Saint-Gervais, just on the eastern edge of the city, schoolchildren went on a march around the neighbourhood, waving hastily made flags (AN 72AJ/62/IV/2, p. 198).

13 Naville (1950f); Bood (1974), p. 334. The Red Cross looked after the women, who were in a diplomatic limbo, until 15 December, when they were finally recognised as prisoners of war.

14 Jay (n.d.), p. 85.

15 Von Choltitz (1969), p. 252; Jay (n.d.), p. 85; von Arnim (1995), p. 250.

16 Von Arnim (1995), p. 250.

17 Martens & Nagel (2006), p. 530.

18 Ritgen (1995), pp. 197–8.

19 AN 72AJ/62/IV/2, p. 188.

20 Ritgen (1995), p. 199.

21 According to FFI leader Vigne, the FFI had taken control of the telephone exchange shortly before the men of the 2e DB arrived on the scene (ML Vigne).

22 AN 72AJ/61/II/2, p. 2.

23 The names of the three fighters were Albert Béal, Henry Kayatti and Marcel Bisiaux. Fournier & Aymard (2009), pp. 184–6.

24 Jacobs (n.d.), p. 37.

25 Pyle (1944), p. 313.

26 AN 72AJ/62/IV/2, p. 182.

27 Chaban-Delmas (1975), pp. 103–104. Chaban paints a typically disarming portrait of his younger self: 'Leclerc recognised me, not only because he was expecting me, but also because my clothes meant that I could not pass unnoticed amid his troops: I was wearing walking boots, jodhpurs belonging to a member of my family, puttees and a sub-lieutenant's jacket onto which I had sewn two stars on each sleeve. To top it all, I was also wearing a khaki cap that was as pointed as anything' (p. 104). Film showing his meeting with de Gaulle a few hours later confirms this comic description. See also Plate 31.

28 AN 72AJ/61/I/17, p. 39.

29 Fournier & Aymard (2009), p. 176. According to de Chézal (1945) p. 235, one of these men was Maclou, the driver of the tank *Le Tromblon*.

30 Pierquin (1983), p. 134. A member of the 2e DB, 'Duc', was also mistaken for a sniper, when he was in fact looking for snipers (Fonde, 1969, p. 104). Colonel Bruce of the OSS was convinced that some of the snipers were indeed either Germans or members of the Milice (Lankford, 1991, p. 174).

31 Berlière & Liaigre (2012), pp. 58–9. For the fate of Madame Goa, who had been in a mental hospital earlier in her life, see chapter 18. There is a novelised account of the death of Max Goa in Boudard (1977), p. 143 – Boudard was a young FFI fighter in the neighbourhood and may have been an eye-witness.

32 de Saint-Pierre (1945), pp. 103–104.

33 de Saint-Pierre (1945), pp. 111–114.

34 Bood (1974), p. 337.

35 Billotte (1972), p. 322. According to Dronne (1970), Luizet and Ely were also present, along with Parodi's aide, Félix Gaillard (p. 300).

36 See the reproduction of the letter in Renoult & West (2010), p. 18.

37 Billotte claimed that his 'promotion' was the work of Gaillard and de la Horie and that he did not notice at the time (Billotte, 1972, p. 323). De Gaulle officially made him a general a few days later.

38 Touche (1946), p. 106. The banner stretched across the road from number 54 to number 61.

39 For details of Gisèle Hasseler's role, including her mention in dispatches by Billotte on 27 August 1944, see Dunan (1945), pp. 313–27. See also Billotte, (1972), p. 323; Dronne (1970), p. 300; Nordling (2002), p. 152.

40 All details from Nordling (2002), p. 153. According to Nordling, von Arnim let it be known that von Choltitz would not put up much of a fight and would surrender as soon as regular troops entered the Hôtel Meurice. However, none of the three key German protagonists who were present in the Hôtel Meurice – General von Choltitz, Lieutenant von Arnim and Colonel Jay – mention any contact with Bender or Nordling in their memoirs, nor do they refer to any ultimatum letter (von Arnim, 1995; von Choltitz, 1969; Jay, n.d.). Walter Dreizner did describe the event in his diary/memoir, but it is not clear where or when he obtained this information (Martens & Nagel, 2006, p. 528, n. 45). According to Dansette (1946), when Bender returned to the Swedish consulate, he told de la Horie that as long as von Choltitz was allowed to make a symbolic 'last stand', he would surrender without much of a fight (p. 373). The war diary of the Groupe Tactique Warabiot, of which Billotte was part, simply states that von Choltitz said 'his military code of honour forbade him from surrendering without a fight' (Fournier & Aymard, 2010, p. 28).

41 Billotte (1972), pp. 323–4.

42 Pierquin (1983), p. 133.

43 See the photograph in Anonymous (1945).

44 A few days later, Paul Tuffrau noted that a placard had been placed on the tank reading: 'There were five Frenchmen and we are all still alive. We'll get the enemy. *Vive de Gaulle.*' (Tuffrau, 2002, p. 127.)

45 Fournier & Aymard (2010), pp. 70–9.

46 Fournier & Aymard (2010), pp. 71–4. This group was known as the 'Lorris maquis'.

47 All details from Castetbon (2004), pp. 211–217. There is a plaque to Michel's memory on the low wall of the right-hand side of the quai d'Orsay, opposite the Chambre des Deputés.

48 Castetbon (2004), pp. 206–209.

49 Fournier & Aymard (2010), p. 79. These figures are based on a cross-referencing of eye-witness accounts and contemporary photographs. For a detailed description of the fighting in this neighbourhood from a civilian point of view, see Tuffrau (2002), pp. 102–109.

50 The commander of one of the 2e DB groups involved in the fighting around

the Jardin du Luxembourg was Commander Putz (1895–1945), who, like Fabien and Rol, had fought with the International Brigades during the Spanish Civil War. He was later largely responsible for the creation of La Nueve, the Spanish battalion within the 2e DB (Mesquida, 2011). There are various versions of the battle for the Senate and the nature of the command structure, although none of them provide contemporary evidence. According to de Boissieu, who was initially in command of the 2e DB attack, 'General Leclerc ordered me to continue the attack on the Luxembourg garrison, and even sent the "Fabien battalion" to help me – the leader of this group, Colonel Fabien, was to remain with General Leclerc to act as a liaison with Colonel Rol-Tanguy, while his deputies were put under my orders. It was thus that in Paris I had the honour of commanding a troop of FFI-FTP in order to neutralise the Jardin de Luxembourg!' (De Boissieu, 1981, p. 254.) According to Albert Ouzoulias, who was one of Fabien's Communist Party comrades, 'An unforgettable thing took place. General Leclerc put seven tanks under the orders of Fabien, one of the commanders of the insurrection of Paris, a 25-year-old engineering worker.' (Ouzoulias, 1972, p. 451.) According to FTP leader Charles Tillon (Tillon, 1977, p. 272), 'the Colonel commanding one of the 2e DB groups promised to put two mechanised platoons under his orders.' Communist leader Jacques Duclos said: 'The attack at Luxembourg was led by Colonel Fabien. Nine tanks, seconded from the 2e DB, worked with him.' (Duclos, 1970, p. 230.) Rol's vision was somewhat different: 'The reality was much less exciting than the legend. Fabien never commanded any armoured vehicles but, as part of a joint operation with a section of the 2e DB, he provided infantry. That does not diminish his worth, but simply sets the story straight.' (Bourderon, 2004, p. 458.) Rol's description is supported by the two earliest accounts of Fabien's involvement. FFI commander Barat described how Fabien's group was one of two that were 'supporting' the attack by the Leclerc division (Barat, 1945, p. 85, n. 1). Commander Dufresne of the FFI wrote: 'Nine tanks attacked while my comrades [of the FFI] acted as accompanying light infantry' (Massiet, 1945, p. 202).

51 Tuffrau (2002), p. 105.
52 Tuffrau (2002), pp. 105–106.
53 There is a plaque to Jean Lavaud's memory at 55, rue d'Assas, on the spot where he was killed.
54 Lankford (1991), p. 172.
55 Fournier & Aymard (2009), pp. 189–98; Billotte (1972), p. 219. In fact, the Germans to the west of Paris were already pulling back.
56 Fournier & Aymard (2010), pp. 4–13 provide a detailed account of the battle for the Majestic, including maps, contemporary photographs and film evidence, and memoirs by participants.
57 This can be seen at around 22:00 in *La Libération de Paris* (1944).
58 Corporal Néri was badly burnt while Commander Mirambeau was wounded. Strikingly different accounts of this event were later provided by Colonel Massu and Colonel de Langlade, both of whom were present. Both are reproduced in Fournier & Aymard (2010), p. 15.

59 de Langlade (1964), pp. 221–2.

60 Fournier & Aymard (2010), p. 15. The exact words were: *'Vacherie, qué cirque!'* A photograph of Desbordes crouching behind the tree can be seen in Plate 31.

61 Accounts of this incident are confused, partly because of its similarity to the earlier grenade attack that severely wounded Corporal Néri and Commander Mirambeau, and to the later killing of the four 'Georgians', all of which took place at the place de l'Etoile within the space of an hour. However, there is no doubt that all three incidents took place, and were all separate in time and space.

62 Photographs of the scene, taken from different angles, show six or seven corpses (Fournier & Aymard, 2010, pp. 14–15). This is also the figure given by de Langlade, who was in the midst of the shooting (de Langlade, 1964, p. 222), and by Colonel Bruce in his diary (Lankford, 1991, p. 173).

63 Boegner (1992), p. 295.

64 The scene with the dead men was included in *La Libération de Paris* (1944). The footage, which can be seen at 0:24:00–0:24:30, confirms Boegner's observation that the four men were not wearing boots. This detail, and the number and location of the bodies, demonstrates that this incident was a separate one from the killing of the seven Germans shortly before.

65 *La Libération de Paris* (1944), 0:24:00–0:24:30. Two stills from the film, showing the four men alive and dead, are in Fournier & Aymard (2010), p. 15.

66 Courdesses (1994), pp. 302–303. The figure of seven tanks is given by Fournier & Aymard (2009), p. 142, on the basis of close examination of the photographic evidence of destroyed and captured tanks.

67 A photograph of the flag can be seen in Fournier & Aymard (2010), p. 3. By the next day, the flag had been suspended from the roof of the arch.

68 Lankford (1991), p. 173.

69 Fournier & Aymard (2010), p. 21.

70 Fournier & Aymard (2010) pp. 16–25 present an exhaustive account of this confrontation, using frame-by-frame analysis of cine film, detailed maps and memoirs. Courdesses (1994), p. 303, gives a slightly different time-course, in which Bizien's tank made the first strike.

71 The soldiers were accompanied by Gisèle Hasseler, Chaban's secretary who had been helping de la Horie find his way round Paris, and who had been allowed by Billotte to join the attack – Dunan (1945), pp. 323–7. Gisèle's apparently unlikely involvement in the attack on the Meurice was mentioned in dispatches by Billotte two days later – the citation concludes: 'During this dangerous attack, she showed calm, sang-froid and a complete disregard for danger; such qualities that even the bravest of men must recognise them.' (Dunan, 1945, p. 327.)

72 Jay (n.d.), pp. 86–7. Von Choltitz (1969) p. 253 provides a simpler, but essentially identical, account.

73 von Choltitz recalls that the first person to enter his office was a civilian FFI fighter, who was 'haggard and excited' (von Choltitz, 1969, p. 253). The man was so excited that he asked the *non sequitur* '*Herr General, sprechen Sie*

Deutsch?' – Karcher then grabbed the civilian by the collar and threw him out (p. 254). Fournier & Aymard (2010), p. 59 report the suggestion that this man was a Spaniard, Antonio Gutierrez. Jay (n.d.) denies that there was a civilian, but states that the first man they saw was 'a laughable figure' (p. 88). Von Arnim says Karcher entered with a man wearing an FFI armband (von Arnim, 1995, p. 251). Dansette (1946), pp. 377–8, does not mention any civilian, and reports that Karcher asked the more reasonable question: 'Does the General speak French?' Jay recognised de la Horie: the two men had met at pre-war equestrian events (Jay, n.d., p. 89).

74 Fournier & Aymard (2010), p. 36. See also the astonishing photographs on pp. 37–41. During the surrender, a German adjutant collapsed to the floor and can be seen in photographs, apparently dead. It is not known whether he was already wounded, or whether he was shot after surrendering, or indeed if he was dead.

75 Kent (1947), p. 210.

76 The time is given on contemporary photographs (Fournier & Aymard, 2010, p. 41).

77 Lankford (1991), pp. 173–4.

78 Bood (1974), p. 336.

79 Bood (1974), p. 336.

80 Roskothen (1977), p. 304. According to a widely circulated story, the gunner was ordered to 'beware of the 5th column' – that is, '5th columnist' snipers. He misunderstood and destroyed the fifth column of the central part of the building, counting from the right.

81 Cumberlege (1946), p. 193.

82 Bourget (1984), p. 372.

83 Touche (1946), pp. 106–113. In the wall of the Tuileries at the end of the rue de Rivoli there are plaques to the memory of Madeleine Brinet, Jean-Claude Touche, Marcel Bizien and seven others who were killed in the fighting.

84 Roskothen, who had been appointed as an intermediary, was taken to the Préfecture in an armoured car, and returned with von Choltitz's surrender order. This can be seen at around 17:00 in *La Libération de Paris* (1944). Roskothen (1977), pp. 306–7; Bourget (1984), pp. 376–7.

CHAPTER 16

1 Pyle (1944), p. 312.

2 Dansette (1946), p. 382.

3 Kriegel-Valrimont's attire can be seen in the colour film of von Choltitz arriving at the Gare Montparnasse, shot by George Stevens and visible at 17:45 on the DVD *D-Day to Berlin* (1998). In 2004, Edgard Pisani recalled how he had seen Chaban and François Mitterrand talking outside the billiard room, and got the impression that this was the first time the two men had met (*Les Témoins de la Libération de Paris*, 2004, 39:30). There is no way of knowing if this actually happened – I have come across no evidence that

Mitterrand was in the building at this time. According to Dansette (1946), p. 381, before von Choltitz was brought into the room, General Barton and 'some US officers' came in, and then left, telling Lecerc that 'You should be alone in Paris at this time.' No other source – including those written by the participants – describes this. Strikingly, Bradley (1951) makes no mention of this at all (p. 392). Indeed, Bradly mistakenly states that the surrender took place at Montparnasse, not at the Préfecture. It seems extremely unlikely that Bradley either came into the room, or uttered these words.

4 Goglin & Roux (2004), p. 182.

5 There is a photograph of a rather disconsolate von Choltitz sitting at a small cluttered desk, signing a paper with two soldiers on either side, one smiling, the other looking at what he is writing (e.g. Fournier & Eymard, 2010, p. 110). This is often presented either as the signature of the surrender order to his troops, or even of the surrender itself. According to the man on the left in the photograph – the 2e DB translator, Captain Alfred Betz – von Choltitz was in fact writing a letter requesting that his personal effects be returned to him (Bourget, 1984, p. 379).

6 AN 72AJ/61/I/17, p. 40.

7 von Choltitz was not consulted over Rol's signature, nor was his copy of the surrender amended. All details in these paragraphs are from Dansette (1946), pp. 383–6; Bourderon (2004), p. 453–4; Kriegel-Valrimont (1964), pp. 222–3. Before the surrender was signed in the Préfecture, von Choltitz objected to the final clause, which stated that any soldiers who continued to fight after the order to surrender had been transmitted would be treated as outside the laws of war. The German commander rightly pointed out that there could be soldiers fighting in Paris who had arrived as reinforcements and were not under his command, and therefore could not be expected to follow his orders. This was accepted by Leclerc. A photograph of the amended surrender document can be found in Rol-Tanguy & Bourderon (1994), p. 289. According to Dansette, Rol demanded to sign the document. However, in Bourderon (2004), Rol claims it was Valrimont's idea; Kriegel-Valrimont also states that it was he who raised the issue, although he situates the whole discussion at the Préfecture. It seems most likely that the razor-sharp political mind of Valrimont would have grasped the potential significance of Rol's signature.

8 This point is made by Blumenson (1961), p. 618.

9 AN 72AJ/61/I/17, p. 40.

10 AN 72AJ/61/II/2. Koenig's 1965 letter to Dansette quotes detailed reports from the Service des Explosifs and is probably the most accurate source for this question. See also Dansette's article in *Le Monde* (Dansette, 1966), in which he states: 'During the insurrection, the administration of Ponts et Chaussées carried out two daily inspections, one in the day, the other at night, under the cover of routine checks, looking for any preparation for destruction of buildings or bridges. It found that the Germans never made any such preparations of any kind.' For details of the importance of the two telephone exchanges, see Gerbier (2007).

11 A facsimile of this document is reproduced at www.choltitz.de/bilder-seiten/redentexte/truemmerfeldbefehl.htm [accessed November 2011] with the reference OKW/WFSt/Up (H) Nr. 772989/44 (23.8.1944, 11.00 Uhr).

·12 This section of film (colourised) can be found on the DVD *Eté 44: La Libération* (2004), at 1:13:50–1:17:00. In his memoirs de Gaulle suggests he gave another reason: 'Above all, the claim that led you to accept this wording is part of an unacceptable trend' (de Gaulle, 1956, p. 306). De Gaulle also claimed he showed Leclerc the CNR declaration published earlier in the day, which did not mention de Gaulle or the Provisional Government. This cannot be seen on film, nor does any independent source support this. De Gaulle does not appear to have remarked then or when writing his memoirs that Parodi also signed the CNR declaration, in the name of the Provisional Government (see above; Dansette, 1946, p. 512). Rol did not recall de Gaulle being so voluble in his annoyance, and rightly pointed out that film of the event does not seem to show more than mild irritation (Bourderon, 2004, p. 455).

13 Chaban-Delmas (1975), p. 106. Photographs and film of the scene show de Gaulle's expression, which is as negative as Chaban describes it. See Plate 31.

14 Bourderon (2004), p. 455.

15 'When he [de Gaulle] heard my pseudonym, he asked me, quite brusquely, what my job was. I replied that it wasn't a relevant question, and I was simply pleased by the outcome symbolised by the fact that von Choltitz was a prisoner in a nearby office. Perhaps my unpleasant attitude had its effect: de Gaulle softened and ended up making a few pleasantries.' (Kriegel-Valrimont, 1964, p. 224.)

16 Bourderon (2004), p. 456.

17 Fournier & Aymard (2010), pp. 64–70.

18 Jay (n.d.), pp. 92–3. Fournier & Aymard (2010), pp. 106–8, summarise the situation at the place de la République but do not refer to Jay's involvement. According to Courdesses (1994), p. 313, and Jauffret (1994), p. 350, n. 4, one of the German officers who carried the surrender order to the Germans at République was a Major Kottrup. It is possible that more than one officer was involved.

19 Darcourt's apparently contemporary account can be found in Breton (1964), pp. 170–2. However, few of the details are corroborated by other sources. See also the accounts of Captain Fenestrelle of the Saint-Just company (Campaux, 1945, pp. 180–1) and of Riffaud (1994), pp. 142–3.

20 For example, Marcel Henriot and Raphaël Bilke were killed at the end of the boulevard Voltaire; Georges Montalbetti was shot dead at 26 rue Faubourg du Temple; 19-year-old student Jeannine Floquet was shot at the end of the avenue Parmentier, and died of her wounds two weeks later.

21 Breton (1964), p. 173; Riffaud (1994), p. 143; Castetbon (2004), pp. 186–93. There is a plaque to Michel's memory where he was killed, at 17 rue du Faubourg du Temple. A long stairway in the 19th arrondissement is now called rue Michel Tagrine. I used to live in an apartment at the bottom of the stairway, with my family.

22 Jay (n.d.), pp. 92–3. The figure of 500 soldiers is taken from Dansette (1946), p. 391, who makes no mention of the involvement of any German officer in the surrender. Rol-Tanguy effectively repeated Dansette's version (Bourderon, 2004, p. 459).

23 BAM VV, 25.8.

24 For the events at Clignancourt, see Campaux (1945), p. 180. Without heavy weapons the FFI were not able to prevent over 100 German soldiers, together with two anti-tank guns and a number of heavy machine guns, from escaping in the early afternoon. This is virtually the only account of this operation. Some of the FFI fighters were apparently based in the nearby Ecole des Garçons, 18 rue Sainte-Isaure, in the 18th arrondissement (AN 72AJ/62/IV/1, pp. 75–6).

25 There are few accounts of this battle. This is taken from Fournier & Eymard (2010), pp. 98–105, which includes many striking photographs and informative maps. Among the FTP fighters who were killed was 19-year-old Henri van Hulst, a Trotskyist; his is the only headstone in the section of the Puteaux cemetery devoted to the Resistance not to be inscribed '*Mort pour la France*'. His mother said to the authorities: 'My son did not die for France, he died fighting fascism' (Broué, 1995, p. 30).

26 AN 72AJ/62/IV/2, p. 142, pp. 143–6.

27 Dupuy (1945), pp. 42–3.

28 Oddly, many of the flower beds remained intact – a photograph of a tank in front of a neat bed of what look like busy lizzie flowers can be seen in Fournier & Eymard (2010), p. 93.

29 Campaux (1945), p. 174.

30 www.gastoneve.org.uk [accessed July 2012].

31 Mesnil-Amar (2009), p. 130.

32 Mesnil-Amar (2009), p. 131.

33 Martens & Nagel (2006), p. 532. Like many prisoners, Dreizner complained that most of his personal effects were removed – his compass, his money and his precious Leica camera – in what was effectively organised theft (for a description of Dreizner's camera and how it had changed his art, see Denoyelle, 2006, p. 91). A virtually identical experience was described by Quartermaster Walraff (Bourget 1984, pp. 377–8).

34 AN 72AJ/62/IV/1, p. 5.

35 AN 72AJ/61/I/17, p. 41. Photographs of this scene can be found in Fournier & Eymard (2010), p. 112.

36 Werth (2007), p. 339.

37 Ritgen (1995), p. 199.

38 Von Arnim (1995), pp. 253–4.

39 Dansette (1946), p. 401.

40 This account of the meeting is based on Dronne (1971), pp. 313–315. Detailed, and not hagiographic, it has the ring of truth, although Dronne's sources are unknown. De Gaulle (1956) gives a brief account and recalls that Parodi and Luizet were both present and they were 'radiant, concerned and tired by the week without rest or sleep that they had just experienced';

he also recalls that they described the 'irritation' of the CPL and the CNR, caused by the fact that he had not gone immediately to the Hôtel de Ville (pp. 306–307).

41 This can be seen on the DVD *Eté 44: La Libération* (2004), at 1:17:00.

42 A photograph can be seen in de Gaulle (1962), p. 342. One of the women was dressed in Alsatian traditional dress. This was presumably Jeanne Borchert, who had been at the Hôtel de Ville the previous day. See chapter 14.

43 AN 72AJ/61/I/1, p. 2.

44 Crénesse (1945), pp. 34–6. For a photograph of the set-up on the place de l'Hôtel de Ville, see Crénesse (1945), opposite p. 34. Some idea of the privations suffered by the Parisians during the occupation can be gained by a photograph of Crénesse and fellow French journalist Charles d'Ydewalle, in the company of Richard Dimbleby and Robin Duff of the BBC. The two Britons are plump and well fed, the Frenchmen gaunt and bony (Crénesse, 1945, opposite p. 46).

45 René Courtin, of the Ministry of Finance, was surprised at how tall de Gaulle was. He expected he would be short, as in the Vichy propaganda cartoons. (Courtin, 1994, p. 44).

46 Campaux (1945), p. 161.

47 Bidault had been President of the CNR for a year. Unlike all the other major Resistance leaders (with the exception of the communists), he did not leave France for London or Algiers during the war. For a perceptive discussion of de Gaulle's antipathy to Bidault, see Elgey (1993), pp. 65–7.

48 Campaux (1945), p. 162.

49 de Gaulle (1956), p. 308 states that the speech was improvised. This is fairly evident from its structure, with its repeated cadences and several false endings. Standing just behind him was the 19-year-old *résistante* Brigitte Servan-Schreiber, watching open-mouthed and wearing a massive pair of earrings (perhaps in red–white–blue); she gave de Gaulle a bouquet of flowers at the end of his speech (Féron, 1945, p. 74 – she had been arrested by the Germans on 16 August and severely beaten – see chapter 5). Also standing next to de Gaulle, exhausted and unshaven, was the Communist Party leader Tollet, who watched the speech grim-faced.

50 Jackson (2001), p. 565. René Courtin was deeply moved by Bidault's speech ('magnificent … it gave me butterflies when he spoke about the suffering of all those who had lived in clandestinity to four years'), but was much less impressed by that of de Gaulle: 'good, but lacked the sense of humanity that made Bidault's speech so beautiful. Nothing for those who had worked for him in France for four years; not even for those who are dead. It was merely an appeal to French greatness. He does not smile. The man appears to be carried about by his destiny, and to follow his path without any attention to anyone else.' (Courtin, 1994, p. 44.) A similar view was expressed by banker Léonard Rist in a note to his brother, Noël: 'Phew! That first contact didn't go so well. A bit more relaxed would have been nice. And that speech at the Hôtel de Ville – brief, authoritarian … Very good, perfect, but still, he could have said "thank you" to the CNR and to Alexander [Parodi] who have made such an

effort for him.' (Rist, 1983, p. 432, n. 38.) These critical reactions to this speech, expressing all the ambiguity that the Resistance felt about de Gaulle, have been forgotten by the French, and even by French historians.

51 There is an intriguing and previously unremarked difference between the contemporary accounts of de Gaulle's speech that appeared in the newspapers (see for example *Le Figaro* (Campaux, 1945, pp. 162–3; see also Dansette, 1946, pp. 403–4) and *L'Aube* (Féron, 1945, pp. 73–5)), and the official version published after the war (de Gaulle, 1970, pp. 439–40). The contemporary versions contain a series of passages about the importance of universal suffrage and the need 'to ensure that in the reconstructed nation no man should fear hunger or misery, and that all French people should enjoy conditions of existence that are worthy of that which they have the right to demand' (Féron, 1945, p. 74), as well as the martial slogan: 'War, unity and grandeur, that is our programme' (Campaux, 1945, p. 163). This is all absent from the official version which is now part of history.

52 de Gaulle (1956), p. 308.

53 It is sometimes said that de Gaulle made his speech from 'the balcony' of the Hôtel de Ville. There is no balcony; the description here is based on contemporary newspaper articles, photographs and newsreel footage.

54 AN 72AJ/42/IV/3, p. 31.

55 The socialist Daniel Mayer declared that de Gaulle had made two mistakes – he had gone first to the Préfecture rather than the Hôtel de Ville, and above all he had refused to declare the Republic. Half a century later, Mayer was still smarting – see his interview in Ragueneau & Florentin (1994), pp. 172–3.

56 Dansette (1946), p. 404.

57 de Boissieu (1981), p. 257–8; de Langlade (1964), pp. 223–4.

58 BAM VV, 24.8.

59 Lankford (1991), p. 174.

60 de Saint-Pierre (1951), p. 78.

61 Boegner (1992), p. 296. Photographs of the aircraft after it landed can be seen in Fournier & Aymard (2010), p. 122.

62 AN 72AJ/62/III/4, pp. 49–50.

63 Pierquin (1983), p. 135; the shootings were also reported with horror by Victor Veau, who knew all three of the victims, and a mere thirty minutes earlier had been in the room where they were shot (BAM VV, 25.8). According to Collins & Lapierre (1965), p. 308, one of the people – Norman Lewis, a US citizen – was killed instantly. This is also recorded by Pasteur Vallery-Radot in his 'diary' which relies heavily for this period on material from Victor Veau (Pasteur Vallery-Radot, 1966, p. 290). I have been unable to verify which version is correct.

64 Dupuy (1945), pp. 40–1.

65 AN 72AJ/62/IV/2, p. 182

66 Groult & Groult (1965), p. 303. The quote is from Mallarmé's poem 'Brise Marine'.

67 Patin (1994), pp. 93–5.

68 Brasillach (1955), p. 290–1.

69 Model & Bradley (1991), p. 267.
70 B-176, p. 5.
71 A-956, p. 16.
72 B-729, p. 21.
73 Model & Bradley (1991), p. 267.
74 AN 72AJ/45/I/6O. General Barton and General Gerow of the US Army both apparently passed through Paris during the day. According to Blumenson (1961), p. 617, Barton disturbed Leclerc at the Préfecture while the Free French general was having lunch. Leclerc, irritated, sent Barton to the Gare Montparnasse, 'where he found General Gerow already taking charge of the enormous responsibility of Paris'. This information is based on a conversation with Barton in 1954. Strikingly, Barton (1951) makes no mention of this. I have been unable to find any verification of what, if anything, Barton and Gerow did on this day. Gerow may have formally held responsibility for Paris according to SHAEF, but General Koenig was the Free French Military Governor of Paris, and everything that happened on 25 August underlined the fact that the Free French were in command of the capital, not SHAEF.
75 Sylvan et al. (2008), pp. 109–10.
76 von Choltitz's memoirs can be taken to imply that he was taken to Britain on the evening of 25 August (von Choltitz, 1969, p. 257). However, this contradicts the evidence in General Hodges' diary that he was questioned in France on 27 August (Sylvan et al., 2008). In his 1949 account of events von Choltitz states that he spent 'days' being interviewed by various American staff officers and travelling through Normandy to Cherbourg (von Choltitz, 1949, 15–26 October 1949). For details of the prison camp at Trent Park, see Neitzel (2007) and chapter 2 n. 16.
77 Lyon (1948), p. 23. Lyon – the T-Force commander – called their journey to Paris 'hazardous'. The hazards he described included French people offering wine, tossing apples and tomatoes as well as 'the ever present danger' of 'getting lost' (p. 22).
78 Lyon (1948), p. 24.
79 Lyon (1948), pp. 35–6.
80 Massu (1969), p. 152.
81 Vilain (1945), p. 23.
82 Massu (1969), p. 155.
83 Boegner (1992), p. 296.
84 Mesnil-Amar (2009), pp. 132–3;
85 Chaigneau (1981), pp. 233–6; for the fate of the deportees, see pp. 250–1.

CHAPTER 17

1 Cumberlege (1946), p. 197. The best accompaniment to this chapter is to watch the last four minutes of *La Libération de Paris* (1944), from 26:45 onwards. This covers the parade and shows some of the sights and the sounds I have tried to describe.

2 Squadron-Leader John Pudney reported from a friend's office: 'The house-keeper explained to me that she was not at her best. She had got drunk when she heard the BBC statement that Paris was free. She sobered up enough to see the Germans still across the road at their HQ, got drunk again from exasperation, and finally had such a hang-over for the liberation that she couldn't enjoy it at all.' Pudney (1944b).

3 Details in this paragraph from: Pyle (1944), p. 316; Tuffrau (2002), pp. 109–10; de Saint-Pierre (1945), p. 118; Lankford (1991), p. 175; AN 72AJ/62/IV/2, p. 198. Later on, Bruce popped into Guerlain's perfumery on the rue Saint Honoré, where Monsieur Guerlain gave him a bottle of Shalimar, to mark the liberation.

4 Tuffrau (2002), p. 112.

5 *L'Humanité* 26 August 1944.

6 Blumenson (1961), p. 619; Dansette (1946), pp. 412–413. A similar invitation was made to the British.

7 Blumenson (1961), p. 620. Lieutenant-Colonel Harold Lyon, who was in command of T-Force and was a stickler for military protocol, described the parade as 'unauthorized' (Lyon, 1948, p. 30).

8 Blumenson (1961), pp. 620–1.

9 See Fenby (2010) for a description of the significance of this parade in de Gaulle's life.

10 AN 72AJ/61/I/17, p. 42. Later that day, Gallois reflected on the tumultuous week he had just experienced, and wondered whether the coming days could be as remarkable. It seems unlikely that anything else in his life turned out to be as amazing.

11 Roy (1944), pp. 61–2. Dukson, with his white sling, can be made out just above the bending figure of de Gaulle on the left-hand page of the photograph of the wreath-laying ceremony reproduced in Conte (1984). US newsreel of the ceremony at the Arc de Triomphe can be seen at www.youtube.com/watch?v=dUVu9lOTkN4 [accessed July 2012]. See also *La Libération de Paris* (1944), at 26:45. Dunan (1946) is the sole source for Dukson's life.

12 According to a contemporary description of the parade published in *Le Figaro* (reproduced in Campaux, 1945, p. 224), de Gaulle was presented with various FFI fighters who had distinguished themselves during the insurrection, and some of these were invited to join the parade; one of those fighters was Georges Dukson. See plate 32. Photographs of the parade shortly after it set off show Dukson being pushed out of the way by an apparently irritated officer (see for example, the frontispiece in Dunan, 1945, or Bourget, 1979, pp. 232–3), which has led me to suggest that Dukson had simply strolled, uninvited, onto the head of the parade, and that he was subsequently ejected without ceremony (Cobb, 2009a and 2009b). This apparently mistaken interpretation of events is also implied by a hasty reading of Dunan (1945) who writes of Dukson: 'He was amazingly audacious. He would do anything for a bet. When General de Gaulle walked down the Champs-Elysées, only Georges Bidault, the future Foreign Minister, stood between Dukson and the head of

government.' (Dunan, 1945, p. 262.) Film of the parade near the place de la Concorde shows Dukson happily involved in the march, keeping the crowd at bay, apparently acting as a steward (at 0:28–0:33 in the US newsreel, which can be seen at www.youtube.com/watch?v=NGR7OnqDYII [accessed July 2012]). My current interpretation is that Dukson was invited to be one of the stewards who were ensuring crowd control by forming a human chain at the sides of the parade. However, with his arm in a sling, he was unable to fulfil this function, and by design or accident, he ended up wandering to the very front of the cortège at the beginning of the march, before being moved back to his function on the edge of the parade. At least one of the scenes was captured on film, and can be seen fleetingly, perhaps more than once. One of those incidents is at 1:20:04 on the DVD *Eté 44: La Libération* (2004). From this angle, the gesture of the officer as he moves Dukson to the side looks positively polite. The fact that even such a minor event remains hard to interpret, despite photographic evidence, underlines the difficulty of historical reconstruction.

13 Kriegel-Valrimont (1964), p. 15.
14 Roy (1944), p. 60.
15 de Gaulle (1956), pp. 310–311; Kriegel-Valrimont (1964), p. 15. The CNR members present were Daniel Mayer (Socialist Party), Joseph Laniel (Alliance Démocratique), Paul Bastid (Parti Radical) and Auguste Gillot (Communist Party) (Noguères & Degliame-Fouché, 1981, p. 565). According to Debû-Bridel (1978), the third member of COMAC, the communist Pierre Villon, was informed too late of the parade (Debû-Bridel, 1978, p. 188). This seems unlikely – he would surely have read his own party's newspaper. There was also a smart group of Free French officers, including Chaban, who by now had been provided with a proper uniform – see the photograph in Rocheteau (2004), p. 70.
16 'The morally prestigious route was physically painful,' wrote Hamon, ruefully. AN 72AJ/42/IV/3, p. 32.
17 AN 72AJ/42/IV/3, p. 32. A photograph of the parade includes Lefaucheux, Hamon and Tollet in the bottom left corner (de Gaulle, 1962, p. 349).
18 There are several photographs of this boisterous moment, which was typical of the whole parade. See for example Conte (1984).
19 de Gaulle's decision to walk down the Champs-Elysées was remarkable, in that this kind of walkabout was completely unheard of. In his diary, Daniel Boisdon called it 'audacious' (AN 72AJ/62/III/4, p. 51).
20 These long paper banners, barred with the tricolour and the words '*Vive de Gaulle*' or '*Vive la République*', were given out to people to hold along the length of the parade (Auroy, 2008, p. 335) – see for example Plate 36. '*De Gaulle au pouvoir*' can be seen on a banner in a photograph in Barozzi (1980) p. 157 and in a series of banners and placards in a colour photograph originally published in *Life* and reproduced in Fournier & Aymard (2010), p. 127.
21 Kriegel-Valrimont (1964), p. 15.
22 Pierquin (1983), p. 135.

23 BAM VV, 26.8. Despite this major obstacle, a journalist next to Professor Veau breathlessly dictated over the phone an entirely fictitious story about what he could see.

24 There is an excellent collection of pictures of the march, and of the huge crowds, in Fournier & Aymard (2010).

25 See for example the photograph in Anonymous (2004), p. 130.

26 Roy (1944), p. 63; Pyle (1944), p. 316.

27 de Saint Pierre (1945), p. 123.

28 Bood (1974), p. 338.

29 Roy (1944), p. 62.

30 Tuffrau (2002), p. 113.

31 Auroy (2008), p. 335.

32 Lankford (1991), p. 175.

33 Groult & Groult (1965), p. 303.

34 AN 72AJ/62/III/4, p. 51.

35 Boegner (1992), p. 299.

36 De Beauvoir (1965), p. 597.

37 AN 72AJ/61/I/14, p. 7.

38 Tuffrau (2002), p. 113.

39 Auroy (2008), p. 335.

40 In film of the parade, '1830' can be seen written on one of the shield-like placards; another placard read '1914' and can be seen in a photograph next to one of the *'De Gaulle au pouvoir'* banners (Barozzi, 1980, p. 157). According to Colonel de Langlade, as soon as de Gaulle began to march down the Champs-Elysées, a crowd of people swept around the Free French leader: 'There were two or three hundred people. The women had their hair down and their breasts out [*'leurs mammelles au vent'*], dressed in tri-colour flags and wearing phrygien bonnets [the symbol of the 1789 revolution]. I had a flashback of the *tricoteuses* [the women who according to myth sat by the guillotine in revolutionary France, knitting]. The sight was both indecent and grotesque ...' (De Langlade, 1964, pp. 224–5.) De Langlade further claimed that both he and his men were 'disappointed and disgusted' by the parade, which they had imagined very differently (de Langlade, 1964, p. 225). The minor collaborationist politician Jacques Bardoux also did not like the parade – it was too disorganised, and he also reported there were women with bare breasts (*'des filles dépoitraillées'*) (Bardoux, 1958, p. 369). René Courtin complained: 'Behind, there was an indescribable throng of official cars, reporters' cars, and various lorries, too often covered with women.' (Courtin, 1994, p. 45.) In his memoirs published in 1956, de Gaulle writes: 'Some people with minor walk-on roles joined the cortège of my comrades, even though they had no right to. But no one paid them any attention' (de Gaulle, 1956, p. 311). However, given de Gaulle's acerbic style, this could be referring to virtually anyone except the Free French.

41 Spanish exile Victoria Kent, excited by the sight of the tanks of La Nueve, wrote in her diary: 'The heat is overwhelming, but the earth is not dark: it

glows red, white and blue. The dark earth has been blown away by the wind: today the streets are red, white and blue ... The sky is no longer the colour of lead: silver aeroplanes, under a new light, are twinkling over the beautiful Arc de Triomphe, wishing everyone welcome and spreading an indefinable calm, based on safety and confidence.' Kent (1947), p. 211. According to Dansette (1946), there was a huge banner in the Spanish republican colours (violet, yellow and red), stretched across the Champs-Elysées (Dansette, 1946, p. 422). I have found no evidence of the presence of this banner; it does not appear on any of the hundreds of photographs of the parade.

42 A cursory comparison of any photographs from the 26 August parade and from Pétain's five months earlier (see prelude) shows that there were many, many more people there for de Gaulle – compare Plate 1 and Plate 33.

43 Auroy (2008), p. 336.

44 Pyle (1944), pp. 316–217.

45 Tuffrau (2002), p. 115.

46 Auroy (2008), pp. 337–8.

47 Galtier-Boissière (1944), p. 284.

48 Cumberlege (1946), pp. 199–201. The full report is remarkably atmospheric. A similar French radio recording of the gunfire can be heard at 2:30 here: www.youtube.com/watch?v=dyKtQyIAzJU [accessed July 2012].

49 Ratcliffe (2011), p. 345. This sentence is not given in the earliest publication of this letter to Wodehouse's friend, W. Townend, written on 30 December 1944 (Wodehouse, 1953, pp. 117–119). Wodehouse had been caught up in the fall of France and had notoriously made some humorous broadcasts on German radio that were later seen as evidence of Nazi sympathies (Sproat, 1981 and 1999). Wodehouse moved to Paris from Berlin in 1943 because his wife was frightened of the air-raids; the couple moved into the Hotel Bristol on the rue du Faubourg Saint-Honoré in September. According to the director of the Bristol, Monsieur Vidal, Wodehouse was 'a particularly quiet man' who did not discuss politics or the war, and 'did not speak to many people' (NA KV/2/3550, p. 46). According to his statement to Major Cussen of MI5 on 9–12 September 1944, while in Paris Wodehouse completed *Joy in the Morning*, and wrote *Full Moon*, *Spring Fever* and *Uncle Dynamite* (NA KV/2/3550, p. 43). As might be expected of Wodehouse, none of these books give the slightest hint of the circumstances under which they were written. In the same 30 December letter to Townend, Wodehouse recognised his detachment from events: 'I always think it such a pity that experiences happen to the wrong people. I don't suppose, for instance, that I shall ever make anything of life in Paris during the liberation, whereas if you had been here then you would have got a wealth of material.' (Wodehouse, 1953, p. 117).

50 Dubois (1944), p. 103.

51 Dubois (1944), p. 104.

52 Bood (1974), p. 339.

53 Lyon (1948), p. 31.

54 Jacobs (n.d.), p. 40. T-Force headquarters was chaotic. British intelligence

officer Malcolm Muggeridge hoved up there and found a scene of 'great confusion' (Muggeridge, 1973, p. 210).

55 Some French historians have devoted a surprising amount of attention to this decision, presumably because of the affront it represented to the Catholic Church, and the potential politico-religious tensions it implied. See for example Dansette (1946), pp. 415–421; Aron (1959), pp. 444–7. For a first-hand account of why the decision was taken, and what exactly was involved, see Closon (1974), pp. 232–5.

56 Cumberlege (1946), pp. 201–204; Crang (2007) reproduces the broadcast and also a later document by Reid describing the event and how he managed to get the recording to London (Crang is Reid's grandson). The dramatic recording – including the alarming break in transmission – can be heard at news.bbc.co.uk/media/audio/40176000/rm/_40176183_9061_25_08_1944 gaulle.ram [accessed July 2012].

57 Courtin (1994), p. 46.

58 See the photograph in Barozzi (1980), p. 180.

59 Cumberlege (1946), p. 203.

60 Courtin (1994), p. 46.

61 See photographs of these incidents in Fournier & Aymard (2010), pp. 146–7.

62 *Manchester Guardian* 12 September 1944.

63 BAM VV, 26.8

64 Cumberlege (1946), p. 204.

65 Bood (1974), p. 339.

66 Bourget (1984), pp. 455–6 and Giolitto (2002), p. 358. Roger Stéphane describes how he ordered Mansuy's arrest on 25 August, and how the captive was executed in cold blood the next day (Stéphane, 2004, pp. 19–22). Aron (1959), p. 441, perhaps basing himself on Stéphane's account, also states that Mansuy was arrested on 25 August. Favreau (1996), pp. 484–5 covers the alternative versions of Mansuy's capture and death.

67 Hazard (1998), p. 395. At the Ministry of Finance, which occupied much of the north side of the Louvre, the Budget Director, Roland Dagnicourt, was killed by gunshot, although whether this was from a sniper or was 'friendly fire' was never known (Courtin, 1994, p. 47).

68 Laborie (1994), p. 383.

69 de Gaulle (1983), p. 297.

70 de Gaulle (1956), p. 315. For an analysis of this change of view, and for how the Communist Party changed its presentation of the shootings in a rather different way from de Gaulle, see Laborie (1994), pp. 381–5. Strikingly (and Laborie does not note this), the shootings do not feature in the extensive coverage of the parade in the thirty-minute newsreel *La Libération de Paris* (1944). Luizet later told his close friend General de Boissieu that he thought the shooting was a genuine attempt on de Gaulle's life and that it was the work of 'dissident elements in the CNR' – in other words, the communists (de Boissieu, 1981, p. 259). At the time, Daniel Boisdon was convinced that there were snipers trying to kill de Gaulle, and that they were thwarted by the size of the crowd, which acted as a kind of human shield. He heard that

a man and two women were responsible for the firing in Notre Dame (AN 72AJ/62/III/4, p. 52). Albert Grunberg thought that the people responsible for the firing were far-right elements: 'The enemy within wants to start a civil war. Let's put an end to their games, by a thorough and exemplary purge.' (Grunberg, 2001, p. 351.)

71 Lankford (1991), p. 177. The 'finally evaded him' is telling.

72 AN 72AJ/61/I/14, p. 7.

73 Christienne & Plancard (n.d.), p. 62. In a dramatic story (Barat, 1945, pp. 87–9) which is impossible to verify, at nightfall, Dogue of the 'Victoire' hit-squad was sent up on the roof of a building in Saint-Germain to find a rooftop sniper. There was no one up there, but they did find an empty cartridge. To try and trick the sniper, most of the group left, making as much noise as possible, leaving Dogue, his comrade Canard and the group's leader up on the roof. Long after midnight there was a noise from near one of the chimneys, a series of bricks was removed, and then a man's head appeared. The group fired two shots and there was a terrific noise as the man fell back into the chimney and down into the building. The FFI men dashed downstairs and smashed down the door of the apartment below and found a wounded man lying in a pool of blood. His gun was nearby, along with a stock of ammunition and a large sum of money. It is not known who he was, what he was hoping to achieve, or even if he existed.

74 Pasteur Vallery-Radot (1966), p. 290.

75 Debû-Bridel (1978), pp. 188–9.

76 Courtin (1994), p. 47.

77 BAM VV, 26.8, 27.8. In his entry for 26 August, Veau suggests that de Gaulle was also present. Given de Gaulle's attitude towards the secretary-generals the next day (see chapter 18), this seems very unlikely. In his own, brief, account, Pasteur Vallery-Radot makes no mention of de Gaulle's presence (Pasteur Vallery-Radot, 1966, p. 290). Veau based his account on his conversation with Pasteur Vallery-Radot's wife, Jacqueline.

78 For the context and implications, see Novick (1968). For an interesting discussion over how to translate the term, inserted into a thriller about the period, see Elkins (2002), p. 189.

79 All details from AN 72AJ/247/I/2.

80 Brasillach (1955), pp. 291–4.

81 Berlière & Liaigre (2012), pp. 155–6 & 314–315.

82 AN 72AJ/62/IV/2, p. 61. A similar story is told by the soldier's mother, Madame Godfroy, AN 72AJ/62/IV/2, p. 65.

83 After Action Report, p. 43.

84 All details from B-308, p. 164.

85 B-728, p. 11.

86 B-729, pp. 15–22.

87 B-546, p. 4.

88 Fournier & Eymard (2010), p. 153.

89 Fournier & Eymard (2010), pp. 154–5.

90 Jauffret (1994).

91 B-176, pp. 5–6.
92 AN 72AJ/62/IV/2, p. 190.
93 See the 1946 report by Louis Marcou of Turma-Vengeance, BDIC FΔ rés 844/03/9, section 9.1.
94 The order to leave for Oissery – initially to take effect at 05:30 on 25 August – is reproduced in Cumont (1991), p. 118.
95 OSS War Diary, 3:768–82.
96 For a detailed, but not particularly clear, account of the various reasons that might explain the delay, and an attempt to outline the chronology, see Cumont (1991). For an even more confusing account, see BDIC FΔ rés 844/03/9. Marcou suggests that the group gathered to receive parachuted British tanks (sections 9.1 and 9.4). This seems unlikely.
97 Cumont (1991), pp. 125–8. See also OSS War Diary, 3:768–82.
98 OSS War Diary, vol 3:768–82 contains the Team AUBREY report. A summary of this report, together with a map and some speculation about the German forces involved, can be found in Lewis (1991), pp. 22–5. In his personal report, Marchant states that the battle took place on 27 August (p. 776); Hooker gives no date, and is unclear (p. 780). At the 1946 Congress of the Vengeance movement that Hildevert belonged to, the date was given as 27 August (see Actes du Congrès de Vengeance, 25 May 1946, chatran.vengeance.free.fr [accessed July 2012]). The obituary of SPIRITUALIST's radio operator, Henry Diacono, also stated that the date was 27 August (*Daily Telegraph* 23 August 2010). However, there is no doubt that the battle took place on 26 August. Furthermore, the major road running past the site of the beet processing plant is called the rue du 26 Août 1944, and the same date is given on the war memorials marking the battle. Gilles Primout's excellent website contains a good summary of events (www.liberation-de-paris.gilles-primout.fr/eoissery.htm [accessed July 2012]), and includes a long list of those who were killed in the fighting or died in deportation, and the names of those few who survived, much of it taken from Cumont (1991). Captain Marchant was killed in April 1945, on an Intelligence Corps operation in the Far East, when his plane crashed on takeoff at Calcutta. He was awarded the Military Cross posthumously (NA WO 373/98). Sergeant Hooker survived the war; he died in Suffolk in June 1988, aged sixty-four (Lewis, 1991, p. 25). Hooker's SOE personnel file can be found at NA HS 9/739/6.
99 For details of Yves Goussard, see www.memoresist.org [accessed July 2012]. In 2009, a school in Martinique was named after Yves Goussard. Yves died at the beginning of March 1945, like Anne Frank.
100 Houssin (2004), p. 234.
101 See chapter 16 and Fournier & Eymard (2010), p. 156.
102 For details of the dead at the Bichat hospital, see Hazard (1998), p. 397.
103 Auroy (2008), p. 339.
104 Tuffrau (2002), pp. 116–117.
105 de Saint Pierre (1945), p. 130.
106 Vilain (1945), p. 26.

107 Massu (1969), p. 156.
108 AN 72AJ/62/III/4, p. 53. One of the few photographs of the destruction taken that night shows Notre Dame silhouetted against the flames from the Halle aux Vins, just the other side of the river. See *Yank* 17 September 1944.
109 Bourget (1984), p. 390. For a list of the sites that were hit, and photographs of the damage caused, see Fournier & Eymard (2010), pp. 157–60.
110 AN 72AJ/62/IV/1, p. 104.
111 AN 72AJ/61/II/1, p. 4.
112 Dreyfus & Gensburger (2003), p. 261.

CHAPTER 18

1 Lankford (1991), pp. 180–1.
2 See chapter 10. For photographs showing the state of Le Bourget, see Fournier & Eymard (2010), pp. 194–7.
3 B-176, pp. 7–8.
4 de Boissieu (1981), p. 260.
5 Fournier & Eymard (2010), pp. 194–5.
6 de Saint-Pierre (1945), pp. 138–9.
7 Model & Bradley (1991), p. 274.
8 ETHINT 30, p. 7.
9 Boegner (1992), p. 314; Cazaux (1975), pp. 232 and 235. Bourget claims that after 3 October Field Marshal Jodl banned attacks on Paris in these terms: 'for political reasons, all attacks on Paris by V2 weapons are suspended' (Bourget, 1984, p. 494, note). Bourget gives no source for this quote.
10 Cazaux (1975), p. 315.
11 Eisenhower (1948), p. 326. See also note 12. There is no mention of this conversation in de Gaulle's war memoirs, which were written eight years after Eisenhower's; indeed, de Gaulle makes no mention of the US march through Paris at all. However, the Americans were clearly not unduly worried about de Gaulle's authority: the day before the march, 28 August, Gerow formally handed control of Paris over to General Koenig, something he would hardly have done had the Americans had any doubts about the ability of the Free French to control the city. Koenig brushed aside the gesture, rightly pointing out that the city had been under French administration since the moment of liberation (Blumenson, 1961, p. 625).
12 Bourget (1984), p. 402.
13 AN 72AJ/61/I/14, p. 8. The march may have produced a different effect in Germany – US newsreel footage of the parade was shown there to indicate that Paris was now under a brutal American occupation (Lindeperg, 1993, p. 139, n. 1).
14 Fonde (1969), pp. 114–115. According to the commentary on the DVD *D-Day to Berlin* (1998), the podium consisted of an upturned Bailey Bridge, covered in drapes.
15 de Gaulle (1956), p. 317. For an examination of whether the situation in

France corresponded to the Trotskyist notion of 'dual power', as suggested by OSS agent Crane Brinton, see Cobb (2009a), p. 385, n. 32.

16 Courtin (1994), p. 48.

17 Hostache (1958), p. 451. In late August, there was still no sign of any of the ministers from Algiers turning up in the newly liberated capital. De Gaulle sent a furious message to Algiers asking why the ministers had not arrived or even communicated with him since he left Algiers over a week earlier (de Gaulle, 1983, pp. 299–300). The Free French leader was now experiencing the isolation and lack of communication that Parodi had suffered for so long. In fact, just as the message was sent, the ministers were leaving Algiers on the *Jeanne d'Arc*. They arrived at Cherbourg on 1 September, and finally got to Paris in the afternoon of Saturday 2 September (Bourget, 1984, p. 415).

18 For the full text of Leclerc's letter see de Gaulle (1956), pp. 710–711.

19 de Gaulle (1983), pp. 301–302; Villon (1984), pp. 117–118.

20 For the full text of Leclerc's letter see de Gaulle (1956), pp. 710–711.

21 Bourget (1984), pp. 418–419; Calvès (1984), pp. 113–114; Riffaud (1994), pp. 143–6; Ouzoulias (1972), pp. 458–62.

22 de Gaulle (1970), p. 441.

23 de Gaulle (1970), p. 442. This alarmed even people who should have been sympathetic to de Gaulle, such as banker Léonard Rist. The sudden arrival of the 'Algerians' with their 'ready-made plans' rankled with those who had been living and fighting inside France. Léonard wrote to his brother: 'Those "brave people" the General mentioned in his broadcast have got their own ideas about what should be done, and those ideas aren't any sillier than those of Georges Boris ... The struggle is now out in the open and the France of the interior feels ignored by the France of Algiers ... We will soon know if de Gaulle is the symbol we thought he was or if he thinks he is some kind of Messiah.' Rist (1983), p. 435, n. 39.

24 Liebling (1944), pp. 44–5.

25 Penrose (2005), pp. 69–71. Miller continued: 'Most were pleased and surprised that the Parisians seemed so beautifully dressed and amiable instead of lean and hungry and sour. As a matter of fact a lot of people were lean and hungry but the sour ones had probably stayed at home and the others were nourished on dreams and stimulated by the adrenalin of joy.'

26 AN 72AJ/61/I/14, p. 9.

27 Penrose (2005), p. 69.

28 Auroy (2008), p. 348.

29 Groult & Groult (1965), p. 309.

30 Groult & Groult (1965), p. 319.

31 Groult & Groult (1965), p. 321. Rudi eventually asked Benoîte to marry him; she turned him down. In 1945 she married a French medical student, who died a few months later.

32 Bood (1974), p. 341.

33 For example John Groth visited Picasso on 27 August. Groth asked Picasso if he had any message for American artists: 'He hesitated and seemed

embarrassed as he walked up and down for a moment while we all waited on his words.' 'Tell them,' he said finally, 'to work hard – like me.' (Groth, 1945, p. 11.) One visitor was photographer Private Francis Lee, who took some excellent photographs of Picasso, including one of the artist with *The Triumph of Pan* (Barr, 1945, p.9). Lee was a pacifist and an artist who initially wanted to be a conscientious objector, but enlisted as an army cameraman. His unit was involved in D-Day, during which he took some memorable film. In 1976 Lee made a short documentary of footage he had shot during the war, including his visit to Picasso: *World War II and Me*.

34 Brassaï (1999), p. 205. The full quote reads in translation: 'Paris was liberated, but I was and still am under siege. Visitors come every day in packs. Again yesterday, there was a huge crowd here. People behave as if I had nothing better to do.' This conversation took place on 12 May 1945.

35 Penrose (2005), p. 73. Miller writes of a series of 'exquisite portraits of an imaginary FFI. The face is exactly that of all the rifle-slinging boys in the street – gentle and ferocious – young but wary and wise, poetic and buoyant. Scarcely bearded but with warm eyes, be he university student or *"chasseur du café"* he is proud and equal and free. He has tasted the blood of the enemy, in private duel and guerilla warfare, and now he awaits joining the real Army to satisfy his appetite' (pp. 73–4). Zervos (1963) pp. 20–1 reproduces four black-and-white portraits of a teenage boy, three in profile, painted on 13–15 August (before the FFI appeared on the streets), and one face on, painted on 31 August. A photograph of Picasso in his studio by Miller shows two of these portraits in the lower part of the image. One of the 13–15 August paintings is in the Art Institute of Chicago: www.artic.edu/aic/collections/artwork/158479?search_id=5 [accessed July 2012].

36 Pudney (1944a), p. 182.

37 Pudney (1944a), p. 183.

38 Bourget (1984), p. 502; Penrose (1962), p. 317. For a photograph of the exhibition, see Barr (1945), p. 7.

39 For the best account of this period in the history of Paris, see Beevor & Cooper (2004).

40 Cazaux (1975), p. 299.

41 Cazaux (1975), pp. 290 and 349. Five of the dailies still survive – *Le Figaro*, *France-Soir* (previously known as *Défense de la France*), *L'Humanité*, *Le Monde* and *Le Parisien*.

42 BAM VV, 2.9.

43 Auroy (2008), pp. 343–4.

44 Cazaux (1975), p. 258.

45 de Saint-Pierre (1945), pp. 144–6.

46 Bourget (1984), p. 473.

47 Cazaux (1975), p. 304.

48 Auroy (2008), pp. 348–9.

49 Tuffrau (2002), pp. 117–118.

50 de Saint-Pierre (1945), p. 141.

51 Rist (1983), p. 433. Charles was the father of banker Léonard Rist.

52 For contrasting views of this period, see Novick (1968), Aron (1967 and 1969) and Vergez-Chaignon (2010). Before the liberation, the Free French had tried to find out what the public thought about punishing collaborators. In July, Yves Morandat, one of Parodi's aides, sent Algiers the results of an opinion poll that the Free French Delegation in Paris had carried out through a network of agents, who obliquely questioned around 500 people. This group was known as the Services de Sondages et Statistiques (SSS). For details of how they carried out their polls, see AN 72AJ/71/VI/2a, pp. 3–5. Examples of the raw responses can be found at AN 72AJ/71/VI/2a, pp. 40–56, and examples of SSS reports, including detailed breakdowns of the answers according to social group, at AN 72AJ/71/VI/2b. On this occasion, nearly one third of respondents were in favour of allowing popular hatred of collaborationists to go ahead, unbridled. Similarly, 30 per cent thought that Pétain merited a death sentence (about the same number disagreed), while 65 per cent thought that Laval should die for his betrayal, against 15 per cent who disagreed. Finally, when asked whether de Gaulle had been right in his handling of the Allies, 77 per cent of those questioned were positive, while 11 per cent did not care and 12 per cent thought he had been maladroit (AN 72AJ/235/II/170–3).

53 Bourget (1984), pp. 433 and 451.

54 Bourdrel (1988).

55 A photograph of the collaborationist prisoners in the Vel' d'Hiv' was printed in Babelay (1945). Much later it was claimed to show the round-up of Jews in 1942; see Bourget (1984), pp. 437–8.

56 Bourget (1984), p. 436; Taittinger (1948), p. 244.

57 Bourget (1984), p. 439.

58 Taittinger (1948), p. 256.

59 Boegner (1992), p. 305; Cazaux (1975), p. 243.

60 Bourget (1984), pp. 442–3.

61 Bourget (1984), p. 433.

62 Cazaux (1975), p. 248. The photograph is reproduced in Bourget (1979), pp. 162–3; of forty-five men, only five were unidentified.

63 Bourget (1984), p. 456.

64 Brasillach (1955), pp. 295–303.

65 For a detailed description of the trial, see Kaplan (2000). For a reproduction of the letter to de Gaulle pleading for clemency, signed by Paul Valéry, François Mauriac, Louis de Broglie and others, see Piketty (2011), p. 175. For a discussion of the issue, see Winock (1994).

66 Buton (1994), p. 391.

67 Pisani provides a dramatic eye-witness account of the sordid events (Pisani, 1974, pp. 11–15).

68 Vergez-Chaignon (2010).

69 Bourget (1984), p. 468.

70 Berlière & Liaigre (2007), pp. 334–7.

71 This did not go unnoticed by the press – in particular the communist news-papers – who organised campaigns against these men (Berlière, 1996, p. 76,

n. 3). For the general context of the police during the occupation, see Berlière (2001). Intriguingly, a substantial portion of the files from the Brigades Spéciales allegedly disappeared from the Préfecture during the insurrection. Some of these allegedly related to interrogations and signed confessions by some communists. Berlière & Liaigre (2007) suggest that these documents provided the leadership of the Communist Party with weapons in its post-war internal struggles (pp. 319–23).

72 Virgili (2000).

73 Tuffrau (2002), pp. 120–1.

74 AN 72AJ/62/IV/1, p. 88.

75 AN 72AJ/62/IV/1, pp. 97–103. The rumours about the headmaster persisted for days afterwards, and when he attempted to find out which FFI group had been involved in arresting him, there was no trace of them. For a discussion of the role of rumour in this incident, see Virgili (2000), p. 196. The FFI group in charge of this area was the Saint-Just company of Madeline Riffaud and André Calvès. The Saint-Just company had no records of any such raid, and neither Riffaud (1994) nor Calvès (1984) mentions any of the FFIers named by the two teachers.

76 Bourget (1984), p. 435. For the fullest treatment of the Institut Dentaire, see the chilling account by Berlière & Liaigre (2012). They point out that there is no evidence that Fabien ever visited the Institut (p. 144).

77 There were unofficial 'prisons' on the rue Beaubourg, at Vitry-sur-Seine and Maisons-Alfort; see Berlière & Liaigre (2012), pp. 358–63.

78 Bourget (1984), p. 464 gives the date as 26 August. Berlière & Liaigre (2012) show that Madame Albertini was arrested on 25 August (p. 158). Her arrest was revealed at the trial of Georges Albertini, who in December 1944 was tried for treason and condemned to the relatively light sentence of five years' hard labour (Vergez-Chaignon, 2010, p. 391). Albertini was arrested on 25 September (Lévy, 1992, p. 21).

79 Berlière & Liaigre (2012), p. 156. For a first-hand account of life inside the Institut Dentaire, see the memoir by collaborationist politician René Chateau, published under the pseudonym of Jean-Pierre Abel (Abel, 1947).

80 Berlière & Liaigre (2012), p. 280.

81 Berlière & Liaigre (2012), p. 173.

82 Berlière & Liaigre (2012), p. 188.

83 Berlière & Liaigre (2012), pp. 292–3. I have been unable to discover if René Sentuc was related to CGT leader Maurice Sentuc, a.k.a. 'Véry' (see chapter 3).

84 Denis (1963), p. 137.

85 Barcia (2003), p. 80. Two of Bucholz's comrades were also kidnapped and beaten by Communist Party members at this time. Barcia, a.k.a. 'Hardy', was a young man who was close to the Communist Party, but was also influenced by Bucholz, who was a member of the tiny group led by David Korner ('Barta'). The shock of Bucholz's assassination led Barcia to join the Barta group; he went on to found and lead Lutte Ouvrière, which from the 1970s onwards became well known in France through its presidential candidate, Arlette Laguiller.

86 Berlière & Liaigre (2012), p. 230.

87 Bourget (1984), p. 443.

88 All details about Petiot from Césaire (2006) and King (2012). Petiot was eventually flushed out following the publication of an article about the case in a Resistance newspaper, which named him and cast a large number of aspersions on his name (as if being a mass killer was not bad enough). This provoked Petiot to write a letter to the press, inadvertently revealing a series of clues as to his new identity and whereabouts. Long after his death, Petiot was defended in a book by the colourful former SOE agent Ronald Seth (in 1942 Seth was arrested by the Gestapo on a mission to Estonia and subsequently worked for the Germans; after the war he became a sexologist and, under the pseudonym Robert Chartham, founded the magazine *Forum* – see his obituary in *The Times* 5 February 1985). Seth accepted Petiot's claim that he was in fact working for the Resistance, and that he had been threatened by the Communist Party (Seth, 1963).

89 Bourget (1984), p. 462. British Intelligence officer Malcolm Muggeridge interviewed 'Laffont' after he claimed that the French police were compromised and unable to deal with his case fairly. Nearly thirty years afterwards, Lafont still left a striking impression on Muggeridge, whose closing recollections are typically unpleasant: recalling that Lafont was guillotined rather than shot, Muggeridge imagined that 'neat, sallow head with the blunt Mediterranean back to it, sliced off like a thistle's' (Muggeridge, 1973, p. 220). Bonny and Lafont were arrested at the end of August, having been betrayed by one of their colleagues, the shadowy Joseph Joanovici, a millionaire scrap metal merchant who worked for the Germans and also claimed to have links with sections of the Resistance in the Paris police. Joanovici was eventually arrested in 1947 and tried for economic collaboration in 1949; the head of French counter-intelligence, Roget Wybot, claimed that Joanovici had not been arrested previously because he was protected by the Préfecture de Police. Whatever the case, the Prefect of Police, Charles Luizet, was forced to resign because of suspicions about the role of the Préfecture in the Joanovici case (Bernert, 1975). Joanovici's double-dealing existence is the subject of a recent multi-volume French comic book series, *Il Etait Une Fois en France*, by Fabien Nury and Sylvain Vallée.

90 Galtier-Boissiere (1944), p. 294.

91 Vergez-Chaignon (2010), pp. 202–74.

92 Berthonnet (2003).

93 Denis (1963), p. 148.

94 The first managing director of the régie Renault, as it was known, was Pierre Lefaucheux.

95 Denis (1963), pp. 147-50; Zvenigorosky (1994).

96 See Minguet (1997) for the view of a Trotskyist working in one of these factories, Caudron. For an overview of this period, written by a participant, see Craipeau (1978); Craipeau was a leader of the Trotskyists, but stepped down during the insurrection, frustrated because most of his comrades were unable or unwilling to seize the moment. On 17 September, the few

hundred Trotskyists in the Parti Communiste Internationaliste (PCI) did their best to talk up the factory occupations, in a leaflet entitled 'Vivent les Comités d'usines!', but it contains few concrete examples of factories actually under the control of factory committees (the exceptions were the Caudron and Jumo factories, where Trotskyist militants had some influence) (www.association-radar.org/spip.php?article1023 [accessed July 2012]). Although the PCI's call for the creation of inter-factory committees and of 'soviets' at this stage may have been programmatically pure, the moment that such demands could catch fire in the popular imagination of workers in the Paris region had passed, if it had ever existed. Indeed, according to the Trotskyists themselves, this orientation may have contributed to their isolation. A year later, one of the leaders of the PCI (Marc Spoulber) publicly stated that their group was 'inexperienced and lacked audacity', and that by concentrating on the question of factory committees ('elected by a very small proportion of the working class') they had been unable to challenge the domination of the Communist Party in the working-class neighbourhoods where the insurrection took place, arms in hand (Marc, 1945, p. 6). Another militant of the time, Claude Bernard ('Raoul'), had a similar analysis: 'Our "soviet" orientation led us to counterpose soviets to everything else.' In Suresnes, when the PCF-led militia decided to take the town hall during the insurrection, recalled Raoul, 'Instead of going with them, we stayed outside, mocking their democratic legalism. All we had to do was to go inside and sit down. But we deliberately remained apart, bewitched by our perspective of creating "pure" soviets.' (Broué, 1995, p. 27.)

97 Marc (1945), p. 6.
98 Hostache (1958), p. 454.
99 The 'Gardes patriotiques' were initially, and confusingly, known as the 'Milices patriotiques'. For fairly obvious reasons, the name was soon changed. There was a struggle with the CPL over who would appoint the mayors in the twenty arrondissements of the city. According to the laws adopted by the Provisional Government earlier in the year, the CPL had the right to appoint the arrondissement mayors. On 30 October the government decided that it would appoint the mayors and that the CPL would merely be consulted on various issues, despite opposition from the whole of the CPL, including Léo Hamon. This was effectively the death-knell of the CPL; in July 1945 it organised a rally ('les États Généraux de la Renaissance Française') calling for the full application of the CNR programme before transforming itself into a society for commemorating its previous role, in which form it still exists today. Denis (1963), pp. 151–9.
100 Bourget (1984), p. 421.
101 Cazaux (1975) pp. 321 and 326. In the second half of November, British intelligence officer Malcolm Muggeridge hung out with one of the last armed groups (he claimed to have met them when Churchill and de Gaulle marched down the Champs-Elysées (Muggeridge, 1973, p. 216); this was on 11 November – Boegner, 1992, p. 319). Muggeridge's recollections were those of a perfect snob: 'They were mostly very young, with that curious

hunted animal look that street life gives … I was never able to decide whether they were just a marauding gang, or whether patriotism and ideological fervour played some part in their activities and antics … Considering their youth, they behaved with a horrifying callousness, arrogance and brutality.' (Muggeridge, 1973, p. 217.)

102 The Communist Party's support for the government was assured – at least temporarily – and this was confirmed when exiled PCF leader Maurice Thorez returned from Moscow and, in January 1945, made a barnstorming speech in front of his comrades, in which he pledged the Party's support for 'One army, one police, one administration' (Buton, 1993, p. 195).

103 Galtier-Boissière (1944), pp. 292–3.

104 ANACR (n.d.), p. 38.

105 Courtin (1994), pp. 72 and 75.

106 Marie-Hélène Lefaucheux wrote down this amazing story – she called it 'a series of miracles' – in August 1945. The section dealing with her successful rescue of Pierre can be found in AN 72AJ/67/IV/18, pp. 16–24. In the text, the names of the key protagonists are indicated by initials; there is a key on p. 9. Although there was no question of a bribe, Madame Lefaucheux gave von Else 10,000 marks as they parted; she regretted this when she returned safely to Paris. For Claire Girard, a farm manager who was not a member of any Resistance group but helped downed Allied pilots, see Girard (1954) and Andrieu (1997) (neither make mention of her link with Marie-Hélène Lefaucheux). The small square in front of the boulangerie in Courdimanche is now called place Claire Girard.

EPILOGUE

1 Rice (1945), pp. 328 and 332.

2 Cazaux (1975), pp. 263 and 273.

3 Tuffrau (2002), p. 129; Matot (2010), p. 261. 'Decour' was the Resistance pseudonym of Jacques Decourdemanche. For a short time after the liberation the school was known as Lycée Decourdemanche.

4 Philippe Castetbon's immensely moving book *Ici Est Tombé* consists of interviews he made in the early 2000s with the surviving relatives of the victims, along with some stunning photographs of the interviewees (Castetbon, 2004). Various websites have sought to list these plaques, providing information about the locations and about the people they commemorate – e.g. www.plaques-commemoratives.org [accessed July 2012].

5 The poster for the exhibition, which took place at the Musée Carnavalet, is reproduced in Darrobers (1989), p. 69. It featured a montage of images, centred on one of Robert Doisneau's photographs of the barricade on the rue de Huchette, opposite the Préfecture.

6 ADM 72A, p. 2. The introduction to the brochure was written by Parodi, and is reproduced in Studer (2003).

7 Merlat (1947).

8 This bold decision to digitise soon fell victim to a failure to 'future-proof': the software that is required to view the images under the best circumstances (Adobe VSG) was discontinued by its maker in 2009 (the most recent versions date to 2005 or even 2001, depending on your operating system, so may no longer work). The images can be viewed, but with difficulty. Good luck. www.archivesdefrance.culture.gouv.fr [accessed July 2012].

9 Among the recently emerged material is some film of the 11th arrondissement, taken in August: www.dailymotion.com/video/x8867e_paris-xie-aout-1944_webcam [accessed July 2012].

10 Debono (2004).

11 There are several accounts of this process. Langlois (1998) is particularly detailed, contrasting the various versions of the film, and the difference between French, US and Soviet newsreel accounts of the liberation of Paris.

12 See chapter 16; Albert Mahuzier, who was not one of the core team of the Comité de Libération du Cinéma Français, recalled that he filmed a member of the Garde républicaine sounding 'Ceasefire' on his trumpet, but that 'this scene, no doubt compromising for some, did not appear in the official film of the Liberation' (Mahuzier, 1961, p. 224).

13 Lindeperg (1993); Debono (2004); Langlois (1997 and 1998).

14 This explains why it has been called a 'Gaullist' film, despite the relative downplaying of the role of the Free French – Debono (2004).

15 See the excellent analysis in Tombs (1995). For a survey of Parisian insurrections, including 1944, see Burton (2001).

16 See Eric Hazan's exploration of the city and its meaning (Hazan, 2010).

17 In a discussion with Marc Boegner, de Gaulle claimed that the communists hoped to seize power after 24 August, but they were hampered by the fact that the masses did not follow them; by mid-September de Gaulle considered that the communists were not a 'present danger' (Boegner, 1992, p. 309). For an overview of the position of the Communist Party in this period, see Buton (1993); for the classic anti-communist view, see Aron (1959). For an account of the overall context in Europe, see Lowe (2012).

18 Cazaux (1975), pp. 227–8.

19 Bourget (1984), p. 477.

20 Bourget (1984), pp. 476–9. See for example the discussions with the participants in Breton (1964) or Crémieux (1971), or the polemical broadside by Rajsfus (2004).

21 NA GRGG 181(C), p. 4.

22 Studer (2003).

23 AN 72AJ/62/VII/3.

24 von Choltitz (1949).

25 *Is Paris Burning?* is based on hundreds of interviews with participants, but it is impossible to verify or cross-reference them, rendering it hard to use as a historical source. In reviews published at the time, British and US historians appear to have taken Collins & Lapierre's statements about the threat to Paris at face value. M. R. D. Foot concluded: 'The General was faced, in the

end, with the choice of obeying orders or saving Paris; he saved Paris, and earned his niche in history' (Foot, 1965), while William Chamberlin stated that 'what impelled von Choltitz to act as he did remains something of a mystery' because the Germans had 'mines and explosives set for massive destruction' (Chamberlin, 1965). There was no mystery, because there were no mines and explosives, and he did not 'save' the city (see chapter 16 and below). The film was directed by René Clément and starred a host of major French and US actors in a style that mixed location reconstructions with documentary footage of the actual events. The actors included Jean-Paul Belmondo, Yves Montand, Alain Delon, Leslie Caron, Orson Welles, Anthony Perkins, Kirk Douglas and Robert Stack, while the screenplay was by Gore Vidal and Francis Ford Coppola. According to Langlois (1998), German viewers were shocked by the presentation of von Choltitz, because it was not favourable enough. The film was nominated for two Academy Awards (Best Art Direction and Best Cinematography), but did not receive an overwhelmingly positive critical reception (one reviewer complained of 'such a mishmash of melodrama and such a dumbfounding lack of suspense' – *New York Times* 11 November 1966). It was also accorded a major accolade – a spoof in *Mad* magazine, under the title 'Is Paris Boring?' (Silverstone & Drucker, 1967). The two-page feature includes the usual *Mad* jokes (e.g. von Choltitz says, 'I luf Paris in ze Springtime! Und I luf Paris in ze Fall! Und I luf Paris in ze Summer ... But mein Fuehrer only lufs Paris ven it sizzles!') The spoof also contains a sharp piece of satire, when Nordling asks von Choltitz: 'You blasted Rotterdam off the face of the Earth without a second thought. Why this sudden change of heart with Paris?' to which von Choltitz replies: 'First, ve vere not at var vit ze Dutch! Ve only did it for kicks! Und second, ve vere vinning ze var zen! Hitler was a genius! Now zat ve are losing, Hitler is mad, und ve gotta save our necks!'

26 von Choltitz (1949); *Le Figaro* 12 October 1949. In his final memoir, published in 1951, von Choltitz merely says that he learnt of the telegram 'by accident' from 'better informed superior officers' (von Choltitz, 1969, pp. 241–2); he does not say when this supposed message was received.

27 Collins & Lapierre state that General Warlimont heard Jodl's aide uttering this phrase on the telephone to Model's headquarters at Margival on 25 August (Collins & Lapierre, 1965, p. 284). Warlimont makes no reference to this in his memoirs written at the same time as Collins & Lapierre's blockbuster, or in interviews he gave closer to the event (ETHINT 1; ETHINT 5; Warlimont, 1964; Crémieux, 1971, pp. 181–4). Because there is no evidence that Hitler ever sent such a message, I have not referred to it here. For an excellent summary of this question, see Dansette (1966). For Hitler's message of 23 August, which did order that if Paris was to fall to the enemy, it should be as 'a heap of rubble', see chapter 12.

28 Alexandre Parodi particularly objected to this interpretation. On 12 August 1965 he wrote to the authors of the film, outlining a series of corrections and criticisms, but beginning with a critique of the book: 'The book is highly contestable in terms of its political interpretation of the major decisions we

took: it presents the insurrection as essentially a communist attempt to seize power, or at least to get close to it, while the cease-fire was a manoeuvre of the "Gaullists".' (Studer, 2003, pp. 733–4). Colonel Jay had little time for Collins & Lapierre: 'The descriptions in this book are for the most part superficial and false. It is a bestseller for the masses, written by two sensationalist journalists with all the imagination and guile that such gentlemen normally possess.' (Jay, n.d., p. 75.)

29 For a pithy summary of von Choltitz's motivations during and after the war, see Dansette (1966). All this had been clearly set out in *Le Franc Tireur* 24 October 1949, under the headline 'Von Choltitz did not have the means to defend or to destroy Paris' (AN 72AJ/62/VII/3, p. 18). In 1954, von Choltitz appears to have admitted as much in the pages of the East Berlin daily *Täglische Rundschau*; under pressure from critics within the army, he stated he had not destroyed Paris solely because he did not have the necessary means (Adler-Bresse, 1955). Alexandre Parodi, writing in *Le Figaro* in 1966, concluded with this explanation of the German commander's behaviour: 'Paris was saved because of von Choltitz's feelings of doubt mixed with fear' (Studer, 2003, p. 738). The apparent enigma of von Choltitz continues to intrigue; at the beginning of 2011 a play called *Diplomatie* was put on in Paris at the Madeline theatre, portraying an imaginary night-time meeting between Nordling and von Choltitz in which the pair discuss whether von Choltitz will destroy Paris. However, the true enigma is that there is still an enigma.

30 Figures given by historians vary substantially, and can rarely be traced back to any original source. Dansette (1946), p. 434 states that 2000 Parisians were killed, alongside 800 *résistants* and over 100 soldiers (2e DB and US). According to de Boissieu (1981), p. 261, 1400 Resistance fighters were killed, and over 2000 wounded, while German casualties were 2,700 dead and nearly 5,000 wounded. Jackson (2001) suggests nearly 1500 FFI and Parisians were killed. Wieviorka (1994) states that there were 1000 FFI fighters killed, 600 civilians and 71 men from 2e DB. According to Burton (2001) p. 243, there were 2887 Germans killed and 1482 Frenchmen (482 were civilians). Burton's figures are taken from Michel (1980), p. 99 who in turn cites the newspaper *La Voix de Paris* (19–20 August 1945). However, there no sources for the figures given in *La Voix de Paris* (AN 72AJ/61/I/22); the numbers do not even add up, and the newspaper also claims that a total of ninety-two German tanks were captured or destroyed, which is a gross overestimate. These figures would appear to be at the origin of the numbers of dead given in *Le Figaro* 25 August 2004) on the sixtieth anniversary: 1483 Parisians, 130 2e DB and 2788 Germans. A contemporary figure was 989 killed and 3859 wounded (AN 72AJ/61/I/14, p. 9).

31 Campaux (1945), p. 229. For the history of *Cadran* see Holman (2005).

Index

Picture credits

1. Gamma-Keystone via Getty Images
2. Gamma-Keystone via Getty Images
3. From Bood (1974)
4. Courtesy of the Lainville family
5. From Denoyelle (2006)
6. From cover of Touche (1946)
7. AFP/Getty Images
8. Illustration by Jean Reschofsky; from Roy (1945)
9. Roger Viollet/Getty Images
10. Gamma-Keystone via Getty Images
11. Getty Images
12. NARA (226-FPL-T-25)
13. Roger Viollet/Getty Images
14. Serge de Sazo
15. Serge de Sazo
16. Serge de Sazo
17. adoc-photos/Corbis
18. Photograph by Zalewski; from Conte (1984)
19. Gamma-Keystone via Getty Images
20. From Rocheteau (2004)
21. Getty Images
22. Franc-Tireur
23. From Fournier & Eymard (2009)
24. Musée du Général Leclerc de Hauteclocque et de la Libération de Paris — Musée Jean Moulin; from Fournier & Eymard (2009)
25. Gamma-Keystone via Getty Images
26. Gamma-Keystone via Getty Images
27. Gamma-Keystone via Getty Images
28. Gamma-Keystone via Getty Images
29. Imperial War Museums (EA 37079)
30. Bettmann/CORBIS
31. Imperial War Museums (BU 158)
32. From Foundation de la Resistance www.fondationresistance.org/pages/rech_doc/dukson-oublie-histoire-liberation_photo10.htm
33. AFP/Getty Images
34. Getty Images
35. Lee Miller Archives, England 2013. All rights reserved. www.leemiller.co.uk
36. US Army/Handout/CNP/Corbis Lee Miller Archives, England 2013. All rights reserved. www.leemiller.co.uk